ARCHAEOLOGICAL VIEWS FROM THE COUNTRYSIDE

VILLAGE COMMUNITIES IN EARLY COMPLEX SOCIETIES

EDITED BY GLENN M. SCHWARTZ
AND STEVEN E. FALCONER

SMITHSONIAN INSTITUTION PRESS
WASHINGTON AND LONDON

© 1994 by the Smithsonian Institution
All rights reserved

Library of Congress Cataloging-in-Publication Data

Archaeological views from the countryside: village communities in early complex societies / edited by Glenn M. Schwartz and Steven E. Falconer.
 p. cm.
 Includes bibliographical references (p.   ) and index.
 ISBN 1-56098-319-1
 1. Mayas—Antiquities. 2. Indians of Mexico—Antiquities. 3. Middle East—Antiquities. 4. Villages. 5. Social evolution. 6. Commerce, Prehistoric. 7. Mexico—Antiquities. 8. Central America—Antiquities. I. Schwartz, Glenn M. II. Falconer, Steven E.
 F1435.A68 1993
 972.81′016—dc20   93-28140

British Library Cataloguing-in-Publication Data is available.

Manufactured in the United States of America
00 99 98 97 96 95 94   5 4 3 2 1

Editor and typesetter: Peter Strupp/Princeton Editorial Associates
Production Editor: Jack Kirshbaum

∞ The paper used in this publication meets the minimum requirements of the American National Standard for Permanence of Paper for Printed Library Materials Z39.48-1984.

For permission to reproduce illustrations appearing in this book, please correspond directly with the owners of the works, as listed in the individual captions. The Smithsonian Institution Press does not retain reproduction rights for these illustrations individually or maintain a file of addresses for photo sources.

Cover illustration: Kurdish village, central western Zagros Mountains, Iran, August 1976 (photo by Harvey Weiss, Yale University). Detail of Colha, Belize, 1980.

To our parents,
Robert and Judith Falconer and Evelyn Schwartz,
and to the memory of Sidney Schwartz,
in gratitude for their love and support

Contents

CHAPTER ONE
Rural Approaches to Social Complexity   1
GLENN M. SCHWARTZ AND
STEVEN E. FALCONER

CHAPTER TWO
Segmentary States and Organizational Variation in Early Complex Societies: A Rural Perspective   10
GIL STEIN

CHAPTER THREE
Rural Economic Specialization and Early Urbanization in the Khabur Valley, Syria   19
GLENN M. SCHWARTZ

CHAPTER FOUR
Urban-Rural Relations in Bronze Age Syria: Evidence from Alalah Level VII Palace Archives   37
BONNIE MAGNESS-GARDINER

CHAPTER FIVE
The Ancient Maya Craft Community at Colha, Belize, and Its External Relationships   48
THOMAS R. HESTER AND HARRY J. SHAFER

CHAPTER SIX
Small Sites in Prehistoric Maya Socioeconomic Organization: A Perspective from Colha, Belize   64
ELEANOR KING AND DANIEL POTTER

CHAPTER SEVEN
Specialized Commodity Production in and around Matacapan: Testing the Goodness of Fit of the Regal-Ritual and Administrative Models   91
ROBERT S. SANTLEY

CHAPTER EIGHT
State Formation and the Organization of Domestic Craft Production at Third-Millennium B.C. Kurban Höyük, Southeast Turkey   109
PATRICIA WATTENMAKER

CHAPTER NINE
Village Economy and Society in the Jordan Valley: A Study of Bronze Age Rural Complexity   121
STEVEN E. FALCONER

CHAPTER TEN
Social Complexity in the Aztec Countryside   143
MICHAEL E. SMITH

CHAPTER ELEVEN
The Classic Maya Collapse at Copan, Honduras: An Analysis of Maya Rural Settlement Trends   160
ANNCORINNE FRETER

CHAPTER TWELVE
Rural Household Diversity in Late Classic Copan, Honduras   177
NANCY GONLIN

CHAPTER THIRTEEN
Village Approaches to Complex Societies   198
BRIAN HAYDEN

CHAPTER FOURTEEN
Scale, Organization, and Function in Village and Town   207
CAROL KRAMER

Contributors   213

Index   215

CHAPTER ONE

Rural Approaches to Social Complexity

GLENN M. SCHWARTZ AND STEVEN E. FALCONER

RESIDENTS OF URBAN CENTERS in a wide range of cultures conceive of city life as inherently superior to life in the countryside. In the Islamic Near East, for example, a clear urban-rural dichotomy typifies local world views: the city is the seat of civilization, the countryside a backwater of ignorance, coarseness, and lack of refinement (Sweet 1960:3, 228; Baer 1982:8–14, 103; Eickelman 1989:55). Near Eastern societies, which have been characterized by extensive mobile animal husbandry, compound this bias with the pastoralist's contempt for agrarian village life. Eickelman (1989:55) notes tellingly that "many classical Middle Eastern scholars divided the region's inhabitants into the two ideal types of town dweller (Arabic ḥadarī) and 'noble' pastoralist (Arabic badawī).... This popular dichotomy has been taken over by many writers on the region, even though it leaves the bulk of the population, the tribal and nontribal peasants (fallaḥūn) as an incomplete realization of one or another of the two ideal types."

A similar "urbanocentric" bias has also been characteristic of the archaeology of many early urban civilizations. Traditionally studies of the development of social complexity have focused on large urban communities, the presumed seats of elite-dominated institutions. The palaces, temples, and high-status burials of the large cities—ostentatious manifestations of social, political, and economic stratification—are thought to be of greater value for studying complex societies than the presumably more mundane and homogeneous communities of the countryside. Implicit in this focus is not only an opportunistic orientation toward sites where more "spectacular" discoveries are likely to be made but also an assumption that research in the countryside is of minimal scholarly interest. Without the bright lights of the big city, it is supposed, we simply cannot illuminate the myriad dimensions along which societies become differentiated. Perhaps the bluntest expression of this perspective is found in Oswald Spengler's (1923:106) global generalization that "Weltgeschichte ist die Geschichte des Stadtmenschen." In regions and time periods that provide ancient written records, this prejudice tends to be reinforced by the urban preoccupations of those texts and the world views of their authors, typically city-dwelling elites and the scribes in their employ (Adams 1982:12; Liverani 1982:250).

At the same time, a sense of the import of rural communities in the development of complex societies has not been completely absent in archaeological quarters. It has been repeatedly stressed that social hierarchies in urbanized societies are dependent on the agricultural surpluses provided by the countryside to support non-food-producing specialists (Redman 1978:216). This urban reliance on the countryside is also thought to have had a pronounced effect on rural social structure, for only with the extraction of surpluses by a ruling elite did farmers first become institutionally subordinated as "peasants" (Wolf 1966:3). Furthermore, it is clear that any attempt to understand early urban or state systems in a holistic sense must include the countryside in its purview, if only because a large percentage, often the majority, of the population lived there. Mann (1986:264), for example, estimates that 80–90 percent of the population of preindustrial societies worked the land to support labor specialists and the elite.

In this volume, we undertake a renewed study of the rural aspect of early complex societies: the villages and villagers that provided the economic and demographic foundations of complex societies but that all too often escape the spotlight of detailed archaeological inquiry. The studies that follow provide a glimpse of the insights into social complexity that may follow from investigations that use the rural community as their focal point.

Rural Communities and Archaeological Research

The issue of urban-rural relations in early complex societies has typically been addressed by archaeological settlement pattern analyses (e.g., Smith 1976). Implicit in such studies are several important preconceptions about the roles played by village populations. Following an intellectual tradition rooted in the argument that population growth leads to craft specialization and social differentiation (e.g., Childe 1942, 1950)—with analyses of early cities as largely nonagricultural "market settlements" (e.g., Wirth 1938; Weber 1958)—archaeologists tend to assume that social, political, and economic diversity in a given community or region is a function of scale. Thus urban centers are characterized by their "large size and diverse inhabitants" (Redman 1978:220) and engage in "fully specialized productive activities" (Wright 1981:278), whereas villages are assumed simply to supply food and raw materials and consume urban goods and services (e.g., Trigger 1972; Clarke 1979).

Archaeologists' assumptions of a correlation between the size of a community and the range of functions performed by it, influenced as well by studies of modern geography (see discussion in G. A. Johnson 1980), have pervaded settlement pattern analyses, despite explicit recognition that the structure of *ancient* hierarchies may not be indicated by relative population sizes (Wheatley 1972; G. A. Johnson 1982). This approach follows logically from the optimizing assumptions of American processual archaeology, which would argue that cities are the most efficient managerial nodes in complex systems (e.g., Wright 1986). In this approach, the rural community is viewed as the antithesis of the urban center, i.e., as the lowest, least diverse element within a large settlement system (e.g., G. A. Johnson 1980). Yet such assumptions are made without the benefit of any detailed information on individual rural communities.

Rather than approaching complex societies from an urban vantage point and assuming that cities and villages are antithetical, this volume addresses social complexity from a rural perspective, without presumptions of urban-rural polarities. Those studies with a regional focus shift our attention to the settlements of lesser size, though not necessarily lesser significance. Several authors employ survey data to tie specific small places into regional systems. Many contributors present detailed assessments of individual villages as case studies that may be extrapolated to a regional scale.

The studies in this volume concentrate on the rural communities in two regions, the Near East and Mesoamerica, for several reasons. First, we restrict our geographic coverage in order to facilitate a comparative study of some depth, rather than presenting a global smorgasbord of village studies that might defy attempts to define shared characteristics. Second, since social complexity developed independently in these early "heartlands" of urban civilization, any regularities in New and Old World rural life should provide insights into the structure of complex human societies generally. Finally, a relatively wide range of relevant data is available from both regions, including excavation results from rural settlements, a vast body of data on early urban development, textual material from ancient sources, and ethnohistoric commentaries.

These contributions, with one exception, were presented in preliminary form at the symposium "Village Communities in Early Complex Societies," organized by the editors and held on April 8, 1989, at the annual meeting of the Society for American Archaeology in Atlanta, Georgia. The inspiration for the symposium arose when we and Bonnie Magness-Gardiner discussed our results from excavations at two Near Eastern village sites. Although the sites were from different spatial, cultural, and temporal contexts, both projects obtained compellingly similar and unexpected results: these rural settlements engaged in specialized activities, leaving an archaeological signature that might otherwise have been termed "urban." A variety of data made it abundantly clear that they were not the simple, undifferentiated agricultural villages we had anticipated. This issue of rural complexity set the tone for the ensuing symposium and resonates in this volume as well.

This volume collectively investigates the nature and extent of the integration of rural communities into developing complex societies: the roles that villages played in urban, state, and economically specialized societies and the effect that societal changes had on the hinterlands. Our emphasis, therefore, is on the social and economic organization of rural communities within developing urban and state systems.

In this context, conventional archaeological models of urban-rural interrelations are tested, the axiomatic concepts "rural" and "urban" are reassessed, and the related issues of what defines a community as "urban" or "rural," or a settlement system as "urbanized" or "nonurbanized," are addressed. These analytical concerns may be considered with reference to a number of facets that define rural-urban relations in modern and ancient societies.

Peasant Communities: Models of Homo- and Heterogeneity

Conventional models of village social and economic structure have been derived largely from ethnographic studies of twentieth-century peasant communities. Because these communities are found in societies affected by colonialism and/or capitalist-industrialist economies (Wolf 1955:453, 462), the models generated from their study must be applied with caution to preindustrial or noncapitalist complex societies. The use of archaeological data for the study of preindustrial rural societies becomes all the more significant, therefore, but it consequently suffers from the absence of unquestionably applicable present-day analogues.

Perhaps the most influential model of villages in complex societies views them as communities dedicated almost exclusively to food production and dependent on cities for products and services. Redfield's pioneering studies of Mexican villages led him to conclude that peasant communities are, as a rule, typically "homogeneous": their populations consist of socially and economically equivalent agricultural producers (Redfield 1953). Wolf's "closed corporate community" expands on this model; these peasant communities are characterized by communal control and redistribution of agricultural land, an insular world view, and leveling mechanisms to maintain economic and social uniformity (Wolf 1955).[1] Because such peasant villages are thought to be "closed" to outside ideas and influences, rural change is typically attributed to external variables.

Peasant dependence on the city is underscored in this model: "There were no peasants before the first cities.... The peasant is a rural native whose long established order of life takes important account of the city" (Redfield 1953:13). Rural villages, therefore, are "part-societies" (Kroeber 1948:284) that must be understood in relation to the larger whole.

Divergences from the model of the homogeneous rural community can be found in the sociological and cultural anthropological literature by the 1960s and 1970s. In the Islamic Near East, for example, many "urban" characteristics—such as religious buildings, craft specialists, and elaborate peasant-based commercial relations—were identified in the nonindustrial countryside (Lapidus 1969). Likewise, historic cities housed large subpopulations that carried out "rural" functions in an urban setting (Abu-Lughod 1969:159; Gulick 1969:124). Nineteenth-century Cairo provides a celebrated metropolitan example in which large proportions of the "economically active population" commuted regularly to fields at the city's fringes (Abu-Lughod 1969:164; Issawi 1969:105–106). Reexaminations of Redfield's work in Mesoamerica revealed a similar lack of fit with the homogeneous peasant model (Goldkind 1965).

Nonetheless, the model of village homogeneity has retained considerable influence in archaeological circles, largely because of the assumption, outlined earlier, that community size is a correlate of functional diversity. This state of affairs may also be attributed to the absence of a significant corpus of archaeological data from rural settlements. However, with the growing body of evidence now available, archaeological studies such as those presented in this volume demonstrate that this model is as often inaccurate or oversimplified for rural communities in early complex societies as it is for twentieth-century peasant communities. These studies reveal varying forms of social complexity, in which cities and villages are not always political and economic complements and in which the rural populace performs unexpectedly diverse functions, often not simply in subordinate roles to the central place interests of cities.

Urban Dependence on the Rural Hinterland

Cities depend, to varying extents, on the agricultural surpluses provided by the countryside; these surpluses support the ruling elite, religious specialists, professional bureaucrats, craft specialists, and all others not directly concerned with food production (Redfield 1953; Wolf 1955:452). Historically, successful urban centers often maintained a parasitic or predatory relationship with their hinterlands, siphoning off as many assets as possible, while stopping short of undermining rural infrastructure. Bureaucrats and members of the elite were particularly adept at "finding ways to rationalize their imposition of arbitrary authority in pursuit of their own self-interest" (Adams 1984:88; see also Gilman 1981). Institutionalized authority provided only mixed blessings (e.g., military protection and economic advantages versus greater tax and corvée labor obligations) for rural commoners tied to cities (Adams 1972:743; Diakonoff 1975:123–124).

The self-interest of paramount authorities inspired compensatory strategies at the lower end of the social hierarchy that illustrate conflicting needs within stratified society. For example, in the Near East, increased pastoralism was adaptive for rural populations, but disintegrative for complex political systems for the same reason: nonsedentary populations are more difficult for authorities to control and tax (Adams 1978). This contradictory tension was reflected in antiquity by the distinct and separate interests of city and countryside ("die Scheidung von Stadt und Land," Marx 1968:373). Villages were in particular jeopardy of being "forcibly incorporated into larger estates and otherwise losing their corporate character" (Adams 1982:11; see also Diakonoff 1975:127). If these separate interests were not reconciled, societal disintegration was the likely result (Yoffee 1979). This rural-urban dialectic challenges archaeologists to isolate and compare the conflicting needs and strategies of the constituent groups that made these societies complex, rather than assume early civilizations to have been coherently adaptive wholes (see Kohl 1981:109).

Toward this end, many of our contributors share a concern for identifying the mechanisms by which rural communities maintained their integrity in the face of urban attempts to coerce or compel the agrarian populace to deliver up needed surpluses. Textual data available from later historical periods in the Near East reveal a diversity of strategies for urban control of the countryside. One of the earliest means for control of rural production called for the state to lay direct claim to land ownership, thereby extracting maximum agricultural surpluses without entirely destroying the productive base. For example, in Late Bronze Age Ugarit in northern Syria (circa thirteenth century B.C.), the royal establishment derived most of its surpluses from agricultural estates worked by unmarried state dependents who were kept at a bare subsistence level (Liverani 1982). In a similar vein, Magness-Gardiner (Chapter 4) notes that although the state could lease land in return for a proportion of the harvest, her data also show that the state of Alalah was not able to tax its entire hinterland but could only acquire surpluses from land it owned directly.

Another strategem for central control of the countryside's resources relied upon a "feudal" organization, or what Wolf (1966:50) terms a "patrimonial" system. In this arrangement, land was controlled by members of a hereditary elite who performed military or administrative duties for the state (e.g., see the discussion of *ilkum* in Chapter 4 by Magness-Gardiner). This system was, at least in theory, the result of the distribution of lands by the state, the nominal owner (e.g., Lambton 1953). In the case of the late Roman Empire, the state apparently parceled out the countryside to local lords because it lacked the ability to collect rural resources effectively on its own (Wickham 1984; Mann 1986:290–291, 356). The disadvantage of this arrangement, from the state's point of view, was the appropriation of a disproportionate "cut" of the surpluses by local authorities. Alternatively, rather than distribute lands itself, the state could distribute tax-collecting privileges in a "prebendal" (Wolf 1966:50) system of tax-farming, such as that found particularly in highly centralized bureaucratic polities such as the Ottoman Empire and Mughal India.

Private or "mercantile" landownership (Wolf 1966:53) developed when land became the private property of a landlord, to be bought and sold as a commodity (Diakonoff 1975; Adams 1982:3). In the Near East, the growth of private landownership probably resulted from urban-based entrepreneurs making loans to peasants on their crops and subsequently appropriating their lands when harvests failed and the peasants defaulted on their debt (Sweet 1960:3; Graham-Brown 1990; see also Datta 1989).

In addition to varieties of urban-dominated land tenure or urban taxation of the countryside, agricultural surpluses might also be obtained from voluntary offerings such as those provided in a religious context (Adams 1979:18). Finally, city dwellers might derive their agricultural surpluses from the exchange of products and services in a market setting (A. W. Johnson and Earle 1987:272).

This volume presents a number of observations on the appropriation of surpluses by nonrural populations. For example, Stein (Chapter 2) points out that the degree of political centralization in early state societies is expressed very directly by the nature of urban interactions with villages. Schwartz (Chapter 3) notes the establishment of grain collection and processing centers in the Khabur River countryside of Syria and hypothesizes that they were installed to ensure the collection of surpluses by burgeoning elites.

In other cases, the development of central communities may depend on means of accumulating wealth other than the exploitation of rural agriculture, such as large-scale craft production and exchange. In general, Mesoamerican centers did not reap agricultural surpluses comparable to those of the Near East. However, Hester and Shafer (Chapter 5) show that even with a moderate resident population, economic nodes like Colha developed on the basis of specialist production of both utilitarian and elite lithic commodities.

Rural community organization in the face of urban demands must have taken a variety of forms, some of which may have predated the intrusion of city and state into the countryside (Adams 1982). As late as the end of the nineteenth century, practically all private land in Palestine and Syria, for instance, was worked communally by corporate villages. This communal landholding system, known as *musha'* in the Arabic-speaking Middle East, characterized villages similar to Wolf's "closed corporate communities" (Wolf 1955; Kramer 1982:35; Graham-Brown 1990). *Musha'* land was held jointly by the members of one family, among several families united in a *hamula,* or by the inhabitants of an entire village (Grannot 1952:174; Sweet 1960:48; Poyck 1962:27; Lutfiyya 1966:104; Antoun 1972:20; Atran 1986). These villages met tax and labor obligations corporately and equalized long-term agricultural risks among farming households by redistributing *musha'* land at regular intervals (Granott 1952:215; Poyck 1962:27; Atran 1986).

Archives from the cities of Ugarit and Nuzi in Syria suggest that the ancient landscape similarly was tilled by corporate agrarian villages, in addition to the royal estates mentioned previously. Both private and collective family ownership of farmlands are attested (Heltzer 1976:84, 95; Zaccagnini 1979:51). The most common rural economic units of the kingdom of Ugarit were approximately 200 villages with collective tax, military, and labor obligations to the crown (Heltzer 1976:18–47). Given such evidence, we have reason to believe that the traditional corporate structure of modern village agriculture had ancient roots, suggesting one possible analogue for the ancient rural countryside.

In contrast to elite-controlled land tenure systems, these arrangements are documented only fleetingly in ancient texts, since those records were concerned almost exclusively with elite affairs. Consequently archaeology has been called upon to contribute to our understanding of such systems (Adams 1982:2). Although no study in this volume presents direct evidence of corporate community structure, those analyses that emphasize village autonomy in the face of urban growth and collapse (e.g., Chapter 9 by Falconer, Chapter 11 by Freter) can look to these ethnographic and historic analogues as examples of how rural communities may respond resiliently to the pressures of central authority.

Ideological Dichotomies

Historical evidence frequently indicates a significant ideological gap between city and countryside, despite their interdependence. As noted earlier, urban populations have often regarded country dwellers pejoratively, considering them unsophisticated and ignorant. Although their attitudes are recorded only rarely, one might presume that peasants viewed city dwellers with equal suspicion and mistrust, especially if one considers the economic and political demands with which central authorities burdened the countryside (Redfield 1953; Wolf 1955).

Religious differences are particularly common between city and country. Peasant religion tends to diverge from the orthodoxy of urban religious specialists (Geertz 1960) and is often viewed with suspicion by the latter group (Weulersse 1946; Wolf 1966:105; Watson 1979:233). Baer (1982:8–10) notes that in Ottoman Egypt the *'ulama* (religious specialists) were exclusively urban based. City dwellers thought peasants had a "paucity of religion" (*qillat al-din*), manifested by an ignorance of even the basic precepts of Islam, such as knowing how to pray correctly or how to maintain ritual cleanliness. Evidence of religious practices presented in this volume (Chapter 3 by Schwartz, Chapter 10 by Smith) offers the beginnings of an archaeological data base with which to test hypotheses on this issue.

Economic Specialization

Economic specialization is considered a fundamental attribute of complex societies, although the reasons for this association should not be considered self-evident (Zeder 1991). Redfield's model of homogeneous peasant villages considers economic specialization to be uncharacteristic of rural settlements (Redfield 1953). As already noted, this model has not been accepted with unanimity by sociologists and cultural anthropologists. For example, in his reexamination of Redfield's data from the *ejido* of Chan Kom, Goldkind (1965) documents the potential significance of village craft specialization. In this community, artisans and shops became so abundant that villagers had little need to visit larger towns for goods and services. Similarly, Baer's review of Ottoman Egypt reveals the presence of artisans and merchants in villages; these rural craftsmen primarily manufactured basic goods intended for rural consumers, again with the result that peasants were only minimally dependent on the cities for manufactured goods (Baer 1982:54–56).

Several studies in this volume (e.g., Chapter 2 by Stein, Chapter 6 by King and Potter, Chapter 9 by Falconer) underscore the prevalence of economic specialization in the rural countryside. Santley (Chapter 7) and Wattenmaker (Chapter 8) show that craft specialists were found in both urban and rural settings and could service elites and commoners alike, and Gonlin (Chapter 12) explores specialized rural settlements, each of which was concerned with a specific variety of production.

Status Differentiation

Two of the most salient characteristics of social complexity are economic and social stratification. Such differentiation derives from variability in access to and control of the means of production, particularly land, in both the Near East and Mesoamerica (Sweet 1960:125; Kramer 1982:52; Graham-Brown 1990; Krantz 1991:101). The model of homogeneous peasant villages emphasizes the classless nature of rural communities in complex societies (Redfield 1953). Characteristic of such homogeneous communities is an economy regulated by leveling mechanisms such as a cult of poverty and the institutionalized envy of those trying to acquire and display more wealth than others (Wolf 1955:459–460; Foster 1972; Adams 1982:3).

But even where collective landholding exists, power and wealth can be distributed unequally (Mintz 1973). Despite the egalitarian ideology and supposedly equal allocation of resources in the Mexican *ejido* studied by Krantz (1991), land had come to be apportioned unevenly. The original members of the village wielded their influence and political power to maintain advantages over later arrivals, while larger families were able to provide extra labor and expand their landholdings into previously uncultivated areas.

In the Chan Kom *ejido,* Goldkind notes economic stratification in the development of private landownership and in the differentiation between villagers with abundant agricultural surpluses and those working only at subsistence level (1965:865). Status differentiation is also observed in variation in size and construction materials among the village houses. Very similar results were obtained from an *ejido* northwest of Mexico City studied by DeWalt (1975), in which economic differences were reflected in household possessions and residential construction, the number of animals owned, and the type of food eaten. Cancian's study of Maya villages in Chiapas, Mexico (1965), reveals economic and social peasant stratification based on a *cargo* system of rotating religious offices. These conclusions contradict earlier interpretations of this system as a leveling mechanism (e.g., Wolf 1955), wherein the "rich" spend more than the "poor." Cancian asserts that both stratifying and leveling mechanisms coexisted in these communities.

Middle Eastern ethnographic data reveal similar evidence of social stratification in the countryside. In Tell Toqaan, Syria (Sweet 1960:110), economic differences again were manifested by disparities in residential architecture. The heads of the most affluent families owned land, flocks, or the monopoly on an important craft service (e.g., carpentry) or were foremen or partners of other landlords. In an echo of Krantz's results, the wealthier peasants tended to have larger families. At the same time, Sweet describes a uniform village life-style and notes that displays of wealth were rare (1960:227). She also emphasizes that class distinctions within the village were far less sharply marked than the class distinction between the urban elite and the villagers (1960:228).

The issue of rural social stratification finds expression in a number of chapters in the present volume. Smith (Chapter 10) discerns architectural evidence of an elite at the rural site of Cuexcomate but not at Capilco, whereas Gonlin (Chapter 12) distinguishes patterns of social stratification even in extremely small communities. Schwartz (Chapter 3) cites differentiation in mortuary data and the emulation of urban elite art as possible evidence of village social heterogeneity.

Villages in Complex Societies: Mesoamerican and Near Eastern Case Studies

Because this compilation of studies is intended to foster comparisons of data and interpretations from two distinct and distant regions, the chapters are not segregated into Mesoamerican and Near Eastern sections but instead are grouped according to common local settings or analytical concerns.

Chapters 2–4 investigate rural agricultural production and the mobilization of surplus by towns and cities in Northern Mesopotamia and coastal Syria. Stein (Chapter 2) uses settlement pattern data from the hinterland of Tell Leilan to infer changes in the third-millennium B.C. rural productive economy, which he suggests are tied to developments in sociopolitical complexity. Schwartz (Chapter 3) discusses a small third-millennium B.C. site in the Khabur River Valley and its participation in a network of villages specializing in grain storage and processing, which he suggests were established by developing complex polities as a mechanism for the collection of agricultural surplus. Second-millennium B.C. texts from the Alalah royal palace provide Magness-Gardiner (Chapter 4) with detailed evidence of the means by which authorities in Alalah extracted surplus production from its surrounding villages. Textual evidence provides a potent source of information on such intangibles as land tenure, which are difficult to observe archaeologically, and thus it can be used to complement archaeological field investigations.

Chapters 5–7 consider the significance and extent of craft specialization in the Mesoamerican countrysides of Belize, the Basin of Mexico, and southern Veracruz. Hester and Shafer (Chapter 5) examine surprisingly substantial Maya lithic production at the specialized workshop community of Colha, Belize, and the distribution of Colha's products to a variety of consumer sites. King and Potter (Chapter 6) reveal that, contrary to expectations, village craft specialization and social stratification fueled many cross-cutting exchange networks in the Maya countryside, with minimal participation of central places. Santley (Chapter 7) reexamines conventional definitions of Mesoamerican urbanism with data from the Basin of Mexico and from Matacapan and the Tuxtlas Mountains, Veracruz. He argues that the center of Matacapan grew primarily in response to political, rather than economic, factors, whereas most specialized craft production was located in hinterland communities, not in principal central places.

Chapters 8–11 explore village structure and economic organization based on small-site excavations in Jordan, southeastern Turkey, and Morelos, Mexico. Wattenmaker (Chapter 8) infers that households at Kurban Höyük, Turkey, became increasingly involved in some, but not all, aspects of the specialized economy of its surrounding region during early state formation. Falconer (Chapter 9) considers evidence for social and economic organization at two Bronze Age villages in the Jordan Valley and suggests a revised paradigm of "rural complexity" rather than "urbanism" for early complex society in the southern Levant. Smith (Chapter 10) infers several unexpected dimensions of social complexity in three recently excavated Aztec rural communities and challenges a variety of urban models for agrarian states generally and for Aztec society in particular.

Chapters 11 and 12 examine the dynamics of Classic Maya rural settlement based on surveys and excavations at the large center of Copan, Honduras, and at numerous small sites in its hinterland. Freter (Chapter 11) adopts a rural perspective to argue that the Classic Maya collapse in the Copan Valley was primarily an urban phenomenon not paralleled in the hinterland. Gonlin (Chapter 12) compares urban and rural evidence to distinguish regional patterns of social stratification and economic diversity, particularly as seen in extremely small communities.

Concluding the volume are two commentaries, one by a Mesoamericanist (Chapter 13 by Hayden) and the second by a Near Eastern specialist (Chapter 14 by Kramer), that review central issues raised by the preceding chapters, pose new queries, and identify directions for subsequent research on the significance of village communities.

This volume proposes that an archaeological perspective from the countryside will illuminate new aspects of those characteristics that define societies as "complex" and the inherent tensions that drive their growth and collapse. Rural studies are compelling not only because they may be unorthodox but also because they allow us to reject, revise, and refine previous interpretations of ancient societies in ways we cannot always anticipate. These studies modestly hope to inspire such new insight by critically reassessing archaeological assumptions of village homogeneity, the dependence of cities on their surrounding countrysides, and the social, economic, and ideological distinctions that mold rural-urban interplay.

Rural studies will contribute to the archaeology of early complex societies not so much by redressing popular and scholarly urbanocentrism or rebutting Spengler's opinion of "Weltgeschichte" as by demonstrating how detailed assessments of the smallest of communities may provide new challenges for our study of the grandest expressions of human organization: socially, economically, and politically complex societies. We hope that the discussions gathered together in this volume represent a substantial collective contribution toward that end.

Acknowledgments

We acknowledge the help and encouragement provided by our acquisitions editor, Daniel Goodwin, and by our production editors, Ruth Spiegel and Jack Kirshbaum, at the Smithsonian Institution Press. We are particularly indebted to Peter Strupp of Princeton Editorial Associates for his remarkably meticulous and prompt copyediting. Thanks are also due to our anonymous reviewer and to Jane Dreyer, Department of Near Eastern Studies, The Johns Hopkins University, for her unstinting administrative assistance.

Notes

The authors wish to thank Betsy Bryan and Sidney Mintz for their helpful comments on an earlier draft of this chapter.

1. The applicability of the closed corporate peasant community model to precolonialist societies has been questioned by some, including its original proponent (Wolf 1957; Skinner 1971), while others reject the concept in toto (Rambo 1977; Popkin 1979). Boomgard (1991) and others maintain that variations in the closed or corporate nature of villages can be linked to vicissitudes in state power. "Open" peasant communities in Wolf's typology are linked more explicitly to colonialist or postcolonialist economies.

References Cited

Abu-Lughod, Janet
    1969 Varieties of Urban Experience: Contrast, Coexistence and Coalescence in Cairo. In *Middle Eastern Cities: A Symposium on Ancient, Islamic, and Contemporary Middle Eastern Urbanism,* edited by I. Lapidus, pp. 157–187. University of California Press, Berkeley and Los Angeles.

Adams, Robert McC.
    1972 Patterns of Urbanization in Early Southern Mesopotamia. In *Man, Settlement and Urbanism,* edited by P. J. Ucko, R. E. Tringham, and G. W. Dimbleby, pp. 735–749. Duckworth, London.
    1978 Strategies of Maximization, Stability, and Resilience in Mesopotamian Society, Settlement, and Agriculture. *Proceedings of the American Philosophical Society* 122:329–335.
    1979 The Natural History of Urbanism. In *Ancient Cities of the Indus,* edited by G. Possehl, pp. 18–26. Vikas, New Delhi.
    1982 Property Rights and Functional Tenure in Mesopotamian Rural Communities. In *Societies and Languages of the Ancient Near East: Studies in Honour of I. M. Diakonoff,* edited by M. A. Dandamayev et al., pp. 1–14. Aris and Phillips, Warminster, England.
    1984 Mesopotamian Social Evolution: Old Outlooks, New Goals. In *On the Evolution of Complex Societies: Essays in Honor of Harry Hoijer, 1982,* edited by T. K. Earle, pp. 79–129. Undena Press, Malibu, Calif.

Antoun, Richard T.
    1972 *Arab Village. A Social Structural Study of a Transjordanian Peasant Community.* Indiana University Press, Bloomington.

Atran, Scott
    1986 Hamula Organisation and Masha'a Tenure in Palestine. *Man* 21:271–295.

Baer, Gabriel
    1982 *Fellah and Townsman in the Middle East.* Frank Cass, London.

Boomgard, Peter
- 1991 The Javanese Village as a Cheshire Cat: The Java Debate Against a European and Latin American Background. *Journal of Peasant Studies* 18:288–304.

Cancian, Frank
- 1965 *Economics and Prestige in a Maya Community: The Religious Cargo System in Zinacantan.* Stanford University Press, Stanford, Calif.

Childe, Vere Gordon
- 1942 *What Happened in History.* Pelican, Harmondsworth, England.
- 1950 The Urban Revolution. *Town Planning Review* 21:3–17.

Clarke, David L.
- 1979 Towns in the Development of Early Civilization. In *Analytical Archaeologist: Collected Papers of David L. Clarke,* edited by N. Hammond et al., pp. 435–443. Academic Press, New York.

Datta, Rajat
- 1989 Agricultural Production, Social Participation and Domination in Late Eighteenth-Century Bengal: Towards an Alternative Explanation. *Journal of Peasant Studies* 17:68–113.

DeWalt, Billie
- 1975 Inequalities in Wealth, Adoption of Technology, and Production in a Mexican Ejido. *American Ethnologist* 2:149–168.

Diakonoff, Igor M.
- 1975 The Rural Community in the Ancient Near East. *Journal of the Economic and Social History of the Orient* 18:121–133.

Eickelman, Dale F.
- 1989 *The Middle East: An Anthropological Approach.* Prentice Hall, Englewood Cliffs, N.J.

Foster, George
- 1972 The Anatomy of Envy: A Study in Symbolic Behavior. *Current Anthropology* 13:165–202.

Geertz, Clifford
- 1960 *The Religion of Java.* Free Press, Glencoe, Ill.

Gilman, Antonio
- 1981 The Development of Social Stratification in Bronze Age Europe. *Current Anthropology* 22:1–23.

Goldkind, Victor
- 1965 Social Stratification in the Peasant Community: Redfield's Chan Kom Reinterpreted. *American Anthropologist* 67:863–884.

Graham-Brown, Sarah
- 1990 Agriculture and Labour Transformation in Palestine. In *The Rural Middle East: Peasant Lives and Modes of Production,* edited by K. and P. Glavanis, pp. 53–69. Zed Books/Birzeit University, London.

Granott, Abraham
- 1952 *The Land System in Palestine: History and Structure.* Eyre and Spottiswoode, London.

Gulick, John
- 1969 Village and City: Cultural Continuities in Twentieth Century Middle Eastern Cultures. In *Middle Eastern Cities: A Symposium on Ancient, Islamic, and Contemporary Middle Eastern Urbanism,* edited by I. Lapidus, pp. 122–158. University of California Press, Berkeley and Los Angeles.

Heltzer, Michael
- 1976 *The Rural Community in Ancient Ugarit.* Ludwig Reichert Verlag, Wiesbaden, Germany.

Issawi, Charles
- 1969 Economic Change and Urbanization in the Middle East. In *Middle Eastern Cities: A Symposium on Ancient, Islamic, and Contemporary Middle Eastern Urbanism,* edited by I. Lapidus, pp. 102–121. University of California Press, Berkeley and Los Angeles.

Johnson, Allen W., and Timothy Earle
- 1987 *The Evolution of Human Societies.* Stanford University Press, Stanford, Calif.

Johnson, Gregory A.
- 1980 Rank-Size Convexity and System Integration: A View from Archaeology. *Economic Geography* 56:234–247.
- 1982 Organizational Structure and Scalar Stress. In *Theory and Explanation in Archaeology,* edited by C. Renfrew, M. J. Rowlands, and B. A. Seagraves, pp. 389–421. Academic Press, New York.

Kohl, Philip L.
- 1981 Materialist Approaches in Prehistory. *Annual Review of Anthropology* 10:89–118.

Kramer, Carol
- 1982 *Village Ethnoarchaeology: Rural Iran in Archaeological Perspective.* Academic Press, New York.

Krantz, Lasse
- 1991 *Peasant Differentiation and Development: The Case of a Mexican Ejido.* Stockholm Studies in Social Anthropology 28. University of Stockholm.

Kroeber, Alfred L.
- 1948 *Anthropology.* Harcourt Brace, New York.

Lambton, Ann K. S.
- 1953 *Landlord and Peasant in Persia.* Oxford University Press, Oxford.

Lapidus, Ira M.
- 1969 Muslim Cities and Islamic Societies. In *Middle Eastern Cities: A Symposium on Ancient, Islamic, and Contemporary Middle Eastern Urbanism,* edited by I. Lapidus, pp. 47–79. University of California Press, Berkeley and Los Angeles.

Liverani, Mario
- 1982 Ville et campagne dans le royaume d'Ugarit. Essai d'analyse économique. In *Societies and Languages of the Ancient Near East: Studies in Honour of I. M. Diakonoff,* edited by M. A. Dandamayev et al., pp. 249–258. Aris and Phillips, Warminster, England.

Lutfiyya, Abdulla M.
- 1966 *Baytin. A Jordanian Village.* Mouton, Paris.

Mann, Michael
- 1986 *The Sources of Social Power.* Cambridge University Press, Cambridge.

Marx, Karl
  1968 *Das Kapital.* Europäische Verlagsanstalt, Leipzig.
Mintz, Sidney W.
  1973 A Note on the Definition of Peasantries. *Journal of Peasant Studies* 1:91–106.
Popkin, Samuel L.
  1979 *The Rational Peasant: The Political Economy of Rural Society in Vietnam.* University of California Press, Berkeley and Los Angeles.
Poyck, A.
  1962 *Farm Studies in Iraq.* Medelingen van de Landbouwhogeschool te Wageningen 62(1). H. Veenman and Zonen, Wageningen, The Netherlands.
Rambo, A. Terry
  1977 Closed Corporate and Open Peasant Communities: Reopening a Hastily Shut Case. *Comparative Studies in Society and History* 19:179–188.
Redfield, Robert
  1953 *The Primitive World and Its Transformations.* Cornell University Press, Ithaca, N.Y.
Redman, Charles L.
  1978 *The Rise of Civilization.* W. H. Freeman, San Francisco.
Skinner, G. William
  1971 Chinese Peasants and the Closed Community: An Open and Shut Case. *Comparative Studies in Society and History* 13:271–281.
Smith, Carol A.
  1976 Introduction: The Regional Approach to Economic Systems. In *Regional Analysis*, Vol. 1: *Economic Systems*, edited by C. A. Smith, pp. 3–68. Academic Press, New York.
Spengler, Oswald
  1923 *Der Untergang des Abendlandes: Umrisse einer Morphologie der Weltgeschichte.* Oskar Beck, Munich.
Sweet, Louise E.
  1960 *Tell Toqaan: A Syrian Village.* Museum of Anthropology, University of Michigan, Anthropological Papers, No. 14. University of Michigan, Ann Arbor.
Trigger, Bruce
  1972 Determinants of Urban Growth in Pre-industrial Societies. In *Man, Settlement and Urbanism,* edited by P. J. Ucko, R. E. Tringham, and G. W. Dimbleby, pp. 575–599. Duckworth, London.
Watson, Patty Jo
  1979 *Archaeological Ethnography in Western Iran.* Viking Fund Publications in Anthropology, No. 57. University of Arizona Press, Tucson.

Weber, Max
  1958 *The City.* Macmillan, New York.
Weulersse, Jacques
  1946 *Paysans de Syrie et du proche-Orient.* Gallimard, Paris.
Wheatley, Paul
  1972 The Concept of Urbanism. In *Man, Settlement and Urbanism,* edited by P. J. Ucko, R. E. Tringham, and G. W. Dimbleby, pp. 601–637. Duckworth, London.
Wickham, Chris
  1984 The Other Transition: From the Ancient World to Feudalism. *Past and Present* 103:3–36.
Wirth, Louis
  1938 Urbanism as a Way of Life. *American Journal of Sociology* 44:3–21.
Wolf, Eric R.
  1955 Types of Latin American Peasantry: A Preliminary Discussion. *American Anthropologist* 57:452–470.
  1957 Closed Corporate Peasant Communities in Mesoamerica and Central Java. *Southwestern Journal of Anthropology* 13:1–18.
  1966 *Peasants.* Prentice Hall, Englewood Cliffs, N.J.
Wright, Henry T., ed.
  1981 *An Early Town on the Deh Luran Plain: Excavations at Tepe Farukhabad.* Museum of Anthropology, University of Michigan, Memoirs, No. 13. University of Michigan, Ann Arbor.
Wright, Henry T.
  1986 The Evolution of Civilizations. In *American Archaeology Past and Future,* edited by D. Meltzer, D. Fowler, and J. Sabloff, pp. 323–368. Smithsonian Institution Press, Washington, D.C.
Yoffee, Norman
  1979 The Decline and Rise of Mesopotamian Civilizations: An Ethnoarchaeological Perspective on the Evolution of Complex Society. *American Antiquity* 44:5–35.
Zaccagnini, Carlo
  1979 *The Rural Landscape of the Land of Arraphe.* Quaderni di Geografia Storica, Vol. 1. Istituto di Studi del Vicino Oriente, University of Rome, Rome.
Zeder, Melinda
  1991 *Feeding Cities.* Smithsonian Institution Press, Washington, D.C.

CHAPTER TWO

Segmentary States and Organizational Variation in Early Complex Societies: A Rural Perspective

GIL STEIN

IN THIS CHAPTER I EXAMINE the relationship between rural economic organization and state structure in the early complex societies of the Mesopotamian world. The first part of the chapter describes the main axes of variation in the organization of early states, suggesting how these factors may affect the relationship between centers and rural hinterlands. In the second part, I outline the ways in which this perspective on village economic organization can help clarify the regional political economy of early state societies in the dry-farming zone of northwest Mesopotamia in the third millennium B.C.

Analytical Approaches to State Centralization

Traditional models of early state organization in the Near East have focused almost exclusively on urban elites and their institutions in reconstructions of ancient Mesopotamian society. These largely implicit models derive from the history of Orientalist archaeological and textual research. For most of the last century, excavations in Greater Mesopotamia (defined as the drainage of the Tigris and Euphrates rivers, comprising modern Iraq, northeast Syria, southeast Turkey, and southwest Iran) have concentrated on large third-millennium urban sites such as Ur, Uruk, Mari, and Nineveh, while ignoring the countryside. Concurrently textual research by Assyriologists used temple and palace archives as the basis for models that viewed virtually all economic and political power as residing within the purview of the Palace and Temple "sectors"—the "Great Institutions" of Mesopotamian society (Deimel 1931; Falkenstein 1974).

This urban-oriented focus is perfectly natural, given the fact that Mesopotamia is the earliest known and best documented ancient urban society. However, more recent research has begun to add balance to this picture by documenting the importance of the rural sector in ancient Mesopotamian state organization. Assyriological studies (Gelb 1969; Diakonoff 1974, 1975) have shown the existence of a surprisingly autonomous rural sector, while Adams (1978, 1982) has convincingly argued for a high degree of volatility and contingency in the extent of urban control over the countryside in Mesopotamian state societies. As a result of this conceptual shift, archaeological research has begun to focus on Mesopotamian rural organization, examining the range of activities that took place in ancient villages, while relating these communities to the wider regional context of complex polities (Wright 1969; Wright, Miller, and Redding 1981; G. Stein 1987; Schwartz and Curvers 1992). We recognize implicitly that some kind of relationship exists between rural economic organization and the political structure of early state societies. However, we need to develop an explicit analytical framework that can link these two systems, explaining the different forms of village economy that we see in the archaeological record in terms of variation in early state organization.

We tend to view "the state" as an internally homogeneous and monolithic entity, implicitly emphasizing the high degree of centralized control in polities of this type. By counterposing the state against simpler sociopolitical entities such as "chiefdoms" or "middle-range societies," we have perhaps overemphasized the state's complexity. Absolute categorizations of this type tend to obscure the range of variation in state-hinterland relations. Excavation and survey in both the

Old and the New World have made it clear that early state societies differ widely in vital structural aspects, such as population, subsistence base, areal extent, degree of urbanization, and extent of political centralization. If early states exhibit such a high degree of organizational variability, then we need to rethink the systems we commonly use to categorize different levels of sociocultural complexity.

In recent studies of the emergence of complex societies in highland Mesoamerica, Blanton and his colleagues have suggested that it might be more useful to think of states as societies whose organization varies along three main axes:

1. Scale (or size): "the number of people incorporated into the society, and/or the size of the area involved" (Blanton et al. 1981:17).
2. Complexity: the extent of functional differentiation between social units (Blanton et al. 1981:21).
3. Integration: the interdependence of units (Blanton et al. 1981:23).

This three-dimensional scale of organizational variation gives us a shared set of variables that can be used to compare different descriptive models of social complexity.

The Segmentary State Model

One can conceptualize this range of variability in the scale, complexity, and integration of complex societies by using Southall's distinction between "segmentary" and "unitary" states based on his ethnographic study of the Alur polity in East Africa (Southall 1956, 1988; B. Stein 1977) (Fig. 1). Segmentary states are fairly primitive polities in which centralized government and specialized administration operate at low levels of scale, complexity, and integration:

> Whereas the unitary state is a structure in which there is a central monopoly of power, exercised by a specialized administrative staff within defined territorial limits, the segmentary state is a structure in which specialized political power is exercised within a pyramidal series of segments tied together at any one level by the oppositions between them at a higher level, and ultimately defined by their joint opposition to adjacent, unrelated groups. (Southall 1956:260)

Territorial sovereignty in these polities is unevenly distributed over the social landscape, forming a series of zones in which authority is most absolute at the center and increasingly restricted toward the periphery. Although a specialized administrative staff exists at the center with administrative foci in the outlying areas, these peripheral nodes simply replicate at a

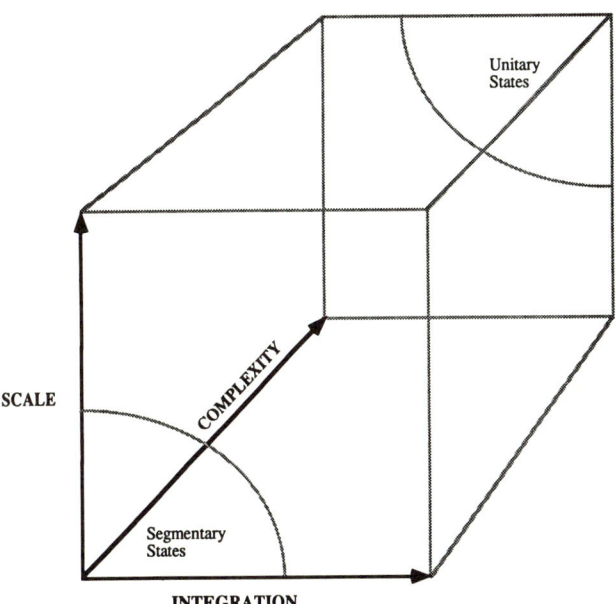

Fig. 1. Proposed relationship of segmentary and unitary states in terms of their relative degrees of scale, complexity, and integration.

smaller scale the powers of the centralized authorities, rather than having internally differentiated decision-making powers. The lack of clear functional differentiation between the different parts of the Alur system led Southall to describe this polity as "segmentary," an analogy with Durkheim's concept of "mechanical solidarity," in which society consists of identical segments (Durkheim 1933:175, cited in Southall 1956:249).

In segmentary states, the centralized authorities exercise only limited control over peripheral foci of administration. As a result, center-hinterland relations form a gradient in which the absolute power of the centralized authority declines with distance from the capital. Rural areas retain a high level of local political and economic autonomy, often reducing centralized authority to an essentially ritual hegemony (Southall 1956:260; Netting 1972; B. Stein 1980:266–267).

This distance decay of centralized power affects the nature and degree of tribute collection from the countryside in segmentary states. Centralized authorities can generally mobilize only low levels of tribute in goods, usually in the form of seasonal surpluses from agriculture or herding; even these forms of tribute-in-goods are rendered as payment for ritual and jural services by the central authorities, rather than being a regular fiscal obligation (Southall 1956:261). Tribute tends to be more frequently in the form of labor rather than goods, since labor can be more easily mobilized through the idiom of either kinship or ritual obligation. Areas close to the center pay higher levels of tribute and provide labor more frequently, since they are more easily subject to coercive force. However, tribute payment drops off with distance from the center so that, for example, the more peripheral settlements in the Alur segmentary state recognized the ritual and political legitimacy of the centralized authority but paid virtually no tribute or labor to the center (Southall 1956:81–82).

Recasting this model in terms of the variables outlined by Blanton and his colleagues, one would expect segmentary state societies to be characterized by spatially variable levels of economic integration and relatively low levels of organizational complexity. Central authority in a segmentary state lacks the power to extract consistently high levels of surplus from the hinterlands. Similarly, the distance decay in centralized power would also make it difficult to maintain consistent, reliable modes of exchange with the countryside. Rural settlements in such polities would thus have few positive or negative incentives impelling them toward economic specialization in the sense of surplus production for exchange. Instead, villages would maintain a generalized, flexible subsistence system aimed at preserving a high degree of local political and economic autonomy.

In contrast to segmentary states, unitary states lie at the upper end of the continuum of scale, complexity, and integration (Fig. 1). Unitary states have a strongly defined hierarchical administrative structure with a centralized monopoly of political, military, and fiscal power exercised by a specialized ruling class. In this hierarchical system, similar powers are not repeated at all levels, but certain powers are reserved at the top of the structure and lesser powers distributed to the lower levels of it. Unitary states exert control within clear territorial limits. The combination of centralized power, monopoly of force, and highly organized bureaucracy can be used by centers in unitary states to maintain access to rural surpluses through tribute, trade, or direct control of village lands and herds. As a result, rural economies in unitary states tend to develop a high degree of productive specialization in response to the demand by centers for agricultural and pastoral products.

The high degree of centralization and the increasing monopoly of military force in unitary states give the centralized authorities the power to extract rural surpluses in any or all of the following three ways: direct control over rural lands and herds, the extraction of tribute, and the maintenance of secure, reliable conditions for the balanced exchange of products between centers and hinterlands. Whichever method is employed, the centers in unitary states gain long-term access to rural resources. At the same time, consistently high levels of demand by centers for agricultural and pastoral products push the rural economies of unitary states toward the specialized production of large-scale food surpluses.

The terms "segmentary" and "unitary" states must not be considered rigid categories but instead convenient labels for opposite ends of a continuum in the scale, complexity, and integration of early polities. The value of the segmentary state model lies in its explicit recognition of variability in the degree of political centralization in state societies. In addition, for a given polity, the segmentary state model gives a spatial component to variation in centralized authority. This framework allows us to describe the political and economic relationships between centers and their hinterlands in geographical terms that can be verified by archaeological survey and excavation.

The segmentary state model is particularly useful in characterizing small-scale ("Podunk") polities or states in the earliest stages of development. Rural organization in these societies should differ markedly from that of the specialized, surplus-producing hinterlands that develop with the emergence of more strongly centralized, highly integrated, unitary states.

Changing Patterns of Rural Organization in the Leilan Hinterlands, Syria

The region around Tell Leilan, on the Khabur Plains in Syria, forms an ideal area in which to study the roles of scale, complexity, and integration in center-hinterland relations of early state societies in the Near East (Fig. 2). Excavations at Leilan conducted by Harvey Weiss of Yale University have shown that in Leilan period II, circa 2500–2200 B.C., the site expanded sixfold from 15 to 90 ha (Weiss 1983, 1990). Shortly afterwards, a large fortification wall was built around the site. With this development, Leilan became one of the largest urban centers on the Khabur Plains. Concurrent with this urban expansion, a major reorganization of craft production took place with the emergence of mass-produced, highly standardized undecorated fineware pottery (Schwartz 1988; Blackman, Stein, and Vandiver 1993; G. Stein and Blackman 1993). The changes in site size and ceramic manufacture argue for a related complex of demographic, economic, and political developments that apparently reflect the emergence of complex societies in this area. The magnitude of these changes forces us to ask how the regional economy of the Khabur Plains developed in order to meet the demand for food and agricultural commodities generated by this newly emergent urban center.

To study the relationship between urban development and rural organization, an intensive regional survey of the Leilan hinterlands was conducted by Gil Stein and Patricia Wattenmaker (Stein and Wattenmaker 1990, in press). The changes observed in the scale, complexity, and integration of the settlement system argue for the development of a centralized,

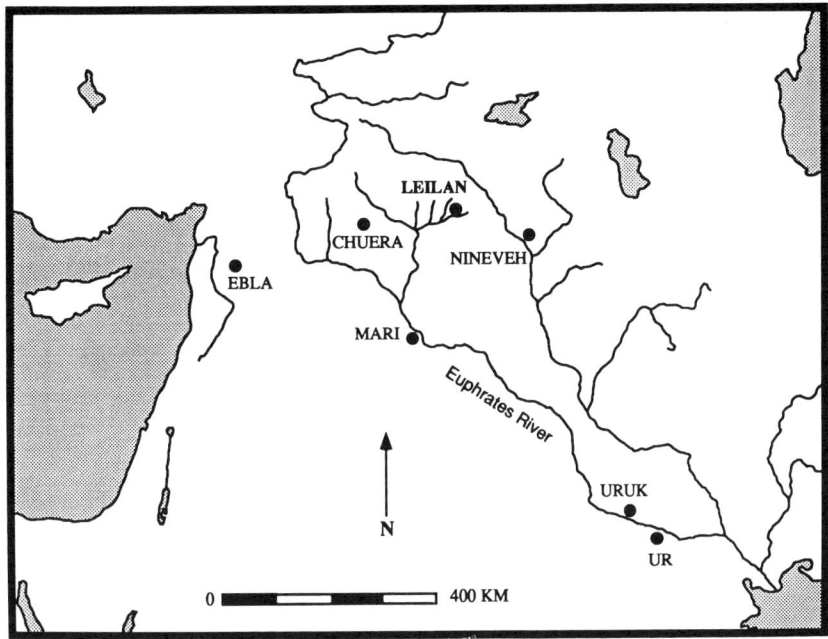

Fig. 2. The Near East, showing location of Tell Leilan and other selected third-millennium sites.

unitary state in this area during the mid–third millennium B.C.

Shifts in site size provide evidence for increasing complexity in the settlement system (Fig. 3). The two-level site size hierarchy of villages and towns in the preurban period III shows clear signs of expansion and differentiation into a four-tiered system with the emergence of centers and secondary centers during the urban period. Changes in the scale and integration of the Leilan regional system were examined by mapping the relationship between population distribution and available agricultural land (Figs. 4 and 5). Population estimates were first derived for each settlement by multiplying site size times Adams's (1981:69) suggested figure of 100 people per occupied hectare in villages, or 60 people per occupied hectare in larger centers such as Leilan. Following Weiss (1986:95), the latter population density is lower because of the larger amount of nonresidential public space in urban settlements. In both cases, these are conservative estimates (cf. Kramer 1982 and Van Beek 1982 for higher figures). For the traditional dry-farming economy of the Khabur Plains, 3 ha per person has been suggested as the minimum amount of agricultural land needed for subsistence (Weiss 1986:95), assuming an alternate-year fallow system and an overall agricultural productivity approximately half that of irrigation agriculture in southern Mesopotamia (Adams 1981:87, but see also Johnson 1973:98 for a lower estimate of minimum amounts of land necessary for subsistence in the irrigation zone). Multiplying the estimated population of each site times 3 ha per person of agricultural land gave the estimated minimum sustaining area for that settlement. These calculations suggest that both the scale of the Leilan regional system and its level of integration increased markedly from the preurban to the urban period.

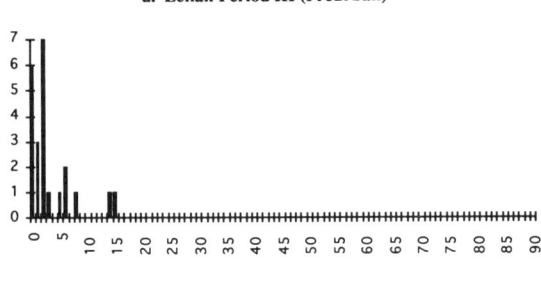

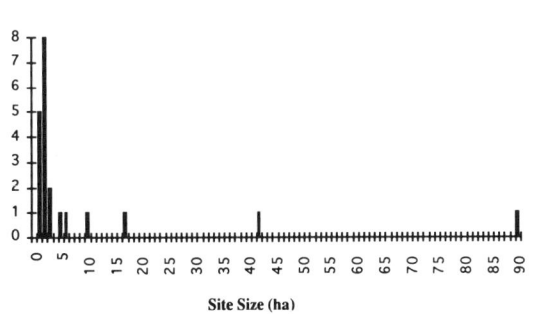

Fig. 3. Leilan Regional Survey site size distributions. (a) Period III (preurban). (b) Period II (urban).

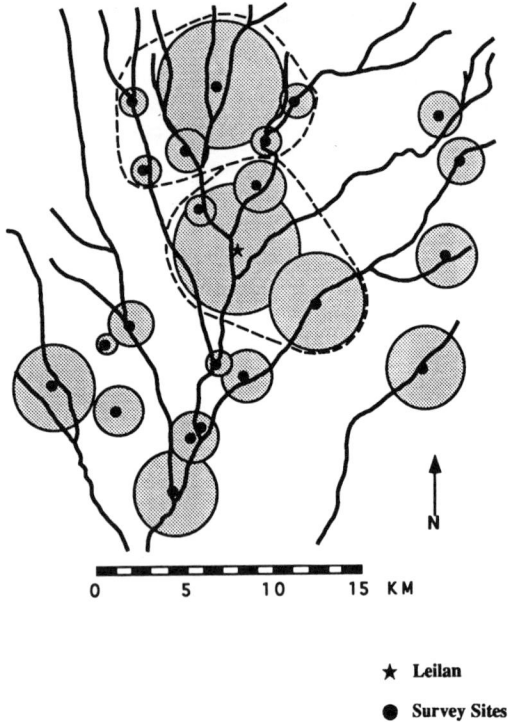

Fig. 4. Period III estimated agricultural sustaining areas in the Leilan hinterlands.

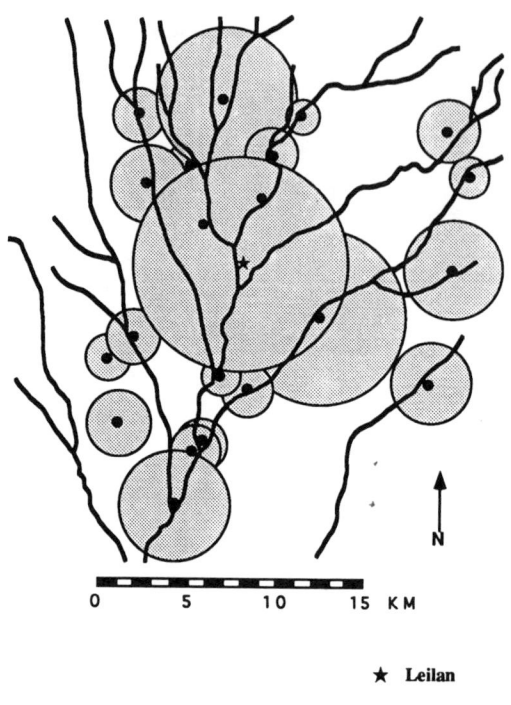

Fig. 5. Period II estimated agricultural sustaining areas in the Leilan hinterlands.

Figure 4 shows the preurban period III sites, with the shaded circles around them indicating their estimated minimum sustaining areas. The circles illustrate the amount of land needed by each settlement, rather than any exact configuration of fields. These estimates indicate that ample agricultural land was available to the period III inhabitants of all sites in the Leilan area. This implies a high degree of subsistence autonomy with little need for the exchange of large-scale agricultural surpluses between the villages and the towns. Equally important, the spacing between sustaining areas suggests a relatively fragmented system of at least two adjacent settlement clusters enclosed by dotted lines on Figure 4: one surrounding Leilan and the other consisting of villages around the center of Dougir.

In the more urbanized period II, there is ample evidence for expansion of settlement size at every level of the system. A large degree of overlap develops between the agricultural sustaining areas of virtually all sites in the Leilan hinterland (Fig. 5). These overlaps point to areas of potential constriction in the amount of land directly available for farming by the inhabitants of Leilan. The sustaining area of Leilan also overlaps markedly with that of at least eight surrounding settlements. This circumscription of the Leilan sustaining area suggests that the urban center lacked sufficient land to meet its subsistence needs. If this was the case, then the surrounding villages and secondary centers must have supplied agricultural surpluses to the urban center at Leilan.

Rank-size distributions also serve to measure regional-level political and economic integration in the Leilan settlement system. A poorly integrated regional system can be expected to have relative autonomy or limited interaction among settlements. In contrast, a high level of regional integration would mean that close linkages exist both horizontally (between different settlements of the same size) and vertically (between different levels of the settlement hierarchy, such as centers, towns, and villages) (Johnson 1980, 1987).

Geographers have found that in many urbanized regional systems there is a relationship between the size of a site and its rank in the settlement hierarchy, such that a double logarithmic plot of these two variables forms a straight-line log-linear or log-normal distribution (Haggett 1966:101). This type of patterning apparently reflects a high degree of regional economic and/or political integration (Fig. 6). Conversely, the degree to which a region's rank-size distribution deviates

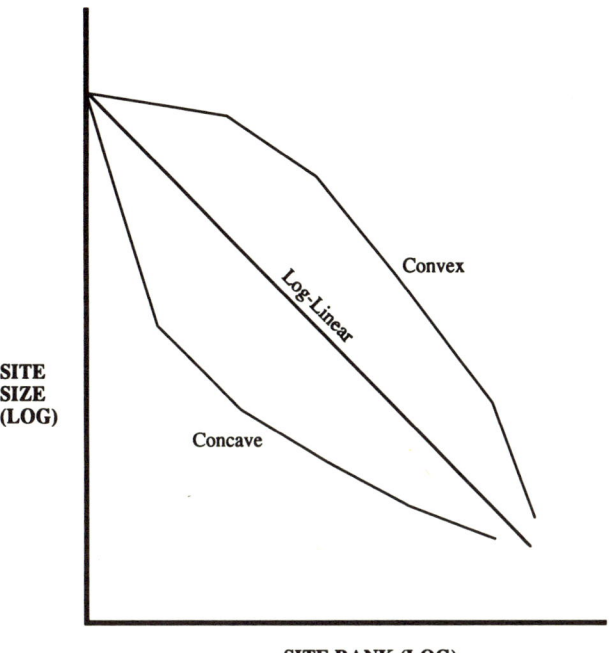

Fig. 6. Types of rank-size distributions.

from this log-linear pattern reflects lower levels of regional integration (Johnson 1980). Rank-size distributions show that the level of regional economic integration increased markedly from the preurban to the urban period, as the expanding center of Leilan extended its control over the countryside.

Figure 7a shows the rank-size distribution for preurban settlements in the Leilan area. These sites clearly deviate from the log-linear distribution; instead they form a convex curve. Convexity of this type suggests low levels of interaction between settlements in the region as a whole. The convexity of the preurban rank-size distribution apparently results from what Robert Paynter has called "pooling" or the "lumping together" (Paynter 1982) in our survey area of at least two complete but independent settlement systems. These results are consistent with the evidence of site location and estimated sustaining areas, which also suggests that at least two distinct settlement clusters existed in the survey area.

In contrast to this fragmented system, during the following period of urban expansion at Leilan, evidence for increasing regional integration can be seen in the emergence of a con-

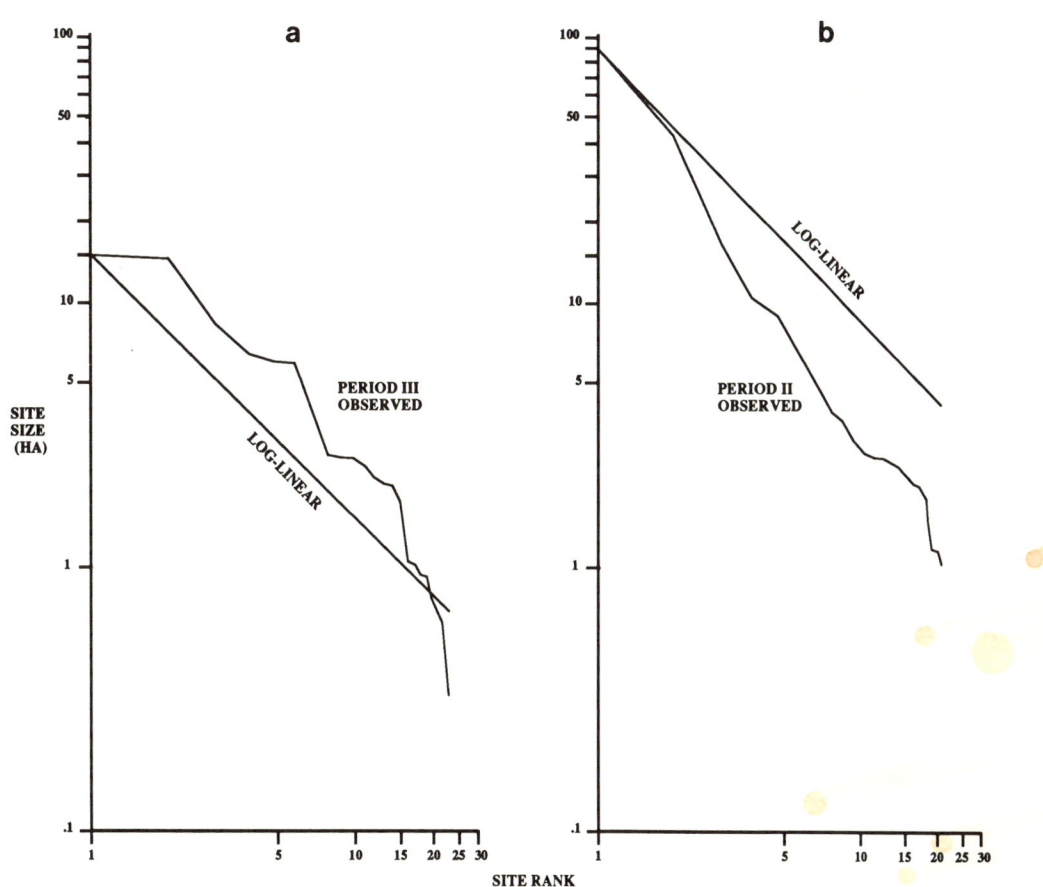

Fig. 7. Rank-size distribution for sites. (a) Period III. (b) Period II.

cave rank-size distribution of site sizes (Fig. 7b). Concave distributions are characteristic of "primate" systems in which a single very large center dominates many small, undifferentiated settlements (Smith 1976:30–32). Primate patterns commonly occur in the regional systems of newly emergent state societies (e.g., Crumley 1976). The concave rank-size pattern of the Leilan area in the period of urbanization seems to reflect a partially integrated, dendritic regional system (Kelley 1976; Smith 1976:34–36; Paynter 1982). Dendritic patterns of site size and location are generally associated with a centralized economy in which one or two large centers dominate the surrounding countryside (Kelley 1976:219). In a dendritic system, the vertical linkages between different levels of the settlement hierarchy are stronger than the horizontal connections between settlements of similar rank (Johnson 1980:242). As a result, goods and information tend to move vertically along the village-center axis, rather than horizontally in village-to-village exchange. The combined evidence of agricultural sustaining areas, site sizes, and site locations suggests that cereal surpluses in the Leilan region were moving upward in this type of dendritic network from the villages to the urban center.

Ceramic Production

Although *agricultural* production was strongly oriented toward the extraction of tribute to supply urban centers, the ceramic evidence suggests that period II craft production was localized, with little evidence so far for regional exchange. Numerous kiln wasters, consisting of large fused stacks of greenish fineware bowls, have been found in the Leilan lower town (see, e.g., Meijer 1986:Fig. 18r; Akkermans 1990:581) and provide clear evidence for the mass production of ceramics during Leilan period II (Senior and Weiss 1992; Blackman, Stein, and Vandiver 1993). The survey found that fragments of stacked kiln wasters for exactly the same ceramic types occurred not only at Leilan but also in at least three of the surrounding village sites. Instrumental neutron activation analyses of these wasters and other survey pottery also suggest that ceramic production took place more or less independently at every level of the settlement hierarchy—centers, secondary centers, and villages (G. Stein and Blackman 1991, 1993). Clearly, ceramics provide just one line of evidence about the regional organization of craft production. However, the available evidence indicates that craft production in period II was oriented toward local consumption rather than regional exchange. Ceramics and cereals seem to have circulated according to different rules, in distinct economic spheres.

The preceding results suggest that the transition from the preurban to the urban period at Leilan involved a set of economic and political changes consistent with development from a system of small-scale segmentary states into a highly centralized, unitary state on the Khabur Plains. The preurban settlement pattern of period III was characterized by a poorly integrated pattern of small-scale competing towns (Leilan and Dougir) and their surrounding villages. These towns appear to have had relatively low levels of control over rural productive resources. Thus the period III locational evidence is consistent with the expectations we have outlined for center-hinterland relations in a segmentary state. However, by the mid–third millennium, in period II, Leilan had expanded to become the largest center in this part of the Khabur Plains, absorbing its onetime rival Dougir into a large-scale, urban-centered, unitary state.

During this urban period, Leilan and its hinterland apparently formed a vertically integrated, regional system in which the center extracted agricultural surpluses from the countryside through a dendritic network of secondary centers and towns. At the same time, each settlement in the system seems to have produced its own ceramics. This contrast between the organization of agriculture and that of craft production suggests that the regional economy of the Leilan area was based on an asymmetric, tributary system, rather than a more balanced relationship of local exchange. The development of a unitary state in the Leilan area clearly involved a shift in center-hinterland relations. Increased levels of urban demand coupled with emergent coercive power allowed the center at Leilan to extract consistently large food surpluses from the countryside. This process, in turn, transformed the Leilan hinterlands into a specialized village sector whose agricultural and possibly pastoral production was largely geared to urban needs.

Conclusions

I have argued here that the degree of regional political integration strongly influences the organization of rural production in early state societies. The cline of variation in scale, complexity, and integration from segmentary to unitary states provides a structural framework to define the relationships between central and peripheral communities. Segmentary states will have a low level of rural productive specialization because of their smaller scale, less centralized structure (lower complexity), and weak control over their hinterlands (lower level of integration). In unitary states, the volume and consistency of demand by centers for rural goods can generate strong incentives for villages to produce surplus agricultural and pastoral products for exchange. At the same time, the degree to which centers can exercise coercive control over their hinterlands can also push the hinterlands toward production of large-scale surpluses in the form of tribute. In either case, the scale, complexity, and high levels of integration in unitary states will elicit a higher level of rural productive specialization; however, as the Leilan example shows, village specialization will generally be limited to those commodities, such as food surpluses, for which there is high demand by the center.

Given the extractive, asymmetric character of center-village economic relations in those unitary states with tribute-based economies, it is only to be expected that villages would attempt to maintain the maximum degree of independence and resilience in the face of an unpredictable, constantly shifting political and economic environment. For this reason, any lapse in the ability of urban centers to extract tribute would be reflected in the countryside by a shift from the specialized production of surpluses back toward more generalized, subsistence-level production (e.g., Adams 1978, 1982).

The analytical framework for complex societies I have outlined here suggests that the opposition between "urban" and "rural" may be less important than the study of changing modes of regional organization. These are best studied through the use of continuous variables (e.g., scale, complexity, integration) rather than through a reliance on categorical differences between settlement types. In this way, village economic organization can provide a sensitive indicator of regional-level political organization in early state societies.

Note

The 1987 Tell Leilan Regional Survey was conducted as part of the Yale University Tell Leilan Project, directed by Harvey Weiss and supported by NEH grant RO-21483. The survey was directed by Gil Stein and Patricia Wattenmaker, assisted by Matthew Adams. In making field identifications of the survey ceramics, we benefited from discussions with Peter Akkermans, Laura Calderone, Jules Frane, Dale Mayo, Ingolf Thuesen, and Harvey Weiss concerning the periodization of material from their excavation areas. John Clark, Lisa Kealhofer, Dan Rogers, Glenn Schwartz, and Carla Sinopoli provided valuable comments on drafts of this chapter. Any remaining errors of omission or interpretation are entirely my own.

References Cited

Adams, Robert McC.
    1978 Strategies of Maximization, Stability, and Resilience in Mesopotamian Society, Settlement, and Agriculture. *Proceedings of the American Philosophical Society* 122:329–335.
    1981 *Heartland of Cities.* University of Chicago Press, Chicago.
    1982 Property Rights and Functional Tenure in Mesopotamian Rural Communities. In *Societies and Languages of the Ancient Near East: Studies in Honour of I. M. Diakonoff*, edited by M. A. Dandamayev et al., pp. 1–14. Aris and Phillips, Warminster, England.

Akkermans, Peter
    1990 Operation 3 in the Lower Town. Pp. 542–547 in H. Weiss, P. Akkermans, G. Stein, D. Parayre, and R. Whiting, 1985 Excavations at Tell Leilan, Syria. *American Journal of Archaeology* 94:529–581.

Blackman, M. James, Gil J. Stein, and Pamela Vandiver
    1993 The Standardization Hypothesis and Ceramic Mass Production: Technological, Compositional, and Metric Indexes of Craft Specialization at Tell Leilan, Syria. *American Antiquity* 58:60–80.

Blanton, Richard, Stephen Kowalewski, Gary Feinman, and Jill Appel
    1981 *Ancient Mesoamerica: A Comparison of Change in Three Regions.* Cambridge University Press, Cambridge.

Crumley, Carole
    1976 Toward a Locational Definition of State Systems of Settlement. *American Anthropologist* 78:59–73.

Deimel, A.
    1931 Sumerische Tempelwirtschaft zur Zeit Urukaginas und seiner Vorgänger. *Analecta Orientalia* 2:71–113.

Diakonoff, Igor M.
    1974 *Structure of Society and State in Early Dynastic Sumer.* Undena Press, Malibu, Calif.
    1975 The Rural Community in the Ancient Near East. *Journal of the Economic and Social History of the Orient* 18:121–133.

Durkheim, Emile
    1933 *The Division of Labor in Society.* Free Press, New York.

Falkenstein, Adam
    1974 *The Sumerian Temple City.* Undena Press, Malibu, Calif.

Gelb, Ignace J.
    1969 On the Alleged Temple and State Economies in Ancient Mesopotamia. In *Studi in Onore di Edouardo Volterra*, pp. 137–154. Giuffre Editore, Milan.

Haggett, Peter
    1966 *Locational Analysis in Human Geography.* St. Martins Press, New York.

Johnson, Gregory A.
    1973 *Local Exchange and Early State Development in Southwestern Iran.* Museum of Anthropology, University of Michigan, Anthropological Papers, No. 51. University of Michigan, Ann Arbor.
    1980 Rank-Size Convexity and System Integration: A View from Archaeology. *Economic Geography* 56:234–247.
    1987 The Changing Organization of Uruk Administration on the Susiana Plain. In *The Archaeology of Western Iran*, edited

by F. Hole, pp. 107–139. Smithsonian Institution Press, Washington, D.C.

Kelley, Klara
- 1976 Dendritic Central-Place Systems and the Regional Organization of Navajo Trading Posts. In *Regional Analysis,* Vol. 1: *Economic Systems,* edited by C. A. Smith, pp. 219–254. Academic Press, New York.

Kramer, Carol
- 1982 *Village Ethnoarchaeology: Rural Iran in Archaeological Perspective.* Academic Press, New York.

Meijer, Diederik
- 1986 *A Survey in Northeastern Syria.* Nederlands Historisch-Archeologisch Instituut te Istanbul, Leiden, The Netherlands.

Netting, Robert McC.
- 1972 Sacred Power and Centralization: Aspects of Political Adaptation in Africa. In *Population Growth: Anthropological Implications,* edited by B. Spooner, pp. 219–244. MIT Press, Cambridge, Mass.

Paynter, Robert
- 1982 *Models of Spatial Inequality. Settlement Patterns in Historical Archaeology.* Academic Press, New York.

Schwartz, Glenn M.
- 1988 *A Ceramic Chronology from Tell Leilan: Operation 1.* Yale University Press, New Haven, Conn.

Schwartz, Glenn M., and Hans H. Curvers
- 1992 Tell al-Raqa'i 1989 and 1990: Further Investigations at a Small Rural Site of Early Urban Northern Mesopotamia. *American Journal of Archaeology* 96:397–419.

Senior, Louise, and Harvey Weiss
- 1992 Tell Leilan "Sila Bowls" and the Akkadian Reorganization of Subarian Agricultural Production. *Orient Express* 2:16–23.

Smith, Carol A.
- 1976 Regional Economic Systems: Linking Geographical Models and Socioeconomic Problems. In *Regional Analysis,* Vol. 1: *Economic Systems,* edited by C. A. Smith, pp. 3–63. Academic Press, New York.

Southall, Aidan
- 1956 *Alur Society.* W. Heffer and Sons, Cambridge.
- 1988 The Segmentary State in Africa and Asia. *Comparative Studies in Society and History* 30:52–82.

Stein, Burton
- 1977 The Segmentary State in South Indian History. In *Realm and Region in Traditional India,* edited by R. Fox, pp. 3–51. Duke University Program in Comparative Studies on Southern Asia, Monograph 14. Durham, N.C.
- 1980 *Peasant State and Society in Medieval South India.* Oxford University Press, New Delhi.

Stein, Gil
- 1987 Regional Economic Integration in Early State Societies: Third Millennium B.C. Pastoral Production at Gritille, Southeast Turkey. *Paléorient* 13:101–111.

Stein, Gil, and M. James Blackman
- 1991 Polities and Potters: Compositional and Metric Evidence for the Organization of Specialized Ceramic Production in Early Complex Societies. Paper presented at the American Anthropological Association Annual Meeting, Chicago.
- 1993 The Organizational Context of Specialized Craft Production in Early Mesopotamian States. *Research in Economic Anthropology* 14:29–59.

Stein, Gil, and Patricia Wattenmaker
- 1990 The 1987 Tell Leilan Regional Survey: Preliminary Report. In *Economy and Settlement in the Near East: Analyses of Ancient Sites and Materials,* edited by N. Miller, pp. 8–18. MASCA Research Papers in Science and Archaeology 7 (supplement). MASCA, University Museum, Philadelphia.
- In press Settlement Trends and the Emergence of Social Complexity in the Leilan Region of the Khabur Plains (Syria) from the Fourth to the Third Millennium B.C. In *The Origins of Northern Mesopotamian Civilization: Ninevite 5 Chronology, Economy, Society,* edited by H. Weiss. Yale University Press, New Haven, Conn.

Van Beek, Gus
- 1982 A Population Estimate for Marib: A Contemporary Tell Village in North Yemen. *Bulletin of the American Schools of Oriental Research* 248:62–67.

Weiss, Harvey
- 1983 Excavations at Tell Leilan and the Origins of North Mesopotamian Cities in the Third Millennium B.C. *Paléorient* 9:39–52.
- 1986 The Origins of Tell Leilan and the Conquest of Space in Third Millennium Mesopotamia. In *The Origins of Cities in Dry-Farming Syria and Mesopotamia in the Third Millennium B.C.,* edited by H. Weiss, pp. 71–108. Four Quarters, Guilford, Conn.
- 1990 Tell Leilan 1989: New Data for Mid-Third Millennium Urbanization and State Formation. *Mitteilungen der deutschen Orient-Gesellschaft* 122:193–218.

Wright, Henry
- 1969 *The Administration of Rural Production in an Early Mesopotamian Town.* Museum of Anthropology, University of Michigan, Anthropological Papers, No. 38. University of Michigan, Ann Arbor.

Wright, Henry T., Naomi Miller, and Richard Redding
- 1981 Time and Process in an Uruk Rural Center. In *L'archéologie de l'Iraq du début de l'époque néolithique à 333 avant notre ère,* edited by M.-T. Barrelet, pp. 265–284. Editions du CNRS, Paris.

CHAPTER THREE

Rural Economic Specialization and Early Urbanization in the Khabur Valley, Syria

GLENN M. SCHWARTZ

Whosoever possesses gold, or silver, or cattle, or sheep,
Shall wait at the gate of him who possesses grain.
    From the Sumerian disputation between "Ewe and Wheat"
                (Alster and Vanstiphout 1987:29–31)

THE IMPORTANCE OF THE RURAL hinterland during the development of early Near Eastern complex societies has been widely appreciated, most particularly in its role as the producer of agricultural surpluses to support urban-based elites and their dependents (Redman 1978:216; Liverani 1982; Adams 1984:95). Among the first to underscore the central role of food surplus in the development of sociopolitical complexity was V. G. Childe:

Society persuaded or compelled the farmers to produce a surplus of foodstuffs over and above their domestic requirements, and by concentrating this surplus used it to support a new *urban* population of specialized craftsmen, merchants, priests, officials and clerks. (Childe 1946:18)

Subsequently, Pearson (1957) and Adams (1966:46) asserted that the crucial issue was not the simple availability of surpluses but the existence of institutional mechanisms and appropriate technologies to extract and administer them. More recently, D'Altroy and Earle (1985) have discussed the possible workings of such mechanisms in the context of systems of "staple finance."

Investigation of the provisioning of cities and of urban-rural interrelations in early Near Eastern complex societies has relied until recently on textual data and on archaeological surface surveys. Third-millennium cuneiform texts from southern Mesopotamia and from Ebla in western Syria have revealed the existence of extensive agricultural holdings controlled by urban-based palaces and temples. These lands were cultivated by dependents or leased out in return for a pre-arranged proportion of the harvest. Occasionally, evidence is also available for agricultural lands controlled by local communities and allotted to community members on the basis of kinship, a system presumed to have preceded the advent of the state and to have persisted alongside it (Diakonoff 1975). But these texts provide only an incomplete picture, since they are written exclusively from an urban, elite perspective and largely date from periods when urbanization was already well established.

In the archaeological sphere, surface surveys such as those conducted by Robert McC. Adams have contributed an essential fund of data and insights on the changing relationship of city and hinterland, particularly in southern Mesopotamia and southwestern Iran (Adams 1966, 1981; Adams and Nissen 1972; Hole 1987). Survey work has allowed for the tracing of broad patterns in the utilization of the southern Mesopotamian and southwest Iranian countrysides, but it is also an incomplete effort, because its wide scope leaves us uninformed about changes in individual rural communities and the extent of their integration into new economic and social systems.

Excavation projects at small rural sites have finally begun in recent years, in part because rescue operations have compelled archaeologists to excavate at smaller sites in threatened areas. Such excavations have produced important new data on the rural Near Eastern landscape, even though few of them have had research programs explicitly framed to investigate urban-rural relationships. Most have concentrated instead on the excavation of the most imposing architectural units or on the documentation of occupation sequences.

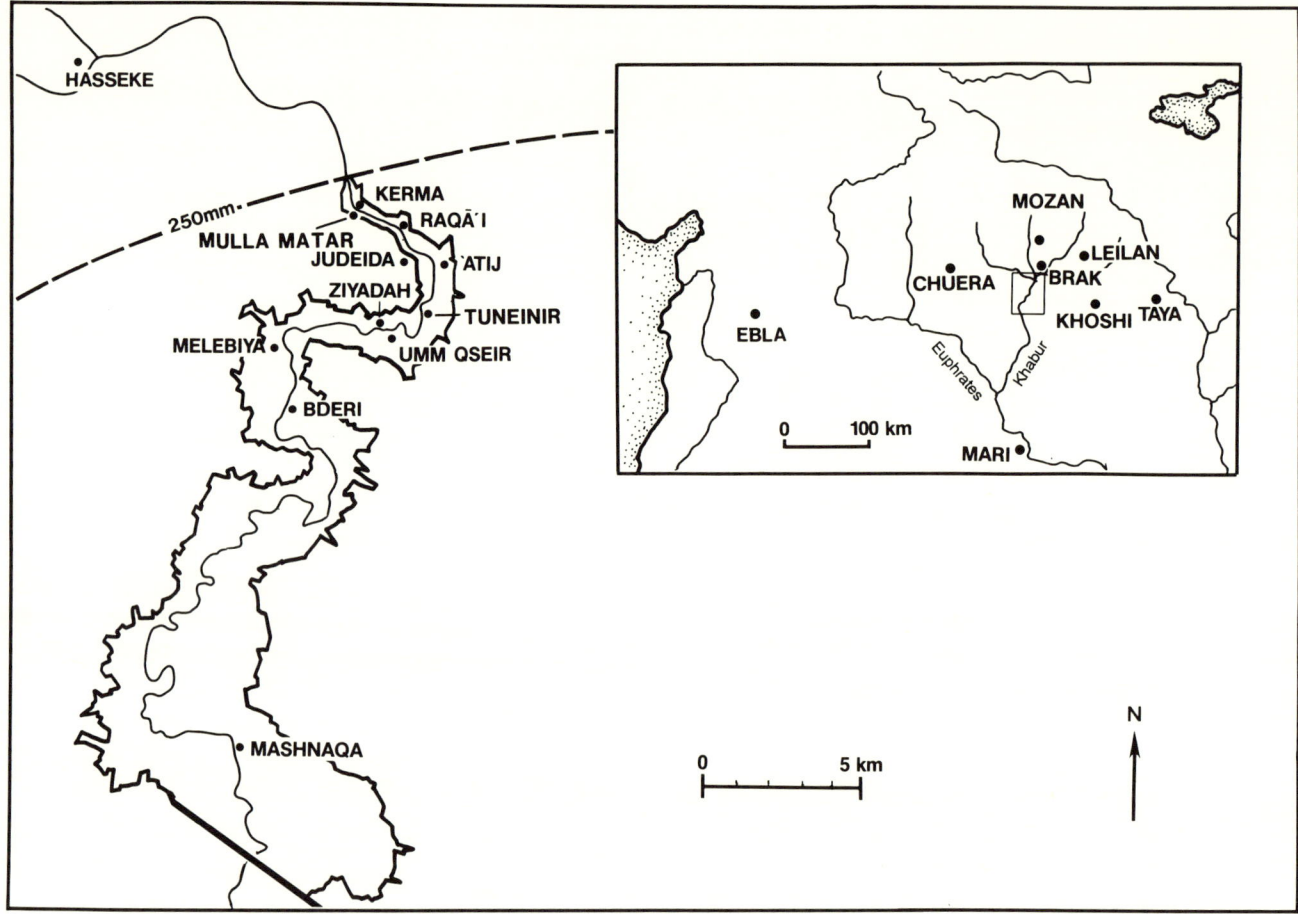

Fig. 8. The Middle Khabur salvage region. Inset: Syria and northern Mesopotamia with excavated third-millennium urban-size sites indicated.

This chapter discusses the results of a recent salvage project, the Johns Hopkins University–University of Amsterdam joint expedition to Tell al-Raqa'i, Syria. The Raqa'i project has aimed specifically at investigating the social and economic organization of a small rural community and the extent of its assimilation into the developing complex polities of the region. Results of the excavations at Tell al-Raqa'i will be briefly outlined, and the implications of these results for understanding early urban-rural interrelationships in Syria and northern Mesopotamia will be discussed. I will argue that Tell al-Raqa'i was one of a set of small riverine communities that specialized in large-scale grain storage and processing for the benefit of developing elites in larger centers elsewhere.

Tell al-Raqa'i: Excavation Results

Tell al-Raqa'i is located in the middle Khabur region of northeast Syria, 12 km downstream from the modern provincial capital of Hasseke on the east bank of the Khabur River (Fig. 8). The site has been excavated as part of an archaeological salvage operation in an area to be flooded by the construction of a hydroelectric dam on the Khabur; the lake created by the dam will inundate sites on either side of the river for a length of some 20 km (Monchambert 1984).

The salvage region is in what is today an agriculturally marginal zone that receives an average of 200–250 mm annual rainfall, too little to sustain a viable rainfall agriculture regime (Wirth 1971). Traditionally, fields on either side of the river have been irrigated with river water, and beyond this irrigated band of a few kilometers stretches the semiarid steppe, utilized historically by pastoralist groups as grazing land for flocks.

Tell al-Raqa'i was primarily occupied in the early to middle third millennium B.C., the period of the earliest indigenous urbanization and state formation in Syria and Northern Mesopotamia. We are aware, by at least the middle of the third millennium B.C., of fortified urban centers 50 to 100 ha in area, such as Ebla (Tell Mardikh), Tell Chuera, Tell Mozan, and Tell Leilan, as well as written evidence affirming the existence of associated state structures. Tell Leilan, which offers the most precise dating of the urbanization process, expanded from a center of some 15 ha to a circumvallated 90-ha community in the Leilan IIId period, approximately corresponding to the twenty-seventh to twenty-sixth centuries B.C. (Weiss 1990; Weiss and Calderone in press).

Five full seasons of excavation and several short study seasons (1986–1993) have revealed seven occupation levels at Tell al-Raqa'i (Curvers 1987; Curvers and Schwartz 1990; Schwartz and Curvers 1992). Level 1, the latest occupation, consists of the minimal remains of a Hellenistic period settlement; earlier contexts, designated levels 2–7, are dated to the early and middle third millennium B.C. Our research design aimed at acquiring a broad horizontal sample from the latest and thus most accessible third-millennium occupations in order to gain a view of the community as a whole. Smaller samples were obtained from the earlier contexts for investigation of temporal changes at the site.

LEVEL 2

Level 2, the latest third-millennium occupation, is dated ceramically to the twenty-sixth to twenty-fifth centuries B.C., contemporary with early period II at Tell Leilan and somewhat earlier than Late Early Dynastic III at Tell Brak. The level was heavily eroded and disturbed by later intrusions. Excavated remains included remnants of small-scale mudbrick rectilinear architecture in the northern and western parts of the mound; in the fill of one of these structures a small clay tablet with apparent numerical notations was recovered. Otherwise, level 2 was primarily composed of child burials distributed in the northwest and eastern parts of the site, dug into level 3 architecture. Some of these graves were in simple pits with few associated burial goods, but others were in mudbrick constructions and were provided with extensive funerary equipment. Burial goods included up to ten ceramic vessels, including examples of Metallic Ware, a presumed luxury item; copper/bronze toggle pins used to attach clothing at the shoulder; copper/bronze spiral ornaments, probably used for hair arrangement; pendants of limestone, shell, and copper/bronze in anthropomorphic, zoomorphic, or other shapes; and stone beads from necklaces, bracelets, and other forms of personal decoration.

The distinction between well-furnished child burials in mudbrick enclosures and child burials in simple pits with few goods may imply the existence of social stratification at the site (Brown 1981:30; Schwartz 1986). The pendants, beads, and copper-bronze toggle pins of the richer burials—which have abundant parallels in elite art from such urban centers as Mari, Chuera, and Brak—indicate that the inhabitants of Raqa'i wore ornaments that either emulated urban art or were obtained directly from urban centers.

LEVEL 3

Level 3 is dated to the end of the Ninevite V period, since its ceramic assemblage included incised Ninevite V sherds comparable to examples from late in the Ninevite V sequence at Tell Leilan (Leilan IIId) and Tell Brak in the upper Khabur Plains (Curvers and Schwartz 1990:15, 17). The Ninevite V period, defined primarily by a pottery assemblage found across northern Mesopotamia from the Khabur drainage to the area east of the Tigris, appears to have included part of the later fourth millennium and most of the first half of the third millennium B.C. (Schwartz 1985; Weiss and Calderone in press). In absolute dates, the level 3 occupation probably should be assigned to the twenty-seventh to twenty-sixth centuries B.C.

The level 3 architectural plan is the most coherent and complete obtained from Tell al-Raqa'i and provides a view of the community in what is perhaps close to its entirety (Fig. 9). Immediately evident from the level 3 plan is the organization of the settlement into a collection of small-scale structures that are arranged in a radial pattern around a thick-walled rounded building (whose south segment is now eroded). The small-scale architecture includes a number of apparent domestic structures consisting of two square or rectangular rooms, one slightly larger than the other (e.g., areas 1–2, 15–16, 18–19, and 20–83), and portions of other architectural units. This architecture often had lime-plastered packed mud or mudbrick features of uncertain function inside the rooms, as well as clay ovens (*tannurs*) and small round surfaces of burned clay on the floors, apparently fireplaces.

A surprising discovery in the north central part of the site was a one-room shrine or temple (area 21) with two stepped altars, isolated from neighboring structures by a thin mudbrick and stone enclosure wall. The temple is so identified on the basis of its plan (comparable to that of small shrines known from urban sites elsewhere in contemporaneous Syro-Mesopotamia), its recessed entry, its elaborate foundations, the stepped mudbrick altars, and the conspicuous divergence of its plan and orientation from those of other structures at the site (Schwartz in press). No religious equipment was found in the structure, which had been cleaned and filled with mudbricks as the foundation for a later (religious?) building that is no longer preserved.

West of the temple (areas 4–6) was a group of three semisubterranean rectangular mudbrick constructions we term "silos," extending down as deep as 3 m. The Rounded Building appears to have been industrial in character; inside

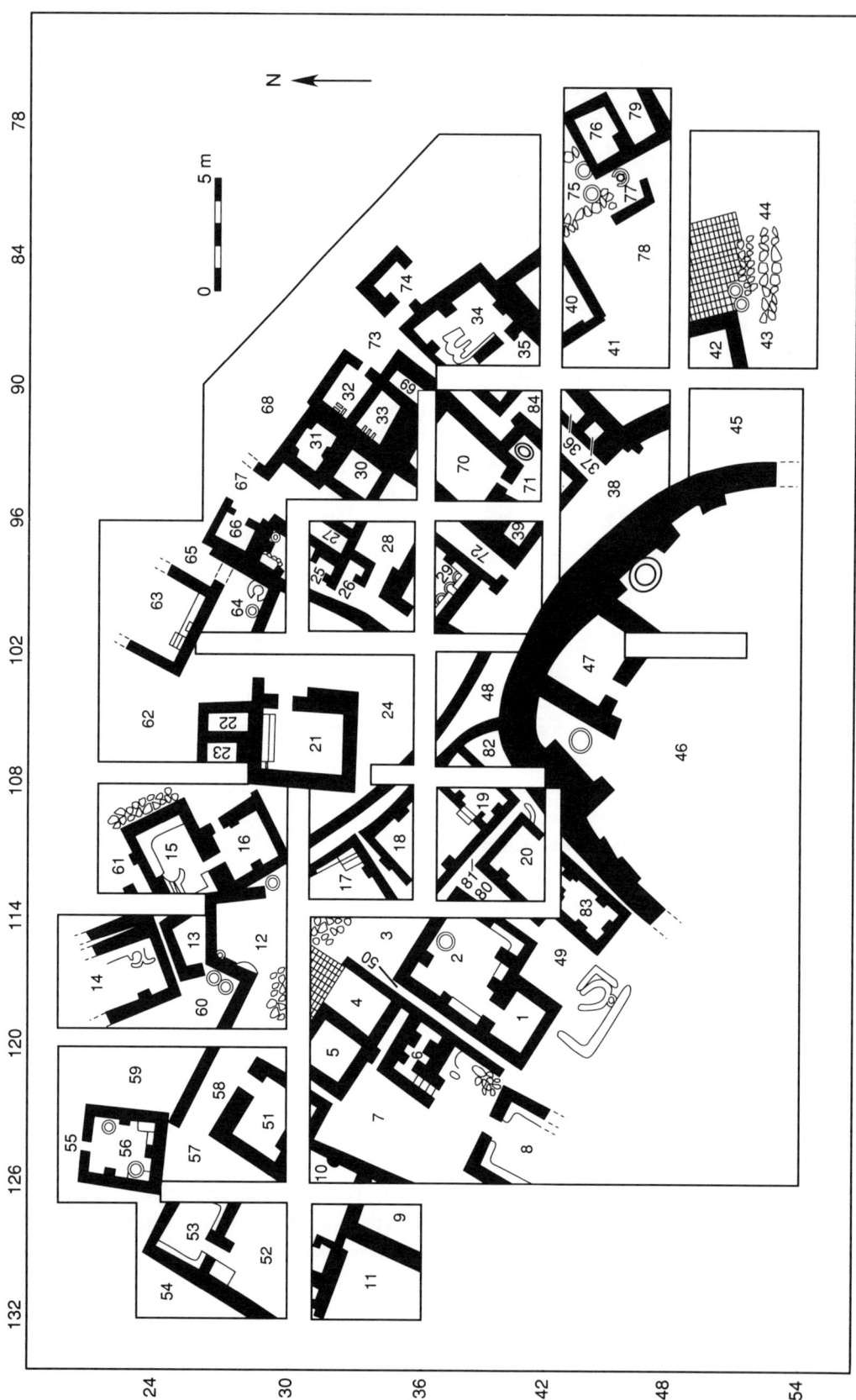

Fig. 9. Architectural plan of Tell al-Raqa'i level 3.

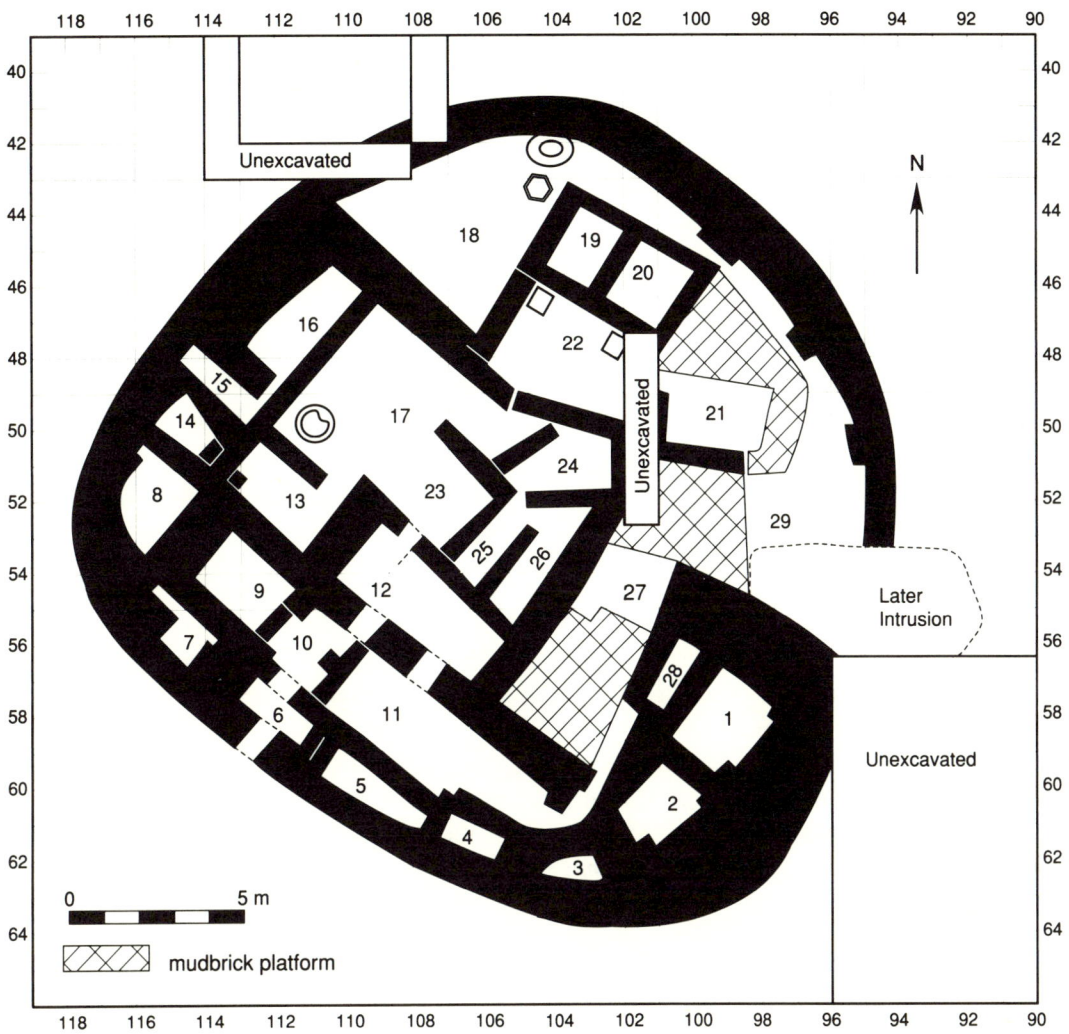

Fig. 10. Architectural plan of Rounded Building, Tell al-Raqa'i level 4 (dashed lines represent blocked doorways).

were mudbrick floors and platforms, ovens, and ash lenses sloping down from the center of the building to the north. A similar "industrial" area was identified in the southeast part of the site, where a concentration of ovens and mudbrick platforms was identified (areas 40–44 and 75–79). A system of streets or alleys separated the smaller buildings from the Rounded Building and divided the blocks of smaller-scale architecture from one another.

A handful of cylinder seal impressions on clay from level 3 contexts provide evidence of the administrative technology in use at the site.

LEVEL 4

The ceramic assemblage of level 4, contemporary with the earlier phases of the Raqa'i Rounded Building, was dominated by handmade cookingware sherds that are difficult to use for relative chronological purposes. The few examples of incised Ninevite V pottery, however, correlate to Leilan IIIb and early IIIc (mid- to late Ninevite V period, perhaps twenty-ninth through twenty-seventy centuries B.C.).

The excavations of level 4 revealed a much better-preserved Rounded Building, extant to a height of 3 m, with small-scale architecture outside it. The Rounded Building included mudbrick platforms and mudbrick semisubterranean "silos" without doors (Fig. 10). In the northern part of the building were two silos (areas 19 and 20) next to an area of ovens, south of which were silos with corbeled vaulted roofs (areas 1, 2, 7, 21, and 27). Room 1 extended down 4 m and had a square window near its top; a vaulted buttress supported the vault of the roof. These doorless vaulted structures may be comparable to the vaulted silos with access from the roof represented on Uruk- and Jemdet Nasr–period seal impressions found at Susa in southwestern Iran (Schwartz 1987:Fig. 2).

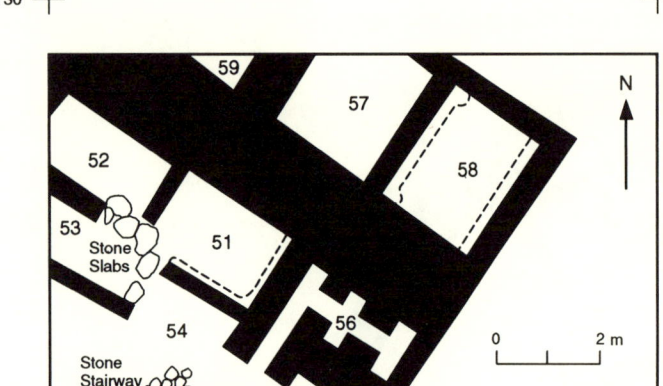

Fig. 11. Schematic plan of northwest silo area, Tell al-Raqa'i level 4.

Excavations in the western part of the Rounded Building revealed a series of small rooms, many of which had doorways with corbeled arches that were later blocked, perhaps to facilitate use of the rooms for storage purposes with access from above. The walls of these rooms, built against the outer wall of the building, often were not bonded to one another, indicating an agglutinative pattern of room construction. One of these small rooms contained scores of clay sealings, two of which had cylinder seal impressions.

In room 9, a piece of painted wall plaster was found on a fragment of collapsed mudbrick in the southeast corner of the room. The fragment bears the depiction of a human figure wearing a short skirt facing left and holding out an object (Dunham 1993). Examples of wall painting are extremely rare from early third-millennium Syria and Mesopotamia, and this one is all the more curious because of its location in a building with apparent industrial and storage functions.

Northwest of the Rounded Building, below the level 3 silos, a complex of as many as six "silos" was exposed, including areas 56–58, which continued to be used in level 3 (=level 3 areas 4–6) (Figs. 9 and 11). A stairway constructed of limestone slabs southwest of the silo complex appears to have allowed access down into the silos from the south. South of the stairway was small-scale rectilinear architecture, including a rectangular room (area 46) with lime-plastered walls, floor, and mudbrick benches as well as a lime-plastered rectangular mud basin leading into a jar sunk into the room floor.

LEVELS 5–7

Soundings to virgin soil at Raqa'i have demonstrated that several occupation levels preceded the construction of the Rounded Building (Schwartz and Curvers in press). These levels yielded grill-like architecture similar to the substructure of the granary excavated at Telul-eth-Thalathat Tell V in northern Iraq (Fukai, Horiuchi, and Matsutani 1974; Schwartz 1987). The small sample of pottery associated with these earliest levels at Raqa'i indicates a date in the early to middle Ninevite V period, equivalent to either Leilan IIIa or IIIb, at the beginning of the third millennium.

The Middle Khabur Network of Specialized Sites

The excavation results indicate that, contrary to our original expectations, Tell al-Raqa'i was not a self-sufficient farming village but a specialized community with probable economic links to larger centers elsewhere. The Rounded Building with its platforms and "silos" in levels 4 and 3, as well as the complex of silos outside it, attests to specialized production and bulk storage at the site, and the seal impressions and numerical tablet indicate the administrative technology employed. A consideration of evidence from nearby contemporaneous sites allows us to comment more specifically on the nature of the specialized activities at Raqa'i.

Excavations at adjacent sites in the middle Khabur reveal that Raqa'i was part of a *complex* of small specialized sites distributed along the river. At 'Atij, 2 km downstream from Raqa'i, excavated under the direction of Michel Fortin of Laval University, the high mound was comprised of facilities interpreted as grain storage emplacements, associated with administrative tools, such as clay tokens or "calculi," a cylinder seal, and a clay tablet with numerical notations (Fortin 1988, 1990). Kerma, 2 km upstream from Raqa'i, excavated by Muntaha Saghieh, provides conclusive evidence that grain storage was a primary concern of these small communities; here the site was dominated by a fortified storage facility filled with a thick deposit of carbonized barley still in situ. Differentiation in the nature of the botanical remains found in the various rooms of the structure suggests that the facilities consisted of a central grain storage area surrounded by rooms for grain processing (Saghieh 1991).

A few kilometers downstream on the other side of the river at Tell Ziyadeh, recent excavations have uncovered an early third-millennium structure with doorless cubicles reminiscent of the Raqa'i "silos"; the building has been interpreted as a grain storage installation (Buccellati, Buia, and Reimer 1991).

Tuneinir (Fuller and Fuller 1991), Mashnaqa (Monchambert 1987), Bderi (Pfälzner 1986–1987), Mulla Matar (Sürenhagen 1990), Rad Shaqrah (Bielinski 1992), and Melebiya (M. Lebeau, pers. comm.) were also occupied in Ninevite V times, but their limited excavated samples do not yet allow for the determination of economic specialization at these sites. At Bderi, perhaps the largest of the middle Khabur Ninevite V sites (circa 5 ha), the excavations have revealed the presence of a town enclosure wall with orthostat gate (Pfälzner 1986–1987).

Because of the nature of the specialized facilities at Raqa'i and the location of the site between two grain storage centers, it appears most likely that the specialized facilities at Raqa'i were devoted to processing and storage of grain as well. The mudbrick platforms, ovens, and predominance of cooking-ware sherds in the Rounded Building, for example, may imply the drying and parching of grain prior to its long-term storage (Hillman 1985:12ff). Parching or roasting of barley, which may have been the predominant cultigen at Raqa'i, is well attested in later Mesopotamian sources (CAD, *qalitu*, p. 59, *laptu* B, p. 96; Postgate 1984:105; Grégoire 1992:332), and Greco-Roman texts also refer to the practice (e.g., Thucydides Book VI, 22); the Roman festival Fornacalia was a celebration of the roasting of grain for purposes of preservation (Dumézil 1970:159–160; Ovid *Fasti* II, 521–532, 693–694; Pliny *Natural History* xviii, 61, 73, 74).[1]

The complex of small economically specialized middle Khabur sites seems to have declined after the close of the Ninevite V period. At Raqa'i, the northwest silo complex was partially rebuilt in the post–Ninevite V level 2 and yielded the numerical notation tablet mentioned previously, but there is no trace of subsequent occupation until the Hellenistic period. Similarly, the latest Bronze Age contexts at 'Atij appear to date to a Raqa'i level 2 time frame (Fortin 1990:Fig. 28), when the silos and other storage facilities of previous levels were apparently no longer in extensive use. The end of the Bronze Age occupation at Kerma and Mashnaqa also appears to fall within the same period (Monchambert 1987; Saghieh 1991). Although occupation continued at other middle Khabur sites later in the third millennium—particularly at the larger settlements of Melebiya and Bderi (Pfälzner 1988; Lebeau 1989) as well as at Judeida (Gudeda), opposite 'Atij on the west bank of the Khabur (Fortin 1990)—there is no evidence for large-scale grain storage or processing at these sites.[2]

MIDDLE KHABUR STORAGE CAPABILITIES

A preliminary estimate of the capacity of the storage facilities of the middle Khabur can give us an idea of the number of people that could have been sustained by their contents. Attempting a very rough calculation of the volume of the Raqa'i level 4 silos, we can estimate at least circa 125 m^3 of storage for the excavated sample (circa 600 m^2 excavated out of perhaps 2,000–3,000 m^2 of level 4 occupation) (Table 1).[3] Moreover, if the rooms in the southwest part of the Rounded Building whose doors were blocked in a later level 4 phase were used as silos, as has been hypothesized (Schwartz and Curvers 1992:407), another 50 m^3 or so would be added to our figure.

Assuming a capacity of some 150 m^3 of storage in Raqa'i level 4, we may attempt to ascertain the size of the population that the stored grain could support. Frank Hole (1991), considering this problem for the storage facilities at 'Atij and Kerma as well as Raqa'i, used figures of 2,500 calories required per person per day and 3,510 calories per kg of grain. In addition, he suggested that 20 percent of the total grain produced would be lost to spoilage, and another 20 percent would be reserved for seed for future crops. Therefore, 433 kg of grain would be required for each person per year on average (Table 2). If we use this figure together with Hole's estimate that 2.25 m^3 will accommodate 1,000 kg of grain, our 150 m^3 of storage would support 154 people.[4] Alternatively, using figures employed by Hunt (1987) (see Table 2), we arrive at 143 kg grain per person per year and, given an estimate of 2 m^3 per 1,000 kg of grain, a total of 524 people who could be supported by 150 m^3 of storage.

It is probable that a more useful estimate will fall between these two. Hole's figure of 2,500 calories assumes that grain was the only source of nutrition, an unlikely scenario (Ellison 1981), whereas Hunt's figure of 15 percent for spoilage and his 10 percent seed ratio might be too low (H. T. Wright 1969:21; Adams 1981:86; cf. also the average of circa 17 percent seed ratio for a traditional Iranian village in Kramer 1982: Table 2.2, note d, and Table 2.3). If, for example, we reduce the number of calories needed for grain per person per day to 1,500 (cf. also Hassan 1981:18) and retain figures of 20 percent for seed and 20 percent for spoilage, although they may still be too high, 150 m^3 would accommodate enough grain for 280 people (given 3,400 calories per kg and 2 m^3 per 1,000 kg grain). Halstead's figures (1981:198), when applied to our data, result in estimates of 375–500 people, and similar numbers are obtained using data from Gentry (1976) and Kemp (1986) (Table 2). Had other grain storage facilities been located in Raqa'i level 4, as is likely, our figures would have to be increased.

If one uses an estimate of 100–200 persons per hectare for an estimated occupied area of 0.3 ha (Kramer 1980), Raqa'i

Table 1. Estimated Storage Capacities of "Silos," Tell al-Raqa'i Level 4

	Estimated area (m²)	Estimated minimum height (m)	Estimated volume (m³)	
Northwest Area				
Area 51				
Lower (with ledge)	3.4	0.1		0.3
Upper (above ledge)	4.4	2.0		8.8
			Total:	9.1
Area 52	3.5	2.0		7.0
Area 53	2.3	2.0		4.6
Area 56	2.4	2.0		4.8
Area 57	5.5	3.0		16.5
Area 58				
Lower (with ledges)	3.8	1.2		4.6
Upper (above ledges)	5.6	1.5		8.4
			Total:	13.0
Area 59	Unclear	Unclear		Unclear
Rounded Building				
Area 1				
Lower (below vault)	5.2	2.5		13.0
Upper (vaulted area, on average)	4.6	1.0		4.6
			Total:	17.6
Area 2				
Lower (below vault)	3.7	2.5		9.2
Upper (vaulted area, on average)	3.4	1.0		3.4
			Total:	12.6
Area 7				
Lower (below vault)	2.3	1.9		4.4
Upper (vaulted area, on average)	1.6	0.7		1.1
			Total:	5.5
Area 19				
Lower (with ledges)	1.8	0.1		0.2
Upper (above ledges)	3.2	1.6		5.1
			Total:	5.3
Area 20				
Lower (with ledges)	1.8	0.1		0.2
Upper (above ledges)	3.2	1.6		5.1
			Total:	5.3
Area 21				
Lower (below vault)	4.8	1.0		4.8
Upper (vaulted area, on average)	4.3	1.4		6.0
			Total:	10.8
Area 27				
Lower (below vault)	4.5	2.0		9.0
Upper (vaulted area, on average)	3.8	0.6		2.3
			Total:	11.3
			Grand total:	123.4
Rounded Building, additional possible storage areas				
Area 6	1.6	1.7[a]		2.7
Area 9	4.5	1.8[a]		8.1
Area 10	3.1	1.8[a]		5.6
Area 11	8.9	2.3[a]		20.5
Area 12	6.2	2.3[a]		14.3
			Grand total:	51.2

[a] Above door blocking.

Table 2. Estimated Grain Requirements per Person per Year, with Reference to Storage Space Capacity

Source	Calories needed per person per day	Calories per kg grain	Spoilage ratio	Seed ratio	kg grain needed per person per year	Storage space needed for 1,000 kg grain (m³)	Persons fed by grain stored in 150 m³ storage space per year
Hole (1991)	2,500	3,510	20%	20%	433	2.25	154
Hunt (1987:165)	1,000 from grain (2,000 from all foods)	3,400	15%	10%	143		524 (given 2 m³ storage per 1,000 kg grain)
Halstead (1981:198)					200	1.5–2.0	375–500
Gentry (1976:23–25)					365 (from Roman military records)	1.3 (wheat) 1.4 (barley)	323 (wheat) 290 (barley)
Kemp (1986:132)					219–365 (from Egyptian ration records)	1.3 (wheat) 1.4 (barley)	290–538
Broshi (1979:7)					200–250		
Clark and Haswell (1967:54)					190–235		
Ellison (1981)	2,200 (adult female) 3,000 (adult male)	3,600 (barley)			A wide range, e.g., 279–558 (from Mesopotamian ration records)		
Hassan (1981:18)	2,140 (!Kung Bushmen average intake) 2,354 (FAO recommended figure)						
Kühne (1990:20)				25–33% average (data from middle Assyrian texts)			
Kramer (1982)				17% average			
H. T. Wright (1969:21)			25%	11% (+16% for animals)	150–250 (average)		
Johnson (1973:97, 137)	1,976 from bread (3,000 from all foods)	3,500 (barley)	25%		278		

level 4 would have had a population of 30–60 persons. Considering the data from Raqa'i level 3, almost completely exposed, we may estimate an area of some 200–300 m² of living space, which would house 20–30 inhabitants if we use the figure of 10 m² of residential space per person (Naroll 1962; Kramer 1980; but see, e.g., Kolb 1985 for a criticism of this figure), or 33–50 inhabitants using a lower figure of 6 m² per person (Marfoe 1980). These calculations suggest that the storage facilities in Raqa'i level 4 would have sustained a population of many times the number of people living on the mound itself. Certainly these figures would be subject to considerable variation if one or more of the variables are altered, but the general pattern of storage facilities far in excess of the local population's needs is nonetheless clear.[5] A similar pattern of storage capacities well in excess of local needs is also apparent at 'Atij (Fortin 1990) and Kerma (Saghieh 1991).

Let us now consider the question of whether the area around Raqa'i was capable of producing enough grain to fill up 150 m³ or more of storage space per year (=75,000 kg of grain). Data available on grain yields from both ancient and modern Near Eastern sources indicate that the production of 75,000 kg of grain would require the cultivation of anywhere from 60 ha (1,254 kg per hectare at pre-Sargonic Girsu) (Adams 1981:86) to 107 ha (700 kg per hectare in Ur III texts) (Adams 1981:146) or even as many as 250 ha (300 kg per hectare in poorer areas of the dry-farming Biqa' Valley) (Marfoe 1979:5). Higher yields are primarily associated with irrigation agriculture in southern Mesopotamia, whereas dry farming is thought to be less productive per unit of area (Weiss 1983).

If the area cultivated in the Raqa'i vicinity was delimited upstream and downstream by fields associated with Kerma and 'Atij, each 2 km distant, the Raqa'i fields would have extended some 2 km along the river. A distance of 2 km is, in fact, quite a convenient figure for the efficient spacing of farming villages (Kramer 1982:246), and farmers typically do not travel farther than 3–4 km to their fields (Chisholm 1962). The possible extent of the fields away from the river is uncertain; if irrigation was employed, as is likely but not yet demonstrable, the fields would have extended as far as river water could be channeled to them (Wirth 1971:Karte 5; Kühne 1990; Hole 1991:23). If the Raqa'i fields stretched 1.5 km from the river, for example, we could reconstruct an area of 2 km × 1.5 km or 300 ha, which would easily provide the requisite amount of grain even given such low yields as those attested from the Biqa'.[6]

COMPLEX POLITIES AND BULK STORAGE

In a review of storage facilities in traditional societies, Earle and D'Altroy (1982) have argued that large-scale centralized storage of staple goods can be interpreted as a material correlate of "staple finance." In this system, characteristic of complex chiefdoms or early states, staples mobilized from the population are stored and used to pay personnel rendering services for the elite (Polanyi 1968; D'Altroy and Earle 1985).[7] Similarly, Hunt (1987:174) emphasizes the tendency for central authorities collecting grain to store the materials in centralized, bureaucratically managed facilities.

The scale of the facilities at Raqa'i and the other middle Khabur specialized centers relative to the small local population indicates that the goods processed or stored in the middle Khabur were intended for consumption elsewhere. The Ninevite V period sites in the middle Khabur Valley are very small settlements, the largest probably being Bderi, perhaps 5 ha in area, and no significant contemporaneous occupation is attested for the steppe zone on either side of the river valley (Hole 1991). Given this conclusion, Earle and D'Altroy's discussion of staple finance, and the administrative technology associated with the middle Khabur facilities (cylinder seals and sealings, numerical tablets, clay tokens), we derive the following working hypothesis: the specialized activities of the middle Khabur sites were conducted for the benefit of elites based at larger centers outside the middle Khabur, who collected agricultural surpluses to support their dependent personnel. If we consider the grain processing and storage activities at Raqa'i to have been conducted in the service of an elite, for example, the Raqa'i temple could be interpreted as evidence for a legitimizing religious context for elite-administered staple collection, a well-documented phenomenon elsewhere (Schwartz 1987:96, in press).

A further argument in favor of the association of the middle Khabur complex with polities elsewhere is the dense settlement of the area in the third millennium. Although only some four or five settlements dating to the fourth millennium have been identified, up to twenty-two third-millennium sites were observed in a surface survey (Monchambert 1984), and Ninevite V period occupation has been confirmed on at least ten of the twelve excavated third-millennium sites. Available evidence indicates that the settlement at Tell al-Raqa'i and associated specialized sites along the middle Khabur were founded in the early to middle Ninevite V period.[8] These data seem to indicate a mass settlement or even a "colonization" of the region in the third millennium, perhaps under the auspices of developing political units in adjacent regions.

Agricultural exploitation of the middle Khabur area might have been conducted by polities in the upper Khabur, for example, in order to maximize the production of agricultural surplus. The upper Khabur "triangle" of tributary wadis was the site of several large third-millennium urban centers, such as Tell Mozan, Tell Brak, and Tell Leilan, with Tell Chuera located to the west of the triangle. All of these centers were occupied to some extent in Ninevite V times and presumably underwent expansion and, at least in some cases, circumvallation toward the middle of the third millennium (Weiss 1990). These communities, most likely the administrative centers of developing advanced chiefdoms or early states, are the closest large centers to the middle Khabur settlements and appropriate candidates for the sites associated with that complex.

It is difficult to explain, however, why the centers of the rainfall farming plains of the upper Khabur would have exploited the marginal agricultural land of the middle Khabur, where irrigation was required, when there would have been ample rain-fed fields in the neighborhood. One possible explanation is political circumscription; the expansion of a polity located in the southern part of the upper Khabur may have been impeded by competing powers to the north, leaving only the marginal lands of the middle Khabur to exploit.

But it must be acknowledged that the middle Khabur specialized sites, founded in early to middle Ninevite V times (=Leilan IIIa or IIIb), were in operation well before the urbanization and circumvallation of the best-dated upper Khabur center, Tell Leilan, at the end of the Ninevite V period (=Leilan IIId). Likewise, survey evidence indicates that even the countryside around Tell Leilan itself was not significantly mobilized for the production of agricultural surplus until the post–Ninevite V period (Chapter 2 by Stein). At present, it is unknown if the urbanization of Leilan was coincident with that of other upper Khabur centers or was a relatively late case.

Alternatively, and perhaps more persuasively, one might propose that the middle Khabur sites were associated with a large southern center such as Mari on the banks of the Euphrates. Mari was located in an area of limited agricultural potential, sustained only by irrigation agriculture in a restricted band on either side of the river. There is evidence in the Ebla archives that grain was sent in large quantities from Ebla to Mari (Archi 1985:68), and the early second-millennium B.C. texts from Mari also refer to large amounts of grain sent by river from the upper Khabur and the middle Euphrates downstream to Mari (Finet 1969, 1983; Margueron 1991; Fortin and Schwartz in press).

The intensification of agriculture by complex polities often takes the form of territorial extension and has been linked to a strategy of short-term maximization of benefits by and for urban elites (Adams 1978). In Sassanid Mesopotamia, for example, the necessity for intensified agricultural productivity compelled the state to exploit lands of marginal productivity at increasing distances from the centers. Adams (1966) specifically argues for an association of the *earliest* complex polities with expansionism, which permitted the collection of ever larger gross agricultural surpluses to support the new sociopolitical order:

> an increase in the gross size of population and territorial unit may offer *at least* as strong an impetus to the Urban Revolution as increases in "efficiency." Trends toward territorial aggrandizement, political unification, and population concentration within the political unit accordingly can be interpreted not merely as expressions of the outcome of the Urban Revolution but as functionally interrelated processes that are central to it. (Adams 1966:46–47)

The recently discovered networks of "colonies" and other manifestations of expansion associated with the earliest states in Late Uruk–period Mesopotamia might be relevant to such a perspective, although this evidence is most often interpreted in the context of large-scale acquisition of raw materials unavailable in southern Mesopotamia (Algaze 1989).[9]

Perhaps also analogous is the recently discovered system of outposts dating to the early third millennium B.C. in the Hamrin region of central Iraq (Tell Razuk, Tell Gubba, Tell Madhhur, and others), which is roughly contemporary with the middle Khabur system and is also composed of a set of small specialized communities in a marginal area probably associated with a complex polity elsewhere. These sites include large circular buildings with vaulted architecture curiously reminiscent of the Raqa'i Rounded Building. Gibson (1986, 1990) interprets the Hamrin sites as military outposts of city-states in the lower Diyala such as Eshnunna, whereas a review by Trümpelmann (1989:72) maintains that the Gubba VII Round Building was used primarily for grain storage.[10]

Expansion of complex polities into previously unexploited, marginal regions for purposes of agricultural intensification is also attested in the New World. Rural specialized "audiencia" sites in the Late Intermediate period Chimu state in Peru (Keatinge and Day 1973) were established in desert settings remote from large urban centers; these sites are construed as administrative centers for the construction of canals and fields and for the storage and redistribution of subsequent agricultural yields. Many of these zones apparently failed to produce, however, and after a great flood wrought havoc on the canal systems, the Chimu rulers abandoned exploitation of marginal areas and concentrated on expansionistic military ventures concerned with the acquisition of tribute (Pozorski 1987).[11]

An important observation derived from the Chimu data is that high agricultural productivity may not have been the most significant variable in the cultivation of marginal territories by early complex societies. The construction of the new Chimu canal systems was partly a strategy employed by members of the ruling elite to maintain high status. Such individuals competed for prestige and political power through the construction of irrigation systems, even in areas that had potentially low productive capabilities (Pozorski 1987:119).

THE MIDDLE KHABUR AS AN INTERMEDIATE COLLECTION POINT

Our discussion thus far has been predicated on the assumption that the material stored and processed in the middle Khabur settlements was grown locally, but this may not have been the case. Another hypothesis to be tested proposes the middle Khabur to have been not the producer of the goods but an intermediary area such as a port of trade (Polanyi 1963) or gateway community (Hirth 1978). Grain harvested in the dry-farming plains of the upper Khabur would be stored in the middle Khabur and then obtained by people from southern areas like Mari. As Earle and D'Altroy (1982:269) note, centralized mass storage in the archaeological record may represent large-scale long-distance exchange in which "the bulking and debulking of goods—related to changing transport modes—are associated with storage at specific transshipment locations . . . recognized by the highly localized and specific nature of their distribution." In such a scenario, grain harvested in the upper Khabur could have been sent overland to the middle Khabur centers, situated at the point where the tributaries of the Khabur join to form a single watercourse, and subsequently loaded onto boats or rafts for the journey downstream. The grain could have been stored in the middle Khabur facilities in quantities large enough to fill boats to be sent down the river (cf. Fortin and Schwartz in press on the navigability of the Khabur in antiquity).

Such an explanation, it must be conceded, will leave several factors unaccounted for. If the middle Khabur sites were established as collection points for grain to be shipped long-distance, one might question why they were distributed along the river at 2-km intervals: large-scale storage would be more easily defended at one spot than at a number of points. A resolution of this problem might be found in the architectural differentiation of the sites (cf. the so far unique Rounded Building at Raqa'i), which could be related to functional differentiation or, alternatively, to different sponsors of individual stations. That defense was an issue in the region is made manifest by the thick walls of the facility at Kerma (Saghieh 1991), the town wall and gate at Bderi (Pfälzner 1986–1987:294), an enclosure wall around the granary area at 'Atij (M. Fortin, pers. comm.), and a thick enclosure wall and glacis at Rad Shaqrah (circa 1–2 km upstream from Kerma) (Bielinski 1992). At Raqa'i, parts of the Rounded Building outer wall were widened in later level 4 and again in level 3, an event that may signal an increasing threat to the operations being conducted at the site.

Furthermore, if the middle Khabur sites were employed in the processing and storage of grain imported from elsewhere, we must also answer the question of why the grain was not processed near its original harvesting site but was instead transported unprocessed to the middle Khabur.

In a thoughtful consideration of the middle Khabur evidence, Hole (1991) has advanced another possible explanation of the function of the middle Khabur centers, suggesting that they processed and stored grain for a relatively small local nomadic pastoralist population. In this interpretation, Hole stresses what he perceives to be the small scale of the middle Khabur storage facilities. First, he proposes that the middle Khabur sites may not have been concurrently occupied, with only one or two sites in operation at any one time and thus with less storage capacity than is immediately apparent. But similar occupational sequences are now observable at eight sites: Raqa'i, 'Atij, Kerma, Melebiya, Mashnaqa, Bderi, Mulla Matar, and Tuneinir. Indications are that these and probably other third-millennium sites were either founded on virgin soil or reoccupied, after a hiatus, in the early third millennium, and there is little reason to presume gaps in their Ninevite V period occupation.

Second, Hole suggests that the facilities within the sites were relatively small-scale. However, it is likely that he has underestimated the storage capacities of the middle Khabur sites, particularly those recently exposed at 'Atij (Fortin 1990) and at Raqa'i level 4 (see earlier discussion).

Finally, Hole submits that administrative artifacts found at the middle Khabur sites may not have been used for administration but as prestige items. But this assertion is contradicted by the clay sealings found at Raqa'i and by the cylinder seals and clay sealings found together in a pit at Mulla Matar (Sürenhagen 1990:151–152). Some of the Raqa'i sealings have been identified as peg sealings, probably used for the sealing of doors (S. Dunham, pers. comm.).

Furthermore, the scale and architectural sophistication of a number of middle Khabur facilities imply a level of organization and labor specialization unlikely in a local agricultural or pastoral nomadic population; architects and perhaps bricklayers from a complex polity were probably involved in the construction projects (cf. Gibson 1990:112). Relevant here are the Raqa'i Rounded Building, the massive retaining wall excavated on the east slope of Mulla Matar (Sürenhagen 1990), the fortified enclosure wall around the Kerma facilities

(Saghieh 1991), the thick outer wall and glacis at Rad Shaqrah (Bielinski 1992), the glacis and mudbrick platform associated with the Ziyadeh storage building (Buccellati, Buia, and Reimer 1991), and a remarkably tall enclosure wall around the 'Atij grain storage area (M. Fortin, pers. comm.).

If the middle Khabur sites were associated with a complex polity elsewhere, one could then suggest that the facilities were established and maintained by the central authorities, but still to service a local pastoral nomadic group: Rita Wright's suggestion that central authorities could have dealt with the conflict for land between agriculturalists and livestock breeders through a strategy of expansion into areas conducive to livestock breeding may be relevant here (R. Wright 1989:600), with the middle Khabur storage intended to feed pastoralists tending the herds in question. Certainly the steppe on either side of the middle Khabur valley has been consistently utilized throughout history as grazing land by migratory pastoral groups. However, the writer is not aware of any analogous ethnographic parallels for a grain storage operation of the scale of the middle Khabur complex operated for or by nomadic pastoralists.

When more archaeobotanical evidence from the middle Khabur sites becomes available, our interpretive powers should increase significantly. At present, analyses indicate that the most common plant remains in the flotation samples taken at Tell al-Raqa'i were waste products (glume bases, rachis internodes) of processed two-row barley, with only small quantities of cereal grain fragments attested (W. van Zeist, pers. comm.).[12] Field weed seeds were also numerous, whereas einkorn, emmer, hard or bread wheat, lentils, and grass-pea seeds (*Lathyrus sativus*) were only minimally represented.

Particularly striking are the chronological patterns observed in the distribution of this material. In levels 5–7 and 2 were very small amounts of plant material, including both wheat and barley, indicative of a subsistence economy. Levels 4 and 3, on the other hand—dating from a time when the Rounded Building and exterior silos were in use—had much larger quantities of cereal remains and a much higher ratio of barley to wheat, a pattern suggestive of surplus production and a specialized concentration on barley.

Barley was also the primary plant material found in situ at the Kerma storage and processing facility, along with some wheat. Inside the storage area was clean, processed grain; outside, near an oven, were waste products of processing that included glume bases and rachises (Saghieh 1991).

Barley generally predominates in areas of lower rainfall, whereas wheat is more prevalent in rainier regions. This dichotomy is supported by evidence from the rainfall plains of the upper Khabur, where dominant cereals include bread wheat at mid-third-millennium Mozan (Galvin 1988) and a mixture of emmer, durum, bread wheat, and some barley at Leilan III (Wetterstrom in press).

There are, however, numerous examples of extensive barley cultivation in ancient Near Eastern rainfall farming areas.[13] Barley apparently was the most common grain in Ebla, if the sign ŠE is to be so interpreted and did not serve as a generic term for grain (Milano 1987), and the Ninevite V granary at Telul-eth-Thalathat Tell V on the Sinjar Plain is said to have contained primarily barley (Fukai, Horiuchi, and Matsutani 1974). Later in the third millennium, barley is mentioned in an Old Akkadian text from Brak (Finkel 1985:190, no. 5), is abundant in the Old Akkadian records from Gasur near Kirkuk in northern Iraq (Foster 1987), and is attested in the archaeological record in the Naram-Sin "palace" at Tell Brak, which yielded carbonized barley and wheat. The early second-millennium B.C. Chagar Bazar 1 tablets also mention barley rather than wheat (Gadd 1937, 1940), and the roughly contemporary archaeobotanical remains from Tell Leilan have likewise indicated the predominance of barley (Weiss 1986).

It has been suggested that a reliance on barley might imply maximization strategies implemented by the dominant elite, since barley is easily storable and transportable on a large scale (Rothman 1985; Weiss 1986). Barley is also important as a cereal used for animal fodder (Watson 1979:68; Kramer 1982:37), and a preference for barley may have been associated with the feeding of ever-increasing state-controlled herds (R. Wright 1989). At Raqa'i and Kerma, the predominance of barley could be interpreted as an employment of the cereal best adapted to dry conditions, if the barley was grown locally; as evidence of large-scale provisioning of herds; or as evidence of agricultural maximization strategies by emerging elites in adjacent regions. Given the apparent specialization in barley in Raqa'i levels 4 and 3, the latter two possibilities appear to be more worthy of serious consideration than the first.

Turning to the Syro-Mesopotamian historical record for comparative material, we find that the texts are disappointingly reticent on the nature of rural specialized centers and on most other aspects of life in the countryside. The best-documented example of a specialized site maintained by central authorities is Puzrish-Dagan (modern Drehem), a late third-millennium southern Mesopotamian collection center that served as a "livestock fund" from which animals were redistributed to different provinces in the Ur III realm (Steinkeller 1987). Occasional reference is also made in Ur III texts to Dusabara, a specialized agricultural center in the Nippur area that, according to Whiting (1979:16, no. 19), was "probably the imperial granary in the same manner that Drehem was the imperial stockyard."

Also relevant are data on the Ur III milling establishments derived from administrative texts (Grégoire 1992). These records indicate that the milling installations were vast complexes employing hundreds of workers; activities conducted there included storage, roasting, and grinding of grain, followed by bread baking and beer brewing. But few details on the nature of these activities or of the associated facilities are supplied.

Conclusions

Having considered the extant evidence from Tell al-Raqa'i and other contemporaneous middle Khabur sites, we may conclude that these results document the existence of a system of rural economic specialization coincident with the development of complex society in northern Mesopotamia, and that the concern of this system was large-scale grain storage and processing.[14] At Raqa'i and the other sites of the middle Khabur complex, there is good reason to believe that we are in possession of direct evidence of elite-administered storage and processing of agricultural surplus, the economic foundation of complex societies.

Adams (1966:46) has noted that the accumulation of agricultural surpluses by early elites must have involved, in addition to improvements in transport technology, the development of institutional mechanisms not only for extracting surpluses but also for storing and redistributing them. Hunt, discussing the specifics of such mechanisms, details how the mobilization of grain by a central authority requires quality control of processing, storage, transport, and distribution activities, which is very likely to entail specialists supervising these procedures: "If . . . the bureaucrats are responsible for some of the processing, and actually organize the work, then it implies a labor force, facilities, and capital assets. Some sort of textual reference (construction costs, inventory of facilities, etc.) and/or archaeological remains could well exist" (1987:176; see also Grégoire 1992). Continued attention to rural site excavation is likely to provide more data to aid in the elucidation of such systems as well as other aspects of the development of complex society hitherto undetected by the traditionally urban-centered focus of archaeology and textual analysis.

Notes

The ideas expressed in this chapter are necessarily preliminary, since much of the archaeobotanical and faunal analysis for the middle Khabur sites discussed remains to be completed, and much of the architectural and artifactual data have not yet been extensively published. Steve Falconer, Betsy Bryan, and this volume's anonymous reviewer read drafts of this chapter and contributed invaluable advice; I am also indebted to Hans Curvers, Robert McC. Adams, Timothy Earle, Sally Dunham, Mitchell Rothman, Wilma Wetterstrom, Roger Woodard, and Hijlke Buitenhuis for their input, although their agreement with what is written here is by no means implied.

Excavations at Tell al-Raqa'i were conducted in 1986 by the University of Amsterdam (Curvers 1987) and jointly by The Johns Hopkins University and the University of Amsterdam (Curvers and Schwartz 1990; Schwartz and Curvers 1992) from 1987 to 1993. Maurits van Loon served as project director for 1986–1988 with Hans Curvers and Glenn Schwartz as field directors; Curvers and Schwartz assumed project co-direction in 1989. The Raqa'i project gratefully acknowledges the support and encouragement of the Directorate-General of Antiquities and Museums of Syria, Damascus, with particular thanks to Dr. Sultan Muhesen, Director-General, Dr. Ali Abu Assaf, past Director-General, and Dr. Adnan Bounni, Director of Excavations; we also warmly thank Jean-Simon Lazar, Department of Antiquities, Hasseke, and our representatives, Ibrahim Nano, Najah Toueir, Ibrahim Murad, and Husayn Yusuf, for their assistance. Funding for the project was provided by the National Endowment for the Humanities, the National Geographic Society, the Dellheim Foundation, Syria Shell Petroleum Development B.V., Damascus, Johns Hopkins University, the University of Arizona, Instituut voor Pre- en Protohistorische Archeologie, Dr. Hendrik Muller's Vaderlandsch Fonds, Stichting Fonds voor de Geld en Effectenhandel, Vereniging van Vrienden van het Allard Pierson Museum, and several private contributors. We are especially grateful to Robert McC. Adams and the Smithsonian Institution for their support of this research.

1. One might also consider whether the circular "kilns" next to the granary at Telul-eth-Thalathat Tell V might have been for the purpose of parching grain (Fukai, Horiuchi, and Matsutani 1974:plates XL and XLI). For other possible grain-processing activities, cf. Hubbard and al-Azm (1990).

2. There may be evidence indicating some kind of post–Ninevite V economic specialization at Judeida (Gudeda), but the facilities excavated there seem to involve a different function than those of the Ninevite V period sites. The duration of third-millennium occupation at the excavated sites of Ziyadah and Umm Qseir is unknown to the writer at present.

3. Although the excavated sample from Raqa'i level 3 was much larger than that from level 4, we consider level 4 here because the Rounded Building, locus of a number of "silos," was more completely preserved in level 4 than in level 3. For doorless grain storage areas outside the Rounded Building in level 3, see areas 4–6 (Schwartz and Curvers 1992); excavation in 1989 revealed that area 4, which contained a large oven in a late level 3 phase (Curvers and Schwartz 1990:8), consisted, in earlier level 3, of a "silo" similar to that of area 5. It appears that silos 4–6 were founded in level 4 (areas 56–58) and reused in level 3; various blocked entrances and

other modifications within these silos indicate the vicissitudes and the duration of use of the features.

4. The daily barley rations allotted to workers in pre-Sargonic and later third-millennium southern Mesopotamia can include such large amounts as 558 kg per year per person (60 silà/month) for adult males, a surprisingly high figure that provides well above the required daily caloric intake; smaller figures are also frequently cited, such as 279 kg per person per year (30 silà/month), which recalls Johnson's figure of 278 kg bread per person per year in modern Khuzistan (Table 2) (Gelb 1965; Johnson 1973:97; Adams 1981:86; Ellison 1981). The ration figures are problematic, however, since the modern equivalents of the ancient measures are not necessarily well fixed, and the figures may or may not represent amounts consumed only by the individual named. Kramer's ethnoarchaeological data suggest a range of 150–250 kg per person per year for cereal consumption in the Zagros-Taurus arc (1980:329).

5. Calculating the total storage capacity of excavated level 4 "silos" assumes, no doubt inaccurately, that all storage spaces were filled to the brim and used concurrently. Although our estimates of grain stored at any one time in the excavated silos may therefore be too high, the observed pattern of storage capacity in excess of community requirements should still hold, particularly if one considers the likelihood of additional silos in unexcavated areas of the level 4 occupation.

6. A related question is the number of agricultural workers required to produce 150 m^3 of grain. There is a wide range of possibilities for this figure, since it is dependent on the number of hectares needed to produce 150 m^3 of grain and the average area one person could cultivate in a year. Estimates for the latter figure range from 1.6 to 4 ha (Oates and Oates 1976:120; Johnson 1987:112; Mazar 1990:128).

7. In the case of the Inka empire, Earle and D'Altroy's primary example, the elite did not mobilize staples directly but mobilized labor to produce them.

8. A ceramic assemblage similar to that from the earliest Raqa'i levels has been identified above virgin soil at 'Atij, Bderi, and Melebiya.

9. Also notable is sponsorship of new communities for purposes of agricultural expansion by early states in Shang and Chou period China (Chang 1980:159–162).

10. The rectilinear cubicles outside the Gubba V Round Building are also quite similar to the "silos" northwest of the Raqa'i Rounded Building in levels 4 and 3, but the former structures are built on parallel "sleeper" wall substructures.

11. Also analogous is the program of agricultural expansions maintained by the Tiwanaku state to reclaim land around Lake Titicaca for the production of agricultural surplus (Kolata 1986). Wari exploitation of virgin territory for irrigation agriculture is also documented (Anders 1986).

12. A report on the archaeobotanical remains from Raqa'i will be published by W. van Zeist in *Tell al-Raqa'i I*. In addition, Dr. Joy McCorriston of the Smithsonian Institution is studying Raqa'i botanical material retrieved from midden deposits for reconstruction of land use patterns.

13. Two-row barley, attested at Raqa'i, can survive in drier conditions than six-row barley and is often associated with rainfall agriculture, but two-row barley can also be the product of irrigation agriculture (Miller 1990:81; W. Wetterstrom, pers. comm.).

14. This statement is made with the full awareness of numerous lacunae in our data and the many problems involved in their interpretation, several of which were discussed earlier in this chapter.

References Cited

Adams, Robert McC.
1966 *The Evolution of Urban Society: Early Mesopotamia and Prehispanic Mexico.* Aldine, Chicago.
1978 Strategies of Maximization, Stability, and Resilience in Mesopotamian Agriculture. *Proceedings of the American Philosophical Society* 122:329–335.
1981 *Heartland of Cities.* University of Chicago Press, Chicago.
1984 Mesopotamian Social Evolution: Old Outlooks, New Goals. In *On the Evolution of Complex Societies: Essays in Honor of Harry Hoijer, 1982,* edited by T. K. Earle, pp. 79–129. Undena Press, Malibu, Calif.

Adams, Robert McC., and Hans J. Nissen
1972 *The Uruk Countryside.* University of Chicago Press, Chicago.

Algaze, Guillermo
1989 The Uruk Expansion: Cross-Cultural Exchange in Early Mesopotamian Civilization. *Current Anthropology* 30:571–608.

Alster, Bendt, and Herman Vanstiphout
1987 Lahar and Ashnan: Presentation and Analysis of a Sumerian Disputation. *Acta Sumerologica* 9:1–43.

Anders, Martha B.
1986 Wari Experiments in Statecraft: A View from Azangaro. In *Andean Archaeology: Papers in Memory of Clifford Evans,* edited by R. Matos Mendieta, S. Turpin, and H. Eling, Jr., pp. 201–224. Institute of Archaeology, University of California, Los Angeles.

Archi, Alfonso
1985 Les rapports politiques et économiques entre Ebla et Mari. *Mari Annales de Recherches Interdisciplinaires* 4:63–84.

Bielinski, Piotr
1992 The First Campaign of Excavations on Tell Rad Shaqrah (Hasake Southern Dam Basin). *Polish Archaeology in the Mediterranean* 3:77–85.

Broshi, Magen
1979 The Population of Western Palestine in the Roman-Byzantine Period. *Bulletin of the American Schools of Oriental Research* 236:1–10.

Brown, J. A.
1981 The Search for Rank. In *The Archaeology of Death,* edited by R. Chapman, I. Kinnes, and K. Randsborg, pp. 25–37. Cambridge University Press, Cambridge.

Buccellati, Giorgio, D. Buia, and Stephen Reimer
- 1991 Tell Ziyada: The First Three Seasons of Excavation (1988–1990). *Bulletin of the Canadian Society for Mesopotamian Studies* 21:31–61.

Chang, Kwang Chih
- 1980 *Shang Civilization.* Yale University Press, New Haven, Conn.

Childe, Vere Gordon
- 1946 *What Happened in History.* Penguin, Harmondsworth, England.

Chisholm, Michael
- 1962 *Rural Settlement and Land Use.* Aldine, Chicago.

Clark, Colin, and Margaret Haswell
- 1967 *The Economics of Subsistence Agriculture.* Macmillan, London.

Curvers, Hans H.
- 1987 The Middle Habur Salvage Operation: Excavation at Tell al-Raqa'i 1986. *Akkadica* 55:1–29.

Curvers, Hans H., and Glenn M. Schwartz
- 1990 Excavations at Tell al-Raqa'i: A Small Rural Site of Early Urban Mesopotamia. *American Journal of Archaeology* 94:3–23.

D'Altroy, Terence, and Timothy K. Earle
- 1985 Staple Finance, Wealth Finance, and Storage in the Inca Political Economy. *Current Anthropology* 26:187–206.

Diakonoff, Igor M.
- 1975 The Rural Community in the Ancient Near East. *Journal of the Social and Economic History of the Orient* 18:121–133.

Dumézil, Georges
- 1970 *Archaic Roman Religion.* University of Chicago Press, Chicago.

Dunham, Sally
- 1993 A Wall Painting from Tell al-Raqa'i, North-east Syria. *Levant* 25:127–143.

Earle, Timothy K., and Terence D'Altroy
- 1982 Storage Facilities and State Finance in the Upper Mantaro Valley, Peru. In *Contexts for Prehistoric Exchange,* edited by J. E. Ericson and T. K. Earle, pp. 265–290. Academic Press, New York.

Ellison, Rosemary
- 1981 Diet in Mesopotamia: The Evidence of the Barley Ration Texts (ca. 3000–1400 B.C.). *Iraq* 43:35–46.

Finet, André
- 1969 L'Euphrate, route commerciale de la Mésopotamie. *Annales archéologiques arabes syriennes* 19:37–48.
- 1983 Le Habur dans les archives de Mari. In *Symposium international. Histoire de Deir-ez-Zur et ses antiquités,* pp. 89–97. Directorate-General of Antiquities, Damascus, Syria.

Finkel, Irving R.
- 1985 Inscriptions from Tell Brak 1984. *Iraq* 47:187–202.

Fortin, Michel
- 1988 Rapport préliminaire sur la première campagne de fouilles (printemps 1986) à Tell 'Atij, sur le moyen Khabour. *Syria* 65:139–171.
- 1990 Rapport préliminaire sur la seconde campagne de fouilles à Tell 'Atij et la première à Tell Gudeda (automne 1987), sur le Moyen Khabour. *Syria* 67:219–256.

Fortin, Michel, and Glenn M. Schwartz
- In press The Middle Habur in the Third Millennium B.C. In *Origins of Northern Mesopotamian Civilization: Ninevite 5 Chronology, Economy, Society,* edited by H. Weiss. Yale University Press, New Haven, Conn.

Foster, Benjamin R.
- 1987 People, Land and Produce at Sargonic Gasur. In *Studies on the Civilization and Culture of Nuzi and the Hurrians,* Vol. 2, edited by D. I. Owen and M. A. Morrison, pp. 89–108. Eisenbrauns, Winona Lake, Ind.

Fukai, Shinji, Kiyoharu Horiuchi, and Toshio Matsutani
- 1974 *Telul eth Thalathat III. The Excavation of Tell V.* University of Tokyo Institute of Oriental Culture, Tokyo.

Fuller, Michael, and Neathery Fuller
- 1991 Tuneinir. Pp. 738–740 in "Archaeology in Syria," edited by H. Weiss. *American Journal of Archaeology* 95:683–740.

Gadd, Cyril John
- 1937 Tablets from Chagar Bazar, 1936. *Iraq* 4:178–185.
- 1940 Tablets from Chagar Bazar and Tell Brak. *Iraq* 7:22–66.

Galvin, Kathleen
- 1988 Paleobotanical Samples from the City Wall. In *Mozan 1: The Soundings of the First Two Seasons,* edited by G. Buccellati and M. Kelly-Buccellati, pp. 83–88. Undena Press, Malibu, Calif.

Gelb, Ignace J.
- 1965 The Ancient Mesopotamian Ration System. *Journal of Near Eastern Studies* 24:230–243.

Gentry, Anne P.
- 1976 *Roman Military Stone-Built Granaries in Britain.* British Archaeological Reports 32. British Archaeological Reports, Oxford.

Gibson, McGuire
- 1986 The Round Building at Razuk: Form and Function. In *Préhistoire de le Mésopotamie,* pp. 467–474. Editions du CNRS, Paris.
- 1990 Remarks on the Round Building. In *Uch Tepe II. Technical Reports,* edited by M. Gibson, pp. 109–120. Akademisk Forlag, Chicago and Copenhagen.

Grégoire, Jean-Pierre
- 1992 Les grandes unités de transformation des céréales: l'exemple des minoteries de la Mésopotamie du sud à la fin du IIIe millénaire avant notre ère. In *Préhistoire de l'agriculture: nouvelles approches expérimentales et ethnographiques,* pp. 321–339. Monographie du CRA, No. 6. Editions du CNRS, Paris.

Halstead, Paul
- 1981 From Determinism to Uncertainty: Social Storage and the Rise of the Minoan Palace. In *Economic Archaeology,* edited by A. Sheridan and G. Bailey, pp. 187–213. BAR International Series 96. British Archaeological Reports, Oxford.

Hassan, Fekri
- 1981 *Demographic Archaeology.* Academic Press, New York.

Hillman, Gordon
- 1985 Traditional Husbandry and Processing of Archaic Cereals in Recent Times. Part II: The Free-Threshing Cereals. *Bulletin on Sumerian Agriculture* 2:1–31.

Hirth, Kenneth G.
- 1978 Interregional Trade and the Formation of Prehistoric Gateway Communities. *American Antiquity* 43:35–45.

Hole, Frank, ed.
- 1987 *The Archaeology of Western Iran*. Smithsonian Institution Press, Washington, D.C.

Hole, Frank
- 1991 Middle Khabur Settlement and Agriculture in the Ninevite 5 Period. *Bulletin of the Canadian Society for Mesopotamian Studies* 21:17–29.

Hubbard, R. N. L. B., and Amr al-Azm
- 1990 Quantifying Preservation and Distortion in Carbonized Seeds; and Investigating the History of *Friké* Production. *Journal of Archaeological Science* 17:103–106.

Hunt, Robert C.
- 1987 The Role of Bureaucracy in the Provisioning of Cities: A Framework for Analysis of the Ancient Near East. In *The Organization of Power: Aspects of Bureaucracy in the Ancient Near East*, edited by M. Gibson and R. Biggs, pp. 161–192. Studies in Ancient Oriental Civilization, No. 46. Oriental Institute, Chicago.

Johnson, Gregory A.
- 1973 *Local Exchange and Early State Development in Southwestern Iran*. Museum of Anthropology, University of Michigan, Anthropological Papers, No. 51. University of Michigan, Ann Arbor.
- 1987 The Changing Organization of Uruk Administration on the Susiana Plain. In *The Archaeology of Western Iran*, edited by F. Hole, pp. 107–139. Smithsonian Institution Press, Washington, D.C.

Keatinge, Richard W., and K. C. Day
- 1973 Socio-Economic Organization of the Moche Valley, Peru, During the Chimu Occupation of Chan Chan. *Journal of Anthropological Research* 29:275–295.

Kemp, Barry J.
- 1986 Large Middle Kingdom Granary Buildings (and the Archaeology of Administration). *Zeitschrift für ägyptische Sprache und Altertumskunde* 113:120–136.

Kolata, Alan
- 1986 The Agricultural Foundations of the Tiwanaku State: A View from the Heartland. *American Antiquity* 51:748–762.

Kolb, Charles C.
- 1985 Demographic Estimates in Archaeology: Contributions from Ethnoarchaeology on Mesoamerican Peasants. *Current Anthropology* 26:581–600.

Kramer, Carol
- 1980 Estimating Prehistoric Populations: An Ethnoarchaeological Approach. In *L'archéologie de l'Iraq du début de l'époque néolithique à 333 avant notre ère*, edited by M.-T. Barrelet, pp. 315–334. Editions du CNRS, Paris.
- 1982 *Village Ethnoarchaeology: Rural Iran in Archaeological Perspective*. Academic Press, New York.

Kühne, Hartmut
- 1990 The Effects of Irrigation Agriculture: Bronze and Iron Age Habitation along the Khabur, Eastern Syria. In *Man's Role in the Shaping of the Eastern Mediterranean Landscape*, edited by S. Bottema, G. Entjes-Nieborg, and W. van Zeist, pp. 15–30. Balkema, Rotterdam, The Netherlands.

Lebeau, Marc, Anne Leyniers, Dominique Martin, Kristien Pillen-Vandermeersch, Malou Schneider, Fabienne Vilvorder, and André Stevens
- 1989 Rapport préliminaire sur la quatrième campagne de fouilles à Tell Melebiya (Moyen-Khabour—printemps 1987). *Akkadica* 61:1–31.

Liverani, Mario
- 1982 Ville et campagne dans le royaume d'Ugarit. Essai d'analyse économique. In *Societies and Languages of the Ancient Near East: Studies in Honour of I. M. Dinkonoff*, edited by M. A. Dandamayev et al., pp. 249–258. Aris and Phillips, Warminster, England.

Marfoe, Leon
- 1979 The Integrative Transformation: Patterns of Sociopolitical Organization in Southern Syria. *Bulletin of the American Schools of Oriental Research* 234: 1–42.
- 1980 Review of A. Kempinski, *The Rise of Urban Cultures*, and R. Amiran et al., *Early Arad. Journal of Near Eastern Studies* 39:315–322.

Margueron, Jean-Claude
- 1991 Mari, l'Euphrate, et le Khabur au milieu du IIIe millénaire. *Bulletin of the Canadian Society for Mesopotamian Studies* 21:79–100.

Mazar, Amihai
- 1990 *Archaeology of the Land of the Bible*. Doubleday, New York.

Milano, Lucio
- 1987 Food Rations at Ebla. *Mari Annales de Recherches Interdisciplinaires* 5:519–550.

Miller, Naomi
- 1990 Archaeobotanical Perspectives on the Rural-Urban Connection. In *Economy and Settlement in the Near East: Analyses of Ancient Sites and Materials*, edited by N. Miller, pp. 79–83. MASCA Research Papers in Science and Archaeology 7 (supplement). MASCA, University Museum, Philadelphia.

Monchambert, Jean-Yves
- 1984 Le futur lac du Moyen Khabour: Rapport sur la prospection archéologique menée en 1983. *Syria* 61:181–218.
- 1987 Mashnaqa 1986. Rapport préliminaire sur la deuxième campagne de fouilles. *Syria* 64:47–78.

Naroll, Raoul
- 1962 Floor Area and Settlement Population. *American Anthropologist* 27:587–589.

Oates, David, and Joan Oates
- 1976 Early Irrigation Agriculture in Mesopotamia. In *Problems in Economic and Social Archaeology*, edited by G. Sieveking et al., pp. 109–135. Duckworth, London.

Pearson, Harry W.
1957 The Economy Has No Surplus: Critique of a Theory of Development. In *Trade and Market in Early Empires,* edited by K. Polanyi et al., pp. 320–341. Free Press, Glencoe, Ill.

Pfälzner, Peter
1986– The Excavations at Tell Bderi 1986. *Annales archéologiques*
1987 *arabes syriennes* 36–37:292–303.
1988 Tell Bderi 1985. Bericht über die erste Kampagne. *Damaszener Mitteilungen* 3:223–386.

Polanyi, Karl
1963 Ports of Trade in Early Societies. *Journal of Economic History* 23:30–45.
1968 *Primitive, Archaic and Modern Economies: Essays of Karl Polanyi* (G. Dalton, ed.). Doubleday, Garden City, N.Y.

Postgate, J. Nicholas
1984 Processing of Cereals in the Cuneiform Record. *Bulletin on Sumerian Agriculture* 1:103–113.

Pozorski, T.
1987 Changing Priorities within the Chimu State: The Role of Irrigation Agriculture. In *The Origins and Development of the Andean State,* edited by J. Haas, S. Pozorski, and T. Pozorski, pp. 111–120. Cambridge University Press, Cambridge.

Redman, Charles L.
1978 *The Rise of Civilization.* W. H. Freeman, San Francisco.

Rothman, Mitchell S.
1985 Barley and Date Cultivation in an Early Southern Iraqi State. Paper presented at the American Anthropological Association Annual Meeting, Washington, D.C.

Saghieh, Muntaha
1991 The Lebanese University Recent Excavations at Tell Kerma: A Salvage Operation on the Middle Khabur, N.E. Syria. In *Actes de la XXXVIème Rencontre Assyriologique International,* pp. 171–184. Mesopotamian History and Environment, Occasional Publications I. University of Ghent, Ghent, Belgium.

Schwartz, Glenn M.
1985 The Ninevite V Period and Current Research. *Paléorient* 11:53–70.
1986 Mortuary Evidence and Social Stratification in the Ninevite V Period. In *The Origins of Cities in Dry-Farming Syria and Mesopotamia in the Third Millennium B.C.,* edited by H. Weiss, pp. 45–60. Four Quarters, Guilford, Conn.
1987 The Ninevite V Period and the Development of Complex Society in Northern Mesopotamia. *Paléorient* 13:93–100.
In press Perspectives on Rural Ideologies: The Tell al-Raqa'i Temple. In *La Djezire et l'Euphrate Syriens de la Protohistoire à la Fin du Sécond Millénaire av. J.-C.: Tendances dans l'Interpretation Historique des Données Nouvelles,* edited by O. Rouault. Éditions Recherche sur les Civilisations, Paris.

Schwartz, Glenn M., and Hans H. Curvers
1992 Tell al-Raqa'i 1989 and 1990: Further Investigations at a Small Rural Site of Early Urban Northern Mesopotamia. *American Journal of Archaeology* 96:397–419.
In press Tell al-Raqa'i Excavations and Analyses: A Progress Report. *Archiv für Orientforschung.*

Steinkeller, Piotr
1987 The Administrative and Economic Organization of the Ur III State: The Core and the Periphery. In *The Organization of Power: Aspects of Bureaucracy in the Ancient Near East,* edited by M. Gibson and R. Biggs, pp. 19–41. Studies in Ancient Oriental Civilization, No. 46. Oriental Institute, Chicago.

Sürenhagen, Dietrich
1990 Ausgrabungen in Tall Mulla Matar 1989. *Mitteilungen der deutschen Orient-Gesellschaft* 122:125–152.

Trümpelmann, Leo
1989 Zum frühgeschichtlichen Silobau im alten Mesopotamien. In *Archaeologica Iranica et Orientalis: Miscellanea in Honorem Louis Vanden Berghe I,* edited by L. de Meyer and E. Haerinck, pp. 67–84. Peeters Press, Ghent, Belgium.

Watson, Patty Jo
1979 *Archaeological Ethnography in Western Iran.* Viking Fund Publications in Anthropology, No. 57. University of Arizona Press, Tucson.

Weiss, Harvey
1983 Excavations at Tell Leilan and the Origins of Northern Mesopotamian Cities in the Third Millennium B.C. *Paléorient* 9:39–52.
1986 The Origins of Tell Leilan and the Conquest of Space in Third Millennium Mesopotamia. In *The Origins of Cities in Dry-Farming Syria and Mesopotamia in the Third Millennium B.C.,* edited by H. Weiss, pp. 71–108. Four Quarters, Guilford, Conn.
1990 Tell Leilan 1989: New Data for Mid-Third Millennium Urbanization and State Formation. *Mitteilungen der deutschen Orient-Gesellschaft* 122:193–218.

Weiss, Harvey, and Laura Calderone
In press The End of the Ninevite 5 Sequence at Tell Leilan. In *The Origins of Northern Mesopotamian Civilization: Ninevite 5 Chronology, Economy, Society,* edited by H. Weiss. Yale University Press, New Haven, Conn.

Wetterstrom, Wilma
In press Ninevite 5 Period Agriculture at Tell Leilan: Preliminary Results. In *The Origins of Northern Mesopotamian Civilization: Ninevite 5 Chronology, Economy, Society,* edited by H. Weiss. Yale University Press, New Haven, Conn.

Whiting, Robert
1979 Some Observations on the Drehem Calendar. *Zeitschrift für Assyriologie* 69:6–33.

Wirth, Eugen
1971 *Syrien: eine geographische Länderkunde.* Wissenschaftliche Länderkunde, Band 4/5. Wissenschaftliche Buchgesellschaft, Darmstadt, Germany.

Wright, Henry T.
1969 *The Administration of Rural Production in an Early Mesopotamian Town.* Museum of Anthropology, University of Michigan, Anthropological Papers, No. 38. University of Michigan, Ann Arbor.

Wright, Rita
1989 Comment on G. Algaze, "The Uruk Expansion." *Current Anthropology* 30:599–600.

CHAPTER FOUR

Urban-Rural Relations in Bronze Age Syria: Evidence from Alalah Level VII Palace Archives

BONNIE MAGNESS-GARDINER

ONE ASPECT OF VILLAGE LIFE that requires clarification is how to identify and characterize the relationships between urban and village communities. The tools at our disposal are archaeological surveys, excavation, and ethnohistory. The first two have been used to define central and peripheral sites by absolute size, function, and distribution over the ancient landscape. Although information derived from surveys allows us to identify the presence of regional site-size hierarchy and the degree of integration (Johnson 1980a,b), it does not give us any information on the nature of the integration and why or how the degree and nature of integration changed over time. Excavation does provide the kind of qualitative and quantitative data necessary to answer these questions: for example, Zeder's recent monograph (1991), based on excavated material from Tall-i Malyan in southwest Iran, supplies a valuable analysis of urban-rural relations and managed economy in an early state system. In the Near East we have another source that describes in some detail the relations between town and country: ancient texts.

In this chapter, I examine the administrative archives from the early second-millennium B.C. palace at Alalah on the Amuq plain of northwestern Syria from the perspective of urban-rural relations. These records are a useful source of information because they are limited in number, cover a fairly short span of time, and concern the purchase, sale, loan, and maintenance of agricultural land and communities in the territory surrounding Alalah.

Early Second-Millennium B.C. Syria: History and Society

During the early second millennium B.C. Syria was organized into a series of territorial states with a capital city at the core and client city-states in the hinterland. Within each state, society was divided into two broad sectors: the government or public sector represented by the palace and temple institutions and the private or communal sector represented by individual families and residents of village communities independent of the palace or temple (Liverani 1975; Diakonoff 1982). Census records document hierarchically organized social classes as well as craft and ritual specialists. The public sector was composed of the king, his immediate family, and his dependents—the nobles, bureaucrats, and priests who ran the government in return for patronage by the king. At a lower level were the craft workers, cooks, housekeepers, guards, and others who served the daily needs of the royal family, and at the lowest level were the agricultural laborers who worked royal land. Class divisions in the private or communal sector paralleled those in the palace sector. At the top were the landed "gentry" who hired or bought labor to work their land, in the middle were the craft specialists and families who worked their own land, and at the bottom were the agricultural laborers, sometimes slaves, who worked other people's land.

The economy of ancient Syria was agrarian, and therefore relations of land and labor played a fundamental role in the definition and continuity of social and political relations (Spriggs 1984:4). Inequality in access to land (the primary agricultural resource) is apparent in land transfer documents and other texts in the palace archives. The question at hand is how this unequal access to land affected the relations between settlements of different sizes and functions. Few of the identifiable second-millennium settlements in the region have been excavated or thoroughly surveyed, so archaeological information will not help us much in characterizing size, function, or interrelations of settlements. State archives, however, provide a wealth of information. The texts I will use here are from a palace archive and as such reflect a point of view and a range of interests restricted to those of the royal family, court, and regional government. For land use and tenure practices within individual families, see family archives at Nuzi (Zaccagnini 1984; Morrison 1987), Babylonia (Charpin 1986), and Assyria (Fales 1981).

The small amount of detail recorded in ancient texts, combined with a lack of explanatory notations, makes it difficult for us to reconstruct land tenure relationships with absolute confidence. The authors of these laconic texts assume the reader is familiar with the system. As has been pointed out a number of times, what is most pervasive in the society is least likely to be recorded (Civil 1980). Like other archaeological evidence, archives suffer from problems of small sample size and incomplete recovery, and care must be taken to evaluate what is present and to be aware of what might be absent. Texts from a particular time and place can be used to construct a general model of relationships among a range of sites within a region, thus paralleling the use of archaeological surveys. Inferences drawn or hypotheses constructed from these texts could then be tested against information derived from independent sources, either other groups of texts or excavation and survey.

Generally in the ancient Near East, the state itself acquired land by military force, treaty, or purchase, whereas individual members of the government acquired land through government service or purchase (Ellis 1976). In the private-communal sector, access to land was achieved through purchase, marriage, inheritance, residence, or group membership (Liverani 1984; Diakonoff 1985). Membership in the two broad groups was not mutually exclusive, and it is often difficult to distinguish between the private and public property transactions of public figures. In both sectors the accumulation of rights and obligations incurred by residence, use, or ownership over time makes the explication of precise rules of use and tenure impossible (Adams 1982:2). However, we should be able to identify broad patterns of use and tenure. The small regional administrative center of Alalah in second-millennium B.C. Syria provides data for a case study in which we will evaluate the interaction between a center and its hinterland and the implications of that interaction for land use and tenure patterns. In the following sections, I will first discuss the archaeological and textual evidence of settlement patterns on the Amuq Plain, where Alalah is located, then the implications of land transactions for the distribution of wealth between the center and peripheral villages. In the concluding section, I will suggest how such interactions might manifest themselves in material remains.

Alalah and Its Hinterland

Alalah was the center of a city-state that formed a part of the large territorial state of Yamhad, whose capital was at Halab, modern Aleppo (Fig. 12). Texts from the level VII palace archives are the primary source for information on Alalah and its hinterland (Tables 3–5). Alalah is located in the Amuq Plain in western Syria, an area of very fertile alluvial soil and over 400 mm of annual precipitation. The Amuq is also the crossroads of major communications routes through passes to the Anatolian Plateau and to the coast. The nearby Amanus Mountains and the local ranges were good sources of timber, and the Amanus was also well known in antiquity for its silver mines. Alalah's subsistence economy was based on dry farming of wheat and barley and herding of sheep, goats, and cattle (Gaàl 1972:279–290). Texts also document Alalah's craft manufacturing capabilities in weaving, metal work, pottery, and carpentry (Gaàl 1972:290–295). Trade, both internal and international, certainly existed as an element of Alalah's economy, but the agrarian subsistence economy undoubtedly was dominant throughout the period of the level VII archives (Gaàl 1972: 295–300). The palace and archive date to the eighteenth century B.C. (Collon 1977) and are roughly contemporary with the First Babylonian dynasty in southern Mesopotamia.

Excavated by Sir Leonard Woolley (1955) and published by D. J. Wiseman (1953, 1954), the archive is composed of approximately 200 texts, most of which come from a series of three interconnected rooms in the palace (Wiseman 1953:119–122). The way the tablets were strewn through these rooms suggested to Woolley (1955:103) that they "had been dropped by people who were trying to save them from the burning building." Although it is clear that the tablets were a deliberate collection (and thus a true archive), we do not know how many and what kinds of documents were in the original collection. I assume that what was retrieved is a representative sample. The level VII archive includes letters, treaties, and legal records, but the majority of the texts are administrative documents: food disbursements and texts relating to the exchange of goods between Alalah and its villages. Although the palace setting of the archive suggests that it relates to the public activities of the king and his family, Klengel (1974:276) sees it as a family archive. Whether or not the archive documents the activities of the royal household in its public or private capacity (or both), it was found in an administrative setting at an urban site and contains information on urban interaction with the settlements in the countryside.

Alalah is only one of many ancient settlements on the Amuq Plain. Therefore, interaction between Alalah, an admin-

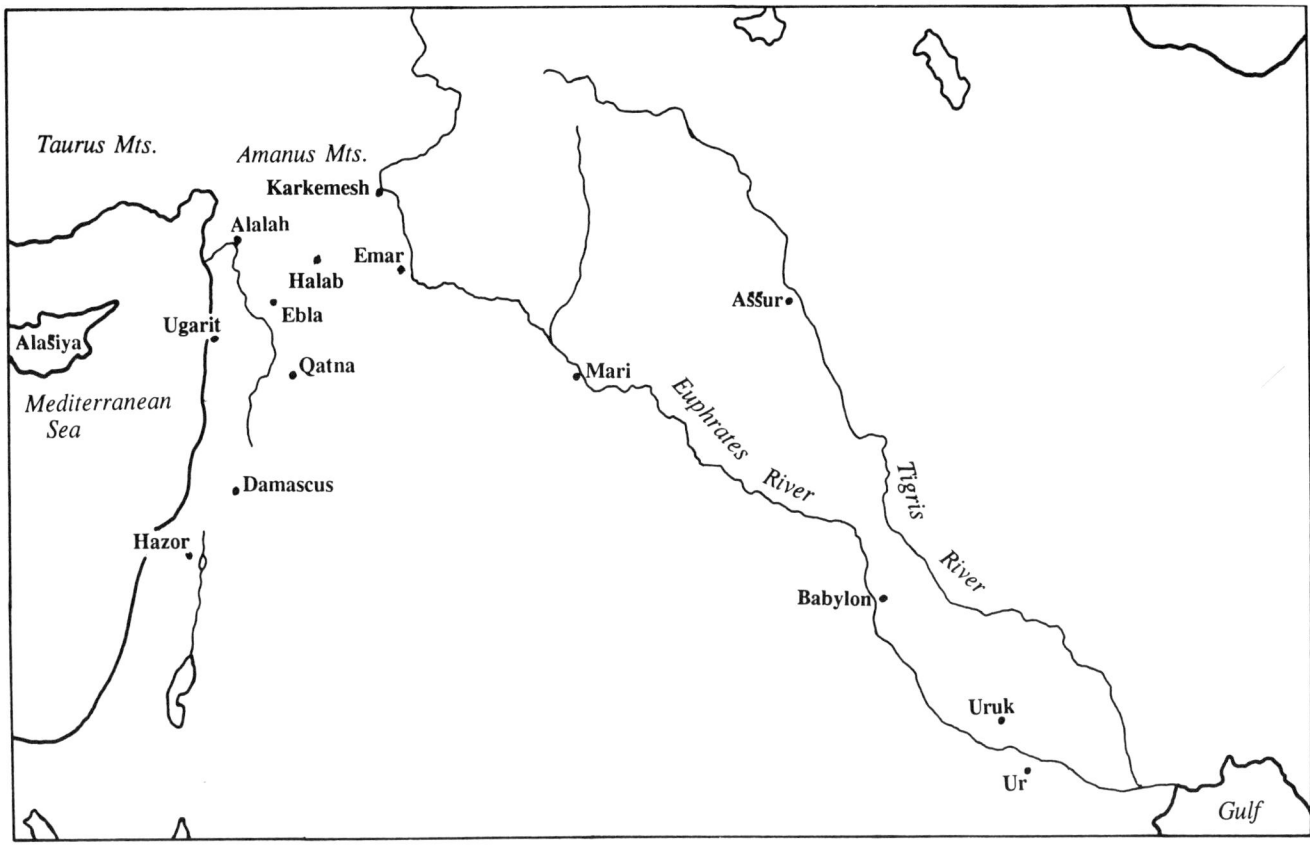

Fig. 12. Northern Syria.

istrative center, and its hinterland villages is potentially reconstructible from settlement patterns, using data from archaeological surveys (Braidwood 1937), analogy with the contemporary Old Babylonian landscape (Leemans 1982), and information from the Alalah archives (Wiseman 1953). Using French cadastral maps, Robert Braidwood and his team located and visited 178 mounds on the Amuq Plain. Sherds were used to date each site: most seem to have been occupied over long periods of time. The placement of sites on the plain does not seem to relate either to defensive requirements or to the need for fresh water (Braidwood 1937:39). At the time of the survey the plain was quite swampy, and Braidwood suggests that the choice of site location was made on the basis of availability of dry, arable land (1937:39). Braidwood's period

Table 3. Sites under Control of Halab, Capital of Yamhad[a]

Annaše (8:38; 58:1)
Arazik (7:49; 8:44; 55:39; 358:4)
Irkilli (21:20; 22:20)
Ituwa (76:3)
Lapana (58:19)
Tadundi (77:3)
  Total = 6

[a] Numbers in parentheses in this table and the following tables are the Alalah text numbers as recorded in Wiseman (1953). The number following the colon is the line in which the place name occurs.

Table 4. Sites Equivalent to Alalah or outside the State of Yamhad

Alašiya (269:33)
Apišal (6:26; 409:45)
Bitin (259:4; 266:4,5; 268:15; 369:8)
Ebla (35:10; 60:3; 269:3; 373:3; 377:4)
Karkemesh (268:11; 349:2)
Kaššu (412:7)
Nihin (11:37)
Nuhašše (96:33)
Qatna (6:37)
Tuba (11:31; 367:14)
Tunip (252:17; 253:27)
Ugarit (358:7)
  Total = 12

Table 5. Sites Politically Subordinate to Alalah

Subordination by treaty	Subordination by legal jurisdiction	
Adrate (456:10)	Adabiq (95:rev+11)	Kuzubia (37:4,9)
Airraše (455:22,25)	Age (54:1; 55:1,21)	Lakka (56:22)
Amame (456:13)	Aime (54:29)	Munnik (455:9,10)
Ammakki (456:7)	Akšiurunne (78:6)	Šallun (56:1)
Aušun (456:14)	Amakwan (56:3)	Šipte (56:6)
Emar (456:1)	Bimi (54:24)	Suharuwa (7:7; 80:3; 86:3)
Halliwa (456:15)	Dimat (76:1; 96:27)	Taradi (55:11)
Kazkuwa (456:6)	Erirambi (56:9)	Tarmannie (56:2)
Madakina (456:3)	Halma (56:7)	Tunid (77:4)
Murar (456:17,38)	Iašul (79:2)	Uniga (45:3)
Naštarbi (456:4)	Iburia (52:1)	Ure (56:8)
Parre (456:8)	Igandan (55:2,22)	Ušuwa (86:7)
Sarbat (456:2)	Igar (56:5)	Warre (78:4)
Uwiya (456:9)	Karše (33:21)	Watikla (80:1)
Zabunap (456:5)	Kubiya (34:3)	Zuzzura (78:5)
Zikir (456:16)	Kunuwa (41:5; 53:1; 78:5)	Total = 31
Total = 16		
Grand total = 47		

VII encompasses level VII at Alalah. For period VII, Braidwood records a fairly dense occupation, evenly distributed over the area (1937:51). The site of Alalah is located on the direct route from the Mediterranean to Aleppo (ancient Halab), close to the wooded foothills at the entrance to the Amuq Plain (Woolley 1968:20–21).

Of the 178 sites surveyed, 53 had sherds belonging to period VII; 28 sites were characterized as "large," 16 were "medium," and 9 were "small."[1] The proportion of large sites seems high (Hodder and Orton 1976:70), but there is substantial alluviation on the plain that may have covered small sites from the second millennium B.C. On the other hand, the total number of sites for this period corresponds well to the number of sites over which Alalah had some control as an administrative center (Table 5). There probably were not very many very small sites.

Information on the composition of rural settlements can be gleaned from Leemans's survey of material concerning the Babylonian countryside (1982). Leemans notes that whereas Hammurabi's law code (Sections 30–41) requires the assignment of field, orchard, and house to eligible soldiers, letters refer principally to fields and date orchards. When there is a reference to a house, the writer complains of its distance from the fields (Leemans 1982:247). In private contracts, houses always border on houses and fields on fields (Leemans 1982:248). This suggests a hinterland of villages rather than individual farmsteads. Although there are fewer texts to consult from the Alalah archives, the situation appears to be the same. Settlements (*âlu*) were transferred from one owner to another as units with their territories (*eperu*) intact.[2] Individual houses also were sold within settlements,[3] but this was a rare occurrence in the Alalah level VII archive, as elsewhere, and may reflect different registration requirements.[4] Thus the settlement size distribution observed in Braidwood's survey data would appear to be correct. People lived in aggregate settlements, rather than on individual farmsteads, and went out to work on surrounding agricultural land.

Interaction

Property in the countryside was bought and sold by the king (Table 6, first column), members of the royal households,[5] and other private individuals resident in the town of Alalah.[6] The king and other wealthy individuals loaned money and material to individuals and groups located in rural villages, and the king provided food for individuals and groups in other hinterland villages (Tables 7, second column, and 6, first column). In order to determine how this state of affairs affected the distribution of agricultural income in Alalah and its hinterland villages, we must look at the general pattern of land tenure relations in the ancient Near East. Two broad categories of labor-land owner relations are relevant to our analysis of Alalah: owners who work the land themselves and owners who have others work the land for them. When the owner of the property worked it himself, usually with the help of his family, there is little documentation. Under normal circum-

Table 6. Sites under Direct Economic Control of the Palace

Sites where the king of Alalah owns property	Sites where grain is delivered
Age (54:1; 55:21; 253:12)	Age (253:12)
Emar (238:19; 253:17,28; 254:12; 269:9,52,74; 275:12; 348:13; 357:6; 456:1)	Alime (245:5; 256:11)
Iašul (79:2,10,23)	Allise (271:8)
Iburia (52:1)	Amame (240:2; 241:3; 456:13)
Igandan (55:2,22)	Ara (253:16; 271:19)
Kunuwa (41:5; 53:1; 78:5; 368:3)	Astakamu (264:9; 268:2; 272:10)
Naštarbi (11:1,6,22,26; 33:29; 269:51,57,69)	Ašuni (271:16)
Suharuwa (7:7; 80:3; 86:3; 98a:x+5)	Hursanu (271:11)
Taradi (55:11)	Murar (261:12; 269:47)
Zibbi (379:4)	Nuranti (376:17)
Total = 10	Šanuka (271:12)
	Warre (78:4; 357:8)
	Total = 12
Grand total = 21[a]	

[a] Age appears on both lists.

stances the palace would not be involved in sales, exchange, or inheritance, and no labor contracts would be necessary. The income from the land was the owner's to dispose of as he pleased. The only institutional claim on that income would have been taxes owed to the government. At Alalah we have knowledge of privately owned and worked property only through the loans made by the king to individuals and groups in various villages (Gaàl 1982–1984:4). The loans imply that the individual or group owned some sort of real property that could be used as collateral for the loan.

When a landowner used agricultural labor outside his own family, he retained the entire income from the property less the expense of production. One production expense was subsistence rations for the workers. Labor contracts and ration texts, then, provide the documentary evidence for the use of nonfamily labor, and they are particularly valuable when other

Table 7. Sites of Individually or Collectively Owned Property

Sites where individuals own property	Sites where individuals or collectives receive loans from the king	Sites where material is purchased by the king
Airreše (33:4,16; 63:2; 64:2,3; 96:9,14; 98d:6; 455:22,25)	Aime (54:29)	Hutamme (376:3)
Akšiurunne (78:6)	Alama (42:3,4; 319:3)	Irta (269:27)
Amakwan (56:3)	Apratik (374:2)	Utiyar (269:36,65)
Dimat (79:1; 96:27)	Kubiya (34:3; 280:9; 224b:9)	Total = 3
Erirambi (56:9)	Kuzubia (37:4,9)	
Halma (56:7)	Uniga (45:3; 376:3)	
Igar (56:5)	Total = 6	
Lakka (56:22)		
Munnik (455:19,20)		
Šallun (56:1)		
Šipte (56:6)		
Tarmannie (56:2)		
Tunid (77:4)		
Ure (56:8)		
Watikla (80:1)		
Zuzzura (78:5)		
Total = 16		

Grand total = 25

ownership documentation is missing. So if individuals or corporate groups at a site received substantial quantities of food from the palace, one can assume that the site belonged to the institution providing the food (Gaàl 1982–1984:4). Whether or not the people receiving the food were free to move off the land is another issue.

Land sales, loans (presumably made against land as collateral), and texts documenting the distribution of food give us some indication of various types of land use relations. The ninety-nine toponyms present in the level VII archives allow us to identify different types of land use relations at individual settlements (Gaàl 1982–1984:2) and to reconstruct a regional pattern of interaction. Not all of the places mentioned were under Alalah's direct control. Gaàl (1982–1984) discusses the documentary evidence for each toponym, as well as the size and status of each entity relative to Alalah. I will use his initial assessment to discuss urban-rural relations in more detail. The types of interaction documented in the texts allow us to sort settlements into three categories: dominant, equivalent, and subordinate. Evidence for these different types of relations is found in treaties, contracts for the sale and exchange of real estate, loans, and food distribution texts.

DOMINANT SITES

Halab (modern Aleppo), capital of Yamhad, was the seat of economic and political power in the region. Many legal and political decisions concerning Alalah and its surrounding sites emanated from the court at Halab. Landownership and labor were central concerns of both the local administration and the regional state. These concerns impinged directly on Alalah's relationships with its surrounding villages (Diakonoff 1982) and with Yamhad's relations with Alalah (Gaàl 1982–1984). That the king of Alalah was subordinate to the king of Yamhad is clearly stated in a legal record of exchange[7] and in a treaty.[8] Abbael, the king of Yamhad, put down a revolt in the town of Irridi, a secondary administrative center under the control of Yarimlim. Yarimlim, who may have been Abbael's brother (Landsberger 1954:51), remained loyal to Abbael during the revolt, but in the course of the fighting the city of Irridi was destroyed. Abbael then gave Alalah to Yarimlim in exchange for the "smashed" city of Irridi. The language of the treaty makes it clear that Alalah was being given to Yarimlim because of his loyalty and that if Yarimlim or any of his descendents rebelled or otherwise "sinned" against the kings of Yamhad, the settlements (*âlu*) and lands (*eperu*) would be forfeited.[9] This is a statement of political patronage, not the simple movement of real estate between two members of a ruling family.

The king of Alalah acquired his right to reside and rule at Alalah from the king of Yamhad. The king of Yamhad also provided sufficient agricultural land and labor (resident in the village settlements) to support the king of Alalah, but the king of Yamhad retained the right of first refusal to purchase land in Alalah.[10]

EQUIVALENT SITES

Twelve places named in our archival texts interact with Alalah on a more or less equivalent level (Table 4). There are royal families at many of the places in Table 4. Some of the sites were more powerful than Alalah. These sites, however, were outside the state of Yamhad and therefore had no power over Alalah. The transactions represented are social, political, and economic exchanges encompassing negotiations for dynastic intermarriage, for example, as well as commercial transactions involving large amounts of goods. Occasionally an individual originating from or going to these places was given rations for travel, but as far as we know from the texts no one from Alalah owned property in these sites.

SUBORDINATE SITES

The treaty AT 456 gave Yarimlim hegemony over Alalah and a number of villages in the vicinity in exchange for the city and towns of Irridi. Fifteen toponyms (lines 1–18) named in the text indicate that these were attached in some formal way to the secondary centers at Alalah and Irridi. Conditions that affected land tenure existed for both parties: Abbael, the king of Yamhad, could not take back his "gift" (without punishment), and Yarimlim would not reveal things said to him by the king, nor commit any offense against him, nor "grasp the hem" of (i.e., be loyal to) any other king (lines 42–49). If Yarimlim did any of these things, then he would lose both the city (Alalah) and the territory (*eperum*) given to him by the king of Yamhad (lines 49–50). Yarimlim's descendants were also required to abide by the same conditions. The implication of the terminology is that the places other than Alalah named in the exchange were part of the territory (*eperum*) of the new state.

Clearly, landed property was central to the political relationship between the rulers of Alalah and Yamhad. Throughout the period of the archives, the "Great King" in Yamhad maintained an interest in, and to some degree control over, the transfer of land within the kingdom of Alalah. The superimposition of this level of control adds to the complexity of town-village relations at the site of Alalah. For example, a number of texts document legal and commercial relations between residents of Alalah and villages under the direct control of Halab (Table 3). That the king of Yamhad also remained in control of tax collection throughout the regional state can be inferred from tax exemption clauses in properties that the king of Alalah bought with the exemption intact.[11] Since the king of Alalah had no need to exempt himself from tax obligations to himself, the taxes must have been due directly to the king of Yamhad at Halab. Perhaps the direct taxation of villages by Yamhad was the reason why the king of Alalah was provided with a number of specific villages. Without any tax base, the king of Alalah would have had to work his own property to provide for the basic subsistence requirements of his family and the administrative apparatus of his court.

Although the role of Yamhad in Alalah's relations with its villages is a factor that cannot be ignored, most relationships and transactions recorded in Alalah's archives reflect purely local interests. Of particular interest to us here are the fifty-seven places that Alalah as a regional center dominated politically and/or economically.[12] Political subordination of sixteen sites is specified in AT 455 and AT 456 (Table 5, first column), in which the king of Alalah received his right to rule from the king of Yamhad. Political subordination of various sites is also recognizable in texts indicating that the king of Alalah has jurisdiction over the settlement of disputes over land or the activities of village residents (Table 5, second column). Within the legal texts themselves the king's jurisdiction is not always made explicit, but the very fact of the texts' presence in the royal archive implies local jurisdiction.

The tradition of domination and taxation is a long one in this region. At Ebla, a regional state of the twenty-fourth century B.C., the city collected crops from the outlying villages on a regular basis (Archi 1992). At Ugarit, a later state on the Syrian coast, political domination over villages entitled the administrative center to extract taxes in money and in kind (Heltzer 1976; Liverani 1979). In Alalah level VII, however, no records of tax collection were found. If the lack of records reflects ancient reality (and it is certainly possible that these records were kept elsewhere), perhaps the taxes were collected directly by the administration at Halab, the capital of the state of Yamhad. In any case, the apparent lack of tax revenue suggests that the continued existence of the administration of Alalah as a unit within the state of Yamhad depended on other methods of extracting agricultural products from its rural settlements.

These alternative methods of economic domination of peripheral villages are inferred on the basis of documented sales, exchanges or inheritance of property, and rationing of inhabitants. The kings of Alalah over several generations acquired by purchase or exchange fields or entire settlements in ten places (Table 6, first column). In one case, the property was obtained by exchange from the king of Yamhad.[13] In three cases the kings of Alalah purchased settlements and fields from individuals,[14] and in one case the palace acquired property through default of a loan.[15] Kunuwa, the property acquired through default, later reentered the private sector when the king exchanged it for other property.[16] Clearly, agricultural land moved back and forth from private to palace sectors easily and, in the case of Kunuwa, frequently. Gaàl (1982–1984) details this movement on a place-by-place basis.

Purchase, inheritance, and exchange documents provide evidence of ownership but not of the method of working the land and distributing its products. We can only infer the organization of agricultural production by the presence or absence of rationing and by analogy with the organization of agricultural production in other ancient Near Eastern states. Texts record the delivery of monthly rations to over 200 individuals and groups in the city of Alalah and twelve of its villages (Wiseman 1959; Goetze 1959). Only for one, Age, is there a record of the king having purchased property (Table 6, second column). In the other rationed villages the king seems to have the rights to property by previous or unrecorded arrangements. The dependency implied by the delivery of foodstuffs suggests that the king purchased or otherwise acquired the services of some of the village residents with the land itself. The amount of food delivered to the inhabitants of a village ranges from 5 *parisu* (1 *parisu* = 8 liters) to 500 *parisu* of grain (Bunnens 1982). Although we have no population figures for the villages under examination, 4,000 liters of grain would certainly seem to be enough to keep a village fed for the month in which the rations were issued (Ellison 1981:38; Chapter 3 by Schwartz). It is very likely that, in the case of the villages where rations were distributed, the palace directly supervised agricultural production, used the inhabitants as laborers, paid them in comestibles, and took the entire harvest minus expenses. This pattern of direct control occurs elsewhere in Syria and Mesopotamia in earlier and later periods (Foster 1983, 1986).

There are no records of rations being distributed to inhabitants of the other nine villages in which the king purchased property. Here the conditions of tenure are unspecified, with one exception: AT 55 records the transfer of property from private hands to the king, with *ilkum* attached. *Ilkum* is a term best known in Old Babylonian Mesopotamia in the context of state service. Ellis defines it as "the service which an individual performed for the state, and which by extension also came to be applied to land held in return for (or subject to) service" (1976:13). The connection of service obligation to land tenure is demonstrable for Mesopotamia proper, but the term itself may have been adopted outside Babylonia without the conditions attached to it in Babylonia itself (Postgate 1982). The one-time use of the term at Alalah seems to imply the transfer of a service obligation to the king with the transfer of the property. The implication is that the inhabitants of the village were to serve the king in some capacity (perhaps in the military), and the village land would serve to support those people while they performed their service.

No other texts mention the *ilkum* service. In the villages where someone (including the king) purchased property but did not provide food for the inhabitants, the villagers probably leased the land from the owner in return for a set percentage of the harvest. This is the case at Ugarit, for example, where the palace expected 25 percent of the harvest on leased property in palace-owned villages and 10 percent of the harvest in taxes from "free" villages (Liverani 1979).

One curious omission in the royal archives is the lack of any records for receipt of harvested grain from property owned and worked directly or sublet by the palace. The palace ordered seed grain and food to be delivered to various villages, but never recorded collection of the harvest. Perhaps this omission may be explained by storage of grain in or near the place of production, where the records were kept. In fact, one ration text[17] ordered that grain be delivered to one village from another site. Since only texts documenting expenditures seem to have been kept at the palace, records of income must have been stored elsewhere, presumably with the grain.

The king was not the only documented property owner in the state sector of Alalah. Officers of the palace also owned fields, houses, and entire settlements. Unfortunately, it is not made clear in the texts whether the "ownership" of land by members of the court was related to their position in the palace organization. Sixteen villages were recorded as being owned wholly or in part by individuals in the state of Alalah (Table 7, first column). Many of them played a role in the administration of the state, and all of them were of the elite. With Gaàl (1982–1984), I believe these individuals acted within the private sector. There are no records to indicate whether the owners resided on and worked the property themselves with wage (or rationed) labor or leased it to the inhabitants under the conditions described earlier, because no private archives were found in Alalah. However, the fact that many of the people who bought property held positions at court suggests that they did not reside on their property and probably worked the property with tenant farmers.

A less dependent relationship is exemplified by the loan of silver or grain by the king to individuals or groups in six villages (Table 7, second column). The loans were made only to individuals or groups at places where the king neither purchased property nor rationed individuals. After a poor harvest or other catastrophe the palace provided loans of seed grain, oil, or silver. Because these six villages were not otherwise recorded in property transfers but received loans from the king, they are considered communally or privately owned (Gaàl 1982–1984). Finally, the palace purchased large quantities of beer[18] and even grain[19] from three villages (Table 7, third column). If the palace owned these villages, then there would have been no reason to pay for produce. Payments were made to the settlements themselves rather than to individuals. Thus these three villages should be considered part of the private, communally organized sector in Alalah (Gaàl 1982–1984:21).

Conclusion

One clear conclusion from this brief look at patterns of land ownership in Alalah is that the economic relationship between the palace and the villages under its political jurisdiction was neither uniform nor static. The palace directly controlled some land in some villages and all the land in other villages, and it sold land from its own land fund as well as purchased and exchanged property from the private sphere. In total, of the places we can identify as politically subordinate to Alalah (Table 8), 56 percent were under direct control of the center.[20] Other individuals resident at Alalah owned property in 28 percent of the subordinate villages (Table 7, first column), and another 16 percent of the villages mentioned in the archive were communally owned (Table 7, second and third columns). Obviously, this does not represent the totality of economic relationships in Alalah level VII. The palace had a greater need to document interaction with people and places under its direct control than with those in the private sector whose needs were sporadic or temporary. The pattern of landownership, however, and our hypothesized organization of agricultural production give us a basis on which to model the distribution of wealth in Alalah and its countryside.

One vital question to an archaeologist is how this pattern of landownership and agricultural production would be reflected in the material culture of the peripheral villages. I propose that a dichotomy of village types would be recogniz-

Table 8. Distribution of Economic Power over Villages[a]

Palace	Private individual	Communal or collective
32 (56%)	16 (28%)	9 (16%)

[a]Total = 57.

able. Where the king or town-based elite owned land in the countryside and worked it with wage or rationed labor, the owners located at Alalah would have had the right of disposal over the entire amount produced on the land minus expenses for seed and labor. Therefore, the village inhabitants would have been kept at subsistence level with little or no possibility of increasing their wealth. On the other hand, communal or privately owned villages and villages owned by the palace but leased to inhabitants would have had a greater percentage of production available for local consumption, storage, transformation, and investment. We would expect these villages to display greater wealth, both in access to exotic goods and in improvement of property or housing.

In fact, this dichotomy of village types was the result of a similar pattern of landownership and use in the Amuq during the late nineteenth and early twentieth centuries, when the Ottoman empire granted land titles to high-ranked members of the Turkmen tribe. Barbara Aswad (1971) conducted her research in this area in the 1950s, and her results have been used by both Adams (1982) and Postgate (1982) to discuss possible land tenure options in other areas of ancient Mesopotamia. Notables of the Turkmen tribe quickly became large landowners, hiring lower-ranked herders and other tribespeople as sharecroppers (Aswad 1971:22). The nobility continued for a time to live in the villages, where they built fine stone houses for themselves and one-room huts of mud and straw for their sharecroppers. Approximately 200 huts and 1 or 2 houses composed a typical Turkmen village.

Shortly after the Turkmen settled down, another group of herders moved into the area and also settled down in a pattern of core and fringe villages. This herding group was less highly ranked than the Turkmen and, rather than individually obtaining property rights from the Ottoman government, maintained property corporately (Aswad 1971:24). Within this group, agriculturally successful lineages expanded at the expense of less successful lineages and developed into core villages. Property was owned by villagers but worked by sharecroppers. Less successful patronymic groups broke up and formed heterogeneous fringe villages in which property was owned elsewhere. Both core and fringe villages, however, were clearly distinguishable from Turkmen villages in their layout and architecture. A core village consisted of 40+ stone houses, with a few mudbrick houses attached for the sharecroppers (Aswad 1971:44–45). I would suggest that the villages in the territory of Alalah would have been similarly differentiated depending on the conditions under which they worked the land during the period of the level VII archives. The only way to confirm, reject, or modify this assessment will be to systematically survey and excavate a sample of the village sites still remaining in Alalah's hinterland.

Notes

I would like to thank Glenn Schwartz, the anonymous reviewer, and Maria deJ. Ellis for their helpful comments on content and form. However, I am responsible for any deficiencies of fact or interpretation in the argument presented here.

1. Absolute dimensions for the sites are not given. "Large" is less than 400 × 250 m (the largest site on the plain) and greater than 25 m in diameter. "Small" is less than 25 m in diameter. "Medium" is everything in between (Braidwood 1937:39).
2. Alalah Text (hereafter AT) 56 and 55. Alalah texts are published by Wiseman: AT 1–454 (1953), AT 455 (1954), and AT 456 (1959).
3. AT 59, AT 60.
4. I would like to thank Maria deJ. Ellis for bringing this possibility to my attention.
5. AT 60, AT 63.
6. AT 58, AT 62, AT 64.
7. AT 1.
8. AT 456.
9. AT 456:47–57.
10. AT 79.
11. AT 52:3, AT 54:3, AT 55:6.
12. Of the rest of the sites named to make up the ninety-nine, some are mentioned in ambiguous contexts, others only as the residence of witnesses to legal texts.
13. AT 79.
14. AT 52, AT 55, AT 80.
15. AT 41, AT 53.
16. AT 78.
17. AT 271.
18. AT 269, AT 376.
19. AT 269.
20. Twenty-one sites exist where the king owned property or rationed the inhabitants (Table 4). Eleven sites not mentioned elsewhere in the archive are given to the king via the treaty documents (AT 455, AT 456).

References Cited

Adams, Robert McC.
   1982 Property Rights and Functional Tenure in Mesopotamian Rural Communities. In *Societies and Languages of the Ancient Near East: Studies in Honour of I. M. Diakonoff*, edited by M. A. Dandamayev et al., pp. 1–14. Aris and Phillips, Warminster, England.

Archi, Alfonso
   1992 The City of Ebla and the Organization of its Rural Territory. *Altorientalische Forschungen* 19:24–28.

Aswad, Barbara
   1971 *Property Control and Social Strategies in Settlers on a Middle Eastern Plain*. Museum of Anthropology, University of Michigan, Anthropological Papers, No. 44. University of Michigan, Ann Arbor.

Braidwood, Robert
1937 *Mounds on the Plain of Antioch*. Oriental Institute, Chicago.

Bunnens, Guy
1982 Quelques aspects de la vie quotidienne au palais d'Alalakh d'après les listes de rations du niveau VII (XVIIIe/XVIIe s.). *Archiv für Orientforschung, Beiheft* 19:72–84.

Charpin, Dominique
1986 Transmission des titres de propriété et constitution des archives privées en babylonie ancienne. In *Cuneiform Archives and Libraries*, edited by K. Veenhof, pp. 121–140. Nederlands Historisch-Archeologisch Instituut te Istanbul, Leiden, The Netherlands.

Civil, Miguel
1980 Les limites de l'information textuelle. In *L'archéologie de l'Iraq du début de l'époque néolithique à 333 avant notre ère*, edited by M.-T. Barrelet, pp. 225–232. Editions du CNRS, Paris.

Collon, Dominique
1977 A New Look at the Chronology of Alalah Level VII: A Rejoinder. *Anatolian Studies* 27:127–131.

Diakonoff, Igor M.
1982 The Structure of Near Eastern Society before the Middle of the 2nd Millennium B.C. *Oikumene* 3:7–100.
1985 Extended Families in Old Babylonian Ur. *Zeitschrift für Assyriologie* 75:47–65.

Ellis, Maria deJ.
1976 *Agriculture and the State in Ancient Mesopotamia*. University Museum, Philadelphia.

Ellison, Rosemary
1981 Diet in Mesopotamia: The Evidence of the Barley Ration Texts (ca. 3000–1400 B.C.). *Iraq* 45:35–46.

Fales, Frederick M.
1981 Il villaggio assiro Bit Abu-Ila'a. *Dialoghi di archeologia* 3:66–84.

Foster, Benjamin
1983 Ebla and the Origins of Akkadian Accountability. *Bibliotheca Orientalis* 40:298–306.
1986 Agriculture and Accountability in Ancient Mesopotamia. In *The Origins of Cities in Dry-Farming Syria and Mesopotamia in the Third Millennium B.C.*, edited by H. Weiss, pp. 109–128. Four Quarters, Guilford, Conn.

Gaàl, Erno
1972 The Economic Life of Alalah in the 18th–17th Centuries B.C. *Annales Universitatis Scientiarum Budapestinensis de Rolando Eotvos Nominatae. Sectio Historica* 13:279–300.
1982– State and Private Sectors in Alalah VII. *Acta Antiqua*
1984 *Academiae Scientiarum Hungaricae* 30:1–44.

Goetze, A.
1959 Remarks on the Ration Lists from Alalakh VII. *Journal of Cuneiform Studies* 13:34–38.

Heltzer, Michael
1976 *The Rural Community in Ancient Ugarit*. Ludwig Reichert Verlag, Wiesbaden, Germany.

Hodder, Ian, and Clive Orton
1976 *Spatial Analysis in Archaeology*. Cambridge University Press, Cambridge.

Johnson, Gregory A.
1980a Spatial Organization of Early Uruk Settlement Systems. In *L'archéologie de l'Iraq du début de l'époque néolithique à 333 avant notre ère*, edited by M.-T. Barrelet, pp. 133–163. Editions du CNRS, Paris.
1980b Rank-Size Convexity and System Integration: A View from Archaeology. *Economic Geography* 56:234–247.

Klengel, Horst
1974 Königtum und Palast nach den Alalah-Texten. In *Le palais et la royauté*, edited by P. Garelli, pp. 273–282. Geuthner, Paris.

Landsberger, Benno
1954 Assyrische Königsliste und "Dunkles Zeitalter." *Journal of Cuneiform Studies* 8:31–106.

Leemans, William F.
1982 The Pattern of Settlement in the Babylonian Countryside. In *Societies and Languages of the Ancient Near East: Studies in Honour of I. M. Diakonoff*, edited by M. A. Dandamayev et al., pp. 246–249. Aris and Phillips, Warminster, England.

Liverani, Mario
1975 Communautés de villages dans le Syrie. *Journal of the Social and Economic History of the Orient* 18:146–164.
1979 Economia delle fattorie palatine ugaritiche. *Dialoghi di Archeologia* 1:57–72.
1984 Land Tenure and Inheritance in the Ancient Near East. In *Land Tenure and Social Transformation in the Middle East*, edited by T. Khalidi, pp. 33–44. American University of Beirut, Beirut, Lebanon.

Morrison, Martha A.
1987 The Southwest Archives at Nuzi. In *Studies on the Civilization and Culture of Nuzi and the Hurrians*, Vol. 1, edited by D. I. Owen and M. A. Morrison, pp. 167–201. Eisenbrauns, Winona Lake, Ind.

Postgate, J. Nicholas
1982 Ilku and Land Tenure in the Middle Assyrian Kingdom. In *Societies and Languages of the Ancient Near East: Studies in Honour of I. M. Diakonoff*, edited by M. A. Dandamayev et al., pp. 304–313. Aris and Phillips, Warminster, England.

Spriggs, Matthew
1984 Another Way of Telling. In *Marxist Perspectives in Archaeology*, edited by M. Spriggs, pp. 1–10. Cambridge University Press, Cambridge.

Wiseman, Donald J.
1953 *The Alalakh Tablets*. British Institute of Archaeology in Ankara, Ankara, Turkey.
1954 Supplementary Copies of the Alalakh Tablets. *Journal of Cuneiform Studies* 8:1–20.
1959 Ration Lists from Alalah VII. *Journal of Cuneiform Studies* 12:19–33.

Woolley, C. Leonard
1955 *Alalakh*. The Society of Antiquaries, Oxford.

1968 *A Forgotten Kingdom.* W. W. Norton, New York.

Zaccagnini, Carlo
1984 Land Tenure and Transfer of Land at Nuzi. In *Land Tenure and Social Transformation in the Middle East,* edited by T. Khalidi, pp. 79–94. American University of Beirut, Beirut, Lebanon.

Zeder, Melinda
1991 *Feeding Cities.* Smithsonian Institution Press, Washington, D.C.

CHAPTER FIVE

The Ancient Maya Craft Community at Colha,
Belize, and Its External Relationships

THOMAS R. HESTER AND HARRY J. SHAFER

SINCE 1979, EXTENSIVE FIELDWORK and laboratory analysis have focused on the archaeological record at Colha in northern Belize (Fig. 13). Numerous published papers, along with doctoral dissertations and master's theses, have provided considerable detail on the chronology, settlement pattern, technologies, and economic focus of this site. Most of the available literature is concerned with the stone tool production at Colha, the craft-specialized activity that this represents, and the distribution of lithic artifacts produced at Colha and at sites in northern Belize and adjacent areas (e.g., Shafer and Hester 1983, 1986, 1991; Hester and Shafer 1984, 1987, 1991b). King and Potter (Chapter 6) address the nature and role of the Colha community through more than 2,000 years of occupation.

This chapter briefly summarizes the lithic technology of Colha and examines the manner in which the lithic commodities from the site were acquired and utilized by Maya consumers outside the Colha settlement area. We have recognized both "primary" and "peripheral" areas of stone tool consumption. The primary area is located in northern Belize, where utilitarian tools are found at sites generally within 60 km of Colha. In the peripheral area, at sites in Guatemala and Mexico, lithic artifacts used for ritual or symbolic purposes are found; these were probably linked to Maya elites.

Settlement History and Lithic Technology at Colha

The site of Colha is located on Rancho Creek and covers an area of about 6 km². Excavations have revealed Maya occupations dating from Middle Preclassic through Middle Postclassic times. At both ends of this spectrum, Colha represented a small village or hamlet. Maximum growth clearly occurred in the Late Preclassic and in the Late Classic. Not only were the chert workshops numerous at these times, but there was also settlement expansion and major attention devoted to the small ceremonial center at the north end of the site. Even at these peaks, Eaton (1980, 1982) estimates that Colha never exceeded a maximum of 5,000 inhabitants.

Even though the site had few elite courtyards, a minor ceremonial center, and no freestanding architecture, Colha clearly functioned, from an economic perspective, as a "central place" that maintained control of lithic production in northern Belize, at least in Late Preclassic times. Despite extensive excavation and surveys by many researchers in northern and central Belize, no other Late Preclassic lithic production sites are yet known. In contrast, during Late Classic times, Colha may have been under the aegis of the major center at Altun Ha, 26 km to the south. Possibly this relationship began in the Early Classic, if we follow Scarborough's (1985:341) argument that northern Belize polities were disrupted by a "coercive elite" in the Early Classic.

During the Late Classic period, several lithic workshops developed in the chert-bearing zone between Colha and Altun Ha.[1] Clearly, Colha's role as a community that dominated certain kinds of chert artifact production is limited largely to the Late Preclassic. However, some distinctive lithic forms, such as small stemmed blade points, were produced in large numbers at Colha in Terminal Classic times, while the other workshops to the south made bifaces or celts.

The stone tool makers of Colha utilized extensive outcrops of high-quality cherts, usually banded and of various colors, including brown, gray, and tan. The site itself was situated on

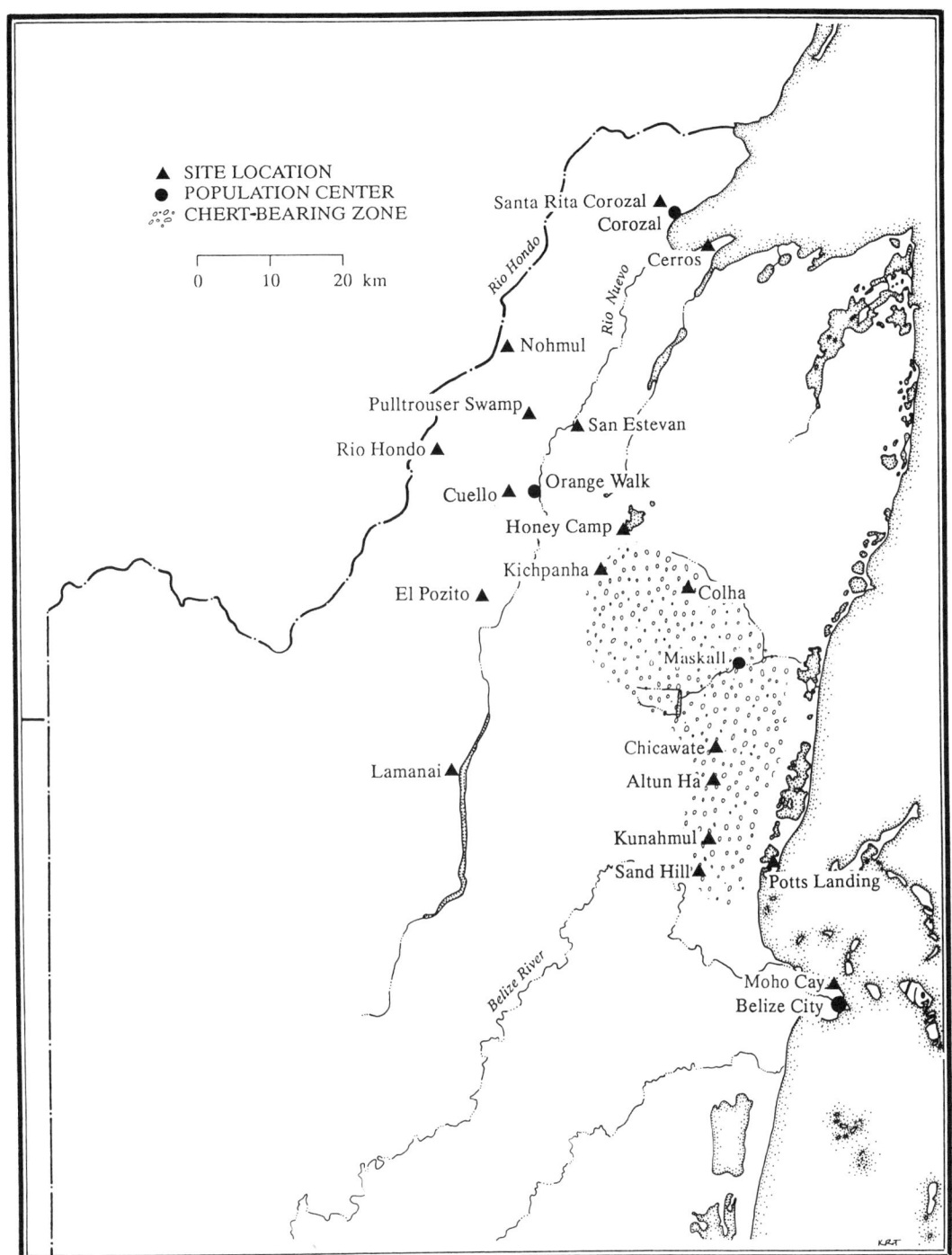

Fig. 13. Northern Belize. The chert-bearing zone is shown, along with the location of many sites noted in the text.

the northern perimeter of what we have called elsewhere the northern Belize chert-bearing zone (CBZ) (Fig. 13). Outside this region, northern Belize lithic resources are primarily poor-quality white/gray chalcedony, although there are areas such as the site of Kichpanha, 12 km northwest of Colha, where good-quality chert has been documented.

Nine excavation seasons at Colha have provided us with an abundance of data on the technology of lithic production and the diagnostic tool forms of each major period at the site. In the Middle Preclassic (900–250 B.C.), there are standardized tool forms that include narrow oval biface celts, bifaces with wedge-shaped bits (Fig. 14a), T-shaped adzes (Fig. 14b), and

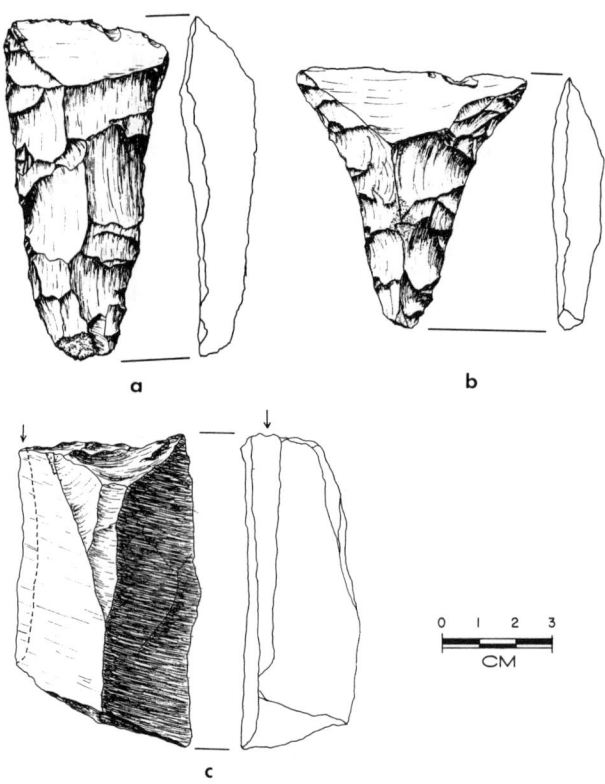

Fig. 14. Middle Preclassic lithics from Colha. (a) Wedge bit biface; (b) T-shaped adze; (c) truncated blade burin spall core (arrow indicates direction of blow).

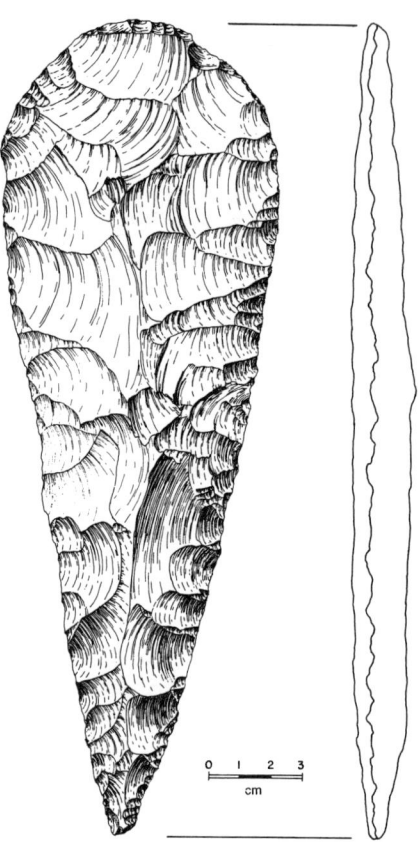

Fig. 15. Late Preclassic large oval biface from Colha.

truncated macroblade cores (Fig. 14c) that produced burin spall drills used in shell-bead making. Although we have not recognized any lithic production areas or incipient workshops, the lithic sample from Cuello, now known to be of this time frame as well (Andrews and Hammond 1990), essentially duplicates the Colha forms. It is our view that stone tool making already was underway at Colha, probably at the cottage industry level, and provided highly specialized forms, such as the T-shaped adze, to Middle Preclassic villages in northern Belize. There is the possibility that such distinctive forms were being even more widely distributed. For example, a large T-shaped adze of Middle Preclassic form on display at the Field Museum in Chicago is attributed to a provenience on the Subin River in southern Belize (collected by J. Eric Thompson, Third Marshall Field Expedition).

The extensive macroblade technology recorded at Colha in the Middle Preclassic may have had its origins in preceramic or Archaic lithic industries. A buried preceramic lithic component at Colha has been reported by Wood (1990) and Lohse (1993).

A wide array of data indicates that the extensive Late Preclassic (250 B.C.–A.D. 250) lithic industry is clearly derived, in technology and form, from the Middle Preclassic. However, unlike the Middle Preclassic, the Late Preclassic occupation at Colha is dominated by stone tool mass production. More than thirty-five large workshops, up to 450 m² in area and consisting of deposits up to 1.75 m thick, are clustered in the central core of the site. The extremely high volume of output, numbering in the hundreds of thousands to millions of tools, has been documented previously by Shafer and Hester (1983, 1986; see also Roemer 1984). Distinctive forms produced in great volume are large oval bifaces (Fig. 15), tranchet bit tools or adzes (see Shafer 1983a) (Fig. 16), and large stemmed macroblade points, often called tanged points or daggers (Fig. 17). These three forms, and a lesser but even more distinctive form produced at Colha, the eccentric (Fig. 18), are found at numerous other sites in a variety of contexts. Although other artifacts were produced in the Late Preclassic workshops, the chert workers specialized in these forms, apparently for export to Maya consumers. We cannot date the end of the workshops precisely, if indeed there was (as we have earlier suggested) a hiatus in manufacture. There is increasing evidence to indicate that the Late Preclassic workshops continued into Terminal Preclassic and even Early Classic times, although the level of production and the variety of forms may have decreased.

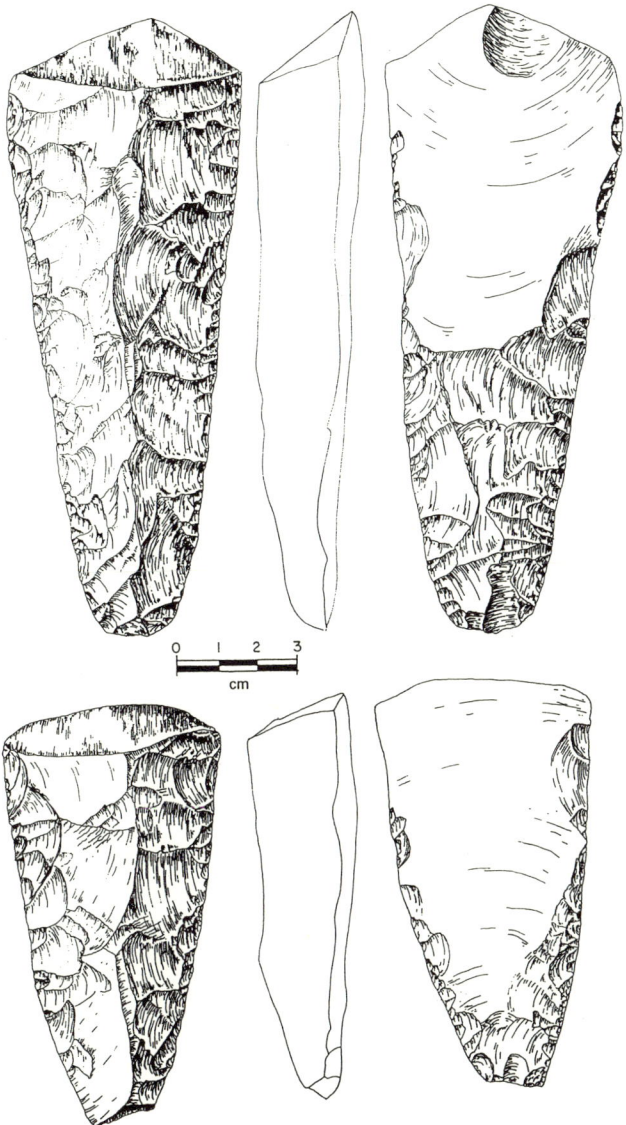

Fig. 16. Late Preclassic tranchet-bit tools from Colha. Both sides and longitudinal cross sections are shown for two specimens.

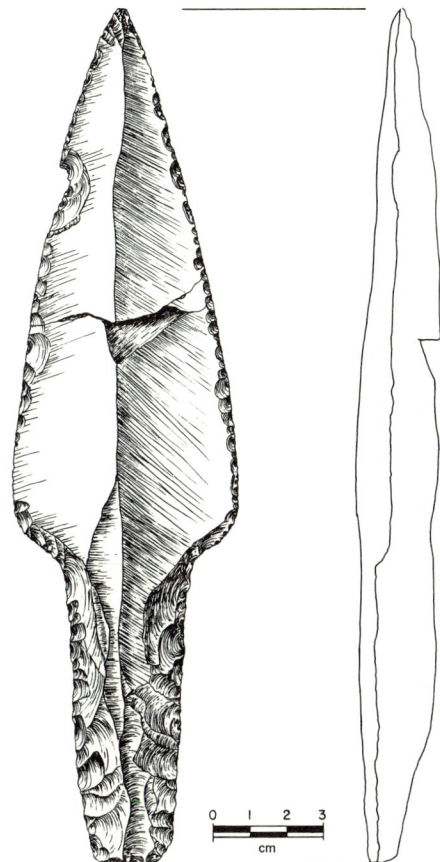

Fig. 17. Late Preclassic stemmed macroblade from Colha.

The Late Classic workshops at Colha are even more numerous and are distributed across the site. The Late Classic was characterized by the manufacture of general utility bifaces (thick, heavy celts with extensive use wear) (Fig. 19a) and smaller oval bifaces, the continuation (perhaps in reduced numbers) of tranchet technology, and the manufacture of eccentrics, particularly smaller effigy-style eccentrics and multinotched blades (Fig. 20).

In Terminal Classic workshops, such as Op 2007, excavated by Roemer (1984), the emphasis was on making blades (Fig. 21), which were used in the production of small stemmed blade points (Fig. 19b–d). Roemer's (1984) quantitative studies revealed a workshop debitage density of more than five million pieces per cubic meter (see Shafer and Hester 1986).

The Postclassic lithic technology at Colha presents a wholly different picture. The long-lived technologies of the Preclassic and Classic were replaced by forms clearly derived from outside the region, including side-notched dart points (Fig. 22a) in the Early Postclassic and lozenge-shaped points in the Middle Postclassic (Fig. 22b). Although the local chert outcrops were still used, the Postclassic flintknappers imported chalcedony into their small village, which had been built over the remains of the earlier ceremonial center (Hester and Shafer 1991a).

Given the size of the Colha community, it seemed likely to us as early as 1976 that the lithic production was of such volume that the majority of the output must have been directed to a market or exchange system moving it to Maya consumers elsewhere. The excavations in 1979–1981 confirmed our hypotheses with respect to the level of production. But where did all the stone tools go—especially those of Late Preclassic and Late Classic times—and how were they uti-

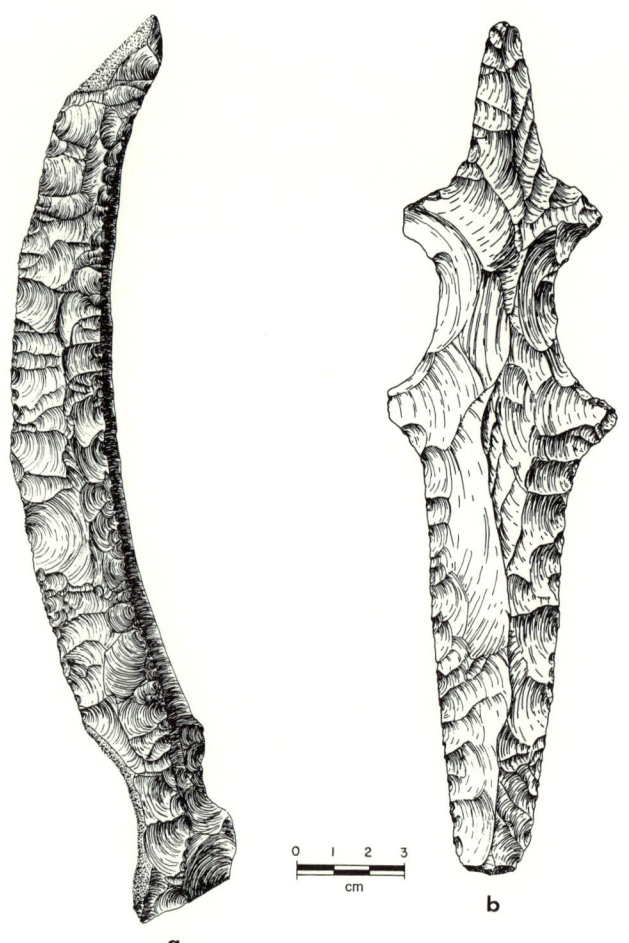

Fig. 18. Late Preclassic eccentrics from Colha.

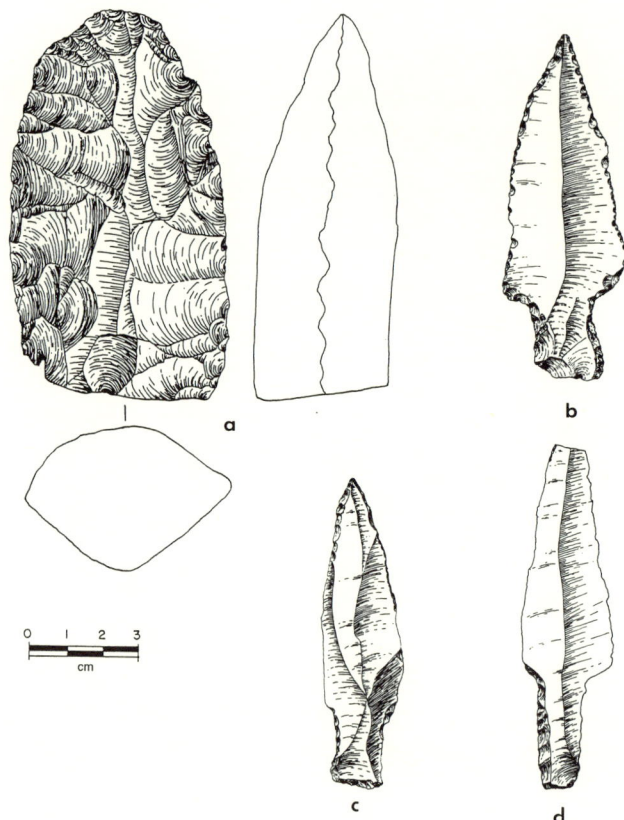

Fig. 19. Late-Terminal Classic artifacts from Colha. (a) General utility biface (cross section); (b–d) stemmed blade points.

lized? A fortunate coincidence of intensive archaeological work in Belize in the 1980s and the cooperation of numerous colleagues who permitted us access to their lithic collections has allowed a fairly accurate picture of Colha tool distribution to emerge.

First, we can say that most of the output was intended to meet the utilitarian needs of consumers at other sites. However, a second level of distribution is also evident. The eccentrics and many of the stemmed macroblades were destined for ritual and/or symbolic use, and were included in caches and elite tombs. These two quite different spheres of consumption are indicated clearly by the contexts in which Colha-produced tools are found. One specific tool form—the large stemmed macroblade—apparently was a highly prized commodity that sometimes went to Maya centers at much greater distances. It also has been suggested (Gibson 1987) that eccentrics, the odd-shaped forms used so widely in Maya culture, originated in Late Preclassic Colha workshops. Gibson's study of the literature and of museum collections (see also Gibson 1986) finds that the earliest documented occurrence of eccentrics (e.g., in caches) is at Colha. Thompson (1970:146) has also reported the "export" of eccentrics from the Maya lowlands into the highlands in Preclassic times.

How were the tools from the craft-specialized community of Colha utilized for utilitarian (sociotechnic) and elite/ritual (ideotechnic or symbolic) needs? We preface this discussion with some comments on the identification of "Colha chert" and "Colha technology."

The term "Colha chert" is used to distinguish a banded tan, golden brown, or gray chert (often speckled white with fossil inclusions) that outcrops in the Rancho Creek watershed. The chert occurs in or is eroded from a limestone marl and is formed in nodular masses varying in size from millimeters to over a meter across. Unweathered cortex is white, whereas weathered cortex is usually light gray. These cherts patinate to a cream-colored surface. The texture of Colha chert varies within large nodules. The outer rind beneath the cortex is the finest grade and ranges from finely banded opaque to faintly translucent. The chert becomes gradually coarser deeper into the nodule and is often very grainy at the center. The flintknappers deliberately quarried the nodules to take advan-

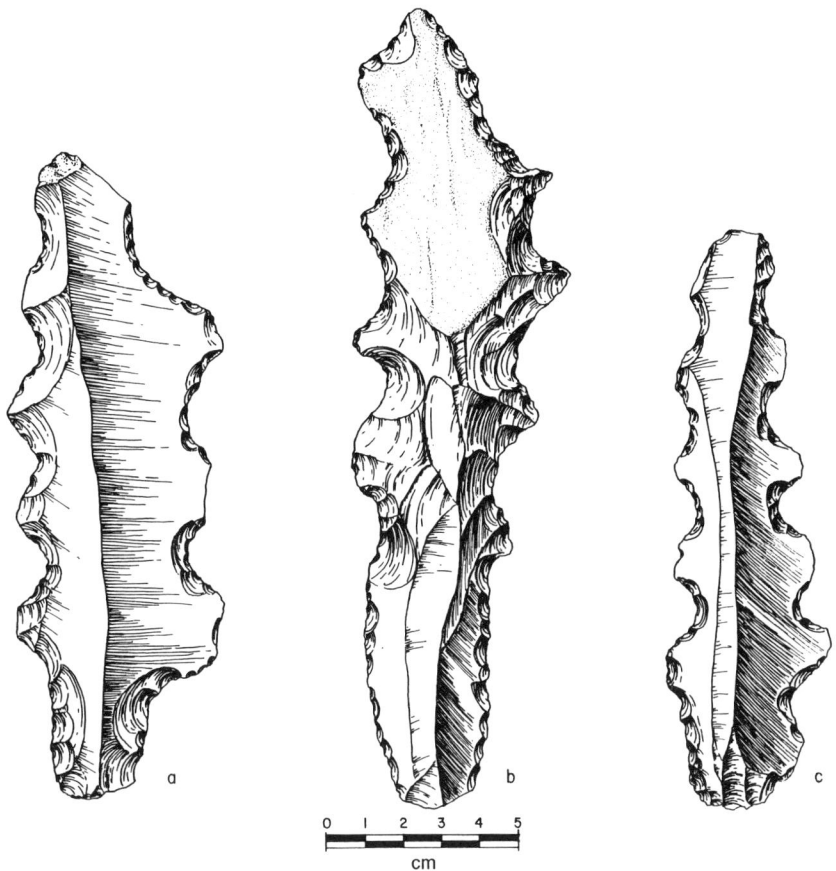

Fig. 20. Late-Terminal Classic notched-blade eccentrics from Colha.

tage of the finer chert, although some macroflakes transect the nodule, and some tools exhibit the entire spectrum of texture.

Our regional surveys have provided samples that demonstrate notable variability in chert texture and form throughout the CBZ of northern Belize. Within the CBZ, the geographic differences in the chert can be distinguished, albeit with some difficulty. For this reason, a large sample of cherts from throughout the zone was subjected to neutron activation analysis. Tobey (1986) was able to recognize two chemically different clusters of chert at Colha and generally to distinguish the Colha cherts from those collected at other localities within the CBZ.

Particularly striking is the difference between Colha cherts and the translucent milky blue or opaque white chalcedonies that occur north and west of the CBZ. Tobey (1986) has shown that these two groups are easily distinguished chemically as well as visually.

"Colha technology" is our term for the distinctive technological systems developed for the mass production of stone tools by Colha craftsmen. Among the technological traits are the unique biconical limestone hammers used in the biface thinning process. Another characteristic is the distinctive pattern of beveling the striking platform at right angles to facilitate thinning flake removal using the stone hammers. This trait is especially notable in thinning flake debitage, dominated by large biface thinning flakes with platforms showing right-angle beveling. A third trait is the use of the tranchet technique (Shafer 1983a) of preparing the bit end for large axe or adze tools. A distinctive by-product is the tranchet flake (Shafer 1976), the removal of which created the faceted bit end of the finished tool. This technique is unknown elsewhere in the New World but was used to produce virtually identical tools in predynastic Egypt (Holmes 1989).

All of these techniques, as well as the formal tools they were used to produce, were first developed in the Late Preclassic community. They became part of the craft tradition that was passed from generation to generation through the Classic period. The Colha lithic tradition has also been documented in the southern end of the CBZ at Kunahmul (Taylor 1980) and Chicawate (Kelly 1980), both in the vicinity of Altun Ha but dating only to the Late Classic.

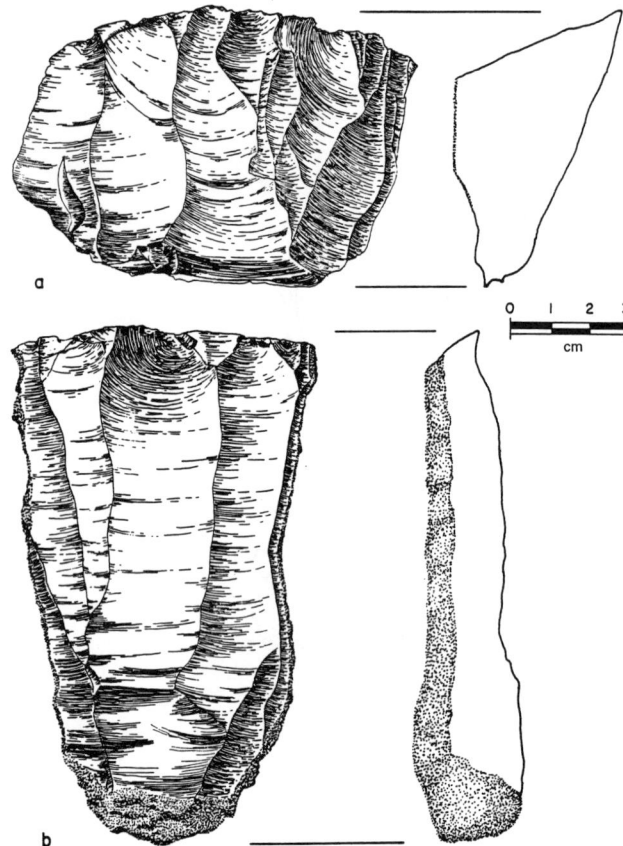

Fig. 21. Terminal Classic blade cores from Colha. Longitudinal cross sections are shown.

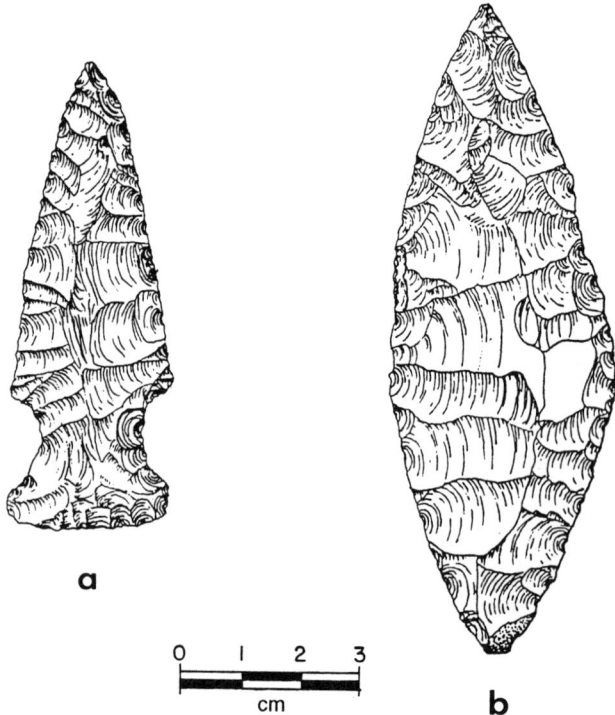

Fig. 22. Early and Late Postclassic points from Colha. (a) Early Postclassic side-notched point; (b) Middle Postclassic lozenge-shaped point.

Colha's External Relationships

Analysis of the distribution and function of Colha lithics must contend with several major issues: (1) How and to what extent were the lithics utilized at consumer sites? (2) Can we document, as postulated earlier, different levels of consumption, and indeed distinctive geographic clusters of consumer sites? (3) In what fashion were Colha lithics traded or exchanged? All of these issues can be addressed, at least in part, with our present data. Fortunately, we can also utilize the intensive research of Patricia McAnany (1986) on both the nature of tool consumption at Pulltrouser Swamp and the processes of exchange that may have imported Colha lithics into the Pulltrouser area.

First, as we have noted earlier, we infer two different levels of tool consumption: a utilitarian level involving the mass-produced tools, such as the large oval bifaces and the tranchet tools, and a ritual/symbolic, and probably elite level involving stemmed macroblades and eccentrics. Do these two levels of tool use have spatial boundaries or do they overlap? We speculate that several geographic areas received Colha tools. In some areas, Colha tools were utilitarian, in some they were ritual/symbolic, and in some they were both.

McAnany has proposed an exchange system that facilitated the export of Colha tools to other communities as an "inter-polity exchange network." In essence, lithic commodities moved between communities as part of a "stable, small-scale sphere of economic interaction" among these communities (1986:253). Some larger sites such as Nohmul or San Estevan might have provided "central marketplaces" (McAnany 1986:269) with "barter as the circulation mechanism" (1986:109). McAnany reconstructs such an exchange system "organized along the lines of petty traders [following Feldman 1978:11], who were responsible for the movement of a single line of goods over short distances" (1986:269). Scarborough (1985) argues for four major Late Preclassic polities in northern Belize, with Colha and its "site level craft specialization" (Scarborough 1985:337) as the dominant center of one of these.

This economic system seems reasonable for what we term our "primary consumer area," the farming areas, villages, and centers of northern Belize and southern Quintana Roo. This primary area also may have extended somewhat into western, central, coastal, and southern Belize. Sites in these areas tend to have a mixture of chert tools, some from Colha but more commonly from other chert sources and production areas. In these areas, as well as in far-flung areas in the Peten, some Colha commodities, especially the elegant stemmed macroblades, were transported by "professional traders—

wealthy merchants . . . who were involved in moving merchandise over long distances" (McAnany 1986:269; see also Feldman 1978). These traders served a "peripheral consumer area" that obtained lithic commodities in the form of the ritual/symbolic artifacts described earlier.

Alternative models may help to explain the distribution of Colha lithics. The Colha flintknappers were probably "independent specialists" (see Brumfiel and Earle 1987:5) with product exchange mechanisms varying "according to economic, social, and political conditions." Utilitarian lithics (the "subsistence goods" of Brumfield and Earle) may have been distributed in Late Preclassic times in response to the increase in population and agricultural production in northern Belize (see Gibson 1989). In the Terminal Classic, the mass production of stemmed blade points may signal a response to the need for weapons during a time of increasing warfare. Lithic artifacts produced for ritual or symbolic purposes were quite probably in the realm of "wealth items" (Brumfiel and Earle 1987:5), made for and exchanged among the regional elite. Based on McAnany's (1986) model, the utilitarian exchange may have been effected by "petty traders" operating among regional communities. The exchange of ritual/symbolic lithics among elites within the region and in an interpolity context may have been handled by the "professional trader/wealthy merchants" (see also Gibson 1989:133).

The exchange of stone axes in the New Guinea highlands also offers some interesting analogies. Recent fieldwork by Hampton (1992) in Irian Jaya suggests that stone axes from the Tagime quarry in the Dani area of the Baliem River Valley are often "custom-ordered" and are carried from village to village by local traders. He notes that there is seldom any contact between the consumers and the toolmakers. Phillips (1979), on the other hand, states that some highland groups "obtain axes by direct trade with those who controlled the quarries," sometimes traveling for four days to effect the exchange. Both Phillips and Burton (1989) note other levels of acquisition and exchange for both "ceremonial" and "bride price" axes.

Hampton's observations at the Una (or Uni) quarries (also known as Langda; see Toth, Clark, and Ligabue 1992) point to two levels of axe trade: trading both axe blades and hafted axes (1) with other Una villages, especially with Una villages "which . . . did not have the right kind of rock for quarrying or did not have quarrying and toolmaking experts" (see also Toth, Clark, and Ligabue 1992:92) (the quarrymen would sometimes go to the user villages and "initiate trade," according to Hampton [1992]); and (2) with select villages located beyond Una-speaking populations. Hampton reports that when the axe trade extended beyond the Una's primary trading sphere, the Una-manufactured tools "were traded still farther away by intermediary traders to still more remote locations." Based on Hampton's maps, the distances involved here exceed 200 km. Hampton's data also provide provocative insights into the exchange of "symbolic stones" (unchipped, decorated tabular stones) that are distributed more broadly than the axes.

The New Guinea data, which we have touched on very briefly, provide examples of different consumer needs for stone tools, different levels of exchange, and varying methods of trade. Direct contact with the tool-making specialists may have occurred between Colha and some of its consumer sites, especially those, to be described shortly, that are in close proximity.

Whatever modes of exchange may have been used in the ancient Maya lowlands, the Colha producer-consumer relationship would have reflected (1) restricted access to chert in the CBZ, (2) the presence of craft specialists at Colha, (3) the need for Colha products at consumer sites that lay outside chert-bearing soils, and (4) the different levels of products required by consumers, both utilitarian and ritual/symbolic, on both an inter- and intraregional basis.

Primary Consumer Sites

Here we describe a number of sites whose inhabitants were the primary consumers of Colha lithic products. They are mainly in northern Belize, within 60 km of Colha.

The nearest documented consumer site to Colha is Kichpanha, 12 km to the northwest. The site is located on the edge of the CBZ, and there are local deposits of good-quality banded cherts and brown chalcedony (Hester and Shafer 1984:164). Formal tools occur from Middle Preclassic through Postclassic times (see also Gibson 1986). At least two lithic workshops are present at the site, and one of these is Late Preclassic in date (J. Cross, pers. comm.).

About 7 km north-northeast of Kichpanha is Honey Camp Lagoon (also known as Laguna de On). In 1950, C. W. Meighan and J. A. Bennyhoff made a surface collection from a beach area. Most of the lithics (Hearst Museum of Anthropology, University of California, Berkeley; Hester notes) are chert (CBZ/Colha), although a small number are made of chalcedony. The assemblage appears to be Late Preclassic to Late Classic in age, and the combination of chert types and technological forms strongly suggests that the artifacts are derived from Colha workshops.

Distinctive forms include stemmed macroblades, oval bifaces, edge-modified macroblades, a tranchet flake, a tranchet-bit tool, narrow parallel-sided bifaces, and several general utility bifaces. Most distinctive of the assemblage, however, is the high frequency of recycled fragments of oval bifaces and macroblades.

The most intensive studies of a chert assemblage from a consumer site have been conducted at Pulltrouser Swamp, 33 km northwest of Colha. Analyses by Shafer (1983b) and McAnany (1986, 1989) have focused particularly on the site of Kokeal. With the exception of eccentrics, all of Colha's Late Preclassic and Late Classic formal tool categories are found at Pulltrouser. McAnany (1986:253) makes special note of the large oval biface form, which was the most intensively recycled tool type at Pulltrouser sites. Shafer's (1983b) research has documented how the Colha tool forms were utilized at Pulltrouser and how, when broken, they were modified and recycled—a pattern that we now recognize at several primary consumer sites.

Nearby is Cuello, about 29 km northwest of Colha. By what is now described as early Middle Preclassic times, Cuello was importing T-shaped adzes and other finished tools. Our examination of the Cuello situation (Shafer et al. 1979) indicates that waste flakes found at the site and related debitage are derived from retouch and recycling of formal tools from the CBZ, almost certainly from Colha. We can also note the great similarity between the Cuello lithic sample and that reported from Pulltrouser localities some 13 km to the north. In the early 1980s, when the earliest Cuello deposits were thought to be Early Preclassic and those at Colha to be Middle Preclassic, it was difficult to explain the presence of such distinctive tools as the T-shaped adze found at both sites. Now that we know these deposits are contemporary, all evidence, particularly technological attributes, points to their manufacture at Colha.

Various studies of Cuello lithics have been published, including Seymour (1982) and McSwain (1982, 1991a,b); macroblades, oval bifaces, tranchet tools, and other Colha forms are represented in the Preclassic assemblage. However, McSwain has taken issue with the producer-consumer model for lithic exchange in northern Belize, basing her critique on data from Cuello. It is her view that "relatively unfinished raw material (such as tool blanks) from the Colha source was brought into Cuello before and during the era of the Colha workshops" (1991b:338). We do not see any evidence in favor of this assertion in our own independent examination of Cuello lithics and debitage (Shafer et al. 1979). We are more in sympathy with McAnany's well-argued observations that "very localized pools of knowledge regarding resource location and *production skills*" (emphasis ours) were the mainstay of interpolity exchange networks. Indeed, she argues further that such localization is "diagnostic of a very stable exchange network" (1986:266). McAnany feels that the data from Pulltrouser, mirrored at Cuello, support the hypothesis that "entrenchment of resources extraction and commodity production skills . . . results in a corresponding lack of such skills at consumer locations" (McAnany 1986:267). The debitage patterns at both Pulltrouser and Cuello provide evidence in support of this hypothesis.

At Nohmul, 38 km northwest of Colha, excavations by Chase and Chase and more recently by Hammond have provided important lithic samples. Nash and Shafer (1986), in their study of the Chases' lithic materials, indicate that the formal tools were predominantly CBZ/Colha chert, although the frequencies are not so high as those at Pulltrouser. In Hester's review of a sizeable sample of Nohmul lithics (3/19/86), he noted many recycled bifaces, Terminal Classic stemmed blades, and even hammerstones, all of CBZ/Colha chert. Nohmul also yielded large thin Early Classic bifaces from ceremonial contexts that were of brown chert and clearly were not made at Colha. Similar specimens found in western and southern Belize will be discussed later. A review of the debitage from Nohmul revealed clearly that CBZ/Colha cherts were dominant; local chalcedonies were also represented heavily. In addition to the utilitarian implements from Nohmul, Hammond et al. (1987; pers. comm.) report two chert eccentrics from a burial in structure B at Nohmul, dated to ca. A.D. 1000. These are described by Hammond (pers. comm.) as "'Colha'-type, honey-colored chert, good quality stuff."

San Estevan, 30 km north-northwest of Colha, yielded oval bifaces and a stemmed macroblade (Bullard 1965:Pl.XVII) that are clearly of banded chert and appear to be of Colha technology. The oval bifaces were associated with all three ceramic complexes, beginning with the Late Preclassic and continuing into the early Late Classic. The stemmed macroblade was from the Barklog complex, probably of terminal Late Preclassic or Protoclassic date. Laura Levi, who has recently tested the site, reported to Shafer (pers. comm.) that she had found much debitage but no lithic workshops. We predict that continuing excavation will yield "consumer" lithic assemblages similar to those at Pulltrouser (only 6 km to the west), Cuello, and Nohmul.

At the site of Cerros, a Late Preclassic center 45 km north of Colha, Mitchum (1985, 1986, 1991) documents lithics from household contexts. In the households, she recognizes a heavy emphasis on recycling of Colha-type formal tools, including bifaces, macroblades, tranchet tools, and hammerstones. Like Shafer (1983b) at Pulltrouser, she found some stemmed macroblades in "household trash" (Mitchum 1991:52). Mitchum's (1991) study indicates that Cerros lithics are made most frequently from CBZ cherts and include considerable debitage from retouch and recycyling of broken tools.

To the northwest at nearby Santa Rita Corozal, Chase and Chase (1986, 1988) have recovered extensive samples of chert artifacts. The Preclassic materials are currently under study at Texas A&M University and are reported to be 90–95 percent CBZ/Colha (Dockall and Shafer 1993). The Late Postclassic lithics are being studied at the University of Texas at Austin. Cherts from fill contexts accompanying the Late Postclassic lots are dominated by Colha tools (see Shafer and Hester 1988) along with local chalcedonies (perhaps from Progresso Lagoon, some 15 km to the south—a locale often erroneously reported as a "chert source"; Andresen 1983).

Lithics recovered from a Santa Rita Early Classic tomb (Chase and Chase 1986) include a huge chert bar eccentric (72 cm long) of CBZ/Colha chert and two stemmed macroblades, with cinnabar residues, also from this same lithic source. We speculate that these lithics, possibly of Late Preclassic date, were curated and and subsequently placed in this tomb. We make this suggestion because the protrusions once present on the bar eccentric had been broken at some earlier date.

The site of Sarteneja, west of Cerros and Santa Rita and about 48 km northwest of Colha, yielded large oval bifaces, macroblades, stemmed macroblades, and Late Classic general utility bifaces of CBZ/Colha chert and technology (Hester and Shafer 1983).

At the major center of El Pozito, 31 km west of Colha, research by Hester, Shafer, and Berry (1991) has demonstrated the occurrence of CBZ/Colha tools, including oval bifaces, general utility bifaces, tranchet tools, blades, and stemmed blades, as well as much evidence of the recycling of all of these. There is also a remarkable set of stemmed macroblades in a Late Preclassic cache (Cache 22; Fig. 23) from the site's ceremonial center. Local white and gray chalcedony was used to make bifaces (mostly with ground bits). Some chalcedony-working scatters are present in nearby sugarcane fields.

For the site of Lamanai, 38 km southwest of Colha, we have a few preliminary observations of lithic materials at the field camp, courtesy of David Pendergast. A cache of Late Classic eccentrics looked very much like Colha chert. Pendergast (pers. comm.) believes, however, that they were made at the Late Classic lithic workshops near Altun Ha. However, there are no eccentric fragments in the debris from the Colha Project tests at workshops in that part of the CBZ (Kelly 1980, 1982).

In far northern Belize, Sidrys (1983:381) notes that the Maya were using "blanks" and "preforms" from Colha and the CBZ. Andresen's (1983) illustrations include oval bifaces and what are clearly recycled bifaces. We suspect that large oval bifaces were being imported into far northern Belize, where they were used as axes and earth-working tools, as seen at Pulltrouser and Rio Hondo (Hester and Shafer notes; courtesy of Mary Pohl) and in the case of the so-called Puleston Axe (Shafer and Hester 1990). Although Andresen (1983:278) states that the majority of the chert collection from the Sidrys survey represents the "work of local chert knappers," he does not describe the kind of chert being knapped (erroneously noting a chert source at Progresso that is actually a source of chalcedony) or the presence of local workshops or lithic concentrations. Interestingly, in this sample, which is largely Classic and Postclassic in date, only two stemmed macroblades were found, one at Sarteneja Beach and a fragment on the beach at Cerros.

We have only general information on the occurrence of CBZ/Colha chert and tools in Quintana Roo. Observations by McAnany (pers. comm.) suggest the presence of these materials at Kohunlich (collection housed in Merida). Heavy bifaces and a slender stemmed biface are made of CBZ/Colha chert.

Lithic data are available from several sites along the central coast of Belize. Collections from Ambergris Cay (Hult and Hester 1994) provided by Tom Guderjan and James Garber are overwhelmingly made of chert in Terminal Classic tool types from Colha, which is 55 km to the northeast. These include general utility bifaces with heavy wear and stemmed blades as well as considerable recycled materials (Hult and Hester 1994). From cache and burial contexts are two stemmed macroblades of Colha material and technology and a cinnabar-coated axelike eccentric of CBZ/Colha material. Intriguingly, at the Northern River Lagoon site, about 20 km southeast of Colha and at the mouth of the Northern River east of Maskall, two similar eccentrics of Colha chert have been found, along with Terminal Classic stemmed blades and other lithics typical of CBZ/Colha cherts and technologies.

About 20 km down the coast, the Hick's Cay site, some 25 km southeast of Altun Ha, has yielded bifaces, macroblades, blades, and debitage of CBZ/Colha and other chert (Hester and Shafer 1983). Although the Colha Project has surveyed this area and recovered typical banded CBZ cherts (Kelly 1982), it is possible that some other cherts are also being worked.

Excavations were conducted at several sites in the vicinity of Potts Landing, south of Hick's Cay, in 1950 by C. W. Meighan and J. A. Bennyhoff (Meighan 1952; collections at the Hearst Museum of Anthropology, University of California, Berkeley). In general, the assemblage appears to be Late to Terminal Classic in age. Distinctive forms include stemmed blade points characteristic of the Terminal Classic, small oval

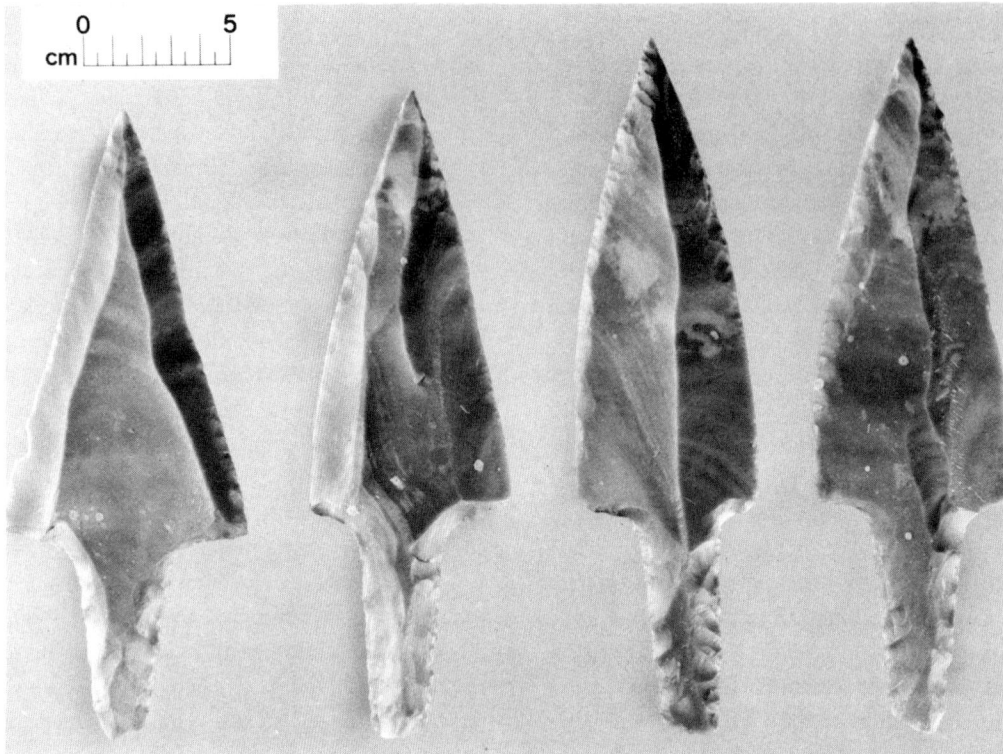

Fig. 23. Selected Late Preclassic stemmed macroblades from Cache 22, El Pozito, Belize.

bifaces, general utility bifaces, a much-reworked tranchet-bit tool, and two bifaces with extensive hoelike polish on their bits. Although most of the artifacts are made of CBZ/Colha chert, a few are of chalcedony, and several others are made of a coarse gray chert that may be local. Though the stemmed blade points and general utility bifaces of CBZ/Colha chert are identical to forms manufactured at Colha in Terminal Classic times, it is possible that they are derived from the nearby stone tool workshops at Kunahmul (Taylor 1980) and Chicawate (Rockstone Pond; Kelly 1980). The Colha Project tested these workshops and they appear to date largely to the Late and Terminal Classic (see Shafer and Hester 1991).

An intriguing lithic assemblage comes from Moho Cay, located at the mouth of the Belize River and thought to have been a trading outlet of some sort (Healy, McKillop, and Walsh 1984). Indeed, there is pristine material that could have been in an exchange "pipeline" and been abandoned or cached at Moho Cay. These include large stemmed macroblades, large oval bifaces, and very large tranchet-bit tools—all typologically Late Preclassic. But Hester's study of the collection also revealed much used or "consumed" material, including utilized macroblades, stemmed macroblades used as cutting tools, and heavily used general utility bifaces—materials of Late Preclassic and Late Classic age. There is some chalcedony in the collection (primarily used for Early Post-classic lithics in the assemblage), which otherwise is overwhelmingly CBZ/Colha brown-tan-gray banded and speckled material. The technology is generally that of Colha. Most of the material is stained black because of manganese oxidation. This coloring led some archaeologists to suggest erroneously that the Moho Cay collection was of black chert.

These central coastal sites are clearly within the primary consumer area. However, along the southern coast of Belize, sites like Placencia (Shafer 1984) and Wild Cane Cay also have considerable amounts of chert and chalcedony. Although some of the chert resembles that of the CBZ, we feel that local chert resources and outcrops must be sought out and studied before any relationship to the north can be postulated.

Peripheral Consumer Area

Sites located more than 60 km from Colha appear to be peripheral consumers. There is little evidence for importation of utilitarian tool forms (although these occasionally occur), but there are eccentrics and stemmed macroblades, the ritual/symbolic tool forms made at Colha, in these distant lithic assemblages.

There are two subareas within the peripheral consumer area: one within Belize and the other outside that country's present political boundaries. Among sites in west and central

Belize, San Jose, about 75 km southwest of Colha (Thompson 1939; Field Museum collections), has several eccentrics of CBZ chert and others of different kinds of chert and chalcedony. Bifaces are made largely from non-Colha chert, including a gray grainy material and a brownish chert. There are large bipoints made of brown chert (as at Nohmul) and of banded gray chert not from the CBZ. A Late Classic general utility biface from the site is of yellow-brown chert, again not from the CBZ.

At Barton Ramie (Shafer 1982), the utilitarian tools, especially Late Classic general utility bifaces and stemmed bifaces, are made of poor-quality chert (non-CBZ) and chalcedony. However, Shafer has studied three stemmed macroblades that are definitely from CBZ sources and are products of Colha technology. Both San Jose and Barton Ramie clearly are consumers only of ritual/symbolic CBZ Colha lithics. Similarly, at Big Falls, about 55 km down the Belize River from Barton Ramie and about the same distance south-southwest of Colha, plowed fields have yielded macroblades and a stemmed blade of CBZ/Colha chert, as well as debitage of CBZ chert; other debitage is gray chert and chalcedony. One stemmed macroblade at Big Falls is of brown chert, not from the CBZ. At Ponce's Site in central Belize, Late Classic burial caches include chalcedony and chert bifacial points and small eccentrics (similar to those reported from Baking Pot by Bullard and Bullard 1965). Some of the stemmed bifaces are made of CBZ chert, but the workshops for these are not yet known. The other chert is not from the CBZ, and the eccentrics are largely of chalcedony. The data from the Belize River and from western and central Belize point to other production locales in that region, especially of Late Classic date.

Archaeological research in the upper Belize River Valley by Anabel Ford (1991) has revealed two debitage mounds at Yaxox (Ford and Olson 1989:195, 197). Shafer's review of the materials indicates that one debitage mound was created by the manufacture of small prismatic chunks used as boring tools, whereas the other produced hundreds of flat oval flakes, perhaps used as wedges. Nearby, in the vicinity of the center of El Pilar, Ford and Olson (1989) report a chert workshop at the LDF site. Its assemblages reflect biface manufacture using local cherts. Indeed, there seem to be little or no CBZ materials represented in this area.

A similar picture is indicated by the few lithics reported from Xunantunich (MacKie 1985). Oval bifaces and stemmed bifaces are illustrated, and none of the illustrations or descriptions sugggest either Colha cherts or technology. Other cherts and chalcedonies appear to have been used.

Farther to the south, at the site of Pacbitun, Paul Healy reports a large stemmed macroblade (Fig. 24) of CBZ/Colha

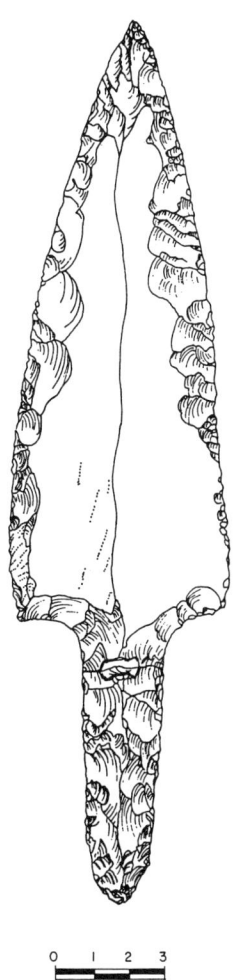

Fig. 24. Stemmed macroblade of CBZ chert from Pacbitun, Belize. (Courtesy of Paul Healy, Trent University.)

chert (Healy 1990:Fig. 10) as well as stemmed bifaces and bipointed bifaces of non-CBZ chert (Cache 15-1; Early Classic).

The second subarea lies outside Belize, at distant sites in the Peten from which we have sketchy but intriguing reports. At El Mirador, Richard Hansen (pers. comm.) has found Late Preclassic stemmed macroblades that are of CBZ/Colha chert and technology. Fowler (1983) reports nineteen artifacts of imported chert, including a Terminal Classic polyhedral blade core, debitage, and stemmed blades, all of CBZ/Colha material. From Tikal, Hattula Moholy-Nagy (pers. comm.) reports stemmed macroblades of CBZ material. John E. Clark (pers. comm.) makes a similar claim for distant Chiapa de Corzo. At Macanche Island in the Peten Lakes, Rice (1987:219) reports that "brown cherts from the northern Belize chert zone were increasingly available in the lakes ... in the Terminal Classic and Postclassic periods." She also notes (1987:213) some leaf-shaped points (possibly Early Postclassic) of "dark flint" that may be of "northern Belize (Colha) chert." There were active Terminal Classic and Postclassic workshops at Colha and perhaps some of the products were distributed this far to the west.

Mark Aldenderfer's lithic reseach in this same area, part of the Central Peten Human Ecology Project (CPHEP), notes the presence of both local cherts and imported chert materials (Aldenderfer 1985). He attributes the imported chert to the CBZ of northern Belize. It is found in housemounds and also in elite contexts, although specific types or forms are not noted. For example, at the site of Yaxha, Kimball, Aldenderfer, and Hohol (1986) report that 80 percent of the mounds contained obsidian and nonlocal ("fine brown"; CBZ?) cherts. In general, Aldenderfer (1985) feels that obsidian was ten times more common than the imported cherts.

Of special interest are five flintworking areas, described as "loci of part-time specialists utility and fine biface production" (Aldenderfer 1985:8). One "station" or "workshop" was found in each of the five basins surveyed. Aldenderfer notes further that the local cherts—gray, white, and yellow in color and medium- to coarse-grained—come from the Sacnab area. All of the lithics from the CPHEP studies are of Late Classic date (Aldenderfer, Kimball, and Sievert 1989). It is difficult for us to evaluate the density or status of the reported CBZ lithics or whether they include tool forms of Colha technology. These lithics may be imported from elsewhere in the CBZ and unrelated to Colha production.

Summary and Conclusions

The site of Colha in northern Belize was a community specializing in chert tool manufacture and export for perhaps 2,000 years. The craft specialists at the site utilized locally abundant chert resources and their own specific technologies and production skills to meet the demands for large volumes of formal tools, beginning in Late Preclassic times or earlier. Although by far the highest level of production went into utilitarian tools, such as large oval bifaces and tranchet bifaces, the Late Preclassic workshops also turned out chert eccentrics for ritual use. Additionally, they manufactured large stemmed macroblade points that were sometimes used within the utilitarian realm as knives, daggers, and spear points. However, these points also had elite appeal and subsequently were distributed more widely than any other lithic commodity from Colha.

The excavations at Colha have demonstrated the character of its lithic industries and a scale of production in excess of local demand. More importantly, a number of excavated lithic assemblages from northern Belize and adjoining areas have been examined. These include numerous examples of tools made of CBZ materials using Colha-style technology. Detailed studies of excavated assemblages in northern Belize indicate that there was a primary consumer area containing sites of many sizes at which varying degrees of Colha tool utilization can be documented. At sites like Pulltrouser, El Pozito, Cuello, Nohmul, and Ambergris Cay, tool consumption formed a distinctive pattern usually involving extensive recycling of tools from the CBZ. At several of these sites, one also sees the importation of eccentrics and stemmed macroblades for ritual use (e.g., at Nohmul and Santa Rita Corozal). As an explanation of the processes of exchange in Colha's external relationships, we favor McAnany's (1986) hypothesized interpolity exchange system, in which traders moved these lithic commodities from Colha to the consumers (see also Shafer and Hester 1991). However, long-distance trade was clearly a part of the picture, given the materials found at the site of Moho Cay and the presence of CBZ/ Colha stemmed macroblades at far-flung sites in southern Belize (e.g., Pacbitun), in southern Quintana Roo, at Tikal and in the Peten Lakes area, and at El Mirador. We have speculated that the long-distance materials that traveled to the peripheral consumer sites were part of the activities of wealthy traders of the type hypothesized by McAnany.

This pattern fits fairly well for the Late Preclassic and into its terminal phases. However, by Late Classic times chert tool workshops were scattered more broadly across the CBZ and included those at Kunahmul and Chicawate, near Altun Ha. We earlier speculated that Colha may have come under the control of Altun Ha during this time and that its monopoly on stone tool production had ceased. Interestingly, small stemmed blade points were made at specialized blade workshops at Colha in the Terminal Classic, and these are fairly widely distributed in northern Belize. Such workshops are not duplicated in the Altun Ha area.

After Colha's abandonment following the Terminal Classic, the site was reoccupied in Early and Middle Postclassic times. The community saw renewed emphasis on production of stone tools (Michaels 1989; Hester and Shafer 1991), particularly projectile points. These are found at a number of Belizean sites and in the Peten Lakes area. No other Postclassic workshops have been documented for the region. In essence, the lithic craft specialization that dominated the Colha locale for almost all of its history proved to be quite adaptable. Stone tool production and export typified the community regardless of political or demographic shifts.

Finally, the research at Colha has demonstrated that a relatively small community, without major monumental or architectural investments, could serve as the focal point for craft-specialized production. Its products were widely dispersed to both rural and urban consumers. These data argue for a complex economic system in the lowlands—uncontrolled by elites at one or more large centers.

Notes

The authors are grateful to Kathy Roemer, Kathryn Reese-Taylor, Pamela Hedrick, and Dennis Knepper for preparing the artifact illustrations. Figure 24 was provided by Paul Healy of Trent University.

We also extend our gratitude to the collaborating institutions involved in the Colha Project: the University of Texas at Austin, Texas A&M University, the University of Texas at San Antonio, and the Centro Studi Ricerche Ligabue (Venice, Italy). Support for Colha field and laboratory analysis has come from many sources, notably the National Endowment for the Humanities, the National Geographic Society, Earthwatch, the American Philosophical Society, faculty research grants from the University of Texas at San Antonio and Texas A&M University, the University Research Institute of the University of Texas at Austin, and a number of private donors. Earlier versions of this chapter were prepared by Geraldine Ross and Kelly Scott. We also thank O. W. Hampton for access to his unpublished notes on ethnographic research in Irian Jaya.

1. Interestingly, Late Classic lithic workshops also appear, for the first time, at sites like Rio Azul in the Peten and in the Rio Bec zone.

References Cited

Aldenderfer, Mark S.
1985 An Analysis of the Production and Uses of Lithic Materials from Domestic Assemblages of the Classic Maya, Central Peten Lakes Region, Guatemala. Manuscript on file with the authors.

Aldenderfer, Mark, Larry R. Kimball, and April Sievert
1989 Microwear Analysis in the Maya Lowlands: The Use of Functional Data in a Complex Society Setting. *Journal of Field Archaeology* 16:47–60.

Andresen, John M.
1983 Chert Artifacts. Pp. 277–293 in Raymond V. Sidrys, *Archaeological Excavations in Northern Belize, Central America.* Monograph XVII. Institute of Archaeology, University of California, Los Angeles.

Andrews, E. Wyllys, V, and Norman Hammond
1990 Redefinition of the Swasey Phase at Cuello, Belize. *American Antiquity* 55:570–584.

Brumfiel, Elizabeth M., and Timothy K. Earle
1987 Specialization, Exchange, and Complex Societies: An Introduction. In *Specialization, Exchange, and Complex Societies,* edited by E. M. Brumfiel and T. K. Earle, pp. 1–9. Cambridge University Press, Cambridge.

Bullard, William R., Jr.
1965 *Stratigraphic Excavations at San Estevan, Northern British Honduras.* Occasional Paper 9. Royal Ontario Museum, Toronto.

Bullard, William R., and Mary Ricketson Bullard
1965 *Late Classic Finds at Baking Pot, British Honduras.* Occasional Paper No. 8. Royal Ontario Museum, Toronto.

Burton, John
1989 Repeng and the Salt-Makers: "Ecological Trade" and Stone Axe Production in the Papua New Guinea Highlands. *Man* (n.s.) 24:255–272.

Chase, Diane Z., and Arlen F. Chase
1986 *Offerings to the Gods: Maya Archaeology at Santa Rita Corozal.* University of Central Florida, Orlando.
1988 *A Postclassic Perspective: Excavations at the Maya Site of Santa Rita Corozal, Belize.* Monograph 4. Pre-Columbian Art Research Institute, San Francisco.

Dockall, John, and Harry J. Shafer
1993 Testing the Producer-Consumer Model for Santa Rita Corozal, Belize. *Latin American Antiquity* 4(3):158–179.

Eaton, Jack D.
1980 Architecture and Settlement at Colha. In *The Colha Project, Second Season, 1980 Interim Report,* edited by T. R. Hester, J. D. Eaton, and H. J. Shafer, pp. 71–85. Center for Archaeological Research, University of Texas at San Antonio and Centro Studi e Ricerche Ligabue, Venice.
1982 Colha: An Overview of Architecture and Settlement. In *Archaeology at Colha, Belize: The 1981 Interim Report,* edited by T. R. Hester, H. J. Shafer, and J. D. Eaton, pp. 11–20. Center for Archaeological Research, University of Texas at San Antonio and Centro Studi e Ricerche Ligabue, Venice.

Feldman, Lawrence H.
1978 Moving Merchandise in Protohistoric Central Quahtemallan. In *Mesoamerican Communication Routes and Cultural Contacts,* edited by T. A. Lee, Jr., and C. Navarrete, pp. 7–17. Papers of the New World Archaeological Foundation 40. New World Archaeological Foundation, Provo, Utah.

Ford, Anabel
1991 Economic Variation of Ancient Maya Residential Settlement in the Upper Belize River Area. *Ancient Mesoamerica* 2:35–46.

Ford, Anabel, and Kirsten Olson
1989 Aspects of Ancient Maya Household Economy: Variations in Chipped Stone Production and Consumption. *Research in Economic Anthropology* (Supplement) 4:185–211.

Fowler, William R.
1983 Analisis de los Artefactos. In *Proyecto El Mirador de la Harvard University, 1982–1983,* edited by A. A. Demarest and W. R. Fowler, pp. 160–195. Instituto de Antropología e Historia de Guatemala, Antigua.

Gibson, Eric C.
- 1986 Diachronic Patterns of Lithic Production, Use and Exchange in the Southern Maya Lowlands. Ph.D. dissertation, Department of Anthropology, Harvard University.
- 1987 The Evolution of Maya Ritual Artifacts. Manuscript on file with the authors.
- 1989 The Organization of Late Preclassic Maya Lithic Economy in the Eastern Lowlands. *Research in Economic Anthropology* (Supplement) 4:115–138.

Hammond, Norman, Sara Donaghey, Colleen Gleason, J. C. Staneko, Dirk Van Tuerenhout, and Laura Kosakowsky
- 1987 Excavations at Nohmul, Belize, 1985. *Journal of Field Archaeology* 14:257–282.

Hampton, O. W.
- 1992 Anthropological Expeditions in Irian Jaya, Indonesia. Vol. II. Summary of Field Notes. Manuscript on file with the authors.

Healy, Paul F.
- 1990 Excavations at Pacbitun, Belize: Preliminary Report on the 1986 and 1987 Investigations. *Journal of Field Archaeology* 17:247–262.

Healy, Paul F., Heather J. McKillop, and Bernetta Walsh
- 1984 Analysis of Obsidian from Moho Cay, Belize: New Evidence on Classic Maya Trade Routes. *Science* 225:414–417.

Hester, Thomas R., and Harry J. Shafer
- 1983 Observations of Lithic Collection from Sarteneja (37/202), Hicks Cay. Manuscript on file with the authors.
- 1984 Exploitation of Chert Resources by the Ancient Maya of Northern Belize, Central America. *World Archaeology* 16:157–173.
- 1987 Observations on Ancient Maya Core Technology at Colha, Belize. In *The Organization of Core Technology,* edited by J. K. Johnson and C. A. Morrow, pp. 239–257. Westview Press, Boulder, Colo.
- 1991a Lithics of the Early Postclassic at Colha, Belize. In *Maya Stone Tools: Selected Papers from the Second Maya Lithic Conference,* edited by T. R. Hester and H. J. Shafer, pp. 155–162. Prehistory Press, Madison, Wis.

Hester, Thomas R., and Harry J. Shafer, eds.
- 1991b *Maya Stone Tools: Selected Papers from the Second Maya Lithic Conference.* Prehistory Press, Madison, Wis.

Hester, Thomas R., Harry J. Shafer, and Thena Berry
- 1991 Technological and Comparative Analyses of the Chipped Stone Artifacts from El Pozito, Belize. In *Maya Stone Tools: Selected Papers from the Second Maya Lithic Conference,* edited by T. R. Hester and H. J. Shafer, pp. 67–84. Prehistory Press, Madison, Wis.

Holmes, Diane L.
- 1989 *The Predynastic Lithic Industries of Upper Egypt.* BAR International Series 469(1). British Archaeological Reports, Oxford.

Hult, Weston, and Thomas R. Hester
- 1994 The Lithics of Ambergris Caye, Belize. In *Maritime Trade, Settlement, and Population on Ambergris Caye, Belize,* edited by T. H. Guderjan and J. Garber. Labyrinthos Press, Culver City, Calif.

Kelly, Thomas C.
- 1980 The Colha Regional Survey. In *The Colha Project, Second Season, 1980 Interim Report,* edited by T. R. Hester, J. D. Eaton, and H. J. Shafer, pp. 51–69. Center for Archaeological Research, University of Texas at San Antonio and Centro Studi e Ricerche Ligabue, Venice.
- 1982 The Colha Regional Survey, 1981. In *Archaeology at Colha, Belize: The 1981 Interim Report,* edited by T. R. Hester, H. J. Shafer, and J. D. Eaton, pp. 85–97. Center for Archaeological Research, University of Texas at San Antonio and Centro Studi e Ricerche Ligabue, Venice.

Kimball, Larry R., Mark S. Aldenderfer, and April S. Hohol
- 1986 Microwear Analysis of Maya Lithic Artifacts from Rural/Center Contexts in the Central Peten Lakes Region, Guatemala. Paper presented at the 51st Annual Meeting of the Society for American Archaeology, New Orleans, April 24–27.

Lohse, Jon
- 1993 Operation 4046, Colha, Belize: A Reconsideration of a Lowland Archaic Deposit. M.A. thesis, Department of Anthropology, University of Texas at Austin.

McAnany, Patricia A.
- 1986 Lithic Technology and Exchange among Wetland Farmers of the Eastern Maya Lowlands. Ph.D. dissertation, Department of Anthropology, University of New Mexico, Albuquerque.
- 1989 Stone Tool Production and Exchange in the Eastern Maya Lowlands: The Consumer Perspective from Pulltrouser Swamp, Belize. *American Antiquity* 54:332–346.

MacKie, Evan W.
- 1985 *Excavations at Xunantunich and Pomona, Belize, in 1959–60.* BAR International Series 251. British Archaeological Reports, Oxford.

McSwain, Rebecca
- 1982 Stone Tools in Secondary Refuse: Lithics from a Late Preclassic Chultun at Cuello, Belize. *Atlatl,* Occasional Papers, Department of Anthropology, University of Arizona, pp. 1–20.
- 1991a Chert and Chalcedony Tools. In *Cuello, An Early Maya Community in Belize,* edited by N. Hammond, pp. 160–169. Cambridge University Press, Cambridge.
- 1991b A Comparative Evaluation of the Producer-Consumer Model for Lithic Exchange in Northern Belize, Central America. *Latin American Antiquity* 2:337–351.

Meighan, Clement W.
- 1952 Excavations in British Honduras. Manuscript on file with the authors.

Michaels, George
- 1987 A Description and Analysis of Early Postclassic Lithic Technology at Colha, Belize. M.A. thesis, Department of Anthropology, Texas A&M University.

1989 Craft Specialization in the Early Postclassic of Colha. *Research in Economic Anthropology* (Supplement) 4:139–183.

Mitchum, Beverly A.
1985 Distribution of Lithic Artifacts and Debris in Late Preclassic Maya Households. Paper presented at the 84th Annual Meeting of the American Anthropological Association, Washington, D.C., December 4–8.
1986 Chipped Stone Artifacts. In *Archaeology at Cerros, Belize, Central America,* Vol. 1: *An Interim Report,* edited by R. A. Robertson and D. A. Freidel, pp. 105–116. Southern Methodist University Press, Dallas.
1991 Lithic Artifacts from Cerros, Belize: Production, Consumption, and Trade. In *Maya Stone Tools: Selected Papers from the Second Maya Lithic Conference,* edited by T. R. Hester and H. J. Shafer, pp. 45–54. Prehistory Press, Madison, Wis.

Nash, Michael A., and Harry J. Shafer
1986 Nohmul Lithics: Preliminary Study. Manuscript on file with the authors.

Phillips, Patricia
1979 Stone Axes in Ethnographic Situations: Some Examples from New Guinea and the Solomon Islands. In *Stone Axe Studies,* edited by T. H. McK. Clough and W. A. Cummins, pp. 108–112. CBA Research Report 23. Council for British Archaeology, London.

Rice, Prudence
1987 Chipped Stone Artifacts. In *Macanche Island, El Peten, Guatemala: Excavations, Pottery and Artifacts,* pp. 210–220. University of Florida Press, Gainesville.

Roemer, Erwin
1984 A Late Classic Maya Lithic Workshop at Colha, Belize. M.A. thesis, Department of Anthropology, Texas A&M University.

Scarborough, Vernon L.
1985 Late Preclassic Northern Belize: Context and Interpretation. In *Status, Structure and Stratification: Current Archaeological Reconstructions,* edited by M. Thompson, M. T. Garcia, and F. J. Kense, pp. 331–344. Archaeological Association of the University of Calgary, Calgary, Canada.

Seymour, Deni J.
1982 Lithic Consumption at Cuello and Its Relation to Production at Colha. Paper prepared for Anthropology 696a lithic seminar, University of Arizona. On file with the authors.

Shafer, Harry J.
1976 Belize Lithics: "Orange Peel" Flakes and Adze Manufacture. In *Maya Lithic Studies,* edited by T. R. Hester and N. Hammond, pp. 28–78. Center for Archaeological Research, University of Texas at San Antonio.
1982 Notes on Barton Ramie Lithics at Peabody Museum, 1982. Manuscript on file with the authors.
1983a The Tranchet Technique in Lowland Maya Lithic Production. *Lithic Technology* 12:57–68.
1983b The Lithic Artifacts of the Pulltrouser Area: Settlements and Fields. In *Pulltrouser Swamp, Ancient Maya Habitat, Agriculture and Settlement in Northern Belize,* edited by B. L. Turner II and P. D. Harrison, pp. 212–245. University of Texas Press, Austin.
1984 Notes on Lithics from Placencia, Belize, 1984. Notes on file with the authors.

Shafer, Harry J., and Thomas R. Hester
1983 Ancient Maya Chert Workshops in Northern Belize, Central America. *American Antiquity* 48:519–543.
1986 Maya Stone-Tool Craft Specialization and Production at Colha, Belize: Reply to Mallory. *American Antiquity* 51:148–166.
1988 Preliminary Analysis of Postclassic Lithics from Santa Rita Corozal, Belize. In *A Postclassic Perspective: Excavations at the Maya Site of Santa Rita Corozal,* edited by D. Chase and A. Chase, pp. 111–117. Monograph 4. Pre-Columbian Research Institute, San Francisco.
1990 The Puleston Axe: A Late Preclassic Hafted Tool From Northern Belize. In *Ancient Maya Wetland Agriculture,* edited by M. D. Pohl, pp. 279–294. Westview Press, Boulder, Colo.
1991 Lithic Craft Specialization and Product Distribution at the Maya Site of Colha, Belize. *World Archaeology* 17:79–97.

Shafer, Harry J., Thomas R. Hester, Thomas C. Kelly, and Norman Hammond
1979 An Analysis of Lithic Artifacts from Cuello, Belize. Manuscript on file with the authors.

Sidrys, Raymond V.
1983 *Archaeological Excavations in Northern Belize, Central America.* Monograph XVII. Institute of Archaeology, University of California, Los Angeles.

Taylor, A. J.
1980 Excavations at Kunahmul. In *The Colha Project, Second Season, 1980 Interim Report,* edited by T. R. Hester, J. D. Eaton, and H. J. Shafer, pp. 241–250. Center for Archaeological Research, University of Texas at San Antonio and Centro Studi e Ricerche Ligabue, Venice.

Thompson, J. Eric S.
1939 *Excavations at San Jose, British Honduras.* Publication 506. Carnegie Institution of Washington.
1970 *Maya History and Religion.* University of Oklahoma Press, Norman.

Tobey, Mark H.
1986 *Trace Element Investigations of Maya Chert from Belize.* Papers of the Colha Project 1. Center for Archaeological Research, University of Texas at San Antonio.

Toth, Nicholas, Desmond Clark, and Giancarlo Ligabue
1992 The Last Stone Ax Makers. *Scientific American* 260:88–93.

Wood, Gregory P.
1990 Excavations at Op. 4046, Colha, Belize: A Buried Preceramic Lithic Deposit. M.A. thesis, Department of Anthropology, University of Texas at San Antonio.

CHAPTER SIX

Small Sites in Prehistoric Maya Socioeconomic Organization: A Perspective from Colha, Belize

ELEANOR KING AND DANIEL POTTER

Maya Small Site Research: Hidden Assumptions

DURING THE PAST THIRTY YEARS, a growing number of sites of various sizes have been investigated in the Maya lowlands. These range from smaller settlements built around central areas containing a few courtyards with monumental architecture to larger settlements that have central areas with numerous courtyards, extensive monumental architecture, and elaborate sculpture. The research strategy used to investigate these sites appears to vary sharply according to site size. In most cases, projects involving small sites have been conducted to solve quite specific research problems. Some notable examples include Barton Ramie (settlement; Willey et al. 1965), the Pulltrouser Swamp sites (agriculture; Turner and Harrison 1983), Colha (lithic manufacturing; Hester and Shafer 1983), and Cuello and Komchen (Maya origins; Andrews et al. 1981; Hammond 1991). At large sites, in contrast, the research goals tend to be broader and the questions posed more numerous. Objectives of the Tikal Project, for instance, included elucidating the growth and development of the site as a major center (Coe 1967; Coe and Haviland 1982), its role in the emergence of lowland Maya civilization (Coe 1965), the settlement of core and peripheral areas (Haviland 1965; Puleston and Callender 1967; Puleston 1983), and Classic Maya sociopolitical organization (Haviland 1968, 1985; Coggins 1980). Equally broad goals have dominated recent research at Copan (W. L. Fash 1988; Webster and Gonlin 1988; B. W. Fash 1992; Schele 1992; Sharer, Miller, and Traxler 1992), Caracol (Chase and Chase 1987, 1989), and other large sites. This difference in approach reflects underlying assumptions about Maya centers that continue to influence research today.

According to Ashmore (1981a:448ff.), one fundamental assumption is that all site centers, regardless of size, performed the same basic functions. Despite striking differences in layout, they are thought to have shared a dual ritual-residential organization, with facilities for both public ceremonies and elite habitation and administration. Small centers are thus viewed simply as less-developed versions of large ones. A corollary to this assumption is that smaller centers and their surrounding settlements are less complex socially and economically than larger ones. Basically, Mayanists believe that the quantity and quality of architecture found at major centers imply that the elite in such places commanded greater concentrations of human energy and natural resources than those in smaller centers. Consequently, it is to the large centers and their surrounding settlements that Mayanists look for indications of social complexity and differentiation, such as the use of writing or the working of exotic raw materials. Smaller centers, often termed "satellites," are thought to have been subservient to and dependent on their larger neighbors, politically, socially, and economically.

This perspective has been formalized in applications of central place theory to Maya settlement patterns (Flannery 1972; Hammond 1974) and in regional rank-size analyses of Maya sites (Adams and Jones 1981; Adams 1982), but it is not restricted to them. Central place theory, in fact, is built on the same kind of bias as the one just outlined. Since it was initially devised to model the location of settlements with respect to the movement of goods to market on an unbounded plain (Christaller 1933, 1966), central place theory assumes that the primary—if not the only—function of settlements is mercantile (Crumley 1987). In its archaeological applications, the political and the economic are often conflated, so that the location of sites involves relative political power as well as redistribution. Nonetheless, the model still posits a nested hierarchy of sites that are functionally similar and differ only in size. Regional rank-size analyses rely on the same kind of assumptions in attempting to find objective, easily measurable criteria by which to order Maya sites. Rather than considering entire settlements, they focus on the scale, configuration, and density of monumental architecture present, particularly in site centers, to establish their hierarchies. However, in so doing they presume that the centers all functioned in the same way and that the most relevant differences among them are precisely those of size and scale.

The pervasiveness of this view in the Maya area can be further demonstrated by looking at another, related assumption about small sites: that they have less of an occupational overburden than large sites. Even casual or tangential references to small sites in the literature suggest that they cannot possibly have the depth or complexity of architectural development that larger sites possess. This perception has been expressed most recently by Moholy-Nagy (1990), who explains the lack of visible chert workshops at large sites like Tikal in terms of these sites' complex constructional history. She argues that such large and densely populated sites must have possessed more complex and efficient patterns of waste disposal than small sites such as Colha, where chert debitage could be left out for all to see. At Tikal, for instance, she suggests that space was at such a premium that all of the site's debitage was reused in construction fill or in special deposits over tombs. We agree that it is possible that sites may well have varied in their approach to the disposal of waste products. But it seems highly improbable that, had Tikal as marked a chert tool specialization as Colha, the resulting residues would not be evident. What seems clearer is Moholy-Nagy's underlying assumption that a large site like Tikal *must* have had everything, and more, than a small site like Colha.

Another example of "large-site" bias can be detected in Mallory's theoretical approach to lithic analysis at Copan (Mallory 1986). Like Tikal, Copan lacks evidence for specialized, full-time lithic production. Mallory has noted a lack of intensive lithic workshops at Copan, but instead of proposing that such workshops were removed for building fill, he has convincingly argued that full-time lithic specialization was never present at the site. Significantly, however, the limited evidence for lithic specialization in the Copan area was found at a small satellite center that Mallory does not name and describes simply as "one out-of-the-way site" (Mallory 1986:153), which we presume to be the small center of El Duende. Mallory seemingly discounts the lithic data from the satellite site because such specialization was *supposed* to occur within Copan itself: "the lack of evidence for specialized production at such a major Maya center.... has led me to be cautious in accepting evidence for specialized production at other Maya sites" (Mallory 1986:153). We find the presence of limited specialized production at the satellite center of El Duende to be significant and will return to this point subsequently.

The same "large-site" preconceptions have also insinuated themselves into recent discussions of urbanism in the Maya area that are directly pertinent to this volume. Ever since the discovery of dense settlements at sites like Tikal and Dzibilchaltun dispelled the idea of the empty ceremonial center over two decades ago, there has been considerable debate on the nature of Maya "cities" (e.g., Haviland 1966, 1970; McAnany 1989). At the core of the argument is the fact that the Maya did not live cheek by jowl but instead spread out across their landscape, with substantial amounts of apparently vacant space between structures. Demographic definitions of urbanism stressing the importance of concentrated, wall-to-wall habitation concluded that the Maya were something less than urban (e.g., Sanders and Price 1968, discussed in Smith 1989). However, functional approaches, which became more prevalent in the 1970s, suggested that the major Maya sites were indeed cities (e.g., Marcus 1983, discussed in Smith 1989), with their own uniquely Maya layout (Haviland 1966; see also Chase, Chase, and Haviland 1990). Additional research at numerous sites, as well as epigraphic evidence on the relationships between sites and on their respective territorial extents, has further bolstered this view (Marcus 1976; Chase, Chase, and Haviland 1990; Culbert 1991).

Sanders and Webster (1988) have recently revived the controversy in attempting to fuse the demographic and functional approaches (Smith 1989). Using Fox's (1977) typology of urban forms, they seek to categorize Mesoamerican cities for purposes of cross-cultural comparison. Most, they find, fall into the category of "regal-ritual centers," that is, central places where "ideological functions are extremely obtrusive" (Sanders and Webster 1988:523) and indeed dominate all else. The only other example of Fox's types that they find strongly represented in Mesoamerica is the "administrative city," whose primary function is political (Sanders and Webster 1988:525). Although the categories are functional, the criteria Sanders and Webster use to distinguish them are essentially demographic (Smith 1989). Thus, their introductory definition of administrative cities describes them as "larger, denser, and more heterogeneous urban communities than regal-ritual ones" (Sanders and Webster 1988:525). Not surprisingly, the only cities that qualify for this category are the densely nucleated settlements of the Mesoamerican highlands such as

Teotihuacan and Tenochtitlan. By virtue of their open configuration, the Maya sites are all lumped together in the regal-ritual type.

Both Smith (1989) and Chase, Chase, and Haviland (1990) have criticized Sanders and Webster's approach for glossing over known variability among Mesoamerican cities and ignoring pertinent archaeological data. Smith (1989:455) also makes the point that Sanders and Webster do not provide for a range of small to large cities in their typology (see also Chapter 7 by Santley, and McAnany 1989). He notes that the cities they cite as examples of Fox's administrative type, Teotihuacan and Tenochtitlan, were primate-type central places, very different from other highland cities dating to the same periods. He suggests that, in Aztec times at least, most people living within the empire turned to their smaller, local urban center for administrative and other purposes rather than to Tenochtitlan. He proposes that the existence of different levels of cities should be recognized by the use of comparative terms such as "town" and "city," which are widely employed in the social sciences and reflect size and organizational differences among urban centers (Smith 1989:456).

Neither Smith nor the other critics, however, draw out the implications of Sanders and Webster's model for settlement levels below the city. In a reply to Smith, Webster and Sanders (1989) appear to differentiate two levels of urban development, but only in areas where their administrative type is found. They note that most Aztec central places outside of Tenochtitlan fit their regal-ritual type. By implication, then, the largest cities in their typology, and the ones that they admit conform best to western views of urbanism (Webster and Sanders 1989:461), are administrative, and the smaller or secondary cities are regal-ritual.

This functional distinction has important implications for the rest of the settlement hierarchy because of the manner in which they define their types. For Sanders and Webster, all regal-ritual cities are equivalent in function, with differences in layout or components due only to local environmental and demographic factors or to regional culture histories (Sanders and Webster 1988:534–535). They add that "the architectural forms found at the centers are often identical to those found in the rural countryside, only writ large" and that "urban-rural settlement contrast is minimally developed" (Sanders and Webster 1988:524). In other words, at and below the level of the regal-ritual urban center, there is no functional variability among sites. In the Maya area, where the regal-ritual city is the solitary urban type found, this means that the only difference among levels of settlement—among "city," "town," "village," and "hamlet"—is one of size, clearly mirroring the set of assumptions outlined earlier. It is worth noting in this context that, although they draw their regal-ritual type from Fox, Sanders and Webster (1988:529–535) are quite obviously thinking primarily of Maya sites when they define the type in Mesoamerica. It is no wonder, then, that their type is imbued with the hidden biases that haunt most other discussions of Maya settlement.

Ball and Taschek (1991) come to conclusions similar to Sanders and Webster's in their research in the upper Belize Valley. They reformulated Fox's (1977) types as models to be tested against the archaeological data, apparently focusing on the administrative and regal-ritual types. They assert that the regal-ritual model, slightly modified to accommodate lower-level central places, best fits their data. They support their argument by presenting the results of a comparative analysis of spatial use at three centers in their survey area. The most detailed information they provide is on Buena Vista, the largest center, where they assign precise percentages to the amount of structural and courtyard space used for each of the following functions: administrative, ceremonial, regal-ritual, regal-residential, nonelite residential, economic, and water storage. However, they have not yet published their data, nor the criteria by which they so exactly defined the function(s) of a given area. It is therefore premature to assess the significance of their findings. They go on to generalize about other sites in the Maya area, with the assertion that although "smaller centers like Colha were without question specialized economically, we do not believe that such centers as Colha or Buena Vista functioned all that differently from Naranjo, Copan, or even Tikal." They add that such "centers differ from the larger ones less in kind than in size and reduced functional redundancy" (Ball and Taschek 1991:157). These observations seem to be based more on the pervasive assumptions about Maya sites discussed previously than on close examination of the evidence.

The myriad problems with these prevailing assumptions begin with their avoidance of real functional differences between settlements, even those of equivalent size. As Ashmore (1981a:453–455) points out, Quirigua, for example, was apparently not a focus for local ritual to the same extent as other major centers. Although there is evidence for incense burning in certain of the large, public areas, only four of the visible or excavated structures could be interpreted as "temples." This picture contrasts starkly with that of sites like Tikal, Palenque, and Copan, where public-ceremonial structures are major components of the architecture. Ashmore (1981a:451ff.) goes on to suggest that Quirigua's function was primarily economic rather than religious. It is likely that other sites, both large and small, had similarly distinct functions reflected in their layout and architecture (see also Chase, Chase, and Haviland 1990).

Equally important, the use of site size as the primary measure of complexity blinds us to the different kinds of functional interdependence that probably existed between settlements, a point also made by Crumley (1987). She suggests that the conflation of "hierarchy" with "complexity" confuses these two distinct concepts and obscures other patterns in the data. In Mesoamerica in general, research on functional variability and interdependence between sites is still in its infancy (Smith 1989; see Blanton 1981 and Marcus 1983). In the Maya area, renewed efforts to analyze the increasingly legible corpus of hieroglyphic texts have further promoted preoccupation with site hierarchies to the exclusion of other views. Focus on political interactions between sites, particularly the largest settlements, has been one of the most fruitful lines of recent research, and the textual evidence certainly suggests that these sites exercised political hegemony over their smaller neighbors during the Classic period (Marcus 1976; Chase, Chase, and Haviland 1990; Culbert 1991). However, little is known concerning intersite social and economic relationships, about which the glyphs remain mute.

The emphasis on site size as a measure of importance also ignores probable changes in status over time. This bias is critical when dealing with the origins of complex society in the lowlands. The genesis of Maya civilization is largely a Preclassic, not a Classic, phenomenon. Establishing that a site is of the first, second, or third settlement rank based on the visible Late Classic remains tells us very little about any role it may have played in the rise of social complexity over 1,000 years earlier.

We have confronted these analytical dilemmas over the course of our research at the site of Colha in northern Belize (Fig. 25), a region where most of even the largest sites are significantly smaller in overall area and density of central structures than major Peten sites such as Tikal, Uaxactun, El Mirador, and Nakbe. Although Colha itself is a small site, craft specialization developed there to a degree unparalleled even at Teotihuacan, judging by the sheer amount of manufacturing residue and by quantified estimates of production (Hester and Shafer 1983, 1986; Clark 1986). In addition, whereas northern Belize has not yielded much of a Classic Period hieroglyphic corpus, Colha and other small sites in this area have produced some of the earliest evidence of writing in the lowlands, dating to the Late Preclassic (Gibson, Shaw, and Finamore 1986; Potter 1991a). These rather surprising aspects of small-site Maya archaeology have led us to reconsider the relationship between site size and socioeconomic complexity and specialization. In brief, we suggest that the picture in the Maya area is much more complicated than the traditional hierarchical settlement models imply. Small sites with a marked sitewide specialization, like Colha, also exhibit important internal variability from early periods onward. We propose that the concept of heterarchy elaborated by Crumley (1987) is more appropriate to the Maya data than any strictly hierarchical model. We also call for more fine-grained studies of both intra- and intersite variability.

The Colha Project: Site Description and Research Overview

COLHA'S CREDENTIALS AS A "VILLAGE" SITE

Most sites in the Maya lowlands, unlike their Southwest Asian counterparts discussed in this volume, are not clearly delimited in space. Since Maya settlements are by nature dispersed, their exact configuration is often ambiguous. Indeed, it is notoriously difficult to determine site boundaries, which are often indicated only by a gradual drop-off in mound density with distance from the site center. Colha is no exception. Nonetheless, its position as a small site within the size range of Maya settlements can easily be established by using several lines of evidence.

Colha is located on approximately 7.5 km^2 of fertile, calcareous soils bordered by swamps and creeks (Hammond 1981:181–184) (Fig. 26). Although the exact limits of the site are unknown, reconnaissance suggests that settlement is not evenly distributed throughout this entire expanse of high ground. Mound density drops off rapidly north of the site center, which contains the monumental construction and specialized architecture typical of Maya administrative and ceremonial cores. The site, in effect, spreads out south and east of the center, with the densest groupings occurring south of Rancho Creek, along the margins of Cobweb Swamp, a vast brackish-water marsh from which there is access, through other swamps, to the sea. The distance between the site center and the farthest reaches of settlement near Cobweb in the south is approximately 3 km. By contrast, Tikal, one of the largest known and most clearly "urban" of Maya sites (Sanders and Webster 1988:534–535; Chase, Chase, and Haviland 1990:499–500), occupies some 123 km^2 of land defined by boundary walls to the north and south and swamps to the east and west (Haviland 1970). Within this area, Haviland (1970:190) differentiates between a peripheral zone of 60 km^2 where settlement is sparse and a central zone of 63 km^2 where settlement is more dense.

Colha can also be fit into traditional settlement and architectural typologies for the Maya area, which rely on the morphology and contents of site centers. J. Eric Thompson, one of the first investigators to call attention to small sites in

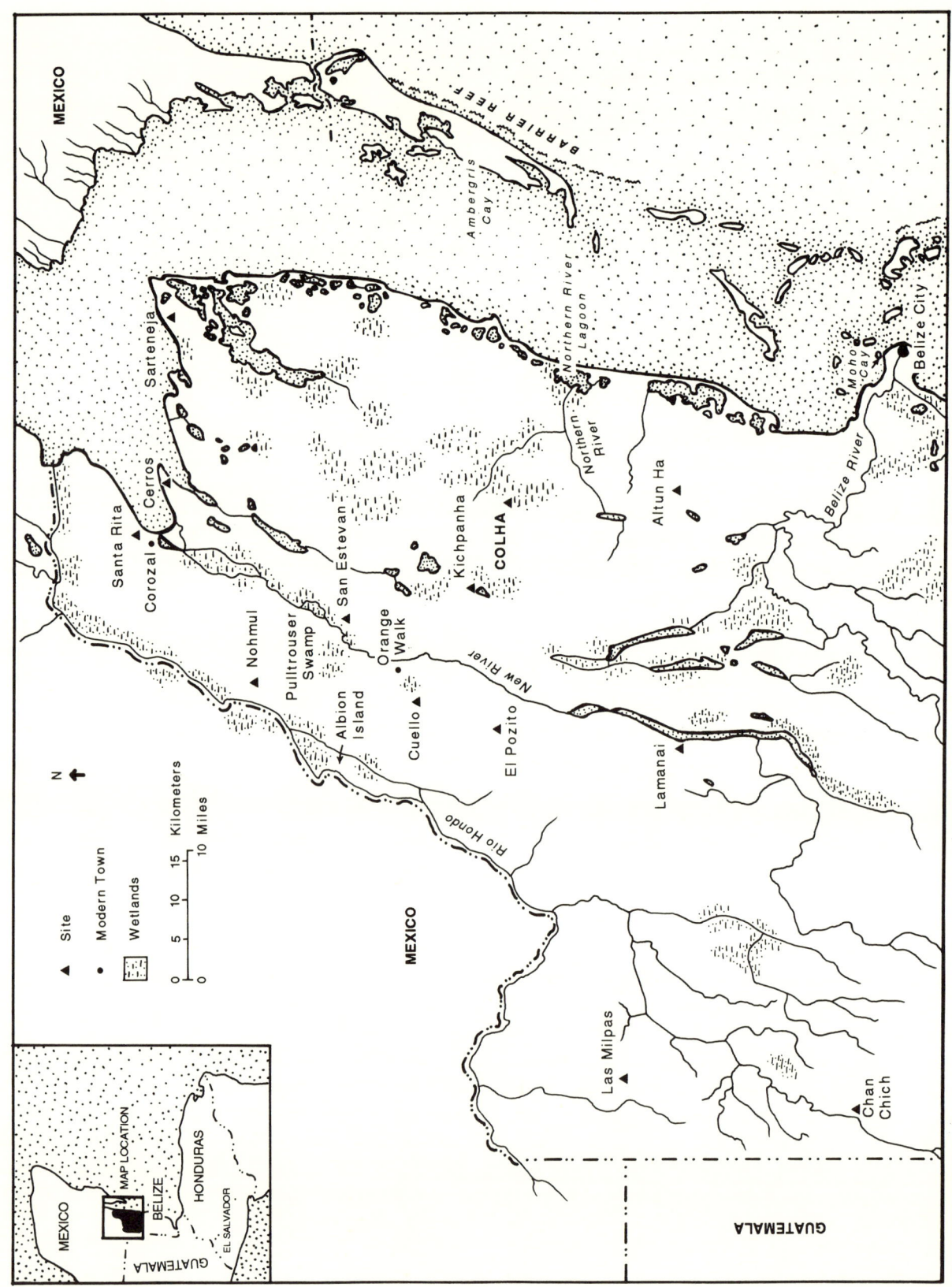

Fig. 25. Northern Belize, showing location of major sites. (Redrawn from Shaw 1991:82.)

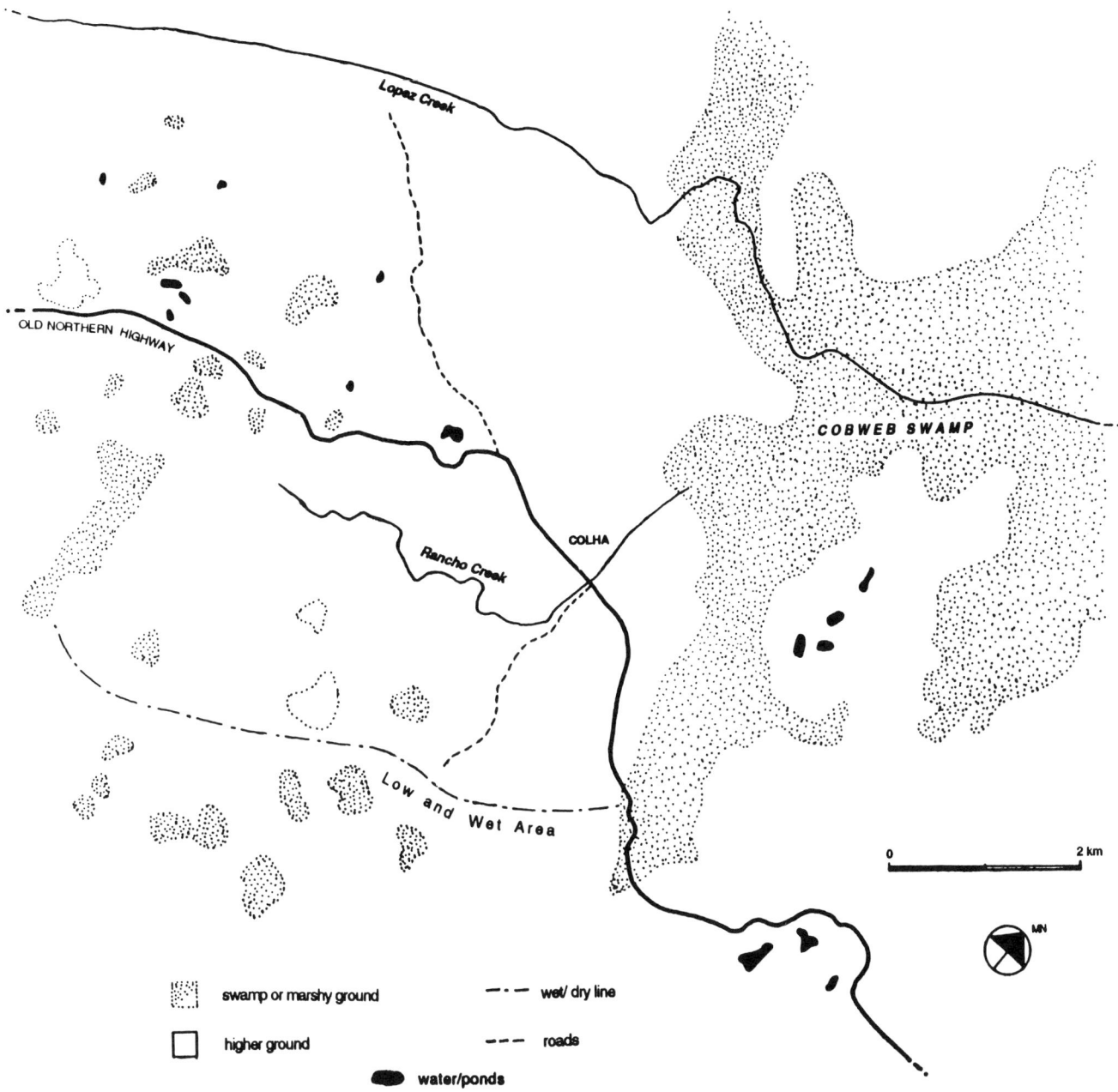

Fig. 26. Location of Colha relative to Rancho Creek and Cobweb Swamp.

the lowlands, viewed San Jose, Belize, where he excavated, as a "simple, primitive village" (Thompson 1939, as described by Haviland 1966:27). He based this interpretation on the fact that the site center boasted only one stela and one ballcourt, had simple mortuary furnishings and caches, and lacked both large structures in complex groupings and fancy local products (Haviland 1966:27). The architectural characteristics just noted would also place San Jose on the low end of the "major ceremonial center" category later devised by Bullard (1960). Colha similarly has only one ballcourt and no complex architectural groupings. Indeed, the central structures are small, with the largest extant mound only 9 m high, as compared to the 20 m or more common for mounds at larger centers. In addition, Colha lacks any stelae, and its mortuary furnishings and caches, like those at Thompson's "village," are not as elaborate as the ones found at larger sites. Indeed, Hammond

(1975), using a modified version of Bullard's (1960) classification, designates Colha as the type site for his "small major ceremonial center" in northern Belize.

More recently, Adams and Jones (1981) have attempted to quantify the hitherto rather subjective determinations of Maya site size. Their method consists of ranking sites by the number of courtyards with major architecture present both in the site center and in the surrounding settlement. Their original article concentrated on the Peten, but Adams (1982) subsequently extended the typology to sites in northern Belize. He ranks Colha on the fifth of eight site levels there, below Nohmul, Lamanai, Aventura, Altun Ha, San Estevan, and El Pozito. Both Hammond (1975) and Adams (1982) note that there are no sites in northern Belize of a size comparable to the large Peten sites like Tikal, a statement that may now be refuted by the rediscovery of the large center of La Milpa in the northwestern corner of the country. Nonetheless, the majority of the large northern Belize sites would fit comfortably in the third or fourth tier of the Peten site hierarchy (Hammond 1975; Adams 1982). We can therefore safely say that Colha is a comparatively small site when considered on either a regional or a pan-lowland scale. We would underscore again that this ranking is based on the site's Late Classic configuration and extent.

OVERVIEW OF INVESTIGATIONS AT THE SITE

Colha was first discovered, mapped, and tested by the Corozal Project, under the direction of Norman Hammond (see Wilk 1973, 1975, 1976; Hammond 1982). From 1979 to the present, investigations have been conducted at the site by the Colha Project, under the direction of Thomas Hester (University of Texas at Austin) and Harry Shafer (Texas A&M University). The focus of research at Colha has typically been on the large worked chert deposits found throughout the site. These deposits have been identified by Hester and Shafer as in situ workshops that produced a limited number of formal tools in massive quantities from the Late Preclassic through the Late Classic. Although used tools in domestic midden and structural fill from these periods indicate that Colha was an important consumer of its own chert products, finds from other sites show that the site also exported large quantities of tools (Chapter 5 by Hester and Shafer).

Investigations in the Colha settlement and center have provided considerable detail about this marked functional specialization and have begun to place workshops within their socioeconomic context. As noted, the settlement extends mainly south and east of the center, following the curve of Cobweb Swamp. Excavations indicate that occupation began in the site center during the Middle Preclassic (circa 900–250 B.C.). By the Late Preclassic (circa 250 B.C.–A.D. 250) settlement had expanded to a zone the outer limits of which were at least 1.5 km distant from the site center. During the Classic (circa A.D. 250–850), the settlement gradually expanded to its full extent. Survey, surface collections, and excavations suggest that the majority of the presently visible mounds at the site date from the Late to Terminal Classic (circa A.D. 600–850).

Before reviewing the lithic industry at Colha, we offer some observations on intrasite functional variability and the beginnings of specialization in the Middle Preclassic.

Middle Preclassic Origins

EARLY SOCIOECONOMIC COMPLEXITY

Regardless of the index used to measure settlement size in the Maya area, the Late Preclassic data from the lowlands are clearly sufficient to demonstrate that site size hierarchies existed by that time. Recently, investigations at Nakbe (Hansen 1990) have produced evidence that reasonably extends the phenomenon of regional settlement hierarchy back to the Middle Preclassic, at least in some parts of the lowlands. This important site, located in the northeast Peten of Guatemala, exhibits Middle Preclassic (late *Ox* phase: 600–300 B.C.) architectural complexes ranging from 5 to 20 m in height (Hansen 1990:12). These are by far the largest constructions dating to this early period anywhere in the lowlands. Also documented at the site were a sophisticated system of aqueducts, monumental sculpture, and a large and complex ceramic assemblage. Although at present we know little about contemporary Middle Preclassic settlements around Nakbe, it is likely that Nakbe was preeminent among them, and that therefore some degree of size hierarchy existed very early on in this part of the Maya area.

Prior to these recent discoveries, Middle Preclassic settlements appeared to be uniformly small, unspecialized, and located so as to provide access to water and good agricultural land. Investigations at Uaxactun, Barton Ramie, Altar de Sacrificios, Seibal, and Tikal contributed to this general impression. However, in most if not all of these cases, data collection was accomplished through very limited testing, either through horizontal trenching or tunneling of structures or vertical "phone booth" testing around them. Because Middle Preclassic remains are typically deeply buried by later deposits, more extensive excavations were at best very difficult and at worst impossible, a problem that continues to plague attempts at reconstructions of this time period to this day. In comparison to the archaeological remains from all later periods, through which fairly impressive vistas have been opened to our view, the Middle Preclassic has been illuminated by only a meager scattering of peepholes. For this reason, it has been difficult to evaluate accurately the adequacy of the "small-village" concept and to put another model in its place.

At Colha, where Middle Preclassic excavations have been more extensive than at most other sites, we have been piecing together data from several parts of a Middle Preclassic settlement since 1979. These data offer tantalizing suggestions that the site already possessed a degree of internal functional specialization along social lines. The evidence includes variability in the following categories across the settlement: architectural form, ceramic assemblages, mortuary program, and caching behavior.

Before considering the evidence for this specialization, we should note that there could be other potential causes for the observed variability across the Middle Preclassic component. In situations like this one in which there has been limited excavation of a sitewide archaeological component, it is sometimes impossible to demonstrate clear stratigraphic (and therefore temporal) continuity between various parts of the site. This lack of precise stratigraphic resolution leaves open the possibility that observed archaeological variability is due to slight differences in chronology between separated areas rather than to socioeconomic or other variables. To address this problem at Colha, we have used a range of radiocarbon and obsidian hydration assays as well as fine-grained comparison of ceramic assemblages.

At operation 2012, located on the southeastern edge of Colha's monumental center (Fig. 27), small block excavations have exposed a total of 47 m² of Middle Preclassic architecture to date, or just over 4 percent of the estimated existing Middle Preclassic architecture at this locale. Although this is a rather small sample, excavations have been sufficiently large to indicate that a shift occurred during the *Bolay* phase (900–400 B.C.) from domestic architecture to large, open platforms of elite or possibly public function. The early *Bolay*-phase structures possessed the wattle and daub superstructures typical of Maya houses, whereas the late-phase *Bolay* platforms have yet to provide evidence that they supported structures. Incorporated within the platforms are a number of Middle Preclassic burials, which were placed while the structures were in use. Ceramics associated with these burials are the most diverse and elaborate of any originating in the Middle Preclassic component at Colha. They include complex animal and human effigies, cylinders, and spouted vessels with strap handles, some of which combined various phytoform modes with a pink stucco wash on black paste (Valdez 1987). It is difficult to ascertain the exact function these late *Bolay* platforms may have served. Nonetheless, given the data at hand, either elite residential or perhaps specialized community-mortuary roles seem reasonable.

Significantly, the operation 2012 deposits were the only Middle Preclassic contexts that produced caches. Two of these were encountered in early *Bolay*-phase deposits here. One of these caches comprised two jade artifacts, one of which is similar in style to some Olmec examples and probably originated from the Motagua Valley jade source in highland Guatemala. A second cache was composed of drilled marine shell-beads in a Consejo Red: Variety Estrella bowl. Both caches indicate that an extensive long-distance trade network was in operation at the time of the earliest settlement at Colha (circa 900 B.C.).

At operation 2006, south of the site center (Fig. 27), test excavations encountered Middle Preclassic deposits underlying a Late Preclassic lithic workshop. These deposits included large features that functioned as hearths, poorly preserved plaster floor remnants, and a very distinctive ceramic assemblage. Over 50 percent of all the sherds recovered were of the Sapote Striated: Variety Unspecified (Valdez 1987:78) type in a thin-walled tecomate form. This type was completely absent at operation 2012, described previously. The finds at operation 2006 suggest the possibility of a specialized Middle Preclassic activity area, or perhaps more probably, portions of a distinctive Middle Preclassic "household cluster" (Winter 1976:25).

A third Middle Preclassic area tested in operations 2011 and 2031 revealed quite different remains underlying the main plaza in Colha's monumental center. Here small platforms with associated middens, domestic features, and burials were found in superimposed household clusters (Anthony 1987; Sullivan 1991). This part of the site during Middle Preclassic times can best be interpreted as a densely settled residential area.

The data thus suggest that a pattern of spatial segregation of activities had evolved at Colha by the end of the Middle Preclassic. This view is bolstered by the evidence for small-scale lithic production at this time.

ANTECEDENTS TO INTENSIVE CHERT PRODUCTION

The chipped stone artifacts of Middle Preclassic *Bolay*-phase deposits are quite distinctive in form but are similar in technology to those of later periods at Colha. The most common lithic tool forms include the celt-form small oval bifaces, T-shaped bifaces, and macroblades (Potter 1991b). Blades were used both as tools and as tool blanks throughout the Middle Preclassic and into the Late Preclassic period. One

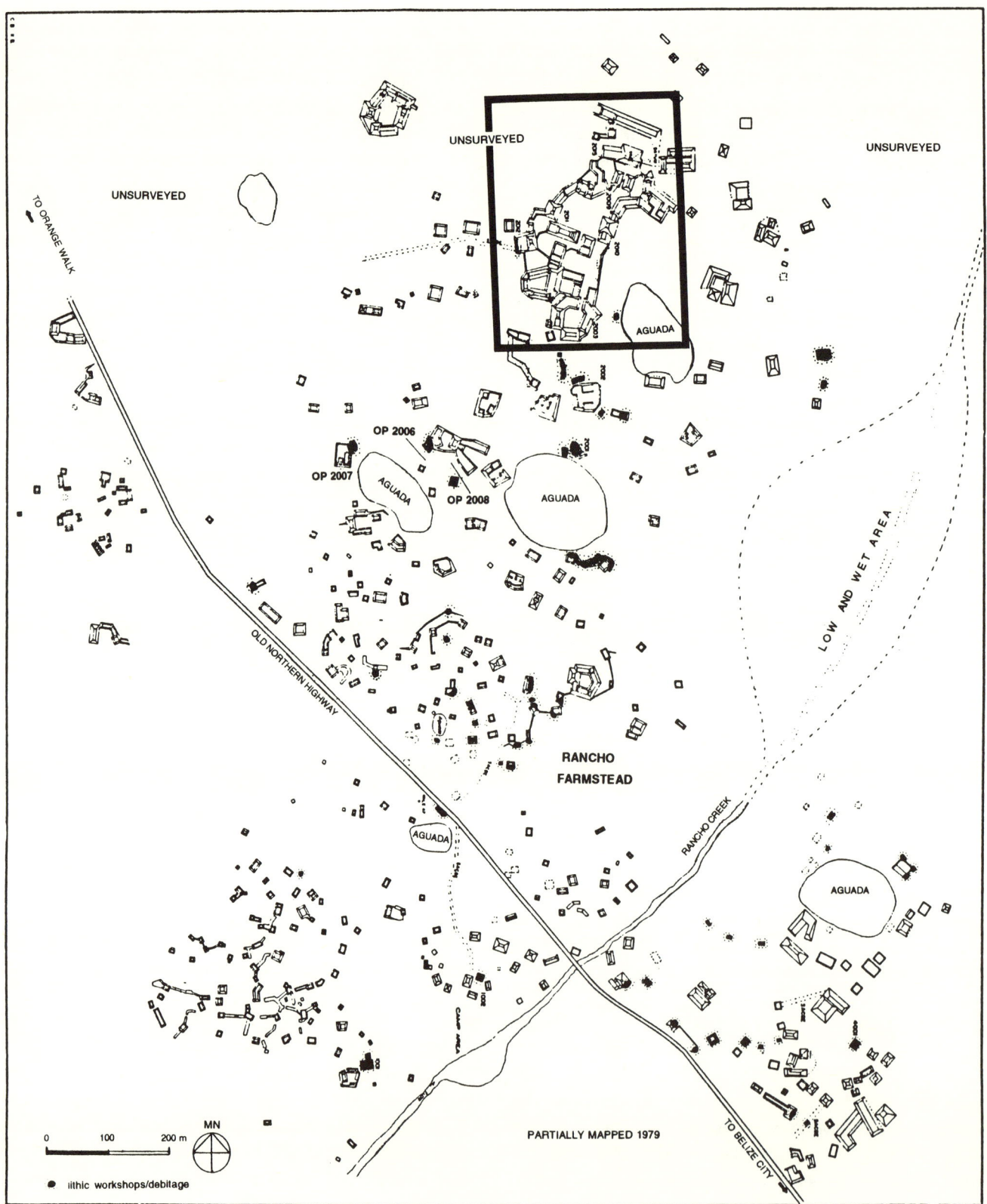

Fig. 27. General map of Colha as of 1980 (Hester, Shafer, and Eaton 1982).

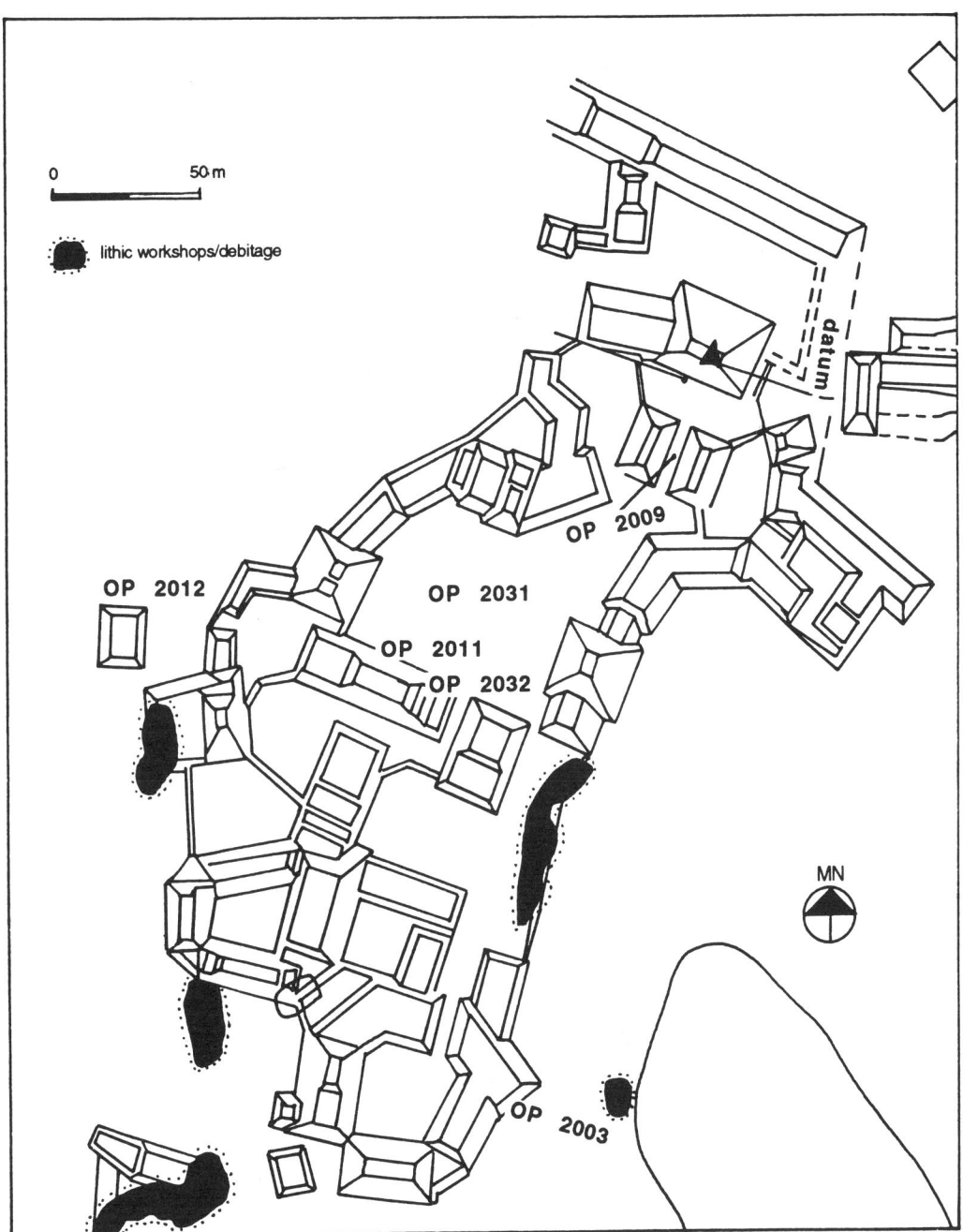

Fig. 27. (*Continued*) Detail of site center and location of operations cited in text.

specialized use of smaller blade forms was in the production of long, narrow burin spalls struck from the truncated ends of the blades. These burin spalls were probably used as drills or perforators and are associated with shell-bead making in *Bolay* deposits at operation 2012 (Potter 1980:180, 1991b). Given the numbers of burin-on-blade artifacts and burin spalls throughout Colha's Middle Preclassic deposits, bead manufacture might have been an important cottage industry at Colha

during this time. The Middle Preclassic deposits at the site have not revealed evidence of intensive production, and no workshops have been encountered within them.

Data from the site of Labpec south of Colha, recorded by Shafer, Hester, and Potter in 1983, support the existence of incipient lithic specialization in the Middle Preclassic. Apparently, the activity taking place here required large numbers of burin spall tools very similar in form and technology to the

Colha lithics just described. Thus, Labpec probably also dates to the Middle Preclassic. It may best be interpreted as a nonresidential locus of some unknown but specialized activity such as the production of marine-shell artifacts.

Regional exchange of chert artifacts made at Colha also began during the Bolay phase, given the evidence of Middle Preclassic stone tools from the site of Cuello, some 29 km northwest of Colha (Shafer et al. 1979; Potter, pers. obs. 1989). Fashioned from Colha chert and identical in form and in technical characteristics to the Colha tools, these Cuello specimens were most probably Colha exports. The likelihood of this scenario is strengthened by the absence of tool production debitage at Cuello. However, in contrast to the situation in the Late Preclassic period, Middle Preclassic chert tools at Colha appear to have been exported only locally, and not in great quantities (Potter 1982:117).

We believe these Middle Preclassic data are substantial enough to indicate that early villages in the Maya lowlands were not as simply organized as has been assumed. Middle Preclassic settlement variability, long-distance and local trade, and perhaps social stratification seem to have evolved in preurban settings in the Maya area, at least in some cases. Nakbe and its surroundings may, of course, present a different picture. Whereas Middle Preclassic lithic production was quite sophisticated and utilized most of the same techniques exhibited in the mass production workshops of later periods, it is suggested here that social and economic conditions prevalent during this period did not evoke a specialized response at the site.

The Context of Functional Specialization at Colha

ORGANIZATION OF LITHIC PRODUCTION

Reconstructions of the lithic industry that flourished from the Late Preclassic through the Late Classic at Colha have been presented in detail elsewhere (Hester and Shafer 1983, 1986; Shafer and Hester 1991). Our goal here is to place this functional specialization within the broad context of life at the site. We will begin by reviewing the organization of production and its evolution over time. We will then comment on the nature of the workshop deposits and on the identity of the chertworkers. We will end by considering the place of chertworking within the framework of other activities at Colha.

LATE PRECLASSIC

Lithic workshops are irregularly interspersed throughout the settlement at Colha from the Late Preclassic onward, indicating that toolmaking was a site-wide specialization (Hester and Shafer 1983). Their distribution is not haphazard, however. In the Late Preclassic, during the first peak of tool production, the spatial segregation of activities already evident at the site in the Middle Preclassic becomes even more clearly marked. The center, which continues to be a locus for settlement, also appears to have developed ceremonial-administrative functions at this time. Excavations in various structures in the site center have shown that the first large-scale monumental construction took place at this point, approximately at the same time that workshops were established at the site. Architectural forms included plastered Late Preclassic platforms (possibly elite residential structures?), pyramids, and a ballcourt (Eaton and Kunstler 1980; Hester et al. 1980, 1982). This ballcourt is among the earliest known for the Maya lowlands.

At operation 2012 (Fig. 27), several superimposed Late Preclassic cemeteries have been recorded by Potter (1980, 1982), containing both burials and cached offerings. Caches placed during the construction of the associated small Late Preclassic pyramid built on a low platform included a pair of bowls with postslip incised glyphs or "protoglyphs." One of these signs has been tentatively identified as an "ahau" glyph by Peter Mathews (pers. comm. to Potter 1984). More recently, Potter has proposed that the glyph might be read as "way," a term related to Maya shamanism, and may be associated with the "promotion" (Flannery 1972) of shamanistic status and power during the Preclassic (Potter 1991a). Regardless of how they might be interpreted, the glyphs can be included among a growing corpus of early Maya writing originating from the lowlands and echo the dynamic nature of the period.

Proceeding hand in hand with these developments was the maturation of economic specialization at the site, evidenced by the growth of Colha's massive lithic workshops. Thirty-six workshops have been identified so far for the Late Preclassic (Hester and Shafer 1986), located for the most part at some distance from the site center. Several seem to cluster in the vicinity of two large *aguadas* (waterholes), one situated about 50 m east of the center, the other one some 400 m south. Other workshops cluster in an area just south of Rancho Creek and east of the modern highway transecting the site (Figs. 26 and 27). The workshops occur either as isolated, discrete entities or as sheet deposits on terraces overlooking the *aguadas*. They range greatly in size from small debitage lenses 20 to 30 cm thick covering about 15 m^2 to large mounded deposits 1.75 m thick and covering some 350 m^2 (Hester and Shafer 1983). Many of these workshops were not buried by subsequent construction and are still visible. However, at least two of the isolated workshops, and perhaps others, were totally buried by unrelated construction at a later date.

Various architectural features have been found associated with the workshops, either in the form of underlying platforms or substructures or in the form of plaster surfaces or floorings lying within the workshop deposits themselves. In some cases, the substructures seem to have served only as work areas, since their plaster surfaces are embedded with debitage but lack other artifacts (Hester and Shafer 1992). In other cases, however, the platforms were not extensively tested to see whether or not they had ever supported a domestic structure in addition to or prior to the workshop.

Reconstructions of the manufacturing process suggest that tool production in the Late Preclassic took place in two stages. The first stage included the production of roughly formed macroflake tool blanks at quarries, as well as the transport of these blanks to the workshops. The second stage involved the thinning of these blanks in the workshops to produce highly standardized, finished tools. All Late Preclassic workshops seem to have produced the same range of goods, with oval bifaces and tranchet-bit implements (an adzelike tool) dominating the output. Other significant products included stemmed macroblades and large bifacial eccentrics, presumed to have served ceremonial functions (Hester and Shafer 1983, 1986; Shafer and Hester 1991; Chapter 5 by Hester and Shafer).

Research has focused mostly on the workshops themselves. As a result, more is known about internal production processes than about the relationship of the workshops to Late Preclassic households. Habitations for this time period are best known from the site center, where extensive excavations have uncovered a number of domestic structures and associated features (e.g., Day and Laurens 1980; Eaton and Kunstler 1980). It is from this area that we have the most substantial data on how Late Preclassic workshops were integrated into the contemporary settlement. The primary information comes from several closely spaced operations in Colha's main plaza: operations 2011, 2031, and 2032 (Fig. 27).

Operations 2011 and 2031 represent several large, contiguous horizontal excavation blocks in the main plaza excavated between 1980 and 1989 (Eaton 1980; Anthony 1987; Sullivan 1991). These two operations have produced clear evidence of at least thirteen separate, partially superimposed domestic structures crammed into a combined area of 143 m². The number of structures estimated here is undoubtedly overly conservative, since approximately half of the excavation area was not taken down to culturally sterile deposits. The structures possessed low circular or apsidal-shaped platforms and date variously to the Middle and Late Preclassic.

Stratigraphy here is complex: remodeling and modification of structures were seemingly constant, and older structures appear to have been consistently "robbed" of various materials for the construction or modification of new or existing structures nearby. Since not all of the thirteen structures are contemporary, it is difficult to ascertain patterning or to assess density for any given time. It is unclear, for instance, whether the platforms were arranged around small patios, like Maya households from later periods (Ashmore 1981b), or whether their layout followed some other pattern. Nonetheless, what is striking here is the intensity, duration, and complexity of settlement (Potter et al. 1984; Anthony 1987; Sullivan 1991). In density, if not in form, the settlement is reminiscent of the nucleated village described by Cliff (1982) at the Late Preclassic site of Cerros.

In 1983, less than 10 m southeast of this habitation area, a chert workshop was discovered in operation 2032, underneath a thick Late Classic flooring. This major workshop (over 1.5 m thick; F. Valdez, pers. comm. to Potter 1993) is unusual in incorporating several superimposed plaster floors. These floors were "sandwiched" between thick lenses of pure workshop debitage and were quite substantial at the northeastern edge of the workshop mound. Fred Valdez, who excavated operation 2032, observed that the floors seemed to become thinner as they continued into the heart of the workshop mound, until they pinched out altogether (pers. comm. to Potter 1993). It is unlikely that the floors represent domestic structures, since the only associated artifactual materials are clearly workshop detritus. Instead, the floors seem to have been laid repeatedly at the edge of the workshop as the debitage mound grew in size. One interpretation of this pattern is that the peripheral floors were the loci of chert tool production and that they were periodically rebuilt as workshop materials accumulated on them and on a mounded deposit off their southwestern edge (cf. Hester and Shafer 1983, 1986, 1992:244 with Moholy-Nagy 1990, 1992).

At present, we cannot be sure how the operation 2032 workshop related to the nucleated Late Preclassic settlement only a few meters away. It may have been associated with a specific Late Preclassic domestic structure or patio group, or perhaps it was related to a number of different nearby structures. Much larger excavations would be required to address this problem decisively. However, the propinquity of this workshop to such a dense and dynamic zone of Late Preclassic settlement is certainly suggestive of some functional relationship between the two.

Outside the site center, excavations in various locations (e.g., Eaton 1982b), particularly around the *aguadas* (H. Shafer, pers. comm. to King 1993), have consistently exposed Late

Preclassic household materials, but we lack a clear overview. As noted, none of the workshops has been found to be associated with domestic remains so far. From what we can observe on a preliminary basis, the workshops tend to be located close to one another within the area of habitation. If the workshops indeed represent independent structures not directly attached to domestic residences, then we might visualize the existence of "manufacturing zones" within the settlement. One such zone, for instance, might comprise the area around and between the large *aguadas* mentioned previously, with the waterholes functioning initially as quarries (Eaton 1982a). Another might comprise the area just south of Rancho Creek. Tool production, with its division of labor into primary and secondary reduction stages, might then have taken place within these zones as a communal activity engaging several possibly related households living nearby. (A discussion of Moholy-Nagy's [1990] alternate interpretation is given later in this chapter.)

EARLY CLASSIC

During the Classic, the organization of production appears to have developed and gradually changed. Though no workshops have yet been identified dating to the Early Classic, the remarkable continuity in manufacturing techniques and products from the Late Preclassic to the Late Classic strongly suggests that they existed (Hester and Shafer 1983). We should note that the Early Classic is weakly represented throughout the site (Adams and Valdez 1980; Valdez and Adams 1982). Furthermore, the paucity of ceramics in the workshops often makes them difficult to date. This problem is compounded by the fact that many common Late Preclassic ceramic types continue unchanged well into the Classic (see Valdez 1987). It is therefore very likely that some of the workshops dated to the Late Preclassic were also in use in the Early Classic (Hester and Shafer 1983). This overlap may help explain why many Late Preclassic workshops are still visible on the surface, whereas coeval domestic structures have all been found buried by later construction or natural deposition.

LATE CLASSIC

In the Late Classic, the workshops are located mostly south of Rancho Creek, well away from the site center, which continued to function as a ceremonial-administrative precinct. Although workshops are often found near each other, they seem to be more widely distributed throughout the settlement and to show less tendency to cluster than the Late Preclassic ones (Figs. 27 and 28). The Late Classic workshops occur both as independent, discrete entities and as talus deposits off single mounds or mound groups (Hester and Shafer 1983). Excavations have shown that both types of workshop are associated with domestic occupations, albeit in different ways. In two of the five known independent workshops, domestic remains seem to underlie and predate the debitage, though still within the Late Classic framework (operations 4026 and 4040/6–10). Two other independent workshops apparently rest on sterile clay or rock (operation 4029 [Roemer 1982] and operation 4040/5 [Masson 1989, 1991]) but are located next to non-workshop mounds presumed to represent domestic residences. Masson (1989) has suggested that these neighboring mounds housed the kin group using the workshop. The fifth independent workshop, located on survey by King in dense forest southwest of the site center, remains unexcavated. In the case of the talus workshops, on the other hand, the associated domestic occupations are found in the adjoining structures and are contemporary. Extensive middens and burials indicate long-term residence and use.

Examination of the Late Classic workshops has shown that production was still organized in two stages but in a different manner than in the Preclassic. Although the Late Preclassic pattern of primary tool reduction at quarries presumably continued (Hester and Shafer 1983), certain Late Classic workshops now specialized in primary and secondary decortication, producing blanks to be finished in nearby tertiary reduction workshops (Masson 1989, 1991). In addition, the tertiary or "finishing" workshops were themselves specialized in making primarily one type of tool—in some cases blades (Roemer 1984; Mason 1989, 1991), in others tranchet-bit implements (King 1986; Masson 1989, 1991; Mitchum and King 1990). Although each workshop exhibits the full range of Late Classic tool types (see Hester 1985), the emphasis on one type above others is quite evident. For example, in one sector of the site some 2 km southeast of the center, excavations in five neighboring workshops show that every workshop had its own characteristic output (Table 9) (see Roemer 1984; Masson 1989, 1991, for other examples).

Masson (1989) has further suggested that workshop specializations changed during the course of the Late Classic. One workshop (operation 4040/6–10), for example, appears to move from a specialization in primary and secondary reduction to one in tertiary reduction emphasizing blades, and then back to primary. Its trajectory seems to complement that of another, nearby workshop (operation 4040/5). This second workshop begins as a locus for finished tranchet production, using blanks that it may have received from the first workshop. It then seems to shift to primary and secondary reduction, making macroflake blanks and blade cores, before switching

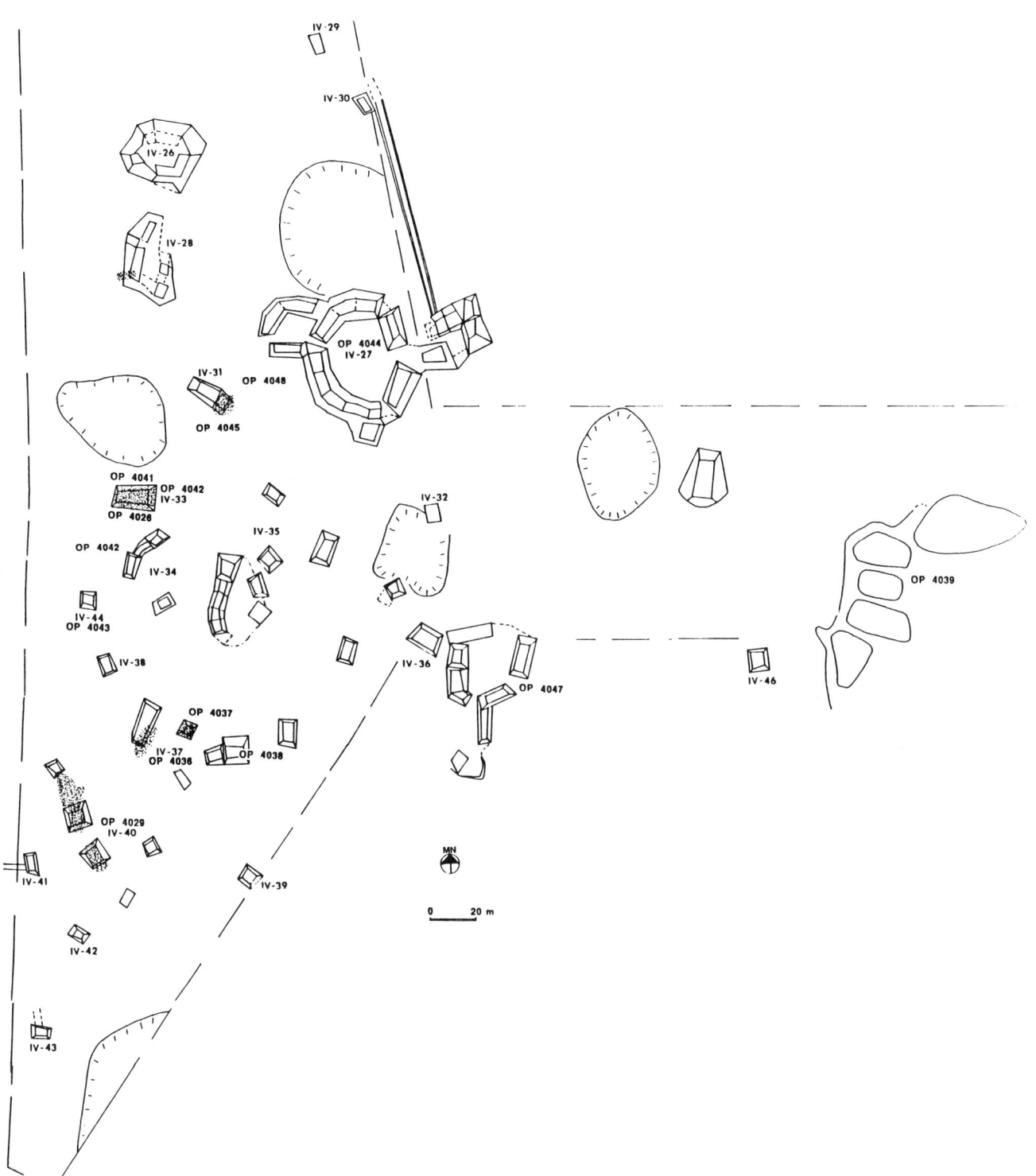

Fig. 28. Southeastern sector of Colha, showing raised fields to the east. Workshops are marked by stippling.

Table 9. Comparison of Tool Inventories in Neighboring Workshops

	Excavation									
	Operation 4026		Operation 4029		Operation 4036		Operation 4037		Operation 4045	
Tool type	No. of tools	Percent of all tools	No. of tools	Percent of all tools	No. of tools	Percent of all tools	No. of tools	Percent of all tools	No. of tools	Percent of all tools
Blades	1,992	74	195	20	288	28	234	36	3,690	81
Bifaces	564	21	132	13	221	21	113	17	600	13
Tranchet-bit tools	134	5	652	67	531	51	307	47	253	6
Total	2,690	100	979	100	1,040	100	654	100	4,543	100

back to tertiary reduction, this time specializing in blades, during its final stages of use (Masson 1989:142–143). It is worth noting that when the two workshops were alternately producing blanks and cores and then blades in their middle and upper levels they may have been shipping blade cores to each other. However, they also must have been dealing with other workshops, since the macroflake blanks would have been used to produce tranchet and oval bifaces, not blades. Masson (1989, 1991) documents similar production changes in other Late Classic workshops. Of particular significance is an observable shift in several workshops from an initial emphasis on mixed production of bifaces and blades to the exclusive production of blades, notably stemmed blades, in the Terminal Classic. Since stemmed blades were used for daggers, spears, and knives, she argues that this switch reflects a rise in consumer demand for weapons caused by the increased warfare associated with the end of the Classic (Masson 1989:146–150; see also Roemer 1984).

A final type of workshop specialization documented at Colha for the Late Classic is mode of production. Analysis of tranchet debitage from operations 4029, 4036, and 4037 has shown that the two workshops represented by operations 4029 and 4037 used two distinct reduction techniques to produce tranchet-bit tools. Tranchet tools from the operation 4037 workshop were made by carefully retouching the bulbar end of a macroflake to form a convex edge before administering the final transverse blow that would peel off a flake, thereby creating the distinctive adzelike bit of the tool (Fig. 29) (see Shafer 1984, for a description of tranchet technique). In the operation 4029 workshop, however, the bulbar end was only grossly shaped before the knapper removed a first tranchet flake to create the bit. The knapper would then have to correct and refine the shape of the bit by removing a second tranchet flake. In the first instance, the extra time used in preparation meant that little material was wasted; in the second, the technique was faster, but more of the bulbar end was lost. In the operation 4036 workshop, both techniques

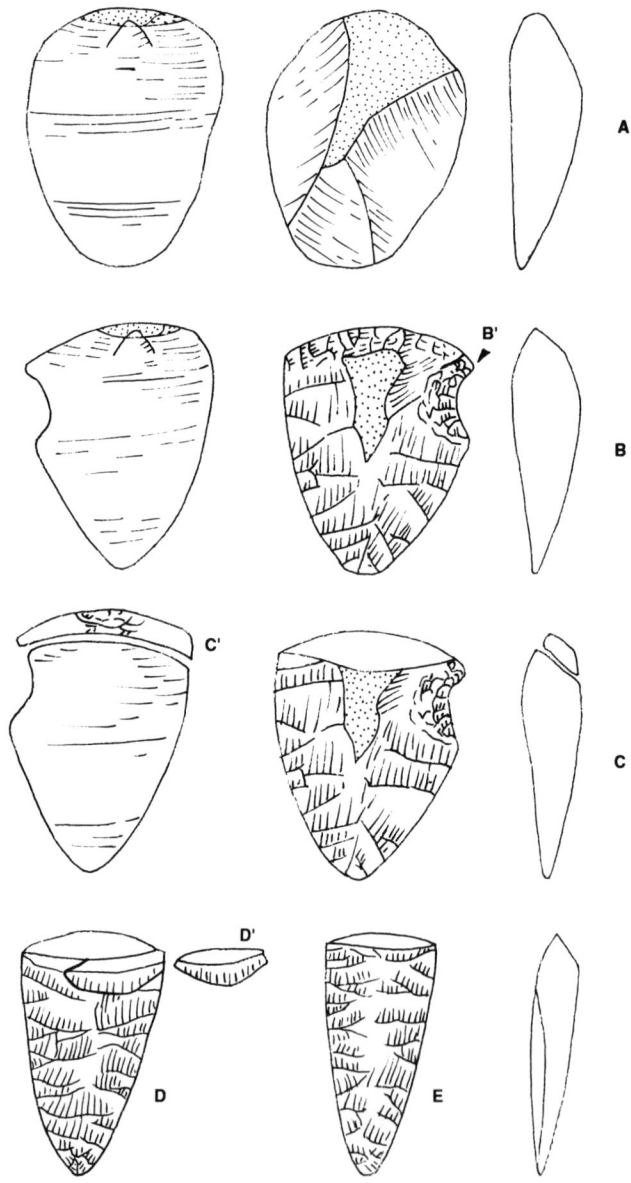

Fig. 29. Reduction sequence for tranchet tools: A, blank; B, preform; B', striking platform preparation; C, removal of tranchet flake (C'); D, final thinning; D', thinning flake intersecting tranchet facet; E, finished form. (Redrawn from Shafer 1984:59.)

were used, though the more precise and sparing method predominates here too in terms of sheer numbers. There are some indications that this mix reflects a change in the workshop's manufacturing technique over time, with the faster method eventually all but replacing the more painstaking one (Mitchum and King 1990).

To summarize, by the Late Classic, chertworking at Colha had evolved into a highly compartmentalized activity, with different workshops specializing in particular stages, types, and modes of production. The individualistic, even idiosyncratic, nature of Late Classic production conforms well to the observed settlement pattern. As noted, workshops, although not distant from each other, do not cluster together in this time period as they did in the Late Preclassic. They are separated by numerous nonworkshop mounds that are presumed to be housemounds. Most Late Classic workshops are thus relatively isolated from each other, suggesting that tool manufacturing was carried out strictly on a household-by-household basis rather than communally, as inferred for the Late Preclassic. We would note, however, that the organization of production in the Late Classic was still sitewide, since it minimally involved the transfer of macroflake blanks from primary to finishing workshops. It may additionally have included the transfer of blanks from quarries to finishing workshops, but the tool-making specialists may have gone to the quarries to extract their own chert, if they owned or had access to them. Comparative ethnographic data suggest that critical resources such as quarries would have been owned and managed by specific people, usually kin groups (H. Shafer, pers. comm. to King 1993; see also Shafer and Hester 1991). Finally, it is also possible that the overall organization of production entailed coordination of individual workshop output, so that enough of each category of tool—biface, blade, tranchet—was produced to meet consumer demand.

WORKSHOP INTERPRETATION AND CHERTWORKER IDENTIFICATION

Moholy-Nagy (1990) has recently suggested that Colha lithic workshops are secondary deposits, probably resulting from the habitual discard of lithic debitage by a number of different nearby households. She uses ethnoarchaeological studies of modern stone and glass-artifact manufacture to argue that the sharp chert debitage, posing a hazard, would have been removed to secondary middens in little-used areas. Her assessment, if correct, would have important implications for the existence of craft specialization at the site. Hester and Shafer's arguments in favor of full-time chertworking have relied on the volume and density of debitage in the workshops along with standardization of production (Shafer 1982; Hester and Shafer 1983, 1986). However, if these workshops were secondary debitage middens created by several households, as Moholy-Nagy proposes, the presence of full-time specialists would be in doubt. Such secondary deposits could well have been produced by numerous part-time or avocational chertworkers (including nonresidents, as implied by Mallory 1986) over an indeterminate period of time. Mallory (1986) has gone further in arguing that chertworking could have been an ancillary activity at the site, rather than its main focus.

Although Moholy-Nagy's concern with the depositional contexts of Colha workshops is important and appropriate, we believe the Colha evidence strongly suggests that the workshops were associated with specific workers or groups of workers and were not community dumps. The evidence also shows persuasively that, although chertworking was the primary activity at Colha, it was certainly not the only one.

For the Preclassic, the clustering of workshops in "manufacturing zones" with no associated domestic remains could be taken to indicate the prehistoric equivalent of landfill areas. The workshops, however, do not occur in a vacuum; the zones are not devoid of habitation. The data on hand are limited, since we lack the settlement context for most workshops, but Late Preclassic occupation has been found in every excavated area in central Colha as well as in areas where modern construction has exposed subsurface deposits. As noted in operation 2032, our best context for this time period, dense settlement and a large workshop occur less than 10 m apart. These data suggest that Late Preclassic workshops and settlement were more closely and specifically linked than previously recognized.

Of course, the mere coexistence of residences and workshops does not preclude Moholy-Nagy's argument that the deposits may be secondary. A few additional points may be made, however. Hester and Shafer (1983, 1986, 1992) have argued that the structure and composition of the workshops (e.g., the presence of microdebitage and lithic dust in the deposits) favors their being located in situ or immediately adjacent to their point of origin. We would point out that in only one instance so far (operation 2006) has a Late Preclassic workshop been found clearly overlying an earlier and apparently abandoned occupation. In this case, the unconformity between the workshop and the underlying Middle Preclassic deposits might indicate secondary deposition, but it could just as easily signify the rapidly evolving function of an in-place settlement.

More important, we note that Late Preclassic workshops have been found in areas where simple waste piles would probably not have accumulated. The operation 2032 workshop, for example, was located in the heart of the site. It was underlain by a Late Preclassic flooring and capped by a second flooring of Late Classic date (Hester and Shafer 1992:244). The sequence of substantial floors within the workshop, interpreted earlier as work surface refloorings, convincingly supports the workshop's status as an in situ activity area. The floors also suggest long-term use and continuity. Of particular interest in this context is the dating of the workshop to the end of the Late Preclassic (Blossom Bank phase, possibly A.D. 150–300; F. Valdez, pers. comm. to Potter 1993), a period during which Colha's first "boom" in monumental construction took place. It is unlikely that an abandoned workshop and its associated waste pile would have been left untended in the ceremonial, administrative, and residential heart of the site. Thus, all the evidence indicates that the workshop was a functional component of life in the center during the latter part of the Late Preclassic, a point to which we shall return.

The evidence from the Late Classic provides a much fuller picture of how chertworking took place at the site. About half of the thirty known (Hester and Shafer 1983:529; Shafer and Hester 1991) Late Classic workshops have been tested. Most were excavated in 1987 under the direction of the senior author, partly to establish their relations with adjacent or underlying structures. As noted, the majority of workshops dating to this period are talus deposits that have formed on specific structures, and, by inference, are associated with specific households. Thus, even if these talus workshops were formed as debitage was swept to one side of an ancient tool-working area, each can still be tied to a specific household (cf. Hester and Shafer 1992). Indeed, in one case (operation 4045) a well-preserved male burial was found within such a workshop, intruded through a thin floor separating two lenses of debitage. This individual is presumed to have lived in the adjoining domestic structure and may himself have been a chertworker, buried in the by-products of his labor.

Although the evidence is not complete, since most workshops were only tested and not thoroughly excavated, it appears that only the five independent workshops might qualify as dumps used by a number of households. As noted, these workshops seem to be situated above earlier residences or sterile surfaces—perfect locations for middens (Moholy-Nagy 1990). However, all but one are closely associated with adjacent mounds, each workshop forming with its neighbors a distinct group within the settlement. Such groups, whether organized informally in a loose aggregation or oriented orthogonally around a central patio (Ashmore 1981b), are conventionally interpreted in the Maya area as the residences of multifamily households (Ashmore and Wilk 1988; Wilk 1988). Thus, if these independent workshops are middens, they represent the lithic waste generated by a single such household unit (Masson 1989; Moholy-Nagy 1990:276; see Wilk and Ashmore 1988 for further discussion of Maya households and their archaeological equivalents).

The exception to this pattern is provided by an independent workshop deposited above an apparently earlier occupation. Operations 4026 (Escobedo 1980; Roemer 1982) and 4041 (Wood 1987; King 1987) (Fig. 28) in the workshop mound uncovered a platform with a midden rich in ceramics that was capped by a blade-producing workshop. Even here, however, interpretation is ambiguous. Excavations did not reveal whether the workshop covered all or only part of the underlying platform, i.e., whether the domestic remains were strictly anterior to the debitage. Since the artifacts from the workshop, the platform, and the midden all date to the Late Classic, a period of some 250 years, the sequence of events is not clear. The workshop could represent the secondary redeposition of lithic debitage on an old, abandoned house platform, as Moholy-Nagy (1990) suggests; the inhabitants of an untested nearby patio group (Fig. 28) might then be good candidates for primary users of the dump. However, the stratigraphy in the independent workshop could also be interpreted to indicate in situ accumulation of lithic debris by a household residing and making tools at that location.

Significantly, in the other independent workshop with underlying earlier remains (operation 4040/6–10) debitage does not cover the entire mound to equal depths. Indeed, a test pit placed away from the main workshop area in that location revealed a cobble platform close to the surface that appears to be contemporaneous with the workshop. If that is the case, both of these workshops could actually represent talus deposits, unrecognized because of the debitage covering their surfaces. It should be emphasized that both mounds are large enough to have supported a domestic structure and a workshop area.

To summarize, the bulk of the data from Colha suggests that the workshops represent either primary contexts or secondary contexts that are closely associated with their points of origin. Although the exact relationship between specialized chertworking and households remains to be resolved for the Late Preclassic, by Late Classic times the craft seems to have been carried out by single households that inhabited the individual mounds or mound groups associated with the workshops. Indeed, chertworking, with its specialized skills, may well have been an inherited, kin-based occupation (Hester and Shafer 1983).

STATUS AND ROLE OF CHERTWORKERS IN COLHA SOCIETY

What was the status of the Colha lithic specialists? What role did they play in Colha society? Perhaps the most intriguing data relevant to these questions come from Late Preclassic deposits at Colha. They come, not from the workshops themselves, but from ritual contexts. First, ritual caches at Colha and elsewhere (Chapter 5 by Hester and Shafer) have yielded Colha-made macroblades and eccentrics, demonstrating that chert workshops produced items for ritual as well as utilitarian use. Furthermore, one Late Preclassic ritual deposit at Colha provides compelling evidence that an experienced flintknapper participated in a bloodletting event on the small pyramid at operation 2012. This cache consisted of two large bowls placed lip to lip in a pit intruded into construction fill from the pyramid's upper flooring. Inside the bowls were marine shells, jade beads, ground cinnabar, shark teeth, and a large macroblade with human blood residue: a bloodletter. Immediately underneath the bowls in the remaining fill of the cache pit were a large macroblade core from which the bloodletter blade had been struck and another blade. The two blades conjoin laterally, and analysis shows that the bloodletter was removed from the core after the underlying blade.

The stratigraphic relationship of the cache contents allows the following reconstruction of ritual events. The blade core was brought to the pyramid and the blades were detached *as part of the caching ritual*. The first blade struck was apparently judged inadequate for the purpose, so a second one was removed. The unused blade and the core were then deposited in the pit, and the remaining blade was utilized, along with the other artifacts recovered from the vessels, in a ceremony that presumably included autosacrifice. How many people took part, what objects other than the bloodletter (e.g., necklaces) were involved, and how they were used remain unclear. Four conjoining jade bead fragments found scattered throughout the lower pit fill have been interpreted by Potter (1992) as the remains of a separate termination ritual probably aimed at the unused blade, the blade core, or both. It is likely that both of these items were thought to possess ritual power.

The presence of the large chert core and the expertise with which the blades were removed suggest that at least one of the participants (indeed, there may have been only one participant) was an accomplished flintknapper. The exotic artifact assemblage found within the cache, on the other hand, points to an elite context. If we assume an elite function for the operation 2012 pyramid and elite participation in the ritual, then we must conclude that at least some craft specialists were included among the elite during the Preclassic. Alternatively, we could start with the assumption that expert flintknappers were somewhat beneath elite status. The conclusion would then be that lower-status individuals had access to—and actively participated in—ritual activities within Colha's monumental center (Potter 1992). The presence of the operation 2032 workshop close to the operation 2012 temple area in the site center further suggests to us that, although our Western perspective may induce us to divorce economic from ritual behavior, the Maya may not have done so. Thus, in our view, the Late Preclassic workshops at Colha cannot be perceived as spatially, temporally, or functionally segregated from contemporary ritual or domestic culture.

In the Late Classic, we have no evidence on the relationship of chertworkers to ritual or other activities in the site center. Perhaps the location of Late Classic workshops primarily at some distance from the monumental core indicates that chertworkers were no longer as directly involved with activities in the site center. We do have good information for this time period, however, on the place of chertworkers within the larger Colha community. Excavations in mounds not associated with workshops have revealed the existence of other occupations, and possibly specializations, at the site. Operation 4044, for example, about 2 km south of the site center (Fig. 28), encompassed a series of excavations in a large patio group consisting of three linked courtyards sharing a raised platform base. Like most of the settlement, this group was built and occupied during the Late to Terminal Classic. The recovery of several poorly preserved burials, primary midden, and artifacts such as mano and metate fragments from different mounds within this large group suggests that it functioned as a residence, probably for a multifamily household. Most interesting, however, was the discovery of a dense concentration of heavily battered general utility and oval bifaces in a primary, sealed floor context (Epstein 1990). These tool types have been associated through use-wear analyses with heavy agricultural tasks such as land clearing (Nash 1986). In 1987, raised fields were discovered at Colha on the margins of Cobweb Swamp and only 100 m from this group. Radiocarbon dates and soil analyses suggest that although wetland modification took place somewhere between the Middle Preclassic and the Early Classic, the fields continued to be used in the Late Classic (Jacob 1992). The presence of eroded Late Classic sherds in soils deposited on the fields and the recovery of a well-used Late Classic oval biface from one of the canals further suggest that the system was still in operation at that time (Epstein 1990; Jacob 1992). In view of the patio group's tool inventory and its proximity to the fields, Epstein (1990) has suggested that the group's occupants were farmers.

Table 10. Comparison of Tool Inventories from Patio Group (Operation 4044) and Blade Workshop (Operation 4045)

	Excavation			
	Operation 4044		Operation 4045	
Tool type	No. of tools	Percent of all tools	No. of tools	Percent of all tools
Blades	146	29	3,690	81
Bifaces	337	67	600	13
Tranchet-bit tools	23	4	253	6
Totals	506	100	4,543	100

It is worth noting in this context that little lithic debitage was found associated with the patio group (Epstein 1990), although chertworking was done in the immediate area at a large Late Classic talus workshop (operation 4045) (Fig. 28) situated less than 25 m away. Furthermore, the type of debitage found in operation 4044 suggests that although the presumed farmers may have resharpened their tools, they clearly did not manufacture them. Despite the proximity of the workshop to the patio group, the orientation of the mounds, off-mound testing, and the material inventory recovered from each operation suggest that the two locales functioned independently of each other (King 1990). This differentiation in affiliation and in function is most strongly supported by comparison of the lithic assemblages from the workshop and the patio group. As Table 10 shows, whereas over three-fourths of the workshop's output consisted of blades, over two-thirds of the tools found in the patio group were bifaces, with blades accounting for less than a third of its total tool inventory. These striking differences indicate that there were differences within the Colha rank and file, not only among chertworkers, as evidenced by production specialization, but between chertworkers and other inhabitants, possibly specialists themselves. Certainly in this case, the strong possibility that the patio group's inhabitants practiced intensive agriculture may indicate that they were farming specialists rather than just subsistence cultivators.

This interpretation is bolstered by evidence from the excavation of another nonworkshop structure, operation 4043 (Fig. 28). This structure was originally thought to form a patio group with the independent workshop previously discussed at length (excavated as operations 4026 and 4041) and another, amorphous mound. Extensive clearing and off-mound testing in the supposed patio area between the structures, however, revealed that the amorphous mound was but the high point of a natural ridge that separated the independent workshop from what proved to be a single, isolated housemound. Material found in midden and in floor contexts in the single mound revealed that the inhabitants of this residence were apparently not as well off as their neighbors. Most striking was the general appearance of the tools found, most of which were bifaces, specifically oval ones. Many were battered and ill- or roughly made. Thus, even though the residence was situated only some 40 m south of the independent workshop and some 50 m northwest of two talus workshops (operations 4036 and 4037) (Fig. 28), its inhabitants did not seem to have had access to the best tools at the site. This observation is particularly striking if one considers that most of the bifaces produced by the independent workshop were oval.

King (1990) has inferred elsewhere that the inhabitants of this isolated mound were small-scale subsistence farmers, perhaps even landless laborers working farmland for others. Certainly, their material goods suggest they were not as well off as the inhabitants of the patio group discussed earlier. In addition, their toolkit was not as complete, since it was noticeably lacking in general utility bifaces and tranchet-bit tools. Thus, although the single mound inhabitants were probably farmers, they do not appear to have been as prosperous as the residents of the patio group. We should add that they were also not as well off as the chertworkers operating the three nearby talus workshops (operations 4036, 4037, and 4045) and the independent workshop (operations 4026 and 4041), who seem to have had access to the same range of goods (ceramics, obsidian, and other finds) as the patio group inhabitants (King 1990).

The difference between the farmers and the chertworkers and between the rich and the poor is further reflected in the layout of the Colha settlement. The pattern of mound distribution at the site is distinctive, with single mounds and informal groups and clusters of five to twelve mounds predominating. Although orthogonally arranged patio groups and clusters occur, they are not as prominent in the Colha settlement as they are at many other Maya sites. King (1990) has argued that this singular pattern reflects Colha's functional specialization. In brief, Wilk (1988:143), using ethnographic analogy, has suggested that informal mound groups are associated with loosely organized multifamily households and patio groups with more cohesive ones. Significantly, only two known Late Classic workshops adjoin patio groups (operations 2007 and 4040/13–20); the others are all attached to or associated with single mounds or informal mound groups. As Epstein (1990) has pointed out, although there is an economy of scale involved in agricultural work that favors cooperation among a large group of people, chert tool production is easily accomplished by one or a few individuals. Chertworking households, therefore, are more likely to have been loosely organized (King 1990). In practical terms, that might mean that the members worked together frequently, but each family retained its own property and made many independent decisions (Wilk 1988).

Conversely, intensive agriculture may have promoted greater cohesion in households in which it was the primary activity. Farming per se is associated with both loosely organized and cohesive households among the modern Kekchi Maya (Wilk 1988:142–143), and this pattern is certainly reflected at Colha in the two farming households already discussed. However, the special requirements of raised field cultivation may specifically have favored larger, more organized households such as the household presumed to have inhabited the patio group (King 1990). Significantly, the other mounds near the Cobweb Swamp fields are part of another large and relatively elaborate patio group also dating to the Late Classic. There seems, therefore, to be a close fit between inferred activities and settlement structure at the site.

Status is also evident in the settlement pattern. Although, as noted, there are no obvious differences in the material inventories from workshop and nonworkshop mounds, Epstein (1990) has pointed out that the patio groups were generally better constructed, with house platforms and basal walls made of finely cut stone. Residences associated with workshops, on the other hand, were usually built on rough cobble platforms. Epstein (1990) suggests that the patio groups represent emerging, lower-level Colha elite. Building on the ideas outlined earlier, he proposes that the farmers at the site were able to improve their position because they controlled a prized Maya commodity, labor (King 1990), and were capable of mobilizing large work forces. Chertworkers, on the other hand, while enjoying a certain status and wealth because of their own expert labor and perhaps through ownership of quarries (H. Shafer, pers. comm. to King 1993), were not able to expand their power base. They were, in fact, constrained from further advance by the very structure and nature of their task (Epstein 1990).

To summarize, chertworking was an important, sitewide occupation from the Late Preclassic through the Late Classic. Organization of work within the primary lithic industry was quite sophisticated and changed over time. In the Late Preclassic, production seems to have taken place in two stages, with macroflake preparation taking place at the quarries and tool finishing occurring in the actual workshops. Workshops during this period seem to be concentrated in "manufacturing zones" that also contained habitations. Specialized chertworking seems to have been integrated with both domestic and ritual activities at Colha and to have been intimately associated with the original monumental buildings of the site center. By the Late Classic, workshops are securely tied to individual households and show specialization not only in the stage of production but also in the type of product and in the mode of manufacturing. Data from nonworkshop contexts, on the other hand, show that although Colha was functionally specialized, it was not a single-purpose site. Its inhabitants carried out diverse activities, including chertworking and other pursuits perhaps as specialized. These activities are linked to specific households and can be mapped out on the settlement. The organization of these activities may in turn have given rise to first-echelon social differentiations within Colha society.

That such distinctions occur at a small site argues for greater socioeconomic complexity at this settlement level than Sanders and Webster's (1988) regal-ritual model or other hierarchical schemes allow. Although Colha is certainly unique in its emphasis on lithics, a comparable diversity of functions can no doubt be found in varying degrees at other small sites. These conclusions are supported by Rice's (1987) analysis of the Late Classic ceramic production system in the Maya lowlands. Reviewing the data on production locales, she suggests that they were geographically dispersed and essentially nonurban, i.e., carried out in small, "village" sites (see also McAnany 1989).

Sanders and Webster (1988), in fact, make a similar point in discussing their model. They suggest that specialized production of utilitarian goods would be found outside the regal-ritual cities, in rural areas where it could be controlled by the local elite. Their model only allows for part-time specialization, however, by people who were essentially peasant farmers. If applied to Colha, we would expect most, if not all, of the households at the site to be associated with small-scale lithic production, as the inhabitants capitalized on their rich local resource under the watchful eye of their overlords. That is clearly not the case. Nonworkshop mounds far outnumber workshop mounds, which are in turn much denser deposits than such casual activity would produce (see Hester and Shafer 1983, 1986; Shafer and Hester 1991). We would add that debitage is consistently present in nonworkshop domestic contexts (e.g., operations 4043 and 4044 discussed previously; see also Gibson 1982). Thus, although many of the Colha inhabitants were adept at flintknapping, they were clearly not as specialized as the resident chertworkers, some of whose tools have yet to be accurately reproduced. Finally, the rural part-time "peasant producer" model does not fit well with our impression of the central role played by lithic specialization at Colha in the Late Preclassic. Indeed, given their participation in important ritual activity, it could be argued that the chertworkers, far from being subservient to the elite, were themselves members of a privileged group, as suggested previously. (See also Shafer and Hester 1991 for a discussion of the chertworkers' control over production, and Chapter 7 by Santley on rural craft specialization.)

Conclusions

We are not arguing against the validity of site size hierarchies in this chapter. Clearly, certain sites in the Maya lowlands were larger and more important than others. The problem lies in defining the exact nature of that importance, which probably varied according to the center's primary function, whether economic, religious, or political. Also critical is a better understanding of the relationship among center function, configuration, and growth, and how these factors coevolved.

Unquestioning acceptance of the assumptions behind the "bigger is better" approach can skew research. By expecting centers to be functionally similar, we fail to explore variability and fail to discern the intricate relations that must have existed among them, particularly the kinds of interactions that are not spoken of in the glyphs. By not expecting social, economic, or political complexity from small sites, we disregard possible important sources of information on the lowland Maya world. This remark seems particularly pertinent to the Middle Preclassic. Now that the discovery of Nakbe has pushed the existence of site size hierarchies further back in time, we are once again in danger of simply looking at the large sites for information on emerging sociopolitical complexity. The data from Colha demonstrate that this approach would be a mistake, since early differentiation began there in the apparent absence of local or regional site hierarchies.

In a thought-provoking article, Crumley (1987) has suggested that the problem with our models of complex societies is that, in the state societies anthropologists usually inhabit, there is a hidden bias that equates structure and order with hierarchy. Following Clarke (1972), she refers to this bias as a "controlling model" that makes it "difficult [for us] to imagine, much less recognize and study, other structures which are not hierarchical" (Crumley 1987:158). She adds that this viewpoint has also impeded our efforts to study process, or more specifically the relation between structure and process—structural change—that she considers the "proper focus of study" (Crumley 1987:156). She proposes instead the concept of heterarchy, borrowed from McCulloch's (1945) research on artificial intelligence. In brief, he suggested that the human brain, though orderly, is not organized hierarchically (Crumley 1987:157) in that different parts are in control depending on the task at hand. Crumley (1987:158) thus defines structures as "heterarchical when each element is either unranked relative to other elements or possesses the *potential* [sic] for being ranked in a number of ways." Heterarchy does not negate hierarchy, it subsumes it. Indeed, Crumley (1987:163) suggests that "the ultimate in complexity is not hierarchy but the play between hierarchy and heterarchy: across space, through time, and in the human mind."

Crumley herself has successfully used the concept of heterarchy in her diachronic regional analysis of land use and settlement in Burgundian France (Crumley and Marquardt 1987). This concept has also been applied to prehistoric time periods in areas such as Southeast Asia where prevailing hierarchical models lack explanatory power (White 1992). We propose that this same concept could fruitfully be applied to both contemporary and diachronic interactions between sites in the Maya area. A similar kind of approach has already been tried with the concept of "peer-polity interaction" (Renfrew and Cherry 1986; see especially Sabloff 1986 and Freidel 1986), but it is a more limited model, since it deals with alliances (Crumley 1987:162) and does not, for example, address interactions between sites of markedly different size.

Adopting a heterarchical approach might be most useful in examining Maya economic relations. The prevalent hierarchically oriented models assume that the larger sites acted as central places, gathering in both utilitarian and elite goods and redistributing them to lower-order centers and thence to the countryside in their surrounding region. The models also assume direct elite administrative and fiscal control over the movement of products (see for example Chase and Chase 1992:13). As Rice (1987) has observed, however, there is a curious lack of archaeological evidence to support this view. A market area has tentatively been identified at Tikal (Jones 1979; Morley, Brainerd, and Sharer 1983:283), and several archaeologists have suggested that the ceremonial plazas doubled as markets (Coe 1967:73; Freidel 1981:378; Folan, Kintz, and Fletcher 1983:49–64, all cited in Rice 1987:77; see also Jones, Ashmore, and Sharer 1983). But there is little physical evidence beyond the presence of the goods themselves to indicate that trade took place through centrally administered exchange. Rice (1987:77) adds that "Nothing suggests that the writing system was used to record transactions, yields, tribute, or other economic affairs. Nor have workshops been found in concentrations in the centers that would indicate barrio-like organization, ... administrative control of production (i.e., taxation), and/or a desire on the part of artisans to establish themselves in proximity of a market."

She also points out, as noted previously, that studies of utilitarian goods, primarily pottery (Fry and Cox 1974; Hammond, Harbottle, and Gazard 1976; Bishop, Rands, and Harbottle 1979; Fry 1980; Rands and Bishop 1980), have shown that production was dispersed in small, "village" communities. They also suggest that distribution was noncentralized and extremely localized (within 15 km; Rice 1987:79). This information complements the data from Colha, where locally produced utilitarian tools seem to travel to a less localized (75 km; Shafer and Hester 1991:94) but still restricted "primary consumer area" within northern Belize (Shafer 1983; Shafer and Hester 1991; Chapter 5 by Hester and Shafer). Rice (1987) concludes that the Maya did not have a hierarchically organized, centrally administered market system. Rather, she suggests independent, noncommercialized exchange of utilitarian goods among communities, probably based on kin relations. She points out that the procurement and distribution of exotic goods such as obsidian, on the other hand, conform much better to a centralized model. Utilitarian and ritual goods thus seem to move in different ways, a point that again seems borne out by the Colha data (Shafer and Hester 1991; Chapter 5 by Hester and Shafer).

Rice's study seems a perfect departure point for a heterarchical look at economic relations in the Maya area. Using such a framework would enable us to model the production and distribution of various goods differentially and to see how patterns of exchange correlate with intersite political and social relationships (see McAnany 1989). What we need, however, is a different class of data. More regional analyses of the kinds noted earlier would help map the movement of different types of goods (see Dreiss and Brown 1989). We must also clarify functional distinctions within classes of items, such as, in the category of exotics, objects that functioned as symbols of elite religious and political authority and objects that served as mere luxury goods (Chase and Chase 1992). Finally, we need more fine-grained analyses of activities within sites to know where goods went and how they were used.

Intrasite studies would also provide us with clearer insight into the variety of functions performed by individual sites, whether large or small. A promising step in this direction has been taken at the large site of Sayil, where intensive surface survey has recently revealed evidence for social differentiation and economic specialization in unsuspected areas (Smyth and Dore 1992). More work of this kind needs to be done, however, before we can speak knowledgeably about the functions of different-sized sites and model their many complex interactions in a heterarchical framework. We should be especially careful not to neglect small sites, because they may hold the answers to any number of questions, from the origins of socioeconomic complexity in the Maya lowlands to Classic patterns of economic relations.

Note

This chapter would not have materialized without the help of a number of people. Glenn Schwartz and Steve Falconer invited us to participate in the original SAA symposium and to revise our paper for this volume. Georgianna Grentzenberg drew all of our illustrations, often on short notice, with precision, grace, and speed. Wendy Ashmore, Dave Brown, Steve Epstein, Steve Falconer, Tom Hester, Beverly Mitchum, Glenn Schwartz, Harry Shafer, Bob Sharer, Fred Valdez, and Joyce White provided useful comments, suggestions, and information. We wish to thank them all for helping to make our contribution much stronger. We reserve the right to claim any errors as our own.

References Cited

Adams, Richard E. W.
   1982 Rank Site Analysis of Northern Belize Maya Sites. In *Archaeology at Colha, Belize: The 1981 Interim Report,* edited by T. R. Hester, H. J. Shafer, and J. D. Eaton, pp. 60–64. Center for Archaeological Research, University of Texas at San Antonio and Centro Studi e Ricerche Ligabue, Venice.

Adams, Richard E. W., and Richard C. Jones
   1981 Spatial Patterns and Regional Growth Among Classic Maya Cities. *American Antiquity* 46(2):301–322.

Adams, Richard E. W., and Fred Valdez
   1980 The Ceramic Sequence of Colha, Belize: 1979 and 1980 Seasons. In *The Colha Project, Second Season, 1980 Interim Report,* edited by T. R. Hester, J. D. Eaton, and H. J. Shafer, pp. 15–40. Center for Archaeological Research, University of Texas at San Antonio and Centro Studi e Ricerche Ligabue, Venice.

Andrews, E. Wyllys, V, William Ringle, Philip J. Barnes, A. Barrera Rubio, and Tomas Gallareta N.
   1981 Komchen: An Early Maya Community in Northwest Yucatan. Paper presented at the 1981 Meeting of the Sociedad Mexicana de Antropología, San Cristobal, Chiapas, June 21–27.

Anthony, Dana S.
   1987 An Analysis of the Preclassic Households Beneath the Main Plaza at Colha, Belize. M.A. thesis, Department of Anthropology, University of Texas at Austin.

Ashmore, Wendy
    1981a Precolumbian Occupation at Quirigua, Guatemala: Settlement Patterns in a Classic Maya Center. Ph.D. dissertation, Department of Anthropology, University of Pennsylvania.
    1981b Some Issues of Method and Theory in Lowland Maya Settlement Archaeology. In *Lowland Maya Settlement Patterns,* edited by W. Ashmore, pp. 37–70. University of New Mexico Press, Albuquerque.

Ashmore, Wendy, and Richard R. Wilk
    1988 Household and Community in the Mesoamerican Past. In *Household and Community in the Mesoamerican Past,* pp. 1–27. University of New Mexico Press, Albuquerque.

Ball, Joseph W., and Jennifer T. Taschek
    1991 Late Classic Lowland Maya Political Organization and Central Place Analysis: New Insights from the Upper Belize Valley. *Ancient Mesoamerica* 2:149–165.

Bishop, Ronald L., Robert L. Rands, and G. Harbottle
    1979 A Ceramic Compositional Interpretation of Incense-Burner Trade in the Palenque Area, Mexico. *Brookhaven National Laboratory Report* BNL-26787. Brookhaven National Laboratory, Upton, N.Y.

Blanton, Richard E.
    1981 The Rise of Cities. In *The Handbook of Middle American Indians* (Supplement), Vol. 1: *Archaeology,* edited by J. A. Sabloff, pp. 392–400. University of Texas Press, Austin.

Bullard, William R., Jr.
    1960 Maya Settlement Pattern in Northeastern Peten, Guatemala. *American Antiquity* 25:355–372.

Chase, Allen F., and Diane Z. Chase
    1987 *Investigations at the Classic Maya City of Caracol, Belize: 1985–1987.* Pre-Columbian Art Research Institute Monograph 3. Pre-Columbian Art Research Institute, San Francisco.
    1989 The Investigation of Classic Period Maya Warfare at Caracol, Belize. *Mayab* 5:5–18.
    1992 Mesoamerican Elites: Assumptions, Definitions, and Models. In *Mesoamerican Elites: An Archaeological Assessment,* edited by D. Z. Chase and A. F. Chase, pp. 3–17. University of Oklahoma Press, Norman.

Chase, Allen F., Diane Z. Chase, and William A. Haviland
    1990 The Classic Maya City: Reconsidering the "Mesoamerican Urban Tradition." *American Anthropologist* 92:499–506.

Christaller, Walter
    1933 *Die Zentralen Orte in Süddeutschland.* Zeiss, Jena, Germany.
    1966 *Central Places in Southern Germany.* Prentice Hall, Englewood Cliffs, N.J.

Clark, John E.
    1986 From Mountains to Molehills: A Critical Review of Teotihuacan's Obsidian Industry. *Research in Economic Anthropology* (Supplement) 2:23–74.

Clarke, David L.
    1972 Models and Paradigms in Contemporary Archaeology. In *Models in Archaeology,* edited by D. L. Clarke, pp. 47–52. Academic Press, New York.

Cliff, Maynard
    1982 Lowland Maya Nucleation: A Case Study from Northern Belize. Ph.D. dissertation, Department of Anthropology, Southern Methodist University. University Microfilms, Ann Arbor, Mich.

Coe, William R.
    1965 Tikal, Guatemala, and Emergent Maya Civilization. *Science* 147:1401–1419.
    1967 *Tikal: A Handbook of the Ancient Maya Ruins.* University Museum, University of Pennsylvania, Philadelphia.

Coe, William R., and William A. Haviland
    1982 *Introduction to the Archaeology of Tikal, Guatemala.* Tikal Report No. 12. University Museum, University of Pennsylvania, Philadelphia.

Coggins, Clemency
    1980 The Shape of Time: Some Political Implications of a Four-part Figure. *American Antiquity* 45:727–739.

Crumley, Carole L.
    1987 A Dialectical Critique of Hierarchy. In *Power Relations and State Formation,* edited by T. C. Patterson and C. W. Gailey, pp. 155–169. American Anthropological Association, Washington, D.C.

Crumley, Carole L., and William H. Marquardt, eds.
    1987 *Regional Dynamics: Burgundian Landscapes in Historical Perspective.* Academic Press, San Diego.

Culbert, T. Patrick
    1991 *Classic Maya Political History: Hieroglyphic and Archaeological Evidence.* Cambridge University Press, Cambridge.

Day, D. William, and Jane C. Laurens
    1980 Excavations at Operation 2003, 1980 Season. In *The Colha Project, Second Season, 1980 Interim Report,* edited by T. R. Hester, J. D. Eaton, and H. J. Shafer, pp. 71–85. Center for Archaeological Research, University of Texas at San Antonio and Centro Studi e Ricerche Ligabue, Venice.

Dreiss, Meredith, and David O. Brown
    1989 Obsidian Exchange Patterns in Belize. *Research in Economic Anthropology* (Supplement) 4:57–90.

Eaton, Jack D.
    1980 Operation 2011: Investigations within the Main Plaza of the Monumental Center at Colha. In *The Colha Project, Second Season, 1980 Interim Report,* edited by T. R. Hester, J. D. Eaton, and H. J. Shafer, pp. 145–162. Center for Archaeological Research, University of Texas at San Antonio and Centro Studi e Ricerche Ligabue, Venice.
    1982a Colha: An Overview of Architecture and Settlement. In *Archaeology at Colha, Belize: The 1981 Interim Report,* edited by T. R. Hester, H. J. Shafer, and J. D. Eaton, pp. 11–20. Center for Archaeological Research, University of Texas at San Antonio and Centro Studi e Ricerche Ligabue, Venice.
    1982b Operation 2025: An Elite Residential Group at Colha. In *Archaeology at Colha, Belize: The 1981 Interim Report,* edited by T. R. Hester, H. J. Shafer, and J. D. Eaton, pp. 123–140. Center for Archaeological Research, University of Texas

at San Antonio and Centro Studi e Ricerche Ligabue, Venice.

Eaton, Jack D., and Barton Kunstler
1980 Excavations at Operation 2009: A Maya Ballcourt. In *The Colha Project, Second Season, 1980 Interim Report,* edited by T. R. Hester, J. D. Eaton, and H. J. Shafer, pp. 121–132. Center for Archaeological Research, University of Texas at San Antonio and Centro Studi e Ricerche Ligabue, Venice.

Epstein, Stephan M.
1990 Operation 4044 Preliminary Excavation Report: Plazuela Group IV-27, Colha, Belize. Manuscript on file with the authors.

Escobedo, James T., Jr.
1980 Notes on Test Excavations at Operation 4026—A Debitage Mound. In *The Colha Project, Second Season, 1980 Interim Report,* edited by T. R. Hester, J. D. Eaton, and H. J. Shafer, pp. 221–224. Center for Archaeological Research, University of Texas at San Antonio and Centro Studi e Ricerche Ligabue, Venice.

Fash, Barbara W.
1992 Late Classic Architectural Sculpture Themes in Copan. *Ancient Mesoamerica* 3:89–104.

Fash, William L.
1988 A New Look at Maya Statecraft from Copan, Honduras. *Antiquity* 62:157–169.

Flannery, Kent V.
1972 The Cultural Evolution of Civilizations. *Annual Review of Ecology and Systematics* 3:399–426.

Folan, William J., Ellen R. Kintz, and Laraine A. Fletcher
1983 *Coba: A Classic Maya Metropolis.* Academic Press, New York.

Fox, Richard G.
1977 *Urban Anthropology.* Prentice Hall, Englewood Cliffs, N.J.

Freidel, David A.
1981 Political Economics of Residential Dispersion among the Lowland Maya. In *Lowland Maya Settlement Patterns,* edited by W. Ashmore, pp. 371–384. University of New Mexico Press, Albuquerque.
1986 Maya Warfare: An Example of Peer Polity Interaction. In *Peer Polity Interaction and Socio-political Change,* edited by C. Renfrew and J. F. Cherry, pp. 93–108. Cambridge University Press, Cambridge.

Fry, Robert E.
1980 Models of Exchange from Major Shape Classes of Lowland Maya Pottery. In *Models and Methods in Regional Exchange,* edited by R. E. Fry, pp. 3–18. S. A. A. Papers, No. 1. Society for American Archaeology, Washington, D.C.

Fry, Robert E., and Scott C. Cox
1974 The Structure of Ceramic Exchange at Tikal, Guatemala. *World Archaeology* 6:209–225.

Gibson, Eric C.
1982 Investigations at Operation 1002, A Late Classic Household Group at Colha, Belize. In *Archaeology at Colha, Belize: The 1981 Interim Report,* edited by T. R. Hester, H. J. Shafer, and J. D. Eaton, pp. 141–151. Center for Archaeological Research, University of Texas at San Antonio and Centro Studi e Ricerche Ligabue, Venice.

Gibson, Eric C., Leslie C. Shaw, and Daniel R. Finamore
1986 *Early Evidence of Maya Hieroglyphic Writing at Kichpanha, Belize.* Working Papers in Archaeology, No. 2. Center for Archaeological Research/University of Texas at San Antonio, San Antonio.

Hammond, Norman
1974 The Distribution of Late Classic Maya Major Ceremonial Centres in the Central Area. In *Mesoamerican Archaeology: New Approaches,* edited by N. Hammond, pp. 313–334. University of Texas Press, Austin.
1975 Maya Settlement Hierarchy in Northern Belize. *Contributions to the University of California Research Facility* 27:40–55.
1981 Settlement Patterns in Belize. In *Lowland Maya Settlement Patterns,* edited by W. Ashmore, pp. 157–186. University of New Mexico Press, Albuquerque.
1982 Colha in Context. In *The Colha Project, Second Season, 1980 Interim Report,* edited by T. R. Hester, J. D. Eaton, and H. J. Shafer, pp. 65–71. Center for Archaeological Research, University of Texas at San Antonio and Centro Studi e Ricerche Ligabue, Venice.
1991 *Cuello: An Early Maya Community in Belize.* Cambridge University Press, New York.

Hammond, Norman, G. Harbottle, and T. Gazard
1976 Neutron Activation and Statistical Analysis of Maya Ceramics and Clays from Lubaantun Belize. *Archeometry* 18:147–168.

Hansen, Richard D.
1990 Investigaciónes Arqueológicas en el Norte del Peten, Guatemala: Una Vista Diacrónica de los Origines Mayas. Paper presented at the symposium "450 Aniversario de la Fundación de Campeche, Mexico." Manuscript on file with the authors.

Haviland, William A.
1965 Prehistoric Settlement at Tikal, Guatemala. *Expedition* 7:15–23.
1966 Maya Settlement Patterns: A Critical Review. *Middle American Research Institute Publications* (Tulane University, New Orleans) 26:21–47.
1968 Ancient Lowland Maya Social Organization. *Middle American Research Institute Publications* (Tulane University, New Orleans) 26:93–117.
1970 Tikal, Guatemala, and Mesoamerican Urbanism. *World Archaeology* 2:186–199.
1985 Population and Social Dynamics. The Dynasties and Social Structure of Tikal. *Expedition* 27:34–41.

Hester, Thomas R.
1985 The Maya Lithic Sequence in Northern Belize. In *Essays in Honor of Don E. Crabtree,* edited by M. Pleuw, J. Woods, and M. Pavesic. University of New Mexico Press, Albuquerque.

Hester, Thomas R., Giancarlo Ligabue, Jack D. Eaton, Harry J. Shafer, and Richard E. W. Adams
1982 Archaeology at Colha, Belize: The 1981 Season. In *Archaeology at Colha, Belize: The 1981 Interim Report,* edited by

T. R. Hester, H. J. Shafer, and J. D. Eaton, pp. 1–10. Center for Archaeological Research, University of Texas at San Antonio and Centro Studi e Ricerche Ligabue, Venice.

Hester, Thomas R., Giancarlo Ligabue, Harry J. Shafer, Jack D. Eaton, and Richard E. W. Adams
   1980 The 1980 Season at Colha, Belize: An Overview. In *The Colha Project, Second Season, 1980 Interim Report,* edited by T. R. Hester, J. D. Eaton, and H. J. Shafer, pp. 1–14. Center for Archaeological Research, University of Texas at San Antonio and Centro Studi e Ricerche Ligabue, Venice.

Hester, Thomas R., and Harry J. Shafer
   1983 Ancient Maya Chert Workshops in Northern Belize, Central America. *American Antiquity* 48:519–543.
   1986 Maya Stone-Tool Craft Specialization and Production at Colha, Belize: Reply to Mallory. *American Antiquity* 51: 158–166.
   1992 Lithic Workshops Revisited: Comments on Moholy-Nagy. *Latin American Antiquity* 3:243–248.

Hester, Thomas R., Harry J. Shafer, and Jack D. Eaton, eds.
   1982 *Archaeology at Colha, Belize: The 1981 Interim Report.* Center for Archaeological Research, University of Texas at San Antonio and Centro Studi e Ricerche Ligabue, Venice.

Jacob, John S.
   1992 The Agroecological Evolution of Cobweb Swamp, Belize. Ph.D. dissertation, Department of Soil and Crop Sciences, Texas A&M University.

Jones, Christopher
   1979 Tikal as a Trading Center: Why It Rose and Fell. Paper presented at the 43rd International Congress of Americanists, Vancouver, Canada.

Jones, Christopher, Wendy Ashmore, and Robert J. Sharer
   1983 The Quirigua Project: 1977 Season. In *Quirigua Reports,* Vol. II, pp. 1–38. University Museum Monographs 49. University Museum, University of Pennsylvania, Philadelphia.

King, Eleanor M.
   1986 Recent Discoveries in the Colha Settlement. Paper presented at the 85th Annual Meeting of the American Anthropological Association, Philadelphia, December 3.
   1987 Overview of the 1987 Field Season at Colha, Belize. *Friends of Archaeology Newsletter* 4:27–34.
   1990 Maya Household Organization and the Problem of Isolated Mounds: A Perspective from Colha, Belize. Paper presented at the symposium "Reconstructing Social Organization at the Household Level in Mesoamerica" at the 55th Annual Meeting of the Society for American Archaeology, Las Vegas, April 20.

McAnany, Patricia A.
   1986 Lithic Technology and Exchange among Wetland Farmers of the Eastern Maya Lowlands. Ph.D. dissertation, Department of Anthropology, University of New Mexico, Albuquerque.
   1989 Economic Foundations of Prehistoric Maya Society: Paradigms and Concepts. *Research in Economic Anthropology* (Supplement) 4:347–372.

McCulloch, Warren S.
   1945 A Heterarchy of Values Determined by the Topology of Nervous Nets. *Bulletin of Mathematical Biophysics* 7:89–93.

Mallory, John K.
   1986 "Workshops" and "Specialized Production" in the Production of Maya Chert Tools: A Response to Shafer and Hester. *American Antiquity* 51:152–157.

Marcus, Joyce
   1976 *Emblem and State in the Classic Maya Lowlands.* Dumbarton Oaks, Washington, D.C.
   1983 On the Nature of the Mesoamerican City. In *Prehistoric Settlement Patterns: Essays in Honor of Gordon R. Willey,* edited by E. Vogt and R. Leventhal, pp. 195–242. University of New Mexico Press, Albuquerque.

Masson, Marilyn
   1989 Lithic Production Changes in Late Classic Maya Workshops at Colha, Belize: A Study in Debitage Variation. M.S. thesis, Department of Anthropology, Florida State University, Tallahassee.
   1991 Craft Specialist Cooperation and Autonomy: An Examination of Late Classic Lithic Workshop Composition at Colha, Belize. Paper presented at the 56th Annual Meeting of the Society for American Archaeology, New Orleans, April 26.

Mitchum, Beverly, and Eleanor King
   1990 Tool Production Strategies at Colha, Belize. Poster session presented at the 55th Annual Meeting of the Society for American Archaeology, Las Vegas.

Moholy-Nagy, Hattula
   1990 The Misidentification of Mesoamerican Lithic Workshops. *Latin American Antiquity* 1(3):268–279.
   1992 Lithic Deposits as Waste Management: Reply to Healan and Hester and Shafer. *Latin American Antiquity* 3:249–251.

Morley, Sylvanus G., George W. Brainerd, and Robert J. Sharer
   1983 *The Ancient Maya.* Stanford University Press, Stanford, Calif.

Nash, Michael A.
   1986 A Functional Analysis of Two Lithic Tool Collections from Colha, Belize. M.S. thesis, Department of Anthropology, East Texas State University.

Potter, Daniel R.
   1980 Archaeological Investigations at Operation 2012. In *The Colha Project, Second Season, 1980 Interim Report,* edited by T. R. Hester, J. D. Eaton, and H. J. Shafer, pp. 173–184. Center for Archaeological Research, University of Texas at San Antonio and Centro Studi e Ricerche Ligabue, Venice.
   1982 Some Results of the Second Year of Excavation at Operation 2012. In *Archaeology at Colha, Belize: The 1981 Interim Report,* edited by T. R. Hester, H. J. Shafer, and J. D. Eaton, pp. 98–122. Center for Archaeological Research, University of Texas at San Antonio and Centro Studi e Ricerche Ligabue, Venice.
   1991a The Emergence of Colha as a Preclassic Maya Center. Paper presented at the 47th International Congress of Americanists, New Orleans.

1991b A Descriptive Taxonomy of Middle Preclassic Chert Tools at Colha, Belize. In *Maya Stone Tools: Selected Papers from the Second Maya Lithic Conference,* edited by T. R. Hester and H. J. Shafer, pp. 21–29. Monographs in World Archaeology, No. 1. Prehistory Press, Madison, Wis.

1992 Strat 55 and the Evolution of Lowland Maya Blood Ritual. Paper presented at the 57th Annual Meeting of the Society for American Archaeology, Pittsburgh.

Potter, Daniel R., Thomas R. Hester, Stephen Black, and Fred Valdez, Jr.
1984 Relationships Between Early and Middle Preclassic Phases in Northern Belize: A Comment on Marcus. *American Antiquity* 49:628–631.

Puleston, Dennis E.
1983 *The Settlement Survey of Tikal.* Tikal Report No. 13. University Museum Monographs 48. University Museum, University of Pennsylvania, Philadelphia.

Puleston, Dennis E., and Donald W. Callender
1967 Defensive Earthworks at Tikal. *Expedition* 9:40–48.

Rands, Robert L., and Ronald L. Bishop
1980 Resource Procurement Zones and Patterns of Ceramic Exchange in the Palenque Region, Mexico. In *Models and Methods in Regional Exchange,* edited by R. E. Fry, pp. 19–46. SAA Papers, No. 1. Society for American Archaeology, Washington, D.C.

Renfrew, Colin, and John F. Cherry, eds.
1986 *Peer Polity Interaction and Socio-political Change.* Cambridge University Press, Cambridge.

Rice, Prudence M.
1987 Economic Change in the Lowland Maya Late Classic Period. In *Specialization, Exchange, and Complex Societies,* edited by E. M. Brumfiel and T. K. Earle, pp. 76–85. Cambridge University Press, Cambridge.

Roemer, Erwin, Jr.
1982 Investigations at Four Lithic Workshops at Colha, Belize: 1981 Season. In *Archaeology at Colha, Belize: The 1981 Interim Report,* edited by T. R. Hester, H. J. Shafer, and J. D. Eaton, pp. 31–38. Center for Archaeological Research, University of Texas at San Antonio and Centro Studi e Ricerche Ligabue, Venice.

1984 A Late Classic Maya Lithic Workshop at Colha, Belize. M.A. thesis, Department of Anthropology, Texas A&M University.

Sabloff, Jeremy A.
1986 Interaction among Classic Maya Polities: A Preliminary Examination. In *Peer Polity Interaction and Socio-political Change,* edited by C. Renfrew and J. F. Cherry, pp. 109–116. Cambridge University Press, Cambridge.

Sanders, William T., and Barbara J. Price
1968 *Mesoamerica: The Evolution of a Civilization.* Academic Press, New York.

Sanders, William T., and David Webster
1988 The Mesoamerican Urban Tradition. *American Anthropologist* 90:521–546.

Schele, Linda
1992 The Founders of Lineages at Copan and Other Maya Sites. *Ancient Mesoamerica* 3:135–144.

Shafer, H. J.
1982 Maya Lithic Craft Specialization in Northern Belize. In *Archaeology at Colha, Belize: The 1981 Interim Report,* edited by T. R. Hester, H. J. Shafer, and J. D. Eaton, pp. 31–38. Center for Archaeological Research, University of Texas at San Antonio and Centro Studi e Ricerche Ligabue, Venice.

1983 The Lithic Artifacts of the Pulltrouser Area: Settlements and Fields. In *Pulltrouser Swamp. Ancient Maya Habitat, Agriculture, and Settlement in Northern Belize,* edited by B. L. Turner, II, and P. D. Harrison, pp. 212–245. University of Texas Press, Austin.

1984 The Tranchet Technique in Lowland Maya Lithic Technology. *Lithic Technology* 12:57–68.

Shafer, Harry J., and Thomas R. Hester
1991 Lithic Craft Specialization and Product Distribution at the Maya Site of Colha, Belize. *World Archaeology* 23:74–97.

Shafer, Harry J., Thomas R. Hester, Thomas C. Kelly, and Norman Hammond
1979 An Analysis of Lithic Artifacts from 1976 Excavations at Cuello, Belize. Manuscript on file with the authors.

Sharer, Robert J., Julia C. Miller, and Loa P. Traxler
1992 Evolution of Classic Period Architecture in the Eastern Acropolis, Copan: A Progress Report. *Ancient Mesoamerica* 3:145–159.

Shaw, Leslie
1991 The Articulation of Social Inequality and Faunal Resource Use in the Preclassic Community of Colha, Belize. Ph.D. dissertation, Department of Anthropology, University of Massachusetts at Amherst.

Smith, Michael E.
1989 Cities, Towns, and Urbanism: Comment on Sanders and Webster. *American Anthropologist* 91:454–460.

Smyth, Michael P., and Christopher D. Dore
1992 Large-Site Archaeological Methods at Sayil, Yucatan, Mexico: Investigating Community Organization at a Prehispanic Maya Center. *Latin American Antiquity* 3:3–21.

Sullivan, Lauren Ann
1991 Preclassic Domestic Architecture at Colha, Belize. M.A. thesis, Department of Anthropology, University of Texas at Austin.

Thompson, J. Eric S.
1939 Excavations at San Jose, British Honduras. Carnegie Reports, No. 528, Contribution 35. Carnegie Institution, Washington, D.C.

Turner, Billy Lee, II, and Peter D. Harrison, eds.
1983 *Pulltrouser Swamp. Ancient Maya Habitat, Agriculture, and Settlement in Northern Belize.* University of Texas Press, Austin.

Valdez, Fred, Jr.
1987 The Prehistoric Ceramics of Colha, Northern Belize. Ph.D. dissertation, Department of Anthropology, Harvard University.

Valdez, Fred, Jr., and Richard E. W. Adams
   1982 The Ceramics of Colha after Three Field Seasons: 1979–1981. In *Archaeology at Colha, Belize: The 1981 Interim Report,* edited by T. R. Hester, H. J. Shafer, and J. D. Eaton, pp. 21–30. Center for Archaeological Research, University of Texas at San Antonio and Centro Studi e Ricerche Ligabue, Venice.

Webster, David L., and Nancy Gonlin
   1988 Household Remains of the Humblest Maya. *Journal of Field Archaeology* 15:169–190.

Webster, David L., and William T. Sanders
   1989 The Mesoamerican Urban Tradition: Reply to Smith. *American Anthropologist* 91:460–461.

White, Joyce
   1992 Prehistoric Roots for Heterarchy in Early Southeast Asian States. Paper presented at the Annual Meeting of the Society for American Archaeology, Pittsburgh.

Wilk, Richard R.
   1973 1973 Operations (Colha). In *British Museum–Cambridge University Corozal Project 1973 Interim Report,* pp. 55–60. Centre of Latin American Studies, Cambridge University, Cambridge.
   1975 Superficial Examination of Structure 100, Colha. In *Archaeology in Northern Belize. British Museum–Cambridge University Corozal Project, 1974–75 Interim Report,* pp. 152–173. Centre of Latin American Studies, Cambridge University, Cambridge.
   1976 Work in Progress at Colha, Belize, 1976. In *Maya Lithic Studies: Papers from the 1976 Belize Field Symposium,* edited by T. R. Hester and N. Hammond, pp. 35–40. Special Reports 4. Center for Archaeological Research, University of Texas at San Antonio.
   1988 Maya Household Organization: Evidence and Analogies. In *Household and Community in the Mesoamerican Past,* edited by R. Wilk and W. Ashmore, pp. 135–151. University of New Mexico Press, Albuquerque.

Wilk, Richard R., and Wendy Ashmore
   1988 *Household and Community in the Mesoamerican Past.* University of New Mexico Press, Albuquerque.

Willey, Gordon R., William R. Bullard, Jr., John B. Glass, and James C. Gifford
   1965 *Prehistoric Maya Settlements in the Belize Valley.* Papers of the Peabody Museum, Harvard University, No. 54. Peabody Museum, Cambridge, Mass.

Willey, Gordon R., A. Leadyard Smith, Gair Tourtellot III, and Ian Graham
   1975 *Excavations at Seibal, Department of the Peten.* Memoirs of the Peabody Museum of Archaeology and Ethnography, Vol. 13, No. 1. Harvard University, Cambridge, Mass.

Winter, Marcus C.
   1976 The Archaeological Household Cluster in the Valley of Oaxaca. In *The Early Mesoamerican Village,* edited by K. V. Flannery, pp. 25–31. Academic Press, New York.

Wood, Gregory
   1987 Report on Operations 4041 and 4046, Colha, Belize. Manuscript on file with the Colha Project.

CHAPTER SEVEN

Specialized Commodity Production in and around Matacapan: Testing the Goodness of Fit of the Regal-Ritual and Administrative Models

ROBERT S. SANTLEY

THE DEVELOPMENT OF URBAN centers is considered to be a hallmark of the emergence of complex societies. Early approaches to the study of cities defined urban centers in a variety of ways (Wirth 1938; Childe 1942; Weber 1958; Sjoberg 1960; Christaller 1966; Jacobs 1969). Many of these studies also stressed the presence of specialists who provided goods and services for the populace of the centers as well as settlements of food producers distributed around them (Wirth 1938; Childe 1950; Jacobs 1969). Indeed, for Childe (1950), one of the dominant prehistorians of his time, the aggregation of specialists was one of the most important processes behind the urban revolution. This view of the urban center was originally derived from studies of historically known Western and Middle Eastern systems, which the literature suggested had a highly differentiated urban component at the core surrounded by a relatively undifferentiated rural hinterland inhabited primarily by food producers (Wirth 1938; Childe 1942, 1950; Christaller 1966).

Because manufacturing leaves detectable archaeological residues, most recent research on specialization has focused on craft production. The results of this research indicate that craft production is a highly variable phenomenon. For example, there appears to be significant variability in the organization of craft production, with some centers or regions emphasizing manufacture on the household level and others maintaining a variety of production modes involving households, workshops, and manufactories (e.g., the Roman Empire [Peacock 1982], Matacapan [Santley, Arnold, and Pool 1989], Teotihuacan [Spence 1981], the Turanian Basin of southwestern Asia [Tosi 1984], and western Europe [Van der Leeuw 1976]).

It has also been pointed out that the economy of a center cannot be divorced from the regional system into which it is structurally integrated (English 1966; Johnson 1973, 1975; Blanton 1976; Smith 1976; Hassig 1985). In some cases, craft production was centralized at the principal centers (e.g., weaving at Vijayanagara, South India [Sinapoli 1988] or in southern Mesopotamia [Adams and Nissen 1972]); in other cases it was dispersed in the countryside (e.g., potterymaking in the Valley of Oaxaca [Feinman, Blanton, and Kowalewski 1984] or saltmaking in northern Yucatan [Andrews 1983]); in still other cases it was administered by or involved goods produced for the ruling elite (e.g., the Aztecs of the Basin of Mexico [Brumfiel 1987] or in the Inka Empire [Earle 1987]).

The results of recent work in Mesoamerica suggest that craft specialization was a weakly developed phenomenon in pre-Columbian times and that the major centers themselves probably contained large numbers of food producers (Millon 1973; Marcus 1983; Sanders and Santley 1983; Webster 1985). According to Sanders and Webster (1988), most pre-Columbian urban centers fall into two types: regal-ritual and administrative. Regal-ritual cities are centers whose primary function is ideological in character. The permanent population of such centers consists of members of the political leadership, their immediate families, and various servants, slaves, and other retainers. The leadership uses religion to justify its goals and legitimize its exalted position, often through the performance of great ceremonies with participation by the elite and commoners alike, hence the label regal-ritual.

Administrative cities, in contrast, are much larger in size, more densely occupied, and more heterogeneous in composi-

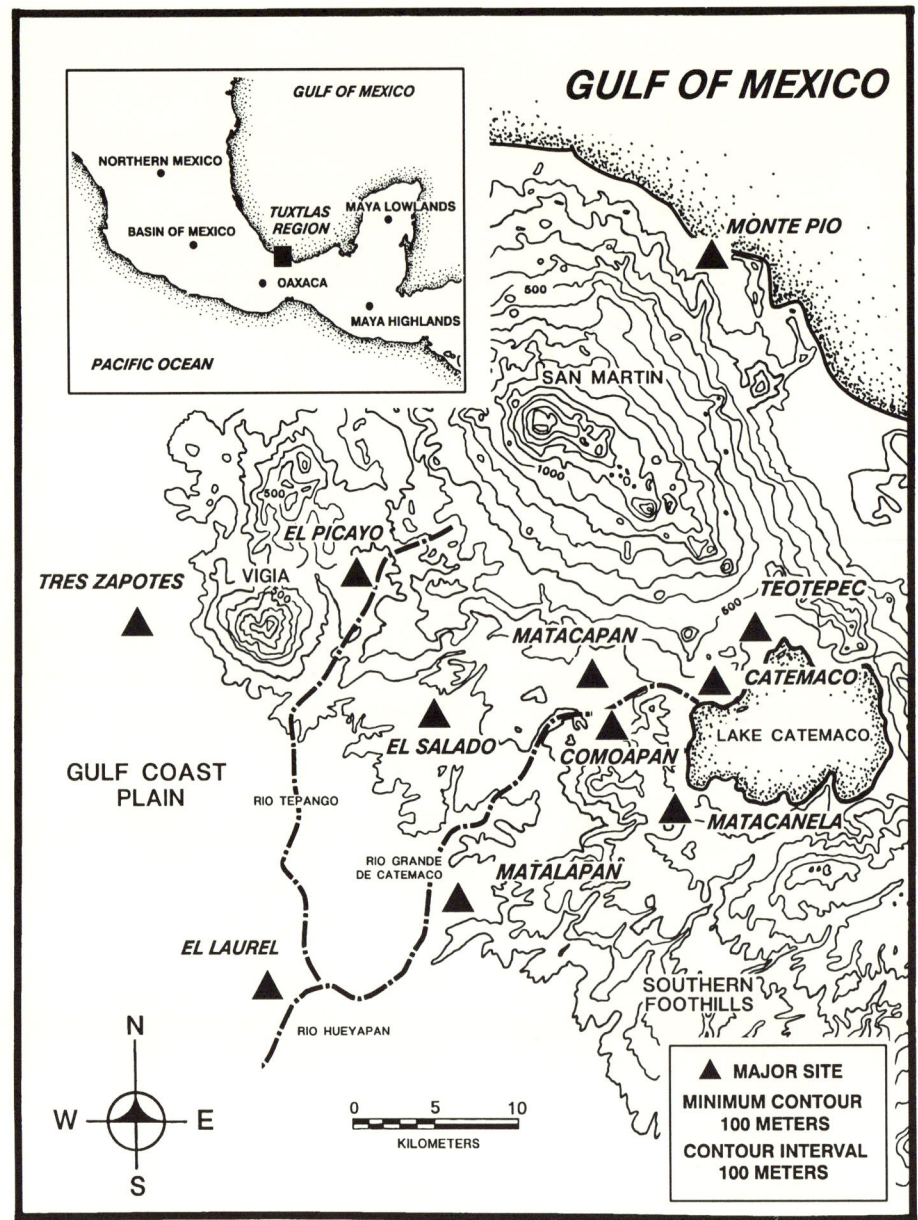

Fig. 30. The Tuxtlas Mountains, showing the location of major archaeological sites.

tion and occupational makeup. Their inhabitants consist of the ruling family, the nobility, government personnel, and a professional military. Because these cities are often the centers of large imperial domains, political decision making is the dominant function of the city. Administrative centers also contain craftsmen, merchants, and traders. "Much of the craft production or trade involves high-status goods but in more developed cases may include a range of more mundane goods and technology as well. The principal customers, however, are still the inhabitants of the center itself, and [consequently] such cities do not produce significant quantities of goods for the rural countryside or for long-distance exchange" (Sanders and Webster 1988:525).

According to Sanders and Webster (1988), the Mesoamerican urban tradition did not favor the development of mercantile cities whose economy was based on specialized craft production and long-distance trade. This was because food production systems were fairly unproductive compared to those that provided the economic basis for centers in the Old World. The limited amounts of surpluses produced thus restricted the number of specialists that could be supported in centers and confined craft production in centers to luxury goods. One way around this constraint is reliance on imported foodstuffs. Thus, whereas individual food producers might not be capable of producing a substantial surplus, the total amount of food aggregated in a center might be very large indeed, provided that transport costs were not excessive.

Pre-Columbian Mesoamerican transportation systems, however, mainly involved human carriers, not boats or draft animals. Transport by human carriers is a very inefficient way to move basic goods across the landscape, because the value of foodstuffs is low but their transport costs are high (Sanders and Santley 1983; Hassig 1985). As a result, systems involving specialization in basic goods and staple finance tend to be relatively small in size (Curtin 1984; Brumfiel and Earle 1987; Santley and Alexander 1992). Major exceptions include salt and obsidian, two goods that were exchanged over long distances in Mesoamerica but apparently were only used in nominal amounts per capita (Bittman and Sullivan 1978; Andrews 1983; Santley 1984).

All of the examples of regal-ritual centers cited in the literature come from the Mesoamerican lowlands. Here dry land food production systems were relatively unproductive, especially under conditions of intensive agriculture, a situation that presumably severely limited center size and degree of craft specialization and favored a dispersed settlement pattern, with most of the population living in small communities. On the other hand, administrative cities appear to have been mainly a highland Mexican phenomenon. In central Mexico, for example, dry land agriculture was capable of producing larger surpluses than systems of land use in lowland Mesoamerica under comparable levels of intensification. This characteristic permitted the aggregation of large populations at highland centers and enabled the support of greater numbers of craft specialists. Large population size also meant that competition for space in major centers in highland Mesoamerica was probably quite high, a circumstance that produced nucleated settlements with a built environment containing relatively little open space.

Although the regal-ritual and administrative models may account for much of the variability known to exist at major centers in the Maya lowlands and central Mexico, data from the Tuxtlas Mountains on the south Gulf Coast of Mexico exhibit a poor fit with these models (see Fig. 30). This chapter addresses this lack of fit. First, the evidence for specialized ceramics production at the site of Matacapan is discussed. That evidence suggests that most production was small scale and geared primarily to urban elites. The next section deals with craft production in suburban contexts. Pottery manufacture here took place on a much larger scale and involved a differentiated production system, suggesting the presence of an economy of scale. Specialized production was not confined to the environs of the principal center but also was widely distributed in rural contexts and involved other goods as well. This patterning blurs the distinction between center and countryside, and calls into question models of regional systems that view craft specialists as primarily residing in urban centers. Finally, the primary good produced, pottery, is a bulky utilitarian commodity that should not be exchanged very far from manufacturing nodes. Archaeological evidence, in contrast, indicates a fairly broad-scale distribution sphere, a finding that suggests that water transport may have been the primary means by which goods were moved.

The Matacapan Site

How were these conclusions derived? To date, we have completed five seasons of fieldwork at Matacapan (Santley et al. 1984, 1985b,c; Santley, Kneebone, and Kerley 1985a; Santley, Kerley, and Kneebone 1986; Santley, Ortiz C., and Pool 1987; Santley 1989; Santley, Arnold, and Pool 1989; Pool 1990). This fieldwork involved a multistaged surface survey, 100 stratigraphic excavations, a program of ethnoarchaeological research, and work on the region's geochronology, plus a variety of ancillary studies. My original reason for initiating fieldwork in the Tuxtlas was to define the character of the Teotihuacan presence at Matacapan, the major site in the region, an objective that required that we undertake a surface survey to select locations for subsequent excavation. Ultimately, an area nearly 23 km^2 in size was systematically surveyed, from which more than 6,700 controlled surface collections were obtained.

The provenience of all collections was tied into the main Matacapan grid so that maps of the frequency distribution of different classes of material could be produced. We also completed a season of field research at El Salado, a salt-making station 9 km southwest of Matacapan (Santley, Ortiz C., and Kludt 1988), as well as a general surface reconnaissance of a 400-km^2 area around Matacapan (Santley 1991).

The major occupation at Matacapan dates to the Middle Classic period, a time when materials produced in Teotihuacan style were widely distributed in Mesoamerica (Parsons 1978; Santley 1983). The Middle Classic period at Matacapan is more protracted than elsewhere in Mesoamerica, beginning around A.D. 300 and lasting perhaps as late as A.D. 800. The central part of the site is dominated by a large complex of public buildings and other mounded architecture covering approximately 2.5 km^2 (Santley, Ortiz C., and Pool 1987). This complex contains seventy-one mounds, many of which are arranged around small plazuelas, which in turn are situated

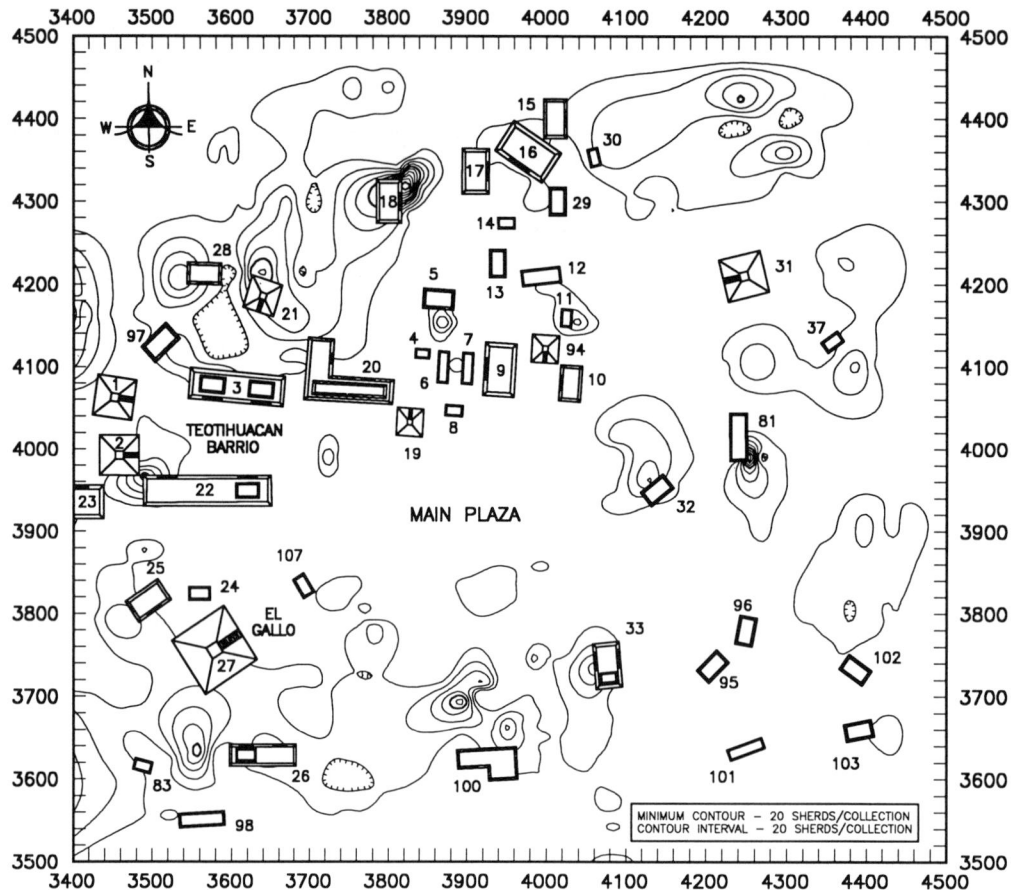

Fig. 31. Central Matacapan, showing the location of major mounded architecture and the distribution of surface refuse.

around a large central plaza (Fig. 31). Two types of buildings are present: multistaged temple mounds and low, rectangular platform mounds that presumably housed the community's top-ranking elite and their retainers. Many of these platforms are quite substantial in size, suggesting the presence of large multifamily residential groups. The excavation of one platform structure (Mound 61) indicates that it consisted of a complex of rooms arranged around patios and separated by intervening corridors.

Distributed around this central core is a large area of suburban occupation covering at least 20 km². Settlement patterns in this area are dispersed, with groups of residential mounds separated by areas of relatively little occupation. Many of these platforms are also quite large, again suggesting the presence of large residential groups. In general, the pattern is one of decreasing density of occupation with greater distance from the site center. Through time the picture is somewhat different (Ortiz Ceballos and Santley in press). In the early Middle Classic (A.D. 300–450), Matacapan was a small, compact community centered on the Teotihuacan Barrio. The middle and late Middle Classic periods (A.D. 450–650), in contrast, were times of explosive growth, with the main occupation zone expanding to cover more than 700 ha. At 463 ha, the terminal Middle Classic settlement (A.D. 650–800) was smaller in size, but apparently it was more densely nucleated.

Areas of artifact accumulation frequently occur near mounds, but often residential structures are not situated near them. Many of these areas of dense occupation were refuse dumps created by specialized ceramics production. Based on the presence of wasters, kiln debris, and high densities of sherd accumulation, the ceramics production areas cover 22 percent of the area defined as the main site (see Santley, Arnold, and Pool 1989 for a more extensive discussion of identification criteria). Matacapan's ceramics industry was also internally differentiated, with some manufacturing occurring in household contexts and other production taking place in specialized workshops and manufactories (Santley, Arnold, and Pool 1989). Locational analysis indicates significant variation in their spatial patterning.

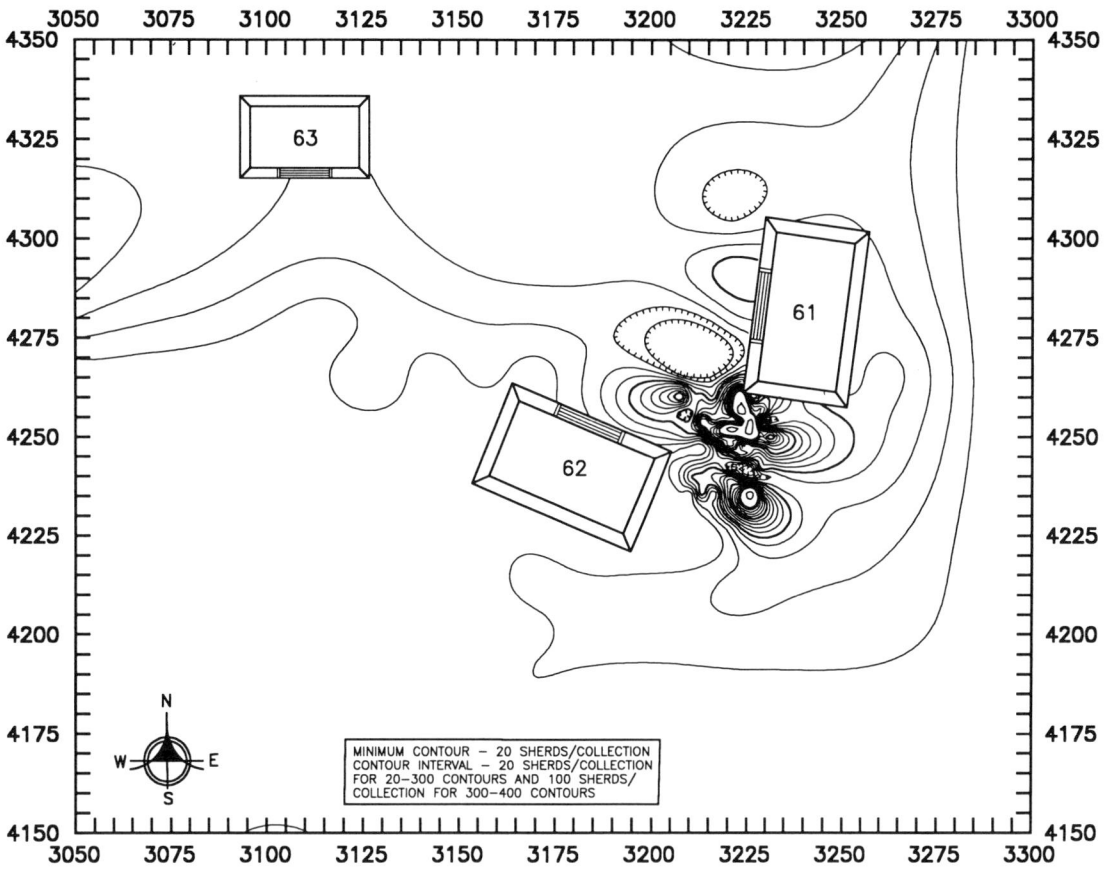

Fig. 32. The Mound 61 ceramics production area, showing the distribution of surface refuse.

Ceramics Production in Urban Contexts

Matacapan's area of urban occupation includes the site's central civic-ceremonial district (see Fig. 31) as well as the area of occupation across the Rio San Joaquin directly to the west. Refuse accumulations in the civic-ceremonial complex are generally quite low, the result of the intentional burial of trash in mounds or in underground pits. Surface refuse densities, however, do increase near the western and northern periphery of the urban zone. Much of this refuse was the result of specialized ceramics manufacture.

Thus far, we have identified fifteen ceramics production areas within the urban zone. Production in all areas took place in domestic contexts: that is, evidence of ceramics manufacture is associated with residential structures or domestic trash. Following Van der Leeuw (1976), each area probably represents a household industry, with pottery production supplying part of the domestic group's income and farming or other activities providing the remainder. Many of these production areas specialized in the manufacture of a few wares, Coarse Orange in particular, but others appear to have produced the full suite of wares and vessel forms.

Of the fifteen production zones identified in the urban core, the Mound 61 locality is the best studied (Santley et al. 1985b; Pool 1990) (Fig. 32). Mound 61 is a large, low structure approximately 44 × 27 m on a side. As mentioned previously, the structure consisted of complexes of rooms arranged around small patios, and the large number of burials in subfloor contexts and substantial quantities of trash present indicate that it was occupied by a large residential group. The proximity of the mound to the civic-ceremonial center and the presence of pottery imported from central Veracruz suggest that the mound's occupants were not members of the site's lowest social stratum.

The ceramics production area is located directly to the southwest of the room complex and consists of a small group of kilns and nearby waster dumps where firing took place (Pool 1990). Also present were a number of small pits filled with domestic trash and one human burial. The major ceramic type produced was Fine Buff; however, other service and utility wares were also present in significant quantities. Mound 61 was occupied throughout the Middle Classic, but most of the evidence of specialized production apparently dates to the middle of the period. The small size of the firing area and low density of refuse during early Middle Classic times imply that only some of the mound's inhabitants were physically involved in the production process and that ceramics manufacture was a part-time endeavor. Although some pottery was apparently produced for use by the mound's inhabitants, other vessels undoubtedly were manufactured for exchange. During the middle part of the period, refuse densities increased markedly, and there were at least three discrete waster dumps, each presumably associated with one or more kilns. This increase in production suggests that either specialization was on a more full-time basis or a greater number of the mound's occupants were involved in ceramics manufacture. Production levels then plummeted toward the end of the period as the mound was abandoned.

Some pottery in "downtown" Matacapan was also made by potters attached to particular households, not by specialists working in the production areas just discussed. This is a form of production that I term "tethered specialization" (Santley, Arnold, and Pool 1989; see also Brumfiel and Earle 1987). The tethered specialist is a craftsman who produces goods for elite use or for consumption by the state, either on a commissioned basis or as a result of obligations owed to high-ranking individuals. On the terrace behind Mound 3, for example, were the remains of a small, circular updraft kiln. Although it is possible that the mound's elite inhabitants manufactured their own pottery, it is more likely that the kiln was built for potters who, living elsewhere, made ceramics on consignment for the occupants of the structure. Although the midden associated with the kiln was rich in Coarse Orange, it also contained relatively large amounts of Red-on-Fine Orange and Red Slipped Fine Orange, two service wares that were common in domestic refuse deposits behind the mound. The elite occupants of other mounds in the main center probably had some of their pottery produced in this fashion as well.

Production in central Matacapan was therefore mainly on the household level. Although some specialists were probably attached to particular high-status residences, most pottery was made by household industries. Some ceramics were made to be used by the potters' own households, with the remainder exchanged beyond the specialist's immediate residential group.

Ceramics Production in Suburban Contexts

Suburban Matacapan includes a large area of dispersed occupation covering at least 20 km^2. Refuse densities generally are much greater than in the site center, and habitation mounds are less common, although they do tend to occur in groups. Refuse middens are often situated near mounds, many of which contain evidence of specialized ceramics manufacture.

To date, thirty-two ceramics production localities have been identified, three of which have been excavated. These production areas vary greatly in size and internal configuration, suggesting major differences in the organization of production (Santley, Arnold, and Pool 1989).

Twenty-five of these production areas are quite small, and the evidence of production comes from middens situated near residential mounds, again suggesting production in domestic contexts. Some of these household production areas manufactured the complete range of utility and service ceramics, whereas others were somewhat more specialized, producing only certain wares (e.g., Coarse Orange or Fine Gray). Analysis of the surface assemblages indicates that most of the pottery produced in them was fired in kilns. Kilns are again associated with waster dumps. These middens either are small in size or, if distributed over larger areas, contain lower densities of material, indicating production on a part-time basis or full-time production for a shorter period of time.

Seven areas are much larger in size and contain more substantial quantities of refuse. Of these, six qualify as workshop industries or nucleated industries (Van der Leeuw 1976; Santley, Arnold, and Pool 1989). Kilns and refuse dumps are again located near structures; however, the function of these buildings was probably not domestic. Refuse disposal at Matacapan involved discard near structures; hence, the types of materials present in middens provide a basis for defining structure function. Most of the refuse present in these middens consists of over-fired sherds, many with evidence of warping and cracking. Moreover, obsidian, figurines, and ground stone, three classes of material that were discarded in dumps near habitation structures, are not well represented in the production middens, suggesting that the platforms supported special workshops and not domestic residences.

The production area near Mounds 69 and 75 is fairly typical of the workshop-industry level of production. Mound 69 is a large structure measuring 56 × 87 m on a side, and it is paired with Mound 75, a smaller platform to the south (Fig. 33). Although direct excavation evidence is lacking, it is probable that these platforms supported workshops. In all likelihood, different phases of the production process (e.g., clay preparation, vessel forming, and drying) took place in different parts of the shop, given the large size of the platforms and the substantial quantities of refuse discarded near them. Immediately to the south and east of the platforms is a 1.1-ha area that was exceedingly rich in refuse. Kiln fragments were also present, indicating that this was the location where the vessels were fired. A number of smaller mounds occur to the southwest. Quantities of refuse here are much lower, suggesting that the potters physically lived in this area. The Mound

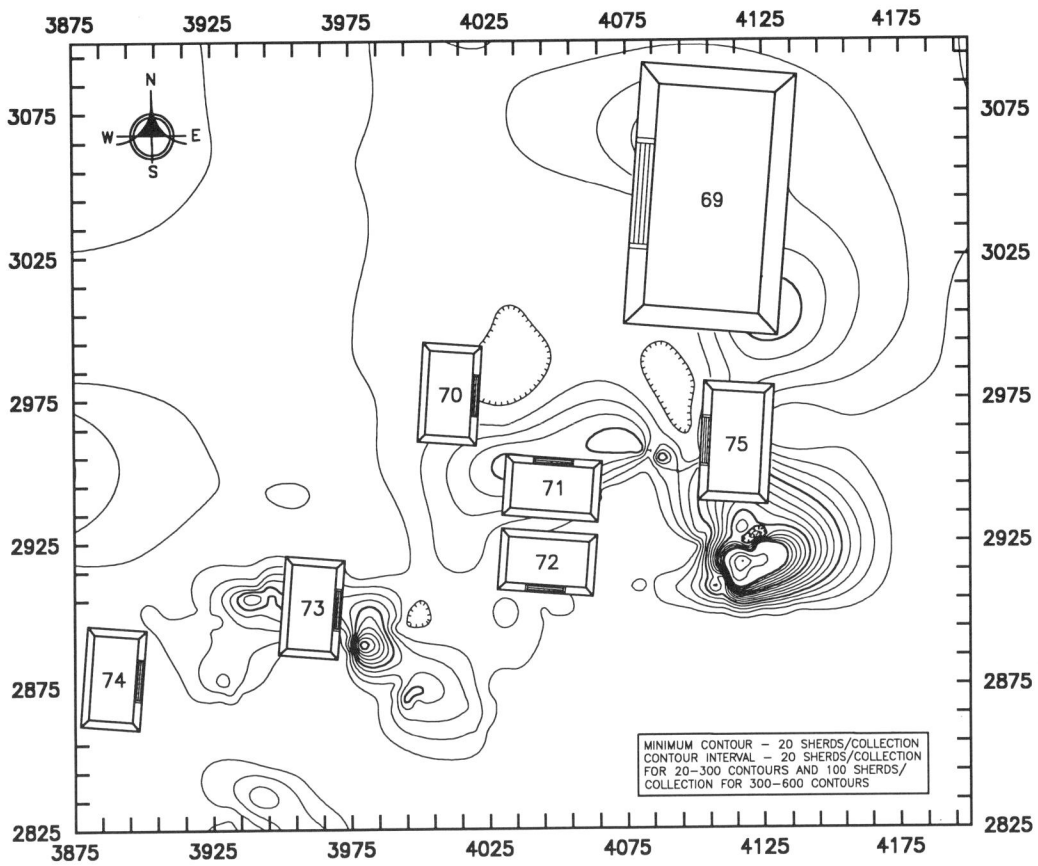

Fig. 33. The Mound 69–75 ceramics production area, showing the distribution of surface refuse.

69–75 workshop complex was highly specialized, emphasizing the production of Fine Gray bowls. This complex is one of five areas in Matacapan's southern suburbs that qualify as workshop industries and that also focused primarily on Fine Gray bowl production (see Fig. 34).

Production near Mounds 88, 89, 90, and 91 in Matacapan's southwest suburbs was even more intensive than in the Fine Gray areas and covered a larger expanse: circa 3.5 ha (Fig. 35). Again, the platforms were comparatively large in size, and three of them were erected directly adjacent to one another. Areas of dense midden accumulation occur near the platforms, as elsewhere at Matacapan. The dense quantity of refuse, combined with the presence of kiln debris, suggests firing as the principal activity. Although the full repertory of ceramic wares is represented in the middens, the focus was definitely on Coarse Orange production, which greatly dominates the surface collections obtained from this locus. The relative lack of refuse indicative of domestic activities again suggests the presence of a set of workshop industries; however, the placement of the platforms next to one another implies that production was organized on a larger scale than a workshop—perhaps as a nucleated industry.

The most intensive level of production took place at Comoapan, a small suburb of Matacapan. The ceramics production area may be divided into two zones (Fig. 36). The eastern part of the site consists of high-density occupation covering an area of about 4 ha. Surface densities typically average above 9 sherds/m^2, with densities reaching as high as 200 sherds/m^2. Seven discrete waster dumps are in evidence, as well as six groups of kilns. The western part of the site also covers about 4 ha, but surface densities there are much lower, and there are only two kiln groups, both of which are situated near waster dumps. Distributed throughout both zones of occupation are clear areas where the density of surface material is very low. This western zone is probably the area where the pottery was physically formed and where vessels were allowed to dry. Little evidence of domestic occupation was recovered from either segment of the Comoapan production area, suggesting that the potters lived elsewhere.

In total, there are eight groups of kilns or other features. Each group (or unit) generally contains several kilns, with one or more trash middens placed nearby. Units 1, 3, and 4 are far larger than the other kiln groups and produced 70 percent of the material obtained from the survey. The composition of the

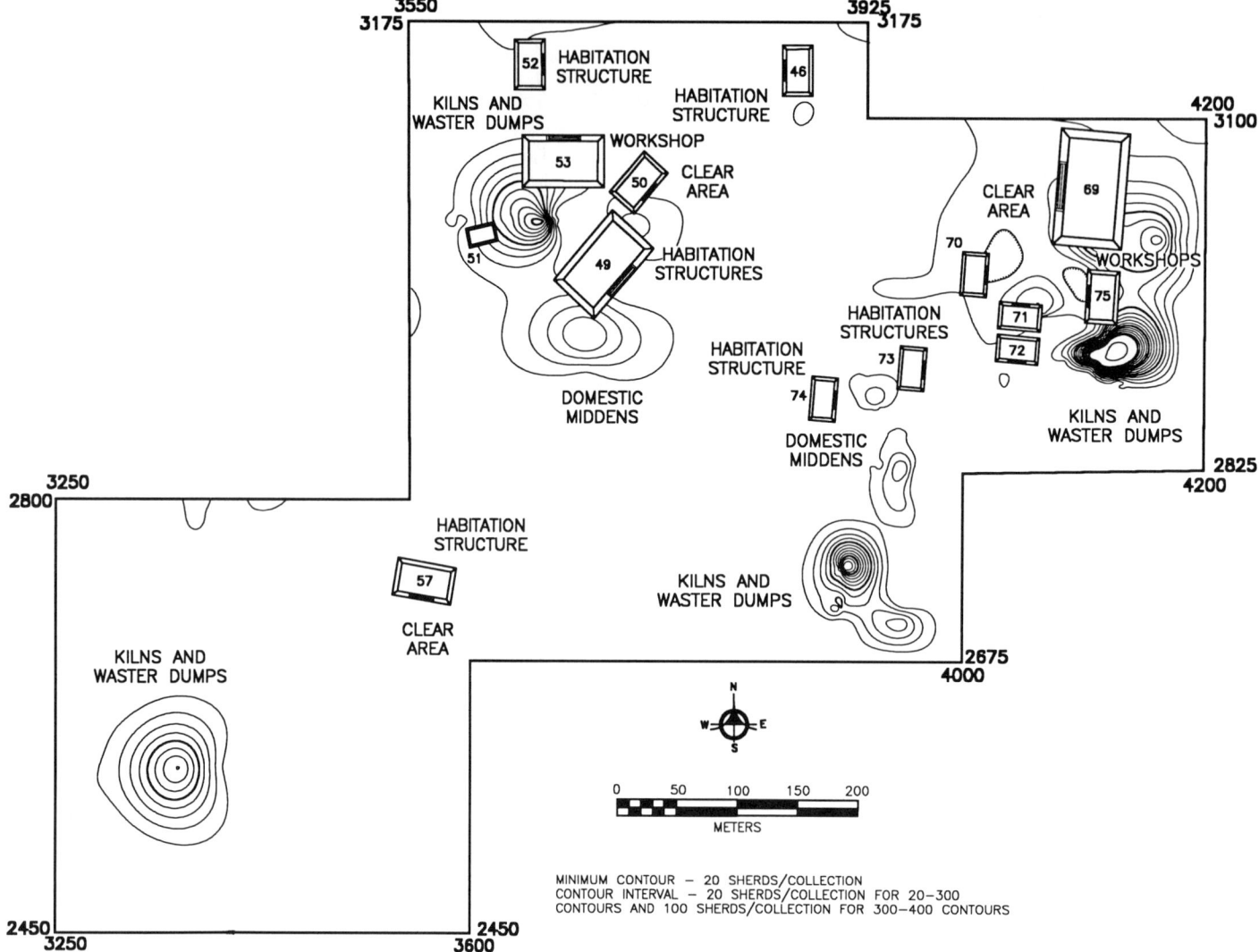

Fig. 34. The southern suburbs of Matacapan, showing the location of several Fine Gray production areas.

assemblage from different units generally matches that from the excavated kiln group. This is especially the case for units 1, 2, 4, 7, and 8, and to a lesser extent unit 3, which collectively account for 89 percent of all of the material discarded at Comoapan.

Except for unit 5, the cumulative frequency plots for different assemblages are extremely flat, indicating a common emphasis on the production of a few wares (see Fig. 37). By and large, Coarse Orange predominates. Unit 5, in contrast, was devoted primarily to Fine Orange production, whereas in unit 6 the focus was on Coarse Brown. No area contained substantial amounts of Fine Gray. Hole-mouth and collared jars constitute most of the Coarse Orange vessels deposited in middens. These two forms are particularly common in units 1, 2, 4, and 8, where they account for 72 percent of the sample of Coarse Orange rims. Bowls make up most of the sample of Fine Orange, the major service ware produced at Comoapan, and 67 percent of the rims in unit 5, the major locus of Fine Orange production. Very few Coarse Brown rims were obtained from the survey, but most appear to be from collared jars.

The Comoapan assemblage is skewed toward few wares and vessel forms. The samples, however, contain the full range of utilitarian wares, service wares, and vessel forms. This range is significantly greater than that present at all other production areas except the Mound 88–91 workshop complex. Correlation-regression analysis suggests that the number of wares and forms present at production areas is primarily a function of sample size ($r = .86$, $t = 9.29$, $p < .001$). Thus, sites with large sherd samples typically have more wares and vessel forms.

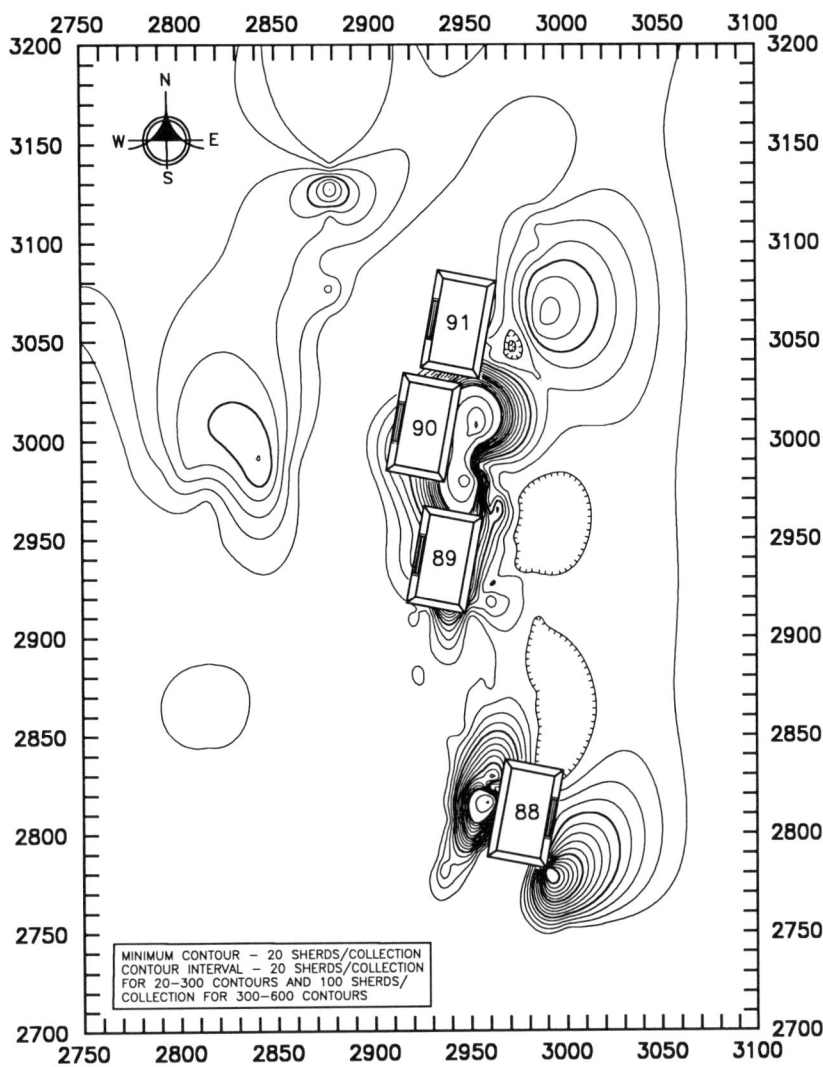

Fig. 35. The Mound 88–91 ceramics production area, showing the distribution of surface refuse.

Computation of a partial correlation coefficient that controls for differences in sample size indicates that large production areas such as Comoapan may have actually produced fewer wares than other areas ($r = -.92$, $F = 482.2$, $p < .001$).

It also appears that certain fine paste wares were fired at specific kilns. We have determined experimentally that Fine Orange was produced using the same clay as Fine Gray, with paste color variation simply a function of firing atmosphere (oxidizing versus reduction). Fine Orange and Fine Gray pottery rarely occur together in kilns. This mutually exclusive distribution indicates that production facilities were segregated according to the technological requirements of certain desired end products. This pattern only holds true for fine paste vessels, however, since sherds from large Coarse Orange storage jars dominate the assemblages from all contexts. Interestingly, although kilns were individually segregated in this manner, kiln groups were not, suggesting the production of a more generic suite of vessel wares and forms for the entire production area, combined with internal variation to accommodate varying technological requirements.

It is difficult to estimate the precise number of vessels produced at Comoapan from the survey data alone, but it is clear that very large numbers of vessels were fired and that production was highly intensive. Technology indicative of raw material preparation, vessel forming, and vessel decoration is also lacking in the dumps near the kilns, implying spatial segregation of disparate activities involved in the production process. The spatial segregation of different production activities, the emphasis on Coarse Orange production and the manufacture of only a few vessel forms, the high degree of vessel standardization, and the lack of variability within the firing area are lines of evidence consistent with the proposi-

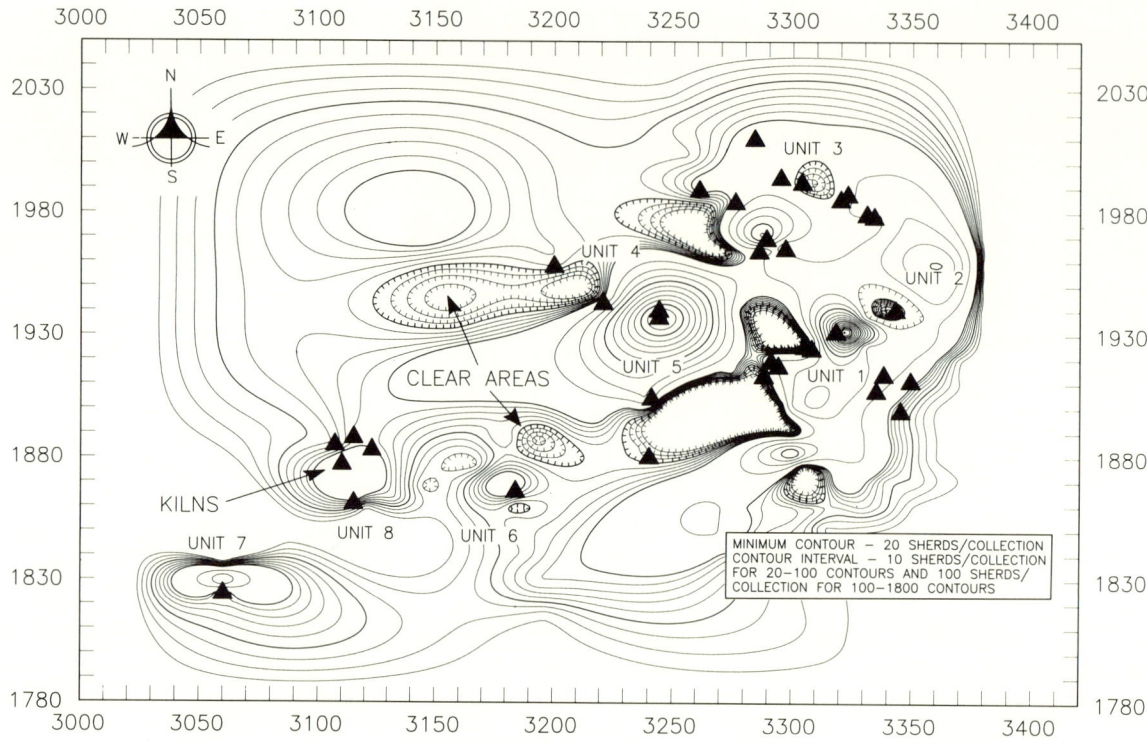

Fig. 36. The Comoapan ceramics production area, showing the location of kilns (triangles) and the distribution of surface refuse.

tion that ceramics production at Comoapan was organized as a large nucleated industry or manufactory (Santley, Arnold, and Pool 1989).

In sum, ceramics production in suburban Matacapan was extremely diversified. Although many production areas were household industries, several areas were much larger in size, covering 1.1–8.0 ha. Intensive survey and excavation indicate that each contained a complex of kilns and waster dumps. Some of these production entities were organized as work-

shop industries, whereas others probably operated as nucleated industries or manufactories. The total volume of production in suburban Matacapan must have been considerable, amounting to tens if not hundreds of thousands of vessels annually. Although service wares were manufactured in some areas, most potteries emphasized the production of Coarse Orange, which was rendered in two main forms: hole-mouth jars and necked jars.

Specialized Production in Rural Contexts around Matacapan

Specialized production of this sort extended well into the countryside. This specialized ceramics production reached a peak in late Middle Classic times, although many sites were occupied throughout the Middle Classic (Santley 1991). Of 180 sites recorded by the settlement survey, 24 were involved in specialized ceramics production (Fig. 38). A number of these sites were situated near Matacapan, but others were located throughout the survey region. Most production in the countryside was fairly low level, involving household industries and occurring at hamlets or in small production areas at larger sites, but manufacturing activities at three settlements (sites 11, 94, and 112) were more intensive. Here were found unusually large amounts of kiln debris and misfired pottery,

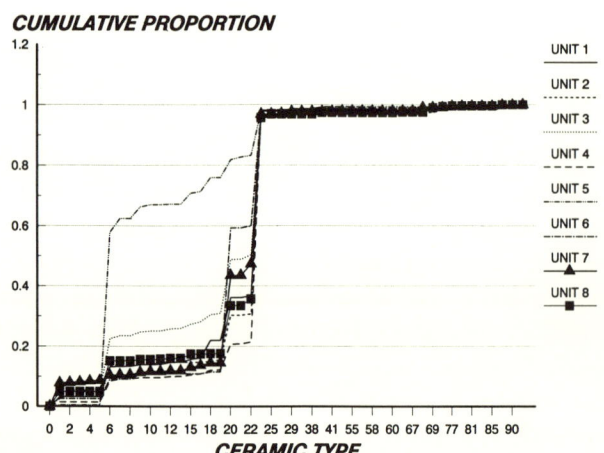

Fig. 37. Cumulative frequency of pottery produced in different spatial units at Comoapan.

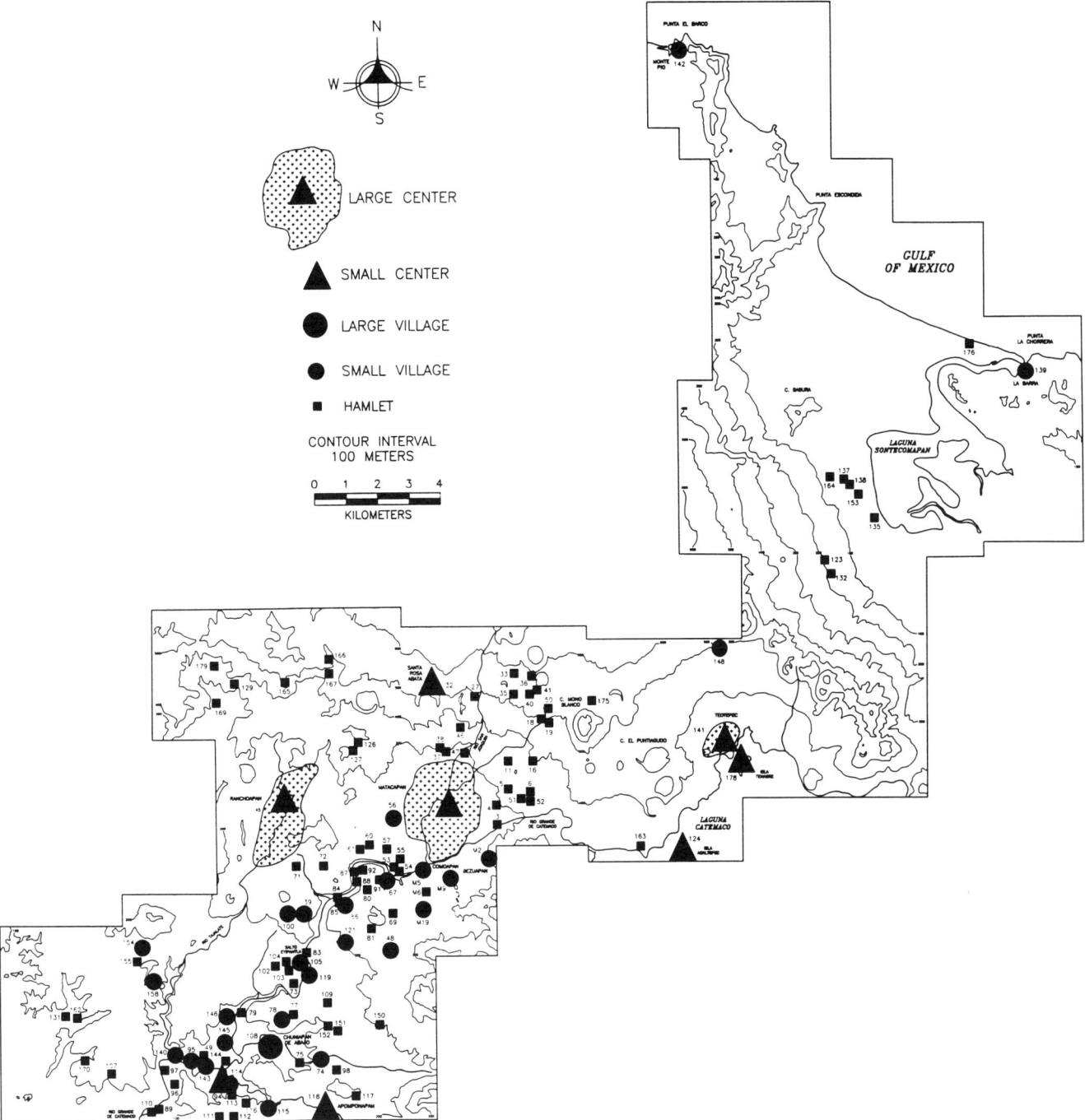

Fig. 38. The Tuxtlas region, showing regional settlement patterns.

including batches of vessels melted together during firing. Moreover, production residues were distributed over large areas 2.2–10 ha in size, implying manufacture in special workshops on a more intensive basis. Fine Orange (27.4 percent) and Coarse Brown (37.2 percent) were the major wares produced at rural sites, wares that apparently were not made in great numbers at Matacapan's larger production entities.

The largest ceramics production area, covering nearly 10 ha, was situated at site 11, several kilometers northeast of Matacapan. This settlement extended over a small hill and the adjacent flatlands. The northern part of the hill was terraced. Each terrace supported groups of circular updraft kilns where firing took place. Middens containing misfired sherds were sometimes placed near the kilns, but wasters were generally

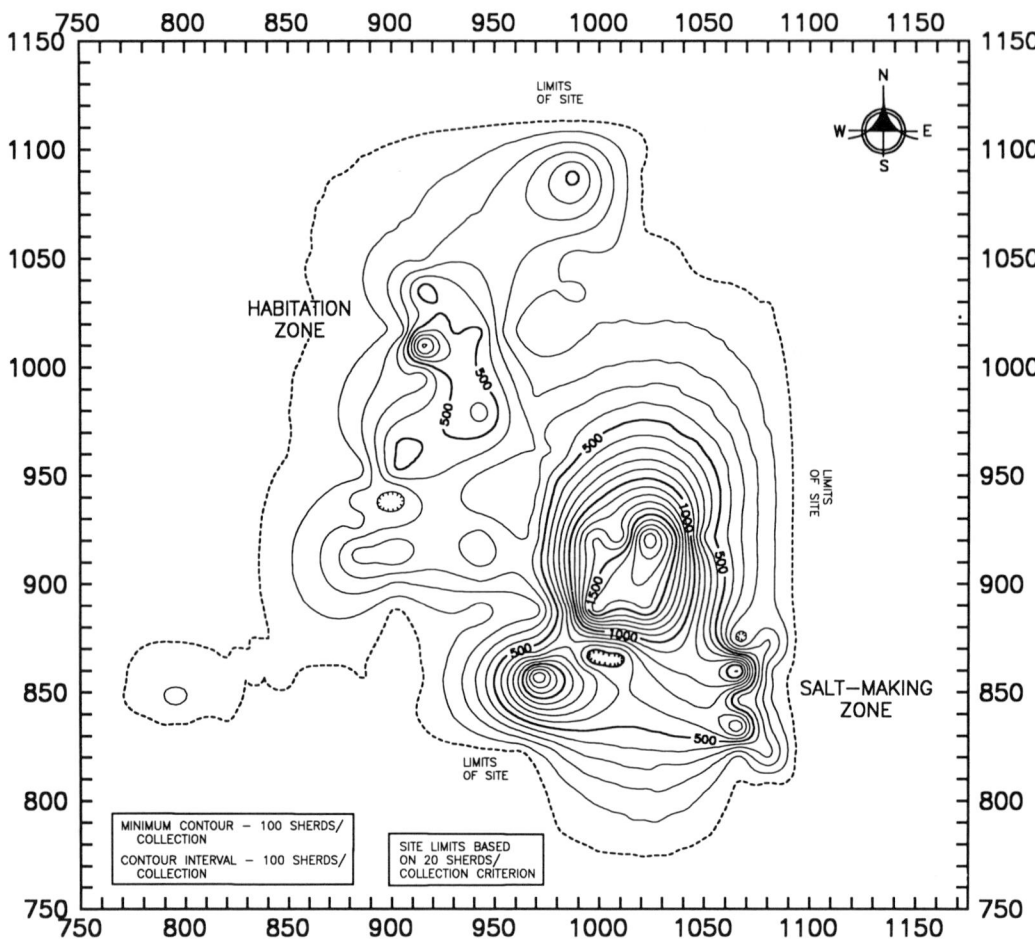

Fig. 39. El Salado, showing the distribution of surface refuse.

discarded on the southern side of the hill and at its base. The large size of the production area indicates that manufacture was on a scale comparable to that at Comoapan or at several of the Fine Gray production zones in southern Matacapan.

The best evidence of rural craft production comes from El Salado, a Classic Period salt-making station. The site is located 9 km southwest of Matacapan on the eastern side of an extinct volcanic cone, Cerro Coxole (Santley, Ortiz C., and Kludt 1988) (Fig. 39). In this area, recent volcanism has upwarped Tertiary marine sediments rich in kaolinite and possessing a comparatively high salt content. These clay sediments underlie all of El Salado and are exposed on the surface at various points throughout the site. A stream leaching salts from this clay effuses at the base of the hill directly north of the site. The stream flows east, ultimately joining the Rio Tajalate to the southeast. Potsherds and other artifacts occur over a broad area but are most abundantly concentrated in the 8.25-ha area defined as the site. Within this area, high densities of surface refuse occur in pockets. The highest densities of material generally occur downslope.

The central part of the site contains a group of irregularly shaped mounds. This mound group consists of one large mound 4 m high and 50 m in diameter in addition to three smaller mounds to the north. A modern roadway bisecting the site indicates that the mounds were refuse middens, not platforms built to support structures. Sherds are literally stacked one atop another with little soil deposited between them. Assemblages from different spatial contexts also vary in composition; some contain substantial numbers of jars, whereas others are dominated by basins, *cazuelas*, or trays. The midden exposed in the roadway profiles was about 1.5 m deep, but it was probably greater than 3 m in depth in areas near the mounds.

Analysis of the distribution of surface refuse indicates that the site may be divided into two zones: a salt-making area where the density of surface refuse is extremely high and a low-density area upslope where the saltmakers probably resided. The high-density area was a concentrated refuse midden where large amounts of trash were dumped in antiquity. Three utility wares account for 85 percent of all materials, and each is dominated by a single vessel form. Different wares are concentrated in different parts of this area, suggesting that ceramics from different activities were deposited in special dumps. The skew in assemblage content implies the presence of a series of highly specialized activities that were probably conducted in the same area. These activities were spatially segregated from one another, to judge from the vessel forms represented, and involved the use of fires, since kiln debris and burned earth are concentrated in this zone. "Domestic" artifacts, such as fine paste pottery, obsidian, figurines, and ground stone, are rare. This evidence implies that the area around the mound group was not a habitation zone.

Sal cocida was apparently the primary method employed to manufacture salt, to judge from the amount of refuse present and the area over which it was distributed (Andrews 1983). Two kinds of vessels were involved in the production process. Jars were used to collect water from the spring or from shallow wells dug nearby. Reducing the salt water to a congealed mass of salt was probably a two-step operation. Because water from the stream is not extremely saline, it was probably boiled first to produce brine. Boiling in jars is a fuel-efficient method for making brine; it requires continuous but low heat and does not use large quantities of wood or charcoal per batch. The brine was then transferred to basins in which loaves of salt were produced by continued boiling. Vessels of medium size with unrestricted orifices were preferred for this activity because they could be reused many times.

These two activities took place at different locations within the salt-making zone. Brine production in jars occurred mainly in the southern part of the zone nearest the stream, where water could be fetched with ease. Evidence of loaf production was mainly confined to the northern part of the zone, where the assemblages are dominated by basins and *cazuelas*. It is also possible that the entire reduction sequence was sometimes conducted in jars, which were broken after the water had evaporated. This production technique, however, was probably not a common practice, given the heavy demands it would have made on ceramic vessels. Most of the pottery used in the salt production process was apparently made on site. This pottery was fired in double-chambered updraft kilns similar to the ones used at Comoapan (Santley et al. 1985b). Kiln debris occurs throughout the *sal cocida* production area, suggesting that saltmakers manufactured their own pottery.

The site's inhabitants probably lived upslope, in the area of lower-density surface occupation. Although no structures were encountered during the survey of the upslope area, domestic artifacts, such as obsidian blades, obsidian reduction material, figurines, and the full range of ceramic service and utility wares, were present. In addition, there are a number of clear areas situated near small refuse middens. Recent ethnoarchaeological work by members of the Matacapan Project has shown that households maintain a clear area free of refuse around a residence, a zone where most of the family's daily activities are conducted (Arnold 1987; Killion 1987; see also Hayden and Cannon 1983). Clear areas are surrounded by refuse middens, where household trash is periodically dumped. A broadcast approach to disposal is often adopted because there are few constraints on space. Garbage is simply swept away from the house, producing a ring of refuse around the patio. Moreover, when given the opportunity, peasants prefer to discard garbage downslope. The area to the northwest of the mound group meets these criteria. It is upslope from the mound group, it contains clear areas surrounded by middens rich in a wide variety of ceramic materials, and it produced most of the obsidian and figurines retrieved from the survey.

From the preceding discussion, it is clear that El Salado produced salt for distribution over a comparatively large area. The mound group may have functioned as one large production zone where salt was processed in a special workshop complex. Our spatial analysis suggests that vessels used in different stages of the production process were deposited in different dumps and that the mound group in general contains comparatively few domestic artifacts. These two characteristics indicate that salt production took place in a workshop context. This specialized production zone was located next to an area where the saltmakers lived. At present, it is difficult to determine if saltmaking was a full-time specialization or to ascertain how many salt-making households existed at El Salado, although an estimate of ten to fifteen residential units seems reasonable.

This patterning in specialization suggests a complex ceramics production system that involved urban, suburban, and rural components. The largest-scale production entities were situated in Matacapan's suburbs or near the center, but others were located in the countryside. Most of this rural pottery production was probably intended for exchange with household ceramics consumers, but some production was also geared to other specialized industries, such as saltmaking, which used pottery in great amounts. Saltmaking at El Salado was a large-scale affair involving production in special workshops while the saltmakers lived in another part of the site. Matacapan, site 94, and site 112 probably shared the Fine Orange market, with each site manufacturing pottery for clienteles living nearby. Matacapan, however, also manufactured large quantities of Fine Gray and Coarse Orange, two wares that were not produced in abundance at rural sites. The market in these wares that Matacapan dominated, therefore, was probably of considerably greater size than that overseen by smaller sites situated in the countryside.

Discussion

The craft industry that Matacapan dominated was large scale and internally differentiated. Ceramics production in the center's civic core took place primarily in household contexts and probably involved the manufacture of goods for specific clienteles, such as the site's elite and its central political and religious institutions. Pottery production in suburban Matacapan was more differentiated, involving household industries as well as larger-scale entities like workshops, nucleated industries, and possibly manufactories. Many of these larger-scale industries emphasized the production of specific ceramic wares and vessel forms, whereas others produced the full range of service and utility wares. At Comoapan, different activities involved in the production process took place in different areas, a work regime that may characterize other larger-scale production localities as well.

This specialized ceramics production system extended well into Matacapan's hinterland. Hinterland specialization involved ceramics as well as other goods. Most ceramics production in the countryside was small scale and occurred at sites distributed throughout the region, suggesting manufacture for rural consumers. Salt production at El Salado, in contrast, took place on a large scale and involved a spatially segregated activity regime. Because of the profuse quantities of refuse generated, the saltmaking zone was situated downslope from the area of residential occupation. Ceramics production at site 11 was on a comparable scale and apparently involved a similar activity regime. The extreme amount of differentiated production in and around Matacapan suggests the presence of an economy of scale, at least as far as ceramics production is concerned.

There were also major changes in the scale and structure of the ceramic production industry through time. With the exception of the ceramics manufacturing areas near Mounds 61 and 69–75 and at Comoapan, which seem to have been devoted to Fine Buff production, evidence of specialized manufacture in the early Middle Classic is quite limited. Despite the fact that two of these production zones, Mounds 88–91 and Comoapan, covered 3.5 and 8 ha, respectively, most were comparatively small in size. Furthermore, the density of refuse in middens rarely exceeded 60 sherds/m^2. Firing areas were generally located either close to house mounds or next to "vacant" areas within the high-density zones, implying production in household contexts or in small workshops. But production expanded greatly during the middle of the period. By late Middle Classic times, most production areas had reached their maximum size, and there were major increases in the intensity of production and degree of specialization. Many of these production entities consisted of virtually continuous concentrations of kilns and waster dumps covering 1.5 to 4 ha each, suggesting manufacture in highly specialized contexts involving groups of workshops or manufactories. Curiously, these developments occurred at a time when the civic-ceremonial center was in the process of being abandoned and when Teotihuacan influence at the site had reached an all-time low.

Most of the pottery produced at Matacapan was probably destined for exchange beyond the local region. This conclusion is based on three lines of evidence. First, the primary ceramic group produced, Coarse Orange, is never very common in domestic assemblages from any time period, yet it is predominant in most production site assemblages at Matacapan. High frequencies of this ware, however, would be expected at producer sites if production was highly specialized but oriented to a broad regional market. Second, ceramic types identical to pottery produced at Matacapan are present throughout the Tuxtlas and in neighboring regions, sometimes in significant amounts. Typologically identical pottery occurs at El Picayo, Tres Zapotes, and sites on the northern side of the Tuxtlas, including Piedra Labrada and Montepio. Similar material occurs in the Mixtequilla (M. T. Stark, pers. comm.) and at Lagunade los Cerros (P. Ortiz Ceballos, pers. comm.). In addition, large quantities of Tuxtlas pottery are present in the Merchant's Barrio at Teotihuacan (Rattray 1987). Represented in the assemblage from Teotihuacan is the full range of Matacapan service wares as well as the major utility wares, including Coarse Orange.

Finally, three settlements are situated at special locations. La Barra (site 139) and Monte Pio (site 142) are located at the intersection of the Gulf Coast and two major routes of water transport into the interior, and the third (site 132) is situated on the route from Laguna Sontecomapan to Lake Catemaco. Their placement at these locations implies that access to the Gulf Coast played a major role in determining site distributions in this area. Monte Pio and La Barra have functioned as ports of entry into the Tuxtlas, whereas site 132 may have operated as an overnight station on the route from Laguna Sontecomapan to Laguna Catemaco, the major route of access from the Gulf of Mexico to Matacapan and its satellites along the Rio Catemaco. The Gulf Coast therefore would have provided the ceramics production system at Matacapan with a convenient means for distributing its goods over longer distances. Since changes in transport mode often require adjustments in lot size, alterations in packing technique, and modifications in routing, sites should have been founded at major break-of-bulk points, such as La Barra and Monte Pio.

Thus, data from Matacapan and its sustaining area do not fit the model of a regal-ritual or administrative center. Craft production levels greatly eclipsed that expected at an elite center, and the principal orientation of this industry was production for export, which would not be expected if the site functioned mainly as an administrative center. The high level of specialized craft production activity is more in line with the commercial center model. Such centers often arise in regions that have a source of wealth other than control over peasant subsistence agriculture and in which government control is weak or poorly developed (Fox 1977:95). The evidence from Matacapan agrees with the former criterion but not with the latter. Although the site was a major center of craft production, Matacapan supported a substantial Teotihuacan enclave that maintained close ties with its homeland in central Mexico. Moreover, specialized craft activity expanded in scale at the same time that Teotihuacan influence reached a peak at Matacapan, implying that control over the local resource base was the major motive behind Teotihuacan's decision to establish a base in the Tuxtlas.

The fact that evidence of craft production extended well into the countryside also indicates that there was no clear boundary between center and hinterland. Ceramics were manufactured in areas of urban occupation near the main mound group as well as in suburban contexts and in the countryside. In addition, proximity to the site center had no impact on the scale or organization of the ceramic production industry. Therefore, the larger, more complex production entities were not confined to the main center, with the smaller, more simply organized industries relegated to rural areas. Rather, the center itself supported the smallest-scale production sites, and larger-scale entities were situated in suburban and rural contexts. Access to raw materials and transportation routes appear to have been the primary factors affecting industry placement. These requirements are best met by locations near the Rio Grande de Catemaco and its tributaries, which bisected clay and temper deposits, supplied important other materials such as water and salt, and also provided a convenient artery for distribution downstream.

Another unusual aspect of craft production at Matacapan is the emphasis on ceramic vessels, which were exchanged in large quantities as far away as Teotihuacan. Pottery, it is often claimed, will not be traded long distances when transport involves human carriers, because the costs of hauling vessels overland are very high and the raw materials necessary to make the vessels are widely distributed. Consequently, ceramics manufacture should be a lower-order specialization, with producers situated near consumers to take advantage of the savings in transport costs. Such a situation applies only so long as the cost of transporting goods remains high and there are no variations in transport efficiency.

Large-scale ceramics production areas at Matacapan, however, were situated in close proximity to the Rio Catemaco, the major transportation route downstream to the Rio San Juan, the Rio Papaloapan, and ultimately the Gulf of Mexico. An alternative path would have involved transit upstream to Lake Catemaco and then to the sites of LaBarra and Monte Pio on the Gulf Coast. Because transport by canoe is forty to fifty times more efficient than carrying goods overland on human backs, the marketing areas associated with production centers linked to consumers by water tend to be much larger in size or to involve the exchange of much larger or more massive objects (Sanders and Santley 1983; Curtin 1984; Hassig 1985; Santley and Alexander 1992). Transport by water thus may have played a vital role in extending the range over which the ceramics industries around Matacapan could distribute their products (Santley 1989; Santley, Arnold, and Pool 1989). This ability to gain access to a large hinterland probably had major effects on the growth of progressively larger-scale production entities and the ultimate development of an economy of scale.

Concluding Remarks

This chapter has dealt with the question of urbanism and ruralism in Mesoamerica. An aspect of the urbanization process is the development of centers occupied by large numbers of specialists. Recent work in Mesoamerica indicates that centers had mainly ritual-ideological, political, and administrative functions and that when craftsmen were present goods were produced primarily for consumption by the inhabitants of the centers and their immediate rural hinterlands, which were occupied largely by food producers.

Although this characterization describes most of the variation known to exist in the largest centers in central Mexico, the Valley of Oaxaca, and the Maya lowlands, it does not account for patterning at Matacapan and in its sustaining area. Here craft specialization was more highly developed and the emphasis was on production for export. Craft production was mainly a suburban and rural phenomenon characterized by production sites situated near raw material deposits and transportation routes leading out of the local region. The development of a large-scale and internally differentiated ceramic production system seems to be linked to two factors: the presence of an efficient transportation system that emphasized travel by canoe and the establishment of the Teotihuacan enclave, which had the capacity to control exchange and to move goods in bulk up and down the Gulf Coast, as well as into the interior.

Whether similar developments are evident at other Gulf Coast sites remains to be seen. I suspect, however, that specialized craft production was more common than the extant archaeological record indicates, for the following reason. Most archaeological research at large sites in lowland Mesoamerica is mound oriented, especially in areas where vegetation obscures the ground surface. Here surface survey strategies have focused on defining the distribution of structures, which are then excavated to determine mound function and date. At Matacapan, in contrast, although some production areas occur near mounds, many others do not. This is the case because most structures were not constructed atop platforms and were built of perishable materials, with kilns and waster dumps placed some distance away from building areas. Thus, because of their design, traditional survey methods would miss many of the ceramic production areas at Matacapan. In addition, the discovered loci would be near residential mounds, suggesting that most ceramics production occurred in household contexts and that specialization did not involve more complex production entities. Reconstructions based on this methodology would consequently generate a very distorted picture of the archaeological record. This bias can only be remedied by intensively surveying intermound areas, both at the principal centers and at sites in the countryside.

Note

A large number of persons assisted in the collection of the information presented in this chapter, including Philip J. Arnold III, Thomas Barrett, Richard E. Diehl, Bob Estes, Barbara A. Hall, Veronica Kann, Janet M. Kerley, Thomas W. Killion, Trevor Kludt, Ronald R. Kneebone, Sara Ladron, Roberto Lunagomez, Raul Olivares, Ponciano Ortiz Ceballos, Martha Osorio, Christopher A. Pool, Zenaido Salazar, Scott Wails, Daniel Wolfman, and Clare Yarborough. I am also indebted to Joaquin Garcia Barcena, Robert H. Cobean, Angel Garcia Cook, Gema Lozano y Nathal, Lorena Mirambell, Daniel Molina, and Daniel Nahmad of INAH, who greatly facilitated the fieldwork efforts and provided a congenial research atmosphere in Mexico. The research summarized in this chapter was generously funded by the National Science Foundation, the Pittsburgh Foundation, and the University of New Mexico, as well as several private donors.

References Cited

Adams, Robert McC., and Hans J. Nissen
 1972 *The Uruk Countryside: The Natural Setting of Urban Societies.* University of Chicago Press, Chicago.
Andrews, Anthony P.
 1983 *Maya Salt Production and Trade.* University of Arizona Press, Tucson.
Arnold, Philip J., III
 1987 The Household Potters of los Tuxtlas: An Ethnoarchaeological Study of Ceramic Production and Site Structure. Ph.D. dissertation, Department of Anthropology, University of New Mexico.
Bittman, Bente, and Thelma D. Sullivan
 1978 The Pochteca. In *Mesoamerican Communication Routes and Cultural Contacts,* edited by Thomas A. Lee, Jr., and Carlos Navarrete, pp. 211–218. Papers of the New World Archaeological Foundation 40. Brigham Young University, Provo, Utah.
Blanton, Richard E. D.
 1976 Anthropological Studies of Cities. *Annual Review of Anthropology* 5:249–264.
Brumfiel, Elizabeth M.
 1987 Elite and Utilitarian Crafts in the Aztec State. In *Specialization, Exchange, and Complex Societies,* edited by E. M. Brumfiel and T. K. Earle, pp. 102–118. Cambridge University Press, Cambridge.
Brumfiel, Elizabeth M., and Timothy K. Earle
 1987 Specialization, Exchange, and Complex Societies: An Introduction. In *Specialization, Exchange, and Complex Societies,* edited by E. M. Brumfiel and T. K. Earle, pp. 1–9. Cambridge University Press, Cambridge.
Childe, Vere Gordon
 1942 *What Happened in History.* Pelican, Harmondsworth, England.
 1950 The Urban Revolution. *The Town Planning Review* 21:3–17.
Christaller, Walter
 1966 *Central Places in Southern Germany.* Prentice Hall, Englewood Cliffs, N.J.
Curtin, Philip D.
 1984 *Cross-Cultural Trade in World Prehistory.* Cambridge University Press, New York.
Earle, Timothy K.
 1987 Specialization and the Production of Wealth. In *Specialization, Exchange, and Complex Societies,* edited by E. M. Brumfiel and T. K. Earle, pp. 64–75. Cambridge University Press, Cambridge.
English, Paul W.
 1966 *City and Village in Iran: Settlement and Economy in the Kirman Basin.* University of Wisconsin Press, Madison.
Feinman, Gary M., Richard E. Blanton, and Stephen A. Kowalewski
 1984 Market System Development in the Prehispanic Valley of Oaxaca, Mexico. In *Trade and Exchange in Early Mesoamerica,*

edited by K. G. Hirth, pp. 157–178. University of New Mexico Press, Albuquerque.

Fox, Richard
1977 *Urban Anthropology*. Prentice Hall, Englewood Cliffs, N.J.

Hassig, Ross
1985 *Trade, Tribute, and Transportation: The Sixteenth-Century Political Economy of the Valley of Mexico*. University of Oklahoma Press, Norman.

Hayden, Brian, and Aubrey Cannon
1983 Where the Garbage Goes: Refuse Disposal in the Maya Highlands. *Journal of Anthropological Archaeology* 2:117–163.

Jacobs, Jane
1969 *The Economy of Cities*. Random House, New York.

Johnson, Gregory A.
1973 *Local Exchange and Early State Development in Southwestern Iran*. Museum of Anthropology, University of Michigan, Anthropological Papers, No. 51. University of Michigan, Ann Arbor.
1975 Locational Analysis and the Investigation of Uruk Local Exchange Systems. In *Ancient Civilization and Trade*, edited by J. A. Sabloff and C. C. Lamberg-Karlovsky, pp. 285–339. University of New Mexico Press, Albuquerque.

Killion, Thomas W.
1987 Infield Gardening Practices in the Sierra de los Tuxtlas: Building a Foundation for Archaeological Inference. Ph.D. dissertation, Department of Anthropology, University of New Mexico.

Marcus, Joyce
1983 On the Nature of the Mesoamerican City. In *Prehistoric Settlement Patterns: Essays in Honor of Gordon R. Willey*, edited by E. Vogt and R. Leventhal, pp. 195–242. University of New Mexico Press, Albuquerque.

Millon, Rene
1973 *Urbanization at Teotihuacan*, Vol. 1: *The Teotihuacan Map*. University of Texas Press, Austin.

Ortiz Ceballos, Ponciano, and Robert S. Santley
In press *La Cerámica de Matacapan*. Museo de Antropología, Jalapa, Veracruz, Mexico.

Parsons, Lee A.
1978 The Peripheral Coastal Lowlands and the Middle Classic Period. In *Middle Classic Mesoamerica: A.D. 400–700*, edited by E. Pasztory, pp. 25–34. Columbia University Press, New York.

Peacock, D. P. S.
1982 *Pottery in the Roman World: An Ethnoarchaeological Approach*. Longman, London.

Pool, Christopher A.
1990 Ceramic Production, Resource Procurement, and Exchange in Southern Veracruz: A View from Matacapan. Ph.D. dissertation, Department of Anthropology, Tulane University.

Rattray, Evelyn C.
1987 Evidencias de un Grupo Etnico de la Costa del Golfo en Teotihuacan. Paper presented at the conference on Balance y Perspectiva de la Antropología en Veracruz, Jalapa, Veracruz, Mexico.

Sanders, William T., and Robert S. Santley
1983 A Tale of Three Cities: Energetics and Urbanization in Prehispanic Central Mexico. In *Prehistoric Settlement Patterns: Essays in Honor of Gordon R. Willey*, edited by E. Vogt and R. Leventhal, pp. 243–291. University of New Mexico Press, Albuquerque.

Sanders, William T., and David L. Webster
1988 The Mesoamerican Urban Tradition. *American Anthropologist* 90:521–546.

Santley, Robert S.
1983 Obsidian Trade and Teotihuacan Influence in Mesoamerica. In *Highland-Lowland Interaction in Mesoamerica: Interdisciplinary Approaches*, edited by A. Miller, pp. 69–124. Dumbarton Oaks, Washington, D.C.
1984 Obsidian Exchange, Economic Stratification, and the Evolution of Complex Society in the Basin of Mexico. In *Trade and Exchange in Early Mesoamerica*, edited by K. G. Hirth, pp. 43–86. University of New Mexico Press, Albuquerque.
1989 Obsidian Working, Long-Distance Exchange, and the Teotihuacan Presence on the South Gulf Coast. In *Cultural Adjustments in Mesoamerica after the Decline of Teotihuacan: A.D. 700–900*, edited by R. A. Diehl and J. C. Berlo, pp. 131–151. Dumbarton Oaks, Washington, D.C.
1991 Final Field Report: Tuxtlas Region Archaeological Survey, 1991 Field Season. A Report to the National Science Foundation, Washington, D.C. Department of Anthropology, University of New Mexico, Albuquerque.

Santley, Robert S., and Rani T. Alexander
1992 The Political Economy of Core-Periphery Systems. In *Resources, Power, and Interregional Interaction*, edited by E. M. Schortman and P. A. Urban, pp. 23–49. Plenum Press, New York.

Santley, Robert S., Philip J. Arnold III, and Christopher A. Pool
1989 The Ceramics Production System at Matacapan, Veracruz, Mexico. *Journal of Field Archaeology* 16:107–132.

Santley, Robert S., Janet M. Kerley, and Ronald R. Kneebone
1986 Obsidian Working, Long-Distance Exchange, and the Politico-Economic Organization of Early States in Central Mexico. *Research in Economic Anthropology* (Supplement) 2:101–132.

Santley, Robert S., Ronald R. Kneebone, and Janet M. Kerley
1985a Rates of Obsidian Utilization in Central Mexico and on the South Gulf Coast. *Lithic Technology* 14:107–119.

Santley, Robert S., Ponciano Ortiz C., Philip J. Arnold, Barbara A. Hall, Veronica Kann, Janet M. Kerley, Ronald R. Kneebone, David Mora M., Raul Olivares M., Carmela Parra U., Christopher A. Pool, Zenaido Salazar B., Michael P. Smyth, and Clare Yarborough
1985b Final Field Report, Matacapan Project: 1984 Season. Final Report to the Instituto Nacional de Antropología e Historia and the National Science Foundation. Department of Anthropology, University of New Mexico, Albuquerque.

Santley, Robert S., Ponciano Ortiz C., Philip J. Arnold, Janet M. Kerley, Ronald R. Kneebone, and Michael P. Smyth
    1985c Reporte Final de Campo, Proyecto Matacapan: Temporada 1983. *Cuadernos del Museo de Universidad Veracruzana* 4:3–98.

Santley, Robert S., Ponciano Ortiz, Thomas W. Killion, Philip J. Arnold, and Janet M. Kerley
    1984 *Final Field Report of the Matacapan Archaeological Project: The 1982 Season.* Latin American Institute, University of New Mexico, Research Papers, No. 15. University of New Mexico, Albuquerque.

Santley, Robert S., Ponciano Ortiz C., and Trevor J. Kludt
    1988 El Salado: A Prehistoric Salt Production Site in the Sierra de los Tuxtlas. Report to the Heinz Trust of the Pittsburgh Foundation. Department of Anthropology, University of New Mexico, Albuquerque.

Santley, Robert S., Ponciano Ortiz C., and Christopher A. Pool
    1987 Recent Archaeological Research at Matacapan, Veracruz: A Summary of the Results of the 1982 to 1986 Field Seasons. *Mexicon* 9:41–48.

Sinapoli, Carla M.
    1988 The Organization of Craft Production at Vijayanagara, South India. *American Anthropologist* 90:580–597.

Sjoberg, Gideon
    1960 *The Preindustrial City, Past and Present.* Free Press, Glencoe, Ill.

Smith, Carol A.
    1976 Exchange Systems and the Spatial Distribution of Elites: The Organization of Stratification in Agrarian Societies. In *Regional Analysis,* Vol. 2: *Social Systems,* edited by C. A. Smith, pp. 309–374. Academic Press, New York.

Spence, Michael W.
    1981 Obsidian Production and the State in Teotihuacan. *American Antiquity* 46:769–788.

Tosi, Maurizio
    1984 The Notion of Craft Specialization and Its Representation in the Archaeological Record of Early States in the Turanian Basin. In *Marxist Perspectives in Archaeology,* edited by M. Spriggs, pp. 22–52. Cambridge University Press, Cambridge.

Van der Leeuw, Sander E.
    1976 *Studies in the Technology of Ancient Pottery.* Organization for the Advancement of Pure Research, Amsterdam.

Weber, Max
    1958 *The City.* Macmillan, New York.

Webster, David L.
    1985 Surplus, Labor, and Stress in Late Classic Maya Society. *Journal of Anthropological Research* 41:375–399.

Wirth, Louis
    1938 Urbanism as a Way of Life. *American Journal of Sociology* 44:3–21.

CHAPTER EIGHT

State Formation and the Organization of Domestic Craft Production at Third-Millennium B.C. Kurban Höyük, Southeast Turkey

PATRICIA WATTENMAKER

THIS CHAPTER EXAMINES ECONOMIC organization among the nonelite population at a rural third-millennium B.C. site in southeast Turkey. Recent research on the economic organization of archaic Near Eastern states has focused on political centers (e.g., Tosi 1984; Zeder 1988; Stone 1990) and regional settlement patterns (Adams 1981; Johnson 1987; Stein and Wattenmaker 1990), but comparatively little work has been done on economic organization among nonelite rural households. The relative lack of interest in rural households may stem from an implicit assumption that rural communities in state societies were similar in economic organization to those in less complex societies, with households producing most of their own goods. However, survey results in both the Old and the New World (Johnson 1973, 1987; Blanton et al. 1982) indicate that state formation was accompanied by increasing specialization in the rural sector as well as at centers. Excavation results from the Near East revealed linkages between village economy and regional economy (H. Wright, Redding, and Pollock 1989:112) and intrasite household variability in consumption patterns at a small town (e.g., H. T. Wright 1981:277). These observations suggest that full understanding of economic organization in archaic states rests on study of both the urban and the rural sectors. This chapter examines craft production and consumption patterns at the rural site of Kurban Höyük, with the aim of documenting the degree of economic specialization among nonelite rural households in early state society. Mid– to late third-millennium B.C. occupational levels provide the data for this study of economic organization during an episode of early state formation in what is now southeastern Turkey.

Ceramics, chipped stone, and spindle whorls from Kurban provide data on the organization of craft production. The roughly contemporaneous palace archives from Tell Mardikh (ancient Ebla), 180 km south of Kurban, provide additional insight into the productive context of craft goods, particularly textiles and metal objects. Determining the range of craft goods produced on a household basis and those produced by specialists (either supported by the state or working independent of state sponsorship) provides the basis for considering factors guiding the organization of production and consumption patterns among nonelite rural households.

The Research Area

Kurban is located near the east bank of the Turkish Euphrates Valley, Urfa Province, 65 km from the Syrian border (Figs. 40 and 41). The region forms a transition zone between the Taurus Mountains and the north Mesopotamian steppe. In terms of both geography and ancient material culture, the area can be tied to the dry farming zone of the north Mesopotamian plain.

Twenty years ago, north Mesopotamia was considered a backwater of civilizational development. However, recent surveys and excavations revealed that in the mid–third millennium B.C., states with urban centers of 40–100 ha, such as Titriş (Algaze 1992), Chuera (Orthmann 1986), and Leilan (Weiss 1983), arose across the dry farming zone of north Syria and north Mesopotamia. The Ebla texts provided strong evidence for a complex, hierarchically organized, specialized economy in northwest Mesopotamia. This restructuring of north Mesopotamian society represents a period of state re-

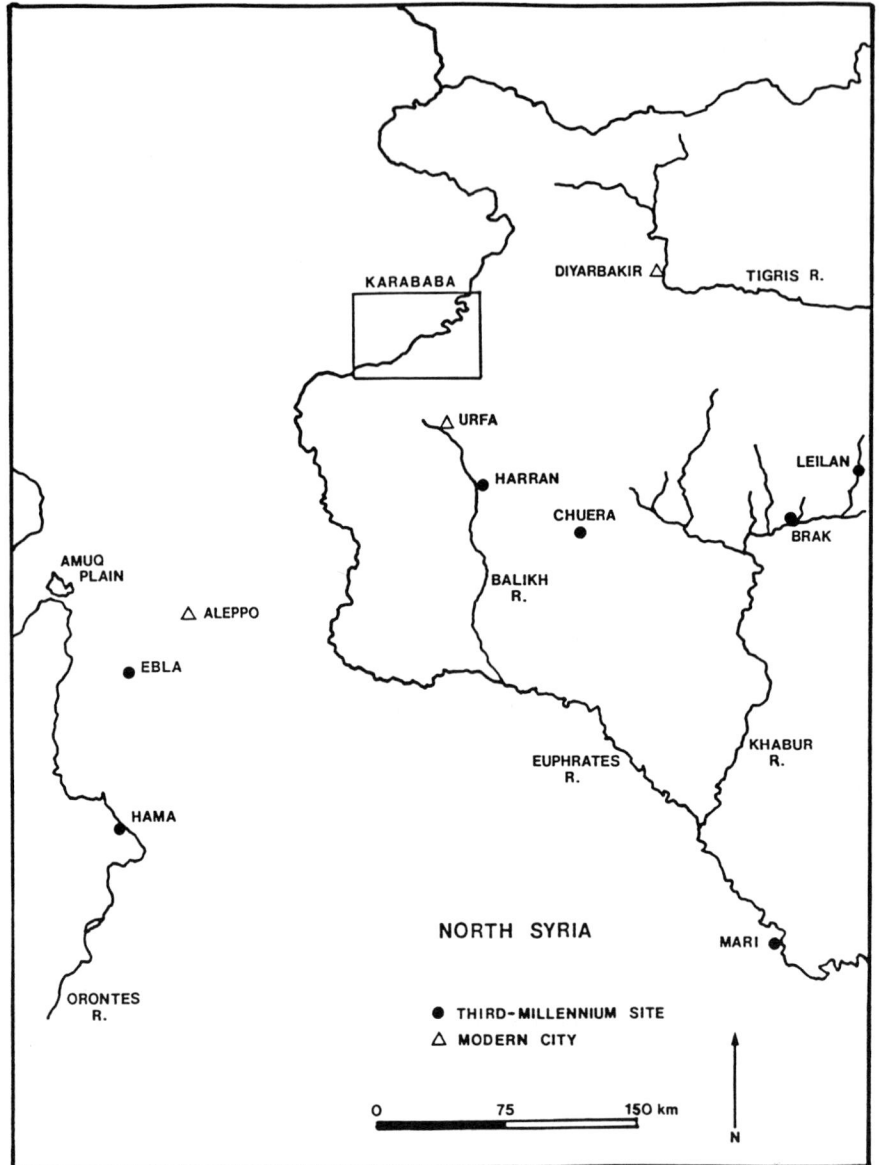

Fig. 40. Location of the Karababa Basin.

surgence following the collapse of earlier and smaller-scale state societies at the end of the fourth millennium B.C.

Third-millennium B.C. settlement trends in the Karababa Basin, where Kurban is located, paralleled trends elsewhere in north Mesopotamia. In the mid–third millennium B.C., the aggregate settlement area in the Kurban region more than doubled. The settlement pattern shifted from a series of small hamlet- and village-sized sites to a more differentiated hierarchy (Wilkinson 1990:94–99) that included a center of 35+ ha (Titriş Höyük; G. Algaze, pers. comm.), towns, and villages (Wilkinson 1986, 1990). Kurban had been occupied almost continuously since ca. 5000 B.C., but in most periods occupation had been limited to one of the two mounds; during the mid–third millennium B.C., Kurban grew from a 1-ha single-mounded site to a double-mounded settlement of at least 6 ha.

Excavation of mid– to late third-millennium B.C. deposits at Kurban indicated that although the site was fairly small, architecture was variable in scale and function. A 5-m-thick fortification wall was located on the higher of the two mounds, and a substantial structure, possibly an administrative building, was situated behind it (Marfoe and Ingraham 1990:43–44). The building was carefully constructed and contained a very large storage jar and two clay door locks. Domestic architecture across the site indicated a degree of socioeconomic variability, with some houses more substantial

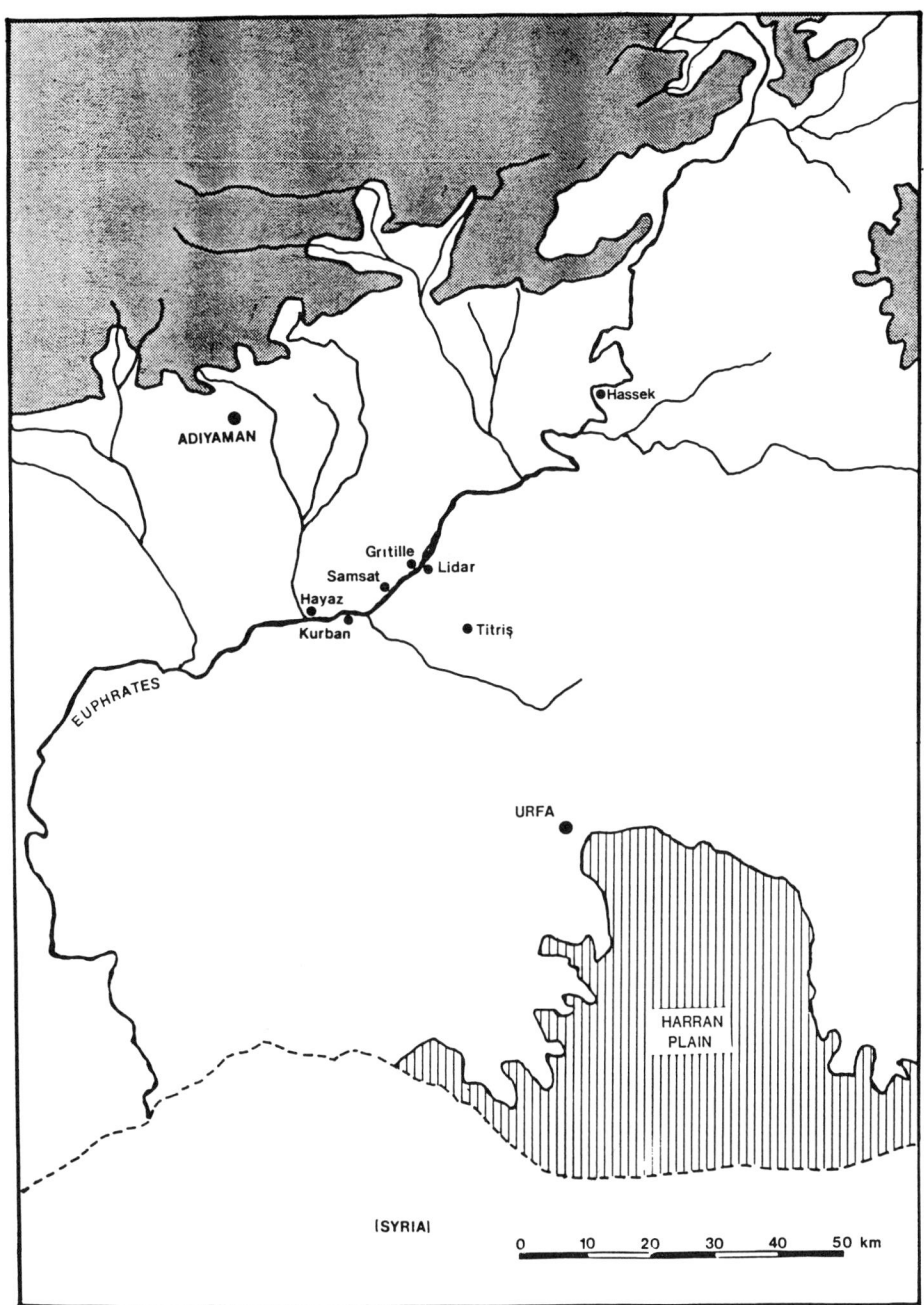

Fig. 41. Kurban Höyük and other sites in the Karababa Basin.

and elaborately constructed and others fairly modest (Wattenmaker 1990). These findings support settlement pattern data indicating that complex societies had emerged in the Karababa Basin by this time.

Throughout most of its history, Kurban was a rural site of 3 ha or less. The mid– to late third-millennium B.C. settlement might be considered a small town; during this time Kurban reached 6 ha in area, and architectural remains suggest socioeconomic diversity. However, it remained one of the smaller sites in the region and, on the basis of relative size, could be characterized as rural even during the mid– to late third millennium B.C., when sites in the region tended to be relatively large (Wilkinson 1990:97). Moreover, archaeological evidence indicates that Kurban was a farming community throughout most of the mid– to late third millennium B.C. Sickle blades used in harvesting were associated with all houses for which data are available until the very last phases of the period (Wattenmaker 1990:208).

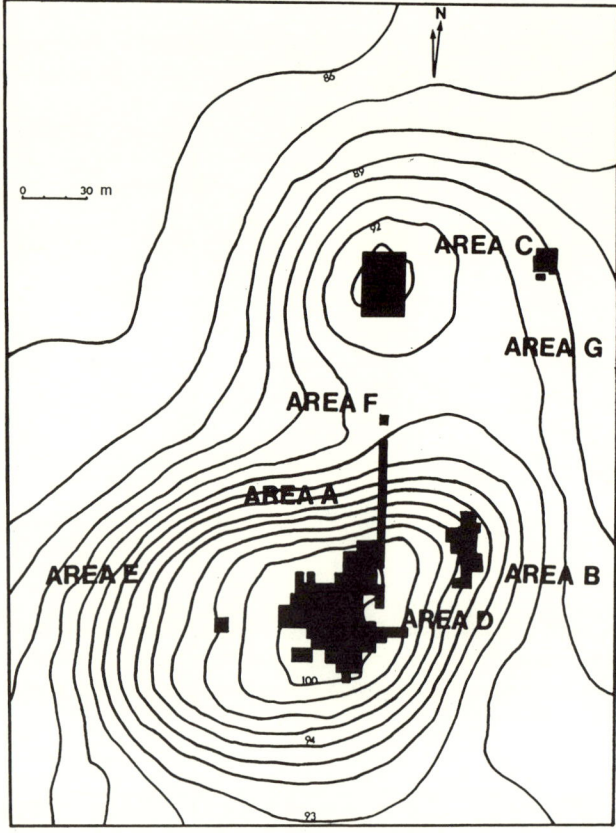

Fig. 42. Plan of Kurban Höyük.

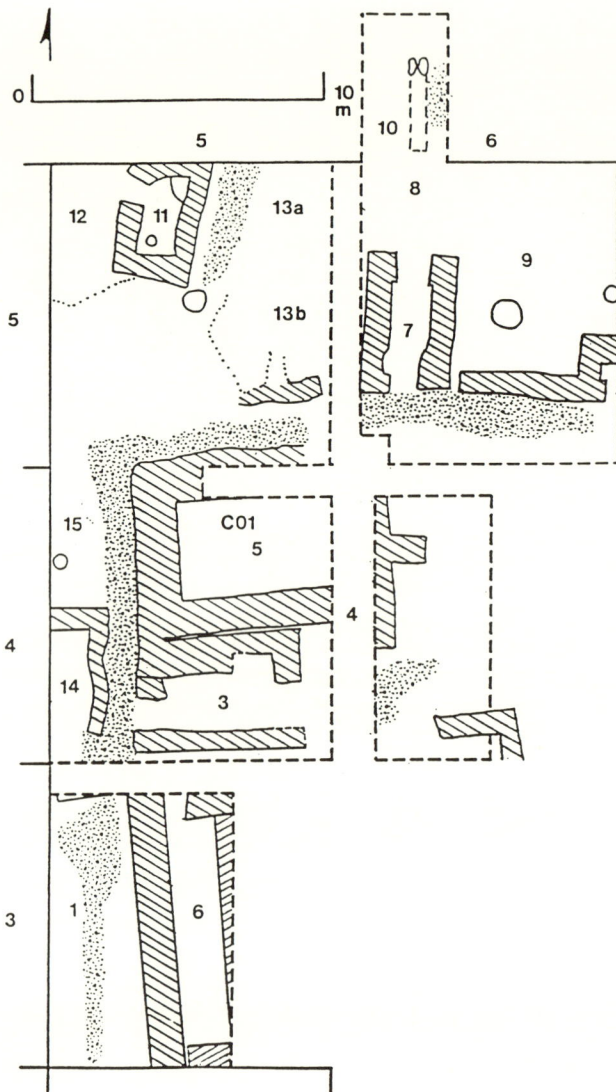

Fig. 43. Plan of area C at Kurban Höyük. Rooms 3–6 represent a relatively large and well-constructed house. The other rooms are part of more modest houses.

The small size of the site, combined with evidence for the involvement of most families in agricultural activities, suggests that Kurban was a rural site even during this period.

Excavations at Kurban were conducted by the University of Chicago. Three excavation areas toward the center of each mound (Fig. 42: areas A, C, and F) yielded fairly elaborate as well as more modest architecture dating to the mid– to late third millennium B.C. (Fig. 43). To investigate nonelite economic organization, two site sectors toward the edge of the site (areas B and G) (Figs. 42 and 44) were excavated. These areas revealed modest houses and associated features. Combining all excavation areas, circa 700 m² from three horizontal areas and circa 200 m² from three soundings were excavated for this study. Occupational deposits in different parts of the site were linked chronologically through a seriation of ceramics (Wattenmaker 1990). The step trench, which spanned the entire period and yielded 8 m of mid– to late third-millennium B.C. remains, provided a chronological anchor for the rest of the site. On the basis of the seriation results, I divided the mid– to late third-millennium B.C. sequence (Kurban period IV) into four subperiods: (4) the earliest village subperiod, (3) the subperiod when the fortification wall was constructed, (2) the subperiod of site expansion, when the site reached its maximum size, and finally (1) the nucleation subperiod, when population density at the site was high and houses were closely spaced. Most probably, construction of the fortification wall and settlement expansion at Kurban (subperiods 3 and 2) date to the period of political centralization and urbanism throughout the region. Having summarized the excavation results, we can now turn to the excavated artifacts and evidence for the organization of craft production during this period.

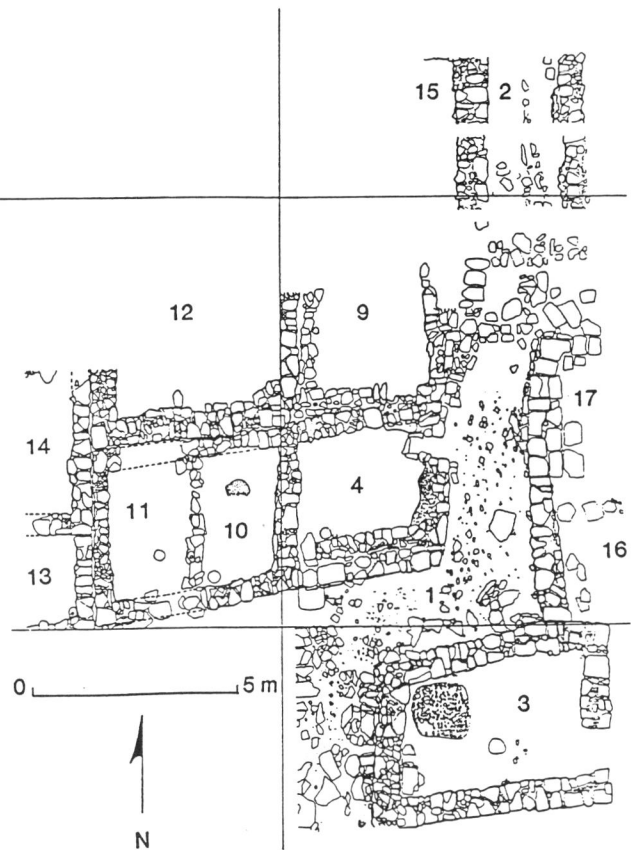

Fig. 44. Plan of area B at Kurban Höyük. All structures in this area were fairly modest.

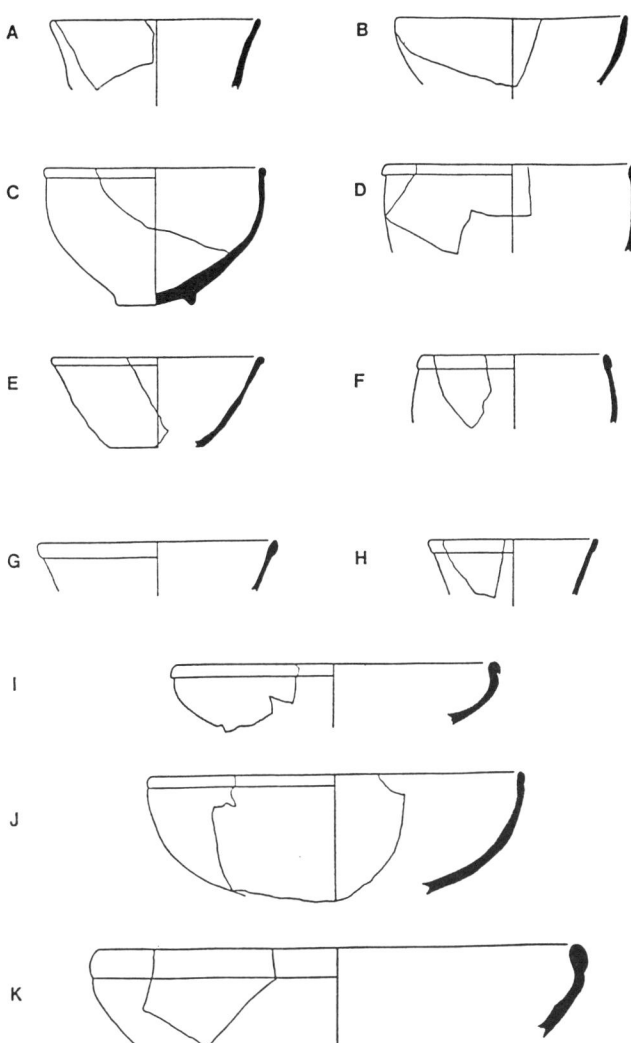

Fig. 45. Undecorated wheel-made pottery from Kurban Höyük (scale 2:5).

Ceramic Production and Consumption

Ceramics were the best-represented class of artifact, used in all parts of the settlement in all mid– to late third-millennium B.C. phases. I examined ceramics excavated at Kurban to determine whether nonelite households in this early state society were producing their own ceramics or procuring ceramics through exchange networks.

Two criteria were used to determine which ceramics were produced by specialists: the technology of manufacture and the degree of standardization. Kilns and potter's wheels have the advantage of enabling one to produce large quantities of standardized products relatively quickly, but they require a high investment of labor and fuel resources. Therefore, they are generally used in connection with specialized production (Peacock 1982:8–11).

Goods produced by specialists are often more uniform than those produced by nonspecialists (Rice 1981:223, 1987:182). This pattern tends to hold true because specialists develop skill through repetition, because goods are usually not produced with individual needs or preferences in mind, and because there are fewer producers relative to products. Therefore, in this study of the ceramics from Kurban, it was expected that pottery produced by individual households or in other relatively informal contexts would be less standardized than that produced by large-scale specialists. In sum, evidence for production techniques and the degree of standardization provided the basis for deciding how the Kurban ceramics were produced.

The Kurban ceramics recovered from domestic contexts can be divided into two major ware groups: fine to medium grit–tempered wares used for wheel-made vessels and coarse grit– and chaff-tempered wares used for handmade vessels (Algaze 1990:311). The first group of pottery was highly standardized and was at least finished on a wheel. Forms include cups, pot stands, bowls of all sizes, and jars (see Figs. 45 and 46). Sherds in this category were classified as specialist-

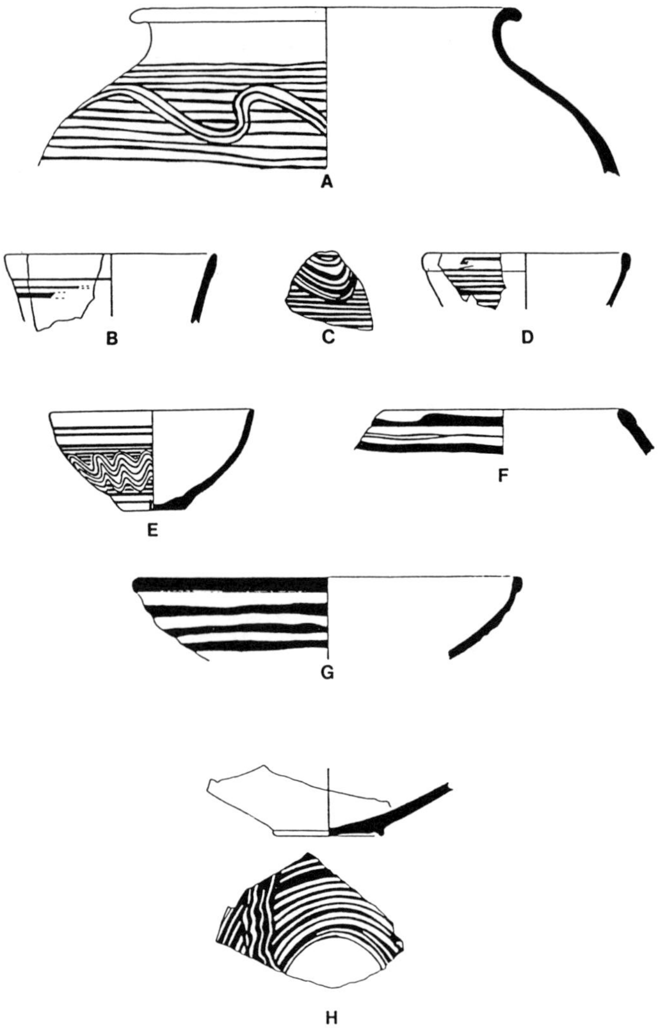

Fig. 46. Decorated wheel-made pottery from Kurban Höyük (scale 2:5).

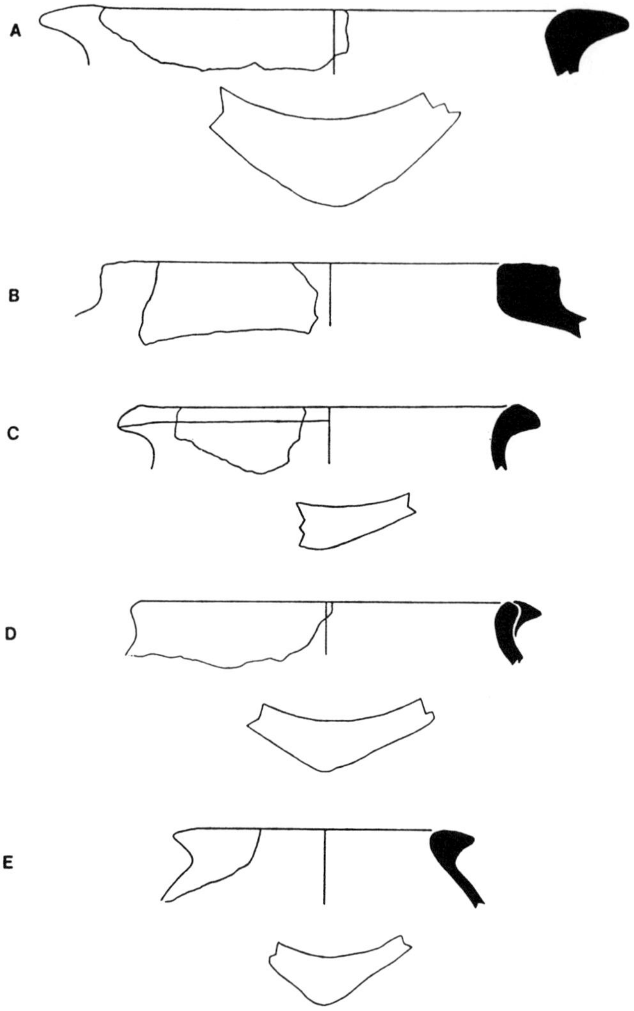

Fig. 47. Variation in hand-made vessels from Kurban Höyük (scale 1:5).(From Algaze 1990.)

produced because they exhibited closely spaced wheel marks resulting from production on a fast wheel.

Although no kilns were found at Kurban, a kiln workshop was found at the larger town of Lidar Höyük, 18 km upstream (Hauptmann 1982). This workshop consisted of some nineteen kilns and had a large quantity of ceramics associated with the kilns. Many of the wheel-made ceramic types from Kurban appeared superficially to be identical to those found next to the Lidar kilns. A neutron activation analysis is currently in progress, so it may be possible in the future to determine whether ceramics found at Kurban were in fact produced at Lidar (M. Evins, pers. comm.); regardless of whether the Kurban ceramics were produced at Lidar, it is likely that similar firing practices would have been employed. The association of these pottery types with a large-scale kiln workshop provides additional evidence that these types were produced by specialists.

The coarseware was used primarily for the production of lugged cooking pots, identified as such since they were often found in hearths and sometimes had fire marks (Algaze 1986; Figs. 47 and 48). Some medium and large bowls and storage jars were also made of this coarseware. Each diagnostic sherd appeared to be unique. The forms were so variable that

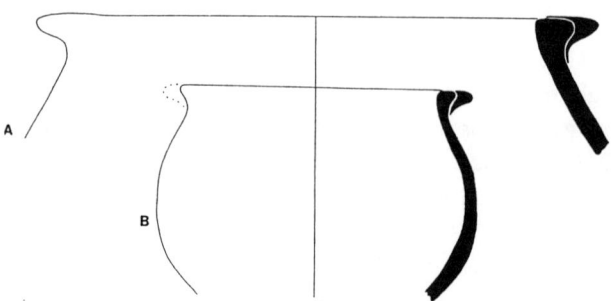

Fig. 48. Variation in hand-made vessels from Kurban Höyük (scale 2:5).

it was difficult to establish a typology; for this reason, I concluded that ceramics of this ware were probably made relatively informally, perhaps by households. Handmade vessels are often produced by specialists, but even specialist-produced handmade wares are relatively standardized compared with those produced by households (Benco 1988). It was the degree of variability in forms, rather than the fact that they were handmade, that led to the conclusion that pots from this group were produced in a relatively decentralized manner. These pots were apparently absent from the Lidar kiln assemblage.

Wheel-made pottery was well represented in all period IV phases, and the proportion of wheel-thrown to handmade pottery increased steadily throughout period IV. In the earlier phases, handmade pottery contributed 46 percent of the assemblage. By the final period of nucleation, handmade pottery made up only 32 percent of the assemblage. At the regional center of Tell Chuera in northeastern Syria, handmade pottery also declined in relative frequency (Orthmann 1986:69). The ceramic data suggests that households became increasingly reliant on ceramics produced by specialists. By the final phase of this period, households obtained almost all their ceramics from exchange networks, with the exception of cooking pots and the occasional bowl or storage jar.

The spatial distribution of wheel-made ceramics suggests that all households at the settlement utilized pottery produced by specialists. Wheel-made pottery was associated with all structures excavated, although more elaborate structures had a higher proportion of wheel-made pottery than did more modest structures.

Less information is available on the organization of pottery production than on consumption patterns. No workshops were found at the site, and only one part of the site yielded any evidence for ceramic production. The presence of ceramic slag toward the center of the small mound and saddle (areas C and F) suggests that a pottery kiln (or smelting area) may have been nearby. The limited evidence for production areas suggests that most residents at the site were consumers, but apparently not producers, of wheel-made, kiln-fired pottery.

Although the extensive workshop at Lidar indicates large-scale production specialization, available evidence from the Karababa Basin suggests that ceramic production was probably not centrally administered by the political elite. A second, smaller pottery workshop at Lidar was associated with a house rather than a public building (Hauptmann 1983:95–96). At Kurban, the ceramic slag was concentrated in a domestic area.

Ceramics may have been manufactured in a number of places, to judge from the presence of two separate workshops at the town of Lidar and possibly a third workshop at Kurban. Given the limited excavation of mid– to late third-millennium B.C. communities in this region, with broad horizontal excavations conducted only at Kurban, it is surprising to have found any ceramic workshops at all. The recovery of at least two workshops through relatively limited excavated samples suggests that ceramics were produced in multiple workshops and that ceramic production was not administered by the political elite. This interpretation is supported by the absence of textual references to ceramic production, collection, or distribution at the center of Ebla.

The tablets recovered from the Ebla palace indirectly provide insight into ceramic production and use in northern Mesopotamia during the mid–third millennium B.C. In this analysis, I use the Ebla tablets only to gain general insights into economic organization and cultural values in northern Mesopotamia, keeping in mind that interregional differences in economic organization may have existed. The Kurban region apparently did not fall under the control of Ebla in the mid–third millennium B.C. (Archi 1980:3), and it is unlikely that inhabitants of the two sites had any direct contact. Both the considerable distance between Kurban and Ebla (circa 180 km) and their asymmetric political rankings (Ebla was an urban center whereas Kurban was a much smaller rural site) argue against direct exchange between the two settlements. However, the ceramic assemblage from Ebla Palace G is similar to that of Kurban period IV (Algaze 1990:346), suggesting interaction between the two regions (although there were local differences). Some ceramics found in the palace apparently came from the Euphrates Valley (Mazzoni 1988:85), and texts indicate that Ebla had exchange relations with sites in the Euphrates Valley.

Another reason for caution in using the Ebla archives arises from uncertainty regarding the degree to which they represent the full range of economic activities carried out by the palace, particularly since publication of the tablets is still in progress. Nonetheless, the abundance of records and the wide range of regions mentioned in published texts indicate that Ebla archives provide a useful source of data for hypotheses on economic organization, both at Ebla and in other areas of the Near East.

The economic texts from Ebla list goods kept in storage areas, goods received by the palace, and goods sent from Ebla to other sites. Published economic texts from Ebla refer to containers (presumably made of clay) only in the course of describing the contents (oil, wine), with minimal information provided about the containers themselves. The lack of attention to ceramics probably reflects the fact that the political elite were not concerned with their production and distribution (e.g., Archi 1982:212, 216, 218), although ceramics were well represented in the palace (Mazzoni 1988).

In summary, available archaeological and epigraphic evidence suggests that although specialist-produced ceramic vessels were important in Syro-Mesopotamian exchange systems, their manufacture was not administered by the political elite. We note that at Kurban, even in the earliest village phases, wheel-thrown pottery produced by specialists was common, and wheel-made pottery became increasingly important through time.

Chipped Stone Production

Chipped stone artifacts provide the second data source on craft manufacture. Although the mid– to late third millennium B.C. is referred to as the "Early Bronze Age," 177 kg of chipped stone (5,000 pieces) were recovered from less than 330 m^2 in area C. The chipped stone assemblage was made almost entirely from flint, readily available from the Euphrates River and from limestone hills less than 2 km away (MacDonald 1986).

The chipped stone assemblage appears to represent an expedient industry (MacDonald 1986), and it is difficult to recognize even basic tool types. Tools probably used for similar purposes (e.g., scrapers) varied in blank forms (including flakes, chunks, and blades), location of working edge, and direction of retouch. The lack of standardization suggests household production, and the spatial distribution of tools and debitage resulting from stone tool manufacture support this conclusion. Debitage was recovered from each room excavated (as well as exterior deposits), indicating that all households under investigation produced most of their own stone tools. Approximately 70 percent of all chipped stone analyzed represents manufacturing debris. The high quantity and ubiquitous distribution of chipped stone debris, combined with the informal nature of the industry, suggests household production. In both of the subperiods of site expansion and nucleation, chipped stone debris from the residential quarters G and B indicated that every nonelite household at Kurban manufactured its own stone tools. Data on chipped stone production in the earliest two subperiods are not yet available, but analyses of chipped stone from the second two periods suggest that patterns of chipped stone production did not change through time.

Large prismatic blades, which are relatively difficult to produce, may have been an exception to this pattern of household stone tool production. Prismatic blades were relatively standardized in appearance. This fact, combined with the absence of large blade cores in parts of the site that were excavated, may indicate that some larger blades were manufactured by specialists.

In summary, the pattern of chipped stone production contrasts with that of pottery; available evidence indicates that most chipped stone tools were produced by households throughout the period.

Weaving and Metallurgy

Whereas pots and chipped stone were prevalent at Kurban but absent from economic records at Ebla, textiles and metals were almost archaeologically invisible at Kurban but were of clear economic importance in northwest Mesopotamia during this time, to judge from the textual evidence. Therefore, I consider evidence for textile production and metallurgy using both archaeological data from Kurban and supporting documentation from the Ebla archives.

The distribution of spindle whorls used to spin fibers into yarn provides one indicator of the organization of textile production at Kurban. The number of terra-cotta or stone spindle whorls at Kurban is low; only two could be positively identified, both recovered from an area with modest domestic architecture dating to the final part of the period. Their absence in other sectors of the site is surprising, given the extensive clearance of occupational remains. If spindle whorls were made of wood, as they are in the Near East today, we would not expect to find them even if they were widely used at the site. However, the recovery of two stone spindle whorls from a deposit dating to the final subperiod suggests that stone spindle whorls had not yet been entirely replaced by wooden ones. Thus, the absence of spindle whorls in most excavated deposits suggests that households did not spin their own yarn, a first step in textile production. Either yarn or textiles themselves may have been imported into these areas.

Given the lack of evidence at Kurban for spinning, it is noteworthy that garments and textiles were among the most frequently listed items in economic texts from Ebla (Pinnock 1984:22; for examples see Archi 1982:211 and Archi 1987:125). Detailed categories of colors, design, and quality of material were used to describe the textiles. At least some weaving took place in administered workshops. The records mention textile factories (Archi 1982:209), rations for state-supported weavers, and inventories of large quantities of garments in storage. References to garment expenditures indicate that substantial quantities were exported as trade items or were distributed as gifts to elites at other centers or as payments to workers (Archi 1982:208, 219). Tablets also record the delivery of garments to palace officials (Archi

1981:12; 1982:218). Textiles and metals are often listed in the same texts.

Metallurgy was at least partially administered, as indicated by the large quantities of unworked precious metals and the high number of metal objects delivered to the Ebla palace (Archi 1980:2), the records of metals in storage (Archi 1982:211), metal objects produced in a workshop (Archi 1982:216), and the records of metal and metal objects distributed (Archi 1981:3,5, 1982:209). At Kurban, however, metal objects were rare and confined to deposits associated with more elaborate architecture. Three copper pins were recovered from a street, in front of a relatively substantial house toward the center of the small mound. Area F, a sounding, yielded another copper pin and a copper ornament in deposits associated with a relatively massive wall. Even if metals were widely used, we would not expect metal objects to be well represented; because of the high value of the raw material, metal objects would generally not be intentionally discarded in domestic contexts. Although the sample size of metal objects is small, the uneven spatial distribution of metal objects reveals variability in consumption patterns within this rural site. A single crucible from the plowzone in area C provides the only evidence for metallurgy in period IV levels at Kurban (Yener 1990:403).

The detail with which textiles and metals are recorded, combined with the frequent references to them in texts, suggests that they were both highly valued. The Ebla archives reveal aspects of the elite political economy at a Near Eastern regional center and are not directly relevant to understanding nonelite production patterns or textile manufacturing at smaller sites such as Kurban. They do, however, reveal the importance of textiles within the North Mesopotamian economy during the mid–third millennium B.C.; although textile production in the private nonelite sector may have been organized very differently, textiles were probably highly valued. Attention to detail in describing the textiles suggests that subtle differences were significant in the social messages they conveyed and in the value of the textiles. The low density of spindle whorls at Kurban suggests that even nonelite households may have relied on specialists during this time. However, they probably utilized lower-quality cloth and obtained textiles from different sources than did the political elite, who apparently received some cloth from palace-sponsored weaving factories (Archi 1982:209).

Summary and Conclusions

The analysis of Kurban artifact assemblages shows that in this early state society considerable specialization existed among the rural nonelite population. Moreover, the Kurban sequence reveals change through time in the degree of household reliance on specialists, with households becoming increasingly reliant on specialists for ceramics. A study of animal production supports the conclusion from ceramic analysis that the economy became increasingly specialized through time (Wattenmaker 1987). These results are in accord with other studies that have asserted that production became increasingly specialized in early state societies, not only at centers but also at smaller sites (Johnson 1973, 1987; Blanton et al. 1982). As political reorganization occurred on a regional level, households became increasingly involved in a specialized economy. This shift in consumption patterns illustrates the dynamic nature of rural economies and suggests that rural household economies were linked to regional-scale political and economic systems.

Households at Kurban appear to have procured several items from specialists: ceramic cups, bowls, and jars, and possibly yarn or woven goods. However, they may have produced their own cooking pots and most stone tools. Textile production and metalworking may have been partially administered by the state, but most nonelite households probably did not receive goods from state-administered workshops.

The range of craft goods produced by specialists provides insights into factors guiding the organization of production and consumption patterns in the rural sector. Why would cups, bowls, and jars be produced by specialists and cooking pots and stone tools be produced by households?

Food-serving vessels have a relatively high degree of visibility when compared with stone tools and cooking pots (see Wobst 1977:328–330). They are items of social display, used when serving guests, and they therefore have symbolic significance. Ethnographically, food containers are often used as ethnic markers or items of competitive display (Hodder 1982). Food serving and consumption often accompany religious rituals, adding another dimension to their social significance.

In contrast to the public, social use of serving vessels, cooking pots and stone tools were probably used inside the home or courtyard and viewed largely by relatives. These household-produced goods seem to have played a minimal role in the communication system. By this time, metal had become an important display item in the Near East and may have replaced chipped stone as a medium for conveying social information such as rank. Ceramics of relatively high social visibility were made by specialists working in formal workshops, but their production does not appear to have been administered by the political elite. This finding may be related to the fact that ceramics are made from clay, which was readily accessible in the vicinity of Kurban. Although the social visibility of ceramics makes them appropriate media for conveying some categories of social information, such as group affiliation, the wide availability of clay would make them less powerful prestige symbols than craft goods made of scarcer materials, such as garments or metal objects.

Garments are of potentially even greater social visibility than ceramic vessels, and the raw materials used to produce textiles (flax, wool, or goat fibers) are limited. Moreover, textile production requires skill and intensive labor. Goods of high visibility made from relatively limited resources—such as textiles and metals—probably served to express rank (along with other kinds of information). The production of textiles and metal objects may have been at least partially supported by the political elite in an effort to control access to these symbols of prestige. Specialized production of these prestige goods may have served to restrict access to them to the elite, since nonspecialists could not duplicate the workmanship of skilled and well-practiced specialists (Rowlands 1973:594; Pollock 1983:19). Specialized production of these goods on the nonelite level may represent efforts by the nonelite population to reproduce the prestige goods used by the elite. Emulation of prestige goods by low-ranking groups has been documented through an analysis of grave goods from the Royal Cemetery of Ur (Pollock 1983).

In summary, nonelite households at Kurban appear to have manufactured goods for their own use if such goods were of minimal significance for bearing social messages. But they apparently obtained goods of greater social importance through exchange. The increased reliance on specialist-produced ceramics among the nonelite population may be related to political centralization, increasing social differentiation, and the increasing role of goods in the communication system as the society increased in size and socioeconomic diversity.

Some goods (such as sickle blades and large storage vessels) might require specialization regardless of their social significance, because of the skill involved in their manufacture. Ceramic vessels found in the Ebla storerooms were probably used as storage containers and perhaps for the transport of goods as well (Dolce 1988:37–38; Mazzoni 1988). Moreover, the need for large numbers of containers to transport goods such as oil or wine may have led to increased demand for ceramic jars. On the household level, however, the demand for specialist-produced goods appears to be closely related to their social significance, as well as to other considerations such as productive efficiency.

The results from Kurban suggest that the social visibility of goods played a key role in creating a demand for specialist-produced goods among both nonelite households and the elite, although the quality and quantities of the goods would be different for each social group, and only small quantities of prestige goods would end up in low-ranking households. For ceramics, the basic pattern of production and consumption was similar for both nonelite and elite contexts at Kurban: both social groups obtained most of their ceramics from workshops. Available evidence indicates that both the nonelite and elite populations at Kurban obtained textiles through exchange systems, although the elite presumably obtained textiles from different sources than the nonelite population.

The variability in production and consumption patterns for different categories of goods highlights the need for archaeologists to consider carefully the productive context and social uses of goods when selecting artifact categories for addressing specific research questions. Ceramics have been utilized to monitor ancient Near Eastern political economy (e.g., Johnson 1973; see R. Wright 1989:147–149, 152), but our results suggest that ceramics may not be as informative about mid-third millennium B.C. political economy in this part of the Near East.

The considerable degree of economic specialization in display goods from domestic contexts at Kurban underscores the fact that rural nonelite households were active participants in the material component of the social system. These results suggest that an understanding of household economic specialization in early state societies may be reached not only through exploration of the modern economic principles involved but also through efforts to understand the social significance of the goods to the people who used them.

Note

Excavations at Kurban Höyük were directed by Leon Marfoe. I wish to thank Paula Bienefield, Jim Blackman, Michelle Hegmon, Emlyn Meyers, Gil Stein, Henry Wright, and Melinda Zeder for comments on a previous version of this chapter. The manuscript benefited from comments by Guillermo Algaze, Glenn Schwartz, and an anonymous reviewer. I am grateful to Guillermo Algaze for unpublished ceramic data. Gil Stein and Kathy Ataman conducted much of the chipped stone analysis, and Gil Stein completed the graphics.

References Cited

Adams, Robert McC.
   1981 *Heartland of Cities.* University of Chicago Press, Chicago.
Algaze, Guillermo
   1986 The Ceramic Sequence. *Anatolica* 13:54–60.
   1990 The Ceramic Sequence and Small Finds. In *Town and Country in Southeastern Anatolia,* Vol. II: *The Stratigraphic*

Sequence at Kurban Höyük, edited by G. Algaze, pp. 211–395. University of Chicago Oriental Institute Publications, Vol. 110. Oriental Institute of the University of Chicago, Chicago.

1992 Excavations at Titriş Höyük, a Small Mid-Late Third Millennium Urban Center in Southeastern Anatolia, 1992. Manuscript on file, Department of Anthropology, University of California, San Diego.

Archi, Alfonso
1980 Notes on Eblaite Geography. *Studi Eblaiti* 2:1–17.
1981 Notes on Eblaite Geography II. *Studi Eblaiti* 4:1–17.
1982 About the Organization of the Eblaite State. *Studi Eblaiti* 5:201–220.
1987 More on Ebla and Kish. In *Essays on the Ebla Archives and the Eblaite Language,* Vol. 1, edited by C. H. Gordon, G. A. Rendsburg, and N. H. Winter, pp. 125–140. Eisenbrauns, Winona Lake, Ind.

Benco, Nancy
1988 Morphological Standardization: An Approach to the Study of Craft Specializaton. In *A Pot for All Reasons: Ceramic Ecology Revisited,* edited by C. Kolb and L. Lackey, pp. 57–72. Temple University, Philadelphia.

Blanton, Richard E., Stephen Kowalewski, Gary Feinman, and Jill Appel
1982 *Monte Alban's Hinterland,* Part I: *The Prehispanic Settlement Patterns of the Central and Southern Parts of the Valley of Oaxaca.* Museum of Anthropology, University of Michigan, Memoirs, No. 15. University of Michigan, Ann Arbor.

Dolce, Rita
1988 Some Aspects of the Primary Economic Structures of Ebla in the Third and Second Millenniums B.C.: Stores and Workplaces. In *Wirtschaft und Gesellschaft von Ebla,* edited by H. Hauptmann and H. Waetzoldt, pp. 35–45. Heidelberger Studien zum Alten Orient, Band 2. Heidelberger Orientverlag, Heidelberg, Germany.

Hauptmann, Harald
1982 Lidar Höyük, 1981. *Anatolian Studies* 32:17–18.
1983 Lidar Höyük, 1981. *Türk Arkeoloji Dergisi* 26:93–110.

Hodder, Ian
1982 *Symbols in Action: Ethnoarchaeological Studies of Material Culture.* Cambridge University Press, Cambridge.

Johnson, Gregory A.
1973 *Local Exchange and Early State Development in Southwestern Iran.* Museum of Anthropology, University of Michigan, Anthropological Papers, No. 51. University of Michigan, Ann Arbor.
1987 The Changing Pattern of Uruk Administration on the Susiana Plain. In *The Archaeology of Western Iran,* edited by F. Hole, pp. 107–139. Smithsonian Institution Press, Washington, D.C.

MacDonald, Mary
1986 The Chipped Stone Sequence. *Anatolica* 13:60–66.

Marfoe, Leon, and Michael Ingraham
1990 Area A. In *Town and Country in Southeastern Anatolia,* Vol. II: *The Stratigraphic Sequence at Kurban Höyük,* edited by G. Algaze, pp. 23–118. University of Chicago Oriental Institute Publications, Vol. 110. Oriental Institute of the University of Chicago, Chicago.

Mazzoni, Stefania
1988 Economic Features of the Pottery Equipment of Palace G. In *Wirtschaft und Gesellschaft von Ebla,* edited by H. Hauptmann and H. Waetzoldt, pp. 81–105. Heidelberger Studien zum Alten Orient, Band 2. Heidelberger Orientverlag, Heidelberg, Germany.

Orthmann, Winfried
1986 The Origin of Tell Chuera. In *The Origins of Cities in Dry-Farming Syria and Mesopotamia in the Third Millennium B.C.,* edited by H. Weiss, pp. 61–70. Four Quarters, Guilford, Conn.

Peacock, David P. S.
1982 *Pottery in the Roman World: An Ethnoarchaeological Approach.* Longman, London.

Pinnock, Frances
1984 Trade at Ebla. *Bulletin of the Society for Mesopotamian Studies* 7:19–36.

Pollock, Susan
1983 The Symbolism of Prestige. Ph.D. dissertation, Department of Anthropology, University of Michigan. University Microfilms, Ann Arbor, Michigan.

Rice, Prudence
1981 Evolution of Specialized Pottery Production: A Trial Model. *Current Anthropology* 22:219–240.
1987 *Pottery Analysis: A Sourcebook.* University of Chicago Press, Chicago.

Rowlands, Michael
1973 Modes of Exchange and the Incentives for Trade, with Reference to Later European Prehistory. In *The Explanation of Culture Change: Models in Prehistory,* edited by C. Renfrew, pp. 589–600. Duckworth, London.

Stein, Gil, and Patricia Wattenmaker
1990 The 1987 Tell Leilan Regional Survey: Preliminary Report. In *Economy and Settlement in the Near East: Analyses of Ancient Sites and Materials,* edited by N. Miller, pp. 8–18. MASCA Research Papers in Science and Archaeology 7 (supplement). MASCA, University Museum, Philadelphia.

Stone, Elizabeth
1990 The Tell Abu Duwari Project, Iraq, 1987. *Journal of Field Archaeology* 17:141–162.

Tosi, Maurizio
1984 The Notion of Craft Specialization and Its Representation in the Archaeological Record of Early States in the Turanian Basin. In *Marxist Perspectives in Archaeology,* edited by M. Spriggs, pp. 22–52. Cambridge University Press, Cambridge.

Wattenmaker, Patricia
1987 Town and Village Economies in an Early State Society. *Paléorient* 13:113–122.

1990 The Social Context of Specialized Production: Reorganization of Household Craft and Food Economies in an Early Near Eastern State. Ph.D. dissertation, Department of Anthropology, University of Michigan. University Microfilms, Ann Arbor, Michigan.

Weiss, Harvey
1983 Excavations at Tell Leilan and the Origins of North Mesopotamian Cities in the Third Millennium BC. *Paléorient* 9:39–52.

Wilkinson, Tony
1986 Environmental Change and Local Settlement History. *Anatolica* 13:69–76.
1990 *Town and Country in Southeastern Anatolia,* Vol. I: *Settlement and Land Use at Kurban Höyük and Other Sites in the Lower Karababa Basin.* University of Chicago Oriental Institute Publications, Vol. 109. Oriental Institute of the University of Chicago, Chicago.

Wobst, H. Martin
1977 Stylistic Behavior and Information Exchange. In *Papers for the Director: Research Essays in Honor of James B. Griffin,* edited by C. Cleland, pp. 317–342. Academic Press, New York.

Wright, Henry T., ed.
1981 *An Early Town on the Deh Luran Plain: Excavations at Tepe Farukhabad.* Museum of Anthropology, University of Michigan, Memoirs, No. 13. University of Michigan, Ann Arbor.

Wright, Henry, Richard Redding, and Susan Pollock
1989 Monitoring Interannual Variability: An Example from the Period of Early State Development in Southwestern Iran. In *Bad Year Economics: Cultural Responses to Risk and Uncertainty,* edited by P. Halstead and J. O'Shea, pp. 106–113. Cambridge University Press, Cambridge.

Wright, Rita
1989 The Indus Valley and Mesopotamian Civilizations: A Comparative View of Ceramic Technology. In *Old Problems and New Perspectives in the Archaeology of South Asia,* edited by J. Kenoyer, pp. 145–156. Wisconsin Archaeological Reports, Vol. 2. University of Wisconsin, Madison.

Yener, Aslihan
1990 The Small Finds. The Ceramic Sequence and Small Finds. In *Town and Country in Southeastern Anatolia,* Vol. II: *The Stratigraphic Sequence at Kurban Höyük,* edited by G. Algaze, pp. 397–410. University of Chicago Oriental Institute Publications, Vol. 110. Oriental Institute of the University of Chicago, Chicago.

Zeder, Melinda
1988 Understanding Urban Process through the Study of Specialized Subsistence Economy in the Near East. *Journal of Anthropological Archaeology* 7:1–55.

CHAPTER NINE

Village Economy and Society in the Jordan Valley: A Study of Bronze Age Rural Complexity

STEVEN E. FALCONER

DURING THE THIRD AND SECOND millennia B.C. the southern Levant (i.e., Palestine and Transjordan) witnessed the initial appearance of town life, its relatively brief abandonment, and its subsequent rejuvenation. The development of large towns in the Early Bronze (circa 3500–2300 B.C.) and Middle Bronze ages (circa 2000–1500 B.C.) is implicit evidence of a long era of urbanism associated with the Canaanites of the Old Testament and other historical sources. Currently prevailing archaeological interpretations hold that Canaanite cities exercised increasingly centralized economic and political functions as Bronze Age society developed to a zenith of pre-Roman urbanism by circa 1500 B.C. (Dever 1987).

The urbanization of Canaanite society is inferred almost entirely from the development of relatively large, often fortified, communities. These Bronze Age towns measured only a fraction of the size of contemporaneous cities elsewhere in the Near East (e.g., in Syria and especially Mesopotamia). The small scale of Canaanite "urbanism" *has* been acknowledged, but only as the natural result of its introduction from distant foreign sources (Lapp 1970; de Vaux 1971).

The theme of this chapter follows Clarke's observation that "ideas about the early stages of urbanism—as about many aspects of prehistory—are often distorted by too limited a set of models, derived from the better-known but atypical situations of the present day.... Archaeology offers an escape from this circularity by providing a vast and continuous time-depth of evidence for study, which stresses the great variety and variability of what have been called 'towns'" (1979:435).

A normative interpretation of Canaanite civilization simply as a scaled-down case of regional urbanism risks "an implicit, and therefore dangerous, assumption of the unity of all urban phenomena" (Adams 1966:10). In particular, it obscures the significance of unexpected *rural* expressions of social complexity, which may be intriguingly characteristic of many nonmetropolitan complex societies. We may do ancient Canaan greater justice, and expand our insight into preindustrial urbanism generally, by reframing Canaanite society in terms of rural complexity, rather than urban preeminence (see Falconer 1993). The nature of Bronze Age villages and their roles in this complex but predominantly rural society are illuminated by regional settlement patterns in Palestine and a localized case study of village economy and society in the Jordan Valley, particularly as seen at Tell el-Hayyat and Tell Abu en-Ni'aj.

Regional Chronology

The Levantine Bronze Age is divided into Early, Middle, and Late components (Table 11). The appearance of sedentary town life in Early Bronze I paralleled the rise of the First Dynasty of Egypt. The subsequent periods of Early Bronze II–III were marked by the growth of numerous sedentary communities atop the mounded *tell* sites of the southern Levant. This era was contemporaneous with the first centralized political authority in Egypt during Dynasties I–V. Likewise, Early Bronze II–III normally is interpreted as the first major expression of Canaanite urbanism (e.g., Richard 1987; Joffe 1991).

As the result of an ongoing debate on archaeological systematics, a bewildering mix of chronological designations has been applied to the time range circa 2300–2000 B.C. in the

Table 11. Bronze Age Chronology for the Southern Levant

Years B.C. (approximate)	Period
1200	
	Late Bronze
1500	
	Middle Bronze II C
1650	
	Middle Bronze II B
1800	
	Middle Bronze II A
2000	
	Early Bronze IV
2300	
	Early Bronze III
2650	
	Early Bronze II
3100	
	Early Bronze I
3500	

southern Levant. This span, referred to most commonly as Early Bronze IV (see discussion in Dever 1980), is characterized as an interlude of nonsedentary pastoral life between periods of urbanism and sedentary agriculture in Early Bronze II–III and the Middle Bronze Age (i.e., Middle Bronze II). Over roughly the same interval Egypt suffered through the First Intermediate Period, during which central political authority collapsed temporarily and international contacts waned (Weinstein 1975).

Following the First Intermediate Period, the dynasties of Egypt's Middle Kingdom reestablished political stability, and the southern Levant developed town life anew. The beginning of this era in Middle Bronze II A witnessed the rebirth of towns and cities, some reoccupying Early Bronze Age sites, some newly founded. Middle Bronze II B and C often are analyzed jointly as the apex of urban city-state development in the southern Levant prior to Roman imperial annexation (see Dever 1987).[1]

Following the Middle Bronze heyday of urbanism, the number and size of Canaanite towns and cities gradually declined during the Late Bronze Age (Gonen 1984). Whereas archaeological data reveal a particularly vibrant international trade that might have nurtured Levantine city life (Leonard 1989), historical texts document serious military incursions that doomed its continued growth, beginning with the expulsion of the Hyksos from Egypt circa 1500 B.C. and ending with the calamitous arrival of the Philistines circa 1200 B.C. (Merrillees 1986).

Measuring Urbanism and Ruralism

Recent compilations of settlement data from Israel and Jordan permit a broad macroscopic critique of prevailing concepts of Bronze Age urbanism. This chapter proposes that ancient settlement systems can be assessed according to the ability or inability of individual communities to provide for their own agricultural subsistence. "Urbanized" settlement systems incorporated communities with populations that exceeded the bounds of agricultural self-sufficiency. Conversely, "rural" villages in these settlement systems *were* agriculturally self-sufficient. These definitions permit the measurement of one aspect of the economic differentiation and interdependence of cities and villages that characterized early urbanized societies.

For the purposes of quantifying ancient agricultural potential, subsistence farming is assumed to have occurred within a sustaining area surrounding any given settlement. The population of an archaeological site can be estimated using the population densities of between 100 and 250 people per hectare reported in ethnographic literature on modern traditional farming villages in southwestern Asia (e.g., Gremliza 1962; Antoun 1972; Sumner 1972, 1979; Kramer 1980, 1982). Ancient productivity of wheat and barley is estimated from ethnographic data (e.g., Granott 1952; Lutfiyya 1966; Allan 1972; Watson 1978, 1979; Kramer 1980, 1982) and studies of Mesopotamian agricultural texts (e.g., Zaccagnini 1975). These data suggest mean subsistence requirements of 1.5 ha per person in regions of rainfall farming like the southern Levant. As an idealized construct for this chapter, sustaining areas are bounded at a radius of 3–4 km, based on Chisholm's (1968) estimates of transportation costs and productive return in traditional agrarian communities in Europe and Asia.

These analogues suggest that even under favorable conditions (i.e., a sparse population [100 persons/ha] and unrestricted access to a large sustaining area [radius = 4 km]) all Levantine settlements measuring 35 ha and larger would have depended on subsidiary villages for their agricultural well-being. They may be considered urban portions of "urbanized" settlement systems in which many communities were economically interdependent. At the other end of the spectrum, even under significant constraints (i.e., a dense population [250 persons/ha] and restricted access to a smaller sustaining area [radius = 3 km]), all settlements smaller than 4 ha could have supported themselves easily. They may be considered potentially independent rural elements of regional settlement systems. The remaining class of settlements, measuring between 4 and 34.9 ha, cannot be judged as agriculturally dependent or independent without reference to their local resource base on a case-by-case basis, an inquiry that is beyond the scope of this analysis (see discussion in Falconer 1987a:49–95).

Bronze Age settlement patterns are summarized on a regional basis using five basic measurements:

1. Site density: the number of sites occupied period by period per 100 km².
2. Population density: estimated using aggregate site area per 100 km².
3. Mean site area: calculated using all sites occupied during each period.
4. Urban population: estimated as the proportion of aggregate site area constituted by sites 35 ha and larger.
5. Rural site frequency: frequency of sites smaller than 4 ha.

When analyzed in this manner, Bronze Age settlement data from the southern Levant describe patterns of development in which cities tend to be geographically peripheral and growth is manifested by a proliferation of small villages, often well removed from these peripheral cities.

The Advent of Town Life in the Early Bronze Age

Data compiled by Joffe (1985) and Broshi and Gophna (1984) from several regional surveys in Palestine describe a trajectory of Early Bronze Age population growth and increasingly abundant settlements (Fig. 49). Joffe (1985) compares the spatial characteristics of Early Bronze I and II sites as they illustrate the growth of towns. Broshi and Gophna (1984) similarly discuss the sizes and distributions of Early Bronze II and III sites, primarily west of the Jordan River and north of the Negev Desert. Broshi and Gophna combine, rather than segregate, the data from these two periods. By doing so they present a "best case" portrait of the apogee of third-millennium urbanism "after the beginning of the Early Bronze Age III, ca. 2600 B.C." (Broshi and Gophna 1984:41). The following discussion also attributes combined Early Bronze II–III settlement data to Early Bronze III, but acknowledges this lumping as a potential source of inprecision. In particular, site and population densities are probably inflated.[2]

During Early Bronze I–III, settlement density grew noticeably while population density increased more modestly. Strikingly, these data describe virtually no change in the relative importance of populations in larger communities. Approximately half of Palestine's inhabitants remained in settlements larger than 7 ha through most of the Early Bronze Age. Significant change *is* noted in mean site size, which drops through this sequence. A drop in rural site frequency is de-

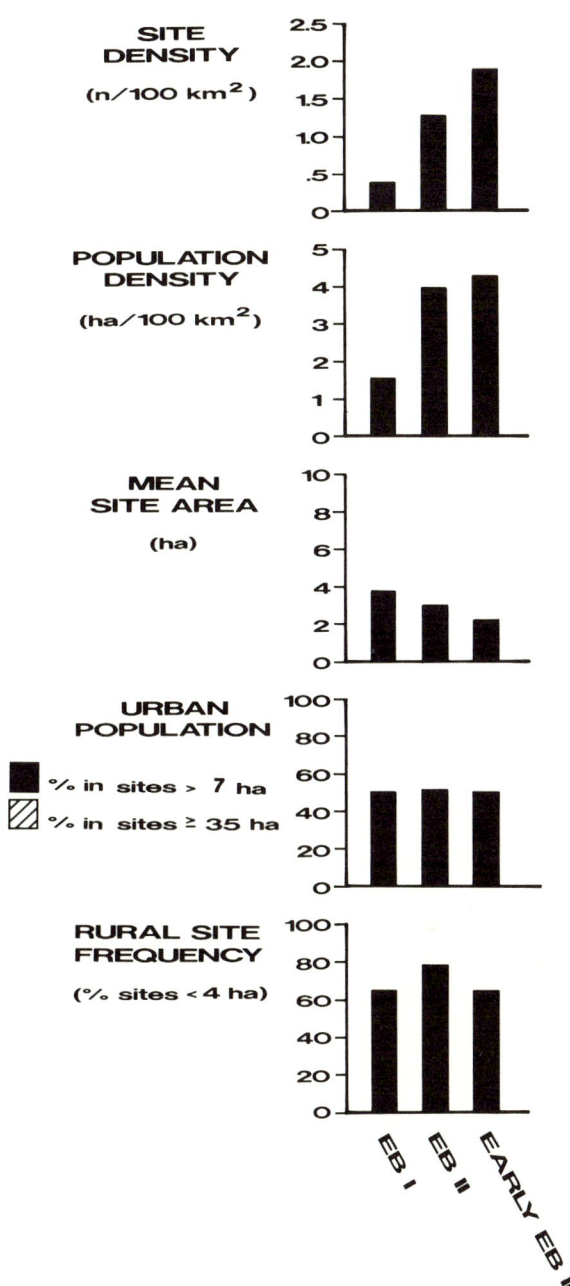

Fig. 49. Settlement data for Early Bronze Age Palestine. (Data from Broshi and Gophna 1984; Joffe 1985)

scribed by Broshi and Gophna's data, but this may be skewed by the problems of chronological lumping noted above.

Significantly, not a single site surpassed the 35-ha urban size threshold suggested here. This single observation does not deny the potential importance of large Early Bronze communities. However, when viewed collectively, these trends reveal a pattern of development that is expressed primarily in the countryside by increasingly abundant small villages.

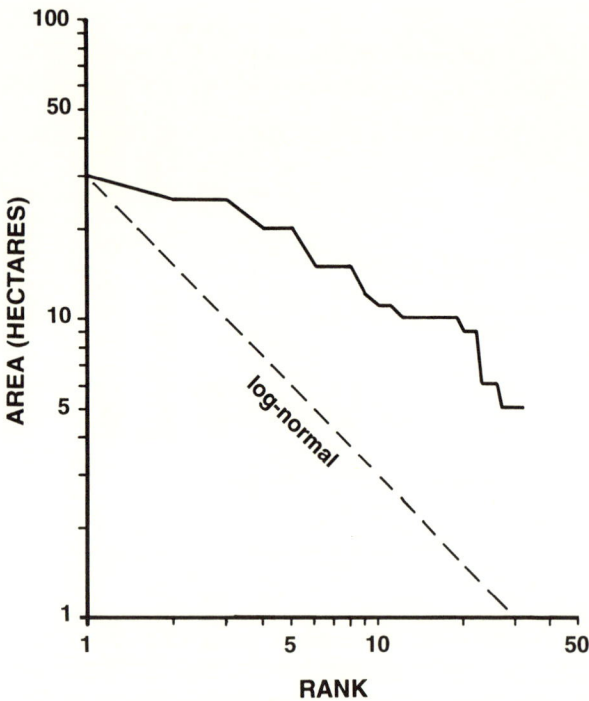

Fig. 50. Rank-size distribution of Early Bronze III sites in Palestine. (Data from Broshi and Gophna 1984.)

This situation is reiterated by an Early Bronze Age rank-size distribution (Fig. 50) that reflects very modest size differences between sites, the lack of large predominant settlements, and the probable lack of strong hierarchical integration among Early Bronze Age settlements (see the discussion of rank-size convexity in Johnson 1980).

Perhaps most important, the data invalidate the argument that the southern Levant experienced substantial urban nucleation during the Early Bronze Age (e.g., Kempinski 1978). Only five Early Bronze II–III settlements, inhabited by perhaps 20 percent of Palestine's sedentary population, grew to 20 ha or larger. Furthermore, the rank-size plot of Early Bronze II–III settlements has a pronounced convex distribution consistent with the limited preeminence of larger towns.

Early Bronze IV Pastoralized Society

The archaeological record for the Early Bronze IV period stands in stark contrast to the episodes of sedentary town life in Early Bronze II–III and Middle Bronze II. By circa 2200 B.C., virtually all *tell* sites in the region had been abandoned, and regional Early Bronze IV settlement patterns imply extensive use of land outside the present limits of dry farming (see also Evenari, Shanan, and Tadmor 1961:982, 1971:97).

The most influential working model of Early Bronze IV society (Prag 1974; Dever 1980) interprets cemeteries and isolated tombs as "the seasonal burying grounds for groups of semi-nomadic pastoralists" who "frequented the abandoned Early Bronze II–III *tell* sites during the latter part of Early Bronze IV but did not settle permanently" (Dever 1980:39, 42). A pervasive element of pastoralism at this time generally is seen as a consequence of urban collapse. Most social reconstructions hypothesize movements of pastoralists in a yearly round between lowland desert winter encampments and summer camps in the hill country of Palestine and Transjordan.

A more recent model for interpreting Early Bronze IV society *does* accommodate sedentism as well as pastoralism. Richard and Long (1989) argue that village agriculture was not abandoned but simply deemphasized. "Specialized" sedentary farming gave way to a mix of "despecialized" opportunistic crop cultivation and mobile animal husbandry. Although this model makes better use of the growing evidence for Early Bronze IV sedentary villages, it carries a strong connotation of a gradual adaptive shift that may not be sufficient to explain the sudden and dramatic dislocations into and out of the Early Bronze IV period. Most sedentary Early Bronze IV villages were not occupied over the Early Bronze III–IV transition, and we have no clear evidence that any persisted into Middle Bronze II. Therefore, the villages of Early Bronze IV cannot be viewed simply as despecialized products of the collapse of Early Bronze II–III towns. Nor can they be viewed as the village-level foundation to which larger, more specialized Middle Bronze II towns were added almost overnight. In other words, sedentary settlement in the Middle Bronze Age did not simply grow in situ but developed anew, particularly in the rural countryside of the southern Levant.

The Rejuvenation of Towns in the Middle Bronze Age

The most celebrated archaeological evidence for Middle Bronze Age society comes from reoccupied *tell* sites that were abandoned during Early Bronze IV. Traditionally, Middle Bronze II A is interpreted as a formative period during which Palestine developed the foundations for "reurbanized" society. This view holds that modest Middle Bronze II A towns expanded into massively fortified Middle Bronze II B–C cities during five centuries of considerable population increase and urban-based economic and political development (Mazar 1968; Kenyon 1973; Dever 1976). This urban preoccupation leads to interpretations of Middle Bronze II B–C urbanism in Palestine as comparable to that found elsewhere

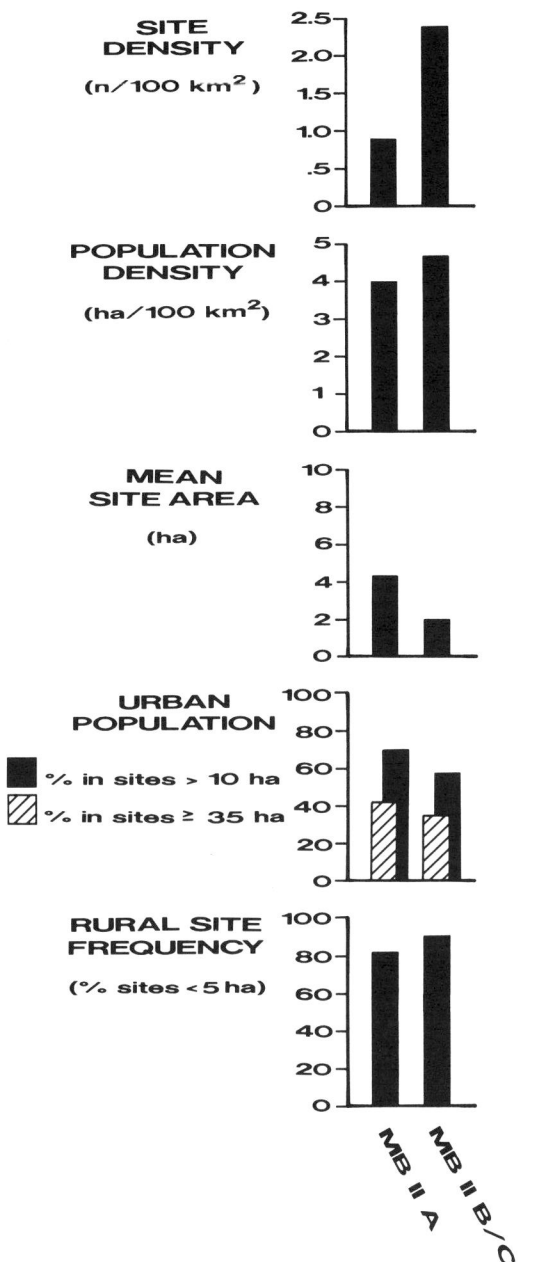

Fig. 51. Settlement data for Middle Bronze II Palestine. (Data from Broshi and Gophna 1986.)

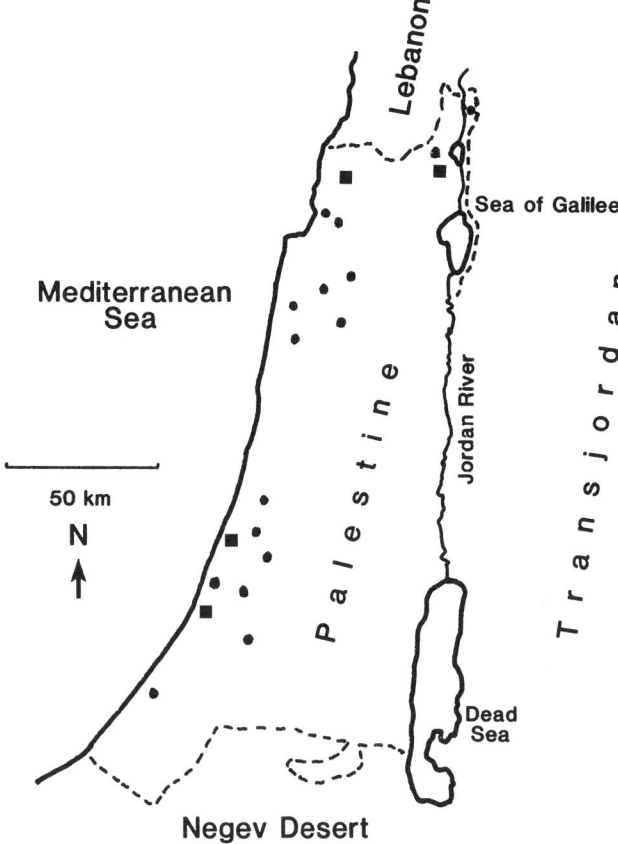

Fig. 52. Middle Bronze Age sites 10 ha and larger. Sites 35 ha and larger are indicated by squares. The dashed line encloses the region covered by the archaeological surveys. (Data from Broshi and Gophna 1986.)

in southwestern Asia (e.g., Syria; Gerstenblith 1983:115), despite obvious differences in scale and probable differences in structure.

Survey data compiled by Broshi and Gophna (1986) describe settlement trends very similar to but more pronounced than those of the Early Bronze Age (Fig. 51).[3] Middle Bronze II B–C site density increased noticeably over that of Middle Bronze II A, but this shift produced only a slight rise in population density. In addition, mean site size dropped sharply.

These characteristics indicate, as already suggested for the Early Bronze Age, a form of growth primarily involving smaller settlements. This inference is corroborated by a substantial drop in the relative size of Palestine's town and city populations, which was accompanied by the development of more abundant villages in the countryside. In a parallel study of regional settlement, Mabry (1984) shows that, by Middle Bronze II B–C, fully two-thirds of Canaanite communities measured 1 ha or smaller. In contrast to the Early Bronze Age, an appreciable Middle Bronze urban population *is* indicated. However, this population *declines* into the presumed urbanized florescence of Middle Bronze II B–C.

Levantine cities were neither sufficiently large nor centrally enough located to provide regional urban dominance (Fig. 52). A rank-size plot of Middle Bronze II B–C settlements (Fig. 53) shows a less convex distribution than the Early Bronze example, but it clearly departs from log-normal. This distribution reflects relatively low vertical integration between higher- and lower-ranking settlements. This convexity also may result from Early Bronze and Middle Bronze analyses

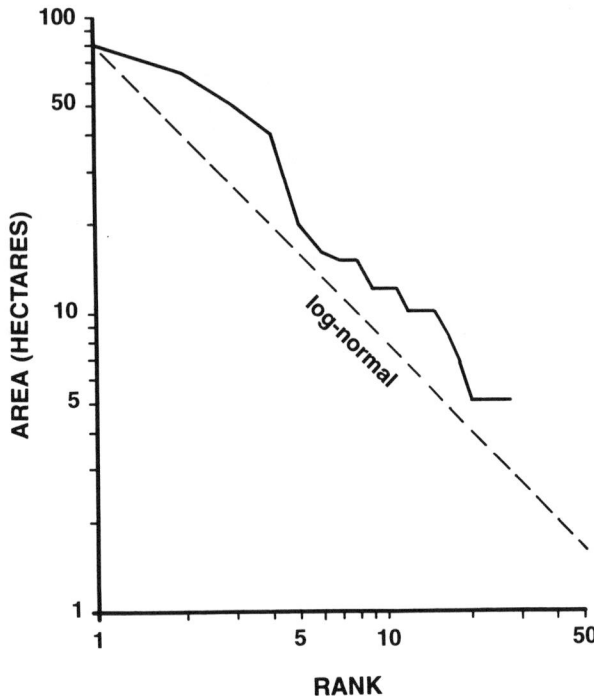

Fig. 53. Rank-size distribution of Middle Bronze II B–C sites in Palestine. (Data from Broshi and Gophna 1986.)

that (1) exclude external economic and political centers (e.g., in Egypt) or (2) pool relatively autonomous settlement systems or subsystems (Johnson 1980). Most important, these convex rank-size patterns cast doubt on normative expectations of cohesive urbanized settlement systems in Early and Middle Bronze Age Palestine.

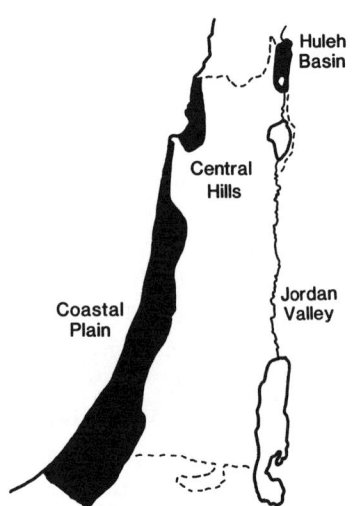

Fig. 54. Regions of Bronze Age settlement in Palestine. (Based on Broshi and Gophna 1984:Fig. 1, 1986:Fig. 1. The Huleh and Coastal Plain comprise their regions 3, 8, and 9.)

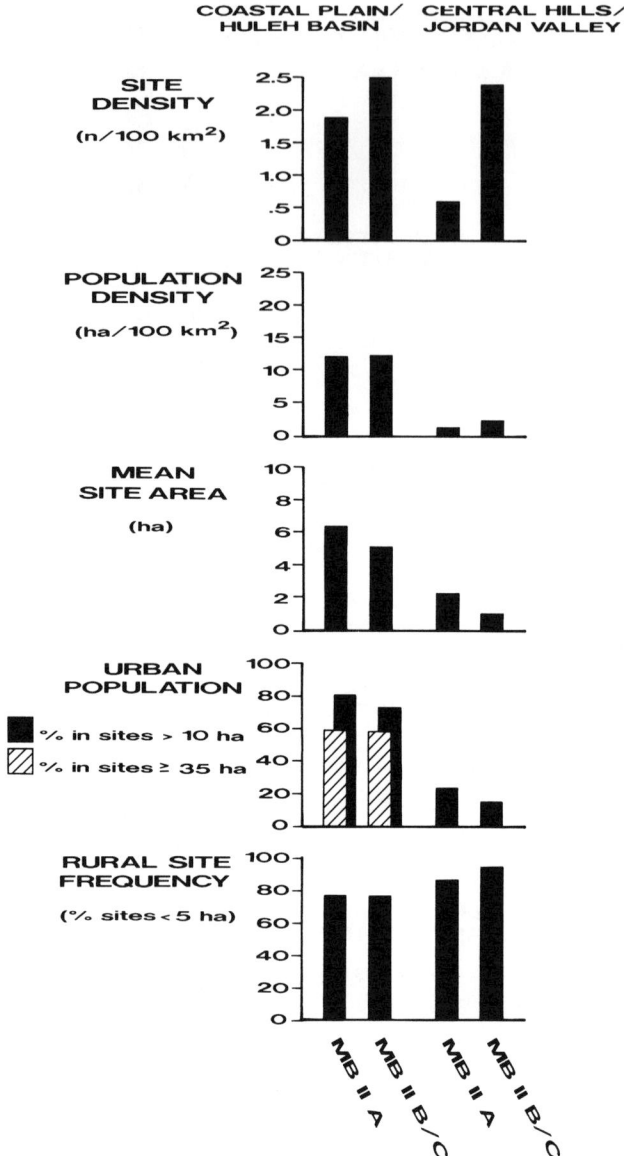

Fig. 55. Settlement data for central and peripheral regions of Middle Bronze II Palestine. (Data from Broshi and Gophna 1986.)

Figure 52 shows that Middle Bronze Age urban settlement was clearly a peripheral phenomenon restricted to the coastal plain and the Huleh Basin. Additional larger towns (i.e., 20 ha and larger) clustered along the coast and in the adjacent Jezreel Valley. Even modestly sized towns (i.e., 10 ha and larger) were exceedingly sparse over most of Palestine's interior landscape, accounting for only 15 percent of the inhabitants of the Central Hills and Jordan Valley by the end of the Middle Bronze Age.

Segregation of settlement data from Palestine's central and peripheral regions (Figs. 54 and 55) shows striking contrasts in pattern and scale of development. The coastal plain and Huleh

Basin encompass only 23 percent of surveyed hectarage in Palestine but contain an inordinate proportion of Middle Bronze Age aggregate site area (71 percent in Middle Bronze II A, 61 percent in Middle Bronze II B–C). Figure 55 shows population densities indicative of this contrast. It also demonstrates only very modest population growth in both regions through these periods.

The most significant arena of growth was a proliferation of settlements, primarily small villages, in the central hills and Jordan Valley. In these central regions, 95 percent of the settlements were rural by Middle Bronze II B–C, and mean size had fallen to 1 ha. Meanwhile, urban population in the peripheries dropped slightly, while rural settlement remained static.

The roles played by cities in these trends may be interpreted according to two generally opposing scenarios: (1) Although Bronze Age population growth did not occur in the immediate hinterlands of Levantine cities, the development of village life may have resulted from the instigation of rural settlement by urban authorities and landowners. This inference would play down the geographical separation of cities and villages in favor of theories of urban-driven rural economic development often derived from the modern world (e.g., Hudson 1969). (2) Alternatively, we might draw on ethnographic and textual accounts of the development of rural communities on a more autonomous basis. Particularly attractive models may be extrapolated from references to independent farming villages in the countryside surrounding ancient Ugarit (Heltzer 1976) and the corporate organization of traditional Middle Eastern agrarian communities that practiced communal ownership of *musha'* land until the early twentieth century (e.g., Kramer 1982:35; Atran 1986; see discussion in Chapter 1 by Schwartz and Falconer).

The remainder of this chapter considers Bronze Age village social and economic organization in light of more detailed evidence excavated from two small sites in the Jordan Valley. This evidence suggests that rural settlements were surprisingly complex, resilient in the face of urban growth and collapse, and potentially independent in a variety of economic capacities. In short, these two hamlets portray rural complexity and autonomy as fundamental characteristics of Canaanite society.

Tell el-Hayyat and Tell Abu en-Ni'aj

Excavated data from Tell el-Hayyat and Tell Abu en-Ni'aj (Fig. 56) illustrate the roles of Bronze Age villages as they affected, and were affected by, the reappearance of towns over the transition between the Early and Middle Bronze ages (Falconer and Magness-Gardiner 1984, 1989). Regional sur-

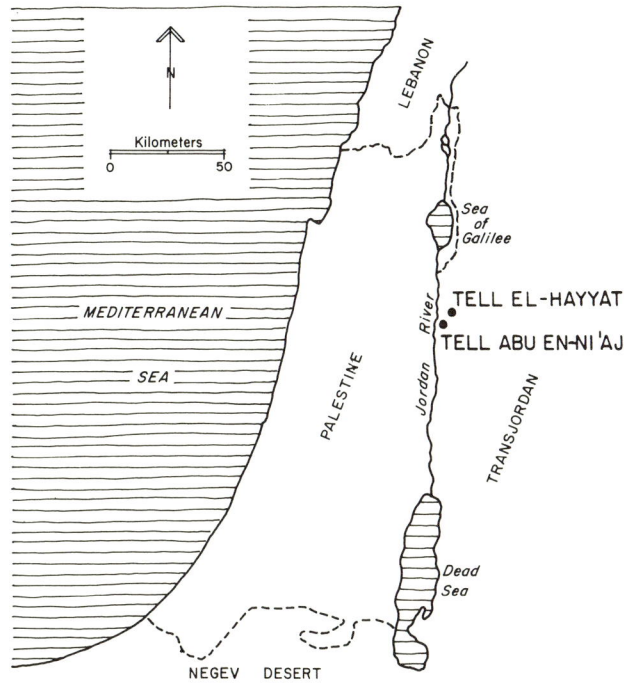

Fig. 56. Southern Levant, showing locations of Tell el-Hayyat and Tell Abu en-Ni'aj in the Jordan Valley.

veys (Glueck 1951:259; Mellaart 1962:144–145; Ibrahim, Sauer, and Yassine 1976) indicated that Ni'aj was inhabited only during Early Bronze IV, whereas Hayyat's occupation spanned Early Bronze IV and Middle Bronze II. Jointly they provide an unusual opportunity to study rural economy and

Table 12. Phases of Occupation at Tell el-Hayyat, Jordan[a]

Years B.C. (approximate)	Phase designation	Archaeological period
1500	Phase 1	Late Middle Bronze II C
1550		
	Phase 2	Middle Bronze II C
1650		
	Phase 3	Middle Bronze II B
1825–1800		
	Phase 4	Middle Bronze II A
1925		
	Phase 5	Early Middle Bronze II A
2000		
	Phase 6	Early Bronze IV
2150[b]		

[a]Periodization based on stylistic ceramic analysis.

[b]No earlier than 2200 B.C., no later than 2000 B.C.

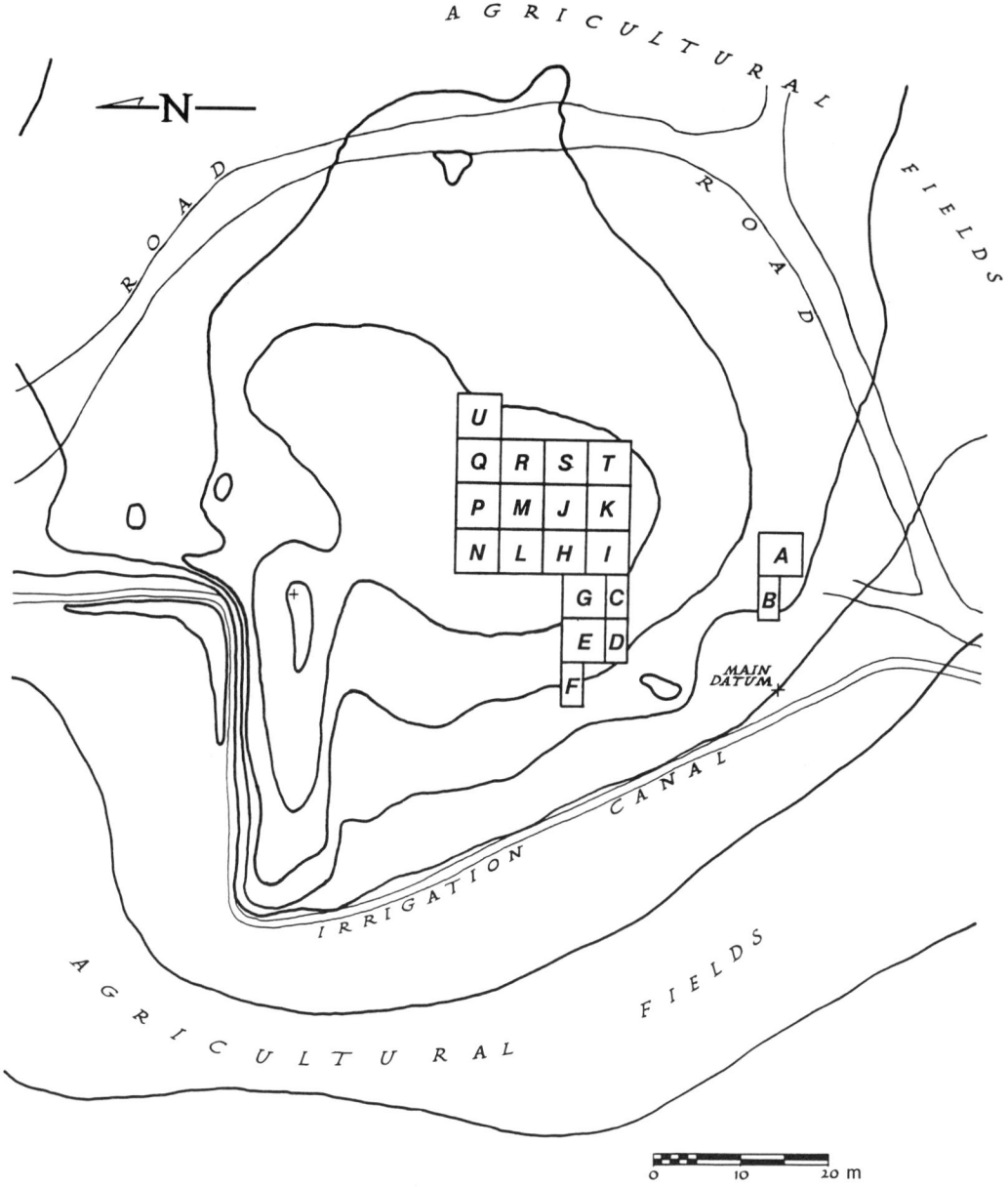

Fig. 57. Topographic plan of Tell el-Hayyat, showing areas of excavation. Contour interval = 1 m; main datum is approximately 240 m below sea level. (Drafted by Robert A. Erskine.)

social organization during periods of both pastoralism and renewed town life.

Floral and faunal assemblages from the two sites were expected to reflect the pervasive pastoralism of Early Bronze IV and a distinct shift to sedentary agriculture in support of Middle Bronze II city-states. These excavations have indeed illuminated village life but in ways unexpected at their outset. Tell Abu en-Ni'aj (2.5 ha in area) exemplifies the importance of sedentary agricultural villages during the supposedly "pastoralized" climax of the Early Bronze Age. Tell el-Hayyat (0.5 ha in area) provides a sequence of four Middle Bronze Age temples in a community that amounted to little more than a farming hamlet. Spatial patterns of animal bone deposition at Hayyat distinguish communal behavior centered on the temples from the domestic practices of individual households. Neutron activation analysis of ceramics from the Jordan Valley (Falconer 1987b) indicates specialized pottery production in both Early Bronze IV and Middle Bronze II A *villages,* not simply in larger urban centers. Collectively, these results suggest an unexpected degree of social and economic diversity and potential independence in such diminutive communities.

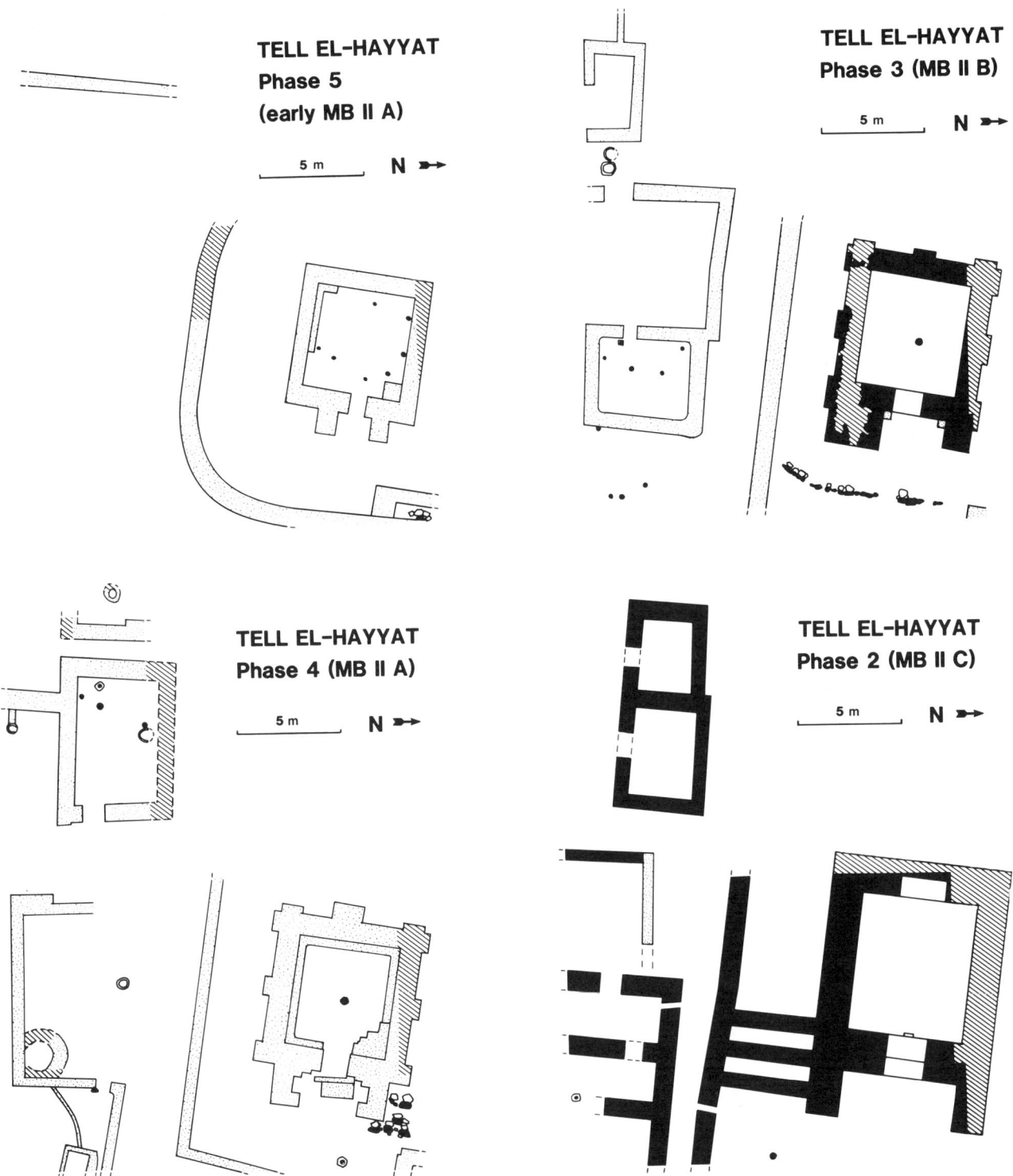

Fig. 58. Plan of Middle Bronze Age temple and domestic architecture, Tell el-Hayyat phases 5–2.

The results of three seasons of fieldwork at Tell el-Hayyat show that habitation there began in late Early Bronze IV and continued without interruption through six stratigraphic/architectural phases to late Middle Bronze II C (Table 12). Three seasons of excavation exposed 400 m² (8 percent of Tell el-Hayyat's surface area) and proceeded through 4.5 m of cultural deposition (Fig. 57).

Any architecture that might have been used in phase 6 was leveled for the subsequent construction of a small temple in early Middle Bronze II A (phase 5), which was the first in a stratified sequence of four mudbrick temples (phases 5–2) (Fig. 58). An enclosure wall was constructed in phase 5 and rebuilt in tandem with each subsequent temple. Aside from a single mudbrick wall toward the western edge of the village, domestic architecture was absent in phase 5. In phases 4–2, single- and multiple-room houses, walled courtyards, and alleyways outside the temple compound characterized the settlement. Isolated remnants of the phase 1 village included stone wall foundations and pebbled floors. This uppermost stratum has been disturbed considerably by Byzantine pits and the activities of modern farmers.

MIDDLE BRONZE AGE TEMPLES

Figure 58 presents four phase-by-phase plan views of the domestic and temple architecture excavated in squares C–T at Tell el-Hayyat. The remains of Hayyat's earliest temple consist entirely of molded earth foundations in a simple rectilinear plan with projecting anterior buttresses. The phase 4 temple is constructed entirely of mudbrick following a more elaborate plan with exterior pilasters and inset-offset niching framing the entry. The phase 3 temple is built on a single-course stone foundation placed directly on the remains of the lower mudbrick courses of phase 4. These two temples are almost identical in plan, aside from the phase 3 buttresses, which are rectilinear, asymmetric, and shifted to the temple's anterior corners. Mudbrick domestic construction in phases 4 and 3 gives way in phase 2 to single-course stone-founded houses and a temple that is simple in plan but rises above massive multicourse stone foundations. The phase 2 temple buttresses are augmented by foundations linking the temple to its enclosure wall.

These temples are interesting in and of themselves, but for this study we must consider why they were part of this tiny hamlet and what they suggest about Bronze Age rural settlement. Temples with this characteristic plan are known primarily from the larger towns and cities of Palestine, Syria (e.g., Ebla temple D [Matthiae 1981:130–132]), and the eastern Nile Delta (e.g., Tell el Dab'a [Bietak 1979:247–253])

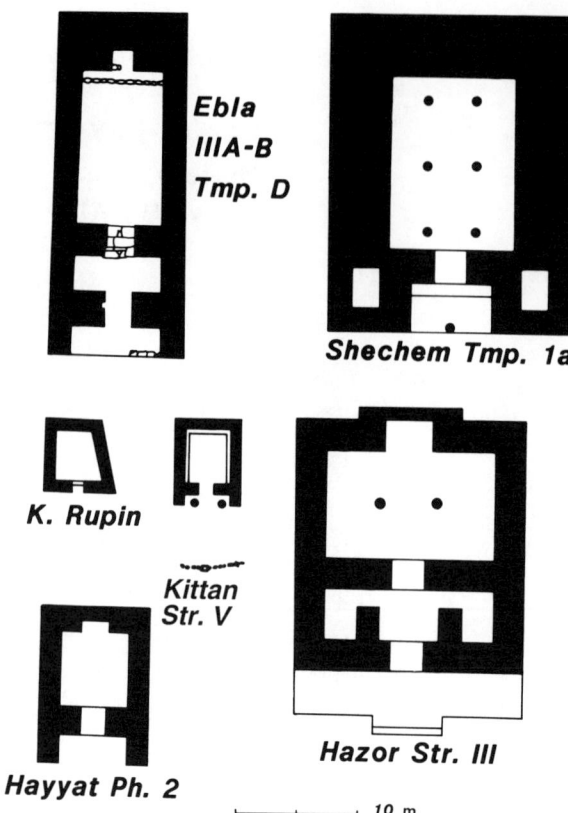

Fig. 59. Examples of temples in antis from towns and villages in Syria and the southern Levant: Shechem temple 1a (after Wright 1965:Fig. 41); Hazor stratum III area H temple (after Yadin 1972:76, Figs. 18, 19); Ebla III A–B temple D (after Matthiae 1981:130, Fig. 30); Kfar Rupin temple (after Gophna 1979:30, Fig. 2); Tell Kittan stratum V temple (after Eisenberg 1977:80); Hayyat phase 2 (after Falconer 1987a:Fig. 32).

(Fig. 59). These edifices normally are seen as manifestations of urban Canaanite religious institutions (e.g., Wright 1974). Therefore, the scaled-down temples at Hayyat present an intriguing juxtaposition of a presumably urban institution in a distinctly rural setting.

Interestingly, Tell el-Hayyat is not an isolated example of a village with temples. The sites of Kfar Rupin (Gophna 1979:29–30; site size < 0.4 ha) and Tell Kittan (Eisenberg 1977; site size = 0.8 ha) have temples of the same architectural form that are contemporaneous with Hayyat's phase 2 temple. Rupin and Kittan are among the very few excavated Middle Bronze Age villages in the southern Levant, and both are relatively near Tell el-Hayyat in the Jordan Valley.

These extremely small sites might be interpreted as isolated shrines or sanctuaries. Although Hayyat's phase 5 temple might be interpreted in this manner, abundant evidence of domestic architecture in Hayyat's subsequent phases and at Tell Kittan and Kfar Rupin suggests that these temples more commonly are central components of residential villages. All three of Tell Kittan's temples (strata V–III; Middle Bronze II B–C to Late Bronze I) were surrounded by houses (Eisenberg 1977:78–80). The Middle Bronze Age architecture at Kfar Rupin lies at the bottom of a fish pond and has been mapped but not excavated. Here again, the clear plan of a village temple is surrounded by the stone foundations of distinct, presumably domestic, buildings (Gophna 1979:Fig. 2).

Alternatively, Hayyat's sequence of increasingly labor-intensive architecture might exemplify long-term investment in rural development by urban estate owners or political authorities. However, administrative texts from the early second-millennium B.C. palace at Alalah, Syria (see Chapter 4 by Magness-Gardiner) reveal a striking pattern in which villages owned by the palace or urban elites were kept at subsistence level, while villages owned communally or leased from the palace had greater potential for improvement of their material well-being. The analogous situation around Alalah suggests that architectural improvements at Tell el-Hayyat are symptomatic of less, rather than more, absentee administration of Hayyat's affairs.

VILLAGE ECONOMY AND SOCIAL STRUCTURE

The architecture of Tell el-Hayyat provides a framework within which to explore the economic base and social structure of Bronze Age villages. Floral and faunal data are particularly valuable in highlighting subsistence practices and distinguishing patterns of household and communal behavior.

Soundings along the site perimeters of both Tell Abu en-Ni'aj and Tell el-Hayyat recovered abundant animal bones and carbonized plant macrofossils, especially from trash deposits. Preliminary analyses of these assemblages reveal more similarities than differences between the subsistence economies of Early Bronze IV Ni'aj and Middle Bronze II Hayyat. The sedentary nature of the Middle Bronze Age farmers at Tell el-Hayyat is indicated by their substantial domestic and temple architecture, by their use of plants requiring relatively long-term cultivation (e.g, grapes, olives; Fall 1983), and by the significant role of nonherding livestock in their animal husbandry (e.g., pigs; Metzger 1983a,b, 1984). The nature of Hayyat's Early Bronze IV settlement is less clear. However, evidence from Tell Abu en-Ni'aj provides supplementary information on Early Bronze IV village life.

Tell Abu en-Ni'aj is a low mound 1.5 km southwest of Tell el-Hayyat (see Ibrahim, Sauer, and Yassine 1976:49, 51). Brief test excavations revealed 2.5 m of cultural deposition containing three phases of Early Bronze IV mudbrick domestic architecture. The lower phases at Ni'aj were investigated in two deep soundings, and the upper phase was excavated in three broader exposures totaling 160 m². The cultural debris excavated from Abu en-Ni'aj is solely Early Bronze IV. The faunal assemblage for Ni'aj's upper phase reflects sedentary agriculture with a reliance on sheep, goat, cattle, and pig similar to that of Middle Bronze Age Tell el-Hayyat (phases 5–2) (Falconer and Magness-Gardiner 1989).

Table 13 shows raw frequencies of major plant taxa identified in flotation samples from the uppermost phase at Ni'aj and collectively from phases 5–2 at Hayyat (see also Fall 1983). All of these taxa are morphologically domesticated. In parallel with post-Neolithic economies in southwestern Asia, the remains of annual cereals and legumes are abundant. Perennial species that required multiyear cultivation also are abundant at both sites. These data do not show the distinctions in plant use expected between Early Bronze IV pastoralism and Middle Bronze II sedentary agriculture.

Likewise, Table 14 shows general intersite similarities in animal exploitation. The remains of sheep and goats, the primary herded species of southwestern Asia, are abundant at both sites (see also Metzger 1983a,b, 1984). More important, the remains of pigs, animals not suitable for pastoral herding, are surprisingly abundant at Tell Abu en-Ni'aj. Therefore,

Table 13. Floral Assemblages Excavated from Tell el-Hayyat and Tell Abu en-Ni'aj[a]

Taxon	Hayyat (N = 53)	Ni'aj (N = 16)
Wheat/barley	96	100
Pea	45	38
Lentil	43	44
Fig	81	81
Grape	15	50
Olive	29	13

[a]Data are expressed as percentages of flotation samples with each taxon present. N refers to the number of flotation samples analyzed. Data combined from all contexts, Hayyat phases 5–2, Ni'aj all phases.

Table 14. Faunal Assemblages Excavated from Tell el-Hayyat and Tell Abu en-Ni'aj[a]

Taxon	Hayyat (N = 35,000)	Ni'aj (N = 1000)
Sheep/goat	63	60
Pig	21	28
Cattle	11	11
Wild	5	1

[a]Data are expressed as raw bone element frequencies. N refers to the number of identifiable bone elements analyzed. Data combined from all contexts, Hayyat phases 5–2, Ni'aj all phases.

these floral and faunal data provide at least circumstantial evidence that the Early Bronze IV inhabitants of Abu en-Niʿaj practiced sedentary agriculture and animal husbandry.

More detailed phase-by-phase analysis of bone deposition at Hayyat suggests general trends in animal exploitation and, indirectly, interaction with animal distribution networks. Trends in these faunal data through the Middle Bronze Age provide a first indication of changing herd management practices and distribution of animal products, particularly in light of Zeder's (1991) exhaustive zooarchaeological analysis of Malyan, Iran, during the fourth through second millennia B.C. Zeder distinguishes "direct distribution" of animal products between herders and consumers from "indirect distribution" involving middleman distributors and managerial bureaucracies (1991:37–38). She argues that managed indirect networks strive for maximimum returns on each transaction. They tend to specialize in distributing species that produce large amounts of meat or secondary products per animal or carry the highest nutritional value per unit volume. Direct distributors (i.e., herders themselves) are more concerned with herd security and growth and therefore favor taxa with high reproductive rates.

Among the domestic taxa at Malyan and Hayyat, cattle carry the most meat per animal, whereas cattle and sheep provide more calories than goats. Pigs provide the highest caloric value but are poorly suited to large-scale centralized management or the seasonal movements of nonsedentary pastoralists. On the other hand, pigs have the highest reproductive capacity and, in light of all these factors, are particularly appropriate for small-scale management by individual households (see discussion in Zeder 1991:37–38).

Approximately 19 percent of Hayyat's total domesticated animal bone assemblage derives from chronologically unmixed primary depositional contexts, including surfaces, occupational debris and ash layers immediately above surfaces, and small domestic pits. When segregated by taxa, the data for phases 5–3 describe relative frequencies of bone deposition that remain fairly static for sheep and goats, increase for pigs, and dwindle for cattle (Table 15). The phase 2 data do not follow this pattern quite so nicely, perhaps because of the small sample size.

These general characteristics demonstrate that the villagers of Hayyat consistently emphasized consumption of sheep and goats, which are conducive to a variety of management schemes. Perhaps more significantly, their increasing supplementary emphasis on pigs, rather than cattle, may reflect greater household animal management and decreased participation in centrally managed distribution networks. As with the architectural characteristics described earlier, these data

Table 15. Relative Frequencies of Domesticated Animal Bones, Tell el-Hayyat[a]

	Sheep/goat	Cattle	Pigs	N
Phase 2	49	20	31	216
Phase 3	72	6	22	1,638
Phase 4	71	12	17	2,568
Phase 5	69	19	12	2,305

[a]Data are expressed as percentages based on raw bone element counts from primary contexts. N refers to identifiable bone elements.

accommodate an interpretation of developing village autonomy somewhat better than one of growing village-town interdependence.

Spatial patterns of bone deposition also distinguish household domestic behavior from village activities in the temple compounds. Table 16 segregates the data from the primary deposits discussed previously into temple contexts (temple interiors and temple courtyards within the enclosure walls), domestic interiors (i.e., roofed interior space), and domestic exteriors (including alleyways and unroofed domestic courtyards). These data reinforce some of the patterns already described.

The very modest amounts of bone from house interiors probably reflect greater cleaning of these floors than of temple

Table 16. Relative Frequencies of Domesticated Animal Bones Segregated According to Associated Architecture, Tell el-Hayyat[a]

	Sheep/goat	Cattle	Pigs	N
	Temple interior and courtyard			
Phase 2	63	14	22	76
Phase 3	92	4	4	1,109
Phase 4	83	11	6	1,903
Phase 5	83	16	2	1,574
	Domestic interiors			
Phase 2	52	17	31	29
Phase 3	10	15	76	62
Phase 4	11	13	76	126
Phase 5	NA	NA	NA	—
	Domestic exteriors			
Phase 2	43	27	30	88
Phase 3	34	10	56	438
Phase 4	47	12	41	488
Phase 5	39	26	35	717

[a]Data are expressed as percentages based on raw bone element counts from primary contexts. N refers to identifiable bone elements. NA, not available.

or alley surfaces. Despite small sample sizes, the high frequencies of pig bones found in house interiors in phases 4–2 may reinforce an interpretation of household consumption of swine products and possibly management of the animals themselves. This emphasis on pigs comes at the expense of sheep and goats, whose relative frequencies in phases 4 and 3 domestic interiors are very modest. Contrary to the sitewide pattern of cattle deposition discussed, cattle bones actually increase slightly through this sequence, suggesting that the general decline in cattle consumption pertains primarily to communal behaviors in and around Hayyat's temples, as discussed shortly. In contrast to these interior contexts, domestic exteriors provide a hodgepodge of relative frequencies that reveal few clear patterns of change other than a decrease in cattle and an increase in pigs during phases 5–3. Once again, the small sample of bones from phase 2 may obscure the later end of some of these trends.

The most dramatic spatial pattern is manifested by tremendously high rates of bone deposition and consistently high frequencies of sheep and goat bones found in temple interiors and courtyards. Akkadian texts from the Syrian site of Meskene (ancient Emar) suggest one form of communal behavior that could have caused this bone deposition. These texts describe the installation of an Entu priestess as the spouse of the Storm God at Emar in the late second millennium B.C. (Arnaud 1982, 1986). Participants included the king and elders of Emar, the designated Entu priestess and her family, prior Entu priestesses and priestesses of other cults, diviners, and singers. Activities over several days centered on sacrifices to the Storm God at temples, at temple gates, and at the home of the Entu priestess. Sacrifices usually involved a cow and several sheep, as well as beer, wine, and bread. In some cases, the participants feasted on cuts of meat after the meat had been offered in sacrifice, whereas at other times these goods were stored, apparently for later consumption (see Arnaud 1982:47–50). The strong correlation of sheep and goat bone deposition with Tell el-Hayyat's public architecture, which stands in distinct contrast to the emphasis on pigs in households and the mixed assemblages in domestic open space, may be an archaeological reflection of communal behavior practiced at temples such as that recorded at Emar.

Tell el-Hayyat and Tell Abu en-Ni'aj are most intriguing as counterintuitive examples of Bronze Age settlement in the countryside. Tell Abu en-Ni'aj is one of a growing number of sedentary villages reported in recent surveys (Ibrahim, Sauer, and Yassine 1976:51, 54) and excavations (Helms 1984, 1986; Rast and Schaub 1984; Richard and Boraas 1984) that formed a significant component of Early Bronze IV society, particularly in the Jordan Valley.

More detailed data from Tell el-Hayyat provide an intriguing glimpse into the inner workings of a Bronze Age agrarian hamlet. Faunal assemblages portray Hayyat as a community with a pronounced potential for agricultural independence. Most important, Hayyat's temples and the associated patterning of animal bone deposition may reflect the social means by which villages survived as autonomous communities or, at the very least, remained cohesive when responding to the demands imposed by urban authorities. The final aspect of this study, again based on unexpected evidence from Tell el-Hayyat, allows us to tie rural communities into regional economic networks, once more as surprisingly independent components.

Village Pottery Production and Exchange in the Jordan Valley

A case study of ceramics from Tell el-Hayyat, Tell Abu en-Ni'aj, and neighboring Jordan Valley sites elucidates local economic ties *between* sedentary Early Bronze IV and Middle Bronze II communities (Falconer 1987b). In particular, the economic roles of small villages before and after the reappearance of towns circa 2000 B.C. are inferred from an investigation of pottery production and exchange.

Excavation of the south slope at Tell el-Hayyat revealed a Middle Bronze II A (phase 4) pottery kiln (Falconer and Magness-Gardiner 1983:Pl. VI, 2, Pl. VII, 1, 1989:345, 1984: 54–55). More important, ceramic manufacturing debris was excavated from phases 5–2 in areas on the southern and western slopes, in and around the temple enclosures and, in greatest abundance, around the kiln itself. This evidence includes pottery wasters, tempered unfired potting clay, unfired clay toys, and handworked clay apparently prepared for potting. Some wasters are from failed storage jars, but the vessel types for most wasters cannot be identified. Two pottery wasters also were excavated from the uppermost phase of Tell Abu en-Ni'aj.

This evidence of pottery manufacturing provides a direct means of inferring patterns of Bronze Age pottery production and exchange in the Jordan Valley through the use of neutron activation analysis. Trace element "fingerprints" characteristic of potting clays used at Tell el-Hayyat and Tell Abu en-Ni'aj are compared with trace element data for pottery from these villages and other carefully selected Bronze Age sites. Statistical assessment of these data permits the inference of pottery manufacturing sites and patterns of distribution. Specifically, this study tests the normative expectations that (1) during the "pastoralized" Early Bronze IV period, manufacture of commodities (e.g., pottery) was decentralized, largely because of the collapse of towns as economic centers, and that (2) with the rejuvenation of town life in Middle Bronze II, towns reemerged as the manufacturing hubs of more centralized local and regional economic systems. The sampling of sites and pottery for this study follows directly from this problem orientation.

Selection of Sites

Although focusing on Tell el-Hayyat and Tell Abu en-Ni'aj, this analysis incorporates comparative pottery samples from Early Bronze IV settlements at Khirbet el-Hammeh, Dhahret Umm el-Marar, and Tell Umm Hammad. In addition to Hayyat, Middle Bronze II samples were analyzed from the village at Tell el-'Arba'in and the town sites of Ṭabaqat Faḥl (ancient Pella) and Tell es-Sa'idiyyeh (Fig. 60). Sherds from Hayyat to be included in the Early Bronze IV analysis were selected as often as possible from unmixed phase 6 contexts. Unfortunately, a paucity of large, clearly recognizable cooking pot and fineware sherds from phase 6 required the use of additional Early Bronze IV samples from phase 5. One clay sample was included from the upper phase at Tell Abu en-Ni'aj. This phase is most likely to be contemporaneous with Hayyat phase 6.

The time frame considered within the Middle Bronze Age was narrowed to Middle Bronze II A. Pottery samples from Tell el-Hayyat were drawn from phase 4, which provides abundant, stylistically homogeneous Middle Bronze II A ceramics. A single additional sample was chosen from a partially restorable Middle Bronze II A storage jar from phase 3. In addition to pottery samples, ten clay and waster samples from phases 5–2 at Tell el-Hayyat were analyzed. Half of these were from the Middle Bronze II stratum of interest, phase 4. The remaining samples were drawn from phases 5, 3, and 2. Unfortunately, no wasters or clays were excavated from phase 6.

Sample contemporaneity is less controllable among the collections from other sites. Middle Bronze II A sherds from Pella provided the only samples from stratified contexts. However, other sites provide many sherds large enough to indicate similar vessel shapes and, therefore, similar ceramic dates within each time period. Table 17 summarizes the sites and sources from which sherd samples were obtained.

SELECTION OF SAMPLE TYPES

Three vessel types were analyzed from the Early Bronze IV and Middle Bronze II A periods: cooking pots, storage jars, and fineware cups and bowls. Tables 18 and 19 specify the numbers and types of samples from each site. Both analyses

Fig. 60. Sites in the Jordan Valley that provided pottery samples for neutron activation analysis. Beth Shan is included only as a reference point. ●, Early Bronze IV; +, Middle Bronze II A.

incorporated the ten clay and waster samples excavated from Tell el-Hayyat.

Cooking pots from both periods were coarsely handbuilt and are good candidates for local manufacture because their weight and morphology preclude easy distribution. Early Bronze IV cooking pots in the Jordan Valley appear in closed globular forms that contribute to vessel strength but make them unsuitable for stacking and transport in quantity. Analyzed samples included everted-rim versions (e.g., Fig. 61, No. 1) from Hayyat, Ni'aj, and Marar plus holemouth specimens (e.g., Fig. 61, No. 2) from Marar and Hammad. Middle Bronze II A cooking pots from Hayyat have the flat bottoms and straight sides characteristic of the period (e.g., Fig. 61, No. 11). This form detracts from vessel strength, again rendering this an unlikely pottery type for regional exchange. The lone comparative Middle Bronze II A cooking pot specimen is an everted-rim pot from Sa'idiyyeh (Fig. 61, No. 3).

Small fineware vessels (Early Bronze IV "trickle-painted" cups and bowls, Middle Bronze II "carinated" bowls) were chosen as more likely candidates for centralized production and broader distribution. These vessels were wheel thrown (in Middle Bronze II A) or at least often wheel finished (in Early Bronze IV). They require greater skill to manufacture and more time for slipped (Middle Bronze II A) or painted (Early Bronze IV) decoration. They may also have been somewhat stackable and therefore could have been reasonable commod-

Table 17. Sites and Sources for Sherd Samples Used in Jordan Valley Case Study

Period/site	Excavation by Tell el-Hayyat Project	Provided by site excavator	Surface collection, Jordan Valley Survey	Surface collection, Tell el-Hayyat Project
Early Bronze IV				
Tell el-Hayyat	×			
Tell Abu en-Ni'aj	×			
Khirbet el-Hammeh			×	×
Dhahret Umm al-Marar			×	×
Tell Umm Hammad				
al-Gharbi		×		×
esh-Sharqi		×		
Middle Bronze II A				
Tell el-Hayyat	×			
Tabaqat Fahl (Pella)		×		×
Tell el-'Arba'in			×	×
Tell es-Sa'idiyyeh			×	×

Table 18. Early Bronze IV Sites and Pottery Samples

Site	Site size (ha)	Cooking pots	Storage jars	Fineware
Hayyat	<0.5	5	5	3
Ni'aj	2.5	2	4	3
Hammeh[a]	2.5	—	6	1
Marar[a]	1.0	2	5	2
Hammad[a]	[b]	2	4	2

[a]Site size estimates are based on maximum length and width as paced off by the author, fall 1985.

[b]Most Umm Hammad samples (seven of eight) come from a 2.0-ha component of Tell Umm Hammad el-Gharbi, part of the overall Early Bronze IV settlement estimated at 44.75 ha (Helms 1986).

Table 19. Middle Bronze II A Sites and Pottery Samples

Site	Site size (ha)	Cooking pots	Storage jars	Fineware
Hayyat	0.5	4	3	3
'Arba'in[a]	1.5	—	3	3
Pella[b]	7.0	—	5	1
Sa'idiyyeh[b]	8.0	1	2	3

[a]Site size estimate is based on maximum length and width as paced off by the author, fall 1985.

[b]Site sizes measured from topographic site maps (McNicoll, Hennessy, and Smith 1980:Fig. 1; Pritchard 1980).

ities for transport in bulk. Early Bronze IV cups were analyzed in both trickle-painted and unpainted versions (e.g., Fig. 61, Nos. 4 and 5). Middle Bronze II A fineware samples come from carinated bowls (e.g., Fig. 61, No. 6) and one double-handled juglet from Tell es-Sa'idiyyeh (not illustrated).

Storage jars from both periods were chosen because they were apparently produced in large quantities. Diagnostic storage jar sherds are abundant in the Hayyat collections and in surface collections from other Jordan Valley sites. Large jars, represented by Early Bronze IV ledge handles (e.g., Fig. 61, No. 8), Early Bronze IV everted and holemouth rims (e.g., Fig. 61, Nos. 9 and 10), and Middle Bronze II A rims (e.g., Fig. 61, No. 7), were the most abundant vessels in the Jordan Valley surface collections. Storage jars in both periods may have been transported from sites of manufacture to sites of deposition through exchange of the commodities they contained. Although it may be troublesome to distinguish exchange in commodities from exchange in pottery per se, analysis of storage jars is a ready means of incorporating Tell el-Hayyat and Tell Abu en-Ni'aj into local Bronze Age pottery production and distribution networks.

EXPECTED RESULTS

The apparent absence of local and regional economic centers (i.e., towns) in Early Bronze IV and the normative interpretation of a "reurbanized" Middle Bronze Age would lead one to expect accompanying contrasts in pottery production and exchange. Data from the Early Bronze IV period would be expected to show minimal economic integration between

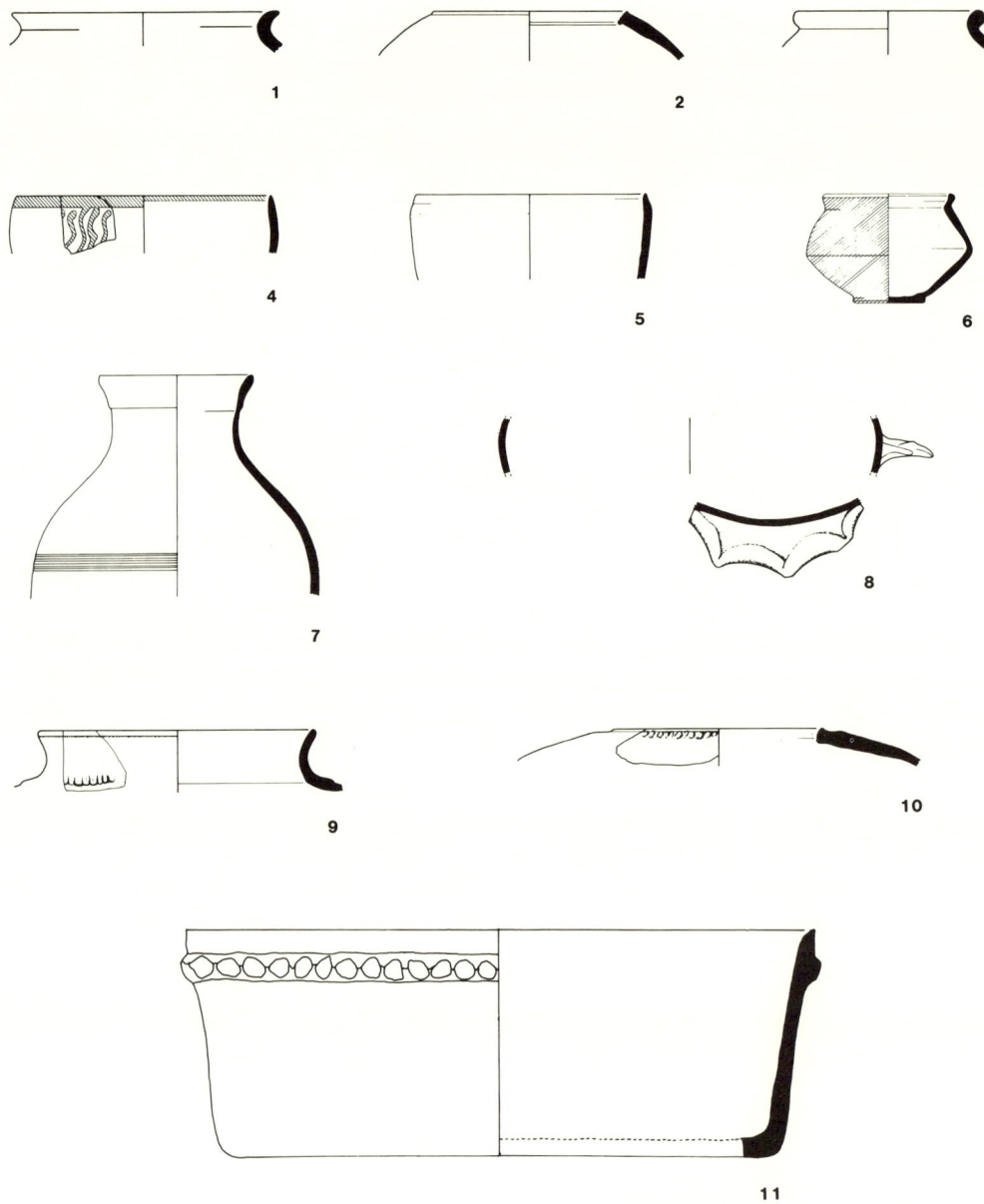

Fig. 61. Pottery types included in neutron activation analysis.

communities in the Jordan Valley. The production of all three vessel types considered here should be redundant from site to site. In contrast, Middle Bronze II A ceramic production was expected to be more centralized. Although smaller villages like Tell el-Hayyat might have produced cooking pots and perhaps jars, manufacture of finewares would have been concentrated in larger towns like Pella.

METHODS OF ANALYSIS

The relative concentrations of eleven trace elements (scandium, chromium, zinc, rubidium, cesium, samarium, europium, ytterbium, lutetium, tantalum, and thorium) were determined using neutron activation analysis. The trace element concentrations in each data set, expressed in parts per million, were standardized to Z scores for centroid-linkage cluster analysis of cases using Euclidean distance as a measure of similarity (Engelman 1983). Cluster analyses of the Early Bronze IV and Middle Bronze II A data measure relative similarities between clays and pots, permitting the grouping of pottery samples made from clays with very similar trace element signatures. The similar signatures within each cluster are hypothesized to indicate a common clay source and site of manufacture.

Cluster analysis, when used alone, lacks any statistical test of whether hypothesized pottery manufacturing groups are significantly different (Christenson and Read 1977; Aldenderfer and Blashfield 1978). In other words, a cluster analysis dendrogram may be subdivided into any number of clusters from 1 to *n*, based on an investigator's prior expectations and ability to explain subdivisions (see Wilson 1978:230–232). As a response to this problem, the results of each cluster analysis were investigated further using stepwise discriminant analysis. Discriminant analysis provides a complementary statistical means of *measuring* differences between hypothesized clusters (Lachenbruch 1975; Morrison 1976). The stepwise discriminant analyses conducted here calculate an F statistic in pairwise tests of differences between group means (Jennrich and Sampson 1983).

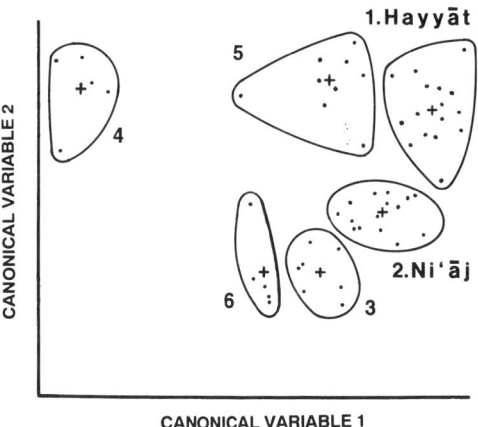

Fig. 62. Discriminant analysis scatter plot of Early Bronze IV samples and groups.

RESULTS AND IMPLICATIONS

This pilot study explores village pottery production using a modest preliminary data base. Not surprisingly, it suggests that Bronze Age pottery was manufactured at a variety of sites in the Jordan Valley. However, there are unexpected patterns in these data that suggest the importance of specialized rural pottery manufacture in periods both with and without large towns and the nodes of exchange they might have provided.

The Early Bronze IV cluster analysis produced seven major clusters that were used as defined strata for a follow-up stepwise discriminant analysis (see discussion of methods in Falconer 1987a:273–313). The first two canonical discriminant functions produced by this analysis account for 96 percent of the variance when these data are recombined into six discriminant analysis groups (Fig. 62 and Table 20). The means for these groups differ significantly from one another at the 99 percent confidence level.

The samples within groups 1 and 2 suggest manufacture at Tell el-Hayyat and Tell Abu en-Niʻaj, respectively, based on the inclusion of seven of Hayyat's clay and waster samples in group 1 and the co-occurrence in group 2 of clay samples from Niʻaj and Hayyat with the majority of pottery samples from Abu en-Niʻaj. The manufacturing locales for groups 3–6 remain conjectural for lack of appropriate clay or waster samples, although suggestions have been offered elsewhere (Falconer 1987b).

The pottery in group 1 includes samples only from Tell el-Hayyat, providing evidence for local manufacture of cooking pots and perhaps storage jars but no indication of distribution of vessels from Hayyat to other sites. On the other hand, one Hayyat clay sample and the Niʻaj clay sample are associated with specimens of all three vessel types from Tell Abu en-Niʻaj, as well as jars and cups sampled from three other sites. This combination provides at least circumstantial evidence of local pottery manufacture, probably at Abu en-Niʻaj,

Table 20. Early Bronze IV Pottery Groups as Inferred from Stepwise Discriminant Analysis ($N = 57$)[a]

1. Hayyat	2. Niʻaj	3	4	5	6
4 TH clays	1 AN clay	4 KH jars	4 DM jars	1 HG CP	1 DM CP
5 TH wasters	1 TH clay	2 TH jars	1 HS jar	3 HG jars	1 DM jar
5 TH CPs	2 AN CPs	1 AN cup (TP)		2 HG cups	1 DM cup
2 TH jars	3 AN jars			1 TH jar	1 AN jar
	2 AN cups (1 TP)			1 KH jar	1 Kh jar
	1 TH jar (TP)			1 DM CP	
	3 TH cups (3 TP)				
	1 DM cup (TP)				
	1 KH cup				

[a]The sample types are labeled according to the site from which they were excavated or collected: AN, Niʻaj; DM, Marar; HG, Umm Ḥammad el-Gharbi; HS, Umm Ḥammad esh-Sharqi; KH, Hammeh; TH, Hayyat. CP, cooking pot; TP, trickle-painted vessel.

and transport of jars (and their contents?) and cups (most of them trickle painted) to other settlements in the Jordan Valley.

The possibility of specialized production of trickle-painted pottery at Tell Abu en-Ni'aj may be in keeping with the production role proposed for the nearby village of Tell 'Artal. Neutron activation analysis of pottery samples from 'Artal, 'En-Hanatziv, and Megiddo, all located west of the Jordan River, suggests "the existence of a potter's workshop where products were manufactured for distribution throughout the Beth-shan area" (Hess 1984:57). Hess offers only the impressionistic and untestable explanation that "an inspired craftsman," presumably at 'Artal, "specialized in producing decorative designs that stood out against the background of monotonous decoration characteristic of the period" (1984:57). However, given the similar results of these two studies, a more intriguing possibility is that manufacture of such energy-intensive specialized products, normally expected in urban settings, may have taken place in new locales in the countryside during Early Bronze IV, a period that lacked large central places altogether.

The Middle Bronze II cluster analysis revealed six major clusters that were defined as strata for subsequent discriminant analysis. The first two canonical discriminant functions produced by this analysis account for 96 percent of the variance when these data are recombined into four discriminant analysis groups, with one outlying sample (Fig. 63 and Table 21). The means for these groups differ significantly from one another at the 99 percent confidence level, except for groups 7 and 10, which differ significantly at the 95 percent confidence level.

Manufacture of the pottery in group 7 may be attributed to Tell el-Hayyat based on the presence of nine Hayyat clays and wasters. The final clay sample failed to group well with other samples and was excluded from the final discriminant analysis. The location of one jar specimen from Pella (P603) far from the other Middle Bronze II samples in Figure 63 suggests its manufacture from a clay source unlike any other reflected in

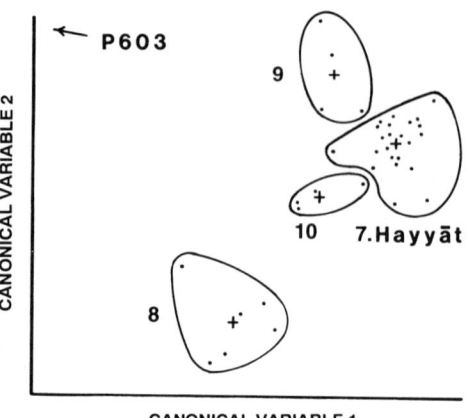

Fig. 63. Discriminant analysis scatter plot of Middle Bronze II samples and groups.

this analysis. The samples in group 7 suggest that Hayyat's potters produced all three Middle Bronze vessel types considered here and distributed jars and well-crafted carinated bowls to other modest villages (e.g., Tell el-'Arba'in) and quite possibly to some of the larger towns in the Jordan Valley (e.g., Pella) as well.

This ceramic analysis suggests that even during the urban hiatus of Early Bronze IV some communities (perhaps including Tell Abu en-Ni'aj and Tell 'Artal) were parts of a differentiated economic network engaged in specialized manufacture at the village level. The Middle Bronze II patterns of exchange imply the active participation of small settlements (e.g., Tell el-Hayyat) in the production of pottery and its distribution to substantially larger towns. Therefore, diversified rural pottery production may have persisted into, rather than arisen in, the urbanized Middle Bronze Age.

The clearest implication here is that Bronze Age villages like Tell el-Hayyat and Tell Abu en-Ni'aj were not necessarily dependent on large central places for manufactured commodities. Rather, in some economic capacities, the countryside of the southern Levant was marked by surprisingly self-sufficient

Table 21. Middle Bronze II A Pottery Groups as Inferred from Stepwise Discriminant Analysis ($N = 37$)[a]

7. Hayyat	8	9	10	Exotic
3 TH clays	1 S CP	2 P jars	2 TA bowls	1 P jar
6 TH wasters	1 S jar	2 TH bowls	1 P bowl	
4 TH CPs	2 S bowls		1 S jar	
3 TH jars	1 S double-handled juglet			
1 TH bowl	1 P jar			
1 P jar				
3 TA jars				
1 TA bowl				

[a]The sample types are labeled according to the site from which they were excavated or collected: P, Pella; S, Sa'idiyyeh; TA, 'Arba'in; TH, Hayyat. CP, cooking pot.

and important *small* places that actually contributed these commodities to much more imposing towns and cities.

Conclusions

This study can only begin to portray Canaanite village life from the vantage points of Tell el-Hayyat and Tell Abu en-Ni'aj in the Jordan Valley. However, even the first elements of this portrait suggest several facets of village independence and complexity not in keeping with orthodox interpretations of small communities in complex societies (see discussion in Chapter 1 by Schwartz and Falconer). Levantine urbanism in the Early and Middle Bronze ages provides a striking regional backdrop for Hayyat and Ni'aj because of two general characteristics. First, Canaanite towns and cities were concentrated largely in the coastal and northern peripheries of Palestine, leaving an overwhelmingly rural heartland in the central hill country and Jordan Valley. Second, demographic growth and the establishment of new settlements occurred primarily in this central heartland, where villages and hamlets proliferated.

To the extent that they typify Canaanite villages, Tell Abu en-Ni'aj and especially Tell el-Hayyat suggest that this landscape was populated by rural communities that were economically more diversified and potentially independent, and socially more complex, than most models of early complex societies would anticipate. Tell Abu en-Ni'aj is one among several newly investigated Early Bronze IV settlements that demonstrate the importance of sedentary villages amid an otherwise largely pastoralized social milieu. Tell el-Hayyat's identity as a sedentary agrarian hamlet is hardly surprising, but several lines of evidence *do* reveal unexpected aspects of village life during the heyday of Middle Bronze Age urbanism. Faunal data suggest increased household livestock management and potentially decreased interaction with more centralized sources of animal products at a time when managerial bureaucracies should be burgeoning. Likewise, Hayyat's village architecture and associated spatial patterns of animal bone deposition reveal rural manifestations of public institutional behavior normally ascribed to towns and cities. Finally, analysis of local pottery production and distribution suggests the potential significance of village manufacture of a variety of vessel types, including finewares probably made by craft specialists, during both the collapse of urbanism in Early Bronze IV and its peak in Middle Bronze II.

Some of this evidence, such as the rural character of Bronze Age demographic growth and the development of Hayyat around its temples, could be attributed to urban investment in the countryside. However, the bulk of the data encourage interpretation of Canaanite villages as potentially independent, perhaps autonomous, communities more in keeping with free or leased settlements around ancient Ugarit or traditional communal landowning villages in the recent Middle East. This view of the countryside argues that Bronze Age society in the southern Levant merits archaeological attention not because of its relatively modest peripheral cities but because of the intriguingly unexpected expressions of rural complexity in its villages. In response to Clarke's (1979) appeal for an escape from normative archaeological interpretation, we may argue that the distinction of Canaanite civilization lies not in its similarity to more metropolitan societies elsewhere but in the complex village life that may distinguish it from those societies and challenge us to reinterpret early complex society on its own, often counterintuitive, terms.

Notes

Special thanks go to my research partners, Pat Fall, Bonnie Magness-Gardiner, and Mary Metzger, for their contributions in data and ideas over the years of the Tell el-Hayyat Project. Glenn Schwartz and this volume's anonymous reviewer suggested numerous helpful revisions. The neutron activation analysis summarized here was conducted at the University of Arizona in the Laboratory of Traditional Technology, Department of Anthropology, and the Gamma Ray Analysis Facility, Department of Space Sciences. Laboratory directors Michael Schiffer (LTT) and William Boynton (GRAF) and laboratory supervisor Dolores Hill (GRAF) provided abundant aid and encouragement, for which I am very grateful.

Fieldwork at Tell el-Hayyat was conducted in 1982, 1983, and 1985 in cooperation with the Department of Antiquities, Hashemite Kingdom of Jordan, and with the generous assistance of the American Center of Oriental Research, Amman. Financial support was provided by the Department of Antiquities, the National Endowment for the Humanities, the National Geographic Society, the Wenner-Gren Foundation for Anthropological Research, the University of Arizona Foundation, the University of Arizona's Department of Anthropology, and the Endowment for Biblical Research. Additional considerations were provided by the Royal Jordanian Airline.

Early Bronze IV surface sherds from Tell Umm Hammad for the Jordan Valley case study were provided courtesy of Svend Helms and Alison Betts. Middle Bronze II A sherds excavated from the "West Cut" at Pella were donated by Robert H. Smith. Samples from the East Jordan Valley Survey were obtained through the courtesy of Moawiyah Ibrahim, James Sauer, Khair Yassine, and the Department of Archaeology, Jordan University. This loan was expedited with the help of Robert Erskine.

1. Many studies, including this one, have abandoned Middle Bronze I nomenclature owing to the confusion generated by the taxonomic debate mentioned previously (cf. Dever 1987).

2. In addition to the urban and rural size classes described, Joffe's (1985) class of sites greater than 7 ha is retained here. Broshi and Gophna's (1984) data are reorganized accordingly.

3. Broshi and Gophna (1986) group data for sites less than 5 ha, and rural site frequencies are presented here accordingly. The proportion of aggregate area in sites larger than 10 ha is used as a tertiary measure of populations in large settlements.

References Cited

Adams, Robert McC.
1966 *The Evolution of Urban Society: Early Mesopotamia and Prehispanic Mexico.* Aldine, Chicago.

Aldenderfer, Mark S., and Roger K. Blashfield
1978 Cluster Analysis and Archaeological Classification. *American Antiquity* 43:502–505.

Allan, William
1972 Ecology, Techniques and Settlement Patterns. In *Man, Settlement and Urbanism,* edited by P. J. Ucko, R. Tringham, and G. W. Dimbleby, pp. 211–226. Duckworth, London.

Antoun, Richard T.
1972 *Arab Village: A Social Structural Study of a Transjordanian Peasant Community.* Indiana University Press, Bloomington.

Arnaud, Daniel
1982 Les textes suméro-accadiens: un florilège. In *Meskene-Emar,* edited by J.-C. Margueron, pp. 43–51. Editions Recherche sur les Civilisations, Paris.
1986 *Emar: textes sumeriens et accadiens.* Editions Recherche sur les Civilisations, Paris.

Atran, Scott
1986 Hamula Organisation and Masha'a Tenure in Palestine. *Man* 21:271–295.

Bietak, Manfred
1979 Avaris and Piramesse, Archaeological Exploration in the Eastern Nile Delta. *Proceedings of the British Academy* 65: 225–290.

Broshi, Magen, and Ram Gophna
1984 The Settlements and Population of Palestine During the Early Bronze Age II–III. *Bulletin of the American Schools of Oriental Research* 253:41–53.
1986 Middle Bronze Age II Palestine: Its Settlements and Population. *Bulletin of the American Schools of Oriental Research* 261:73–90.

Chisholm, Michael
1968 *Rural Settlement and Land Use.* Aldine, Chicago.

Christenson, Andrew C., and Dwight W. Read
1977 Numerical Taxonomy, R-Mode Factor Analysis, and Archaeological Classification. *American Antiquity* 42: 163–179.

Clarke, David L.
1979 Towns in the Development of Early Civilization. In *Analytical Archaeologist: Collected Papers of David L. Clarke,* edited by N. Hammond et al., pp. 435–443. Academic Press, New York.

Dever, William G.
1976 The Beginning of the Middle Bronze Age in Syria-Palestine. In *Magnalia Dei: The Mighty Acts of God. Essays on the Bible and Archeology in Memory of G. Ernest Wright,* edited by F. M. Cross, W. E. Lemke, and P. D. Miller, Jr., pp. 3–38. Doubleday, Garden City, N.Y.
1980 New Vistas on the Middle Bronze I Horizon in Syria-Palestine. *Bulletin of the American Schools of Oriental Research* 237:35–64.
1987 The Middle Bronze Age: The Zenith of the Urban Canaanite Era. *Biblical Archaeologist* 50:149–177.

Eisenberg, Emmanuel
1977 The Temples at Tell Kittan. *Biblical Archaeologist* 40:77–81.

Engelman, L.
1983 Cluster Analysis of Cases. In *BMDP Statistical Software, 1983,* edited by W. J. Dixon et al., pp. 456–463. University of California Press, Berkeley and Los Angeles.

Evenari, Michael, L. Shanan, and N. Tadmor
1961 Ancient Agriculture in the Negev. *Science* 133:979–996.
1971 *The Negev: The Challenge of a Desert.* Oxford University Press, London.

Falconer, Steven E.
1987a Heartland of Villages: Reconsidering Early Urbanism in the Southern Levant. Ph.D. dissertation, Department of Anthropology. University of Arizona, Tucson. University Microfilms, Ann Arbor, Mich.
1987b Village Pottery Production and Exchange: A Jordan Valley Perspective. In *Studies in the History and Archaeology of Jordan,* Vol. 3, edited by A. Hadidi, pp. 251–259. Routledge and Kegan Paul, London.
1993 The Development and Decline of Bronze Age Civilization in the Southern Levant: A Reassessment of Urbanism and Ruralism, in *Development and Decline in the Mediterranean Bronze Age,* edited by C. Mathers and S. Stoddart. Sheffield Academic Press, Sheffield, England.

Falconer, Steven E., and Bonnie Magness-Gardiner
1983 The 1982 Excavations at Tell el-Hayyat. *Annual of the Department of Antiquities, Jordan* 27:87–104.
1984 Preliminary Report of the First Season of the Tell el-Hayyat Project. *Bulletin of the American Schools of Oriental Research* 255:49–74.
1989 Bronze Age Village Life in the Jordan Valley: Excavations at Tell el-Hayyat and Tell Abu en-Ni'aj. *National Geographic Research* 5:335–347.

Fall, Patricia L.
1983 La flore. Pp. 309–310 in Steven E. Falconer and Bonnie Magness-Gardiner, Recherches archéologiques à Tell el-Hayyat dans le nord de la vallée du Jourdain, 1982–1983. *Syria* 60:306–310.

Gerstenblith, Patricia
1983 *The Levant at the Beginning of the Middle Bronze.* American Schools of Oriental Research Dissertation Series, No. 5. American Schools of Oriental Research, Winona Lake, Ind.

Glueck, Nelson
  1951 Explorations in Eastern Palestine IV. *Annual of the American Schools of Oriental Research* 25–28.

Gonen, Rivka
  1984 Urban Canaan in the Late Bronze Period. *Bulletin of the American Schools of Oriental Research* 253:61–73.

Gophna, Ram
  1979 A Middle Bronze II Village in the Jordan Valley. *Tel Aviv* 6:28–33.

Granott, Abraham
  1952 *The Land System in Palestine: History and Structure.* Eyre and Spottiswoode, London.

Gremliza, F. G. L.
  1962 *Ecology of Endemic Diseases in the Dez Irrigation Pilot Area.* Development and Resources Corporation, New York.

Helms, Svend W.
  1984 Excavations at Tell Umm Hammad esh-Sharqiya in the Jordan Valley. *Levant* 16:35–54.
  1986 Excavations at Tell Umm Hammad, 1984. *Levant* 18:25–50.

Heltzer, Michael
  1976 *The Rural Community in Ancient Ugarit.* Ludwig Reichert Verlag, Wiesbaden, Germany.

Hess, Orna
  1984 Middle Bronze I Tombs at Tel 'Artal. *Bulletin of the American Schools of Oriental Research* 253:55–60.

Hudson, John C.
  1969 A Location Theory for Rural Settlement. *Annals of the Association of American Geographers* 59:365–381.

Ibrahim, Moawiya, James Sauer, and Khair Yassine
  1976 The East Jordan Valley Survey, 1975. *Bulletin of the American Schools of Oriental Research* 222:41–66.

Jennrich, R., and P. Sampson
  1983 Stepwise Discriminant Analysis. In *BMDP Statistical Software, 1983,* edited by W. J. Dixon, et al., pp. 519–537. University of California Press, Berkeley and Los Angeles.

Joffe, Alexander H.
  1985 Settlement Patterns and Social Organization in Early Bronze I and II Canaan. Paper presented at the symposium "New Perspectives in Early Bronze Age Society," at the Annual Meeting of the American Schools of Oriental Research, Anaheim, Calif.

Johnson, Gregory A.
  1980 Rank-Size Convexity and System Integration: A View from Archaeology. *Economic Geography* 56:234–247.

Kempinski, Aharon
  1978 *The Rise of an Urban Culture.* Israel Ethnographic Society Studies, No. 4. Israel Ethnographic Society, Jerusalem.

Kenyon, Kathleen
  1973 Palestine in the Middle Bronze Age. In *Cambridge Ancient History,* third edition, Vol. 2, Part 1, edited by I. E. S. Edwards, C. J. Gadd, N. G. L. Hammond, and E. Sollberger, pp. 77–116. Cambridge University Press, Cambridge.

Kramer, Carol
  1980 Estimating Prehistoric Populations: An Ethnoarchaeological Approach. In *L'Archéologie de l'Iraq du début de l'époque Néolithique à 333 avant notre ère,* edited by M.-T. Barrelet, pp. 315–334. Editions du CNRS, Paris.
  1982 *Village Ethnoarchaeology: Rural Iran in Archaeological Perspective.* Academic Press, New York.

Lachenbruch, P. A.
  1975 *Discriminant Analysis.* Hafner, New York.

Lapp, Paul W.
  1970 Palestine in the Early Bronze Age. In *Near Eastern Archaeology in the Twentieth Century,* edited by J. A. Sanders, pp. 101–139. Doubleday, Garden City, N.Y.

Leonard, Albert, Jr.
  1989 The Late Bronze Age. *Biblical Archaeologist* 52:4–39.

Lutfiyya, A. M.
  1966 *Baytin: A Jordanian Village.* Mouton, Paris.

Mabry, Jonathan B.
  1984 Political and Economic Centralization in the Northern Central Hill Country of Palestine During Middle Bronze II. Paper presented at the symposium "Economy and Society in the Middle Bronze Age of the Levant," at the Annual Meeting of the American Schools of Oriental Research, Chicago.

McNicoll, Anthony W., J. Basil Hennessy, and Robert H. Smith
  1980 The 1979 Season at Pella of the Decapolis. *Bulletin of the American Schools of Oriental Research* 240:63–84.

Matthiae, Paolo
  1981 *Ebla: An Empire Rediscovered.* Doubleday, New York.

Mazar, Benjamin
  1968 The Middle Bronze Age in Palestine. *Israel Exploration Journal* 18:65–97.

Mellaart, James
  1962 Preliminary Report on the Archaeological Survey in the Yarmuk and Jordan Valley for the Point Four Irrigation Scheme. *Annual of the Department of Antiquities, Jordan* 6–7:126–157.

Merrillees, Robert S.
  1986 Political Conditions in the Eastern Mediterranean during the Late Bronze Age. *Biblical Archaeologist* 49:42–50.

Metzger, Mary C.
  1983a Faunal Remains at Tell el-Hayyat: Preliminary Results. Pp. 98–99 in Steven E. Falconer and Bonnie Magness-Gardiner, The 1982 Excavations at Tell el-Hayyat, *Annual of the Department of Antiquities, Jordan* 27:87–104.
  1983b La faune. P. 310 in Steven E. Falconer and Bonnie Magness-Gardiner, Recherches archéologiques à Tell el-Hayyat dans le nord de la vallée du Jourdain, 1982–1983. *Syria* 60:306–310.
  1984 Faunal Remains at Tell el-Hayyat: Preliminary Results. Pp. 68–69, in Steven E. Falconer and Bonnie Magness-Gardiner, Preliminary Report of the First Season of the Tell el-Hayyat Project. *Bulletin of the American Schools of Oriental Research* 255:49–74.

Morrison, D. F.
　1976　*Multivariate Statistical Methods,* second edition. McGraw-Hill, New York.

Prag, Kay
　1974　The Intermediate Early Bronze–Middle Bronze Age: An Interpretation of the Evidence from Transjordan, Syria and Lebanon. *Levant* 6:69–116.

Pritchard, James B.
　1980　*The Cemetery at Tell es-Sa'idiyyeh, Jordan.* University Museum Monograph No. 41. University Museum, University of Pennsylvania, Philadelphia.

Rast, Walter, and R. Thomas Schaub
　1984　Preliminary Report of the 1981 Expedition to the Dead Sea Plain, Jordan. *Bulletin of the American Schools of Oriental Research* 254:35–60.

Richard, Suzanne
　1987　The Early Bronze Age. The Rise and Collapse of Urbanism. *Biblical Archaeologist* 50:22–43.

Richard, Suzanne, and Roger S. Boraas
　1984　Preliminary Report of the 1981–82 Seasons of the Expedition to Khirbet Iskander and Its Vicinity. *Bulletin of the American Schools of Oriental Research* 254:63–87.

Richard, Suzanne, and Jesse Long
　1989　Specialization-despecialization: A Model to Explain Cultural Change and Continuity at the End of the Early Bronze Age, ca. 2350–2000 B.C. Paper presented at the Annual Meeting of the American Schools of Oriental Research, Anaheim, Calif.

Sumner, William M.
　1972　Cultural Development in the Kur River Basin, Iran. Ph.D. dissertation, Department of Anthropology, University of Pennsylvania. University Microfilms, Ann Arbor.
　1979　Estimating Population by Analogy. In *Ethnoarchaeology: Implications of Ethnography for Archaeology,* edited by C. Kramer, pp. 164–174. Columbia University Press, New York.

de Vaux, R.
　1971　Palestine in the Early Bronze Age. In *Cambridge Ancient History,* third edition, Vol. 1, Part 2, edited by I. E. S. Edwards et al., pp. 208–237. Cambridge University Press, Cambridge.

Watson, Patty Jo
　1978　Architectural Differentiation in Some Near Eastern Communities, Prehistoric and Contemporary. In *Social Archaeology: Beyond Subsistence and Dating,* edited by C. L. Redman et al., pp. 131–158. Academic Press, New York.
　1979　*Archaeological Ethnography in Western Iran.* Viking Fund Publications in Anthropology, No. 57. University of Arizona Press, Tucson.

Weinstein, James M.
　1975　Egyptian Relations with Palestine in the Middle Kingdom. *Bulletin of the American Schools of Oriental Research* 217:1–16.

Wilson, A. L.
　1978　Elemental Analysis of Pottery in the Study of Its Provenience: A Review. *Journal of Archaeological Science* 5:219–236.

Wright, G. Ernest
　1965　*Shechem: The Biography of a Biblical City.* McGraw-Hill, New York.
　1974　The Tell: Basic Unit for Reconstructing Complex Societies in the Near East. In *Reconstructing Complex Societies,* edited by C. B. Moore, pp. 123–130. American Schools of Oriental Research, Cambridge, Mass.

Yadin, Yigal
　1972　*Hazor.* The Schweich Lectures of the British Academy. Oxford University Press, London.

Zaccagnini, Carlo
　1975　The Yield of the Fields at Nuzi. *Oriens Antiquus* 14:181–225.

Zeder, Melinda
　1991　*Feeding Cities.* Smithsonian Institution Press, Washington, D.C.

CHAPTER TEN

Social Complexity in the Aztec Countryside

MICHAEL E. SMITH

AZTEC SOCIETY AT THE TIME of the Spanish conquest was highly complex. Inequality was pronounced, with commoner and noble classes each divided into a number of ranks. Occupational specialization was common, and goods were exchanged through a variety of channels, including markets, professional merchants, and tribute. The political system was based upon a multilevel hierarchy of power and authority, and religion was also highly differentiated, both conceptually and organizationally. The Aztec capital Tenochtitlan, one of the largest cities in the world in A.D. 1500, was entirely representative of this complexity in all of its forms.

This co-occurrence of urbanism and social complexity, coupled with a traditional archaeological dichotomy between urban and rural, has led scholars to an implicit assumption that the inhabitants of nonurban or rural areas in ancient central Mexico were simple and homogeneous peasants. This chapter suggests that this characterization is not only oversimplified but also highly inaccurate. In fact, the Aztec countryside was a setting for small, rural communities with socially complex populations. Results of archaeological excavations of Late Postclassic (Aztec period) sites in a rural area in Morelos, Mexico, reveal the presence of both horizontal and vertical social complexity. These findings have important implications for our understanding of Aztec society and economy.

Social Complexity

ARCHAEOLOGY AND COMPLEXITY

Complexity is an attribute of open systems, and the concept has been discussed in the literature of general systems theory in relation to physical, biological, and social systems (Simon 1962; Pattee 1973). Although most authors have avoided formal definitions of complexity or complex systems, the general sense of the concept is given by Herbert Simon:

Roughly, by a complex system I mean one made up of a large number of parts that interact in a nonsimple way. In such systems, the whole is more than the sum of the parts, not in an ultimate, metaphysical sense, but in the important pragmatic sense that, given the properties of the parts and the laws of their interaction, it is not a trivial matter to infer the properties of the whole. (Simon 1962:468)

Archaeologists, for whom whole cultures traditionally have been important units of analysis, apply this concept most commonly in terms of "cultural complexity." Evolutionary research has long been concerned with the origin and development of complex societies and cultures (e.g., Wenke 1981; Kowalewski 1990), generally as manifested in states and chiefdoms. Recently, a number of archaeologists have concluded that many prehistoric cultures previously described as simple or egalitarian in fact were more complex. Cultures in the American Southwest, formerly viewed as egalitarian tribes, are now interpreted by some as complex (Lightfoot and Upham 1989). Even some hunter-gatherer societies are now described in this manner (e.g., Price and Brown 1985).

The status of agrarian states, like the Aztec or Maya, as complex cultures is not at issue. Countless archaeological and ethnohistorical studies of these societies have demonstrated that they satisfy almost any operational definition of the term. Nevertheless, the spatial configuration of social processes and institutions in complex societies has received little attention.

Linked to the archaeological tendency to view complexity as an attribute of whole cultures is a common association of specific manifestations of complexity (e.g., social stratification, craft specialization) with urbanism. This supposition produces models, both explicit and implicit, of rural areas inhabited by simple, homogeneous peasant farmers.

If, however, we shift our focus from complexity as an attribute of whole cultures to complexity as a feature of specific areas, settlements, or other social components, we may reveal important aspects of rural complexity. Specific material manifestations of social complexity can be investigated to determine empirically the extent to which rural society in ancient states may have been simple or complex. This approach focuses on social organization and institutions and uses the concept of "social complexity" rather than the more common "cultural complexity." The following section discusses three components of social complexity in rural areas: heterogeneity, inequality, and connectivity.

HETEROGENEITY, INEQUALITY, AND CONNECTIVITY

McGuire (1983) presents a particularly useful archaeological treatment of social complexity that discusses the horizontal and vertical dimensions of complexity under the terms "heterogeneity" and "inequality" (following Blau 1977). In this approach, *heterogeneity* "deals with the frequency of individuals among social parameters" (McGuire 1983:101). McGuire identifies three components of heterogeneity: the number of hierarchical levels in a society, the number of dimensions that differentiate groups and statuses, and the degree of independence between social parameters.

Hierarchical levels are inferred most commonly by archaeologists from settlement patterns. Less complex cultures tend to have fewer discrete levels of settlement, whereas states tend to have many levels in their settlement hierarchy (Wright and Johnson 1975). Within ancient Mesoamerica, the lowland Classic Maya categories of house, patio group, cluster, minor center, and major center make up one of the best-documented examples of a complex settlement hierarchy (Ashmore 1981). This approach, rather than the whole-culture applications of McGuire and others (e.g., Lightfoot and Upham 1989), can be applied easily to specific regions. The second component of heterogeneity is the number of dimensions of differentiation. The dimension most frequently analyzed by archaeologists is craft production. The degree of specialization and the number of specialized crafts provide measures of heterogeneity. McGuire (1983:107, 127) discusses dimensions of differentiation in terms of non-kin institutions, which can include sodalities, and religious and political organizations, in addition to economic institutions.[1]

McGuire's second dimension of complexity, *inequality*, "refers to how unequal the distribution of a population is along graduated parameters" (McGuire 1983:102). Archaeologists traditionally have investigated inequality along the classic Weberian dimensions of wealth, status, and power, based on architecture, portable domestic artifacts, and burials. Architecture generally is the strongest indicator of inequality because it embodies all three dimensions and reflects the greatest energetic investment (signaling power and wealth) of any artifact category (see Abrams 1989).

In addition to McGuire's dimensions of heterogeneity and inequality, a third can be added, one that I call *connectivity*. This term denotes the extent to which households are connected with nonlocal economic and political institutions. Although connectivity could be subsumed under heterogeneity and inequality, I separate it here because of its importance in considerations of rural complexity. The traditional model of homogeneous peasants (e.g., Redfield 1941) assumes that rural farmers were isolated from many of the large-scale political and economic currents of their time, except perhaps in their role as producers of tribute for foreign lords. However, archaeological evidence shows that rural Aztec populations not only exhibited features of heterogeneity and inequality but also participated heavily in long-distance trade systems.

RURAL SOCIAL COMPLEXITY AND ANCIENT MESOAMERICA

As commonly used, the concept "rural" has two connotations. First, it is sometimes used to describe individual settlements or small areas where agricultural activities predominate. In this approach, rural settlements are distinguished from urban settlements (see Chapter 9 by Falconer). In a second sense, one employed in this chapter, rural is an attribute of regions, not settlements. Thus, a rural area can be defined as either a region with a low level of urbanization (i.e., few towns, or a low proportion of the population living in towns and cities) or an area far away from large cities. Whichever connotation of the term is used, scholars should avoid placing too much emphasis a priori on the distinctions between rural and urban contexts or settings. An overemphasis on the rural-urban dichotomy often leads to the characterization of urban areas as complex and rural areas as simple, a misleading interpretation. In an important paper, Anthony Leeds (1980) suggests that

any society which has in it what we commonly call "towns" or "cities" is in *all* aspects an "urban" society, including its agricultural and extractive domains ... the terms "urban" and "rural" come to stand to each other not as opposites and equivalents. Rather, the inclusive term describing the whole society is "urban" while the term "rural" refers only to a set of specialties of an urban society characterized by being inherently linked (under any technology known) to specific geographical spaces. (Leeds 1980:6–7)

Leeds's functional approach to rural and urban phenomena allows for the possibility of social complexity in rural areas, a situation reported in many of the chapters in this volume. This line of thought is compatible with the French rural history approach (e.g., Bloch 1931; Braudel 1981), which analyzes peasant society and rural areas on their own terms rather than as the simple homogeneous food-producing sectors of state societies. Graffam's (1992) study of agricultural production in the Lake Titicaca area after the collapse of the Tiwanaku state demonstrates the archaeological relevance of the rural history approach and provides a concrete example of the need to analyze rural areas on their own terms in order to appreciate the nature of rural society and its complexities.

Traditional approaches to ancient Mesoamerican states have tended to ignore the possibility of rural social complexity for several reasons. First, both of the major theoretical approaches to urbanism used by Mesoamericanists—the demographic-sociological approach (e.g., Sanders and Webster 1988) and the functional approach (e.g., Blanton 1976; Kowalewski 1990)—define urbanism at least partly in terms of social complexity. Neither approach rules out the possibility of rural complexity. Nevertheless, their heavy focus on urban settlements themselves tends to divert attention from the countryside, unlike Leeds's (1980) more inclusive approach to urban and rural issues.

A second reason for the neglect of rural complexity is that some of the most archaeologically influential works by Mesoamerican ethnologists describe peasant populations as simple homogeneous societies. Robert Redfield's *The Folk Culture of Yucatan* (1941) is quite explicit about the association between cities and complexity, and between peasants and simplicity, while Eric R. Wolf's *Peasants* (1966) does not deal with the possibility of significant social variation within rural populations. The more recent regional approach of Carol Smith (1976), Leeds (1980), and others helps correct this bias by examining the spatial distribution of economic and social institutions and activities.

The regional approach has been applied in Mesoamerican archaeology by Blanton (1976), Kowalewski (1990), and others, but this work highlights a third reason for the neglect of rural complexity. Even large-scale surveys that include a focus on rural areas cannot investigate rural complexity without the excavation of rural sites. Some information on the distribution of elites or the location of craft production can be generated with surface archaeology (e.g., Brumfiel 1980; Kowalewski 1990), but confident identifications of complex institutions, their controlled dating, and quantitative analyses of their configurations require excavated data, particularly from domestic deposits (Hendon 1992). In other words, we need more excavations of rural sites employing the approach of "household archaeology," as exemplified by many of the chapters in this volume (see also the papers in Santley and Hirth 1993).

Late Postclassic Central Mexico

RURAL AND URBAN IN THE BASIN OF MEXICO

Aztec society usually is described as socially complex and highly urbanized. Indeed, the Aztec capital, Tenochtitlan, was a huge primate city with nearly 200,000 inhabitants and a high degree of social differentiation (Rojas 1986). Most Aztec urban settlements were considerably more modest in size and complexity, however. The predominant urban form was the city-state capital, a small settlement with low-level urban functions that is more properly described as a town than a city (Hicks 1982; M. E. Smith 1989:456–457; M. E. Smith et al. in press). The primary institutions in Aztec city-state capitals were political (the palace of the king) and religious (the central temple-pyramid). These settlements incorporated social complexity into the political and religious dimensions (Sanders and Webster 1988). Palaces, as elite residences and administrative buildings, provide evidence of both inequality and heterogeneity, whereas the religious complexity signaled by temples is an example of heterogeneity.

There is some variation in the extent to which Aztec city-state capitals were scenes of economic heterogeneity in the form of craft specialization. Brumfiel's (1987) ethnohistoric research suggests that the production of luxury or elite crafts (e.g., goldsmithing, lapidary production, feather art) was centered on urban palaces, whereas utilitarian crafts were produced by part-time rural artisans. However, her intensive surface collections at Huexotla yielded little evidence for specialized production at this city-state capital (Brumfiel 1980). On the other hand, recent surface collections and excavation at Otumba, another city-state capital, reveal evidence for intensive production of both utilitarian (cloth, ceramic figurines, obsidian tools) and luxury (obsidian jewelry) items in the urban core of the site (Charlton, Nichols, and Charlton 1991). Data from these Aztec city-state capitals, the only two studied intensively by archaeologists, suggest highly variable economic roles for these settlements.

The extent to which rural areas of the Aztec Basin of Mexico were socially complex is difficult to judge, given the limited state of current archaeological knowledge. Surface collections document the presence of at least some craft production outside the city-state capitals, but the intensity or scale of these industries is difficult to gauge (e.g., Sanders, Parsons, and Santley 1979:172–181; Brumfiel 1980, 1987; Spence 1985). Excavations at the village site of Siguatecpan uncovered an elite residence, an obsidian workshop, and a household textile industry (Evans 1988). Unfortunately, this is the only Aztec rural site extensively excavated in the Basin of Mexico.

Comparative data suggest that the Aztec countryside should have been the setting for a high level of social complexity. Rural population was quite dense (Sanders, Parsons, and Santley 1979:163–171), and, in most cases, social complexity is correlated strongly with population density. Carol Smith's (1976) comparative research suggests that the highly commercialized Aztec economy, integrated by extensive marketplace exchange (Berdan 1985; Hodge 1992), should have favored the presence of elites in rural, as well as urban, settings. Therefore, the palace at Siguatecpan probably is typical of rural settlements. The rapidly growing population and the accompanying probability of land shortages led to agricultural intensification (Sanders, Parsons, and Santley 1979:249–281; Evans 1990). These same forces are linked cross-culturally to the development of rural craft industries (Thirsk 1961; Arnold 1985:171–196). In the absence of excavations at more sites in rural areas, these suggestions cannot be evaluated. However, recent research in a rural area outside the Basin of Mexico provides more complete evidence for rural social complexity in Late Postclassic central Mexico.

EXCAVATIONS AT CAPILCO AND CUEXCOMATE IN MORELOS

The Postclassic Morelos Archaeological Project undertook excavations at the Cuauhnahuac phase (Late Postclassic) sites of Capilco and Cuexcomate in Morelos, Mexico, in part to investigate the possibility of rural social complexity in this area. Ethnohistoric documents and prior archaeological research suggested that western Morelos had dense rural populations that were well integrated into Aztec period exchange networks. Preliminary surface work at these sites by the Xochicalco Mapping Project (Hirth in preparation) had revealed residential architecture with high surface visibility and artifact collections that showed interhouse variation, suggesting differences in wealth and cotton textile production.

Capilco and Cuexcomate were excavated in 1986 with a research design intended to gather data on household conditions (including wealth levels and craft production), residential architecture, and community organization. A random sample of houses at each site was tested to investigate sitewide patterns of variability. Selected houses and large exterior areas were completely cleared to address domestic conditions and activities in greater detail, and a number of nonresidential structures and features were excavated, including a temple-platform, possible granaries, ritual deposits, and agricultural terraces. The excavations and architectural remains are described in M. E. Smith (1992).

Three chronological phases are represented at Capilco and Cuexcomate. The Temazcalli phase (A.D. 1200–1350) is only present in two refuse deposits at Capilco. The Early Cuauhnahuac (EC) phase (A.D. 1350–1430) saw the founding of Cuexcomate and a pattern of growth at Capilco, and both sites continued to grow in the Late Cuauhnahuac or (LC) phase (A.D. 1430–1550). Both sites were abandoned early in the Spanish colonial period, probably in response to Spanish administrative decree. This chronology is discussed in M. E. Smith and Doershuk (1991).

Demographic estimates, based upon our random sample of houses and ethnohistoric data on household size in Morelos, are presented in Table 22. Capilco was a small nucleated

Table 22. Demographic Data for Capilco and Cuexcomate

	Phase		
Site	Temazcalli	Early Cuauhnahuac	Late Cuauhnahuac
Number of houses			
Capilco			
Elite	—	—	—
Nonelite	5	13	21
Cuexcomate			
Elite	—	4	7
Nonelite	—	35	132
Number of persons			
Capilco, nonelite	28	72	116
Cuexcomate			
Elite	—	44	77
Nonelite	—	193	726
Total	—	237	803
Settlement area (ha)			
Capilco	0.14	0.60	1.15
Cuexcomate	—	9.94	14.58
Population density (persons/ha)			
Capilco	197	121	101
Cuexcomate	—	24	55

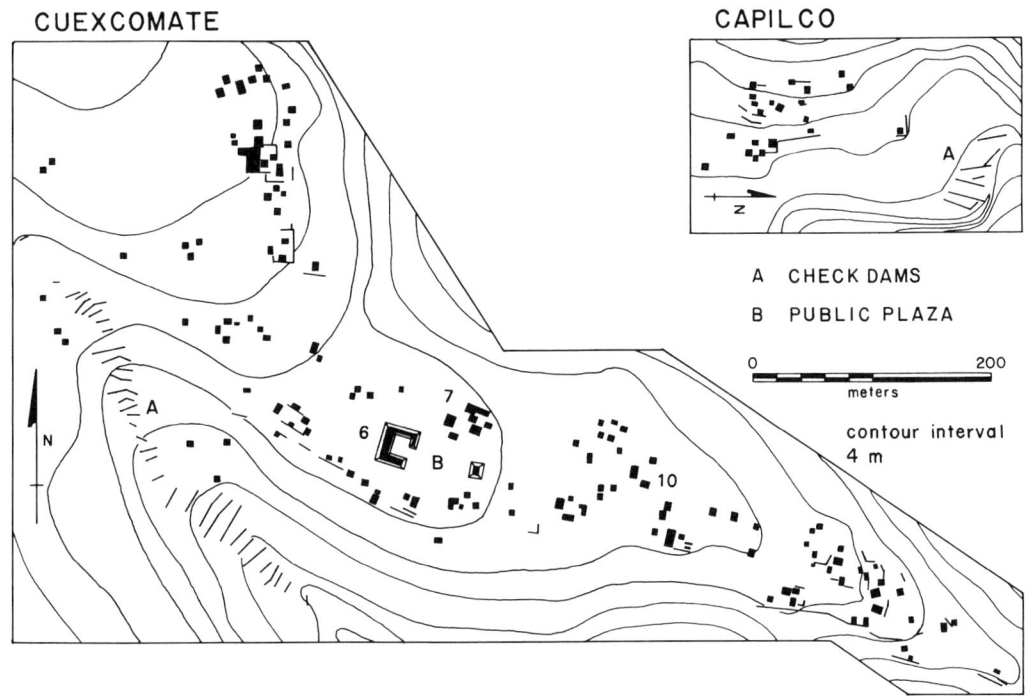

Fig. 64. Cuexcomate and Capilco, showing the maximal extent of settlement (Late Cuauhnahuac phase). The locations of three patio groups discussed in the text, Nos. 6, 7, and 10, are indicated.

village, growing from about five initial houses to a maximum size of 21 houses in the LC phase. Cuexcomate was a larger and more complex town settlement in both the EC and the LC phases, with a centrally located public plaza defined by a temple-platform, an elite residential compound (there were separate compounds in each phase), and another special residence of some sort. The patterns of demographic growth indicated in Table 22 also appear to characterize the larger region around the excavated sites, suggesting a massive population expansion in the fourteenth and fifteenth centuries (M. E. Smith 1992). Figure 64 shows plans for the two sites during the LC phase, the time of their maximum size. As discussed later, the distinction between the village and the town accounts for much of the variation in social complexity at the sites, with Cuexcomate showing considerably more evidence for complexity, although a number of attributes of heterogeneity also are present at Capilco.

Heterogeneity

THE SETTLEMENT HIERARCHY

Excavations and mapping by the Postclassic Morelos Archaeological Project resulted in the identification of four hierarchical classes or levels of settlement: the house, patio group, house cluster, and macrocluster. Early colonial census documents from five towns in Morelos also describe four settlement levels that correspond to groups with important social and economic functions. These are the *calli* (household), the *ithualli,* the *chinamitl,* and the *calpulli* (see Carrasco 1976). Formal comparisons between the archaeological and ethnohistoric hierarchies reveal that they are identical, permitting the use of ethnohistory for social interpretations of the archaeological categories and the use of archaeology for economic interpretations of the ethnohistoric groups. This four-level hierarchy is described briefly here; the reader is referred to M. E. Smith (1992, 1993) for more detailed descriptions and analyses.

Figure 65 is a schematic representation of the settlement hierarchy. The *house* is the basic level of residence. Most houses were small adobe structures with stone foundations, although some elevated platform houses also were present (see the discussion of inequality later in this chapter). Census documents reveal the presence of many joint family households inhabiting single structures in contact-period Morelos. Many houses were arranged in *patio groups* with two to four houses around a plaza or patio, sometimes with a circular structure (probably a granary), or a rock pile that denotes a ritual artifact dump. Archaeological evidence indicates that each house was a separate residence rather than a specialized struc-

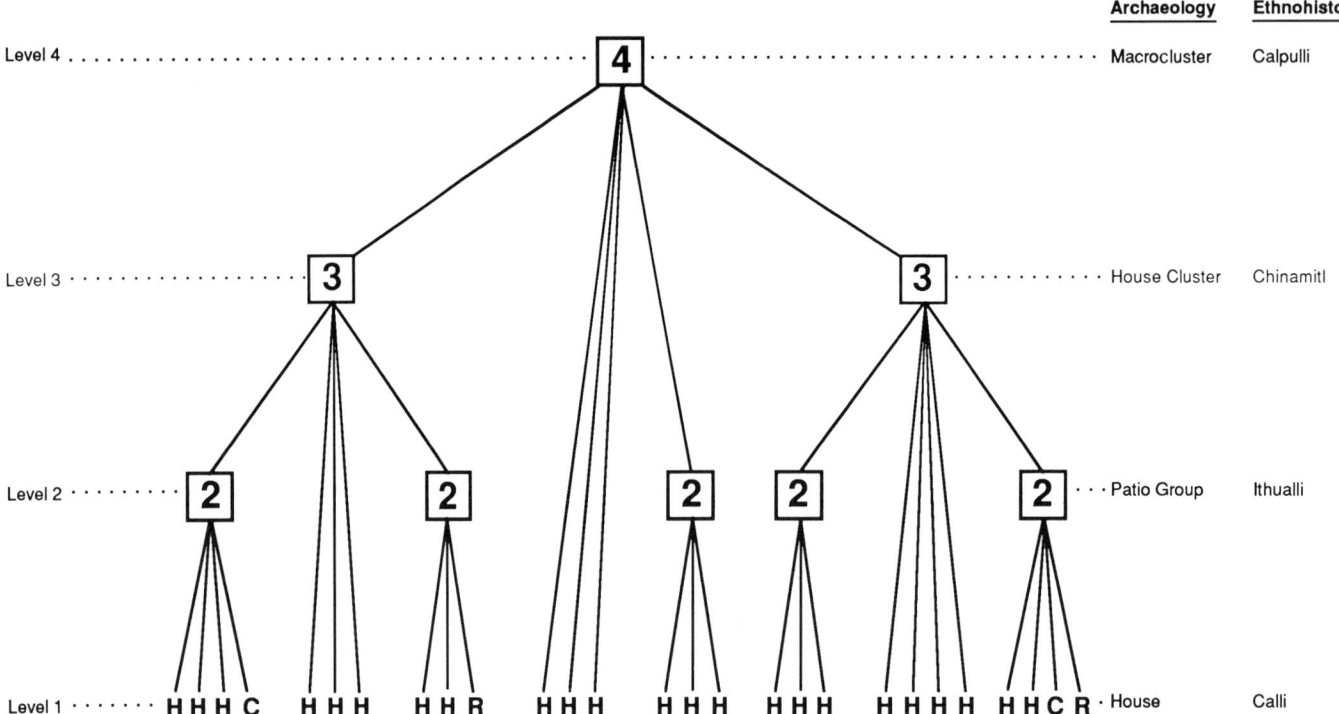

Fig. 65. Cuauhnahuac phase settlement hierarchy in western Morelos. C, circular structure; H, house; R, rock pile.

ture, such as a kitchen or dormitory. These compounds are designated historically by the Nahuatl term *ithualli* ("houses around a courtyard"), and their constituent households were linked by kinship bonds in about half of the cases. Each patio group had a compound head with greater wealth and status than the other household heads. Typically he distributed land to the other households for their cultivation in exchange for tribute payments in goods and services. Both the archaeological and the ethnohistorical data show that the patio group was a widespread unit of great economic and social importance. Carrasco (1976:63) argues that land tenure and tribute obligations played a larger role than kinship in shaping settlement and social organization at this level.

The *house cluster* consists of ten to fifty houses located in close proximity to one another. The site of Capilco consists of a single house cluster, whereas Cuexcomate is composed of three or four clusters (see Fig. 64). The central and northern clusters at Cuexcomate have central patio groups that are large and complex, whereas Capilco and the eastern portion of Cuexcomate are without such nuclei. The census documents use two terms for this unit, the *chinamitl* and the *calpulli*. Since the latter term is also used for larger units, I use the former to denote the house cluster. The *chinamitl* had resident nobles who maintained political and economic control over the other residents. The complex patio groups at Cuexcomate provide archaeological evidence for these cluster heads.

The site of Cuexcomate forms a *macrocluster* that is nucleated around a central public plaza (area B in Fig. 64). The size of Cuexcomate during the LC phase (139 houses) is within the range of *calpulli* units described in the Morelos census documents (120 to 188 houses). The *calpulli* were all under the strict control of a noble who lived among the other residents. Again, the site of Cuexcomate provides a good archaeological illustration of such a unit. In sum, a four-level settlement hierarchy is indicated clearly by the archaeological remains (except for the definition of clusters at Cuexcomate, which must remain subjective until quantitative spatial analyses are carried out), and the social significance of its hierarchial levels is established firmly by census documents (see M. E. Smith 1993).

RITUAL

Three dimensions of heterogeneity beyond that of the settlement hierarchy are evident in the archaeological record. One of these, ritual, exhibits hierarchical variation, and two others, agriculture and craft production, have nonhierarchical patterns of variation.

Archaeological evidence points to a series of ritual activities that pertain to three of the settlement levels already discussed: the house, the patio group, and the macrocluster. Ritual activities are inferred from the formal properties and spatial contexts of artifacts, features, and buildings, using functional analogies based on Aztec ethnohistoric evidence (see M. E. Smith 1992 for details). Domestic rituals, centered in and around houses, are signaled by long-handled ("frying pan") incense burners, ceramic figurines, and infant burials. The incense burners are quite abundant, making up between 2 percent and 5 percent of all ceramic vessels in most domestic middens.[2] Figurines are less abundant, but they do occur in nearly all houses. Burials are not common, but seven of the nine excavated burials occur either under the house floor ($N = 3$) or adjacent to a house ($N = 4$). Only five of the forty-four excavated houses have burials (although most houses were only tested and were not excavated completely). The evidence thus points to two kinds of domestic ritual: offerings involving incense and perhaps figurines, and burials of infants.

Patio group rituals are signaled by "ritual dumps" or rock piles. These features consist of extremely dense unstratified deposits of domestic artifacts 1–2 m in diameter, capped by a layer of large rocks. They are located in the patio areas of five of the twenty-five patio groups at Cuexcomate (there are no ritual dumps at Capilco). Ethnohistoric parallels suggest that these features were the remains of cycle-ending calendrical rituals in which household possessions were broken and discarded every 52 years. Their locations in patio areas suggest that the rituals pertain to the whole group, not to individual houses.

The existence of a temple platform on the east side of the Cuexcomate public plaza points to ritual activities that pertain to the entire settlement and probably to nearby smaller villages as well. Refuse deposits associated with this structure have high frequencies of incense burners and fine serving vessels for food and drink. Ethnohistoric data suggest the presence of professional priests at Cuexcomate, who may have resided in a distinctive patio group along the south side of the public plaza.

CRAFT PRODUCTION

The major craft industry at Capilco and Cuexcomate, cotton textile manufacture, is visible archaeologically in the form of spindle whorls and spinning bowls (Fig. 66). These artifacts are ubiquitous in the excavated midden deposits. The graphs in Figure 67 (see end note 2 on artifact quantification) show that (1) all excavated houses have spinning artifacts, (2) the overall frequencies are high, (3) these artifacts are not any more common in elite contexts than in nonelite contexts, and (4) a few houses stand out with very high frequencies. Cotton textiles were important items of trade and tribute in this area (Berdan 1987; M. E. Smith and Hirth 1988), and much of the

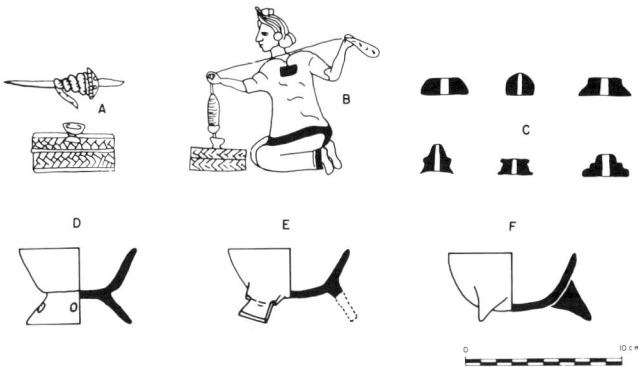

Fig. 66. Ceramic cotton spinning artifacts. A, Aztec spinning equipment (Sahagún 1950–1982, book 8:Fig. 75); B, woman spinning (Codex Mendoza 1992:f.68r); C, small ceramic spindle whorls from Postclassic sites in Morelos; D and E, imported Aztec III Black on Orange spinning bowls from Coatetelco; F, local Morelos spinning bowl from Coatetelco.

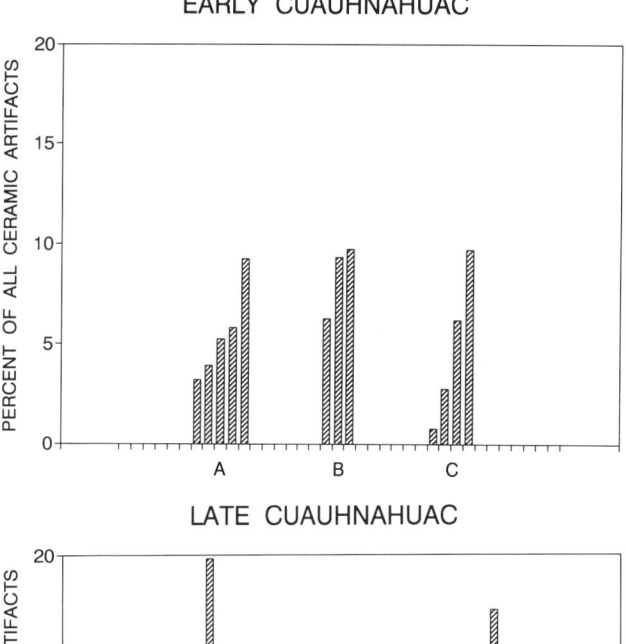

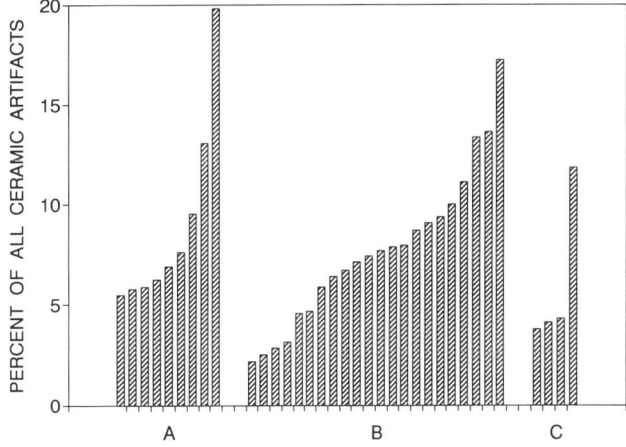

Fig. 67. Frequencies of cotton spinning artifacts in domestic refuse deposits. Each bar represents one house. Houses are grouped into three categories: A, houses at Capilco; B, nonelite houses at Cuexcomate; C, elite houses at Cuexcomate.

cotton production must have been destined for export. Cotton textile production would fit Peacock's (1982:8–11) category of "household industry," which is based on domestic production for both use and exchange, usually by part-time producers. Surface collections at other Late Postclassic sites in Morelos usually include many spindle whorls and spinning bowls, a finding that suggests that textile manufacture was widespread (Smith and Hirth 1988).

Although obsidian artifacts are quite abundant in the excavated deposits (most contexts produced two to four pieces per 100 sherds), there is almost no evidence for the manufacture of obsidian tools at Capilco or Cuexcomate (Sorensen 1988). However, the nearby site of El Ciruelo has a localized heavy concentration of blade production debris suggestive of workshop activity (Sorensen, Hirth, and Ferguson 1989), and it is likely that the artifacts at the excavated sites were manufactured at El Ciruelo. In contrast to the textile industry, obsidian production was specialized by settlement, although the volume of production at El Ciruelo and the intensity of labor (full-time versus part-time) cannot be assessed with current data.

Chert tool manufacture and bark paper production were minor craft industries at Capilco and Cuexcomate. Low-grade chert is present in the immediate vicinity of the sites, and most houses have some chert tools (generally between 0.5 and 1.0 artifact per 100 sherds). Tool production debris is present in many deposits, suggesting "household production" in Peacock's (1982) scheme (i.e., low-level domestic production for immediate household use). The manufacture of paper from the bark of the *amate* or wild fig tree is indicated by the presence of grooved rectangular basalt tools known as "bark beaters." Although these tools are rare, they occur in 70 percent of the houses with large excavated samples (i.e., >5 m³ of excavated midden). Thus it appears that most houses engaged in low levels of paper production. Much of this production probably was for export, since the paper needs of these rural sites would have been low, and bark paper was among the tribute goods paid by western Morelos to the Aztec empire.

Finally, there is evidence for two unidentified types of craft activities. First, a number of copper-tin bronze awls and chisels were recovered in domestic middens. They are quite rare and lack a concentrated distribution pattern. We can only speculate that these tools were used for woodworking. Another rare category includes mineral paint pigments in three colors: red (hematite), yellow (limonite), and black (graphite). Among all of the rare artifact categories, these pigments show the highest degree of concentration. In the EC phase, four of the twelve pigment stones are associated with the elite compound, whereas in LC deposits 5 percent of the forty-three examples are from the elite patio group and 67 percent are from patio group 10 at Cuexcomate. The uses of the pigment are not known (body painting or manuscript painting are possibilities), but painting activities do appear to be concentrated in key patio groups.

INTENSIVE FARMING METHODS

Comparative data from the Late Postclassic Basin of Mexico and modern local ethnography suggest that four types of agriculture probably were employed in the vicinity of the excavated sites: rainfall agriculture, irrigation, terracing, and house gardens (Sanders, Parsons, and Santley 1979). Rainfall agriculture was the dominant method prior to the Late Postclassic period (Hirth in preparation). Probably by EC times, and certainly by the LC phase, the regional population exceeded the carrying capacity of rainfall cultivation in the area (M. E. Smith 1992:Chapter 10), leading to intensification in the form of terracing and possibly irrigation. Only very small plots could be irrigated, and this method made only a minor contribution to subsistence, if it was practiced at all.

Terracing was the dominant form of agriculture for the inhabitants of Capilco and Cuexcomate. Two types of terraces were built in the Cuauhnahuac phase: contour terraces on hill

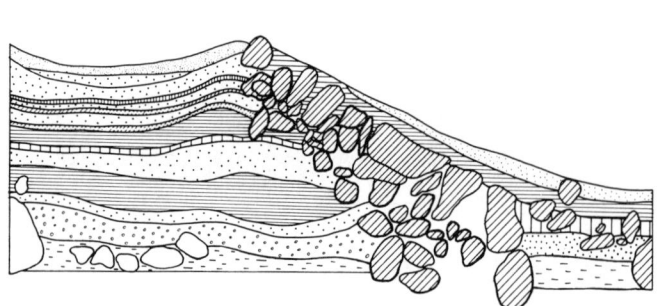 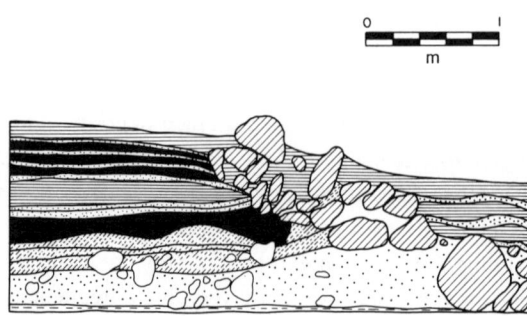

Fig. 68. Cross-channel terraces at Cuexcomate.

slopes and cross-channel terraces or check dams in small drainages (see Donkin 1979 on these types in general). The Postclassic Morelos Archaeological Project excavated a number of cross-channel terraces (M. E. Smith 1992: Chapter 10; M. E. Smith and Price in press), some of which are illustrated in Figure 68. The stone terrace walls were built up gradually. As eroding sediments filled in the area behind the terrace, the wall was built higher, and each incremental addition produced a larger planting surface with deeper soils. Capilco and Cuexcomate both have areas of cross-channel terracing adjacent to the settlement areas (Fig. 64). Contour terracing is far more extensive in the region than cross-channel terracing, but we were able to excavate only one small area of contour terraces, and their construction and use remain poorly understood. Although the slopes surrounding the eastern half of Cuexcomate are covered with contour terraces, none were located in the immediate vicinity of Capilco. The cultivation of house gardens within these settlements may be inferred from similar agricultural features elsewhere (e.g., Evans 1990), but positive evidence is lacking.

DIMENSIONS OF HETEROGENEITY

The three dimensions of heterogeneity discussed previously —ritual, craft production, and farming methods—provide evidence for different types of social complexity. The existence of three levels of ritual activity, each involving different kinds of artifacts and features, lends support to the notion that the hierarchical levels of settlement correspond to important social groups or categories.

The evidence for craft production shows the existence of economic differentiation, again at a variety of levels. All or most households were involved in the production of low levels of chert tools and perhaps wooden objects for domestic use, low levels of paper for exchange, and high levels of cotton textiles for both use and exchange. The only strong evidence for more intensive household craft production came from two houses dating to the LC phase (unit 102 at Capilco and unit 262 at Cuexcomate) that have frequencies of spinning artifacts more than two standard deviations above the mean for the phase (see Fig. 67). The use of paint stones appears to have been organized on a patio group level, since one patio group at Cuexcomate stands out above all others in each phase: patio group 6, the elite compound, in the EC phase, and patio group 10 in the LC phase. Finally, obsidian tool production was apparently specialized by settlement, with El Ciruelo probably providing most of the 12,000 pieces of obsidian recovered at Capilco and Cuexcomate.

Although the simple presence of intensive agricultural practices like terracing does not necessarily indicate social complexity, I consider these methods to be manifestations of complexity for several reasons. First, a number of different cultivation practices were in use, and this diversity is an example of complexity. Second, agricultural intensification makes significant demands on household labor, often leading to more complex forms of household organization and work scheduling (Maclachlan 1987). Third, agricultural intensification has a functional association with both high population density and complex social institutions (Turner 1983; Maclachlan 1987). The ratio of total terraced area at Cuexcomate to that at Capilco far exceeds the ratio of their populations, a fact that might signal that the expansion of terracing was not due to demographic growth alone. The elite at Cuexcomate may have promoted terracing for their own gain. If so, the distribution of terracing may be another signal of social complexity on a regional scale; further fieldwork is required to explore this notion more fully.

Inequality

ARCHITECTURAL MEASURES

Residential architecture provides a relatively direct measure of socioeconomic inequality in energetic and symbolic dimensions. Figure 69 contains reconstruction drawings of a typical nonelite house of adobe bricks and the EC elite compound (patio group 6). The elite compound clearly represents a much higher energetic investment than the nonelite house, implying a greater degree of control over labor (Abrams 1989). Symbolically, patio group 6 conveys a message about the power and status of its inhabitants: it is larger than normal patio groups; it is enclosed, unlike the open configuration of other groups; the rooms are built on top of raised platforms; and the compound is located on the public plaza at Cuexcomate, opposite the temple.

Energetic measures are more appropriate than symbolic factors for assessing the extent or degree of inequality because control over labor is a direct manifestation of elite power, and energetic inputs are easier to quantify. It is not yet possible to estimate the labor required to construct Postclassic houses, because comparative data on adobe house construction are lacking. As a substitute for labor estimates, I have calculated the total architectural volume of walls, foundations, and platforms at Cuexcomate and Capilco (assuming a constant wall height). Ground-level houses, the predominant type of nonelite residence, are small single-room structures with an aver-

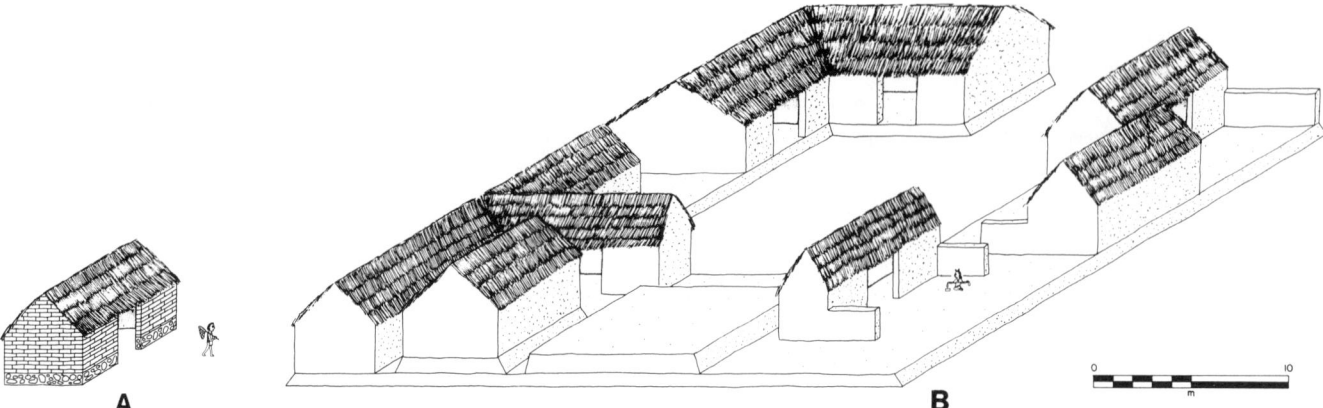

Fig. 69. The Early Cuauhnahuac elite compound at Cuexcomate (patio group 6) compared to a typical ground-level house.

age of 14 m² of interior area (in both phases), and they have a mean architectural volume of 24 m³. A typical patio group of three houses therefore has a total volume of 72 m³. The Cuexcomate EC elite compound pictured in Figure 69 has an architectural volume of 781 m³, which is over ten times the mean figure for nonelite patio groups.

In the succeeding LC phase patio group 6 was abandoned, and its role was assumed by patio group 7, which is located on the north side of the public plaza (see Fig. 64). Although architectural, artifactual, and locational data all support the interpretation of patio group 7 as an elite compound, it is a far more modest group of structures than group 6. The total

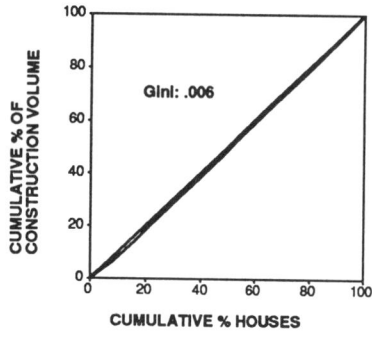
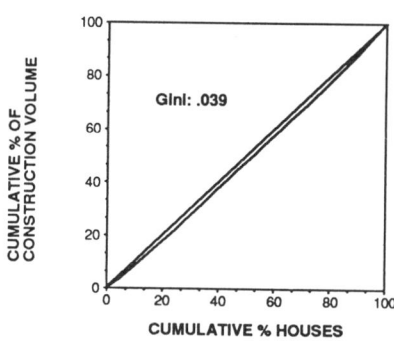
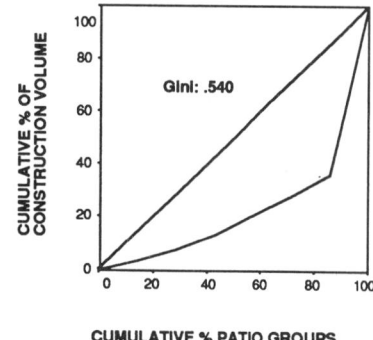
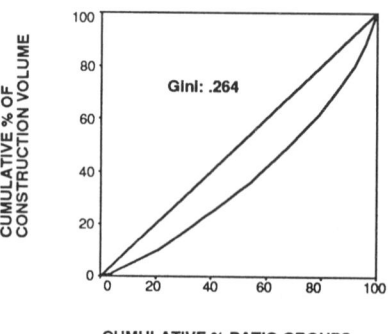

Fig. 70. Lorenz curves illustrating the degree of inequality by site and phase. Inequality is measured by the architectural volume of houses.

architectural volume of group 7, 277 m³, is less than four times the nonelite mean.

The extent of inequality in architectural volume is illustrated by the Lorenz curves in Figure 70. These graphs portray the extent to which a finite good (architectural volume) is concentrated among a small segment of the population. A diagonal line indicates an even distribution in which all houses are the same size (i.e., no inequality), and uneven distributions are signaled by curves dropping below the diagonal; the lower the curve, the greater the inequality. The Gini index is an index of concentration, measuring the area between the diagonal and the curve (see Shryock, Siegel, and Stockwell 1976:98–100 on these measures). The data from Cuexcomate are plotted by patio group; the small size of Capilco necessitates calculations based on individual houses.

The Lorenz curves show that there is virtually no inequality in housing at Capilco in either phase (although there is some variation in architectural volume, from 18.9 m³ to 29.1 m³). Cuexcomate shows a moderately high degree of concentration in the EC phase, with a lower level of inequality in the LC phase. In other words, the site of Cuexcomate has clear evidence for inequality in residential architecture in both phases, with more extreme differentiation in the EC phase than in the LC phase.

ARTIFACTUAL MEASURES

After architecture, domestic artifacts are the next strongest archaeological indicator of household wealth (M. E. Smith 1987). The distributions of artifact categories among houses show that no single type of artifact has an exclusive association with the elite compounds in either phase. Even categories like jade beads, copper bells, and stone sculptures, which might be expected to show a positive association with elite residences, are found in equivalent amounts in all types of residences at both sites. However, a number of ceramic categories do show significant statistical associations with the elite compounds. In other words, there are no clear sumptuary goods (among the excavated artifacts) that were used exclusively by the elite, although some ceramic types are present in elite middens in consistently higher frequencies. This observation is confirmed by discriminant analysis, in which combinations of ceramic variables can distinguish effectively among three categories of residence (Capilco, Cuexcomate nonelite, and Cuexcomate elite) in each phase.

In order to examine the distribution of wealth among households, I have calculated wealth indices for the houses in each phase. The measure discussed here, called wealth index 1, is a phase-specific measure based upon the five ceramic cate-

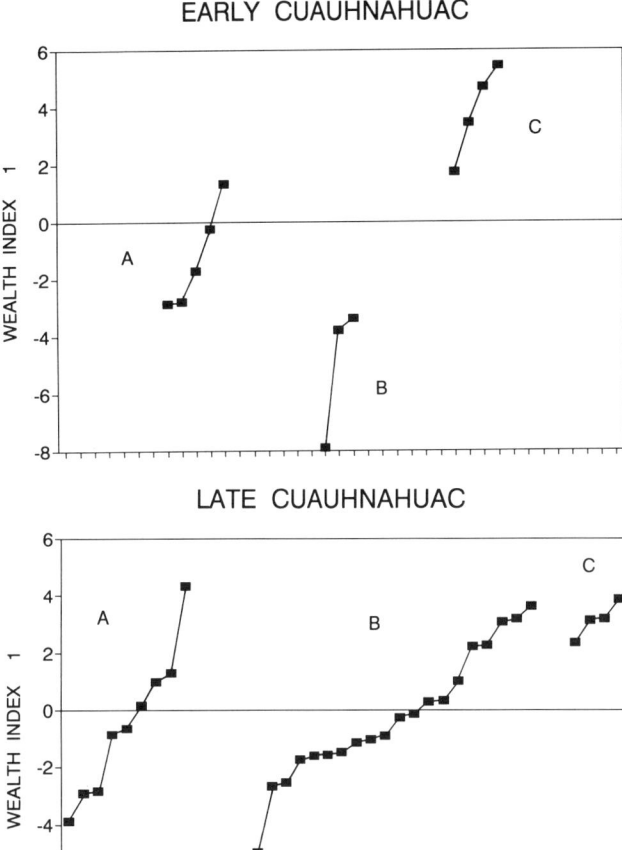

Fig. 71. Wealth variation as measured by wealth index 1, an index constructed from frequencies of wealth-sensitive ceramic categories. Each symbol represents one house. Houses are grouped into three categories: A, houses at Capilco; B, nonelite houses at Cuexcomate; C, elite houses at Cuexcomate.

gories most strongly associated with the elite compound in each phase (as determined by analyses of variance and comparisons of means). Three ceramic types are used for both phases: total bowls, Aztec III Black-on-Orange imports, and polished red bowls. The other two types are other decorated bowls and Morelos imports for EC, and Tlahuica polychrome bowls and incense burners for LC. For each house within each phase, the frequency for each of the five variables (expressed as a percentage of all ceramic vessels) is standardized (converted to a Z score), and the standardized values are summed to produce wealth index 1. This variable has a range of −8 to +6, with a mean of 0 for each phase.

Figure 71 shows the values of wealth index 1 for all excavated houses. These graphs illustrate two important findings. First, the elite residences (category C) are more easily distinguished from the nonelite houses in EC than in LC. This pattern (also reflected in the analyses of variance and the discriminant analysis) parallels the architectural evidence discussed earlier. Second, there is a wide range of wealth values, particularly within the nonelite categories.

PATTERNS OF INEQUALITY

Three important patterns are revealed by these architectural and artifactual data on inequality. First, there is considerable variation in wealth in both the EC and LC phases. This is evident in the Lorenz curves for Cuexcomate (Fig. 70) and in the wealth index distributions for both sites (Fig. 71). This pattern includes not only elite-nonelite differences but also a high degree of wealth variation within the nonelite populations of both sites.

A second pattern is the decline in the magnitude of elite-nonelite differences from EC to LC times. Again, both the architectural and artifactual data show this trend (Figs. 70 and 71). The residents of the LC elite compound were far less differentiated from the rest of the population than were their EC antecedents.

A third important pattern is an apparent overall reduction in wealth levels, probably signaling a lowered standard of living in LC times. The data already discussed are relative measures describing architectural and artifactual patterns within each phase, and therefore they reflect absolute changes between phases only indirectly. The lowering of wealth is signaled by an independent measure, wealth index 2, a phase-independent measure calculated as the percentage of local decorated ceramics plus two times the percentage of imported ceramics. This index is less sensitive to wealth variation within phases, but it does permit comparisons between phases. The nonelite mean values decline from 51.4 in the Temazcalli phase to 43.2 in EC to 35.3 in LC. The elite means decline from 62.5 to 48.3 from EC to LC. This pattern is not apparent in the architectural data beyond the fact that the single largest and most costly residential group, patio group 6 at Cuexcomate, was abandoned in the LC phase. In other words, the nonelite population was living in similar kinds of houses in each phase, whereas the elite were living in far more modest quarters in the LC phase. However, the level of affluence as measured by wealth index 2 declines in all types of contexts, suggesting possible conditions of increasing poverty.

Connectivity

Interaction between rural Morelos populations and the outside world, as measured by material culture, was structured by two general processes: stylistic interaction and exchange.

STYLISTIC INTERACTION

Stylistic interaction refers to the process by which spatially separated populations produce material items that are stylistically similar because of contact or communication between the populations. At Capilco and Cuexcomate, high levels of stylistic interaction with other central Mexican Late Postclassic populations are evident in two realms: elite housing and ritual practices. Aztec palaces, as documented by ethnohistory and archaeology, conformed to a standard architectural pattern (Evans 1991). Many of the major characteristics (such as large size, many rooms that open onto an enclosed courtyard, and the elevation of rooms and structures on low platforms) are features of patio group 6 and, to a lesser extent, group 7 at Cuexcomate (M. E. Smith 1992). The location of these compounds on a public plaza is another standard feature of Late Postclassic palaces. These two patio groups conform to a geographically extensive pattern of elite architecture, indicating that the Cuexcomate elite participated in a widespread network of elite communication.

The material expressions of rituals at all levels also correspond to general central Mexican practices. The figurines and long-handled incense burners used in domestic ritual are nearly identical to Late Aztec artifacts excavated in the Basin of Mexico and depicted in the codices. The rock piles, if interpreted correctly, exemplify another widespread expression of ritual. Finally, the temple platform at Cuexcomate conforms to general Late Postclassic conventions in its stepped profile, the high quality of construction and materials, and its location on the east side of a public plaza.

Apart from elite architecture and ritual artifacts, most of the material remains at Capilco and Cuexcomate either are locally distinctive (e.g., nonelite housing, circular structures, ceramic decoration) or resemble other Late Postclassic items merely because of technological or utilitarian constraints (e.g., obsidian tools, food preparation items). In contrast, elite architecture and religious practices follow widespread cultural patterns whose manifestation in rural Morelos shows the participation of these populations in wider cultural or stylistic networks.

EXCHANGE

The evidence suggests that some domestic manufacture of cotton textiles and bark paper was destined for export, since output would have exceeded the modest demands of rural consumption. Grains or other foodstuffs grown in the extensive terraced fields also may have been exported. All three of these items appear as tribute goods from western Morelos in

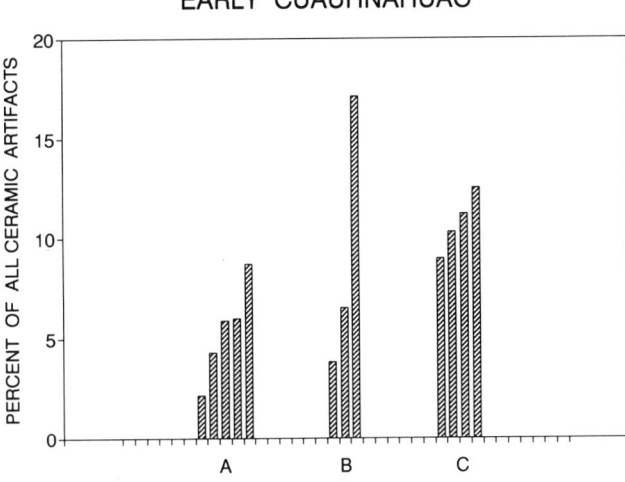
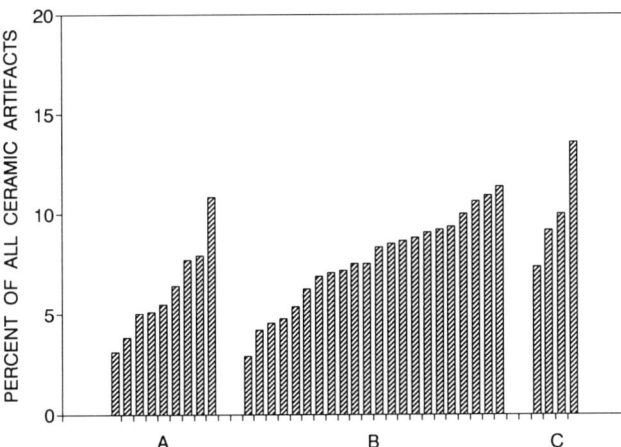

Fig. 72. Frequencies of ceramics imported from the Basin of Mexico. Each bar represents one house. Houses are grouped into three categories: A, houses at Capilco; B, nonelite houses at Cuexcomate; C, elite houses at Cuexcomate.

the Aztec imperial tribute lists (Codex Mendoza 1992:23r–23v), and the importance of cotton textiles in both tribute networks and marketplace exchange (Berdan 1987) suggests that goods produced at rural sites may have moved through a variety of distribution channels.

Imported goods recovered in the excavations may be classified in three categories according to probable place of origin: those from Morelos, the Basin of Mexico, and other areas. The only likely imports from other parts of Morelos are Tlahuica polychrome ceramics from the Cuernavaca area (pertaining to the Teopanzolco ceramic complex), the Yautepec region, and eastern Morelos (in descending order of abundance). These are quite abundant in the two Temazcalli-phase deposits (8.6 percent of all ceramics). The frequency drops off somewhat in EC, when they are most common in elite contexts at Cuexcomate (3.0 percent) and at Capilco

(3.1 percent), while very rare in nonelite houses at Cuexcomate (0.3 percent). The present inability to distinguish the LC polychrome ceramics of the study area from those of the Cuernavaca area (Tecpan phase) makes it difficult to evaluate regional ceramic exchange at that time.

The modest frequency of ceramics imported from the Basin of Mexico (primarily Aztec Black-on-Orange and Texcoco Fabric Marked) in Temazcalli times (3.0 percent) jumps to 7.3 percent and 7.2 percent in the EC and LC phases, respectively. All excavated refuse deposits have examples of these imports (household frequencies are shown in Fig. 72). Thus, whereas elite contexts have slightly more Basin of Mexico imports than nonelite contexts, these ceramics certainly are not limited to the elite. Obsidian imported from the Basin of Mexico also is abundant and ubiquitous, although there is no elite association in the obsidian-to-ceramic ratios. The ceramic and obsidian data together demonstrate an overall high frequency of exchange with populations in the Basin of Mexico and the widespread access of households to exchange networks. The former conclusion accords well with data from other parts of Mesoamerica and indicates a high volume of exchange in ceramics and obsidian from the Basin of Mexico in Late Postclassic times (M. E. Smith 1990). Imports from other areas, including ceramics, jade, and copper, are not abundant.

Discussion

RURAL SOCIETY IN THE CUAUHNAHUAC PHASE

The excavations of domestic contexts at Capilco and Cuexcomate point to a densely settled, socially complex, and economically active population in rural western Morelos during the EC and LC phases. Population density was quite high, not only within settlements (see Table 22), but also on a regional scale. An area of 6 km^2 around the excavated sites had population densities of 80, 280, and 670 persons/km^2 for the Temazcalli, EC, and LC phases, respectively. Even though this zone does not include nearby uninhabitable mountains that would reduce densities, the figures are high, and this situation appears to characterize many parts of Western Morelos in Cuauhnahuac times. Regional population was growing in these phases, and this growth was accompanied by agricultural intensification in the form of contour and cross-channel terracing.

The expansion of terracing may not have kept up with the rapidly growing rural population, leading to lowered standards of living and general conditions of poverty in the study area, as suggested by the decline in wealth index 2. In cross-cultural perspective, growing rural population, land shortages, and

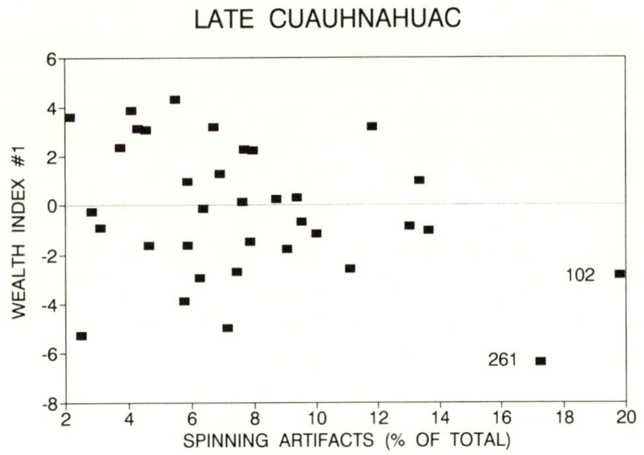

Fig. 73. Plot of wealth index 1 against the frequency of cotton spinning artifacts.

poverty often lead to increased peasant craft production as rural households try to supplement their dwindling agricultural income with cottage industries (Thirsk 1961; Miller and Hatcher 1978; Arnold 1985:171–196). The increased frequency of cotton spinning artifacts through the three phases, coupled with a decrease in wealth index 2, agrees with this interpretation, but does not necessitate it, since increasing tribute demands could also generate this pattern. Nonetheless, the house-to-house distribution of spinning artifacts does support the poverty–cottage industry model. In the EC phase, no single house stands out with excessive frequencies of spinning artifacts, whereas in LC times one nonelite house at each site exceeds the mean value by more than two standard deviations. When the LC data are plotted against wealth level (Fig. 73), it can be seen that both houses with high textile frequencies have low wealth values. Spinning artifacts make up 20 percent and 17 percent, respectively, of the total ceramic inventories of houses 102 at Capilco and 261 at Cuexcomate, suggesting that the inhabitants of these structures may have been specializing in textile manufacture, perhaps to compensate for economic hard times.

The cotton textiles and bark paper that were produced for export at Capilco and Cuexcomate could have moved through the tribute system or marketplace channels. Imperial tribute demands were relatively modest when figured on a per capita basis (M. E. Smith in press). Therefore, many of these manufactured goods probably were traded through market exchange. Ethnohistoric data indicate that many settlements in Morelos the size of Cuexcomate or smaller had regular markets (M. E. Smith in press), and Goodfellow's (1990) study of Cuauhnahuac-phase ceramic petrography points to active regional market exchange of ceramics in western Morelos. In addition, the high volume of ceramic and obsidian exchange supports the notion that these sites were well integrated into central Mexican exchange systems (M. E. Smith 1990).

Architectural, artifactual, and locational data show that elite groups were resident at Cuexcomate in both the EC and LC phases. Whereas the proximity of the elite compounds to the temple platform suggests that the elite played a role in public ritual, we found little evidence of an economic role for the elite. They clearly did not monopolize or strongly control exchange activities, and there is no evidence for elite involvement in craft production beyond the normal domestic production that all households carried out. It is possible that the elite played an economic role by sponsoring or promoting agricultural expansion and intensification, as documented in other agrarian states (e.g., Polgar 1975; Gilman 1981), but existing data do not permit this notion to be evaluated. The census documents from Morelos suggest that nobles controlled most of the farmland and played important political roles as leaders and tribute collectors.

In summary, the Cuexcomate elite appear to have had important social functions in the realms of politics, religion, and perhaps agriculture, with only minimal direct involvement in the control or management of exchange or craft production. Cross-culturally, rural elites often are present in regions with extensive marketplace trade and highly commercialized interlocking market systems (C. A. Smith 1976). This description fits the evidence for Cuauhnahuac-phase Morelos.

CAPILCO, CUEXCOMATE, AND RURAL COMPLEXITY

The study area of the Postclassic Morelos Archaeological Project was characterized initially as a rural area because it is not close to any of the ethnohistorically identified city-state capitals of Morelos. The results presented in this chapter clearly document several dimensions of social complexity at Capilco and Cuexcomate, leading to the general conclusion that rural complexity existed in this area. However, by applying the functional approach to urbanism (Blanton 1976), it is possible to classify Cuexcomate as a low-level urban center or town (as suggested in M. E. Smith 1989). Since Cuexcomate is more complex than Capilco, does this mean that Cuauhnahuac-phase complexity is really an urban phenomenon after all, with small rural sites that were homogeneous settlements of simple peasants? The evidence indicates that this would not be an accurate description of the situation.

Table 23 presents a subjective summary of the archaeological evidence for social complexity at Capilco and Cuexcomate. Although Cuexcomate was the larger settlement, Capilco had a higher population density. Some measures of

Table 23. Comparisons between Capilco and Cuexcomate

Attribute	Capilco	Cuexcomate
Function and size		
Functional classification	Village	Town
LC population	120	800
LC population density (persons/ha)	100	55
Maximal settlement level	Cluster	Macrocluster
Intensive agriculture		
Contour terraces	No	Yes
Check-dams	Yes	Yes
Craft production levels		
Textiles	High	High
Paper	Moderate	Moderate
Paints	Low	Moderate
Presence of textile specialists	Yes	Yes
Levels of ritual		
Domestic	Yes	Yes
Patio group	No	Yes
Public	No	Yes
Inequality		
Elite residence	No	Yes
Nonelite wealth variability	Yes	Yes
Connectivity		
Elite and religious stylistic interaction	No	Yes
Widespread access to trade goods	Yes	Yes

heterogeneity indicate greater complexity at Cuexcomate (more agricultural terraces per capita, possible specialized use of paints, and, especially, more religious complexity), whereas most indicators of craft production are the same at the two settlements. Probably the greatest social distinction between the settlements (apart from size) is the presence of an elite at Cuexcomate, but not at Capilco. The third dimension of complexity, connectivity, shows greater complexity at Cuexcomate in terms of elite and religious stylistic interaction, but no greater access to trade goods among the elite.

In summary, Cuexcomate manifests far more evidence of social complexity than Capilco, although the smaller site exhibits an equivalent level of economic complexity and variability in nonelite wealth levels. Thus, even if Cuexcomate is categorized as a small urban settlement, it does not monopolize the manifestations of social complexity in this area. Irrespective of how one characterizes that site, I believe it is still useful to call this area a rural zone (relative to the major cities of Cuauhnahuac-phase Morelos), and, as such, the excavations at Capilco and Cuexcomate provide evidence for rural social complexity in Late Postclassic central Mexico. The other studies in this volume reach similar conclusions for other societies in ancient Mesoamerica and the Near East. Clearly, rural complexity must be added to our repertoire of archaeologically useful social concepts.

Notes

The Postclassic Morelos Archaeological Project was supported by the National Science Foundation (grants BNS-8507466 and BNS-8804163), the National Endowment for the Humanities, and Loyola University of Chicago. Fieldwork permits were granted by the Instituto Nacional de Antropología e Historia in Mexico City, and the research was aided in many ways by the Centro Regional Morelos, INAH. I thank Elizabeth Brumfiel, Steven Falconer, Mary Hodge, and Glenn Schwartz for helpful comments on an earlier version of this chapter.

1. McGuire's third component of heterogeneity, the degree of independence between social parameters, is difficult to address with archaeological data, and his archaeological example, the ratio of residential to nonresidential built space (McGuire 1983:127), appears to be associated only indirectly with this factor.

2. All quantitative data on artifact distributions in this chapter describe materials from well-phased domestic midden deposits associated with individual houses. Ceramic artifacts are quantified in terms of minimum numbers of vessels per type per context (based upon rim sherds), expressed as percentages for each context. These measures are discussed in M. E. Smith (1992).

References Cited

Abrams, Elliot M.
  1989 Architecture and Energy: An Evolutionary Perspective. *Archaeological Method and Theory* 1:47–86.

Arnold, Dean E.
  1985 *Ceramic Theory and Cultural Process.* Cambridge University Press, New York.

Ashmore, Wendy
  1981 Some Issues of Method and Theory in Lowland Maya Settlement Archaeology. In *Lowland Maya Settlement Patterns,* edited by W. Ashmore, pp. 37–69. University of New Mexico Press, Albuquerque.

Berdan, Frances F.
  1985 Markets in the Economy of Aztec Mexico. In *Markets and Marketing,* edited by S. Plattner, pp. 339–367. University Press of America, Lanham, Md.
  1987 Cotton in Aztec Mexico: Production, Distribution, and Uses. *Mexican Studies/Estudios Mexicanos* 3:235–262.

Blanton, Richard E.
  1976 Anthropological Studies of Cities. *Annual Review of Anthropology* 5:249–264.

Blau, Peter M.
  1977 *Inequality and Heterogeneity: A Primitive Theory of Social Structure.* Free Press, New York.

Bloch, Marc
   1931 *Les caractères originaux de l'histoire rurale française.* H. Aschehoug, Oslo.

Braudel, Fernand
   1981 *The Structures of Everyday Life: The Limits of the Possible.* Harper & Row, New York.

Brumfiel, Elizabeth M.
   1980 Specialization, Market Exchange, and the Aztec State: A View from Huexotla. *Current Anthropology* 21:459–478.
   1987 Elite and Utilitarian Crafts in the Aztec State. In *Specialization, Exchange, and Complex Societies,* edited by E. M. Brumfiel and T. K. Earle, pp. 102–118. Cambridge University Press, New York.

Carrasco, Pedro
   1976 The Joint Family in Ancient Mexico: The Case of Molotla. In *Essays on Mexican Kinship,* edited by H. Nutini, P. Carrasco, and J. M. Taggert, pp. 45–64. University of Pittsburgh Press, Pittsburgh.

Charlton, Thomas H., Deborah L. Nichols, and Cynthia Otis Charlton
   1991 Aztec Craft Production and Specialization: Archaeological Evidence from the City-State of Otumba, Mexico. *World Archaeology* 23:98–114.

Codex Mendoza
   1992 *Codex Mendoza.* 4 vols. Edited by F. F. Berdan and P. Anawalt. University of California Press, Berkeley and Los Angeles.

Donkin, R. A.
   1979 *Agricultural Terracing in the Aboriginal New World.* Viking Fund Publications in Anthropology, No. 56. University of Arizona Press, Tucson.

Evans, Susan T.
   1988 *Excavations at Cihuatecpan, an Aztec Village in the Teotihuacán Valley.* Vanderbilt University Publications in Anthropology, No. 36. Department of Anthropology, Vanderbilt University, Nashville, Tenn.
   1990 The Productivity of Maguey Terrace Agriculture in Central Mexico during the Aztec Period. *Latin American Antiquity* 1:117–132.
   1991 Architecture and Authority in an Aztec Village: Form and Function of the Tecpan. In *Land and Politics in the Valley of Mexico,* edited by H. R. Harvey, pp. 63–92. University of New Mexico Press, Albuquerque.

Gilman, Antonio
   1981 The Development of Social Stratification in Bronze Age Europe. *Current Anthropology* 22:1–24.

Goodfellow, Susan T.
   1990 Late Postclassic Period Economic Systems in Western Morelos, Mexico: A Study of Ceramic Production, Distribution, and Exchange. Ph.D. dissertation, Department of Anthropology, University of Pittsburgh.

Graffam, Gary
   1992 Beyond State Collapse: Rural History, Raised Fields, and Pastoralism in the South Andes. *American Anthropologist* 94:882–904.

Hendon, Julia A.
   1992 The Interpretation of Survey Data: Two Case Studies from the Maya Area. *Latin American Antiquity* 3:22–42.

Hicks, Frederic
   1982 Tetzcoco in the Early 16th Century: The State, the City and the Calpolli. *American Ethnologist* 9:230–249.

Hirth, Kenneth G.
   In prep. *Ancient Urbanism at Xochicalco, Morelos.*

Hodge, Mary G.
   1992 The Geographic Structure of Aztec Imperial-Period Market Systems. *Research and Exploration* 8:428–445.

Kowalewski, Stephen A.
   1990 The Evolution of Complexity in the Valley of Oaxaca. *Annual Review of Anthropology* 19:39–58.

Leeds, Anthony
   1980 Towns and Villages in Society: Hierarchies of Order and Cause. In *Cities in a Larger Context,* edited by Thomas W. Collins, pp. 6–33. University of Georgia Press, Athens.

Lightfoot, Kent G., and Steadman Upham
   1989 Complex Societies in the Prehistoric American Southwest: The Debate. In *The Sociopolitical Structure of Prehistoric Southwestern Societies,* edited by S. Upham and K. G. Lightfoot, pp. 3–32. Westview Press, Boulder, Colo.

McGuire, Randall H.
   1983 Breaking Down Cultural Complexity: Inequality and Heterogeneity. *Advances in Archaeological Method and Theory* 6:91–142.

Maclachlan, Morgan D.
   1987 From Intensification to Proletarianization. In *Household Economies and Their Transformations,* edited by M. D. Maclachlan, pp. 1–27. University Press of America, Lanham, Md.

Miller, Edward, and John Hatcher
   1978 *Medieval England: Rural Society and Economic Change, 1086–1348.* Longman, New York.

Pattee, Howard H., ed.
   1973 *Hierarchy Theory: The Challenge of Complex Systems.* George Braziller, New York.

Peacock, D. P. S.
   1982 *Pottery in the Roman World: An Ethnoarchaeological Approach.* Longman, New York.

Polgar, Steven
   1975 Population, Evolution, and Theoretical Paradigms. In *Population, Ecology, and Social Evolution,* edited by S. Polgar, pp. 1–26. Mouton, The Hague.

Price, T. Douglas, and James A. Brown, eds.
   1985 *Prehistoric Hunter-Gatherers: The Emergence of Cultural Complexity.* Academic Press, New York.

Redfield, Robert
   1941 *The Folk Culture of Yucatan.* University of Chicago Press, Chicago.

Rojas, José Luis de
   1986 *México Tenochtitlan: Economía e Sociedad en el Siglo XVI.* Fondo de Cultura Económica, Mexico City.

Sahagún, Fray Bernardino de
   1950– Florentine Codex: General History of the Things of New
   1982 Spain. A. J. O. Anderson and C. E. Dibble, transl. and ed. School of American Research and University of Utah Press, Santa Fe and Salt Lake City.

Sanders, William T., Jeffrey R. Parsons, and Robert S. Santley
   1979 *The Basin of Mexico: Ecological Processes in the Evolution of a Civilization.* Academic Press, New York.

Sanders, William T., and David L. Webster
   1988 The Mesoamerican Urban Tradition. *American Anthropologist* 90:521–546.

Santley, Robert S., and Kenneth G. Hirth, eds.
   1993 *Prehispanic Domestic Units in Western Mesoamerica: Studies of the House, Compound, and Residence.* CRC Press, Boca Raton, Fla.

Shryock, Henry S., Jacob S. Siegel, and Edward G. Stockwell
   1976 *The Methods and Materials of Demography,* condensed edition. Academic Press, New York.

Simon, Herbert
   1962 The Architecture of Complexity. *Proceedings of the American Philosophical Society* 106:467–482.

Smith, Carol A.
   1976 Exchange Systems and the Spatial Distribution of Elites: The Organization of Stratification in Agrarian Societies. In *Regional Analysis,* Vol. 2: *Social Systems,* edited by C. A. Smith, pp. 309–374. Academic Press, New York.

Smith, Michael E.
   1987 Household Possessions and Wealth in Agrarian States: Implications for Archaeology. *Journal of Anthropological Archaeology* 6:297–335.
   1989 Cities, Towns, and Urbanism: Comment on Sanders and Webster. *American Anthropologist* 91:454–461.
   1990 Long-Distance Trade under the Aztec Empire: The Archaeological Evidence. *Ancient Mesoamerica* 1:153–169.
   1992 *Archaeological Research at Aztec-Period Rural Sites in Morelos, Mexico,* Vol. 1: *Excavations and Architecture.* Memoirs in Latin American Archaeology, No. 4. Department of Anthropology, University of Pittsburgh, Pittsburgh.
   1993 Houses and the Settlement Hierarchy in Late Postclassic Morelos: A Comparison of Archaeology and Ethnohistory. In *Prehispanic Domestic Units in Western Mesoamerica: Studies of the House, Compound, and Residence,* edited by R. S. Santley and K. G. Hirth, pp. 191–206. CRC Press, Boca Raton, Fla.
   In press Economies and Polities in Aztec-Period Morelos: Ethnohistoric Introduction. In *Economies and Polities in the Aztec Realm,* edited by M. F. Hodge and M. E. Smith. Institute for Mesoamerican Studies, Albany, N.Y.

Smith, Michael E., and John Doershuk
   1991 Late Postclassic Chronology in Western Morelos, Mexico. *Latin American Antiquity* 2:291–310.

Smith, Michael E., C. Heath-Smith, R. Kohler, J. Odess, S. Spanogle, and T. Sullivan
   In press The Size of the Aztec City of Yautepec: Urban Survey in Central Mexico. *Ancient Mesoamerica* 5.

Smith, Michael E., and Kenneth G. Hirth
   1988 The Development of Prehispanic Cotton-Spinning Technology in Western Morelos, Mexico. *Journal of Field Archaeology* 15:349–358.

Smith, Michael E., and T. Jeffrey Price
   In press Agricultural Terraces in Aztec-Period Morelos, Mexico: Evidence for Household-Level Agricultural Intensification. *Journal of Field Archaeology* 20.

Sorensen, Jerrel H.
   1988 Rural Chipped Stone Technology in Late Postclassic Morelos, Mexico. Paper presented at the 1988 Annual Meeting of the American Anthropological Association, Phoenix, Arizona.

Sorensen, Jerrel H., Kenneth G. Hirth, and Stephen M. Ferguson
   1989 The Contents of Seven Obsidian Workshops around Xochicalco, Morelos. In *La Obsidiana en Mesoamérica,* edited by M. Gaxiola and J. E. Clark, pp. 269–276. Instituto Nacional de Antropología e Historia, Mexico City.

Spence, Michael W.
   1985 Specialized Production in Rural Aztec Society: Obsidian Workshops of the Teotihuacan Valley. In *Contributions to the Archaeology and Ethnohistory of Greater Mesoamerica,* edited by W. J. Folan, pp. 76–125. Southern Illinois University Press, Carbondale.

Thirsk, Joan
   1961 Industries in the Countryside. In *Essays in the Economic and Social History of Tudor and Stuart England, in Honor of R. H. Tawney,* edited by F. J. Fisher, pp. 70–88. Cambridge University Press, Cambridge.

Turner, B. L., II
   1983 *Once Beneath the Forest: Prehistoric Terracing in the Río Bec Region of the Maya Lowlands.* Westview Press, Boulder, Colo.

Wenke, Robert J.
   1981 Explaining the Evolution of Cultural Complexity: A Review. *Advances in Archaeological Method and Theory* 4:79–127.

Wolf, Eric R.
   1966 *Peasants.* Prentice Hall, Englewood Cliffs, N.J.

Wright, Henry T., and Gregory A. Johnson
   1975 Population, Exchange and Early State Formation in Southwestern Iran. *American Anthropologist* 77:267–289.

CHAPTER ELEVEN

The Classic Maya Collapse at Copan, Honduras:
An Analysis of Maya Rural Settlement Trends

ANNCORINNE FRETER

THIS CHAPTER CONSIDERS THE collapse of the Classic Maya site of Copan, Honduras, from a rural perspective. For nearly a century, the process of the Classic Mayan collapse has been conceptualized as a rather sudden and catastrophic event. This perspective, however, has been developed almost exclusively from data derived through excavations within large Maya centers, focusing on the ruling elite. The goal of this chapter is to present extensive rural settlement data on the Copan Valley that demonstrate that the massive depopulation of the Main Center during the collapse is best characterized as a process of rural out-migration and community formation. This chapter will emphasize the important role played by rural settlement data in reconstructing regional evolutionary patterns.

The Maya civilization developed in southern Mexico, Guatemala, Belize, El Salvador, and Honduras during the first millennium A.D. By A.D. 800, the collapse of this complex civilization is apparent in the archaeological record. Few historical monuments (stelae) were erected by the Maya after this time, most construction within the major Maya centers ceased, and the population within the Southern Lowland Maya region decreased rapidly. Based on these observations, the Maya collapse has been characterized as a period in which the elite class structure of society totally disintegrated, resulting in the rapid depopulation of the major Maya centers and their associated rural communities within the brief period between A.D. 800 and 900 (Thompson 1954; Willey 1956).

This collapse of the Classic Maya civilization has been investigated for over a century. The explanations posited by scholars have been summarized in the literature on several occasions (Morley 1946; Thompson 1954; Cowgill 1964; Willey 1964; Adams 1973; Culbert 1973; Sabloff 1973; Lowe 1985) and so need not be reviewed here in detail. The most commonly cited reasons for the Maya collapse have included ecological or environmental degradation (Cooke 1931; Morley 1946; Sanders 1973; D. Rice 1978); natural catastrophic disasters, such as earthquakes (MacKie 1961) or hurricanes (Webb 1964); the large-scale spread of an indigenous epidemic disease (Saul 1973; Shimkin 1973); internal sociopolitical conflicts (Thompson 1954, 1966; Sharer 1977; Hamblin and Pitcher 1980); external pressure through foreign invasions (Cowgill 1964; Sabloff and Willey 1967); and interregional trade disruptions (Rathje 1973; Webb 1973). However, it has been recognized for many years that a single "prime mover" explanation is unlikely to explain such a complex process completely and that a series of interactive causal factors probably all contributed to the breakdown of Maya society to some degree.

These models are predicated upon the reconstruction of a sudden, dramatic, and rapid depopulation of the Southern Maya Lowlands over a relatively short time period. However, recent demographic data based on regional settlement surveys (Willey 1973; Chase 1979; Ford 1986; P. Rice 1986; Dixon 1992) suggest that the degree of depopulation postulated to have taken place between A.D. 800 and 900 in the Maya Lowlands may have been exaggerated and that substantial rural populations remained well after the collapse of at least some of the major Maya centers. Although most of the potential causes of the Classic Maya collapse have probably been identified, more detailed research on the actual form, demographic extent, and timing of the collapse is needed before an interactive causal model can be solidified.

This chapter focuses on the Classic Maya collapse as it was manifested at the site of Copan. It employs data from rural

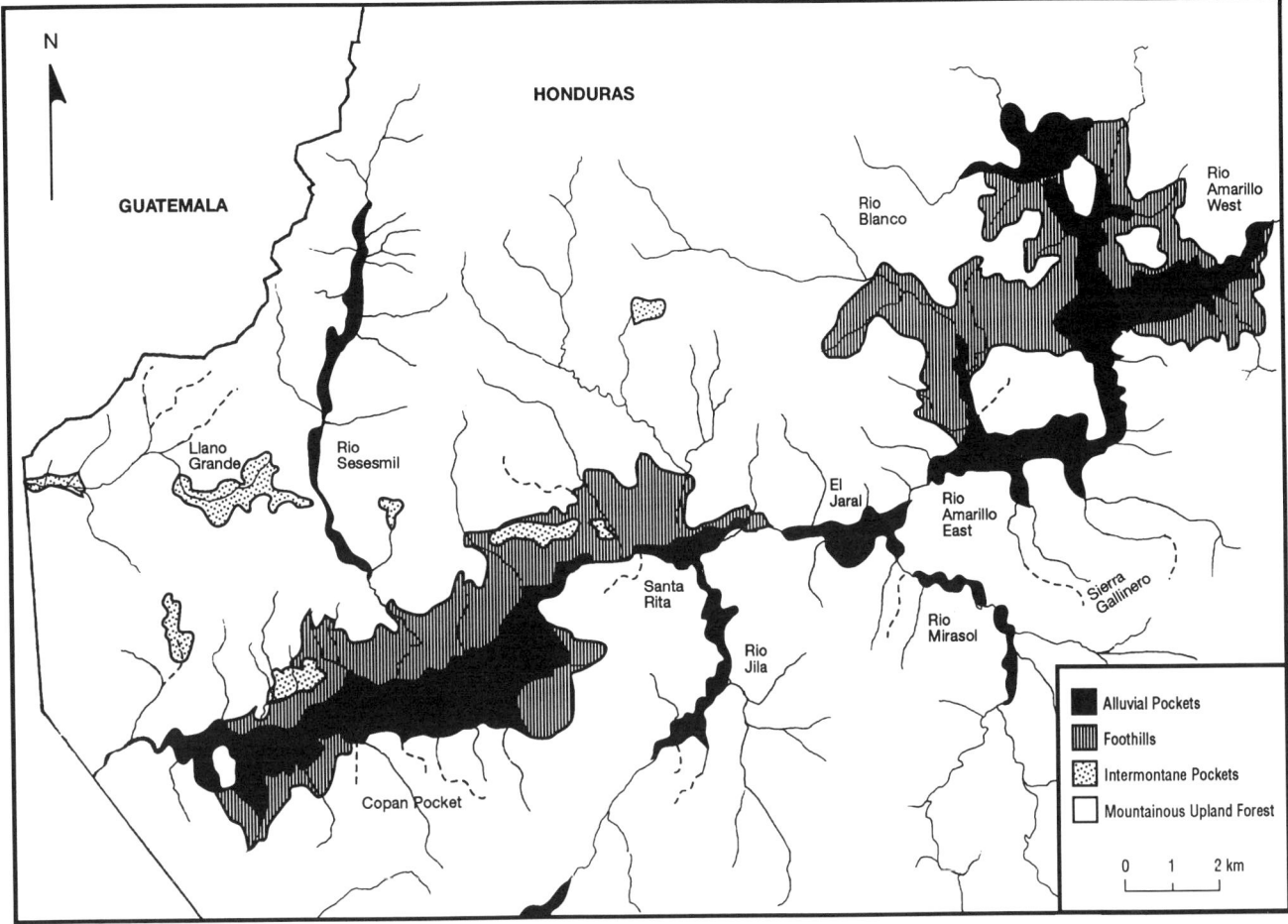

Fig. 74. Copan Valley environmental zones.

settlement surveys (Leventhal 1979, 1981; Fash 1983a,b; Webster 1985; Vlcek and Fash 1986; Freter 1988) and rural test pit excavations (Fash 1983a; Freter 1988; Webster and Freter 1990a,b; Freter 1992), in conjunction with data from extensive excavations within the Main Center (Fash 1983a, 1991; Andrews and Fash 1992; Fash et al. 1992; Sharer, Miller, and Traxler 1992; Stuart 1992), in the surrounding urban barrios (Sanders 1986; Hendon 1987, 1991; Ashmore 1991; Diamanti 1991; Sheehy 1991), and from ten excavated rural sites (Webster and Gonlin 1988; Gonlin 1993; Chapter 12 by Gonlin). These combined rural and urban settlement data indicate that the Classic Maya collapse at Copan began very quickly, between A.D. 800 and 850, but primarily affected the Copan ruling elite, who appear to have lost much of their authority and power during this time. This initial decentralization of the Copan polity was followed by 200 years of rural out-migration and community formation, complete with secondary elite positions and rural administrative centers. The Copan settlement data suggest that the process of collapse involved several phases, some leading to the direct failure of the political system, others involving responses to that failure by various other sociopolitical segments. The data indicate that the ruling elite were affected first and most directly, a situation reflected in a sudden abandonment of the Main Group and its associated structures in the Urban Core. The remaining sizeable population responded more gradually to systemic problems, forming small rural communities that survived until about A.D. 1150. This protracted and relatively detailed demographic history allows for a more refined reconstruction of the processes that may have contributed to the Copan collapse.

Introduction to the Copan Valley

Copan, the largest Maya archaeological center in the southeast periphery of the Maya Lowlands, is located in Honduras about 14 km east of the Guatemalan border. The Copan Valley is defined by the drainage of the Copan River, which covers an area of approximately 400 km^2 (Fig. 74). Surrounding the valley floor's alluvial bottomlands (590–700 m ASL) are zones

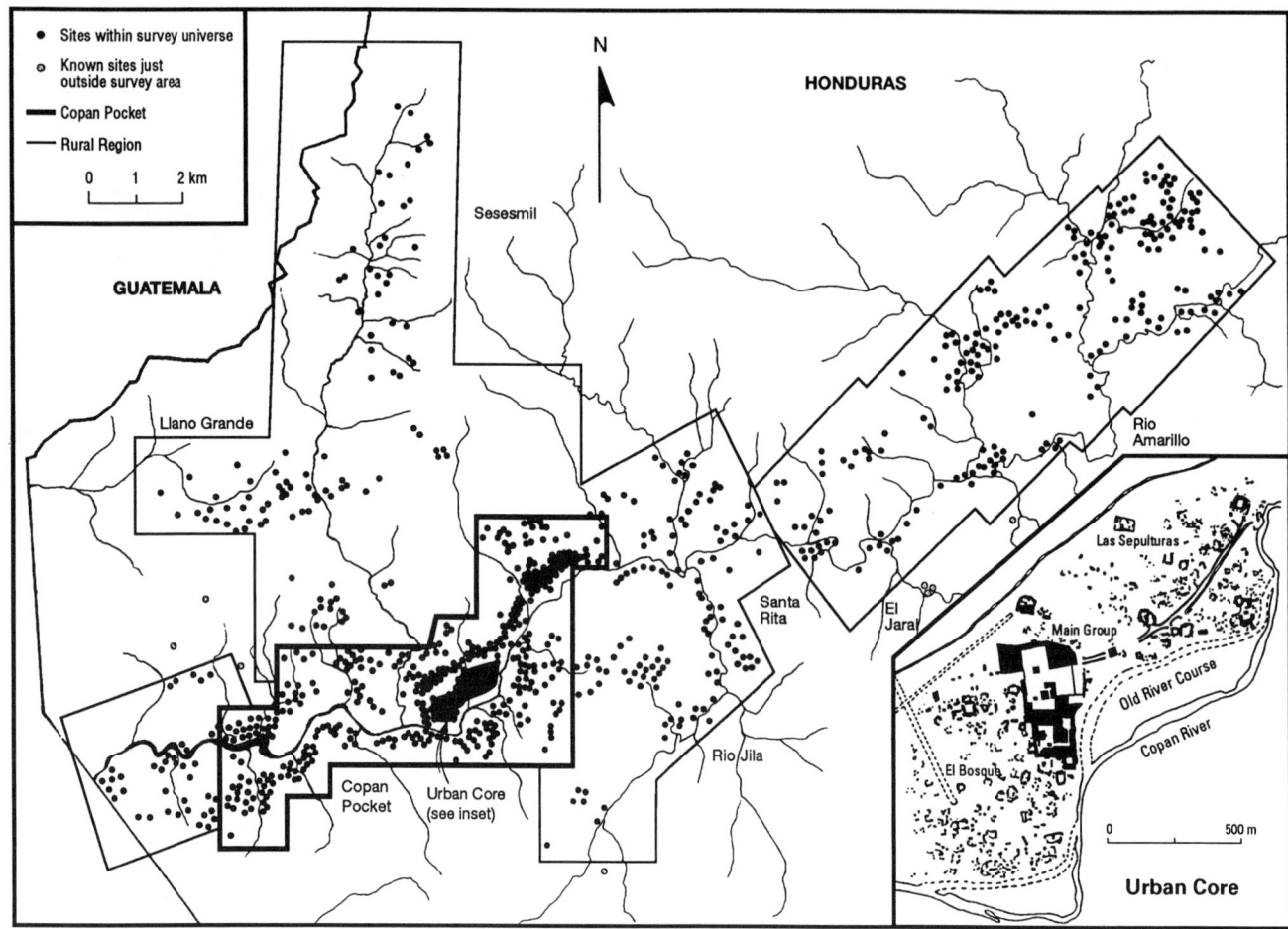

Fig. 75. Copan Valley site distribution.

of foothills (700–900 m ASL) that rise in some areas to rugged mountains (1,100–1,300 m ASL) interspersed with intermontane valleys (800–1,100 m ASL). The environmental setting of the Copan Valley is therefore unlike that of the majority of sites in the Maya Lowlands. The complex hydrologic and topographic valley conditions produce a variety of significantly different ecological zones within a comparatively small region, with a corresponding variety of agricultural potentials and resource availabilities (Turner et al. 1983; Webster, Sanders, and Van Rossum 1992; Wingard 1992). These diverse environmental conditions have clearly had a major impact on the location and distribution of Copan Mayan settlements through time.

The history of archaeological investigation at Copan reflects the changes in research focus and methodology that have occurred in Mesoamerican archaeology over the last century. The initial mapping of the Copan Main Group (Fig. 75 inset) was conducted by John Stephens in 1841. The Main Group was later the subject of research conducted by the Peabody Museum (1891–1895) and the Carnegie Institution (1935–1946). The first attempt to map the settlements surrounding the Main Group was not begun until 1975–1977, when the Harvard University Copan Pocket Mapping Project, directed by Gordon Willey, mapped all the visible mounds within the Copan Pocket, the 24-km² area surrounding the Main Group (Leventhal 1979; Fash 1983b). A preliminary investigation of rural sites elsewhere in the valley followed (Vlcek and Fash 1986).

Systematic regional settlement studies continued to be a primary research focus at Copan after the Harvard project. Phase I of the Proyecto Arqueologico Copan (PAC I), conducted from 1977 to 1980 and directed by Claude Baudez, continued the Copan Pocket Mapping Project and eventually test-pitted 1 percent of the mounds within that area (Fash 1983a). During PAC phase II, directed by William T. Sanders and David Webster from 1980 to 1988, rural settlement surveys were expanded to include a 135-km² area within the Copan River drainage (Webster 1985; Freter 1988, 1992). Toward the end of the PAC II project, in 1985, the Copan Mosaics Project was designed by William and Barbara Fash to

Table 24. Copan Valley Site Counts and Test Pit Samples by Settlement Area

Area	Number of sites	Number of mounds	Number of sites tested	Percentage of sites tested
Urban Core	140	1,068	8	0.5
Copan Pocket	735	2,369	102	13.9
Copan River (rural)	330	762	94	28.4
Sesemil River (rural)	152	225	48	31.5
Jila River (rural)	68	119	0	0
Totals	1,425	4,543	252	17.7

study and record systematically the sculpture within the Main Group. The Mosaics Project later become incorporated into the larger Copan Acropolis Archaeological Project (PAAC) in 1988. PAAC is an ongoing multidisciplinary research project focused on the excavation and restoration of several of the Acropolis structures in the Main Group (Andrews and Fash 1992; Fash et al. 1992; Sharer, Miller, and Traxler 1992) and their associated hieroglyphic texts (Fash and Stuart 1991; Schele 1992; Stuart 1992). This century-long history of archaeological investigation at Copan has produced a wealth of data that allows Copan researchers to integrate the archaeological and hieroglyphic data bases to produce an extremely detailed reconstruction of Late Classic Copan Maya society.

The PAC II Rural Settlement Survey and Test Excavation Methodology

The PAC II Copan Rural Settlement Survey was modeled methodologically after the Basin of Mexico survey (Sanders, Parsons, and Santley 1979). Total survey coverage of the 400-km² contained in the Copan Valley was not feasible given the time and resources available; accordingly, survey efforts were concentrated on the ecological zones most suited for human settlement—the alluvium and foothills located along the larger river systems. Aerial photographs (1:16,000) covering the alluvium and foothill zones along the Copan, Sesesmil, and Jila rivers were selected and enlarged to a scale of 1:5,000 (Fig. 75). This 135-km² area was defined as the survey universe. The team walked the entire area, covering all locations that could be physically surveyed. Tracings over the aerial photographs were used to record site location. This survey methodology was possible because the valley is largely deforested today, and surface visibility was generally quite good. In addition to recording the basic location of sites, each site was individually mapped, a sample of the surface artifacts was collected, the types of construction materials used for each mound were noted, and ecological data on each survey unit were recorded. To date, between the Harvard, Copan Pocket, and Rural settlement surveys, 1,425 archaeological sites have been located and mapped over an area of 135 km² in the Copan Valley.

In conjunction with the PAC II Rural Survey, a comprehensive test excavation program was conducted by Webster and Freter (1990a,b) from 1983 to 1988. The first phase of this project (1983–1986) focused on testing the 482 rural sites located in the Copan and Sesesmil river valleys and resulted in the excavation of 420 test pits at 142, or 29.5 percent, of these sites (Table 24).[1] The sites selected for test pitting were stratified on the basis of geographic area (aerial photo quadrant) and site type, following a modified version of the Willey and Leventhal (1979) site classification (Table 25). Ranked from simple to complex, the typology includes nonmound sites, which consist of artifact scatters only; single mound sites, which are small isolated mounds; aggregate mound sites with two or three mounds but no formal courtyard arrangement; and type 1 through type 5 sites, which become gradually larger in size and more complex in configuration. The test pit sample was stratified to ensure that a statistically representative sample of all social levels of the Late Classic Copan Maya and all settlement and ecological zones within the rural region was obtained. When feasible, selected sites were tested by placing a 2 × 2-m unit in front of or behind each mound and, if possible, within the plaza, a methodology designed to determine general site function and chronology.

After the rural test pitting project was completed in 1986, it became clear that the rural test pit sample far exceeded that available from the 24-km² Copan Pocket settlement region, from which only a 1 percent sample had been recovered during PAC I (Fash 1983a). This severely limited our ability to compare the variations through time between these very different settlement zones. In 1988, an additional field season was conducted in which 268 test pits were excavated at 102 sites within the Copan Pocket (Table 24). This test pitting yielded a 13.9 percent sample of the sites within this settlement zone, a sample again stratified on the basis of site type and geographic area. The Urban Core zone was not selected

Table 25. Summary of Copan Valley Site Typology

Site type	Description
Nonmound	Surface concentration of artifacts with no associated building debris
Single mound	Isolated mound not associated with any other structures; usually cobble construction less than 1 m in height
Aggregate	2–3 mounds with no formal courtyard grouping; mounds less than 1 m in height, usually of cobble construction
Type 1	3–5 mounds with courtyard; mounds less than 1 m in height, cobble or dressed stone construction
Type 2	6–8 mounds with 1–2 courtyards; mounds less than 3 m in height, cobble or dressed stone construction
Type 3	6–20 mounds with 1–3 courtyards; mounds less than 5 m in height, dressed stone construction, vault stones and sculpture usually present; an elite complex
Type 4	8–100+ mounds with multiple courtyards; some mounds over 5 m in height, dressed stone construction, vault stones and sculpture present; an elite complex
Type 5	The Main Group complex; the ruling elite complex

for test pitting since numerous sites within this settlement zone had received extensive excavations over the last 10 years (Sanders 1986; Sheehy 1991; Andrews and Fash 1992). Unfortunately, because of time constraints, the test pitting of sites in the Jila River Valley, also planned during the 1988 season, could not be conducted. In summary, of the 1,425 archaeological sites identified in the Copan Valley, 244 have been tested by the excavation of 688 2 × 2-m units, and an additional eight sites in the Urban Core have received extensive excavation. In total, we have collected data from a stratified random sample of 17.7 percent of the survey universe, representative of all social levels and—except for the Rio Jila—all geographic areas.

Given these data, three zones of prehistoric settlement in the Copan Valley can be identified:

1. The Urban Core, although small in area (0.75 km^2), is the most densely occupied zone, containing 1,425 structures/km^2, almost 45 percent of which are associated with type 3 or higher-ranked sites. This area includes the Main Group and its two flanking barrios, El Bosque and Las Sepulturas (Fig. 75 inset).
2. The Copan Pocket is defined as the 24-km^2 area surrounding the Urban Core but exclusive of it. Within this settlement zone, an average of 102 structures/km^2 are present, 10 percent of which are associated with type 3 or 4 residential units.
3. The Rural Region outside the Copan Pocket boundaries covers the largest geographic area but contains the lowest settlement density (10 structures/km^2) and the fewest (4 percent) elite structures.

The Copan Chronology

Any attempt at interpretation of Copan Valley site distribution must first address the primary problem encountered by the Copan rural settlement projects, that of chronology (see Webster and Freter [1990a] and Freter [1992] for a detailed discussion of this issue). The Late Classic ceramic phase at Copan, the Coner Phase (Viel 1983), has not been subdivided and therefore subsumed 99 percent of all sites in the Copan Valley. This clearly made the ceramic phasing too broad for reconstructing the settlement dynamics in the valley during the critical Late Classic period. Obtaining independent chronological data that could provide a means to subdivide the Late Classic period became essential. Although a limited number of radiocarbon and archaeomagnetic dates have been produced from Copan, inadequate samples from rural sites and the substantial costs of the procedures vitiate the utility of these techniques for dating a large and representative sample from rural Copan settlements. Obsidian hydration dating became the logical alternative, since obsidian was abundant at Copan Valley sites and the technique could produce a large number of dates economically.

The Copan Obsidian Hydration Dating Project was initiated in 1984 and is still in progress. A total of 2,300 obsidian hydration dates from 202 sites—14 percent of the sites in the Copan Valley—have been processed from associated middens, floor deposits, or features. The Copan hydration dates have been extensively cross-checked with other chronological data and agree quite well with ceramic associations, radiocarbon dates, iconographic data, and archaeomagnetic dates (Ashmore 1991; Sheehy 1991; Andrews and Fash 1992; Freter 1992).

Reconstruction of the Demographic History of the Copan Valley

The goal of the PAC II rural settlement survey was to provide the archaeological data necessary to reconstruct the demographic changes that occurred in the Copan Valley during the Late Classic–Postclassic transition—the critical time of the collapse. Population estimates for each area of the valley by 150-year time phases were calculated employing the methodology outlined in Freter (1988) and Webster and Freter (1990b). They are based on an estimated range of 4–5 persons/residential room occupied during that time phase. Corrections were made for nonresidential room functions, nonresidential sites, hidden structures, site abandonment, and areas that were not surveyed. It should be noted that, as with all population reconstructions based on archaeological data, the population estimates presented here should not be taken as absolutes and will differ slightly from other estimates that are based on shorter time periods (Webster, Sanders, and Van Rossum 1992), different techniques to estimate population growth (Paine 1993), or a slightly smaller data base (Freter 1992). The estimates presented here were designed to yield conservative population figures that are internally consistent and can be realistically compared to valley agricultural carrying capacity estimates (Rue 1986; Freter 1988; Webster, Sanders, and Van Rossum 1992; Wingard 1992). Thus, although the absolute population numbers presented should be viewed as only estimates, the population trends that they depict should be highly informative.

Copan Demography: A.D. 550–700

The size of the Middle Classic (Acbi) period population in the Copan Valley is currently difficult to estimate because Acbi remains are clearly underrepresented, owing to problems of preservation and sampling. The area covered by the PAC II Rural Survey ended at the Guatemalan border, an arbitrary modern political boundary, yet a recent settlement survey on the Guatemalan side of the Copan Valley indicates that a sizeable Acbi population resided just outside our current survey universe (C. Murdy, pers. comm. 1990). In addition, there is strong evidence that Acbi-phase constructions were dismantled and reused as construction fill in Late Classic period structures, particularly in the Urban Core: the vast majority of obsidian hydration dates from the construction fill of Late Classic (Coner)–phase buildings date to the Acbi period. It is hoped that the combined efforts of Murdy's Guatemalan survey, the continued work by William Fash (Fash et al. 1992) and Robert Sharer (Sharer, Miller, and Traxler 1992) in the Main Group's East Court, and a detailed examination of the Acbi fill deposits encountered in the Coner-phase Urban Core structures will shortly provide the data necessary to refine our demographic understanding of this important time period.

From the data currently available, it appears that the Late Acbi–period population within the Copan Valley was at least 5,000–7,000 people (Table 26). The PAC II settlement data also indicate that this population was strongly nucleated within the Copan Pocket and Urban Core zones, where about 80 percent of the population resided (Fig. 76).[2] Few rural sites contained evidence of occupation during this time period; the majority of those that did have such evidence, however, were located within the Sesesmil River Valley or out toward the Guatemalan border, a distribution quite consistent with Murdy's preliminary findings.

Interestingly, several of the sites occupied in the Sesesmil River Valley during the Late Acbi period probably functioned as agricultural fieldhuts and not as permanent residences because (1) the artifact inventories of these sites contained very limited domestic remains; (2) their architecture was quite crude, usually consisting of only a rough boulder foundation; (3) they were located in isolated foothill or forest ecological zones; and (4) their hydration dates indicated very short ranges of occupation. These fieldhuts indicate that land in the foothill and forest zones of the Sesesmil was being cleared for agricultural purposes as early as A.D. 600–700. The relatively early expansion of the rural population into the Sesesmil drainage—rather than the alluvial pockets along the Copan River—may be due to such factors as the close proximity of the Sesesmil to the Urban Core and the Sesesmil's excellent pottery clay sources (Turner et al. 1983; Freter 1991).

Table 26. Copan Valley Population Estimates by Time Period and Settlement Zone

Time period	Urban Core	Copan Pocket	Rural Region	Totals
A.D. 550–700	1,500–2,500	2,500–3,000	1,000–1,500	5,000–7,000
A.D. 700–850	5,000–7,000	9,000–10,000	4,000–5,000	18,000–22,000
A.D. 850–1000	3,000–3,500	5,000–6,000	5,000–5,500	13,000–15,000
A.D. 1000–1150	1,000–2,000	2,000–3,000	2,000–3,000	5,000–8,000
Post–A.D. 1150	500–1,000	500–1,000	500–1,000	1,500–3,000

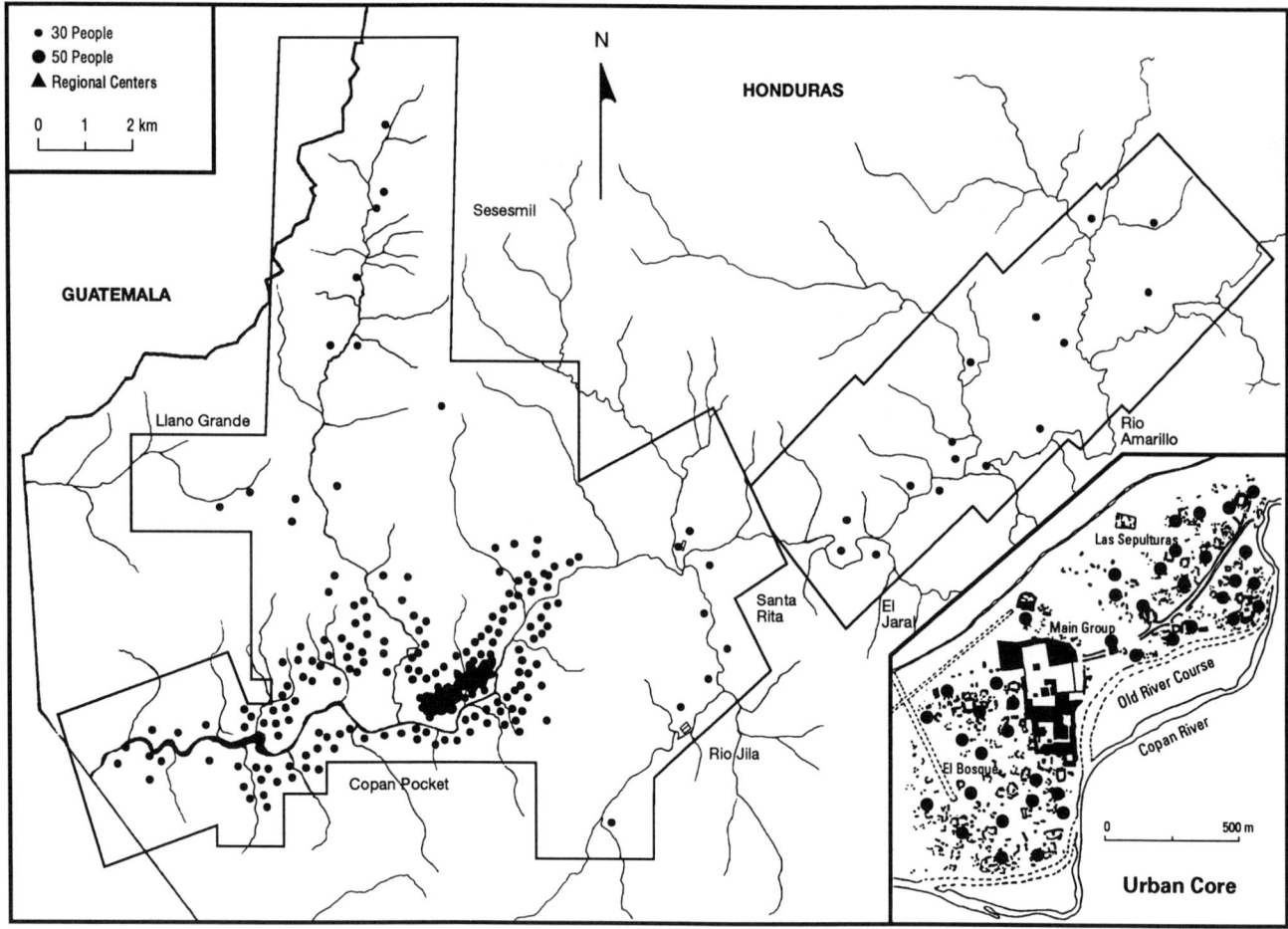

Fig. 76. Copan Valley population distribution, A.D. 550–700.

Toward the end of this phase, by A.D. 650–700, the entire Copan polity was expanding, a phenomenon demonstrated by the concentration of population in the Copan Pocket and Urban Core, the founding of larger elite type 3 and 4 sites in those areas, and the increase in historical monuments dedicated to dynastic rulers (Fash 1983a; Fash and Stuart 1991; Schele 1992). The small rural population at this time was widely scattered over the remainder of the valley, and there is clear evidence of rural expansion and gradual pioneering settlement in the Sesesmil drainage.

Copan Demography: A.D. 700–850

By A.D. 700–850, the Copan Valley had reached its height in sociopolitical complexity, possessing a well-established royal lineage (Fash and Stuart 1991; Schele 1992; Stuart 1992) and a stratified system of elite and commoners (Sanders 1989; Hendon 1991). During this period, the population in the Copan Valley increased rapidly to 18,000–22,000 people (Fig. 77). Excluding the possibility of in-migration, these figures suggest that the population was doubling every 80–100 years, a rapid but not impossible internal growth rate for a preindustrial society (Baker and Sanders 1972). As in the previous phase, the majority of the population, about 80 percent, was concentrated in the Copan Pocket and Urban Core zones. Rural settlement expanded outward along the valley floor; rural sites still consisted primarily of single mound and type 1 sites, although a single rural elite type 4 site was occupied in Rio Amarillo by the end of the phase.

Although the settlement distribution in the Copan Pocket and Urban Core changed little from that of the preceding period, a significant expansion from the alluvial plain into the surrounding foothills did occur. In addition, the densities of structures occupied and the number of people concentrated in the Copan Pocket and Urban Core zones increased dramatically. The Urban Core now had a population density of over 8,000 persons/km^2, and the Copan Pocket reached a population density close to 500 persons/km^2. Thus, by A.D. 800 a conservative estimate would have between 14,000 and 17,000 people residing in the Copan Pocket and Urban Core,

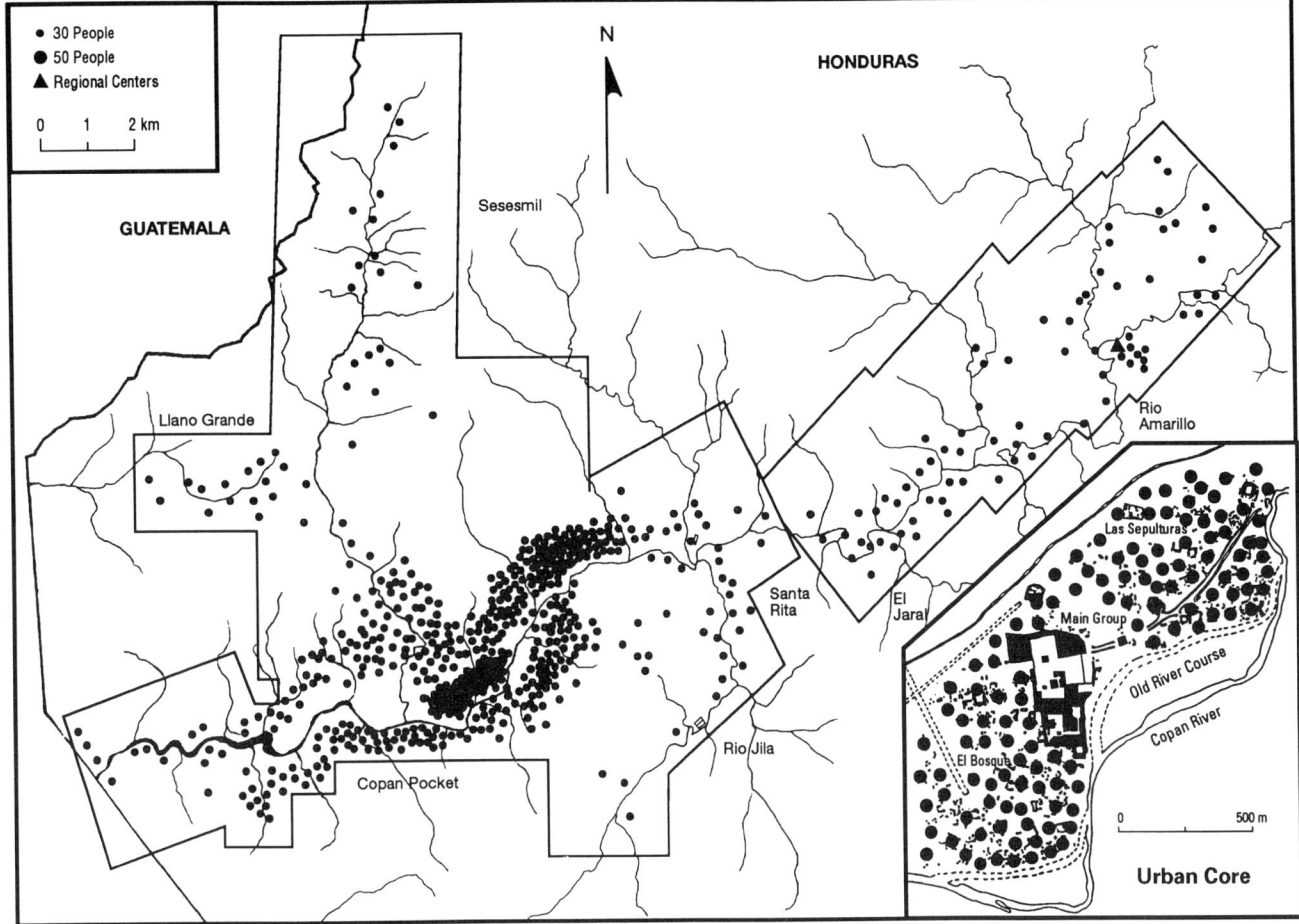

Fig. 77. Copan Valley population distribution, A.D. 700–850.

yet the agricultural carrying capacity of this area, assuming double-cropping on the alluvial plain, was at most 9,000–12,000 people (Rue 1986; Freter 1988; Webster, Sanders, and Van Rossum 1992; Wingard 1992). The rural population lived in widely scattered settlements with densities of about 40–50 persons/km² and was probably producing an agricultural surplus to sustain the nucleated Copan Pocket population by the end of the period.

During this most complex stage of the Copan sociopolitical system, about 82 percent of the population resided in relatively lower-status single mound, type 1, or type 2 sites, whereas only 18 percent lived in higher-status type 3 and 4 sites. This is an important statistic, for it demonstrates that even during the height of Copan's sociopolitical complexity, the majority of the population resided in lower-status dwellings. The actual percentage of the elite population was probably much lower than the estimated 18 percent, since many of the type 3 and 4 courtyard groups also contained residences of lower-status retainers or clients (Sanders 1989). Thus, the number of elite individuals, even during Copan's sociopoliti-

cal height, was probably less than 10 percent of the total population.

Copan Demography: A.D. 850–1000

After A.D. 850, depopulation and outward rural settlement migration occurred, representing the onset of the Copan collapse. The dynastic sequence at Copan ends quite abruptly around A.D. 810 (9.19.0.0.0)—the last date associated with Copan Ruler 16 (Stuart 1992). Interestingly, recent iconographic evidence indicates that there was an increase in subordinate elite texts toward the end of Ruler 16's reign, just prior to the disintegration of ruling elite power. Furthermore, at least three additional nobles, Personage A, Yax K'am Lay, and U K'it Tok', became subsidiary Lords (Stuart 1992). Obsidian hydration dates from test excavations within three residential courtyards in the Urban Core Bosque barrio indicate that this elite residential zone, closely associated with the rulers at the Main Group, ceased to be heavily occupied by A.D. 900 (Andrews and Fash 1992; Freter 1992). Thus, the

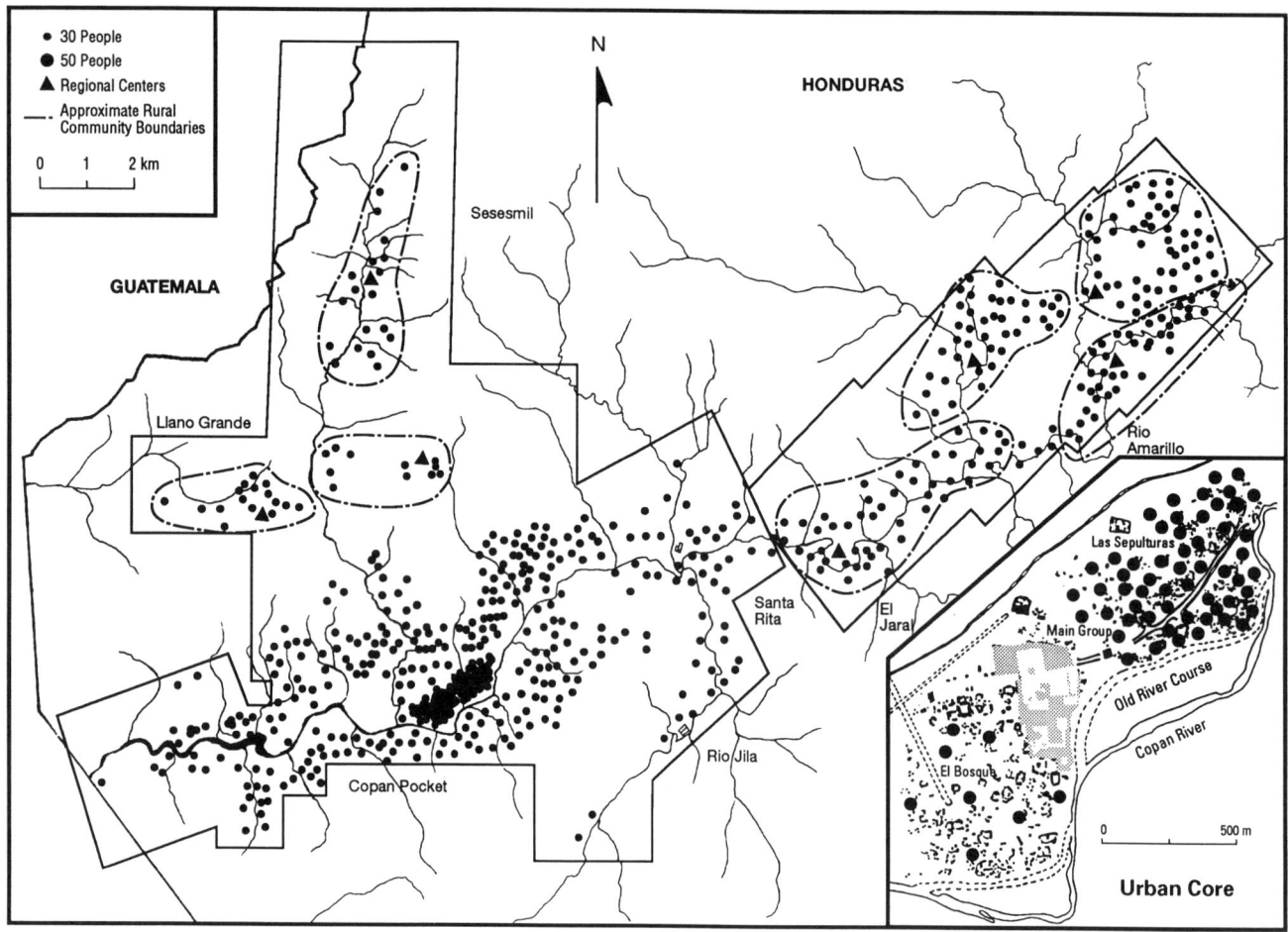

Fig. 78. Copan Valley population distribution, A.D. 850–1000.

archaeological and iconographic data from Copan are in excellent accord and strongly support the model of a sudden elite collapse of the Copan polity between A.D. 810 and 850.

Environmental reconstructions of the Copan Valley have also yielded significant data relevant to this political collapse. An energetic analysis of wood consumption costs (Abrams and Rue 1988) suggests that deforestation in the Copan Pocket foothill and upland mountain zones caused by firewood harvesting, agricultural expansion, and demand for construction materials reached levels that would have caused severe soil erosion by A.D. 800–850. An independent agricultural computer simulation based on the soil characteristics of the Copan Valley (Wingard 1992) also indicates that large-scale sheet erosion probably occurred circa A.D. 800–830, caused by the expansion of the population into the foothills and upland forest for agricultural purposes. Recently, two obsidian blades from Coner-phase deposits in the Copan Pocket alluvium buried under 2.5 m of eroded soil were dated to A.D. 792 and 819 ± 70 years, perfectly matching the population peak and heavy occupation of the foothills indicated by the settlement data and predicted by Wingard's computer simulation (Webster, Sanders, and Van Rossum 1992). In addition, the preliminary results of Rebecca Storey's (1992) analysis of Copan skeletal materials indicate that malnutrition and the incidence of disease increased during the Late Classic period; these data suggest that the overall population was experiencing significant health stress during this period. A palaeoethnobotanical analysis of deposits from the rural test pitting and Urban Core zones also indicates that the Late Classic–period population was under stress, since there is an increased utilization of previously marginal foods such as coyol at this time (Lentz 1991).

Responses to these combined political, health, and environmental stresses are clearly reflected in the population distributions after A.D. 850. The total population decreased to 13,000–15,000 people. More significant than this decrease, however, is the change in spatial distribution (Fig. 78). The population in the Copan Pocket and Urban Core zones decreased by about 50 percent from that during the previous period, while the rural population actually *increased* by almost

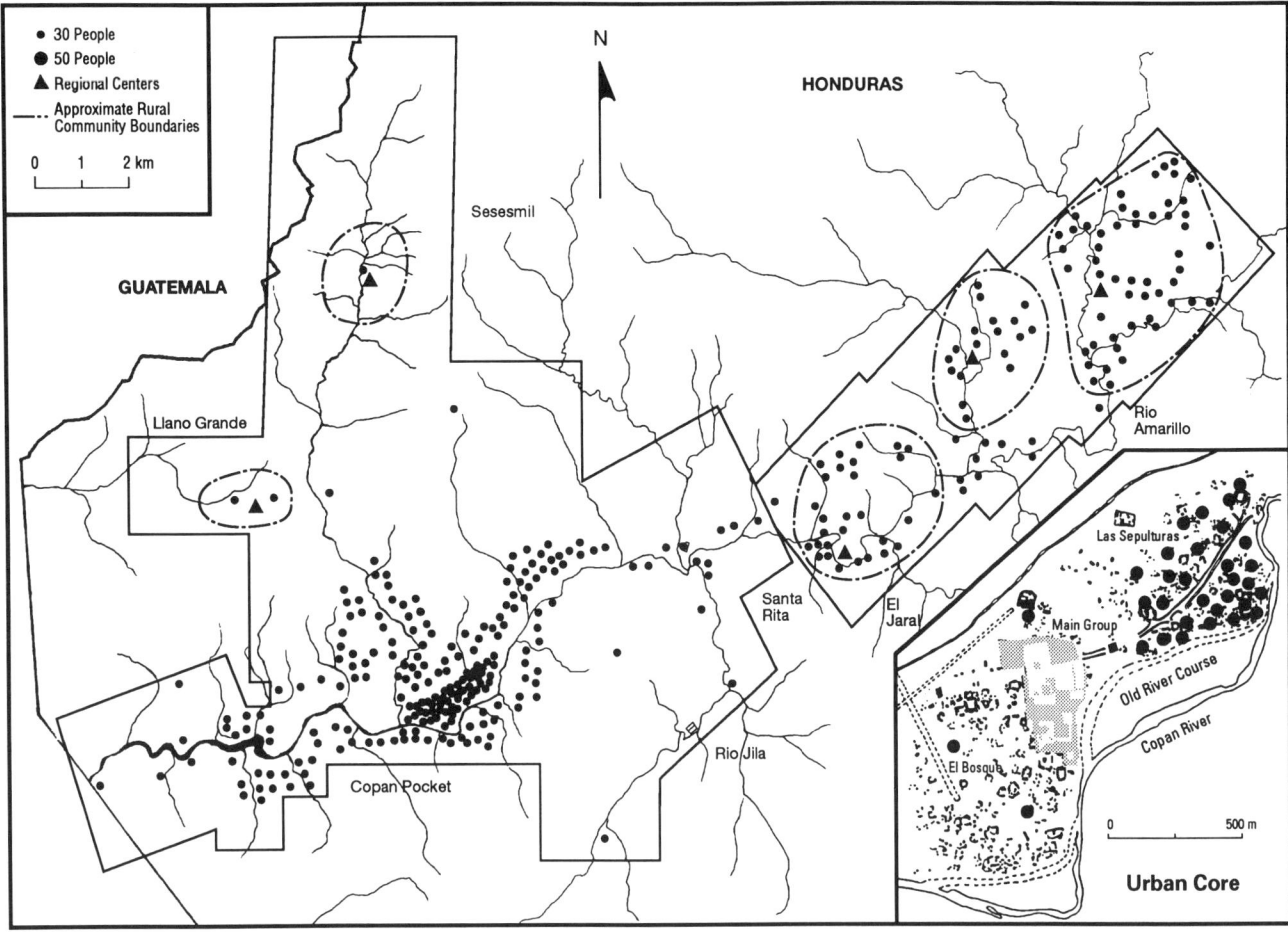

Fig. 79. Copan Valley population distribution, A.D. 1000–1150.

20 percent. Given the PAC II settlement data, it appears that a period of rural out-migration and rural community formation occurred subsequent to the collapse of the Copan ruling elite structure.

This increase in the rural population is clearly correlated with changes in the form and distribution of rural settlements. Clusters of rural settlements started to develop, and regional ceremonial centers were founded within these rural communities (Fig. 78). In addition, most of the larger type 2, 3, and 4 sites in the Rural Region were founded. Thus, both the form and focus of the rural population changed substantially after A.D. 850, with smaller, relatively independent regional settlement clusters developing to serve the rural population's administrative and religious needs—in effect replacing the royal households of the Main Center that no longer functioned effectively in this capacity. It is interesting that these rural settlements are concentrated in those areas of the valley that have the best agricultural potential outside the Copan Pocket alluvial bottomlands (Abrams and Rue 1988; Webster, Sanders, and Van Rossum 1992; Wingard 1992). The same areas accommodate the modern rural population of the valley, and contemporary Honduran farmers use much the same technology and crop complexes as their prehistoric predecessors.

Copan Demography: A.D. 1000–1150

The settlement trends that began during the previous period continued during the interval A.D. 1000–1150 (Fig. 79). The overall population in the valley decreased to 5,000–8,000 people, of whom only 60 percent resided within the Copan Pocket and Urban Core, while about 40 percent lived in the Rural Region. This phase exhibits essentially the same patterns as the preceding one, with the important exception that the overall population density in all settlement zones decreased by almost 50 percent.

The majority of the rural population resided in dispersed, small communities in the Rio Amarillo and El Jaral pockets rather than the agriculturally marginal Sesesmil drainage or the Rio Jila (Fig. 79). The alluvial pockets along the Copan River, especially along Rio Amarillo, provided small areas of

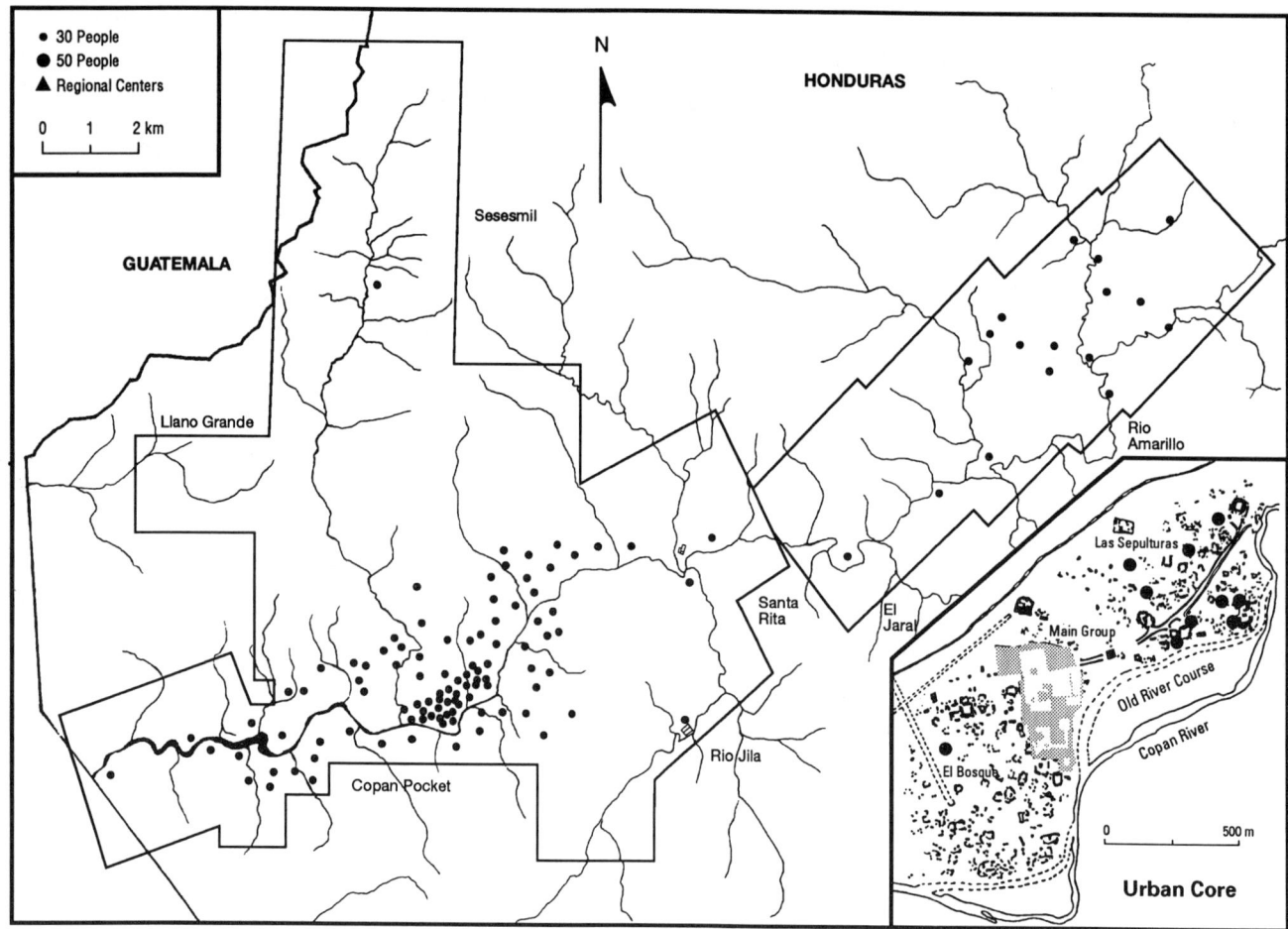

Fig. 80. Copan Valley population distribution after A.D. 1150.

flat, fertile bottomlands (*vega*) that could be double-cropped because of the higher annual rainfall in this part of the valley (Turner et al. 1983). It is thus likely that the agricultural potential of areas outside the Copan Pocket had a major effect on the settlement distribution in the Rural Region after A.D. 1000.

The population within the Copan Pocket and Urban Core remained much the same as that during the previous period, but the process of central collapse continued. The vast majority still resided in the smaller single mound, type 1, and type 2 sites, with only about 15 percent of the population living in the remains of the type 3 and 4 elite residential complexes.

Interestingly, the Obsidian Hydration Dating Project found that several of the courtyards within the type 4 site 9N-8 and the type 3 site 9M-22 showed evidence of reuse and reoccupation after A.D. 1000. It appears that people, probably from outside these elite complexes, began to reoccupy or at least reuse some of the abandoned rooms. For example, one individual was interred on top of the roof collapse in room 1, structure 9N-82, prior to the complete collapse of the building (Webster, Fash, and Abrams 1986). Such data are consistent with the political breakdown, the relatively low population densities, and the lack of evidence of ongoing major construction within the Copan Pocket and Urban Core at this time.

Copan Demography: Post–A.D. 1150

Settlement in the Copan Valley after A.D. 1150 was very sparse. The population numbered somewhere between 1,500 and 3,000 people, of whom about 70 percent lived in the Copan Pocket, while the remaining 30 percent resided in the Rural Region (Fig. 80). The data for this time period, however, are sketchy at best and often involve obsidian hydration dates from disturbed contexts. The available settlement and obsidian hydration data suggest that there was no occupation in the valley after A.D. 1200–1250. An independent study of the pollen from swamp sediments in the Copan Pocket and Rio Amarillo showed that, circa A.D. 1200–1250, the forest in these areas had started to return, and no further evidence of land clearing or agricultural activities is present until the recolonization of the valley in the nineteenth century (Rue 1986, 1987). In short, the settlement data, the obsidian hydration data, and the palynological data indicate a final Maya abandonment of the valley by A.D. 1200–1250.

This outline of Copan's demographic history indicates that the Maya collapse at Copan was more protracted than originally conceived. Although there was a sudden exodus of the ruling elite early in the ninth century, marking the onset of a major decrease in the valley's population, the ensuing demographic decrease occurred gradually over approximately 300–400 years. The rural settlement reconstruction and hydration dates are in excellent agreement with ceramic phasing (Viel 1983; Freter 1992), carbon-14 and archaeomagnetic dates (Freter 1992), the Long Count dates (Andrews and Fash 1992), internal site stratigraphy (Ashmore 1991; Sheehy 1991; Andrews and Fash 1992), energetic (Abrams and Rue 1988) and computer (Wingard 1992) simulations of the agricultural system, palaeodemographic reconstructions (Storey 1992), pollen data (Rue 1987), and palaeoethnobotanical data (Lentz 1991). These diverse, independent lines of investigation, pursued by a large number of scholars, converge upon the same conclusion and provide an excellent example of the value of a conjunctive approach. What the PAC II rural settlement and obsidian hydration research has contributed is a more detailed understanding of the demographic extent and timing of the Copan collapse. As a result, the period of collapse at Copan and the complex processes that contributed to it may now be summarized.

The Copan Maya Collapse

In order to understand better the process of Copan's political decentralization, a clearer picture of its sociopolitical structure is necessary. Perhaps the most cogent model of Maya sociopolitical organization has been proposed by Kurjack (1974), based on his settlement data from Dzibilchatun. Kurjack noted that the settlements around Dzibilchatun ranged in size and complexity from large centers to small hamlet clusters. Kurjack proposed that all of these site types served as residential units, but that varying degrees of social rank influenced the sites' elaboration, size, and form. Citing these observations, Kurjack suggested that the Maya were hierarchically organized as ranked household units.

Kurjack's preliminary model builds on Emile Durkheim's (1933) concept of early state formation. Durkheim viewed the beginnings of state formation as a stage in which society was still held together by mechanical solidarity—a society represented by a likeness of parts or homogeneous segments connected to each other through kinship ties. Durkheim proposed that this early state society would eventually develop into a society based on organic solidarity, in which the development of a division of labor created dissimilar parts that had unique, dissimilar functions. It is certainly recognized that these two "types" represent idealized forms in a continuum of increasing sociopolitical and economic complexity. Nonetheless, the ranked household model of Maya social organization suggested by Kurjack is organized more in terms of mechanical solidarity.

This ranked household lineage model has been expanded recently by Sanders (1989) and Diamanti (1991), who draw ethnographic support for this model from West African societies. Sanders (1989) suggests that Maya polities contained several noble lineages, either autonomous or semiautonomous, that ruled over a specific district and were ranked according to their differential access to resources (primarily land). Thus, Sanders proposes that the population within each Maya polity was socially and politically organized within economically self-sufficient lineage units. Economic specialization and market exchange are thought to play only a marginal role in Late Classic Maya society, inhibited in effect by the organizational efficiency of the lineage.

This collective model of Classic Maya sociopolitical organization is strongly supported by the archaeological data from Copan. Specific studies on Copan lithic production (Mallory 1984), ground stone production (Spink 1983), utilitarian ceramic production (Freter 1991), plaster production (Abrams and Freter 1988), and the architectural labor system (Abrams 1987) all suggest that economic specialization at Copan was not well developed and that most utilitarian production was conducted within each domestic courtyard.

In summary, the Copan polity during the Late Classic period appears to have been a society composed of ranked lineage household compounds, each to a great degree economically self-sufficient. This polity was integrated through the leadership of maximal lineage heads, who administered or controlled the economic, social, political, and ideological agenda of their respective social corporate units. Controlling the total Copan polity was a "king" from the royal lineage who resided in the Main Center and exercised some degree of political control over the maximal lineage heads and their respective populations (Sanders 1989; Hendon 1991; Stuart 1992). The importance of this sociopolitical model to the Copan collapse lies in its emphasis on mechanical solidarity—replicated units connected by social and ideological forces rather than articulated through vital economic ties. Logically, societies structured on this basis are more susceptible to fragmentation, since each unit is economically independent and should remain functionally coherent when disarticulated from other similar units (Fried 1967). It is highly probable that this type of fragmentation would occur gradually, since each lineage unit may dissociate itself from the polity independently of the others.

This gradual process of decentralization or collapse is reflected in the general change from a three-tiered political hierarchy (royalty–lineage heads–commoners) to a two-tiered system (lineage heads–commoners). This change in the structure of power relations explains the sudden diversity of site types in the Rural Region after A.D. 850 (Fig. 78). As lineage heads and their respective populations started to move from the Copan Pocket to the Rural Region, they founded the relatively larger type 2, 3, and 4 sites and regional ceremonial centers. Paradoxically, the size of these architectural compounds and their concomitant large populations suggest that some lineage heads not only survived the political decentralization but possibly even gained status during and after the royal collapse, as witnessed by the recent identification of subelite offices formed just prior to the decentralization of the Copan Polity (Stuart 1992). In effect, new political and economic roles may have been assumed by these lineage heads as a consequence of the void created by the demise of the royal elite.

These demographic and rural settlement data have provided a more detailed reconstruction of the form and extent of the collapse at Copan than was previously possible, and this new reconstruction bears upon the possible factors that contributed to Copan's decline. Ecological explanations of the Maya collapse have been primarily criticized because environmental degradation is a gradual process, not in keeping with a sudden collapse. The data from Copan, however, clearly indicate that, whereas some stages of the collapse—sheet erosion, agricultural failure in the Copan Pocket, the demise of the ruling elite—were relatively sudden, other stages were more gradual, specifically involving the out-migration of lineage units to rural communities. This view of a protracted process of systemic failure and response bolsters the possibility of a central role for environmental factors in explaining the collapse.

As noted previously, recent environmental reconstructions of the Copan Valley suggest that deforestation in the foothill and upland mountain zones of the Copan Pocket reached levels that would have caused severe soil erosion and nutrient depletion by A.D. 800–850 (Rue 1987; Abrams and Rue 1988; Wingard 1992). These conditions would have drastically reduced the agricultural productivity of the Copan Pocket, thereby contributing to the erosion of the power base of Copan's political rulers. Since the size of the nucleated Copan Pocket population by A.D. 800 was at least 14,000–17,000 people, whereas the agricultural carrying capacity of that area was at most 9,000–12,000 people (Rue 1986; Freter 1988; Webster, Sanders, and Van Rossum 1992; Wingard 1992), we can observe that the agricultural system was operating at its maximal limit and generating considerable stress on the physical environment.

By this time, not only had the population in the Copan Pocket exceeded the carrying capacity of the area, but long-term soil degradation had started to affect the productivity of the region—even as the population continued to expand. This type of environmental stress, once begun, cannot be reversed quickly. The densely nucleated population in the Copan Pocket would have required reduced fallow periods to support itself agriculturally. Yet this short-term solution would have accelerated the long-term depletion of the soil resources even further. Eventually, the most viable option, and the one selected, was rural out-migration, which clearly began by A.D. 850.

This ecological stress on the Copan political system is also evident during the reign of the sixteenth and last known ruler of Copan, who commissioned more public monumental construction than any other ruler in Copan's history (Fash 1983a). The radical increase in the construction of public architecture just before the fragmentation of the Copan political system and the increase in subelite texts associated with the end of Ruler 16's reign (Stuart 1992) may represent an attempt by this ruler to create more political solidarity within the Copan Valley. It has been suggested by David Webster (1976) that the construction of large-scale public architecture may reflect a strategy to increase political and social unification. Webster suggests that extensive public works are often constructed when a political system is disrupted and faced with a period of instability or stress. This strategy may have been employed by Ruler 16 in an attempt to hold the Copan polity together under the stressful environmental conditions and consequent lowering of the quality of life that prevailed during his reign. The archaeological data, however, indicate that he was unsuccessful in doing so, the result being the decentralization of the Copan polity.

Conclusion

Several important conclusions have been offered concerning the Classic Maya collapse at Copan, Honduras, based on many years of settlement research. Most directly, the settlement history of both the elite barrios and the rural regions of the Copan Valley has been presented. Although a relatively sudden abandonment of some of the elite urban areas is evident between A.D. 800 and 850, a more gradual abandonment of the center of the Copan polity—the Copan Pocket—is also evident. This finding immediately suggests that the process of systemic collapse at Copan proceeded at different rates when affecting different segments of society and that characterizations such as "sudden" and "gradual" are too simplistic to convey the complexity of the collapse process.

A model drawn from Emile Durkheim involving an idealized dichotomy between mechanical and organic solidarity as characteristic of the structure of early states was presented. Based on the empirical data from Copan, it was suggested that the sociopolitical structure of this early state was organized hierarchically in replicated lineage units, more characteristic of mechanical solidarity. The importance of this Durkheimian model is that societies structured as mechanical units are economically self-sufficient and can exist independent of the larger social unit. Thus, with the relatively sudden departure of the ruling elite, a complete societal failure was not imminent; rather, lineage units of varying rank continued to function, gradually and independently abandoning the center of the now-defunct polity.

The array of ecological data from Copan strongly implicates agricultural mismanagement and failure as the ultimate rather than the proximate cause for the collapse of the Copan polity, in effect precipitating both the sudden departure of the ruling elite and the gradual abandonment of each lineage unit. Thus far, only the process of collapse at the stage when the population was forced to respond through sudden or protracted out-migration has been considered. Yet the process of collapse begins with ecological and demographic stress that occurs well before the actual "failure." The demographic data presented in this chapter clearly reflect that stress, with population growing significantly in the eighth century. Furthermore, carrying capacity data were presented that indicate that the early ninth-century population could not readily be fed from the fields of the Copan Pocket. Although this hypothesis is untested, it is possible that outlying pockets of alluvial soil—the rural pockets—were exploited for surplus production that would have been transported into the Copan Pocket. These rural pockets may have been under heavy cultivation at the time of agricultural failure in the nucleated Copan Pocket. The implication is that these outlying pockets, targeted for out-migration and colonization, may have been heavily exploited for some decades as a means of offsetting the agricultural stress within the Copan Pocket.

It has been suggested (Abrams and Rue 1988) that a series of smaller collapses occurred between A.D. 1000 and 1250 in these outlying pockets, paralleling in both cause and effect the major collapse in the Copan Pocket. If this is the case, then the strategy of exploiting the outlying regions in an attempt to delay (if not end) agricultural and nutritional stress by the ruling elite may have set the stage for subsequent collapses by the descendants of the Late Classic Copanecos, a pattern that may be endemic to cyclical cultural systemic failure (Willey 1991).

This consideration of Copan's collapse, by including the rural settlement data, necessarily implies the critical analytical role played by the nonelite segment of society in our understanding of the complete process of collapse. Considerations of this complex process based only on data pertaining to the ruling elite fail to recognize the total societal effect of economic failure and, importantly, fail to take account of the varied responses available to distinct segments of society. Studying the process of collapse requires a detailed understanding of the material conditions and decisions made by the rural or commoner component of any society.

Notes

The field and laboratory research providing the settlement and obsidian hydration data was generously funded by the Instituto Hondureño de Antropología e Historia, by several National Science Foundation grants (BNS-8219421, BNS-8419933, and BNS-8720027), and by an Ohio University Research Committee grant (853-1990). I am indebted to William T. Sanders and David Webster for their support and insights during the fieldwork and to Joseph Michels for his technical expertise and permission to use the Vickers M-17 microscope for the Copan Obsidian Hydration Dating Project. It was through the diligence of Mike Davis, Melissa Diamanti, Joseph Guiliano, Patricia Miller, John Seldomridge, Thomas Sussenbach, Stephen Whittington, and John Wingard that the PAC II Rural Survey was completed; Valerie Gates, Nancy Gonlin, Richard Paine, David Reed, David Rue, and Glenn Storey contributed their assistance to the test pit excavations. I am also indebted to Elliot Abrams, E. Wyllys Andrews V, Wendy Ashmore, William Fash, Andrea Gerstle, Julia Hendon, John Mallory, James Sheehy, Mary Spink, Rebecca Storey, Randolf Widmer, and Daniel Wolfman, along with many other Copan veterans, for their advice, insights, and criticism. As always, I bear sole responsibility for all errors of fact, logic, and interpretation.

1. These figures differ slightly from those previously published (Freter 1992) because sites identified as "modern" have been removed from the sample, and sites identifed by the PAC II survey that overlapped with the Copan Pocket survey have been reassigned to the Copan Pocket settlement zone.

2. The settlement distribution maps presented here are revised, updated versions of those previously published (Freter 1992). The more refined population trends within the Urban Core settlement zone presented here are based on over 800 obsidian hydration dates from eight sites that have been subject to extensive excavations or test

pitting over the last 10 years. This site sample, however, is quite small, representing only 0.5 percent of Urban Core sites. Therefore, whereas the Urban Core population trends depicted in this chapter are based on all the currently available data, our demographic understanding of this important settlement zone will surely undergo further refinement in the future.

References Cited

Abrams, Elliot M.
  1987 Economic Specialization and Construction Personnel in Classic Period Copan, Honduras. *American Antiquity* 52: 485–499.
Abrams, Elliot M., and AnnCorinne Freter
  1988 Intra-Polity Economics at the Maya Center of Copan, Honduras. Paper presented at the 54th Annual Meeting of the Society for American Archaeology, Phoenix.
Abrams, Elliot M., and David Rue
  1988 The Causes and Consequences of Deforestation among the Prehistoric Maya. *Human Ecology* 16:377–395.
Adams, Richard E. W.
  1973 The Collapse of Maya Civilization: A Review of Previous Theories. In *The Classic Maya Collapse,* edited by T. P. Culbert, pp. 21–34. University of New Mexico Press, Albuquerque.
Andrews, E. Wyllys, V, and Barbara W. Fash
  1992 Continuity and Change in a Royal Maya Residential Complex at Copan. *Ancient Mesoamerica* 3:63–88.
Ashmore, Wendy
  1991 Site-Planning Principles and Concepts of Directionality among the Ancient Maya. *Latin American Antiquity* 2:199–226.
Baker, Paul, and William T. Sanders
  1972 Demographic Studies in Anthropology. *Annual Review of Anthropology* 1:151–178.
Chase, Arlene
  1979 Regional Development in the Tayasal-Paxcaman Zone, El Peten, Guatemala: A Preliminary Statement. *Cerámica de Cultura Maya* 11:86–119.
Cooke, C. Wythe
  1931 Why the Mayan Cities of the Peten District, Guatemala, Were Abandoned. *Journal of the Washington Academy of Sciences* 21:283–287.
Cowgill, George L.
  1964 The End of Classic Maya Culture: A Review of the Recent Evidence. *Southwestern Journal of Anthropology* 20:145–159.
Culbert, T. Patrick, ed.
  1973 *The Classic Maya Collapse.* University of New Mexico Press, Albuquerque.
Diamanti, Melissa
  1991 Domestic Organization at Copan: Reconstruction of Elite Maya Households through Ethnographic Models. Ph.D. dissertation, Department of Anthropology, The Pennsylvania State University.

Dixon, Boyd
  1992 Prehistoric Political Change on the Southeast Mesoamerican Periphery. *Ancient Mesoamerica* 3:11–26.
Durkheim, Emile
  1933 *The Division of Labor in Society.* Free Press, New York.
Fash, William L., Jr.
  1983a Maya State Formation: A Case Study and Its Implications. Ph.D. dissertation, Department of Anthropology, Harvard University.
  1983b Reconocimento y Excavaciones en el Valle. In *Introducción a la Arqueología de Copan, Honduras,* Tomo III, edited by C. F. Baudez. Proyecto Arqueologico Copan. Trejos Hermanos, San José, Costa Rica.
  1991 *Scribes, Warriors, and Kings: The City of Copan and the Ancient Maya.* Thames and Hudson, London.
Fash, William L., Jr., and David Stuart
  1991 Dynastic History and Cultural Evolution at Copan, Honduras. In *Classic Maya Political History: Hieroglyphic and Archaeological Evidence,* edited by T. P. Culbert, pp. 147–179. Cambridge University Press, Cambridge.
Fash, William L., Jr., Richard V. Williamson, Carlos Rudy Larios, and Joel Palka
  1992 The Hieroglyphic Stairway and Its Ancestors: Investigations of Copan Structure 10L-26. *Ancient Mesoamerica* 3:105–115.
Ford, Anabel
  1986 *Population Growth and Social Complexity: An Examination of Settlement and Environment in the Central Maya Lowlands.* Anthropological Research Papers, No. 35. Arizona State University, Tempe.
Freter, AnnCorinne
  1988 The Classic Maya Collapse at Copan, Honduras: A Regional Settlement Perspective. Ph.D. dissertation, Department of Anthropology, The Pennsylvania State University.
  1991 A Reconstruction of the Late Classic Rural Ceramic Production System in the Copan Valley, Honduras. Paper presented at the 56th Annual Meeting of the Society for American Archaeology, New Orleans.
  1992 Chronological Research at Copan: Methods and Implications. *Ancient Mesoamerica* 3:117–133.
Fried, Morton H.
  1967 *The Evolution of Political Society.* Random House, New York.
Gonlin, Nancy
  1993 Rural Household Archaeology at Copan, Honduras. Ph.D. dissertation, Department of Anthropology, The Pennsylvania State University.
Hamblin, Robert L., and Brian L. Pitcher
  1980 The Classic Maya Collapse: Testing Classic Conflict Hypotheses. *American Antiquity* 45:246–267.
Hendon, Julia
  1987 The Uses of Maya Structures: A Study of Architecture and Artifact Distribution at Sepulturas, Copan, Honduras. Ph.D. dissertation, Department of Anthropology, Harvard University.

1991 Status and Power in Classic Maya Society: An Archaeological Study. *American Anthropologist* 93:894–918.

Kurjack, Edward B.
1974 *Prehistoric Lowland Maya Community and Social Organization—A Case Study at Dzibilchultun, Yucatan, Mexico.* Middle American Research Institute Publication No. 38. Tulane University, New Orleans.

Lentz, David
1991 Maya Diets of the Rich and Poor: Paleoethnobotanical Evidence from Copan. *Latin American Antiquity* 2:269–287.

Leventhal, Richard M.
1979 Settlement Patterns at Copan, Honduras. Ph.D. dissertation, Department of Anthropology, Harvard University.
1981 Settlement Patterns in the Southeast Maya Area. In *Lowland Maya Settlement Patterns,* edited by W. Ashmore, pp. 187–209. University of New Mexico Press, Albuquerque.

Lowe, John W. G.
1985 *The Dynamics of Apocalypse.* University of New Mexico Press, Albuquerque.

MacKie, Euan W.
1961 New Light on the End of Classic Maya at Benque Viejo, British Honduras. *American Antiquity* 27:216–224.

Mallory, John K., III
1984 Late Classic Maya Economic Specialization: Evidence from the Copan Obsidian Assemblage. Ph.D. dissertation, Department of Anthropology, The Pennsylvania State University.

Morley, Sylvanus G.
1946 *The Ancient Maya.* Stanford University Press, Palo Alto, Calif.

Paine, Richard R.
1993 Population Dynamics at Copan, Honduras, A.D. 450–1250: A Study in Archaeological Demography. Ph.D. dissertation, Department of Anthropology, The Pennsylvania State University.

Rathje, William L.
1973 Classic Maya Development and Denouement: A Research Design. In *The Classic Maya Collapse,* edited by T. P. Culbert, pp. 405–454. University of New Mexico Press, Albuquerque.

Rice, Don
1978 Population Growth and Subsistence Alternatives in a Tropical Lacustrine Environment. In *Pre-Hispanic Maya Agriculture,* edited by P. Harrison and B. L. Turner, pp. 35–62. University of New Mexico Press, Albuquerque.

Rice, Prudence
1986 The Peten Postclassic: Perspectives from the Central Peten Lakes. In *Late Lowland Maya Civilization: Classic to Postclassic,* edited by J. Sabloff and E. W. Andrews, pp. 251–300. University of New Mexico Press, Albuquerque.

Rue, David
1986 A Palynological Analysis of Prehispanic Human Impact in the Copan Valley, Honduras. Ph.D. dissertation, Department of Anthropology, The Pennsylvania State University.

1987 Early Agriculture and Early Postclassic Occupation in Western Honduras. *Nature* 326:285–286.

Sabloff, Jeremy A.
1973 Continuity and Disruption during Terminal Late Classic Times at Seibal: Ceramic and Other Evidence. In *The Classic Maya Collapse,* edited by T. P. Culbert, pp. 107–131. University of New Mexico Press, Albuquerque.

Sabloff, Jeremy A., and Gordon R. Willey
1967 The Collapse of the Maya Civilization in the Southern Lowlands: A Consideration of History and Process. *Southwestern Journal of Anthropology* 23:311–336.

Sanders, William T.
1973 The Cultural Ecology of the Lowland Maya: A Re-Evaluation. In *The Classic Maya Collapse,* edited by T. P. Culbert, pp. 325–366. University of New Mexico Press, Albuquerque.
1989 Household, Lineage, and State at Eighth-Century Copan, Honduras. In *The House of the Bacabs, Copan, Honduras,* edited by D. Webster, pp. 89–105. Studies in Precolumbian Art and Archaeology, No. 29. Dumbarton Oaks, Washington, D.C.

Sanders, William T., ed.
1986 *Excavaciones en el Area Urbana de Copan: Proyecto Arquelogico Copan, Fase II.* Secretaría de Cultura y Turismo, Instituto Hondureño de Antropología e Historia, Tegucigalpa, Honduras.

Sanders, William T., Jeffrey R. Parsons, and Robert S. Santley
1979 *The Basin of Mexico: Ecological Processes in the Evolution of a Civilization.* Academic Press, New York.

Saul, Frank P.
1973 Disease in the Maya Area: The Pre-Columbian Evidence. In *The Classic Maya Collapse,* edited by T. P. Culbert, pp. 301–324. University of New Mexico Press, Albuquerque.

Schele, Linda
1992 The Founders of Lineages at Copan and Other Maya Sites. *Ancient Mesoamerica* 3:135–144.

Sharer, Robert J.
1977 The Maya Collapse Revisited: Internal and External Perspectives. In *Social Process in Maya Prehistory: Studies in Honor of Sir Eric Thompson,* edited by N. Hammond, pp. 532–552. Academic Press, London.

Sharer, Robert J., Julia C. Miller, and Loa P. Traxler
1992 Evolution of Classic Period Architecture in the Eastern Acropolis, Copan, Honduras: A Progress Report. *Ancient Mesoamerica* 3:145–159.

Sheehy, James
1991 Structure and Change in a Late Classic Maya Domestic Group at Copan, Honduras. *Ancient Mesoamerica* 2:1–19.

Shimkin, Demitri B.
1973 Models for the Downfall: Some Ecological and Culture Historical Considerations. In *The Classic Maya Collapse,* edited by T. P. Culbert, pp. 117–143. University of New Mexico Press, Albuquerque.

Spink, Mary Louise
- 1983 Metates as Socioeconomic Indicators during the Late Classic Period at Copan, Honduras. Ph.D. dissertation, Department of Anthropology, The Pennsylvania State University.

Storey, Rebecca
- 1992 The Children of Copan: Issues in Paleopathology and Paleodemography. *Ancient Mesoamerica* 3:161–167.

Stuart, David
- 1992 Hieroglyphs and Archaeology at Copan. *Ancient Mesoamerica* 3:169–184.

Thompson, J. Eric S.
- 1954 *The Rise and Fall of Maya Civilization,* University of Oklahoma Press, Norman.
- 1966 *The Rise and Fall of Maya Civilization,* second edition. University of Oklahoma Press, Norman.

Turner, Billie Lee, William Johnson, Gail Mahood, Frederick M. Wiseman, and Jackie Poole
- 1983 Habitat y Agricultura en la Region de Copan. In *Introducción a la Arqueología de Copan, Honduras,* Tomo I, edited by C. F. Baudez, pp. 35–142. Proyecto Arqueologico Copan. Trejos Hermanos, San José, Costa Rica.

Viel, Rene
- 1983 Evolución de la Cerámica de Copan: Resultados Preliminares. In *Introducción a la Arqueología de Copan, Honduras,* Tomo I, edited by C. F. Baudez, pp. 471–550. Proyecto Arqueologico Copan. Trejos Hermanos, San José, Costa Rica.

Vlcek, David T., and William L. Fash
- 1986 Survey in the Outlying Areas of the Copan Region, and the Copan-Quirigua Connection. In *The Southeast Maya Periphery,* edited by P. Urban and E. Schortman, pp. 102–113. University of Texas Press, Austin.

Webb, Malcolm C.
- 1964 The Post-Classic Decline of the Peten Maya: An Interpretation in the Light of a General Theory of State Society. Ph.D. dissertation, Department of Anthropology, University of Michigan.
- 1973 The Peten Maya Decline Viewed in the Perspective of State Formation. In *The Classic Maya Collapse,* edited by T. P. Culbert, pp. 367–404. University of New Mexico Press, Albuquerque.

Webster, David L.
- 1976 On Theocracies. *American Anthropologist* 78(4):812–828.
- 1985 Recent Settlement Survey in the Copan Valley, Honduras. *Journal of New World Archaeology* 5:39–51.

Webster, David L., William L. Fash, and Elliot M. Abrams
- 1986 Excavaciones en el Conjunto 9N-8 Patio A (Operación VIII). In *Excavaciones en el Area Urbana de Copan: Proyecto Arqueologico Copan,* Tomo 1, edited by W. T. Sanders, pp. 155–317. Secretaria de Cultura y Turismo, Instituto Hondureño de Antropología e Historia, Tegucigalpa, Honduras.

Webster, David L., and AnnCorinne Freter
- 1990a Settlement History and the Classic Collapse at Copan: A Refined Chronological Perspective. *Latin American Antiquity* 1:66–85.
- 1990b The Demography of Late Classic Copan. In *Precolumbian Population History in the Maya Lowlands,* edited by T. P. Culbert and D. S. Rice, pp. 37–62. University of New Mexico Press, Albuquerque.

Webster, David L., and Nancy Gonlin
- 1988 Household Remains of the Humblest Maya. *Journal of Field Archaeology* 15:169–190.

Webster, David L., William T. Sanders, and Peter Van Rossum
- 1992 A Simulation of Copan Population History and Its Implications. *Ancient Mesoamerica* 3:185–197.

Willey, Gordon R.
- 1956 The Structure of Ancient Maya Society: Evidence from the Southern Lowlands. *American Anthropologist* 58:777–782.
- 1964 An Archaeological Frame of Reference for Maya Culture History. In *Desarrollo Cultural de los Mayas,* edited by E. Vogt and A. Ruz, pp. 135–175. Universidad Nacional Autonóma de Mexico, Mexico City.
- 1973 Altar de Sacrificios Excavations: General Summary and Conclusions. Papers of the Peabody Museum, Vol. 64, No. 3. Harvard University, Cambridge, Mass.
- 1991 Horizontal Integration and Regional Diversity: An Alternating Process in the Rise of Civilizations. *American Antiquity* 56:197–215.

Willey, Gordon R., and Richard M. Leventhal
- 1979 Prehistoric Settlement at Copan. In *Maya Archaeology and Ethnohistory,* edited by N. Hammond and G. R. Willey, pp. 75–102. University of Texas Press, Austin.

Willey, Gordon R., and Demitri Shimkin
- 1973 The Maya Collapse: A Summary View. In *The Classic Maya Collapse,* edited by T. P. Culbert, pp. 457–501. University of New Mexico Press, Albuquerque.

Wingard, John
- 1992 The Role of Soils in the Development and Collapse of Classic Maya Civilization at Copan, Honduras. Ph.D. dissertation, Department of Anthropology, The Pennsylvania State University.

CHAPTER TWELVE

Rural Household Diversity in Late Classic Copan, Honduras

NANCY GONLIN

RURAL OCCUPATION IS MORE often equated with homogeneity and simplicity than with heterogeneity and complexity. But, as many of the contributions to this volume illustrate, the hinterlands of complex societies often provide as much information on diversity as do the urban components of a system. "Rural complexity" is seen in both the Old (Chapter 9 by Falconer) and New worlds (Chapter 7 by Santley; Chapter 10 by Smith).

This chapter examines the nature of rural diversity within the context of the Classic Maya of Copan, Honduras. The information presented here is a subset of the data summarized by Freter (in Chapter 11) but differs in that it offers an in-depth perspective on several small rural households. Freter provides background information on the polity of Copan, the tradition of archaeological research in the region, the definition of rural and urban zones of habitation, and the analysis of settlement in the valley as a whole.

The intent here is to demonstrate the chronological, sociocultural, and functional variation of small households in the three zones of settlement (Urban Core, rural Copan Pocket, Rural Region) and to examine rural life-style through comparison with the urban zone. Rural-urban relations in Classic Maya society will be discussed with respect to a rural-urban dichotomy that is observable in the Copan area in such aspects as architecture, artifacts, and burial treatment as well as spatial proximity to the civic-ceremonial center and to prime agricultural land. The resiliency of the rural population and its relative independence from the center will be examined.

Small Group Size, Commoner Status, and the Type 1 Classification at Copan

Small groups at Copan have been identified as type 1 complexes (see Freter's description of the Copan classification system in Chapter 11 and Willey and Leventhal 1979). Type 1 groups have mounds no higher than 1.00 m and were constructed of cobble masonry with earthen fill; above the substructures were perishable superstructures. Type 2 units may contain as many as six to eight mounds arranged in one or two courtyards, with mound remains as tall as 2.5 or 3 m. Although dressed stone may be present, most mound stone is still unworked, with only a few flat surfaces. A type 3 unit differs from a type 2 unit in the quality of mound construction and sometimes in the quantity of mounds and plaza groupings; some mounds in a type 3 unit may reach heights of 4.75 m. Type 4 units are complex groupings with numerous mounds, some reaching a height of 10 m. These multiplaza groups contain large amounts of dressed stone, sculpture, and sometimes vaulted roofs and hieroglyphic benches. Type 4 units are the largest of the site types outside the Main Group but also the least numerous, making up only 1 percent of all types of sites in the Copan polity (see Webster and Freter 1990a for a breakdown of site types and their distribution in the Copan Valley). Likewise, type 3 units are not very numerous (2 percent) in the Copan polity. Suffice it to say that type 1 and 2 groups are equated with a commoner status and are numerous in the Urban Core, the rural Copan Pocket, and the rural hinterland, with type 1 sites dominating the rural hinterland. This

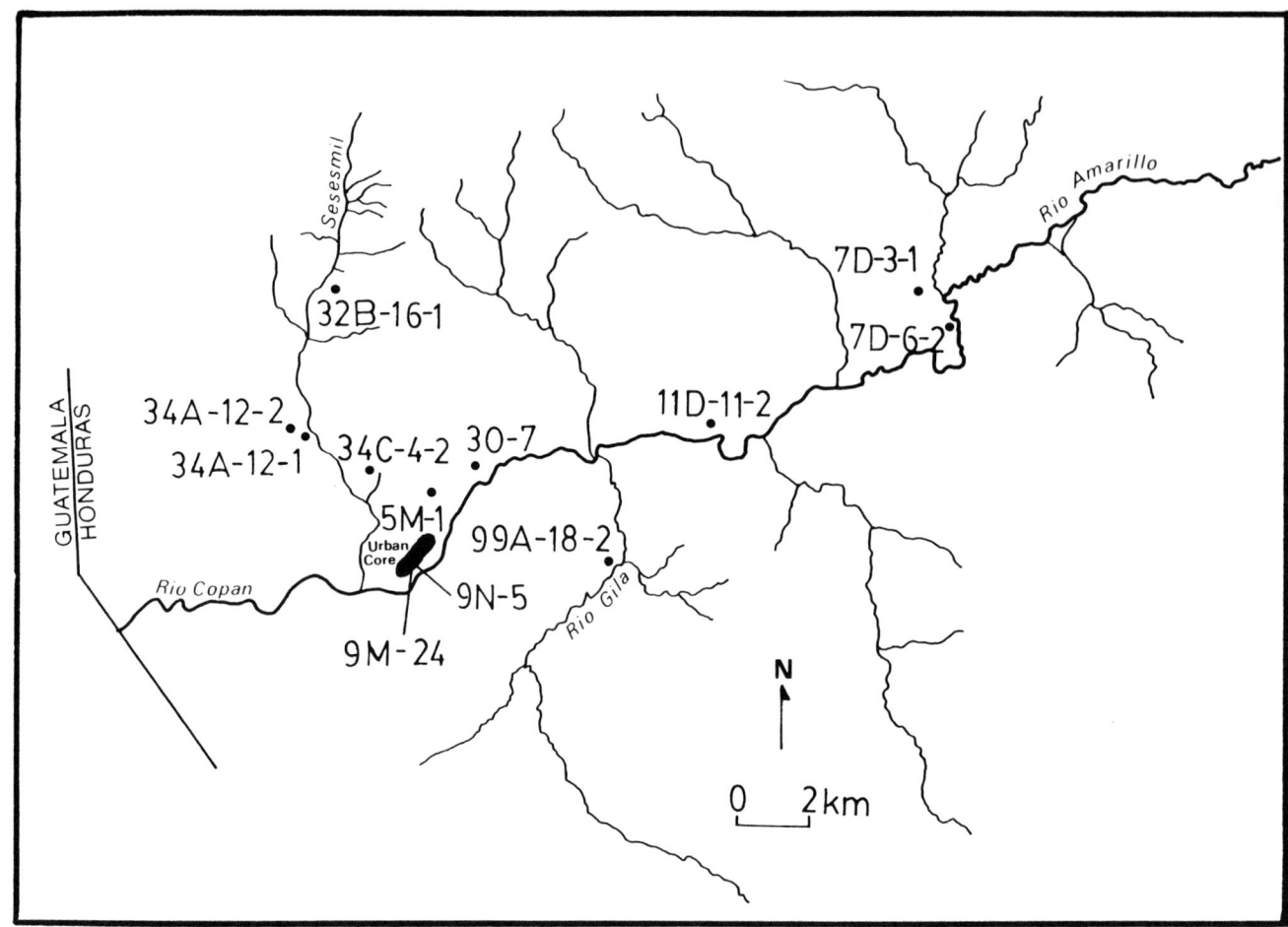

Fig. 81. Location of excavated type 1 sites in the Copan polity.

analysis concentrates on type 1 sites because, at this point, type 1 sites constitute our largest data base of commoner habitations.[1]

At Copan, commoners resided in houses resembling those of many present-day Maya groups. A low stone platform, the substructure, served as a foundation for a perishable superstructure of wattle and daub or pole and thatch. Only the low stone platform survives in the archaeological record. Generally, the substructure and superstructure dimensions are coextensive, or nearly so. The basal platforms common at some Yucatec Maya sites (Kurjack 1974) are extremely rare in lower-class dwellings at Copan.

Many of the structures that form part of higher-ranking groups are of type 1 scale. For example, a type 4 compound may be so identified because of one elaborate constituent building alongside many other simpler structures. The site classification, however, does not take note of the smaller structures, since they are directly connected to and integrated with the other, more elaborate buildings composing the group. These dependent type 1 structures, of which there are many, are not included in the bulk of this analysis, but they are discussed in terms of the role their inhabitants played in commoner-elite ties.

It would be erroneous at this point for the reader to assume homogeneity within the type 1 classification. Even a cursory glance at the site plans (Figs. 82–93) shows differences in site configuration and structure size. Although commoner status is assigned to all type 1 groups, I will discuss the wide variability within this category. Furthermore, status variations will be observed within the rural hinterland and between the rural and urban zones.

The Data Base

Twelve small groups at Copan have been excavated (Mallory 1981, 1983; Murillo 1983; Fash 1985; Gonlin 1985; Whittington 1985; Webster and Gonlin 1988), of which two are in Copan's Urban Core, two fall within the rural Copan Pocket, and eight are located in the Rural Region (i.e., outside the Copan Pocket) (Fig. 81).[2]

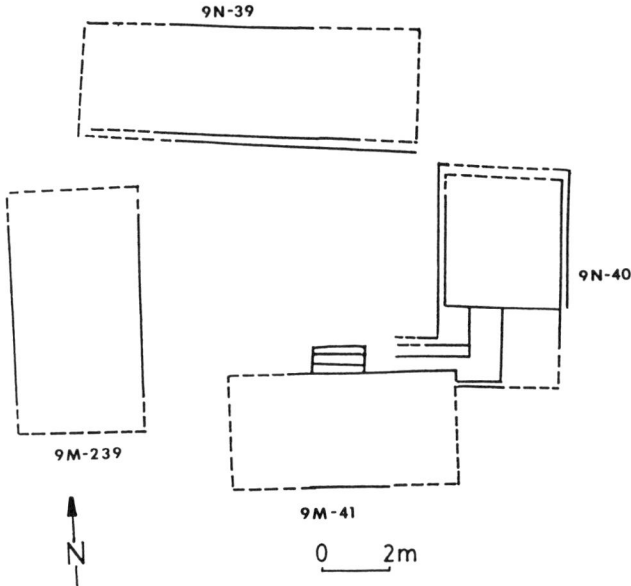

Fig. 82. Plan of group 9N-5, Copan. (Original by W. Fash.)

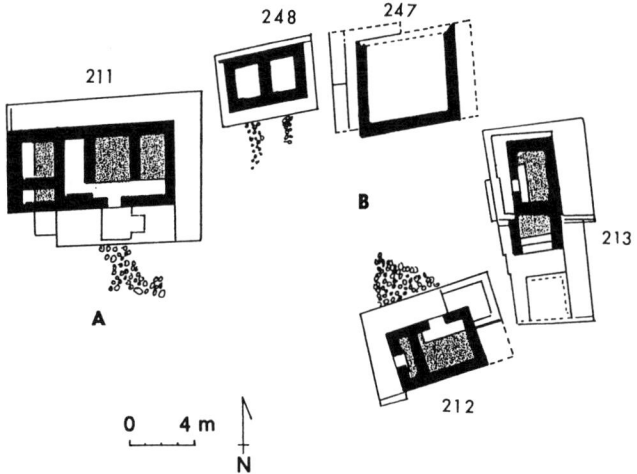

Fig. 83. Plan of group 9M-24, Copan.

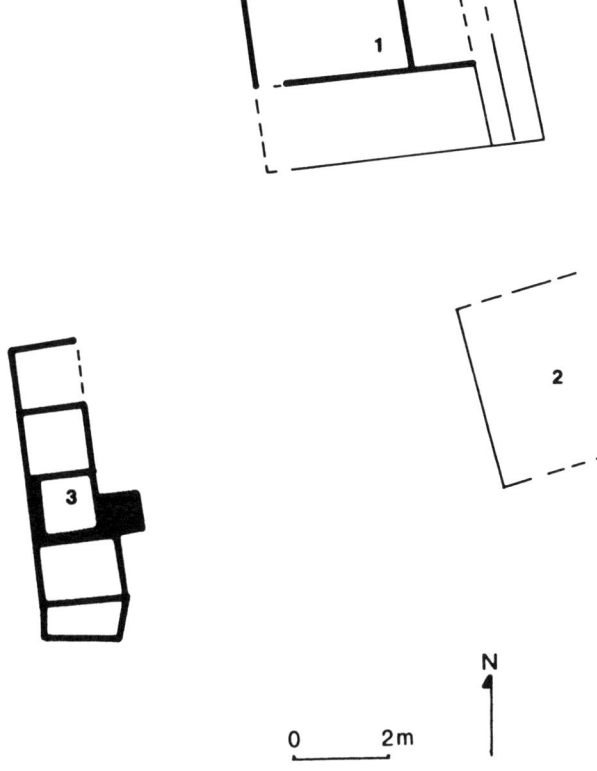

Fig. 84. Plan of group 5M-1, El Duende, Copan. (Original by J. Mallory.)

The two urban type 1 groups, 9N-5 and 9M-24, are located within the residential zone of Las Sepulturas. Group 9N-5 consists of four structures and was excavated in 1977 by the Harvard University Copan Mapping Project, directed by Gordon Willey (Fash 1985) (Fig. 82). The second urban type 1 group, 9M-24, was investigated by the Proyecto Arqueologico Copan, Phase II (PAC II), directed by William T. Sanders and David Webster. Group 9M-24 (Fig. 83) is a

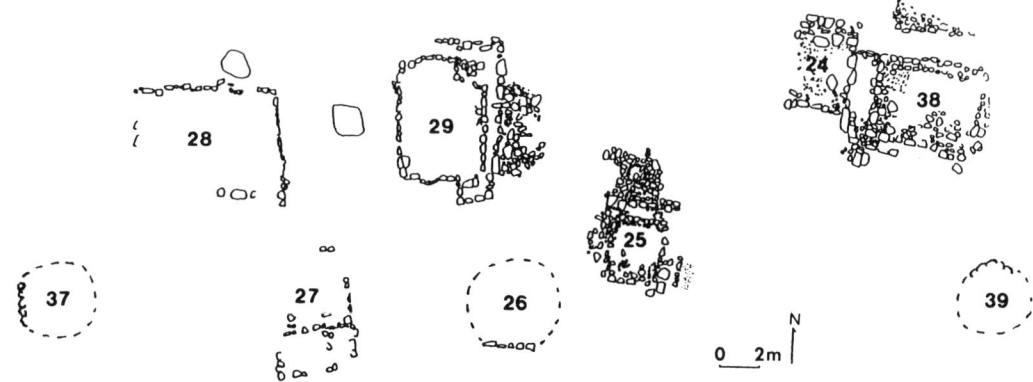

Fig. 85. Plan of group 3O-7, Copan.

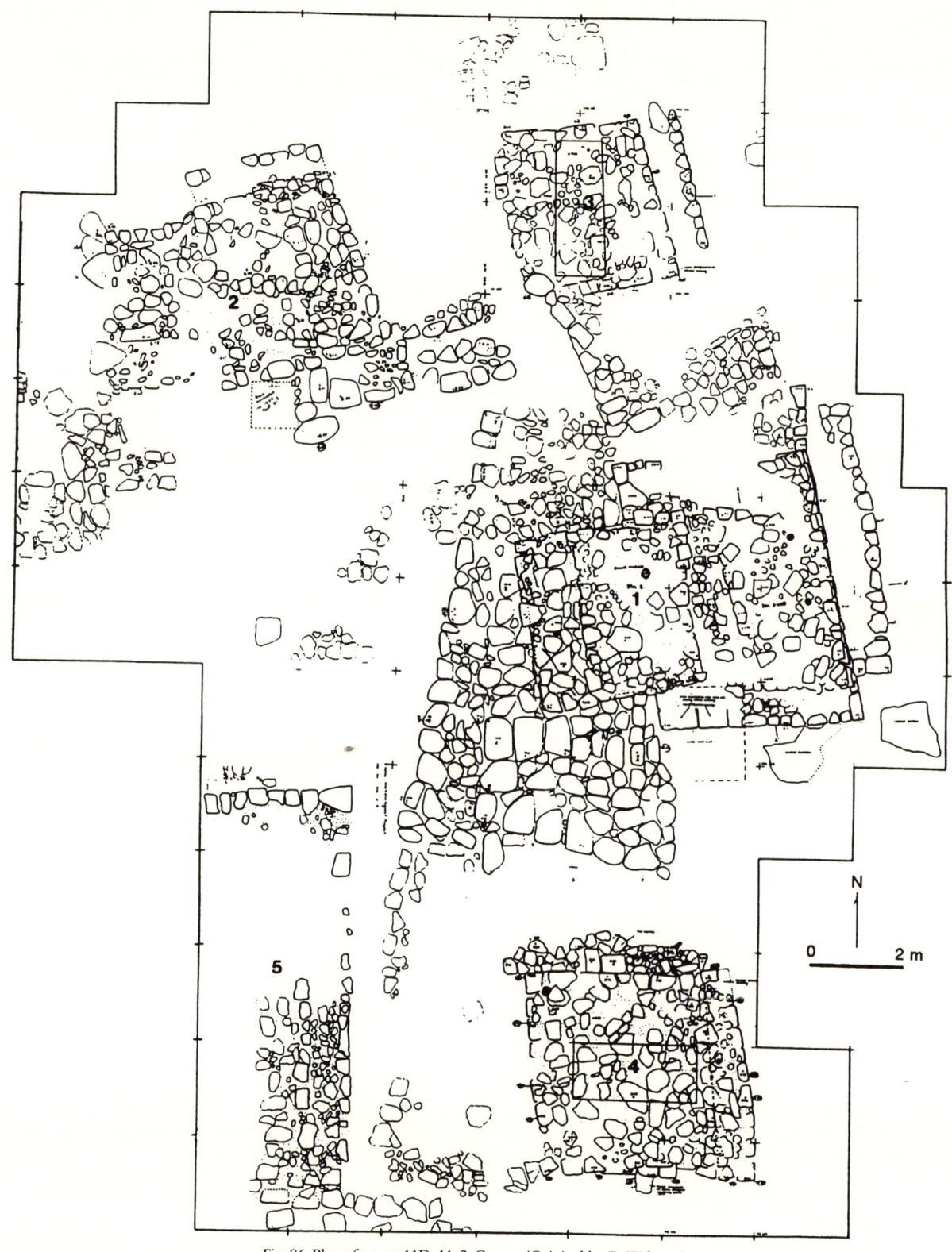

Fig. 86. Plan of group 11D-11-2, Copan. (Original by D. Webster.)

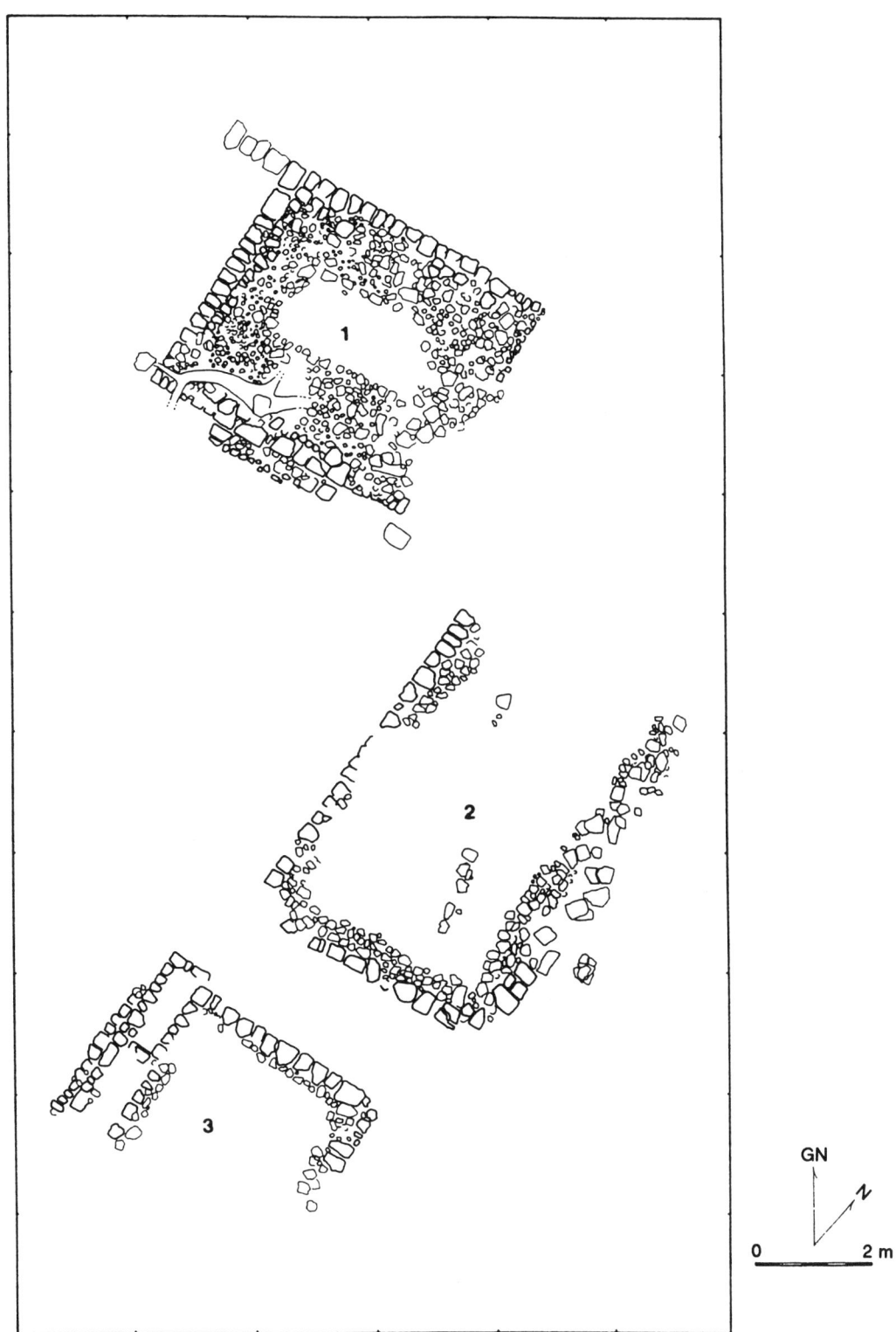

Fig. 87. Plan of group 7D-3-1, Copan. (Original by D. Webster.)

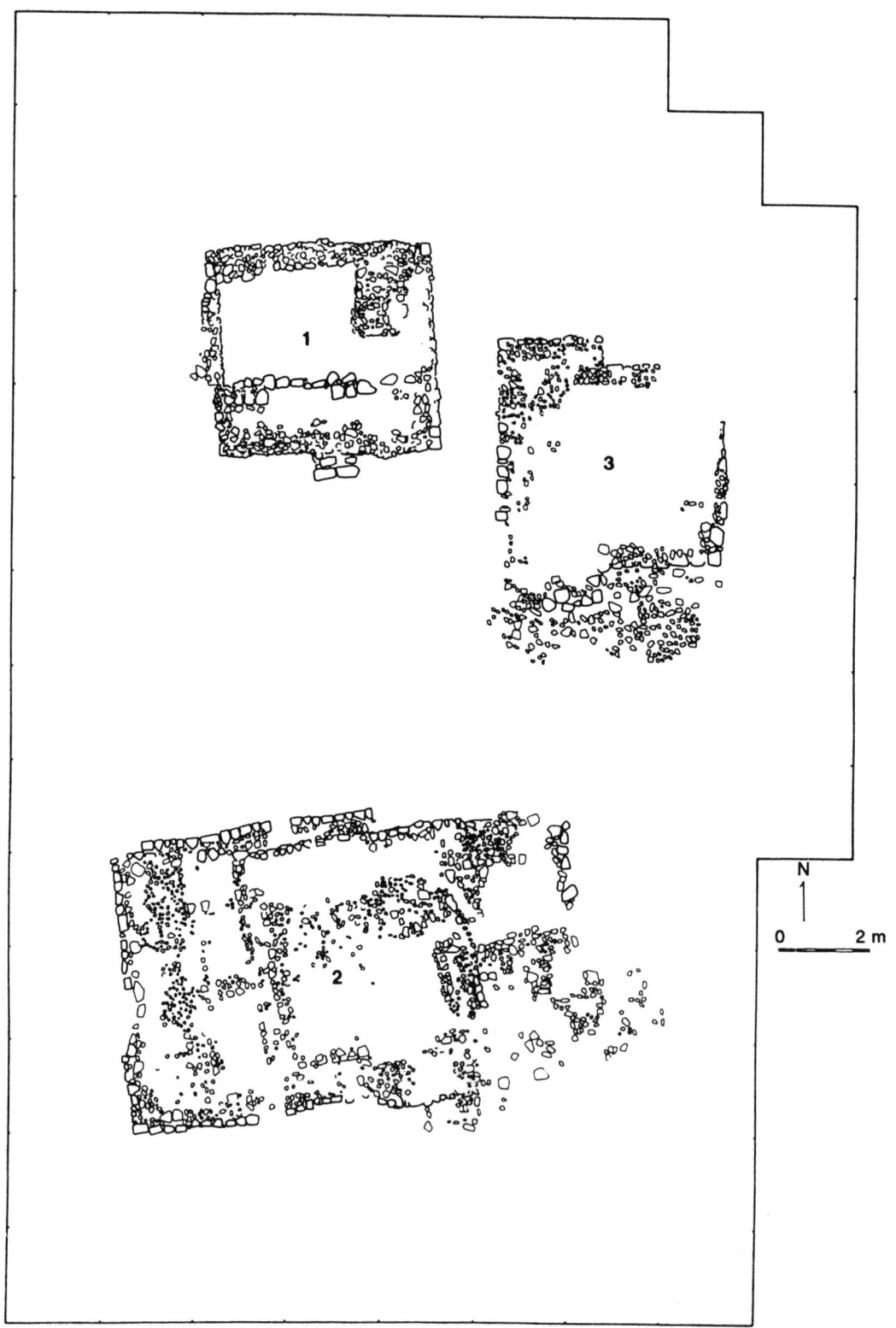

Fig. 88. Plan of group 7D-6-2, Copan. (Original by D. Webster.)

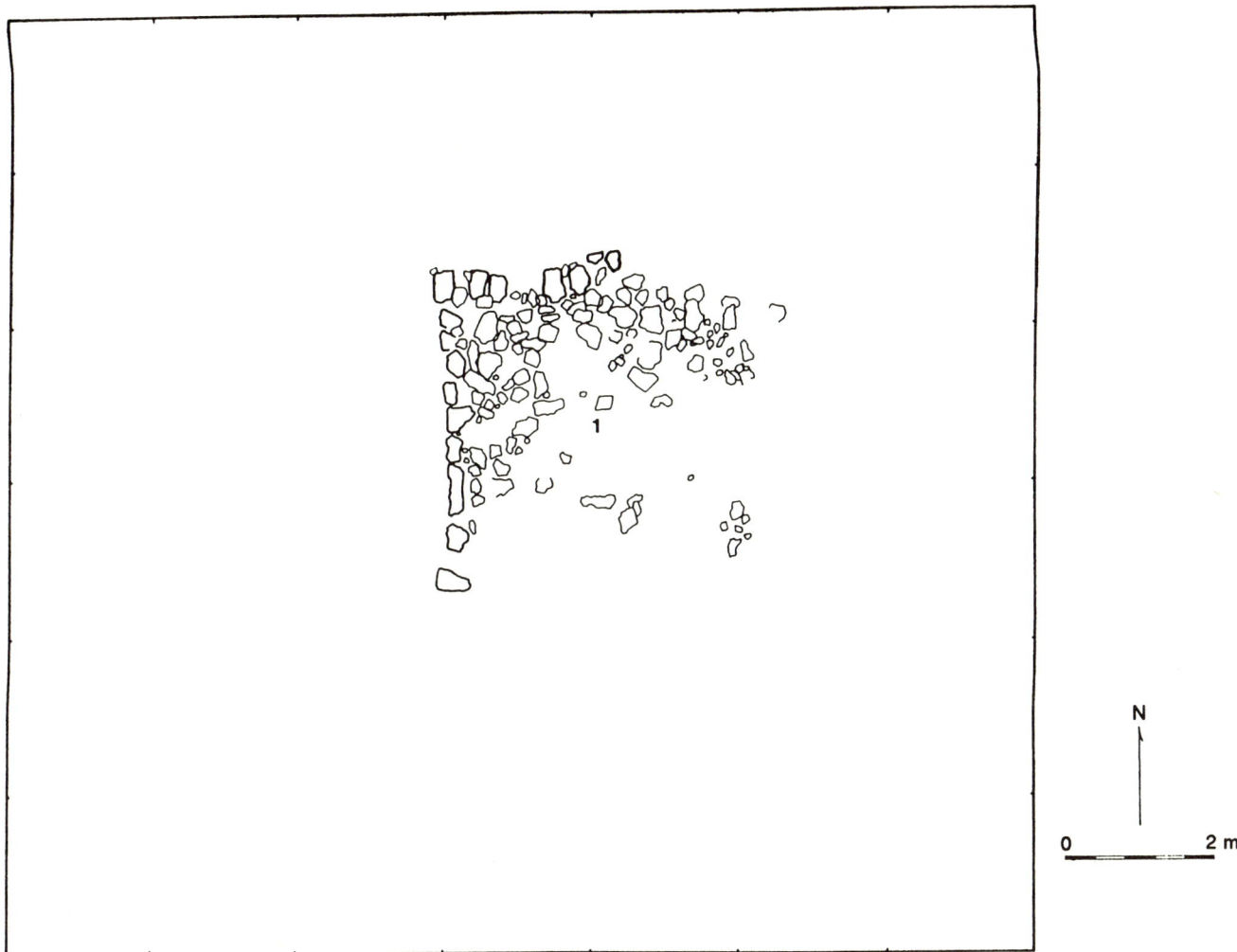

Fig. 89. Plan of group 34A-12-1, Copan. (Original by D. Webster.)

five-mound residential complex (Murillo 1983). Both groups are within meters of the highest-ranking group, 9N-8, outside the Main Group.

Two type 1 groups in the rural Copan Pocket were investigated during PAC II. Group 5M-1, better known as El Duende (Fig. 84), is a three-mound compound located 2.7 km northeast of the Main Group in the steep foothills of the valley. El Duende was excavated by Mallory (1983), who investigated the abundance of obsidian tools at the group (Mallory 1984). In the Petapilla area of the Copan Pocket, 3O-7, a ten-mound type 1 group, was partially excavated in 1984 (Whittington 1985) to obtain a rural burial sample, and further examination of the group was conducted in 1990 by Paine and Webster (Webster 1990) (Fig. 85).

In the Rural Region, eight type 1 groups were excavated during 1985 and 1986 (Webster and Gonlin 1988; Gonlin 1993). David Webster, director of the project, sampled type 1 groups of various sizes located in different geographic and topographic regions of the Copan Valley, six of which had been previously tested by Freter (1988). Three of these groups are in the main valley, the area drained by the Copan River. The El Jaral group, 11D-11-2 (Fig. 86), is a five-mound complex 11 km from the Main Group. The other two main valley groups, 7D-3-1 and 7D-6-2, are located in Rio Amarillo (Figs. 87 and 88). Each has three structures and is at a distance of over 20 km from the core.

Four groups are situated north of the Urban Core in the Sesesmil tributary drainage. The smallest of these, 34A-12-1 (Fig. 89), is a single-mound site located 65 m distant from its neighbor, 34A-12-2 (Fig. 90). Both are approximately 5.8 km from the Urban Core. Group 32B-16-1, located at an elevation of 950 m above sea level in the pine forests of the mountains, is a five-mound group that is 10 km distant from the Urban Core (Fig. 91). One rural group, 34C-4-2,

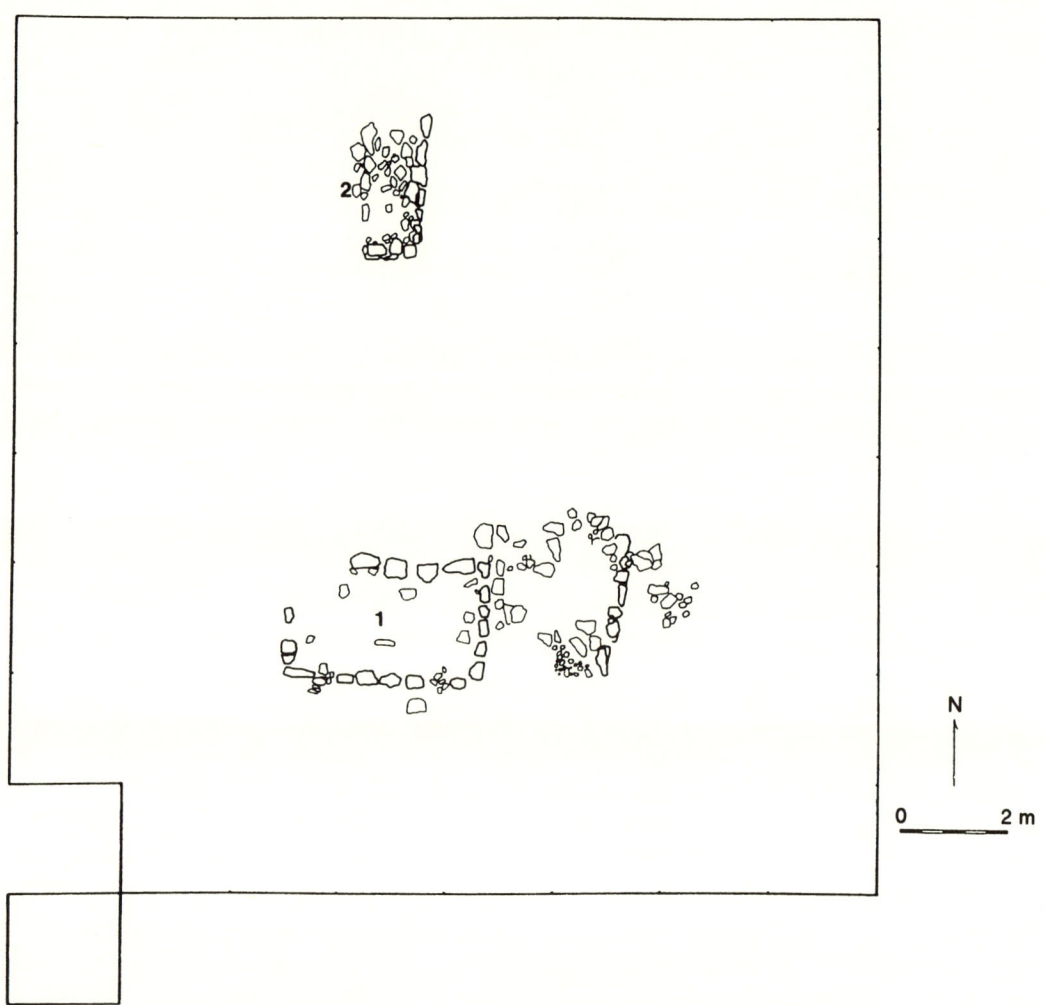

Fig. 90. Plan of group 34A-12-2, Copan. (Original by D. Webster.)

Fig. 91. Plan of group 32B-16-1, Copan. (Original by D. Webster.)

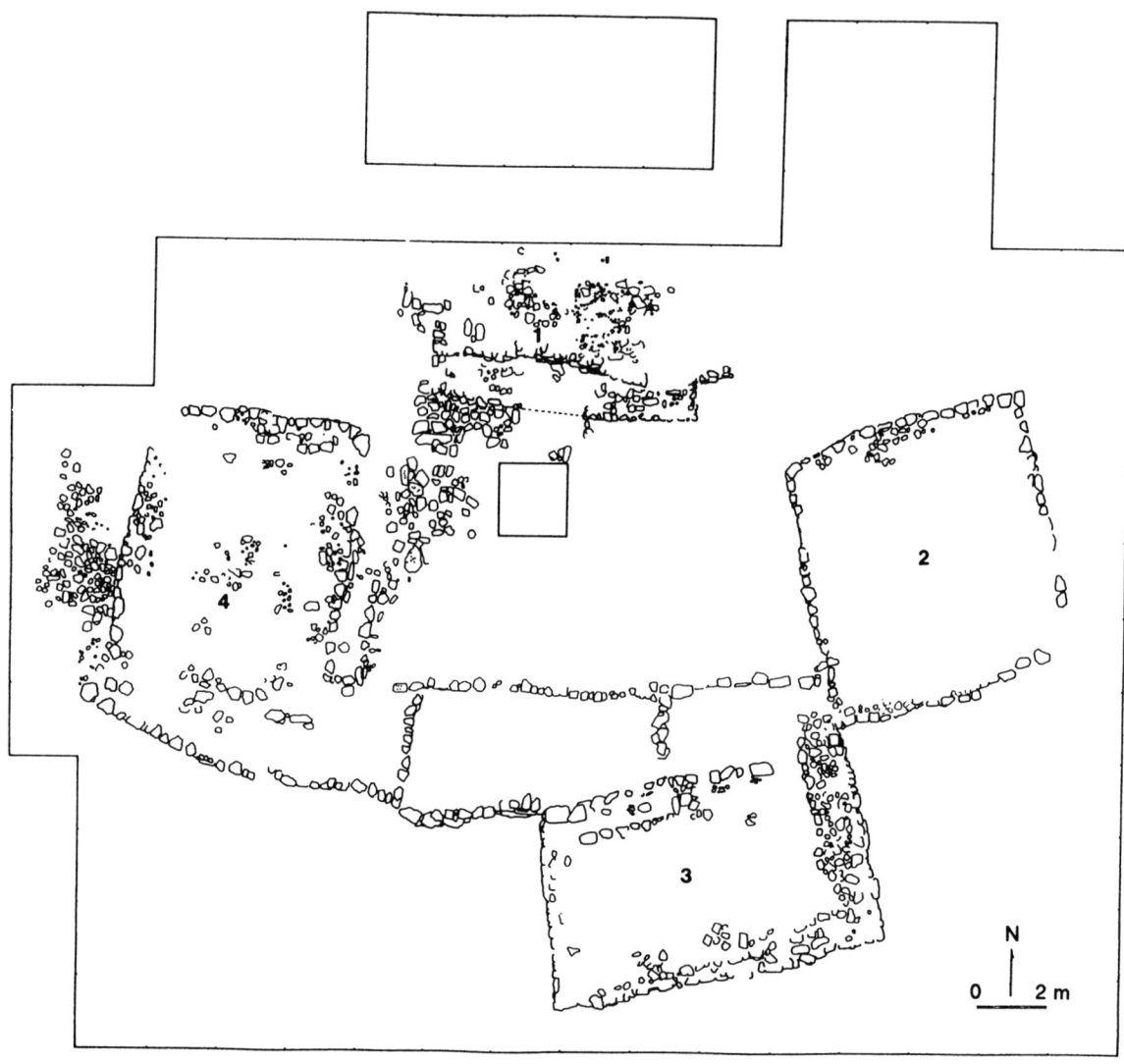

Fig. 92. Plan of group 34C-4-2, Copan. (Original by D. Webster.)

Fig. 93. Plan of group 99A-18-2, Copan. (Original by D. Webster.)

with a typical courtyard arrangement of structures (Fig. 92), is just 2.2 km from the core, yet it falls outside the environmental zone of the Copan Pocket. An eighth group consisting of two structures, 99A-18-2, is located in the Rio Jila drainage, the southern tributary of the Copan River (Fig. 93). It lies 7–10 km from the Main Group, depending on the route taken.

The excavations at these small groups have generated a large corpus of information on variability in architecture, artifacts, burial patterns, and building function. Extensive excavations of large groups in Copan's urban core provide the data with which to make rural-urban comparisons (Sanders 1986; Gerstle 1987; Hendon 1987; Webster 1989; Diamanti 1991). This broad data base facilitates analysis of similarities and differences among small households and between urban and rural areas.

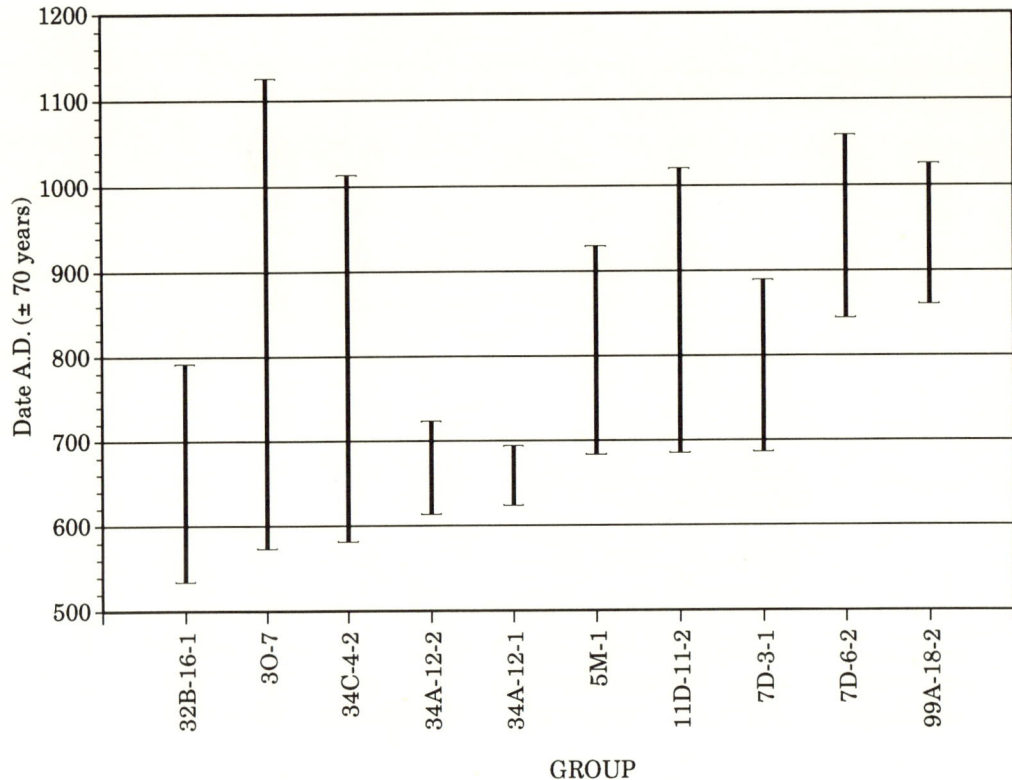

Fig. 94. Time span of ten type 1 groups, Copan, based on obsidian hydration dating.

Chronology

One of the first dimensions of variability that must be addressed for settlement in the Copan Valley is chronology. From Freter's work (1988, Chapter 11; Webster and Freter 1990a,b), it is clear that the Maya collapse at Copan was a protracted affair. The traditional range of the Late Classic ceramic phase at Copan, known as the Coner phase, is circa 700–900 A.D. (Viel 1983). Obsidian hydration dating has been instrumental in altering the view of the collapse and accordingly in extending the range of the Coner phase to 1250 A.D., when the Copan Valley was finally abandoned. The traditional range of earlier phases largely coincides with the range based on obsidian dating. For example, the Acbi phase, or Middle Classic, at Copan ranges from 400 to 700 A.D. whether it is defined by ceramic chronology or by obsidian dates. The revised chronology of the Coner phase and the aforementioned interpretation of the collapse will be used in this discussion.

The presentation here offers a detailed view of a few specific sites of the polity in order to complement Freter's comprehensive work on the settlement system. Data are derived from both published (Freter 1988) and unpublished (A. Freter, pers. comm. 1992) sources. Ten of the twelve type 1 groups (9M-24 and 9N-5 are excluded) provide 318 obsidian hydration dates spanning 590 years, from 535 to 1125 A.D. (Fig. 94). These ten groups have mainly produced Coner-phase ceramics, demonstrating that the ceramic sequence is only a gross indicator for periods of occupation at Copan. Group 9N-5 was probably occupied sometime during the Coner phase, given such evidence as structure fill (Fash 1985), but the precise date of the occupation cannot be established without obsidian hydration dates. Likewise, the date of the occupation of 9M-24 is uncertain, although both Acbi- and Coner-phase ceramics were recovered from this group.

Within the Coner phase, several significant events in the history of the region occurred, including the culmination of demographic and sociocultural development, followed by the political decline and dissolution of the Copan polity. Through the combination of obsidian hydration dates and epigraphy (Schele and Freidel 1990; Fash 1991), we can directly tie the small groups into major political events and comment on the nature of rural-urban relations.

The obsidian hydration dates show that small groups had a wide range of occupation, from very short (70 years at 34A-12-1) to very long (551 years at 3O-7). The development cycle of domestic groups (Goody 1962) has been cited by archaeologists as one of the three reasons, along with group status and function (Tourtellot 1988:98), for variation in the configuration of Maya courtyard groups. At Copan, it has been observed that the length of occupation and the site size (determined by the number of structures) closely correlate ($r = .934$), indicating that the family growth model may have strong explanatory power when considering differences in type 1 group sizes. Those type 1 units with a high number of mounds and lengthy occupations may be seen as more successful than sites with fewer mounds and shorter occupations, or the type of occupation may have been of a different nature.

Architecture

Although type 1 structures are characterized as small, low mounds, they vary, especially between rural and urban areas, in size, height, and architectural features. Based on the data about to be presented, I propose that rural residences represented a basic house form—the most common of the Copan polity—and that simple urban structures were elaborations of this form, mimicking higher-ranking groups. Both qualitative and quantitative comparisons will demonstrate the existence of status differences.

Type 1 residences (excluding kitchens, storehouses, shrines, or special-function buildings) in the Urban Core tend to be larger and taller than those in rural areas. Seven urban residential buildings average 45.5 m^2, or roughly 5 × 9.1 m. For fourteen Rural Region residences for which complete dimensions are known, the average residence size is 34 m^2, or approximately 5 × 6.8 m. In general, substructures in the urban area tend to be much higher (0.5–1 m) than those in the rural area (0.15–0.5 m), although there are exceptions. For instance, the ancillary substructures of 9M-24 are barely 20 cm in height, consisting of one or two courses of cobbles. In Rio Amarillo, several kilometers away from the urban area, structure 1 at 11D-11-2 has a substructure 1 m tall. Likewise, each of the buildings at 34C-4-2, a group close to the Copan Pocket, has substructure heights ranging from 0.5 to 1 m.

Other notable differences exist in the degree of elaboration, expressed in the number and kinds of architectural features present at urban and rural type 1 groups. Residences in the urban area tend to exhibit traits of the improved house form. Relevant criteria, such as a higher substructure platform and dressed stone instead of cobble construction, usually indicate increased energetic input (Abrams 1984:54–55). Additionally, the improved house form exhibits more architectural feature—such as stairs, benches, doorjambs, plaster, partial stone superstructures, internal divisions of superstructures, terraces, and stone-paved floors and courtyards—than the basic form at Copan. Both 9M-24 and 9N-5 have many features of the improved form, which are also common to higher-ranking groups in the Urban Core.

Rural type 1 residences are most often single-room structures with no discernible internal divisions (although divisions made of perishable materials may have existed). Low terraces are the most common architectural modification, but these terraces are not finished with plaster as they are in urban groups. Only one rural Copan Pocket group, 3O-7, has remains of plaster in the plaza area. Some of the higher rural platforms require stairs for access but lack elaborate entranceways. A few of the rural buildings have low stone wall bases for the superstructure, the remainder of which consisted of perishable wattle and daub.

Quantification of Architectural Differences

Because architectural differences are often a function of socioeconomic differences, quantitative analysis of architectural variation can yield important insights into social differentiation. Smith (Chapter 10), for example, utilizes volume of construction as a measure of inequality in the Aztec countryside. At Copan, energetic studies can be carried further through the in-depth work conducted by Abrams (1984, 1987, 1989), allowing for investigation of varying access to labor within type 1 households. I have quantified construction costs for ten of the twelve groups, following the procedures designed by Abrams (pers. comm. 1992), and Abrams (1984, 1987, 1989) has quantified costs for urban groups. The results illuminate the organization of domestic labor for construction events.

Complete structures for which all dimensions, architectural features, and composition are available permit the most accurate energetic calculations. Some structures were only partially revealed because they lacked a wall line, had been robbed for construction material, or were incompletely excavated owing to time constraints. In these cases, the complete dimensions were extrapolated on the basis of comparison with the size and style of other buildings of the group.

These calculations show that the urban group 9M-24 required 461 person-days to build (Fig. 95). Building episodes were probably spread out over a number of years, and a familial-reciprocal work force probably fulfilled the labor requirements, even for a group as large as 9M-24. However, access to additional labor sources, such as a hired worker, might have been required. It should be emphasized that the entire cost cannot be as accurately assessed for this group as for the rural groups, since these structures had been rebuilt once or twice; therefore, the actual cost of this plaza group could easily have been higher.

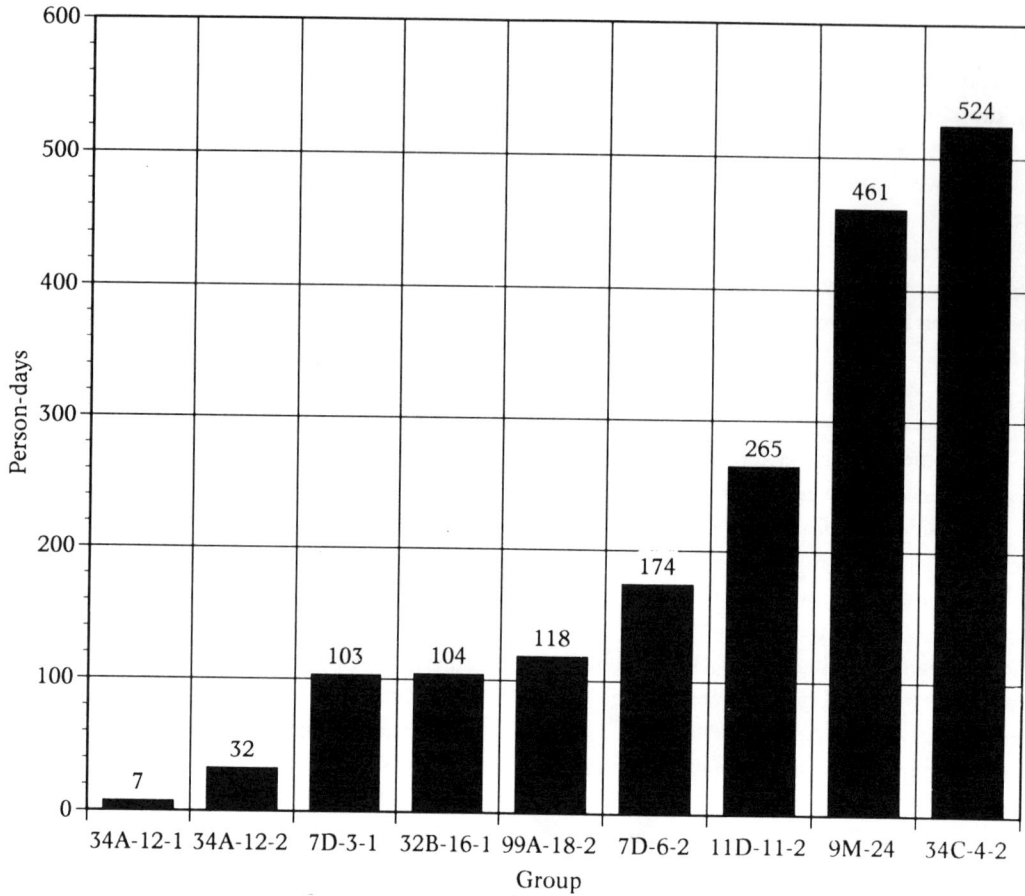

Fig. 95. Energetic input in person-days of type 1 groups, Copan.

Among the rural groups, energetic inputs range from 7 to 524 person-days. The platform and superstructure each account for approximately half of the energy invested in type 1 structures. In the Urban Core, larger and taller substructures required a substantially higher amount of energy than the perishable parts of superstructures.

The type 1 construction figures in Figure 95, combined with the qualitative information on architectural features, indicate that there was a continuum of low-status construction input in the rural area and an overlap between urban and rural type 1 architecture. There is a great deal of variation from group to group in terms of total energetic input.

Smaller excavated type 1 groups in the rural area separate out from the construction cost of an urban type 1 group and the largest rural type 1 group (34C-4-2). Rural groups do not exhibit most features of the improved house form, common in the Urban Core. Since the architecture was small and simple, unspecialized laborers could construct all components of the structures. Abrams (1989:73) estimates that construction of a commoner residence could be accomplished by two to five workers. The nature of the architecture, the lack of multiple construction phases, and the inferred small labor group size collectively suggest that rural buildings were constructed within a short period of time and used for short periods of time.

When comparing type 1 groups to higher-ranking urban groups, we find that the energetic estimates for two patios of a type 3 group in the Urban Core far exceed those for any type 1 group, rural or urban. Abrams (pers. comm. 1992) estimates that it took 17,201 person-days for the construction of 9M-22, plazas A and B; five patios of the type 4 complex, 9N-8, have an estimated energetic cost of 64,532 person-days.

The implications for Maya society are clear. Obvious status differences, reflected in architecture and access to energy, existed within the urban zone and beyond it. Although most of the structures in the Copan polity would have been built within a familial reciprocal work group (Abrams 1984), the construction of some larger, more elaborate buildings required access to larger work forces and different modes of organization. High-status individuals or families were able to command a wide range of kinspeople or hired workers for construction of private residences.

Measures of Wealth

Several measures of wealth, including architecture, will be used to assess household wealth among Rural Region type 1 groups and between rural and urban type 1 groups. This approach is based on Smith (1987), who conducted research on wealth in agrarian states through the examination of household possessions. Archaeologists have traditionally used residential architecture, burials, and household artifacts for the determination of wealth differences.

Smith convincingly argues that in an archaeological context, valuable servingware and food preparation equipment may be the best indicators of wealth. In wealthier households, one would expect to find greater numbers of valuable vessels and differentiation in food preparation artifacts, which would reflect differences in diet. In addition, wealthier households possess more material goods (a quantitative measure), and thereby consume more on a daily basis, producing more domestic refuse. One type of diversity measure, richness (Jones and Leonard 1990), a count of the variety of goods, may indicate that wealthier households tend to have more types of material goods (a qualitative measure). Finally, an object's place of origin may offer clues to wealth, since wealthier families typically possess more "exotic" goods than poorer ones.

For consideration of these variables, the most detailed information comes from the eight Rural Region groups. The following measures of wealth at Copan are used: total energetic input to architecture per site; percent of fineware rims; weight of all ceramics (divided by length of occupation as determined through obsidian hydration dates); number of obsidian blade fragments (divided by length of occupation); and richness measures of ceramic form, lithics, and ground stone. These represent both quantitative (energetics, percentage of fineware, ceramic weight, and obsidian blades) and qualitative (richness measures) assessments of wealth in rural Copan. In addition to the results of the quantitative analysis, I will comment on other unquantified but relevant variables when possible.

Table 27 was computed in the following manner: each of the variables was quantified and then ranked, with the lowest rank receiving one point and the highest rank receiving eight points. In the case of variables for which two or more sites had the same quantity (e.g., lithic richness), those quantities were given a similar rank, and the total points were adjusted accordingly. The highest possible point score is 50. The quantity is given in parentheses below the rank for that item. This approach deemphasizes architecture as a measure of wealth by giving equal weight to all variables.

Table 27. Relative Wealth Ranking of Rural Region Copan Sites[a]

	Group							
	34C-4-2	11D-11-2	7D-6-2	99A-18-2	34A-12-2	7D-3-1	32B-16-1	34A-12-1
Quantitative measures								
Architectural energetics	8	7	6	5	2	3	4	1
(person-days)	(558)	(186)	(160)	(147)	(34)	(307)	(108)	(12)
Percent fineware ceramics	8	6	3	5	7	4	1	2
	(30.8)	(24.6)	(12.4)	(19.3)	(28.6)	(12.6)	(8.9)	(10)
Ceramic weight per year	7	4	8	6	5	2	3	1
	(0.95)	(0.62)	(1.07)	(0.87)	(0.66)	(0.23)	(0.33)	(0.03)
Obsidian blades per year	8	4	6	7	5	3	2	1
	(5.43)	(1.32)	(2.60)	(2.97)	(1.43)	(0.73)	(0.62)	(0.13)
Qualitative measures								
Ceramic richness	6	7	5	4	3	2	3	1
	(23)	(24)	(22)	(18)	(15)	(14)	(15)	(4)
Ground stone richness	5	6	5	2	3	4	3	1
	(9)	(14)	(9)	(3)	(6)	(9)	(6)	(1)
Lithic richness	3	4	4	5	3	2	2	1
	(5)	(6)	(6)	(7)	(5)	(4)	(4)	(3)
Overall rank (points)[b]	8	7	6	5	4	3	2	1
	(45)	(38)	(37)	(34)	(28)	(20)	(18)	(8)

[a]Raw data for each measure are presented in Gonlin (1993). The quantity of each item (expressed in the units given in the first column) is given in parentheses below the rank for that item. Rank 1 = lowest, rank 8 = highest.

[b]Total possible points = 50. Cumulative points for each group are given in parentheses.

Results of Wealth Indices

According to the quantitative analysis, the wealthiest of the Rural Region groups is 34C-4-2. This group also had the highest number of "exotic" items (jade jewelry, earspools, green obsidian, and most ceramics imported from the Ulua Valley, Honduras), although the overall quantity of these items was low. This group is located in foothills just outside the Copan Pocket and is nearest geographically to the Urban Core. Limestone-based soils surrounding the site would have been agriculturally productive for years.

The second highest-ranked Rural Region residence, 11D-11-2, had the highest diversity of ceramic and ground stone artifacts, a long occupation, and the second highest energetic input of the rural residences. A few exotic items, such as jade and imported ceramics, were recovered from this group, which is located on a narrow expanse of bottomland in an area that would have been favorable for agriculture.

The two groups that date exclusively to the late Coner phase at Copan, 7D-6-2 and 99A-18-2, are ranked near 11D-11-2, which was inhabited throughout Copan's rise and fall. Their occupations are one or two centuries shorter than that of 11D-11-2, yet they have some of the highest artifact consumption rates. Structures at 7D-6-2 and 99A-18-2 have more architectural features of the improved house form than do other rural structures. Freter (Chapter 11) has described the out-migration of inhabitants of the Urban Core to the peripheries of the Copan Valley, and it appears that these two residences may represent postcollapse pioneering populations. Both sites are located on foothill lands in outlying pockets of the valley.

The lowest-ranking Rural Region Copan households are 34A-12-2, 7D-3-1, and 32B-16-1. Architecturally, their structures are the simplest, their consumption rates are low, and their assemblages are not as diverse as those of higher-ranking groups. No exotic items were found at 34A-12-2 or 32B-16-1, but a pyrite mirror, an obsidian eccentric, and a small piece of jade were recovered from 7D-3-1. Both 34A-12-2 and 32B-16-1 are located on steep slopes of the Sesesmil Valley, whereas 7D-3-1 is in the transitional bottomland-foothill region of Rio Amarillo. The poorest of the groups, 34A-12-1, represents a nondomestic site exhibiting a paucity of materials.

Wealth in the Rural Region

Rural wealth is closely connected to the agricultural potential of the landscape. The agricultural potential of soils in the Copan Valley varies widely (Wingard 1992), but in general those soils underlain by limestone have greater productivity. Although this was the case for groups 34A-12-2 and 32B-16-1, the slope of the land was the most significant factor in the sustainability of the soils.

Generally, larger households are those with greater wealth and access to resources and are longer lived than smaller households of the Copan Valley. Such wealth differentiation within the Rural Region type 1 category parallels recent ethnographic work on peasant Maya populations, for which status differences have been observed (Wilk 1983; Hayden and Cannon 1984) but not always acknowledged (Redfield 1941).

Urban versus Rural Household Assemblages

Although we do not have as rich a data base for urban type 1 groups as for rural type 1 groups, some comments on wealth and status differences between all urban and rural households may nevertheless be made. First, we consider ceramic distribution, for which our results are affected by several variables. Freter (1988) has noted that a higher degree of erosion in the Rural Region has rendered many sherds unrecognizable; on average, 12 percent of the rim sherds are not diagnostic because of these conditions, as opposed to only 3 percent in the urban area (Gonlin 1993). Therefore, large indeterminate frequencies may in some cases alter the ratios discussed here, since the painted wares are differentially affected.

Our results show that there is considerable variability in the amount of fineware from group to group and from area to area. On the average, all types of urban groups (9M-24, 9M-22, 9N-8) have more finewares (32 percent) than Rural Region groups (22 percent), a result that correlates with such other factors as architectural costs and proximity to the Main Group and prime agricultural land.

The polychrome pottery for which Copan is known, Copador, has been recovered in small quantities at all excavated rural groups that were residences. Only the nonresidential site 34A-12-1 failed to produce this ware. This pattern supports the conclusions of Beaudry (1985), who suggests that Copador was accessible to all inhabitants of the Copan Valley. Although Copador is present throughout the Copan Valley, it is more predominant in the core residences (Diamanti 1991).

Overall, the ceramic assemblages for the type 1 groups exhibit variability in the amount of finewares and in the total number of ceramics recovered, but not in the types that are present. The commoner class as a whole had access to all local wares, both fine-pasted and utilitarian ceramics. Thus the mere presence of finewares does not seem indicative of high status, although the overall quantities may be more revealing, especially when combined with other indices.

Burial Patterns

An examination of burial patterns within the type 1 category reveals that Copan Maya were treated differentially in death and that burial practices were not consistent throughout the polity within this category. Throughout the Maya region, burials are associated with housemounds of all sizes. In our study, both urban type 1 groups produced burials, as did the rural Copan Pocket group, 3O-7, and two of the Rural Region groups, 34A-12-2 and 99A-18-2. But burials were not recovered at five of the Rural Region residences, indicating significant sociocultural variation. Elsewhere in Mesoamerica, Smith (Chapter 10) has also noted that burials are not common in rural Aztec groups.

Whittington (1989) has analyzed skeletal traits of low-status burials at groups 9M-24, 9N-5, and 3O-7, along with several other burials from tested type 1 and 2 groups in the Copan area. The following discussion is taken from his work. Seventeen individuals ranging from infants to adults were recovered at group 9M-24 in the Urban Core. Grave goods were comparatively rich, and some skeletons exhibited traits usually associated with elite practices. For example, a few individuals had artificial cranial deformation, jade-inlaid teeth, and filed teeth. One individual was buried in a grave covered with cobbles. Although not all burials were accompanied with grave goods, some contained fineware ceramic vessels, jade, and deer bone. At group 9N-5, also in the Urban Core, six individuals were recovered. Two were accompanied by ceramic vessels, and one burial was covered with unworked stones. Three individuals had modified teeth, which were either inlaid or filed. Group 3O-7 in the rural Copan Pocket produced eight burials. Two of the burials were interred in rough cists, and one individual had filed teeth. One burial contained a Copador vessel, and another individual with inlaid teeth was interred with two jade pendants.

On the basis of osteopathological analysis, Whittington concludes that "the low status population at Copan was highly stressed and unhealthy during the periods leading up to and following the political collapse of the polity.... Protein, calories, and some B-complex vitamins are the aspects of diet most likely to have been deficient" (Whittington 1989:370). Low-status individuals in rural and urban areas seem to have had equally poor diets. In the urban zone, however, infectious diseases were more prevalent, presumably because of higher population density.

Burial material from the Rural Region excavations is currently under analysis by Rebecca Storey. Field observations on burial treatment reveal that simple pit burials, some of which were marked with a stone, predominated. Grave contents might include, at most, one ceramic vessel (Gonlin 1993).

An analysis of burial treatment in the core, including groups 9M-24, 9M-22, and 9N-8, is provided by Diamanti (1991:Tables 3.27 and 3.30). Most (62 percent) of the graves were simple pits, but other grave types included dressed stone tombs, rough stone tombs, cists, and graves with capstones or cobbles. Many (62 percent) graves had no offerings, but the remaining 38 percent included ceramic vessels or other material. This diversity within the core represents variation in status.

Although most rural and urban graves are simple pit burials, the hierarchy of grave types is not present at small rural households. Although intra-household differences may have existed, this issue is not explored here.

Rural groups that did not contain burials may have had a different relationship with Urban Core relatives than those groups who buried their own people. A lineage structure has been proposed for Copan by several researchers (Fash 1983; Sanders 1989; Diamanti 1991). Given such a model, we might suggest that rural relatives were buried in lineage grounds in the core of Copan and are not found in the hinterland for this reason.

Site Function

From the examination of architecture, artifacts, and burial patterns, various functions can be assigned to the type 1 groups. The majority of them were residences, and their artifact assemblages show that activities such as cooking, food preparation, and storage were characteristic (Hendon 1987; Gonlin 1993). Burials, commonly associated with residences in the Maya region, were recovered from five of the excavated type 1 groups.

Craft specialization on the household level is seen in three groups. Group 5M-1 was the locus for manufacture of wooden artifacts, the production of which consumed thousands of obsidian blades (Mallory 1984). One of the three buildings of the group contains five small enclosed rooms and probably functioned exclusively for storage of finished products. The ceramic inventory is low when compared to those of other groups with similar time spans, perhaps indicating that group use was intermittent.

Two other residences showed signs of economic specialization. In the Urban Core, group 9M-24 has an abundance of chert artifacts that were used to produce a final unknown product, which was perhaps stored in structure 248, having two enclosed rooms much too small for habitation.

Investigations at two groups near rhyolite outcrops in the Petapilla area of the Copan Pocket (Whittington 1989), 3O-7 (a type 1 group) and 3O-8 (a type 2 group), suggest the possibility of mano and metate manufacturing and storage (Spink 1983). Large quantities of these artifacts were found on the surface even before excavation began, including blanks and unfinished manos and metates.

Groups 5M-1, 9M-24, and 3O-7, all with some degree of economic specialization, were occupied during Copan's sociopolitical peak and continued on well after the royal collapse. Two of the groups had primarily residential functions, although the low artifact inventory of 5M-1 suggests that it was occupied on only an intermittent basis.

The distinctive artifact assemblage at site 34A-12-1, a small single-mound type 1 site in the Sesesmil drainage area, is relevant here. Although the architecture of this site does not differ much in style or size from that of its type 1 neighbor 34A-12-2, the absence of artifacts common to type 1 residences, such as manos and metates, as well as the small number of ceramics and lithics (Table 27), indicates that the site was unique; furthermore, no burials were recovered, even though the site was completely excavated. The site has a time span of only 70 years, the shortest of any type 1 group dated by obsidian hydration.

These data indicate that the structure was not used on a permanent basis. Given the documentation of fieldhuts in the outlying areas beyond the core and the Copan Pocket (Freter 1988), we might suggest that this structure served such a function. Alternatively, it may have served as a storage facility for its very close neighbor, 34A-12-2. In either scenario, its function was ancillary.

In summary, although it is safe to assume that the bulk of type 1 groups at Copan represent residences for the common people who were farmers of the Copan Valley, considerable status, wealth, and economic heterogeneity can be observed. Some type 1 inhabitants produced craft items on a part-time basis in both core and rural locations, and some of the single-mound sites were nonresidential in outlying areas.

Rural Articulation with the Center

Chronology and geography play a very important role in defining commoner-elite ties in the Copan polity. The settlement data from survey, testing, and excavation (Webster and Freter 1990a) indicate that during the political centralization of Copan the Maya elite were concentrated in the Urban Core along with many commoners, whereas commoners predominated in outlying regions.

Table 28 shows the meshing of the obsidian hydration dates with epigraphically attested reigns of the rulers of Copan and the occupation of ten of the small households in this study. These data reveal that many of the sites in the Rio Amarillo area were not founded until the period after the political collapse at A.D. 800 (Freter 1988). These commoners would have had no ties to the Main Group but may have been subject to local elites who occupied newly founded higher-ranking sites (Freter 1988:174). In the Sesesmil area, type 1 settlement occurred primarily between A.D. 550 and 850 (Freter 1988:153). The rural Copan Pocket and Urban Core were occupied continuously throughout the rise and fall of Copan, but the population dispersed to more rural areas after A.D. 800. Most small households weathered the rise and fall of the royal dynasty and continued for decades after these events,

Table 28. Correspondence of Rulers' Reigns and Dated Copan Type 1 Sites

Ruler[a]	Time period[a]	Occupied sites[b]								
No centralized ruler	823–1125		3O-7	34C-4-2			5M-1	11D-11-2	7D-3-1	7D-6-2	99A-18-2
Ruler 17	?–822		3O-7	34C-4-2			5M-1	11D-11-2	7D-3-1		
Ruler 16 (Yax-Pac)	763–820	32B-16-1	3O-7	34C-4-2			5M-1	11D-11-2	7D-3-1		
Ruler 15	749–?	32B-16-1	3O-7	34C-4-2			5M-1	11D-11-2	7D-3-1		
Ruler 14	738–749	32B-16-1	3O-7	34C-4-2			5M-1	11D-11-2	7D-3-1		
Ruler 13 (18-Rabbit)	695–738	32B-16-1	3O-7	34C-4-2		34A-12-2	5M-1	11D-11-2	7D-3-1		
Ruler 12	626–695	32B-16-1	3O-7	34C-4-2	34A-12-1	34A-12-2	5M-1	11D-11-2	7D-3-1		
Ruler 11 (Butz'-Chan)	578–626	32B-16-1	3O-7	34C-4-2	34A-12-1	34A-12-2					
Ruler 10	553–578	32B-16-1	3O-7								
Ruler 9	551	32B-16-1									
Ruler 8	?	32B-16-1									
Ruler 7	504–544	32B-16-1									

[a]From Schele and Freidel (1990).

[b]Based on the obsidian hydration method (Freter 1988; A. Freter, pers. comm. 1992).

and some of the small households in the valley (7D-6-2, 99A-18-2) were founded as a result of the migration from the center.

Two models help to assess the kind of relationship that prevailed among rural and urban areas and among commoners and elite before the royal collapse. First, Abrams (1989) shows through energetic reconstructions that, on average, a commoner may have had to supply labor for royal construction events perhaps every ten or eleven years. Rural kinsfolk may also have been called upon for construction of residences of higher-ranking relatives who resided in the core.

The second complementary model that elucidates rural-urban relations is the agricultural production model proposed by Wingard (1992), which asserts that the urban area gradually became dependent on the rural Copan Pocket and the Rural Region to supply it with food. As environmental degradation became more severe toward the end of the Late Classic (900 A.D.), the situation became more intense, with production in Rio Amarillo, El Jaral, Sesesmil, and Rio Jila contributing substantially to the food requirements of the Urban Core. Stripping of the forests, particularly in the Copan Pocket (Abrams and Rue 1988), would have necessitated a greater reliance on outlying regions to provide wood for cooking, heating, and construction as well as other forest products.

The data presented here and the two models discussed all present a picture of urban dependence on the hinterlands of the Copan Valley, contrasting with the relative self-sufficiency of the rural sector. Unless people lived very near or in the Urban Core, as did the inhabitants of 9M-24 and 9N-5, their lives were probably not significantly affected by central authorities on a daily basis, although they formed part of the Copan polity. This reconstruction coincides with Falconer's (Chapter 9) interpretation of Bronze Age villages as economically independent communities that were only modestly affected by cities and urban authorities. Nonelite urbanites who resided in the independent type 1 groups such as 9M-24 and 9N-5 may have led a very different life than the rural inhabitants. Given their proximity to higher-ranking groups, their lives may have been affected on a daily basis; constant demands may have been placed on them,[3] and they would have been exposed to the different types of diseases common to urban life.

Conclusions

A rural-urban dichotomy has long been assumed to exist for the Maya and for other early complex societies as well. For the Copan Maya, at least, it has been demonstrated that this assumption is valid. We can divide the type 1 groups into urban groups (i.e., those in the Urban Core) and rural groups that existed in the rural zones of the Copan Pocket as well as the other pockets and drainage systems of the valley. Urban groups of any type have more elaborate architecture, with many of the features of an improved house form requiring higher construction costs, as well as a high percentage of fineware ceramics, burials that contain finer grave goods, and perhaps a longer episode of occupation.

What is unexpected is the diversity revealed in small rural households. Although, in general, the rural type 1 groups had simpler architecture, simpler graves, less fineware, fewer exotic goods, and restricted access to prime agricultural land, there were wide wealth differences within this category. It should no longer be assumed that rural areas of complex societies are homogeneous in either chronology, function, or sociocultural dimensions.

Our evidence has indicated the various roles that commoners played in Classic Maya society. The bulk of the population consisted of food producers, upon whom the elite were dependent. Agricultural produce may have been sent into the core (Wingard 1992), and rural commoners may have served as part of the work force that constructed the monuments of Copan (Abrams 1987). Some commoners were directly attached to the elite as retainers or servants.

The wide variety of evidence that we have been able to cite would not have been available without the complete excavation of rural households. As Smith (Chapter 10) points out, the issue of rural complexity cannot be resolved without excavation of rural sites. And if we do not fully understand rural complexity, we cannot convincingly speak of complexity in general for the ancient Maya.

Notes

I thank the Instituto Hondureño de Antropología e Historia, the National Science Foundation (BNS-8419933), and the Pennsylvania State University for their support. I appreciate the input of Steve Falconer, Glenn Schwartz, David Webster, William Sanders, Joseph Michels, James Sheehy, David M. Reed, and the anonymous reviewer on drafts of this chapter. I wish to thank all of the researchers who have worked at Copan and have contributed to this large data base, including Elliot Abrams, Eloisa Aguilar, Ricardo Agurcia, Claude Baudez, Melissa Diamanti, William Fash, AnnCorinne Freter, Andrea Gerstle, Julia Hendon, Richard Leventhal, John K. Mallory, Saul Murillo, William Osmore, Jaime Pacheco-Orozco, David M. Reed, David Rue, William Sanders, James Sheehy, Glenn Storey, Rebecca Storey, David Webster, Steve Whittington, Randolph Widmer, Gordon Willey, and John Wingard. I am grateful to the Honduran excavators for their expertise. Thanks also go to David Reed for preparation of the graphs. The conclusions are my own, and any errors are my responsibility.

1. A type 2 group in the rural Copan Pocket was excavated by Whittington (1985) but is not included here.

2. The general term "rural" is used collectively to refer to groups in both the Copan Pocket and the Rural Region.

3. Although the dependent low structures that are part of higher-ranking groups of types 2, 3, and 4 have not been the subject of this chapter, we may remark that some of these platform structures were kitchens or storage areas, whereas other low structures were houses of dependent commoner inhabitants who may have served as retainers for elite relatives or those who were not kinspeople of the Urban Core.

References Cited

Abrams, Elliot M.
  1984 Systems of Labor Organization in Late Classic Copan, Honduras: The Energetics of Construction. Ph.D. dissertation, Department of Anthropology, The Pennsylvania State University.
  1987 Economic Specialization and Construction Personnel in Classic Period Copan, Honduras. *American Antiquity* 52:485–499.
  1989 Architecture and Energy: An Evolutionary Approach. In *Archaeological Method and Theory*, Vol. 1, edited by Michael B. Schiffer, pp. 47–87. University of Arizona Press, Tucson.

Abrams, Elliot M., and David Rue
  1988 The Causes and Consequences of Deforestation at the Late Classic Maya Polity of Copan, Honduras. *Journal of New World Archaeology* 16:377–395.

Beaudry, Marilyn
  1985 Late Classic Painted Ceramics as Indicators of Social Class. Paper presented at the 50th Annual Meeting of the Society for American Archaeology, Denver.

Diamanti, Melissa
  1991 Domestic Organization at Copan: Reconstruction of Elite Maya Households through Ethnographic Models. Ph.D. dissertation, Department of Anthropology, The Pennsylvania State University.

Fash, William L., Jr.
  1983 Maya State Formation: A Case Study and Its Implications. Ph.D. dissertation, Department of Anthropology, Harvard University.
  1985 Excavations at CV-16 (9N-5). Manuscript on file, Department of Anthropology, The Pennsylvania State University.
  1991 *Scribes, Warriors, and Kings: The City of Copan and the Ancient Maya*. Thames and Hudson, London.

Freter, AnnCorinne
  1988 The Classic Maya Collapse at Copan, Honduras: A Regional Settlement Perspective. Ph.D. dissertation, Department of Anthropology, The Pennsylvania State University.

Gerstle, Andrea
  1987 Maya-Lenca Ethnic Relations in Late Classic Period Copan, Honduras. Ph.D. dissertation, Department of Anthropology, University of California, Santa Barbara.

Gonlin, Nancy
  1985 The Architectural Variation of Two Small Sites in the Copan Valley, Honduras: A Rural/Urban Dichotomy? Master's thesis, Department of Anthropology, The Pennsylvania State University.
  1993 Rural Household Archaeology at Copan, Honduras. Ph.D. dissertation, Department of Anthropology, The Pennsylvania State University.

Goody, Jack
  1962 *The Development Cycle in Domestic Groups*. Cambridge University Press, Cambridge.

Hayden, Brian, and Aubrey Cannon
  1984 *The Structure of Material Systems: Ethnoarchaeology in the Maya Highlands*. Society for American Archaeology Papers, No. 3. Society for American Archaeology, Washington, D.C.

Hendon, Julia
  1987 The Uses of Maya Structures: A Study of Architecture and Artifact Distribution at Sepulturas, Copan, Honduras. Ph.D. dissertation, Department of Anthropology, Harvard University.

Jones, George T., and Robert D. Leonard
  1990 The Concept of Diversity—An Introduction. In *Quantifying Diversity in Archaeology*, edited by R. D. Leonard and G. T. Jones. Cambridge University Press, Cambridge.

Kurjack, Edward B.
  1974 *Prehistoric Lowland Maya Community and Social Organization—A Case Study at Dzibilchultun, Yucatan, Mexico*. Middle American Research Institute Publication No. 38. Tulane University, New Orleans.

Mallory, John K., III
  1981 Especialización Economica en el Valle de Copan: Excavaciones en "El Duende." *Yaxkin* 4:171–178.
  1983 El Duende: A Specialized Workshop Site in the Copan Valley. Manuscript on file, Department of Anthropology, The Pennsylvania State University.
  1984 Late Classic Maya Economic Specialization: Evidence from the Copan Obsidian Asscmblagc. Ph.D. dissertation, Department of Anthropology, The Pennsylvania State University.

Murillo, Saul
  1983 Excavaciones en Sepulturas del Complejo 9M-24. Manuscript on file, Department of Anthropology, The Pennsylvania State University.

Redfield, Robert
  1941 *The Folk Culture of Yucatan*. University of Chicago Press, Chicago.

Sanders, William T.
  1989 Household, Lineage, and State at Eighth-Century Copan, Honduras. In *The House of the Bacabs, Copan, Honduras,*

edited by D. Webster, pp. 89–105. Studies in Precolumbian Art and Archaeology, No. 29. Dumbarton Oaks, Washington, D.C.

Sanders, William T., ed.
  1986 *Excavaciones en el Area Urbana de Copan: Proyecto Arqueologico Copan, Fase II.* Secretaría de Cultura y Turismo, Instituto Hondureño de Antropología e Historia, Tegucigalpa, Honduras.

Schele, Linda, and David Freidel
  1990 *A Forest of Kings—The Untold Story of the Ancient Maya.* William Morrow, New York.

Smith, Michael E.
  1987 Household Possessions and Wealth in Agrarian States: Implications for Archaeology. *Journal of Anthropological Archaeology* 6:297–335.

Spink, Mary Louise
  1983 Metates as Socioeconomic Indicators during the Late Classic Period at Copan, Honduras. Ph.D. dissertation, Department of Anthropology, The Pennsylvania State University.

Tourtellot, Gair, III
  1988 Development Cycles of Households and Houses at Seibal. In *Household and Community in the Mesoamerican Past: Case Studies from the Maya Area and Oaxaca,* edited by R. R. Wilk and W. Ashmore, pp. 97–120. University of New Mexico Press, Albuquerque.

Viel, Rene
  1983 Evolución de la Cerámica de Copan: Resultados Preliminares. In *Introducción a la Arqueología de Copan, Honduras,* Tomo 1, edited by C. F. Baudez, pp. 471–550. Proyecto Arqueologico Copan. Trejos Hermanos, San José, Costa Rica.

Webster, David L.
  1990 Preliminary Report on the 1990 Excavations of the Pennsylvania State University/Annenberg Project. Report submitted to the Instituto Hondureño de Antropología e Historia.

Webster, David L., ed.
  1989 *The House of the Bacabs, Copan, Honduras.* Studies in Precolumbian Art and Archaeology, No. 29. Dumbarton Oaks, Washington, D.C.

Webster, David L., and AnnCorinne Freter
  1990a The Demography of Late Classic Copan. In *Precolumbian Population History in the Maya Lowlands,* edited by T. P. Culbert and D. S. Rice, pp. 37–62. University of New Mexico Press, Albuquerque.
  1990b Settlement History and the Classic Collapse at Copan: A Refined Chronological Perspective. *Latin American Antiquity* 1:66–85.

Webster, David L., and Nancy Gonlin
  1988 Household Remains of the Humblest Maya. *Journal of Field Archaeology* 15:169–190.

Whittington, Stephen L.
  1985 Site Report of 3O-7. Manuscript on file, Department of Anthropology, The Pennsylvania State University.
  1989 Characteristics of Demography and Disease in Low Status Maya from Classic Period, Copan, Honduras. Ph.D. dissertation, Department of Anthropology, The Pennsylvania State University.

Wilk, Richard
  1983 Little House in the Jungle: The Causes of Variation in House Size among Modern Kekchi Maya. *Journal of Anthropological Archaeology* 2:99–116.

Willey, Gordon R., and Richard M. Leventhal
  1979 Prehistoric Settlement at Copan. In *Maya Archaeology and Ethnohistory,* edited by N. Hammond and G. R. Willey, pp. 75–102. University of Texas Press, Austin.

Wingard, John
  1992 The Role of Soils in the Development and Collapse of Classic Maya Civilization at Copan, Honduras. Ph.D. dissertation, Department of Anthropology, The Pennsylvania State University.

CHAPTER THIRTEEN

Village Approaches to Complex Societies

BRIAN HAYDEN

IT IS NO LONGER SUFFICIENT simply to document the most dramatic changes that typify the major advances in cultural complexity. It is also essential to understand and explain such changes. In order to understand early urbanism, we must understand how these complex communities attracted so many people and structured their interactions into a spatially coherent functioning body, and we must also understand how such a manifestly un-self-sufficient concentration of people ensured adequate provisioning of food, shelter, and nonlocal supplies for all citizens. Except in the rare cases in which administrative texts have been recovered, it is evident that the answer to the latter question is to be found largely in the archaeology of the hinterland households and villages—a source of data sorely neglected until quite recently. I am aware of less archaeological work in this area for the Near East (except for the survey work of Adams [1965; Adams and Nissen 1972]) than for Mesoamerica, where comparable survey projects of urban areas and their hinterlands have been carried out (Sanders, Parsons, and Santley 1979; Kowalewski and Finsten 1983). There have also been important attempts to wrestle with the question of relationships between outlying Mesoamerican communities and urban centers (Kowalewski and Finsten 1983). Specialization and economic, political, or military control have been explored in Mesoamerica by numerous researchers (e.g., Spence 1981; Santley 1989; Feinman, Nicholas, and Fedick 1991). However, the contributions to this volume have made one of the first, long overdue, concerted efforts to focus specifically on village and household hinterland archaeology, especially at the very small end of the settlement spectrum.

Before discussing some of the issues of particular importance on which the previous contributors have touched, I emphasize that this volume represents but an exploratory foray into the archaeology of urban hinterlands. There are many potentially important facets to a comprehensive understanding of hinterland relationships with urban centers, some of which I will highlight in the following comments. Yet at this stage of research, there is still no consensus within the archaeological community on the most fundamental question: what makes urbanism happen? My own bias is to view urbanism as a response to high volumes of trading activity, although in special cases defense considerations, resource concentrations, and administrative requirements can also clearly lead to concentrations of people in urban proportions. Rather than become ensnared in the problem of urban causality, I will turn instead to the empirical question of what urban relations were like with hinterlands.

Specialization

One aspect that many of the foregoing analyses have in common is their emphasis on the degree of craft specialization present in both Mesoamerican and Near Eastern hinterland communities (e.g., the chapters by Stein, Hester and Shafer, King and Potter, Santley, Wattenmaker, Falconer, and Smith). The outcome of this somewhat surprising, although not unforeshadowed (e.g., Rice 1987), result is the explicit or implicit suggestion that specialization and urbanism might be more profitably viewed as independent phenomena. This seems to be one of the most productive issues for future research raised in the volume. However, as a number of contributors have noted, the question requires some additional focus. In order to address the issue intelligently, I would suggest, along with King and Potter, that we really need a better understanding of what degrees and kinds of specialization exist in Big Man tribal and chiefdom communities prior to the emergence of urban centers or state-level economic organizations.

There are certainly a number of ethnographic indications of such specialization in one form or another, such as the production of salt, axes, and pottery in certain areas of New Guinea (Hughes 1977), the Philippines (Stark 1991), and the Maya Highlands (McBryde 1947; Reina and Hill 1978). Although it might be objected that some cases, such as the Maya, actually represent colonial or state-managed economies, the examples from New Guinea clearly represent relatively good examples of pristine Big Man levels of specialization. Unfortunately, little information is generally available about the degree of household economic reliance on these specializations, how widespread within communities they are, or the degree to which Big Men underwrite some of the more elaborate kinds of specialist products. The archaeological studies undertaken at Colha by Hester, Shafer, and King and Potter may support the notion that specialization begins in small communities before there is any inkling of urbanism or states. Thus the notion that specialization begins at the prestate village level (or before) is one of the more likely conclusions inferable from the research presented in this volume, as supported by ethnographic and other archaeological studies. Once we can establish what independent rural communities are like in terms of specialization and other parameters, then, and only then, is it meaningful to ask how hinterland settlements are affected by the presence of urban centers.

The issue of specialization, however, also raises another set of questions involving not only the intensity of (or degree of dependence on) specialization but also the type of specialization involved. Both Smith and Wattenmaker (and to a lesser extent Santley) have argued that there are distinct types of specialization, although the dimensional characteristics of their distinctions are somewhat different.

PRESTIGE SPECIALIZATION

Impressionistically, the most distinctive of these types of specialization appears to be the development of status crafts (Clark and Parry 1990), or what I have referred to as "prestige technologies" (Hayden 1993:203, 254). These technologies occur among complex hunter-gatherers as far back as the Upper Paleolithic in Europe, and become increasingly more common in the Mesolithic and Neolithic. Even among relatively recent complex hunter-gatherers such as those on the Northwest Coast and Interior, part-time specialized hunters who produced meat for elite potlatches, shamans, and probably nephrite workers existed; the elites themselves were the specialist carvers of prestige totems. There can be no question about the need for urbanism for this type of specialization; all that is required is the need to express socioeconomic inequality and the ability to underwrite prestige technologists. These requirements are met in all Big Man– and chiefdom-level societies (Clark and Parry 1990), and Wattenmaker's lucid comments about specialized prestige items are as appropriate for these societies as they are for urban ones. As Smith suggests, prestige specialists are probably domiciled at the elite centers, although this has yet to be demonstrated on a wide scale.

Another dimension of specialization considered by many contributors is the question of whether it was engaged in on a part-time or a full-time basis. Whereas prestige technology would not be expected to involve full-time specialists in Big Man societies, it might begin to appear in chiefdom societies, and it certainly becomes well established in urban communities and states. Peregrine (1991) has shown that the complexity of and labor investment in prestige items systematically increases with political centralization. It is clear that elites regularly use specialized prestige technologies to differentiate themselves from the rest of society and to provide incentives for aspiring administrators or productive members of the hierarchy. Thus, because of the great differences between hinterland and urban political centralization, we should see major differences between rural and urban centers in terms of full-time prestige technological specialists.

UTILITARIAN SPECIALIZATION

A second type of specialization has been termed "utilitarian specialization" for rural domestic consumption (Wattenmaker, Smith). This type of specialization involves some households or even communities in the hinterland producing pottery vessels, scraped hides, stone tools, or other items for barter or exchange with other hinterland inhabitants (and perhaps some urban households). These items are generally examples of what I have referred to as "practical technology," and they tend to exhibit the most cost-effective production techniques available (in contrast to prestige technologies, which generally seem wasteful of labor and materials). Some decoration may be present, but it generally does not involve unusual labor costs. This kind of specialization also appears to occur among Big Man societies in the ethnographic record of New Guinea and may even begin to appear among complex hunter-gatherers at least at the level of intergroup exchanges of such items as nuts, berries, roots, fish, hides, bows, mats, baskets, and cordage (e.g., Teit 1900:258–262; Anastasio 1972:120, 136). In cases in which this kind of specialization exists at the hunter-gatherer and Big Man level, it is evident that it is a part-time supplement to an otherwise normal subsistence base for the household. At what point it becomes viable or necessary to transform part-time utilitarian specializations into full-time specializations, as exemplified by the potters recorded by Reina and Hill (1978), and probably by the later flintknapping occupants of Colha, is a question yet to be settled.

At the community level, Arnold (1985) has demonstrated a strong relationship between full-time community pottery specialization and resource-poor areas. This can also be extended to San Mateo Ixtatan, the Guatemalan salt-producing community at 2,500 m ASL where I have worked. San Mateo is one of the least agriculturally productive communities in Guatemala because of its rough terrain and high altitude. Yet prior to the introduction of roads it was one of the wealthiest communities in the highlands owing to its productive salt mines. The vast majority of the food for its 300 inhabitants was imported. Similarly, individual household specialists, such as the metate maker that I worked with in Guatemala, often became specialists because they had little or no land. The occurrence of unusually high numbers of spindle whorls in the poorest households in Smith's communities and the increasing reliance on craft specialization with declining living standards in these communities fit this model well. In more attenuated forms, this same kind of causality (regional or local lack of important resources) can be viewed as the underlying factor behind both the need for producers who have no resources to specialize and the need for consumers lacking important items to support specialists, whether part or full time. The reduction of land area under community control resulting from the introduction and intensification of agriculture undoubtedly restricted the range of resources to which community members had direct access and for which they therefore had to trade. General lack of skill to manufacture the more complex technological items is another facet of the demand for specialist products (Wattenmaker). These factors provide a working model for utilitarian domestic rural specialization that appears to operate independently of the presence of urban communities, except perhaps for the most highly administered and integrated types of state systems, such as those of the Inka. Theoretically, this kind of specialization should be able to exist in communities without elites as well as in those with incipient elites or well-entrenched urban elites. However, the empirical data that address such issues are only now beginning to be gathered, as illustrated by the examples already mentioned.

INDUSTRIAL SPECIALIZATION

A third type of specialization suggested in these papers, especially in the chapter by Santley, might be termed "industrial" specialization. In this case, large-scale manufactories are created for the production of specific types of crafts that are exported in bulk to regional markets. In many respects, this variety of specialization may simply be the logical extension of utilitarian rural specialization, with the added availability of large-scale markets that might only emerge in developed market economies typical of states. Whether or not the peak production of flint at Colha should be considered "industrial" is an interesting question. Such manufactories constitute a scale of archaeological phenomena clearly distinct from independent household manufacturing and thus merit some distinct treatment. One would expect this kind of specialization to be full time in all cases. Although there is no a priori reason to assume it would be confined to elite or urban centers, especially if it required large amounts of materials (such as firewood) not easily available in urban centers, specialized manufactories might be expected to be concentrated near major marketing centers, or at least near major transport routes, as in the case of Matacapan. They would thus be at least indirectly associated with state or urban settlement systems.

TRIBUTE SPECIALIZATION

Smith identifies a fourth type of specialization as "tribute" specialization. Superficially, this may resemble utilitarian rural craft production (e.g., the cotton spinning in Smith's examples) or, more likely, prestige craft production. In the former case, it would be difficult to distinguish tribute specialization from utilitarian rural craft production archaeologically; in the latter case, one might find the production of prestige items in a quality or quantity disproportionate to the size of a community, but the total amounts involved as well as the need to produce normal subsistence items would probably obscure most archaeological patterning. Prestige technologists might be retained by local elites responsible for collecting tribute to send up the hierarchy; or such goods (e.g., quetzal feathers, jaguar skins, jade beads) might be produced on an occasional basis by individual households. Nevertheless, the underlying mechanism behind this type of specialist production (imposed elite demands) is fundamentally different from the previous ones discussed, and, although problematical, it merits further attention. Tribute specialization may only occur in state-level societies.

INVESTMENT SPECIALIZATION

Finally, there is a fifth type of specialization that is just beginning to be recognized archaeologically. This can be termed "investment specialization." Essentially, this type of specialization has the character of the "company town." In the cases presented in this volume, there is considerable variability. In the most clear-cut examples documented by Magness-Gardiner, entire communities or parts thereof were purchased by elites as productive investments. Under the terms of tenure, tenants had to produce the surpluses required by owners and had little time or energy to produce other items at levels beyond those sufficient to meet subsistence needs. The archaeological signatures of this kind of specialization—lower general standards of living and greater inequality between commoners and elite administrators in investment communities—appear clear. Other signatures include the urban architecture used for temples, elite residences, and granaries, as well as the presence of large central granaries and record-keeping in small communities. One of the most intriguing of the excavated examples is Tell al-Raqa'i in Syria (Schwartz). The marginal value of the land for dry farming, the necessity of introducing substantial irrigation, the sudden appearance of sites throughout the area, and the urban architecture for the large central granary all indicate heavy investment on the part of an elite bent on increasing grain production. Schwartz's arguments are well documented and convincing. I cannot help but wonder if some of the examples Falconer cites from Jordan, in which urban-style temples are the first buildings at rural sites, might not represent similar investment colonies set up by elites at a distance. Clearly, this type of specialization is intimately linked to urban or state elites that have the capital and incentive to underwrite expensive agricultural or other developments. Numerous examples of elite-founded specialist communities occur archaeologically, historically, and in the present-day world. Archaeologically, Linda Schele and David Freidel (1990:93–94) have argued that the Maya elites underwrote the construction of canals and ridged fields to drain swamps and turn them into productive farming and fishing lands. Historically, people from the Egyptians to industrial elites have established mining towns and enterprises. Today, the diversity of specialized communities underwritten by elites as investments to increase energy or generate profits ranges from uranium mines to ocean drilling rigs to logging camps. Investment specialization is perhaps one of the easiest types of specialization to identify archaeologically and to understand.

Before turning to other issues, it is worth noting that use-wear studies are playing increasingly important roles in the monitoring of specialization in state-level societies (e.g., Lewenstein 1987; Aldenderfer, Kimball, and Sievert 1989). They increasingly are helping archaeologists determine the nature of specialized production, the specific locations of production (in some cases near elite compounds or ritual areas), and the relative degree of specialization.

Political Complexity

King and Potter, Smith, Falconer, and others suggest that political complexity—like specialization—also varies independently in hinterland communities. More specifically, they view the occurrence of hinterland elites as an indication that rural communities were not simply populated by peasants producing surpluses for urban consumption. Like the issue of specialization, the issue of political complexity is not well focused. It is important to define carefully what size settlements are involved, how much inequality is involved, and how widespread or heterogeneous inequality is. The use of rank-size graphs (Stein) is a useful (but still underutilized) technique for dealing with regional complexity. Smith makes an important contribution in breaking down the facets of complexity into archaeologically meaningful measures following McGuire's (1983) dimensions of complexity. I was particularly gratified to see Lorenz curves, Gini coefficients, and wealth indices used to quantify inequality between households within archaeological communities. Although I used the same approach to quantify inequality in contemporary Maya communities (Hayden and Cannon 1984), this is the only archaeological application of this approach of which I am aware.

However, equally important in considering claims of independently varying political complexity is the consideration of community size and the degree to which communities of various sizes might be expected to support elites independently of urban influence. I have often wondered what the minimal size of a community would have to be in order to support internally generated elites. Stein suggests that elites form about 10 percent of a community's population. Smith's data appear to be of the same order of magnitude, as are most other estimates that I have ever seen (circa 5–10 percent). This value also agrees with basic trophic-level ratios in ecological studies, which indicate that ten to twenty producers or more are required to support a single nonproducer. Thus, if a community only has ten households, how likely is it that an elite would indigenously appear in such a community, be supported, and constitute a stable community element? Such a question has not been seriously dealt with in the literature, but

I suspect that elites would not be very viable on their own in such small communities for very long. Impressionistically, it seems that pristine ethnographic powerful Big Men and chiefs only begin to emerge in substantially larger communities with several hundred inhabitants; however, I have never looked at this issue in detail and I may be overstating the case. If it can be shown empirically that a community size of 100–200 is generally requisite for the formation of a Big Man or a chiefly elite, then we need to consider the presence of elite residences in some of the smaller communities discussed in this volume (e.g., Capilco [Smith], some Copan rural sites [Gonlin], Tell al-Raqa'i [Schwartz], and a number of the Jordanian sites mentioned by Falconer) that might not be expected to harbor elites on their own. In these cases, some kind of influence might be expected from urban centers, whether of a direct managerial nature (as seems probable in Tell al-Raqa'i and Capilco) or of an indirect nature, such as via economic ties and support (as may have been the case in the Jordanian communities). From this perspective, Falconer's claim that urban settlements had no effect on the Jordanian hinterland may be overstated, especially since he notes that the initial construction at many hinterland sites consisted of temples and that these temples were scaled-down versions of urban counterparts—a point to which I shall return.

At the other extreme, relatively large hinterland settlements could be expected to include resident elites, whether because of the simple structural need of large communities to have administrators (Naroll 1956; Carneiro 1967; Hassan 1981:81; Kosse 1990), or because of the administrative needs of investors or higher-level dominant elites to maintain control over subordinate communities. It is difficult for me to see clearly how independent political complexity as compared to urban-influenced complexity can be evaluated archaeologically except in cases in which there are clear urban elite styles imposed on local styles or cases in which there is an elite presence in small communities—both of which are counter-examples. In the case of Colha, although the communities may begin as small hamlets, the peak of the community population was estimated at 5,000, a level that might almost be considered as constituting an urban community in itself, depending on actual density. In fact, Hester and Shafer state that Colha was a dominant center in northern Belize in the Late Classic. As such, we expect to find elites present, irrespective of whether Colha was part of a larger state or part of an urban hinterland.

Certainly, by the time agricultural or pastoral chiefdoms exist in either the Middle East or Mesoamerica, considerable elite development is already present, and if these groups entered into cooperative relations with urban elites, or were even subjugated by urban elites, there would have been continued needs for administrative personnel. Thus the question of political autonomy and independent development in the hinterlands may be a more thorny issue than specialization. Perhaps, in order to deal with the issue adequately, it will be necessary to deal with the nature of the relationship between urban centers and hinterlands directly—the ultimate goal of all of the studies in this volume. I therefore turn to the question of such relationships.

Urban-Hinterland Relationships

Several authors working independently in the Near East and in Mesoamerica (Stein, Freter, Santley; see also Sanders and Webster 1988 and Ball and Taschek 1991) have used Fox's (1977) distinctions for categorizing states and urban centers (segmentary versus unitary; regal-ritual versus administrative). Stein and Freter also imply that unitary types of states are more robust and resilient in the face of pressures. I am not sure how such premises can be demonstrated, especially since virtually all archaeological cases have eventually succumbed to adverse conditions. Moreover, most of these classifications have been developed from the vantage point of the urban centers or state centers. Rather than follow this logic, it may be more pertinent to build on some of the distinctions that have already been made at the hinterland level and then see how these might relate to various types of state organizations.

INVESTMENT COLONIES

Probably the most distinctive relationship is the founding of investment colonies, in which the land and land improvements are owned from the outset by urban elites and in which production is geared to the needs and profits of the urban elites. Once again, the textual evidence of Magness-Gardiner and the excavations of Schwartz provide important support for this type of relationship. It is less clear whether this type of hinterland settlement is restricted only to unitary or administrative states, or whether such settlements might also occur in segmentary states. There is good evidence that Minoan states were actively establishing colonies in their maritime hinterland (Van Andel and Runnels 1988), and it is at least conceivable that Aztecs could have established such colonies to produce food for elites and temples, although I have not looked for specific hinterland examples. Presumably, the Aztec empire would be classed as a segmentary state. Similarly, the prevalent view that Maya elites invested in hinterland production by underwriting canal and ridged field construction to reclaim swamps (Schele and Freidel 1990) implies that the investment-colonization type of relationship probably also existed in these regal-ritual, and presumably segmentary, states.

TRIBUTE RELATIONSHIPS

A second distinctive type of relationship is the conquest-tribute relationship, which grades imperceptibly into the defense–protection racketeering type of relationship. In these cases, hinterland communities—with their elites where they exist—are allowed to remain as more or less independent economic and political units on the condition that they pay tribute to a central authority. As Stein has noted, the farther hinterland communities are from urban centers, the more autonomous they should tend to be. Whether tribute-protection relationships with hinterland communities occur uniquely among segmentary states, as Stein suggests, or whether they can also occur on the fringes of unitary states is a question worth examining further. Certainly, in the core of unitary states, one would logically expect to find more direct control and integration than simple tribute relationships. Stein's case of Leilan provides one good example of the tribute relationship; Smith and Wattenmaker and perhaps King and Potter provide additional examples.

SYMBIOTIC RELATIONSHIPS

A third possible type of relationship is a mutually advantageous one between relatively independent urban and hinterland communities, i.e., a symbiotic relationship. In this case, hinterland communities interact with urban centers in situations that the hinterland communities view as favorable, e.g., for trade. Considerable exchange of prestige, practical, and subsistence goods seems to have occurred with periodically friendly barbarian tribes along the Roman frontier. As with distant tribute relationships, relative independence of the hinterland is preserved. The evidence for local specialization in pottery and other crafts as well as the retaining of local elite styles might be some of the archaeological indicators of this or the previously discussed tribute-protection relationship. Zeder (1991) has shown that hinterland providers of animals to urban centers in third- to fourth-millennium Iran maintained considerable autonomy in the management and trading of herd animals. Given the nomadic and peripheral life of herders, this situation might be expected, although they might also have been in a tribute relationship with local urban centers. Similarly, Rice (1987) documents a surprising degree of local pottery autonomy in Maya hinterlands, and Gonlin shows that households in the Copan hinterland did profit (in terms of polychrome vessels, obsidian blades, and other exotics) from their interactions with the Copan center. Although it is difficult to conceive of independent communities existing within the core of a *unitary* state, the above examples indicate that frontiers can exist as independent hinterlands. Thus independent relationships with hinterland communities may exist in both segmentary and unitary states, although they may perhaps take on different geographical distributions.

TAKEOVER RELATIONSHIPS

A fourth category of relationship might be called the takeover relationship; in this arrangement dominant urban or state elites take over an independent community and administer it directly because they view it as being profitable to do so. In these cases, there should be obvious changes in elite architectural styles and prestige items and possibly even reductions in populations with removal of wealth from the community to higher-level elites (or increases in populations if production is intensified by higher-level elites). There are numerous examples of small independent communities developing specialized extractive or manufacturing operations (centered on, e.g., obsidian, salt, ground stone, or flint) only to have their profits and success cut short by takeovers on the part of more powerful neighboring elites in chiefdoms or states. Hester and Shafer imply that this was the history at Colha vis-à-vis Altun Ha (although a simple tribute relationship might have existed instead); the obsidian mining communities in Pachuca were taken over by Teotihuacan; and the metate-manufacturing community of Pucal in Guatemala appears to have been taken over by the more populous neighboring chiefdoms and states of Malacatancito and Zaculeu (Hayden 1987:107–110). Rome also expanded by taking over profitable trading ports and other centers. Obviously, this type of relationship does not appear restricted to either segmentary, unitary, or any other categories of states. Such relations may grade into tribute relationships, the difference being found in the magnitude of centralized control and profit taking.

There may be yet other types of relationships (it is, for example, difficult to characterize the relationship between hinterland and urban communities described by Santley), but this list seems to encompass the most important set of relationships. Having briefly examined these, it seems that the segmentary (mechanically consolidated) versus unitary (organically consolidated) distinction only helps us to understand the relationship between state elites and hinterland communities in the cases of tribute-protection and independent relationships, since neither type of relationship might be expected to occur in unitary state core areas. Thus the unitary/segmentary construct does not provide a master key for understanding urban and hinterland relationships, but it does clarify the situation somewhat.

In contrast, the regal-ritual versus administrative urban distinction does not seem to provide much clarification of the situation at all. Nevertheless, independent relationships with the hinterland might not be expected to occur in the core of an administrative center hinterland. I also feel uncomfortable with the "regal-ritual" label, since it seems to imply that these factors, rather than economics, were the basis for urban existence. In fact, lowland Mesoamerican cities and centers were usually strategically located on major trade routes, either by water or by land. This arrangement indicates that their main concern was trade and that the benefits and profits from trade were what motivated people to agglomerate around those centers. If the centers were regal centers, it is probably because the elites controlled trade (as in the historic case of Acalan; Scholes and Roys 1948) and because profitable trade primarily consisted of prestige goods rather than utilitarian goods of importance to a broader spectrum of the population, as perhaps was the case in administrative centers. Thus I am skeptical that the regal-ritual versus administrative distinction will greatly clarify our understanding of how early states functioned or what their relationship was with the hinterland communities.

Motivations for Interacting with Urban Centers

These considerations lead to a related issue: if some hinterland communities were as independent, complex, and self-sufficient as Falconer and others suggest, what motivated them to interact with urban centers or states? Here is perhaps the pivotal point of the studies in this volume. It is clear that hinterland communities could in most cases exist without urban centers, as Freter's documentation of rural life after the collapse of Copan shows and as the almost universal presence of villages existing before the emergence of urban centers demonstrates. However, it is equally clear that the large, dense populations of the urban centers could not exist without food, supplies, and other goods obtained from the hinterland surrounding them. The question then becomes: how did the urban elites induce hinterland communities to surrender foodstuffs and other goods? Falconer seems to overstate his case, implying that hinterland communities had minds of their own and operated independently of urban centers. If this was completely so, how did the urban centers survive?

The previous discussion and the chapters in this volume clearly indicate that there was no one answer to this question. Possibilities include the use of military threats and tribute; the purchase of land; the establishment of colonies (often with capital-intensive land improvements) for the production of food or other necessary products; and the exchange of goods at solar markets established in urban centers, where goods could be obtained that were desired by hinterland households but were unobtainable elsewhere. It is not clear whether rural solar markets existed prior to the development of states or urban centers (see Smith), although their pervasiveness in rural peasant communities throughout the world today makes this possibility seem likely, as does the existence of yearly trading aggregations among complex hunter-gatherers (Teit 1900; Burch 1988). Today, temple and church courtyards are often used for markets, and the same may have been true in early state hinterland communities.

I suggest that the specific strategy pursued by urban elites depended upon the relative costs and returns of the various options for obtaining food from hinterland communities, as well as on the relative risks. Investment colonization clearly required substantial capital and competent administrators. Military takeovers and tribute required higher investment in military personnel and arms. Solar markets required little investment or military enforcement, but might have been more risky because of the possibility of hinterland crop failures or interruptions in trade supplies. High levels of economic management might have reduced the risks but would have been bureaucratically costly and difficult to manage. This is probably why there is such a high incidence of autonomy in local hinterland utilitarian economies, including local utilitarian specialization, exchange, and markets—even in investment colonies.

Some of the variables that might affect the relative weight of these alternatives could be the length of trade routes; the lack of key resources, such as salt, stone, or metals, in the hinterlands; or the suitability of unused areas for capital-intensive food production. In addition, the magnitude of profits from trade or other investments undoubtedly determined the feasibility of various options, as did competition from outside and inside urban centers, the amount of manpower available (i.e., the size of the settlement), and the magnitude of the need for foodstuffs and other goods by the urban citizenry (also largely determined by the size of the community). Nor must it be forgotten, as Godelier (1978) has pointed out, that hinterland populations can rarely be kept in subservient positions by force, threat, or ownership alone. Even in situations in which hinterland communities are owned outright by elites or have been conquered, elites must provide some minimal benefits to hinterland households if residents are to be expected to remain in place rather than abandon the community and move elsewhere or, even worse, engage in revolts or simply fail to reproduce. These then are some of the variables that I would suggest warrant further modeling and investigation.

Supplementary Considerations

Although Freter suggests that ecological degradation was responsible for urban collapse at Copan, it seems to me that there remain a number of other viable alternate explanations. Especially relevant is her observation that the best alluvial soils in the Copan Pocket would have always been quite productive. If this was the case, then why did everyone eventually leave the region? She suggests that wider political opportunities drew them away from the Copan region. It seems that wider *economic* opportunities would have had a stronger pull, just as remote rural areas in North America today are being abandoned for the higher salary prospects and greater job opportunities of the urban centers. If this was in fact the case during the gradual abandonment of the Copan region, then it might well be asked what initially motivated people to congregate around Copan and other Maya Lowland centers in such dense numbers. Clearly, it seems as though most of the hinterland population was drawn to these centers, rather than being coerced into farming for the elites there. The centers, after all, were not imposed upon a densely settled landscape, but grew up in thinly settled areas. I suggest that it was the benefits (or the potential benefits) of trade and the sharing in luxury items (among which were obsidian, polychrome vessels, occasional jewelry, and exotic foods such as cacao) that drew rural households toward the elite trade centers and into relationships that were initially symbiotic and subsequently based upon tribute. When trade broke down, there was no longer any reason to stay in these centers, and they were eventually abandoned. Instead of using prestige polychrome ceramic vessels for their lineage rituals, households reverted to more easily procured painted, carved, or special sized gourds, which are still used today in these contexts (Hayden and Cannon 1984:172–173).

Although I may take issue with certain of their conclusions, the preceding chapters all represent significant advances in the exciting new comparative quest to understand urbanism. There are remarkable and unexpected parallels involving village specialization in the Middle East and Mesoamerica. The data point to some intriguing directions for future research and prompt us to ask the next series of pertinent questions. Yet one of these questions has been with us from the beginning and has still not, in my view, been satisfactorily answered. That question concerns the role and functioning of the village temple. In both Mesoamerica and the Middle East, the temple is the earliest type of specialized architecture to appear in the evolution of complex communities; in the case of Jordanian hinterland settlements, it is the first structure to appear in newly founded communities. It is difficult for me to believe that such a strong pattern of occurrence is simply related to people's religiosity. Rather I suspect (Hayden 1990, 1993) that these early temples were implicated in the economics, the running, and the organization of small communities. I have suggested that they were originally built by aspiring Big Men for the ritual and privileged component of competitive feasts. In this role, they would have been central features of surplus production, assuming that competitive feasts provided trade and investment returns that motivated people to produce and surrender surpluses. Much later, when state and urban elites sought to extend their direct control to the hinterland, elites may have continued to use temples in their investment communities to serve as arenas of local economic exchange, feasting, and help, just as temples were used even up to Roman times. Falconer's faunal results showing a strong emphasis on consumption of prestige animals at temples (in contrast to household consumption of pigs) indicate that something of this nature was taking place. Thus temples may have provided many of the perks and advantages that motivated villagers to remain within the system and to support incipient or developed elites. Such issues have rarely been addressed, much less studied, in the archaeology of the Middle East and Mesoamerica. I suggest that it is time to take a closer look.

References Cited

Adams, Robert McC.
  1965 *Land behind Baghdad*. University of Chicago Press, Chicago.
Adams, Robert McC., and Hans Nissen
  1972 *The Uruk Countryside*. University of Chicago Press, Chicago.
Aldenderfer, Mark, Larry Kimball, and April Sievert
  1989 Microwear Analysis in the Maya Lowlands: The Use of Functional Data in a Complex Society Setting. *Journal of Field Archaeology* 16:47–60.
Anastasio, Angelo
  1972 The Southern Plateau: An Ecological Analysis of Intergroup Relations. *Northwest Anthropological Research Notes* 6:109–229.
Arnold, Dean
  1985 *Ceramic Theory and Cultural Process*. Cambridge University Press, Cambridge.
Ball, Joseph, and Jennifer Taschek
  1991 Late Classic Lowland Maya Political Organization and Central-Place Analysis. *Ancient Mesoamerica* 2:149–165.

Burch, Ernest, Jr.
   1988 Modes of Exchange in North-west Alaska. In *Hunters and Gatherers 2: Property, Power, and Ideology*, edited by T. Ingold, D. Riches, and J. Woodburn, pp. 95–109. Berg, New York.

Carneiro, Robert
   1967 On the Relationship between Size of Population and Complexity of Social Organization. *Southwestern Journal of Anthropology* 23:234–243.

Clark, John, and William Parry
   1990 Craft Specialization and Cultural Complexity. *Research in Economic Anthropology* 12:289–346.

Feinman, Gary, Linda Nicholas, and Scott Fedick
   1991 Shell Working in Prehispanic Ejutla, Oaxaca (Mexico). *Mexicon* 13(4):69–77.

Fox, Richard
   1977 *Urban Anthropology*. Prentice Hall, Englewood Cliffs, N.J.

Godelier, Maurice
   1978 Infrastructures, Societies, and History. *Current Anthropology* 19:763–771.

Hassan, Fekri
   1981 *Demographic Archaeology*. Academic Press, New York.

Hayden, Brian
   1987 Traditional Metate Manufacturing in Guatemala Using Chipped Stone Tools. In *Lithic Studies among the Contemporary Highland Maya*, edited by B. Hayden, pp. 8–119. University of Arizona Press, Tucson.
   1990 Nimrods, Piscators, Pluckers, and Planters: The Emergence of Food Production. *Journal of Anthropological Archaeology* 9:31–69.
   1993 *Archaeology: The Science of Once and Future Things*. W. H. Freeman, New York.

Hayden, Brian, and Aubrey Cannon
   1984 *The Structure of Material Systems: Ethnoarchaeology in the Maya Highlands*. Society for American Archaeology Papers, No. 3. Society for American Archaeology, Washington, D.C.

Hughes, Ian
   1977 *New Guinea Stone Age Trade*. Terra Australis, No. 3. Department of Prehistory, Research School of Pacific Studies, Australian National University, Canberra.

Kosse, Krisztina
   1990 Group Size and Societal Complexity: Thresholds in the Long-Term Memory. *Journal of Anthropological Archaeology* 9:275–303.

Kowalewski, Stephen, and Laura Finsten
   1983 The Economic Systems of Ancient Oaxaca. *Current Anthropology* 24:413–442.

Lewenstein, Suzanne
   1987 *Stone Tool Use at Cerros*. University of Texas Press, Austin.

McBryde, Felix
   1947 *Cultural and Historical Geography of Southwest Guatemala*. Smithsonian Institution, Institute of Social Anthropology, Publication 4. U.S. Government Printing Office, Washington, D.C.

McGuire, Randall
   1983 Breaking Down Cultural Complexity: Inequality and Heterogeneity. *Advances in Archaeological Method and Theory* 6:91–142.

Naroll, Raoul
   1956 A Preliminary Index of Social Development. *American Anthropologist* 58:687–715.

Peregrine, Peter
   1991 Some Political Aspects of Craft Specialization. *World Archaeology* 23:1–11.

Reina, Ruben, and Robert Hill, II
   1978 *The Traditional Pottery of Guatemala*. University of Texas Press, Austin.

Rice, Prudence
   1987 Economic Change in the Lowland Maya Late Classic Period. In *Specialization, Exchange, and Complex Societies*, edited by E. Brumfiel and T. Earle, pp. 76–85. Cambridge University Press, Cambridge.

Sanders, William T., Jeffrey Parsons, and Robert Santley
   1979 *The Basin of Mexico: Ecological Processes in the Evolution of a Civilization*. Academic Press, New York.

Sanders, William T., and David L. Webster
   1988 The Mesoamerican Urban Tradition. *American Anthropologist* 90:521–546.

Santley, Robert
   1989 Economic Imperialism, Obsidian Exchange, and Teotihuacan Influence in Mesoamerica. In *La Obsidiana en Mesoamerica*, edited by M. Gaxiola and J. Clark, pp. 321–329. Instituto Nacional de Antropología e Historia, Mexico City.

Schele, Linda, and David Freidel
   1990 *A Forest of Kings—The Untold Story of the Ancient Maya*. William Morrow, New York.

Scholes, France, and Ralph Roys
   1948 *The Maya Chontal Indians of Acalan-Tixchel*. Carnegie Institution of Washington, Washington, D.C.

Spence, Michael
   1981 Obsidian Production and State in Teotihuacan. *American Antiquity* 46:769–788.

Stark, Miriam T.
   1991 Ceramic Production and Community Specialization: A Kalinga Ethnoarchaeological Study. *World Archaeology* 23:64–78.

Teit, James A.
   1900 *The Thompson Indians of British Columbia*. American Museum of Natural History Memoirs, Anthropology, 2(4). American Museum of Natural History, New York.

Van Andel, Tjeerd, and Curtis Runnels
   1988 An Essay on the "Emergence of Civilization" in the Aegean World. *Antiquity* 62:234–247.

Zeder, Melinda
   1991 *Feeding Cities*. Smithsonian Institution Press, Washington, D.C.

CHAPTER FOURTEEN

Scale, Organization, and Function in Village and Town

CAROL KRAMER

DIVERSE IN THEIR GEOGRAPHIC and temporal focus, but broadly based in Mesoamerica and Greater Mesopotamia, the thought-provoking chapters in this volume use archaeological data (felicitously supplemented, in many cases, by information drawn from historic, ethnohistoric, and ethnographic sources) to consider the nature and roles of rural components of early urban and urbanizing systems. The following brief comments consider but a few of the many issues raised or suggested by these contributions.

Settlement Variability

Substantial scalar, morphological, and functional variability exists within and among the settlements of early complex societies. The internal organization of sites rural and urban, small and large, varies, and structures designed to house their residents vary in size, floor plan, building materials, and contents. Nor are rural sites today either internally undifferentiated communities of peasants (a concept usefully discussed by Schwartz and Falconer), or necessarily similar one to another. Ethnoarchaeological work in Middle Eastern villages (e.g., Watson 1979; Kamp 1982; Kramer 1982), for example, reveals clear material differentiation among and within even ideologically egalitarian rural settlements. That contemporaneous small-scale communities varied in the past is amply documented in most of the chapters in this volume. "Specialized" production occurs in many rural settlements; some small rural settlements have "special" structures like shrines or temples, massive walls, cisterns, and large-scale storage facilities; there is evidence of record-keeping activities associated with the administration of relations between "centers" and settlements in their hinterlands; artifactual, architectural, and mortuary data reveal differences even among rural households. Ethnographic and historical data from a variety of geographic areas suggest that villages sometimes house major shrines; are burial places of holy persons cum pilgrimage centers; are rural seats of well-placed part-time urbanites, nobles, and administrators; and are production centers for a variety of finished products in demand in urban settings. It should, therefore, not surprise us that some small-scale prehistoric settlements appear to have been more complex than we might have anticipated. Recognizing that functional, formal, and scalar attributes of contemporaneous ancient sites were diverse, we can begin to develop means with which to identify and evaluate a wide range of differences within and among their remains.

Some differences within and between sites relate to their functions. King and Potter suggest that Colha was characterized by internal functional specialization organized along social lines. They, Freter, and others have noted that site function[1] can change over time; such terms as "center," applied cavalierly to multicomponent sites, can obfuscate both areal and functional transformations within sites, as well as processes that affect numbers, sizes, and distributions of sites within regions. Archaeologists often use site area as one measure of site function (e.g., Adams 1981); we also need to develop measures of site function independent of size. For example, functional size and difference can be reflected in part by artifactual type and diversity, and in the number and distances of the sources from which artifacts derive. There is some ethnographic documentation of variation in artifact assemblages at different kinds and sizes of sites in various geographic regions (e.g., Yellen 1977; Kramer 1991), and some archaeological studies (e.g., Conkey 1980) are predicated on the assumption that sites at which affiliated but independent social groups occasionally gather will have a more diverse artifact assemblage than the base camp of any single participating group. Schwartz and Falconer note the common assumption that site size correlates with "functional diversity," but the studies collected here demonstrate that small sites sometimes played more important economic, ritual, or administrative roles than their size alone might imply. For example, specialized textile production for export (including tribute?) is suggested by the large numbers of spindle whorls at large as well as small sites described in Smith's study of rural Aztec socioeconomic organization. Small clay wall cones found at sites in Turkey and Iran, but better known from monumental structures in Mesopotamia proper, suggest the existence of provincial administration, which might not have been anticipated on the basis of these "peripheral" sites' small sizes.

Rural settlements may be economically (comparatively) self-sufficient, but they are not isolated. They both produce and consume such important resources as differentially distributed organic and inorganic raw materials, agricultural products and products derived from wild and domesticated animals, finished craft items, mates, knowledge, and news. Archaeological evidence of at least some of these resources is potentially retrievable, and ethnoarchaeological research could be designed to clarify the nature of interactions between rural settlements and the relationships of such settlements with functionally larger centers, to consider what "villages" receive from "centers," and to develop measures by which the archaeological signatures of partners in these diverse relationships might be identified.

Stein argues that the circulation of different commodities (e.g., cereals and ceramics) between village and city in northern Syria operated according to different rules. The loci of rural Aztec manufacture (and possibly distribution) of textiles and obsidian tools seem to have varied (Smith), and the same seems to have been the case with objects made of a variety of materials at Kurban Höyük (Wattenmaker). Such differences may well occur frequently and cross-culturally. The palace archive from Syria reviewed by Magness-Gardiner illuminates relationships between large centers as well as between cities and villages, and it reveals that goods flowed in both directions: the king provided some villages with rations and occasional loans of both perishable and imperishable goods, and he obtained beer and grain from others. It may be incorrect to assume that, in general, ancient villages provided but did not receive goods and ideas from larger settlements. Falconer suggests that ancient Levantine villagers imported and adapted such urban notions as temple floor plans. Today, Mesoamerican and Middle Eastern villagers visit larger centers for a variety of goods and services and for news of the wider world.

Scale and Sampling

The scale of interaction among ancient settlements, particularly in the absence of the wheel, extensive water transport, or draft animals, may often have been fairly small. A round-trip walk with a radius of as much as 10 or 15 km typifies daily or other short-term interaction between inhabitants of settlements of varying size (Kramer 1982); such scalar information can be useful in defining regional boundaries of archaeological projects. Sampling within regions frequently focuses on more readily identifiable larger sites, which can too easily become the investigator's point of reference. King and Potter note that research strategies used in the Maya area vary with site size, and the same could be said for work in the Middle East. As many of the chapters gathered here indicate, our view of the archaeological record is clouded by substantial sample bias: research on early "civilizations" in various geographic areas has been markedly skewed in favor of their larger sites, leaving us an inadequate and unrepresentative sample of rural settlements with which to monitor systemic interaction and change on a regional scale. Hester and Shafer show that small sites can mass-produce commodities desired by larger communities; they also suggest that different types of exported commodities (e.g., utilitarian tools and more exotic eccentric blades) can function differentially at sites of differing size and distance. Their study, and the studies of Stein, Schwartz, Freter, and Gonlin, make a very strong case for the utility of moving beyond the individual site to the larger region.

Sites of differing size present different sampling problems. Short-term field programs at small, shallow sites can effectively yield much information about site structure; larger, deeper, multicomponent sites pose daunting challenges. Many questions posed by archaeologists can only be answered by work at both small and large sites. These chapters hint at a wide range of financial, logistical, methodological, and analytical issues inherent in working at sites of varying size, occupational duration, and organizational complexity. Regardless of sites' sizes, archaeologists must consider the ramifications of their on-site sampling behavior: How large and numerous must trenches (or cores) be to represent adequately the variability present in any site? Where on (or off) the site should they be located? Should they be contiguous or freestanding squares, rectangles, or transects? Should they be randomly placed or located where the archaeologist has some reason to believe that work will produce more "bang for the buck" than at other locations? Data presented here reinforce the widespread view that some Mesoamerican sites, although enormous, encompass vast areas with little or no archaeological debris; similarly, many Middle Eastern sites are characterized by high percentages of open area with comparatively little payoff for archaeologists bent on exposing huge areas (Kramer 1984). The authors represented here are to be congratulated for spelling out the criteria by which they developed (and sometimes modified) their sampling strategies, for those strategies, after all, enormously affect the "product" on the basis of which analyses and interpretations are built.

Specialization

Among several additional issues relating to sampling, specilization is a recurring theme in several of these chapters. Almost every study refers to "specialization," often (but not exclusively) in relation to "craft" production. Several authors draw the time-honored (albeit elusive) distinction between "part-time" and "full-time" specialization. But not all crafts are created equal; for example, in terms of mastery over raw materials and related transforming technology (such as the use of fuels, fluxes, tempers, pigments, glues, or resins) as well as demand for labor and organization of production, the manufacture of basketry, textiles, and utilitarian earthenwares is probably a phenomenon of a different order than, for example, bronze or iron metallurgy, or the carving of stone for Mesopotamian glyptic or Near Eastern and Maya stelae and reliefs. One wonders whether the same skills were required for the production of Aztec knapped obsidian blades, Elamite carved chlorite bowls and drilled carnelian beads, the pre-Columbian gold jewelry made in many parts of Central and South America, Mayan painted pottery and walls, Hittite carved ivories, and Sumerian bronzes. Related questions (among others) involve the ways in which skilled artists and artisans acquired their specialized skills (and how such knowledge is related to the organization of specialized social groups and relations within and among them), the ways in which they acquired the requisite raw materials (some of which traversed hundreds or thousands of kilometers), and the composition and organization of various targeted groups of consumers.

Obviously, specializations of various sorts exist and are of considerable anthropological and historical import. (For example, time and labor investment and volume of output vary in the production of ceramics as a cottage industry or in a more factorylike setting [see Peacock 1982].) Such variation in productive activity seems to have existed at Matacapan (Santley). Some settlements specialize in relation to consumer demand elsewhere (and Santley argues that this was so at Matacapan). Today, some urban centers in Rajasthan (India) import pottery from villages in their hinterlands (Kramer 1992). Although potters in several villages make many of the same ceramic types, villages typically export only a few types to the same city, so that different types are imported from different villages, which are thus not in competition with one another.

If we are thinking of specialization as a proxy measure of some other more fundamental states or processes (such as the alienation of some from the means of production [D. Arnold 1975], increasing socioeconomic differentiation, or political centralization), we should develop means for locating and identifying the products and work places of specialists and, when it may matter, of specifying the nature and extent of differences among them. Whereas Hester and Shafer document specialization at Colha, reflected in an impressive quantity of chipped stone tools and debitage, Santley notes, importantly, that specialized activities are sometimes carried out in precisely those site areas ignored by most archaeologists; they may thus slip through the average surveyor's or excavator's net.

Ethnographic observations are also salient; they show that specialization (as in craft production and other forms of occupational diversity) exists in both rural and urban settings, and also that some specialists (e.g., potters, leatherworkers) are sometimes locationally marginalized because of such unpleasant characteristics of their craft as noxious fumes (such as those produced by smoke or animal hides). Some specialists reside neither in cities nor in villages, but move between a variety of settlement types; itinerant rug- and quiltmakers, potters, and metalworking tinkers, for example, are found in many regions of the Middle East. Studies of village-based Filipino (Kalinga) potters and basketmakers (Longacre, Skibo, and Stark 1991), Amazonian artisans whose craft specializations vary with linguistic affiliation (Chernela 1992), itinerant and village brass casters in West Bengal (Horne 1983), rural Mexican metate makers (Cook 1982; Hayden 1987), Hong Kong woodcarvers (Cooper 1980), and diverse artisans in the large Indian city of Banaras (Kumar 1988) clearly indicate that craft specialists can be found today in both villages and cities throughout the world. They also suggest that time and labor allocation, and division of labor by age and sex, may vary with the craft.

The Comparative Perspective

A few final comments pertain to some obvious differences between the two geographic areas on which this volume focuses. Post-Pleistocene Middle Eastern settlements investigated most frequently have assumed mounded form. It has been noted that the sizes of large Middle Eastern mounds vary from one region to another; although the reasons for such variation are not considered here, Falconer and others have noted that, for example, the largest Mesopotamian mounds are consistently far larger than their Levantine counterparts. Within Matacapan, at least two pottery-manufacturing areas exceed—by more than ten times—the size of several of the Middle Eastern sites discussed here. Partly because of their modest dimensions, these small (in Mesoamerican terms) but densely settled mounds are defined as "villages." Gargantuan in comparison with most (modern) Middle Eastern villages (Kramer 1984), as well as with some of the larger and best-known Mesopotamian sites, Colha, Copan, and Matacapan were dispersed settlements whose "cores" evidently differed in both organization and density from their peripheral or suburban areas. However, despite differences in site size and morphology, surveys and sampling in both areas are subject to bias. For example, few archaeologists working in the Middle East explore areas beyond their mounds, and Mesoamericanists often fail to identify prehistoric occupation in unmounded areas.

Long-term work at sites with long, deeply stratified, and complex occupation (e.g., Uruk [Iraq], Boğazköy [Turkey], Copan [Honduras], and Tikal [Guatemala]) makes for a richly textured and highly detailed view of parts of entire systems and the ways in which they changed. But extended research at the regional level is also crucial. Documentation through exhaustive survey and numerous excavations in the rural components of the extensively occupied Copan Valley system permitted Freter and her colleagues to monitor demographic and locational variation and changes in various types of settlements. On the basis of these data, she suggests that the sites' inhabitants played differing roles in a process of increasing ruralization (reminiscent of that described by Falconer) in the protracted Maya collapse.

Archaeologists working in different areas sometimes use different terms for sites of differing size. It would appear that, for a variety of reasons, marked differences exist in prehistoric settlement structures and systems, in building materials and site formation processes, and in site morphology within and between Mesoamerica and Mesopotamia. I suggest that these differences constrain archaeological sampling strategies that, in turn, can affect archaeologists' generation of typological and interpretive labels for prehistoric sites and their thoughts about interactions between, and changes in, such remains. The critical discussion by King and Potter of Mesoamericanists' typologies and their conceptual underpinnings, and Santley's evaluation of their (in)applicability at Matacapan, are good beginnings. Recent work in so-called off-site archaeology (see, for example, Rossignol and Wandsnider 1992) and efforts to locate prehistoric occupation in unmounded areas with little or no surface debris (Pyburn 1988) are also promising developments that should lead to a more nuanced and comprehensive appreciation of the wide spectrum of site types and functions. Such research directions will in turn facilitate modifications of currently favored systems of classification that both reflect and shape our thinking about the past.

Another clear difference in archaeological practice in the two areas relates to methods for estimating prehistoric population sizes; this variation may be related to archaeologists' views of the structure of ancient sites and patterns of land use. At large settlements with dispersed habitation areas, Mesoamericanists tend to use different kinds of (and sometimes lower) estimators than their Mesopotamian counterparts. For example, Hester and Shafer claim that the population at Colha probably never exceeded 5,000 (the 600-ha site would have had a density of about 83 people per hectare); other contributors fail to indicate the criteria on which their population estimates are based, although most note differing densities within sites. Using ethnographic and ethnohistoric data, Mesopotamianists commonly assume 100–250 persons per hectare of occupied (usually mounded) site area. Stein adopts the lower of the two figures to consider the population of Tell Leilan; he also uses the generous estimator of 3 ha per person of (dry-farmed) sustaining area to consider whether Leilan had sufficient arable hinterland to support its population. Discussing storage facilities, and local population size at Tell al-Raqa'i, Schwartz uses, in addition, volumetric estimates of silos to consider the size and food requirements of the local population and the possibility that it engaged in surplus production. Together, these examples demonstrate that several lines of evidence can be brought to bear in evaluating such vexing but important issues as population size and change therein, economic relationships among settlements, and variations and changes in land use.

Conclusions

The studies collected here depart emphatically from a depiction of small, self-contained farming villages with cottage industries targeting local consumers as evolving gradually into organizationally more complex, densely inhabited cities or sprawling ritual or administrative centers, just as they reject the equally simplistic notions that rural and urban populations are either independent of, or greatly interdependent on, one another. Such dichotomies do not accurately reflect either recent research in Mesoamerica and Greater Mesopotamia or what actually happened in antiquity. It seems almost paradoxical that research on the period of earliest and subsequent Mesopotamian urbanism—which was evidently characterized by (among other things) increasingly complex size hierarchies of functionally and formally differentiated sites—has until recently focused almost exclusively on the largest sites rather than exploring the full range of sites responsible for this increasing complexity. Work at Uruk-period sites like Hacinebi in Turkey (Stein 1993) and Abu Salabikh in Iraq (Pollock 1990) should illuminate the hitherto poorly known rural components of the world's earliest urbanized society and improve our understanding of the ways in which smaller communities articulated with larger ones. Increasing work at late prehistoric and historic villages should also substantially increase our knowledge of the ways in which rural settlements themselves may have changed since the eighth millennium.

An interest in prehistoric rural life has stimulated several archaeologists to carry out ethnographic work in contemporary Middle Eastern villages; such studies have provided detailed information about material culture, social organization, architecture, and land use. For the most part, however, they lack extended consideration of similar aspects of life in neighboring towns and cities, or of relationships between villages and towns. More ethnoarchaeological work in such complex settings as cities, as well as an explicit focus on urban-rural interactions, could generate data that would usefully complement the kinds of archaeological analyses reported here, as would further ethnoarchaeological work with craft specialists. Several studies of artisans grew out of work that was originally archaeological; examples include Philip Arnold's (1991) work with Veracruz potters, inspired partly by his participation in the Matacapan project, and that of Kenoyer, Vidale, and Bhan (1991), who work at Harappa, with Indian beadmakers. Some research on potters provides details of the scale and mechanisms of ceramic distribution in rural landscapes (e.g., Balfet 1981; Stark 1992), and other studies consider relationships between potters and vendors in both rural and urban settings (e.g., Vossen 1984; Kramer 1991). Further historical and ethnoarchaeological research on the rural components of urban societies, and the ways in which villages and cities articulate in such systems, would surely complement the kinds of archaeological studies that this collection represents. Such studies make a compelling case for more, and more explicitly comparative, cross-cultural research on the form, organization, and function of diverse settlements, and on relationships among them.

Note

1. Functional size refers to the range of available goods and services in a place. Cities are typically viewed as characterized by larger functional size than villages in the same system.

References Cited

Adams, Robert McC.
   1981 *Heartland of Cities*. University of Chicago Press, Chicago.

Arnold, Dean
   1975 Ceramic Ecology of the Ayacucho Basin, Peru: Implications for Prehistory. *Current Anthropology* 16:183–206.

Arnold, Philip
   1991 *Domestic Ceramic Production and Spatial Organization: A Mexican Case Study in Ethnoarchaeology*. Cambridge University Press, Cambridge.

Balfet, Hélène
   1981 Production and Distribution of Pottery in the Maghreb. In *Production and Distribution: A Ceramic Viewpoint,* edited by H. Howard and E. Morris, pp. 257–269. BAR International Series 120, British Archaeological Reports, Oxford.

Chernela, Janet
   1992 Social Meaning and Material Transaction: The Wanano-Tukano of Brazil and Colombia. *Journal of Anthropological Archaeology* 11:111–124.

Conkey, Margaret
   1980 Identification of Prehistoric Hunter-Gatherer Aggregation Sites: The Case of Altamira. *Current Anthropology* 21:609–630.

Cook, Scott
   1982 *Zapotec Stoneworkers: The Dynamics of Rural Simple Commodity Production in Modern Mexican Capitalism*. University Press of America, Washington, D.C.

Cooper, Eugene
   1980 *The Wood-Carvers of Hong Kong: Craft Production in the World Capitalist Periphery*. Waveland Press, Prospect Heights, Ill.

Hayden, Brian
   1987 Traditional Metate Manufacturing in Guatemala Using Chipped Stone Tools. In *Lithic Studies among the Contemporary Highland Maya,* edited by B. Hayden, pp. 8–119. University of Arizona Press, Tucson.

Horne, Lee
   1983 The Brasscasters of Dariapur, West Bengal. *Expedition* 29: 39–46.

Kamp, Kathryn A.
   1982 Architectural Indices of Socio-Economic Variability: An Ethnoarchaeological Case Study. Ph.D. dissertation, Department of Anthropology, University of Arizona.

Kenoyer, J. Mark, Massimo Vidale, and Kuldeep Kumar Bhan
   1991 Contemporary Stone Beadmaking in Khambhat, India: Patterns of Craft Specialization and Organization of Production as Reflected in the Archaeological Record. *World Archaeology* 23:44–63.

Kramer, Carol
1982 *Village Ethnoarchaeology: Rural Iran in Archaeological Perspective.* Academic Press, New York.
1984 Spatial Organization in Contemporary Southwest Asian Villages and Archaeological Sampling. In *The Hilly Flanks and Beyond: Essays on the Prehistory of Southwestern Asia,* edited by T. C. Young, Jr., P. E. L. Smith, and P. Mortensen, pp. 347–368. The Oriental Institute, Studies in Ancient Oriental Civilization 36. University of Chicago Press, Chicago.
1991 Ceramics in Two Indian Cities. In *Ceramic Ethnoarchaeology,* edited by W. A. Longacre, pp. 205–230. University of Arizona Press, Tucson.
1992 Ceramics in Rajasthan: Distribution and Scalar Variation. In *Ethnoarchéologie: Justification, Problèmes, Limites,* pp. 127–133. Editions Association pour la Promotion et la Diffusion des Connaissances Archéologiques, Juan-les-Pins, France.

Kumar, Nita
1988 *The Artisans of Banaras: Popular Culture and Identity, 1880–1986.* Princeton University Press, Princeton, N.J.

Longacre, William A., James M. Skibo, and Miriam T. Stark
1991 Ethnoarchaeology at the Top of the World: New Ceramic Studies among the Kalinga of Luzon. *Expedition* 33:4–15.

Peacock, D. P. S.
1982 *Pottery in the Roman World: An Ethnoarchaeological Approach.* Longmans, London.

Pollock, Susan
1990 Political Economy as Viewed from the Garbage Dump: Jemdet Nasr Occupation at the Uruk Mound, Abu Salabikh. *Paléorient* 16:57–75.

Pyburn, K. Anne
1988 Nohmul: The Settlement Pattern of a Small Urban Center in Northern Belize. Ph.D. dissertation, Department of Anthropology, University of Arizona.

Rossignol, Jacqueline, and LuAnn Wandsnider, eds.
1992 *Space, Time, and Archaeological Landscapes.* Plenum Press, New York.

Stark, Miriam T.
1992 From Sibling to Suki: Social Relations and Spatial Proximity in Kalinga Pottery Exchange. *Journal of Anthropological Archaeology* 11:137–151.

Stein, Gil
1993 Uruk Expansion and Local Communities in the Euphrates Valley: Excavations at Hacinebi, Turkey. Manuscript on file with the author.

Vossen, Rudiger
1984 Towards Building Models of Traditional Trade in Ceramics: Case Studies from Spain and Morocco. In *The Many Dimensions of Pottery: Ceramics in Archaeology and Anthropology,* edited by S. E. van der Leeuw and A. C. Pritchard, pp. 339–397. Cingula VII. University of Amsterdam, A. E. van Giffen Institute of Pre- and Protohistory, Amsterdam.

Watson, Patty Jo
1979 *Archaeological Ethnography in Western Iran.* Viking Fund Publications in Anthropology, No. 57. University of Arizona Press, Tucson.

Yellen, John
1977 *Archaeological Approaches to the Present.* Academic Press, New York.

Contributors

Steven E. Falconer
Department of Anthropology
Arizona State University
Tempe, Arizona 85287

AnnCorinne Freter
Department of Sociology and Anthropology
Ohio University
Athens, Ohio 45701

Nancy Gonlin
Department of Anthropology
Kennesaw State College
Marietta, Georgia 30064

Brian Hayden
Department of Archaeology
Simon Fraser University
Burnaby, British Columbia V5A 1S6

Thomas R. Hester
Department of Anthropology
University of Texas at Austin
Austin, Texas 78712

Eleanor King
Department of Anthropology
University of Pennsylvania
Philadelphia, Pennsylvania 19104

Carol Kramer
Department of Anthropology
University of Arizona
Tucson, Arizona 85721

Bonnie Magness-Gardiner
National Endowment for the Humanities
Washington, D.C. 20506

Daniel Potter
Department of Anthropology
Harvard University
Cambridge, Massachusetts 02138

Robert S. Santley
Department of Anthropology
University of New Mexico
Albuquerque, New Mexico 87131

Glenn M. Schwartz
Department of Near Eastern Studies
Johns Hopkins University
Baltimore, Maryland 21218

Harry J. Shafer
Department of Anthropology
Texas A&M University
College Station, Texas 77843

Michael E. Smith
Department of Anthropology
State University of New York, Albany
Albany, New York 12222

Gil Stein
Department of Anthropology
Northwestern University
Evanston, Illinois 60208

Patricia Wattenmaker
Department of Anthropology
University of Virginia
Charlottesville, Virginia 22903

Index

Entries suffixed by an f denote citations within figure captions; those suffixed by a t, within tables.

Abbael, king of Yamhad, 42
Abu Salabikh, 211
Acalan, 204
Acbi phase, 165, 188
Administrative artifacts, 30
Administrative center models, 202
　in Matacapan, 91–93, 105
　in Maya society, 65–66, 74, 76
　takeover relationships and, 204
Adobe houses, 151
Adzes, 49, 50, 50f, 53, 56
Age (village), 43
Aggregate mound sites, 163
Agricultural labor, 37, 41–42
Agricultural surpluses. *See* Surplus production
Agriculture, 6
　in Alalah, 37, 41–42
　in Aztec society, 150–151, 155–156
　in Copan, 192, 195
　dry. *See* Dry farming
　irrigation, 20, 28, 29, 150
　in Jordan Valley, 122, 131–132
　in Khabur Valley, 20, 28, 29, 31
　sedentary, 131–132
Aguadas, 74, 75–76
Ahau glyphs, 74
Akkadian texts, 133
Alalah, 4, 37–45
　hinterland of, 38–40
　interaction in, 40–42
　sites dominant to, 42
　sites equivalent to, 39t, 42
　sites subordinate to, 40, 42–44
Alalah level VII palace archives, 6, 37–45, 131
　described, 38
　Text 55, 43
　Text 56, 45

Text 455, 43
Text 456, 42, 43
Aleppo. *See* Halab
Alluvium deposits, 163, 168, 169–170, 205
Altar de Sacrificios, 70
Altun Ha, 48, 53, 57, 60, 70, 203
Alur polity, 11, 12
Amanus Mountains, 38
Ambergris Cay, 57, 60
Amuq Plain, 38–40
Analysis of variance, 154
Anatolian Plateau, 38
Animal effigies, 71
Animal husbandry, 124, 131–133
Animal sacrifices, 133
Archaeomagnetic dating, 164, 171
Architectural labor
　in Aztec society, 151–152
　in Copan, 171, 189–190, 195
Architecture
　in Aztec society, 144, 146, 151–153
　in Colha, 71
　in Copan, 171, 189–190, 191, 192, 195
　investment specialization and, 201
　in Jordan Valley, 131
　in Kurban Höyük, 110–111
　monumental, 64, 65, 74, 172
　settlement variability and, 207
　in Tell al-Hayyat, 129f, 130
　in Tell al-Raqa'i, 21
Artifacts. *See also specific types*
　in Aztec society, 153–154
　in Copan, 163
　settlement variability and, 207–208
'Atij, 24, 25, 28, 30
Aventura, 70
Awls, 150
Axes, 53, 55, 57, 199

Aztec society, 6–7, 66, 143–157, 202, 208
　burials in, 193
　connectivity in, 144, 154–155
　heterogeneity in, 144, 147–151
　inequality in, 144, 151–154
　rural aspects of, 145–146, 155–157
　urban aspects of, 145–146

Baliem River Valley, 55
Ballcourts, 74
Barbarian tribes, 203
Bark beaters, 150
Barklog complex, 56
Bark paper, 150, 151, 154–155
Barley, 25, 31, 33, 38, 122
Barter, 54
Barton Ramie, 59, 64, 70
Basin of Mexico, 6, 145–146, 150, 154, 155, 163
Basins, 102, 103
Basket-makers, 209
Bderi, 25, 28, 30
Beer, 44, 208
Belize. *See* Colha
Belize River, 59
Bifaces, 48, 53, 82
　bipointed, 59
　general utility, 51, 52f, 55–56, 57, 58, 59, 81, 82
　oval. *See* Oval bifaces
　parallel-sided, 55
　stemmed, 57, 59
　tranchet, 60
　T-shaped, 71
　wedge-bit, 49, 50f
Bifacial eccentrics, 75
Big Falls, 59
Big Man societies, 199–200, 202, 205
Bipoints, 59
Biqa' Valley, 28

215

Black-on-Orange spinning bowls, 149f, 153, 155
Blade cores, 54f, 59, 76, 78, 116
Blade points, 48, 51, 52f, 55, 57–58, 60
Blades
 in Aztec society, 150
 in Colha, 57, 76, 78, 80, 82
 in Kurban Höyük, 116
 multinotched, 51
 obsidian. *See* Obsidian blades
 prismatic, 116
 sickle, 111, 118
 stemmed, 56, 57, 59, 78
Blanks. *See* Tool blanks
Bloodletting, 81
Blossom Bank phase, 80
Bolay phase, 71, 73, 74
Bosque barrio, 167
Bowls
 in Jordan Valley, 134
 in Kurban Höyük, 113, 114, 117
 in Matacapan, 98
Brass casters, 209
Bride price axes, 55
Brine production, 103
Bronze Age, 195
 Alalah in, 37–45. *See also* Alalah
 'Atij in, 25
 early. *See* Early Bronze Age
 Jordan Valley in, 121–140. *See also* Jordan Valley
 late, 4, 121, 122
 middle. *See* Middle Bronze Age
Bronze ornaments, 21
Buena Vista, 66
Burial goods. *See* Grave goods
Burials, 1, 207
 in Aztec society, 149
 child, 21
 in Colha, 56, 57, 59, 71, 74, 76, 80, 81
 in Copan, 183, 191, 193, 195
 infant, 149, 193
 in Jordan Valley, 124
 in Matacapan, 95
 pit, 193
 in Tell al-Raqa'i, 21
Burin-on-blade artifacts, 73
Burin spalls, 50f, 73

Cacao, 205
Caches, 52, 57, 59, 69, 71, 74, 81
Cairo, 3
Calendrical rituals, 149
Calli, 147
Calpulli, 147, 148
Canals, 30, 201, 202–203
Canoe transportation, 105, 106
Capilco, 6, 146–147, 148, 149, 155, 156–157
 architecture in, 152f, 153
 craft production in, 150
 intensive farming methods in, 151
 political complexity and, 202
 stylistic interaction in, 154
Caracol, 64

Carbon-14 dating, 171
Cargo system of religious offices, 6
Carinated bowls, 134, 135, 138
Carnegie Institution, 162
Cattle, 38, 131, 132
Cazuelas, 102, 103
Celts, 48, 49, 71
Cemeteries, 74, 124. *See also* Burials
Central Hills, 126
Centralization, 4. *See also* Unitary states
 analytical approaches to, 10–11
 in Copan, 194
 distance decay of, 11–12
 in Kurban Höyük, 118
 in Leilan hinterlands, 12–13, 16
Central Mexico, 145–147
Central Peten Human Ecology Project (CPHEP), 60
Central place theory, 64–65
Ceramic phasing, 171
Ceramics
 in Alalah, 38
 in Aztec society, 153–154, 155, 156
 in Colha, 71, 76, 83
 in Copan, 171, 188, 191, 192, 194
 in Jordan Valley, 128, 133–139
 in Kurban Höyük, 109, 112, 113–116, 117–118
 in Leilan hinterlands, 16
 in Matacapan, 94, 104, 210
  in rural contexts, 100–104
  in suburban contexts, 96–100, 105
  in urban contexts, 95–96
 in Tell al-Raqa'i, 21, 23, 24
Ceramics manufactories, 94, 104
Ceramics specialization, 95, 199, 200, 209
 in Kurban Höyük, 113–114, 115, 116, 117–118
 in Matacapan, 94, 100–104
Ceramics standardization, 113–114, 115
Ceramics workshops
 in Kurban Höyük, 115
 in Matacapan, 94, 96–97, 104
Cereals, 131
Ceremonial centers
 in Colha, 48, 51, 57, 70, 74, 76
 in Copan, 169, 172
 in Matacapan, 95, 104
 in Maya society, 65, 66, 69
Cerro Coxole, 102
Cerros, 56–57
Chaff-tempered wares, 113
Chagar Bazar 1 tablets, 31
Chalcedony, 49, 51, 53, 55, 56, 57, 58
Chan Kom *ejido*, 5, 6
Chert
 in Aztec society, 150, 151
 in Colha, 48–49, 50, 51, 52–53, 54, 55–60, 65, 70, 75
 antecedents to intensive production of, 71–74
 in Copan, 193
Chert-bearing zones, 48, 49, 49f, 53, 55, 56–57, 58, 59, 60
Chertworkers, 50
 identification of, 79–80

 status and role of, 81–84
Chert workshops, 59, 60, 65
Chiapa de Corzo, 59
Chiapas, 6
Chicawate, 58, 60
Chiefdom societies, 199, 202
Child burials, 21
Chimu state, 29–30
Chinamitl, 147, 148
Chipped-stone artifacts, 71, 109, 116, 117, 209
Chisels, 150
Chuera, 109
Cists, 193
Civic-ceremonial centers. *See* Ceremonial centers
Classic period. *See also* Early Classic period; Late Classic period; Middle Classic period; Terminal Classic period
 Colha in, 48, 50, 53, 56, 57, 67, 76, 81
 Copan in, 160–174. *See also* Copan
 Matacapan in, 102
 Maya society in, 144
Clay door locks, 110
Clays
 in Jordan Valley, 134, 136, 137, 138
 in Kurban Höyük, 117–118
Clay sealings, 30
Clay tokens, 28
Closed corporate communities, 3, 4–5
Cluster analysis, 136, 137
Coarse Brown ware, 98, 101
Coarse Orange ware, 95, 96, 97, 98, 99, 100, 104
Coarseware, 114
Cobweb Swamp, 67, 69f, 70, 81, 83
Colha, 4, 6, 48–61, 64–85, 207, 210
 chertworker identification in, 79–80
 chertworker status and role in, 81–84
 credentials as village site, 67–70
 external relationships of, 54–55
 functional specialization in, 74–84
 lithics in. *See under* Lithics
 map of, 72–73f
 overview of investigations in, 70
 political complexity and, 202
 settlement patterns in, 48–53, 83
 specialization in, 199, 200, 209
 takeover relationships in, 203
Colha chert, 52–53, 59, 70
Colha Project, 57, 67–70
Colha technology, 52, 53
Collared jars, 98
Collectively owned property. *See* Communally owned property
Commercial center models, 105
Commoners. *See also* Peasant society
 in Copan, 177–178, 190, 192, 194–195
 investment specialization and, 201
Communally owned property, 4–5, 41t, 44, 45
Comoapan, 97–100, 102, 103, 104
Complex polities, 28–30, 31
Computer simulations, 168, 171
Concave rank-size distributions, 15–16
Coner phase, 164, 165, 168, 188, 192

Connectivity, in Aztec society, 144, 154–155
Consejo Red bowls, 71
Contour terraces, 150–151, 155
Cookingware
　in Jordan Valley, 134, 135t, 136, 137
　in Kurban Höyük, 114–115, 117
　in Tell al-Raqa'i, 23, 25
Copador vessels, 192, 193
Copan, 64, 66, 160–174, 177–196, 210
　chronology of, 164, 188–189
　data base used in studies, 178–187
　group 34A-12-1 in, 183, 183f, 188, 191t, 194
　group 34A-12-2 in, 183, 184f, 191t, 192, 193, 194
　group 99A-18-2 in, 187, 187f, 191t, 192, 193
　group 32B-16-1 in, 185f, 191t, 192
　group 34C-4-2 in, 183, 186f, 187, 189, 190, 191t, 192
　group 7D-3-1 in, 181f, 183, 191t, 192
　group 7D-6-2 in, 182f, 183, 191t, 192, 195
　group 11D-11-2 in, 180f, 183, 189, 191t, 192
　group 5M-1 in. See El Duende
　group 9M-22 in, 190, 192, 193
　group 9M-24 in, 179, 179f, 183, 188, 189, 192, 193, 194, 195
　group 9N-5 in, 179, 179f, 188, 189, 193, 195
　group 9N-8 in, 183, 190, 192, 193
　group 3O-7 in, 179f, 188, 189, 193, 194
　group 3O-8 in, 193
　hinterlands of, 177
　lithics in, 65, 171, 191, 194
　Main Group in. See Main Group, Copan
　Maya society collapse in, 171–172, 204, 210
　political complexity in, 202
　Rural Region in. See Rural Region, Copan
　site functions in, 193–194
　small groups at, 177–178
　symbiotic relationships in, 203
　type 1 sites in, 163, 167, 170, 177–178, 178f, 189, 190, 191, 192, 193–194, 195
　type 2 sites in, 167, 169, 170, 172, 177, 193
　type 3 sites in, 166, 167, 169, 170, 172, 177, 190
　type 4 sites in, 166, 169, 172, 177, 178, 190
　type 5 sites in, 163
　Urban Core in. See Urban Core, Copan
　wealth measures in, 191, 192, 195
Copan Acropolis Archaeological Project (PAAC), 163
Copan Mosaics Project, 162–163
Copan Pocket, 164, 165t, 166–167, 168–170, 172, 173, 177, 178, 183, 194, 195, 205
　architecture in, 189
　burials in, 193
　wealth in, 192
Copan Pocket Mapping Project, 162, 163, 179
Copan polity, 168, 171, 172, 173, 188, 194, 195
Copan River, 163, 165, 169, 183, 187
Copan Ruler 16, 167, 172
Copan Valley, 161–163, 183
　demographic history of, 165–171
　environmental zones of, 161f
　site distribution in, 162f
Copper ornaments, 21, 117

Corozal Project, 70
Correlation-regression analysis, 98
Cotton textiles, 146, 149–151, 154–155, 156
Courtyards, 204
　in Colha, 48, 64, 70
　in Copan, 167, 189
　in Tell al-Hayyat, 130
Coyol, 168
Craft production, 4. See also specific crafts
　in Alalah, 37, 38
　in Aztec society, 144, 149–150, 151, 156
　in Colha, 54
　in Copan, 193
　in Matacapan, 91–93
Craft specialization, 2, 5, 6, 37, 54, 193, 198, 203, 209
Cross-channel terraces, 151, 155
Cuauhnahuac phase. See Early Cuauhnahuac phase; Late Cuauhnahuac phase
Cuello, 50, 56, 60, 64, 74
Cuernavaca, 155
Cuexcomate, 6, 146–147, 148, 149, 154, 155, 156–157
　architecture in, 152, 152f, 153
　craft production in, 150
　intensive farming methods in, 151
　stylistic interaction in, 154
Cultural complexity, 144
Cups, 113, 117, 134
Cylinder seals, 28, 30

Debitage
　in Colha, 51, 56, 57, 59, 65, 79, 82, 83–84
　in Kurban Höyük, 116
　in Matacapan, 100–101
Debris. See Debitage
Deer bone, 193
Deforestation, 168, 172, 195
Demographic approach, 65, 145
Demographic history, of Copan Valley, 165–171
Dhahret Umm el-Marar, 134
Direct distribution of animal products, 132
Discriminant analysis, 137, 138, 154
Domestic groups, 188–189
Double-mounded sites, 110
Dougir, 14, 16
Dry farming, 93, 201
　in Alalah, 38
　in Biqa' Valley, 28
　in Jordan Valley, 124
　in Leilan hinterlands, 13
Durum, 31
Dusabara, 31–32
Dzibilchaltun, 65

Early Bronze Age
　Jordan Valley in, 121, 123–124, 125–126
　Kurban Höyük in, 116
Early Bronze I period, 121, 123
Early Bronze II period, 121, 122, 123, 124
Early Bronze III period, 121, 122, 123, 124
Early Bronze IV period, 122, 124, 127, 128, 130, 131, 133, 134–139

Early Classic period, 48, 50, 56, 57, 76, 81
Early Cuauhnahuac (EC) phase, 146, 147, 150, 155, 156
　architecture in, 151, 152
　artifacts in, 153–154
Early Postclassic period, 51, 58, 60
Early Preclassic period, 56
Earspools, 192
Ebla, 20, 31, 43, 118
Ebla archives, 19, 109, 115, 116–117
Ebla palace, 115, 117
Ebla temple, 130
Eccentrics, 208
　bifacial, 75
　in Colha, 50, 51, 52, 52f, 54, 56, 57, 58, 59, 60, 75, 81
　effigy-style, 51
　notched-blade, 53f
　obsidian, 192
Economic specialization, 5
　in Copan, 171, 193–194
　in Khabur Valley, 19–33. See also Khabur Valley
Edge-modified macroblades, 55
Effigies, 71
Effigy-style eccentrics, 51
Egypt, 5, 53, 121, 122
Einkorn, 31
El Bosque, 164
El Ciruelo, 150, 151
El Duende (Copan group 5M-1), 65, 183, 193, 194
Elites
　of Alalah, 44, 45
　of Aztec society, 150, 151, 153–154, 155, 156, 157
　chertworkers as, 81
　of Chimu, 30
　of Colha, 52, 54, 55, 60, 71, 81
　of Copan, 160, 161, 166, 167, 168, 170, 172–173, 194–195
　grain storage and, 28
　hinterland dependence of, 3
　investment specialization and, 201
　of Jordan Valley, 131
　of Khabur Valley, 31
　of Kurban Höyük, 115–116, 118
　landownership and, 5
　of Matacapan, 94, 96
　political complexity and, 202
　prestige specialization and, 199
　takeover relationships and, 203, 204
　temples used by, 205
　tribute specialization and, 200
　utilitarian specialization and, 200
El Jaral, 169, 183, 195
El Mirador, 59, 60, 67
El Picayo, 104
El Pilar, 59
El Pozito, 57, 60, 70
El Salado, 93, 102–103, 104
El Salvador, 160
Emar, 133
Emmer, 31

Energetic input studies, 171, 189, 190, 191, 195
'En-Hanatziv, 138
Entu priestesses, 133
Epigraphy, 188
Eshnunna, 29
Euclidean distance analysis, 136
Euphrates River, 116
Euphrates Valley, 109, 115
Everted rims, 134, 135
Exchange systems. *See also* Exports; Imports; Trade
   in Alalah, 43
   in Aztec society, 154–155, 156
   in Colha, 54, 60
   in Jordan Valley, 133–134, 138
   in Kurban Höyük, 118
Expansionism, 29, 31
Exports, 209. *See also* Exchange systems; Imports; Trade
   Aztec, 150, 154–155
   Colha, 50, 56, 74

Family growth model, 189
Farmers, chertworkers compared with, 82–83
Fauna, in Jordan Valley, 128, 131–133, 139
Feudalism, 4
Figurines, 96, 103, 145, 149, 154
Fine Buff ceramics, 95, 104
Fine-grained analyses, 71, 85
Fine Gray ware, 96, 97, 98, 99, 102, 104
Fine grit-tempered wares, 113
Fine Orange ware, 98, 99, 101, 103
Fine-paste ceramics, 99, 103, 192
Fineware
   in Copan, 191, 192, 193, 195
   in Jordan Valley, 134, 135, 135t, 136
   in Leilan hinterlands, 12, 16
Finishing workshops, 79
First Babylonian Dynasty, 38
First Egyptian Dynasty, 121
First Intermediate Period, 122
Flint artifacts, 60, 116, 200
Flintknappers, 51, 52, 55, 78, 81, 84, 200
Flora, of Jordan Valley, 128, 131–132
Folk Culture of Yucatan, The (Redfield), 145
Food preparation equipment, 191. *See also* Cooking ware
Food production, 91–93
Food-serving vessels, 117, 191
Fornacalia festival, 25
French rural history approach, 145
Frying pan incense burners, 149
Full-time specialization, 199, 200, 209
Functional approach, 65, 145, 156
Functional diversity, 208
Functional specialization, 74–84

Garments, 116–117, 118
Gasur, 31
General utility bifaces, 51, 52f, 55–56, 57, 58, 59, 81, 82
Gini index, 153, 201
Glyphs, 67, 74, 84
Goats, 38, 131, 132, 133

Gourds, 205
Grain, 208
   in Alalah, 41t, 44
   in Aztec society, 154–155
   calories in, 25, 27t
   seed ratios in, 25, 27t
   spoilage ratios in, 25, 27t
Grain storage/processing, 3, 4, 6, 20, 24–33
Grass-pea seeds, 31
Grave goods, 21, 118, 193, 195
Grazing land, 20, 31
Grit-tempered wares, 113
Ground-stone artifacts, 96, 103, 171, 191
Guatemala, 70, 71, 160, 200
Gulf Coast of Mexico, 93, 104–105

Hacinebi, 211
Halab, Yamhad, 38, 39t, 40, 42–43
Hammers, 53
Hammerstones, 56
Hammurabi's law code, 40
Hamrin region, 29
Hamula, 4
Handmade vessels, 113, 114f, 115
Harappa, 211
Harvard University, 162, 163, 179
Hazor temple, 130f
Hearths, 71
Hellenistic period, 21, 25
Herding, 12, 38, 45, 203
Heterarchy, 84, 85
Heterogeneity
   in Aztec society, 144, 147–151
   in peasant communities, 2–3
Hick's Cay, 57
Hierarchies, 2
   in Bronze Age Syria, 37
   in Colha, 67
   in Copan, 171, 172
   heterarchy and, 84
   in unitary states, 12
Hieroglyphic benches, 177
Hieroglyphics, 67. *See also* Glyphs
Hinterlands, 127, 198, 199
   Alalah, 38–40
   Copan, 177
   Leilan, 12–16
   Matacapan, 104, 105
   political complexity in, 201
   urban relationships with, 3–5, 202–205
Hole-mouth jars, 98, 100
Hole-mouth rims, 135
Homogeneity, in peasant communities, 2–3, 144
Honduras. *See* Copan
Honey Camp Lagoon, 55
Household artifacts, 191, 192
Household clusters, 71, 75, 147–148
Houses, 6, 40, 151. *See also* Architecture
Huexotla, 145
Huleh Basin, 126–127
Human carriers, 93, 105
Human effigies, 71
Hunter-gatherer societies, 143, 199, 204

Hyksos, 122

Iconographic data, 164
Ilkum, 4, 43–44
Imports, 209. *See also* Exchange systems; Exports; Trade
   in Aztec society, 153, 154, 155
   in Copan, 192
   in Matacapan, 93, 95
Incense burners, 66, 149, 153, 154
Indirect distribution of animal products, 132
Individually owned property. *See* Private landownership
Industrial specialization, 200
Inequality, in Aztec society, 144, 151–154
Infant burials, 149, 193
Informal groups, 82–83
Inka, 200
In-migration, in Copan, 166
Integration, in segmentary states, 11, 12–13, 14–17
Intensive farming methods, 150–151, 155–156
Interaction
   in Alalah, 40–42
   peer-polity, 84
   stylistic, 154
Internal site stratigraphy, 171
Investment colonies, 202–203, 204
Investment specialization, 201
Iran, 19, 32, 203, 208
Iraq, 29
Irian Jaya, 55
Irridi, 42
Irrigation agriculture, 20, 28, 29, 150
Islam, 5
Israel, 122
Ithualli, 147, 148

Jade artifacts, 71, 153, 192, 193
Jars
   in Jordan Valley, 134, 135, 136, 137, 138
   in Kurban Höyük, 110, 113, 114, 117
   in Matacapan, 98, 100, 102, 103
Jezreel Valley, 126
Jila River (Rio Jila), 163, 164
Johns Hopkins University, 20
Jordan Valley, 6, 121–140, 205
   ceramics in, 128, 133–139
   pastoralism in, 122, 124, 131
   political complexity and, 202
   regional chronology of, 121–122
   ruralism in, 122–123
   sample selection at, 134–135
   town life advent in, 123–124
   town rejuvenation in, 124–127
   urbanism in, 121, 122–123
   village economy and social structure of, 131–133
Judeida, 25, 32

Karababa Basin, 110, 115
Kerma, 24, 25, 28, 30, 31
Kfar Rupin temple, 130–131
Khabur River, 20

Khabur Valley, 4, 6, 19–33. *See also* Middle Khabur; Tell al-Raqa'i; Tell Leilan
Khirbet el-Hammeh, 134
Kichpanha, 49, 55
Kilns
 in Jordan Valley, 133
 in Kurban Höyük, 113
 in Leilan hinterlands, 16
 in Lidar Höyük, 114, 115
 in Matacapan, 95, 96, 97–98, 99, 100f, 100–101, 103, 104
 in Telul-eth-Thalathat Tell V, 32
Kings, 208
 of Alalah, 37, 38, 40, 41, 42, 43, 45
 Aztec, 145
 of Copan, 171
 of Yamhad, 42, 43
Kinship, 80, 148, 171
Kohunlich, 57
Kokeal, 56
Komchen, 64
Kunahmul, 53, 58, 60
Kunuwa, 43
Kurban Höyük, 6, 109–118, 208
 ceramics in, 109, 112, 113–116, 117–118
 chipped-stone artifacts in, 109, 116, 117
 location of, 111f
 metallurgy in, 109, 116–117, 118
 plan of, 112, 113f
 site description, 109–112
 weaving in, 116–117
Kurban period IV, 112, 115, 117

La Barra, 104, 105
Labor, 83
 agricultural, 37, 41–42
 architectural. *See* Architectural labor
Labpec, 73–74
Laguna Catemaco, 104
Laguna de los Cerros, 104
Laguna de On, 55
Laguna Sontecomapan, 104
Lake Catemaco, 104
Lake Titicaca area, 145
Lamanai, 57, 70
La Milpa, 70
Landownership, 19, 204
 in Alalah, 37–45, 44
 in Aztec society, 148
 communal, 4–5, 41t, 44, 45
 private. *See* Private landownership
 in unitary states, 12
Las Sepulturas, 164, 179
Late Acbi period, 165
Late Bronze Age, 4, 121, 122
Late Classic period
 Colha in, 48, 51, 53, 55, 56, 57, 58, 59, 60, 67, 70, 76–79, 80, 81, 82, 83–84
 Copan in, 163, 164, 165, 168, 171, 173, 177–196. *See also* Copan
Late Cuauhnahuac (LC) phase, 146, 147, 148, 150–151, 153–154, 155, 156
Late Early Dynastic III period, 21

Late Intermediate period, 29
Late Postclassic period
 Aztec society in, 143, 145–147, 150, 155
 Colha in, 57
Late Preclassic period, 70
 chert deposits from, 81
 chertworkers in, 83
 lithics in, 48, 50, 51, 52, 53, 54, 55, 56, 57, 58, 59, 60, 71, 74–76, 79–80
Late Uruk period, 29
LDF site, 59
Leaf-shaped points, 60
Legumes, 131
Leilan hinterlands, 12–16
Leilan period II, 12, 14, 15f, 16, 21
Leilan period III, 13–14, 15f, 16, 31
Leilan period IIIa, 24, 29
Leilan period IIIb, 23, 24, 29
Leilan period IIIc, 23
Leilan period IIId, 21, 29
Lidar Höyük, 114, 115
Limestone hammers, 53
Limestone pendants, 21
Lineage units, 171–172, 173, 193
Lithics
 in Colha, 6, 48–61, 64, 65, 71, 73–80, 82
  peripheral consumer area for, 55, 58–60
  primary consumer sites for, 54, 55–58
 in Copan, 65, 171, 191, 194
Lithic specialization, 73–79
Lithic workshops, 71, 74–79, 82
 comparison of tool inventories in, 78t
 interpretation of, 79–80
Livestock, 31, 131, 139
Loans, 4, 40, 41, 42, 43, 44, 208
Log-linear distributions, 15
Log-normal distributions, 125
Long Count dates, 171
Lorenz curves, 152f, 153, 154, 201
Lozenge-shaped points, 51, 54f

Macanche Island, 59
Macroblade cores, 50
Macroblades, 55, 56, 57, 58, 81. *See also* Stemmed macroblades
Macroclusters, 147–148
Macroflake tool blanks, 75, 76, 78, 79
Main Group, Copan, 161, 162, 163, 164, 167, 169, 177, 183, 187, 192, 194
Malacatancito, 203
Malnutrition, 168
Malyan, 132
Manos, 81, 194
Manufacturing zones, 76, 79, 83
Mari, 29, 30
Mashnaqa, 25, 30
Matacapan, 6, 91–106, 200, 211
 ceramics in. *See under* Ceramics
 hinterlands of, 104, 105
 site description, 93–94
 site 94 in, 103
 site 112 in, 103
 site 132 in, 104

Matacapan Project, 103
Maya society, 6, 105, 143, 144, 202–203, 208
 in Colha. *See* Colha
 collapse of, 171–172, 204, 210
 in Copan. *See* Copan
 investment specialization in, 201
 small sites from, 64–85
 socioeconomic complexity in, 70–71
 specialization in, 199
 symbiotic relationships in, 203
Mechanical solidarity, 11, 171, 173
Medium grit-tempered wares, 113
Megiddo, 138
Melebiya, 25, 30
Meskene, 133
Mesoamerica, 65–66, 93, 144–145, 198, 205, 211. *See also specific sites*
 heterogeneity in, 3
 interdependence between sites in, 67
 Mesopotamia compared with, 210
 Pre-Columbian transportation in, 93
 scale of sites in, 209
 villages in, 6–7
Mesolithic period, 199
Mesopotamia, 19, 38, 208, 211. *See also specific sites*
 expansionism in, 29
 ilkum in, 43–44
 Mesoamerica compared with, 210
 recent discoveries in, 109–110
 segmentary states in, 10–17
Metallic Ware, 21
Metallurgy
 in Alalah, 38
 in Kurban Höyük, 109, 116–117, 118
Metates, 81, 194, 209
Mexico, 3, 160. *See also specific sites*
 central, 145–147
 regal-ritual and administrative models in sites, 93
 social differentiation in, 5, 6
Middens
 in Aztec society, 149, 150
 in Colha, 70, 71, 76, 80, 81, 82
 in Matacapan, 96–97, 101–102, 103, 104
Middle Bronze Age, 121, 122
 rejuvenation of towns in, 124–127
 temples of, 130–131
Middle Bronze II period, 122, 124, 127, 131, 133, 134–139
Middle Bronze IIA period, 125, 127, 128
Middle Bronze IIB period, 122, 124–125, 127, 131
Middle Bronze IIC period, 122, 124–125, 127, 130, 131
Middle Classic period
 Copan in, 165, 188
 Matacapan in, 93–94, 95–96, 100, 104
Middle East, 6, 205, 209, 210, 211. *See also specific sites*
Middle Khabur
 as intermediate grain collection point, 30–32
 specialized site network in, 24–32

Middle Postclassic period, 48, 51, 60
Middle Preclassic period, 70–74, 84
    antecedents to chert production in, 71–74
    Colha in, 48, 49, 50, 55, 56, 75, 79, 81
    Cuello in, 56
    socioeconomic complexity in, 70–71
Military force, 3, 38, 204
Mineral paint pigments, 150
Minoan states, 202
Mixtequilla, 104
Moho Cay, 58, 60
Monte Pio, 104, 105
Monumental architecture, 64, 65, 74, 172
Morelos, 6, 143, 155
Mortuary furnishings, 69
Motagua Valley, 71
Mounds, 210
    aggregate, 163
    in Copan, 163
    double, 110
    in Kurban Höyük, 110
    in Matacapan, 93–94, 95–97, 98, 102, 104
    single. *See* Single-mound sites
Mughal India, 4
Mulla Matar, 30
Multinotched blades, 51
Musha', 4

Nakbe, 67, 70, 84
Naram-Sin palace, 31
Naranjo, 66
Near East, 198. *See also specific sites*
    heterogeneity in, 3
    urban dependence on hinterland in, 4
    villages in, 6–7
Necked jars, 100
Neolithic period, 199
Neutron activation analysis
    of Jordan Valley ceramics, 128, 133, 136, 138
    of Kurban Höyük ceramics, 114
    of Leiland hinterland ceramics, 16
New Guinea, 55, 199
Nile Delta, 130
Ninevite V period, 21, 23, 24, 25, 28, 29, 30, 31
Nohmul, 54, 56, 60, 70
Nonherding livestock, 131
Nonsedentary pastoralism, 122
Northern River Lagoon, 57
Notched-blade eccentrics, 53f
Nucleated industries, 97, 100, 104
Nucleation, 115, 124
Numerical tablets, 24, 25, 28
Nuzi, 4–5

Obsidian artifacts, 93, 205
    in Aztec society, 145, 146, 150, 155, 156
    in Colha, 60
    in Copan, 192
    in Matacapan, 96, 103
Obsidian blades
    in Copan, 168, 191, 193, 203
    in Matacapan, 103
Obsidian eccentrics, 192

Obsidian hydration dating
    in Colha, 71
    in Copan, 164, 165, 170, 171, 188, 191, 194
Obsidian Hydration Dating Project, 164, 170
Obsidian jewelry, 145
Obsidian tools, 208
    in Aztec society, 145, 150, 151
    in Copan, 183
Obsidian workshops, 146
Off-site archaeology, 210
Old Akkadian texts, 31
Olmec, 71
Operation 2006, 71, 79
Operation 2007, 51, 83
Operation 2011, 71, 75
Operation 2012, 71, 74, 81
Operation 2031, 71, 75
Operation 2032, 75, 79, 80, 81
Operation 4026, 78t, 80, 82
Operation 4029, 78
Operation 4036, 78–79, 82
Operation 4037, 78, 82
Operation 4040/13–20, 83
Operation 4041, 82
Operation 4043, 82, 84
Operation 4044, 81, 82t, 84
Operation 4045, 78t, 82
Organic solidarity, 173
Ottoman Empire, 4, 5, 45
Out-migration, in Copan, 161, 169, 172, 192
Outpost system, 29
Oval biface celts, 49
Oval bifaces, 50, 50f, 51, 54, 55, 56, 57–58, 59, 60, 71, 75, 78, 81, 82
Ovens, 21, 23, 25

PAAC. *See* Copan Acropolis Archaeological Project
PAC. *See* Proyecto Arqueológico Copan
Pacbitun, 59, 60
Pachuca, 203
Palace archives, 10, 208
    Alalah. *See* Alalah level VII palace archives
Palaces, 10
    Aztec, 145, 154
    Ebla, 115, 117
    land ownership controlled by, 19
    Naram-Sin, 31
Palaeodemographic reconstructions, 171
Palaeoethnobotanical data, 171
Palenque, 66
Palestine, 4, 139
    in Early Bronze Age, 123, 124
    in Middle Bronze Age, 124–125, 126–127, 130
Paper production, 150, 151, 154–155
Parallel-sided bifaces, 55
Part-time specialization, 199, 200, 209
Pastoralism, 122, 124, 131
Patio groups
    in Aztec society, 147–148, 149, 150, 151, 152, 152f, 153, 154
    in Colha, 75, 80, 81, 82, 83
    in Copan, 190

    in Matacapan, 94, 95
Patrimonial systems, 4
Peabody Museum, 162
Peasant society, 1, 145, 207. *See also* Commoners
    in Copan, 192
    heterogeneity in, 2–3
    homogeneity in, 2–3, 144
    religion and, 5
Peasants (Wolf), 145
Peer-polity interaction, 84
Peg sealings, 30
Pella, 134, 136, 138
Personage A (Copan noble), 167
Peru, 29–30
Petapilla area of Copan Pocket, 183, 193
Peten, 54, 59, 67, 70
Peten Lakes, 59, 60
Phone booth testing, 70
Piedra Labrada, 104
Pigs, 131–132, 133, 205
Pit burials, 193
Placencia, 58
Plaster production, 171, 189
Platforms, 71, 75, 94, 97, 147, 151, 154, 190
Plaza groupings, 177
Plazuelas, 93–94
Podunk polities, 12
Points, 51, 54f, 60
Polished red bowls, 153
Political centralization. *See* Centralization
Political complexity, 201–202
Polychrome pottery, 192, 203, 205
Polyhedral blade cores, 59
Ponce's Site, 59
Population density, 13, 155
Postclassic Morelos Archaeological Project, 146, 147, 151, 156
Postclassic period
    Colha in, 48, 51, 55, 56, 57, 58, 59, 60
    Copan in, 165
    early, 51, 58, 60
    late. *See* Late Postclassic period
    middle, 48, 51, 60
Pot stands, 113
Potter's wheels, 113–114
Potter's workshops, 138
Pottery. *See* Ceramics
Potts Landing, 57
Practical technology, 199
Precipitation, 38. *See also* Rainfall
Preclassic period
    Colha in, 50, 52, 56, 57, 67, 74
    early, 56
    late. *See* Late Preclassic period
    middle. *See* Middle Preclassic period
    terminal, 50, 56
Pre-Columbian period, 93
Preforms, 57
Prestige specialization, 199
Priestesses, Entu, 133
Priests, Aztec, 149
Primate systems, 16, 66
Prismatic blades, 116

Private landownership, 4–5
  in Alalah, 37, 41t, 44, 45
  social differentiation and, 6
Productive specialization, 12, 16
Progresso Lagoon, 57
Projectile points, 60
Protoglyphs, 74
Proyecto Arqueológico Copan, Phase I (PAC I), 162, 163
Proyecto Arqueológico Copan, Phase II (PAC II), 162, 165, 169, 171, 179, 183
  excavation methodology in, 163–164
Public sector, 37
Pucal, 203
Puleston Axe, 57
Pulltrouser Swamp, 54, 56, 57, 60, 64
Puzrish-Dagan, 31–32
Pyramids, 74, 145
Pyrite mirrors, 192

Quintana Roo, 57, 60
Quirigua, 66

Radiocarbon dating, 71, 81, 164
Rad Shaqrah, 30, 31
Rainfall, 20, 31, 150, 170
Rajasthan, 209
Rancho Creek, 52, 67, 69f, 74, 76
Rank-size distributions, 201
  in Colha, 65
  in Jordan Valley, 124, 125–126
  in Leilan hinterlands, 14–16
Rations, 43, 44, 45, 116, 208
Recycled tools, 56, 57
Red-on-Fine Orange ware, 96
Red Slipped Fine Orange ware, 96
Regal-residential functions, 66
Regal-ritual models, 202, 203
  in Matacapan, 91–93, 105
  in Maya society, 65–66, 83
  takeover relationships and, 204
Religion, 5, 6, 91, 117, 143, 145, 154
Retouched tools, 57
Ridged fields, 201, 202–203
Rims, 98, 134, 135, 192
Rio Amarillo, 166, 169, 170, 183, 189, 194, 195
Rio Catemaco, 104, 105
Rio Hondo, 57
Rio Jila (Jila River), 187, 195
Rio Papaloapan, 105
Rio San Joaquin, 95
Rio San Juan, 105
Rio Tajalate, 102
Ritual practices, 148–149, 154
Roman Empire, 4, 91, 122, 203
Rounded Building
  in Tell al-Raqa'i, 21–24, 23f, 25, 29, 30, 31, 32–33
  in Tell Gubba, 29, 33
Royalty, 169, 172, 194–195
Rural Region, Copan, 164, 165t, 169, 172, 177, 178, 195
  architecture in, 189

burials in, 193
  wealth measures in, 191, 192
Rural society
  Aztec, 145–146, 155–157
  in Copan, 187, 188, 191, 192, 194–195. *See also* Rural Region, Copan
  in Jordan Valley, 122–123
  in Matacapan, 100–104

Sacnab, 60
Salt-making, 91, 93, 102–103, 104, 105, 199, 200
Sampling, 208–209
San Estevan, 54, 56, 70
San Jose, 59, 69
San Mateo Ixtatan, 200
Santa Rita Corozal, 57, 60
Sapote Striated ceramics, 71
Sarteneja, 57
Sayil, 85
Scale, 208–209
  in segmentary states, 11, 12–13, 16–17
Scrapers, 116
Sculpture, 64
Seal impressions, 23, 24
Sedentary agriculture, 131–132
Sedentary pastoralism, 124
Segmentary states, 10–17, 202. *See also* Centralization
  complexity in, 11, 12–13, 16–17
  integration in, 11, 12–13, 14–17
  scale in, 11, 12–13, 16–17
  takeover relationships in, 203–204
  tribute relationships in, 203
Seibal, 70
Sesesmil drainage, 166, 169, 183, 194
Sesesmil River, 163
Sesesmil Valley, 163, 165, 192, 195
Settlement patterns, 2
  in Alalah, 40
  in Aztec society, 144, 147–148
  in Colha, 48–53, 83
  in Jordan Valley, 122–123
  in Kurban Höyük, 111
  in Tell Leilan, 6
  variability in, 207–208
Shamanism, Mayan, 74
Sharecroppers, 45
Shechem temple, 130f
Sheep, 38, 131, 132, 133
Shell ornaments, 21, 71, 73, 74
Shrines, 21, 207
Sickle blades, 111, 118
Side-notched points, 51, 54f
Siguatecpan, 146
Silos, 21, 24, 26t, 31, 32–33, 210
Silver mines, 38
Single-mound sites
  in Colha, 82–83
  in Copan, 163, 166, 167, 170, 183, 194
  in Kurban Höyük, 110
Social differentiation, 2, 5–6
  in Copan, 189, 190, 192
  in Jordan Valley, 131–133

  in Kurban Höyük, 118
  in Tell al-Raqa'i, 21
Social visiblity, 117–118
Socioeconomic complexity, 70–71
Soil erosion, 168, 172
Spanish colonial period, 146
Specialization, 198–201, 207, 209
  in ceramics. *See* Ceramics specialization
  craft. *See* Craft specialization
  economic. *See* Economic specialization
  full-time, 199, 200, 209
  functional, 74–84
  industrial, 200
  investment, 201
  lithic, 73–79
  part-time, 199, 200, 209
  prestige, 199
  productive, 12, 16
  tethered, 96
  tribute, 200–201
  utilitarian, 199–200
Spindle whorls, 200, 208
  in Aztec society, 149, 149f, 150
  in Kurban Höyük, 109, 116, 117
Spinning artifacts, 151, 156
Spinning bowls, 149f, 150
Staple finance, 19, 28, 93
State centralization. *See* Centralization
Status differentiation. *See* Social differentiation
Stelae, 69, 160
Stemmed bifaces, 57, 59
Stemmed blade points, 48, 51, 52f, 55, 57–58, 60
Stemmed blades, 56, 57, 59, 78
Stemmed macroblades, 50, 51f, 52, 54, 55, 56, 57, 58, 58f, 59, 59f, 60, 75
Stone beads, 21
Storage vessels, 118, 134, 135, 137
Storm God, 133
Stylistic interaction, 154
Subin River, 50
Subsistence economies, 12, 14, 17, 38
Suburban areas, in Matacapan, 94, 96–100, 105
Surplus production, 4, 6, 205
  in Khabur Valley, 28, 29
  in Matacapan, 92–93
  in segmentary states, 14, 16–17
  significance of, 19
Susa, 23
Symbiotic relationships, 203
Symbolic stones, 55
Syria, 39f, 208. *See also specific sites*
  in Bronze Age, 37–45
  temples of, 130

Tabaqat Fahl (ancient Pella), 134
Tagime quarry, 55
Takeover relationships, 203–204
Tall-i Malyan, 37
Talus deposits, 80, 82
Taurus Mountains, 109
Taxation, 3, 4, 43, 44
Tecpan phase, 155
Teeth, modified, 193

Tell Abu en-Ni'aj, 121, 127–133, 139
  ceramics in, 133–134, 135, 137–138
  location of, 127f
  village economy and social structure of, 131–133
Tell al-Raqa'i, 20–28, 29, 30, 31, 201, 210
  grain storage in, 20, 24–28, 32–33
  level 1 of, 21
  level 2 of, 21, 25, 31
  level 3 of, 21–23, 22f, 28, 31, 32–33
  level 4 of, 23–24, 25, 28, 31, 32–33
  level 5-7 of, 24, 31
  political complexity and, 202
Tell 'Artal, 138
Tell Brak, 21, 29, 31
Tell Chuera, 20, 29, 115
Tell el-'Arba' in, 134, 138
Tell el Dab'a, 130
Tell el-Hayyat, 121, 127–133, 139
  architecture of, 129f
  ceramics in, 133–134, 135, 136, 137, 138
  excavation samples from, 135t
  location of, 127f
  phases of occupation at, 127t
  temples of, 129f, 130
  topographic plan of, 128f
  village economy and social structure of, 131–133
Tell es-Sa'idiyyeh, 134, 135
Tell Gubba, 29, 33
Tell Kittan temples, 130–131
Tell Leilan, 12, 13f, 20–21, 29, 31, 109, 210
  hinterlands of, 12–16
  settlement patterns in, 6
Tell Madhhur, 29
Tell Mardikh, 20
Tell Mozan, 20, 29, 31
Tell Razuk, 29
Tell Toqaan, 6
Tell Umm Hammad, 134
Tell Ziyadeh, 24, 31
Telul-eth-Thalathat Tell V, 24, 31, 32
Temazcalli phase, 146, 154, 155
Temple archives, 10
Temples, 128, 202, 204, 207, 208
  in Aztec society, 145, 147, 154
  centralization of power in, 10
  Colha, 66
  Ebla, 130
  Hazor, 130f
  investment specialization and, 201
  Kfar Rupin, 130–131
  land ownership controlled by, 19
  Matacapan, 94
  role and function of, 205
  Shechem, 130f
  Tell al-Raqa'i, 21, 28
  Tell el-Hayyat, 129f, 130
  Tell Kittan, 130–131
Tenochtitlan, 66, 143, 145
Teopanzolco ceramic complex, 155
Teotihuacan, 66, 67, 91, 93, 104, 106, 203
Teotihuacan Barrio, 94, 104

Terminal Classic period, 70
  chertworkers in, 81
  lithics in, 48, 51, 55, 56, 57, 58, 59, 60, 78
Terminal Preclassic period, 50, 56
Terracing
  in Aztec society, 150–151, 155
  in Copan, 189
  in Matacapan, 101
Tertiary "finishing" workshops, 76–78
Tethered specialization, 96
Texcoco Fabric Marked, 155
Textiles, 208
  in Aztec society, 146, 149–151, 154–155, 156
  in Kurban Höyük, 109, 116–117, 118
Tikal, 59, 60, 65, 66, 67, 70, 84
Tikal Project, 64
Titriş, 109, 110
Tiwanaku state, 145
Tlahuica polychrome, 153, 155
Tombs, 52, 124, 193
Tool blanks
  in Colha, 56, 57, 71, 76, 78
  in Copan, 194
  in Kurban Höyük, 116
  macroflake, 75, 76, 78, 79
Towns, 207–211
  in Jordan Valley Early Bronze Age, 123–124
  in Jordan Valley Middle Bronze Age, 124–127
  scale and sampling in, 208–209
  settlement variability in, 207–208
Trace element analysis, 133, 136
Trade, 205. *See also* Exchange systems; Exports; Imports
  in Alalah, 38
  in Aztec society, 149
  in Colha, 54–55, 60
  in Copan, 160
  elite control of, 204
Tranchet bifaces, 60
Tranchet-bit tools, 50, 51, 51f, 53, 54, 55, 56, 57, 58, 75, 76, 78, 78f, 82
Transjordan, 124
Transportation
  in Jordan Valley, 134–135, 138
  in Matacapan, 93, 105
Trays, 102
Trenches, 208–209
Tres Zapotes, 104
Tribute, 204
  in Aztec society, 148, 149, 150, 155
  in Chimu, 29
  in goods, 11
  in labor, 11–12
  in segmentary states, 11–12, 16, 17
Tribute relationships, 203
Tribute specialization, 200–201
Trickle-painted ceramics, 134, 135, 138
T-shaped adzes, 49, 50, 50f, 56
T-shaped bifaces, 71
Tuneinir, 30
Turanian Basin, 91
Turkey, 208. *See also specific sites*

Turkmen tribe, 45
Tuxtlas Mountains, 6, 92f, 93
Tuxtlas region, 101f, 104

Uaxactun, 67, 70
Ugarit, 4–5, 43, 44, 127, 139
U K'it Tok', 167
Ulua Valley, 192
Una (Uni/Langda) quarries, 55
Unitary states, 11, 202. *See also* Centralization
  in Leilan hinterlands, 12–13, 16
  takeover relationships in, 203–204
  tribute relationships in, 203
University of Amsterdam, 20
University of Chicago, 112
Upper Paleolithic, 199
Ur, 31–32, 118
Urban art, 21
Urban Core, Copan, 161, 163–164, 165, 166–167, 168–170, 177, 178, 183, 194, 195
  architecture in, 189, 190
  burials in, 193
  wealth in, 192
Urban nucleation, 124
Urban society
  Aztec, 145–146
  in Copan, 187, 188, 191, 192, 194–195. *See also* Urban Core, Copan
  hinterland relationships with, 3–5, 202–205
  in Jordan Valley, 121, 122–123
  in Matacapan, 95–96
  specialization and, 198–201
Urfa Province, 109
Uruk period, 29, 211
Use-wear studies, 201
Utilitarian specialization, 199–200

Valley of Oaxaca, 91, 105
Veracruz, 6, 95, 211
Vijayanagara, 91
Village approaches, 198–205
Villages, 6–7, 207–211
  in Alalah, 40
  Colha credentials as, 67–70
  economy of in Jordan Valley, 131–133
  scale and sampling in, 208–209
  settlement variability in, 207–208
Volcanism, 102

Wall paintings, 24
Wasters
  in Jordan Valley, 133, 134, 137, 138
  in Leilan hinterlands, 16
  in Matacapan, 96, 97, 100, 101–102, 104
Waterholes. *See Aguadas*
Water storage, 66
Water transportation, 93, 104–106, 208
Wealth indices, 153–154, 155, 201
  in Copan, 191, 192, 195
  takeover relationships and, 203
Weaving, 38, 91, 116–117
Wedge-bit bifaces, 49, 50f

Wheat, 31, 38, 122
Wheel-made pottery
  in Jordan Valley, 134
  in Kurban Höyük, 113, 113f, 114f, 115, 116
Wild Cane Cay, 58
Woodcarvers, 209
Wood consumption, 168, 195
Wooden artifacts, 151

Writing, 67

Xochicalco Mapping Project, 146
Xunantunich, 59

Yamhad, 38
Yarimlim, 42
Yarn, 116, 117

Yautepec, 155
Yaxha, 60
Yax K'am Lay, 167
Yaxox, 59
Yucatan, 91
Yucatec Maya sites, 178

Zaculeu, 203